PROTECTING VULNERABLE GROUPS

The concept of vulnerability has not been interpreted unequivocally either in regional or universal international legal instruments. This book analyses the work of the EU and the Council of Europe in ascertaining a clear framework or a set of criteria suitable to determine those who should be considered vulnerable and disadvantaged. It also explores the measures required to protect their human rights. Key questions can be answered by analysing the different methods used to determine the levels of protection offered by the two European systems. These questions include whether the Convention and the case law of the Strasbourg Court, the monitoring mechanisms of the Council of Europe, EU law and the case law of the European Court of Justice enhance the protection of vulnerable groups and expand the protection of their rights, or, alternatively, whether they are mainly used to fill in relatively minor gaps or occasional lapses in national rights guarantees. The analysis also shows the extent to which these two European systems provide analogous, or indeed divergent, standards and how any such divergence might be problematic in light of the EU accession to the ECHR.

Volume 51 in the series Modern Studies in European Law

AF721896

Modern Studies in European Law
Recent titles in this series:

Services and the EU Citizen
Edited by Frank S Benyon

The Accession of the European Union to the European Convention on Human Rights
Paul Gragl

Normative Patterns and Legal Developments in the Social Dimension of the EU
Edited by Ann Numhauser-Henning and Mia Rönnmar

The European Neighbourhood Policy and the Democratic Values of the EU: A Legal Analysis
Nariné Ghazaryan

EU Security and Justice Law: After Lisbon and Stockholm
Edited by Diego Acosta Arcarazo and Cian C Murphy

EU Environmental Law, Governance and Decision-Making
Maria Lee

Shaping the Single European Market in the Field of Foreign Direct Investment
Philip Strik

Nationalism and Private Law in Europe
Guido Comparato

EU Asylum Procedures and the Right to an Effective Remedy
Marcelle Reneman

The EU Accession to the ECHR
Edited by Vasiliki Kosta, Nikos Skoutaris and Vassilis P Tzevelekos

The European Court of Justice and External Relations: Constitutional Challenges
Edited by Marise Cremona and Anne Thies

A Critique of Codification
Leone Niglia

For the complete list of titles in this series, see 'Modern Studies in European Law' link at www.hartpub.co.uk/books/series.asp

Protecting Vulnerable Groups

The European Human Rights Framework

Edited by
Francesca Ippolito
and
Sara Iglesias Sánchez

• HART •
PUBLISHING
OXFORD AND PORTLAND, OREGON
2017

Hart Publishing
An imprint of Bloomsbury Publishing Plc

Hart Publishing Ltd
Kemp House
Chawley Park
Cumnor Hill
Oxford OX2 9PH
UK

Bloomsbury Publishing Plc
50 Bedford Square
London
WC1B 3DP
UK

www.hartpub.co.uk
www.bloomsbury.com

Published in North America (US and Canada) by
Hart Publishing
c/o International Specialized Book Services
920 NE 58th Avenue, Suite 300
Portland, OR 97213-3786
USA

www.isbs.com

HART PUBLISHING, the Hart/Stag logo, BLOOMSBURY and the Diana logo are trademarks of Bloomsbury Publishing Plc

First published in hardback, 2015
Paperback edition, 2017

© The Editors and Contributors severally 2015

The Editors and Contributors have asserted their right under the Copyright, Designs and Patents Act 1988 to be identified as the Authors of this work.

All rights reserved. No part of this publication may be reproduced or transmitted in any form or by any means, electronic or mechanical, including photocopying, recording, or any information storage or retrieval system, without prior permission in writing from the publishers.

While every care has been taken to ensure the accuracy of this work, no responsibility for loss or damage occasioned to any person acting or refraining from action as a result of any statement in it can be accepted by the authors, editors or publishers.

All UK Government legislation and other public sector information used in the work is Crown Copyright ©. All House of Lords and House of Commons information used in the work is Parliamentary Copyright ©. This information is reused under the terms of the Open Government Licence v3.0 (http://www.nationalarchives. gov.uk/doc/open-government-licence/version/3) except where otherwise stated.

All Eur-lex material used in the work is © European Union, http://eur-lex.europa.eu/, 1998–2017.

British Library Cataloguing-in-Publication Data
A catalogue record for this book is available from the British Library.

ISBN: PB: 978-1-50991-548-4
HB: 978-1-84946-685-1

Typeset by Compuscript Ltd, Shannon
Printed and bound in Great Britain by
Lightning Source UK Ltd

To find out more about our authors and books visit www.hartpublishing.co.uk. Here you will find extracts, author information, details of forthcoming events and the option to sign up for our newsletters.

Contents

III. NON-NATIONALS

IV. VICTIMS OF ILLEGAL ACTS

V. CIRCUMSTANTIAL VULNERABILITY

About the Contributors

Tawhida Ahmed is senior Lecturer in Law at City Law School, City University London, UK. She researches minority rights protection in Europe and international law, specialising on the European Union. She is the author of *The Impact of EU Law on Minority Rights* (Oxford, Hart, 2011). She is an Associate of the UK Network on Human Rights and Minority Groups and an Associate Fellow of the Human Rights Consortium, School of Advanced Studies, University of London.

Jessica Almqvist, BA, LLM (Lund), PhD (European University Institute) is Lecturer in International Law and International Relations, Faculty of Law, Autonomous University of Madrid. She studied international relations at University of California Berkeley (1994–95). Dr Almqvist has held research positions in the Centre for Political and Constitutional Studies in Madrid (2006–09), the Centre for International Cooperation at New York University (2002–04), and FRIDE (Fundación para Relaciones Internacionales y el Diálogo Exterior) in Madrid (2004–06). She is the author of several books and articles in the area of international human rights. She has participated in the EURESTE Pilot Project, funded by the European Commission VICT programme 'Preparatory Action Project for Victims of Terrorism–2006' as a member of the working group that prepared a publication entitled *Meeting Needs in a Crisis. Responding to Those Affected (including by Terrorist Attacks)* (Brussels, Belgian Red Cross, 2008).

Julinda Beqiraj, JD, PhD (Trento) is a Research Fellow at the Bingham Centre for the Rule of Law, British Institute for International and Comparative Law (BIICL). Before joining the Bingham Centre, Julinda obtained a PhD from the School of International Studies in Trento; her doctoral dissertation focused on the international protection of the economic and social rights of migrant workers. In 2010 she was a member of the Research Centre of The Hague Academy of International Law, working on International Migrations under the direction of Professor Goodwin-Gill. Julinda has lectured on courses and held seminars on public international law, EU law and international economic law at the universities of Trento and Bolzano. Among others, she has also been a visiting scholar at the Institute for the Study of International Migration, ISIM (Washington DC), a visiting fellow at the Max Planck Institute for Social Law and Social Policy (Munich) and a visiting lecturer at the Yeditepe University (Istanbul).

Ulrike Brandl is Associate Professor at the Department of International Law and International Organisations, Faculty of Law, University of Salzburg. She has been National Coordinator of the European Legal Network on Asylum (ELENA) since 1989. She is co-editor of the online journal *Fremden und Asylrechtliche Blätter* (*FABL*), available at www.fabl.at. She has written extensively on Aliens Law, Refugee Law and Human Rights Law. She was Visiting Professor at McGeorge School of Law, Sacramento in August/September 2008, and regularly teaches at the University Paris X, Nanterre and at Viadrina University, Frankfurt (Oder). She regularly teaches tutorials on Public International Law, European Union Law, International Institutional Law, International and National Human Rights Protection, Refugee and Asylum Law, Protection of Women in Public International and European Law and also International Trade and Business Law.

Catherine-Amélie Chassin, PhD (Paris II) has been Assistant Professor at the Faculty of Law, University of Caen (France) and Co-Director of the Master 'Fundamental Rights' since 2007. She is Associate Judge in the Cour nationale du droit d'asile (UNHCR's representative) and has given lectures in 2012 and 2013 on 'The European policy toward asylum and refugees' at the Institut international des droits de l'homme, Summer Courses in Refugee law, Strasbourg. In 2010 she was selected to be a participant at the Centre for Studies and Research in International law, Academy of International Law, The Hague in 2010 on the topic of 'International migrations'.

Philip Czech studied law and history at the University of Salzburg. He holds a Mag iur and a DPhil degree. Since 2002 he has been a researcher at the Austrian Institute for Human Rights and editor of the *Newsletter Menschenrechte*, a periodical reporting on the current case law of the European Court of Human Rights (ECtHR). He is mainly engaged with publishing and teaching in the field of fundamental rights, especially with the case law of the ECtHR and its transposition in Austria. Further main fields of interest are asylum and aliens law, family law and media law. He is currently writing his dissertation on freedom of reproductive choice.

Olivier Dubos is Professor of Public Law at the University of Bordeaux and holds a Jean Monnet Chair in European Public Law. He is the coordinator of the Forum Montesquieu and director of the collection *Droits européens* (Paris, Pédone). He is a member of the Scientific Council of the European Organization of Public Law and of the Maison des Sciences de l'Homme d'Aquitaine. Professor Dubos lectures at the Bordeaux School of Law and the Sciences Po Bordeaux, as well as abroad. He primarily researches European Public Law and the European Convention of Human Rights, and has published in many peer-reviewed international journals on these topics.

Peggy Ducoulombier is Professor of Public Law at the University of Strasbourg, previously at Perpignan. She holds a PhD from the University of Strasbourg. She previously worked as a Lecturer at the universities of Keele (UK), Aberdeen (UK) and Strasbourg (France), where she taught UK Constitutional and Administrative Law, UK Civil Liberties, EU Law, Legal Systems of the World and Human Rights. Her main area of expertise is the European Convention on Human Rights. In this field, she has written several articles on conflicts between rights, the hierarchy of Human Rights and the procedure of pilot cases. Her PhD thesis, *Les conflits* *de droits fondamentaux devant la Cour européenne des droits de l'Homme*, was published by Bruylant in 2011.

Francette Fines is Associate Professor in Public Law and has been Associate Vice President of Research at the University of Bordeaux where she directs the Research Masters course in Community and European law. Her research is divided into three main themes, primarily law of the European Union, Institutional Innovations in the European Union legal systems of the Member States, and Fundamental Rights. She is the author of numerous works on issues of non-discrimination. She co-edited with M Gautier and C Gauthier a book on non-discrimination between Europeans, published by Pedone in 2012. She has published a study on 'Gender and Community law' in *Gender and European Law* edited by O Dubos (Paris, Pedone, 2006), and wrote the section on equality between man and woman for the *Dictionary of Human Rights*, edited by J Andriantsimbazovina, S Rials, F Sudre and H Gaudin (Paris, PUF, 2008).

Steve Foster, PhD (Coventry University), LLM (University of London) is a Principal Lecturer in Law at Coventry Law School, teaching domestic and European human rights, constitutional law and research skills. He is the author of *Human Rights and Civil Liberties* (Harlow, Longman, 2011), and for over 20 years has written in various journals, mostly on prisoners' rights in UK law and under the European Convention on Human Rights.

Victor Guset is a Lecturer in Constitutional Law and a PhD student in Public Law at the University of Bordeaux. He is currently working on his thesis 'The National Implementation of the European Charter for Regional or Minority Languages'.

Erica Howard is Associate Professor of Law at Middlesex University, London. She obtained her PhD in European discrimination law at the University of London. She has conducted extensive research in the area of freedom of religion, religious discrimination and other forms of discrimination, including multiple discrimination, and has published a book and a number of articles on these subjects. Her second book is entitled *Law and the Wearing of Religious Symbols: European Bans on the Wearing of Religious Symbols in Education* (Abingdon, Routledge, 2012).

Francesca Ippolito JD (Bologna), Phd (Milan) is currently Senior Lecurer in International Law and the European Union at the University of Cagliari, Italy. She served as Consultant in European Union Law at the Foreign Affairs Ministry in Rome, and is currently the project leader of two international research projects on Cooperation Agreements in the Mediterranean and on Asylum-seekers in Mare Nostrum: a French and Italian appraisal of judicial practice. She was chosen to be a member of the Research Centre of The Hague Academy of International Law on International Migrations in 2010 (Directors: G Goodwin-Gill and P Weckel) and has been Visiting Fellow at the School of Law, University of Glasgow as well as Visiting Professor in European Union law in France at the University Montesquieu-Bordeaux IV. Dr Ippolito has written extensively in the area of EU migration law, the Common European Asylum System, non-discrimination, EU competences and the subsidiarity principle. Her most recent publications include A Abass, F Ippolito (eds), *Regional approaches to asylum seekers protection: an international law perspective* (Farnham, Ashgate, 2014).

Alessandra Lang is Associate Professor of European Union Law at the University of Milan, Italy, where she lectures on EU Law. She has been a member of the Free Movement of Workers Network, coordinated by the Centre for Migration Law of University of Nijmegen (The Netherlands), as an expert for Italy. In this capacity, she wrote the annual reports on Italian implementation of EU law on the free movement of workers and specific reports on different subjects according to the requests submitted by the Commission of the European Union. Drawing from the 27 national reports, the Centre for Migration Law wrote the European Reports, published yearly on the website of the European Commission. Professor Lang's main research areas are: free movement of persons and EU citizenship, EU enlargement, and EU external relations, and she has published widely on these topics.

Valsamis Mitsilegas is Head of the Department of Law, Professor of European Criminal Law and Director of the Criminal Justice Centre at Queen Mary, University of London. His interests and expertise lie in the areas of EU law (with particular focus on the evolution of the Union into an Area of Freedom, Security and Justice), global security governance and human rights. He has published widely in the fields of European criminal law, immigration and asylum, and security and counter-terrorism law. Professor Mitsilegas is a member of the Management Committee of the European Criminal Law Academic Network (ECLAN), a Europe-wide network which brings together academic experts from the 27 EU member states and beyond. He was General Rapporteur to the 2012 Congress of the International Federation for European Law (FIDE), and he is currently the Queen Mary Principal Investigator on a multinational interdisciplinary research project on EU Action to Fight Environmental Crime (EFFACE) funded by the European Commission under the 7th Framework Programme for Research (2012–2016). Professor Mitsilegas is also a regular consultant to the UK Government and the Judiciary of England and Wales, the House of Lords, EU institutions and international organisations. He is the first contributor of a specific chapter on the relationship between EU law and domestic criminal law in *Blackstone's Criminal Practice*. He is member of a team drafting case commentaries for the *Criminal Law Review*. He is also Consultant Editor to *EU Law in Criminal Practice* (Oxford, OUP, 2013) and he is the author of *EU Criminal Law* (Oxford, Hart, 2009).

Jacobo Ríos Rodríguez is 'Maître de Conférences' in Public Law at the University of Perpignan Via Domitia (Associate Professor/Senior Lecturer, french civil servant). He holds a PhD in Law from the Universities of Paris I \Panthéon-Sorbonne (France) and La Coruña (Spain), and an 'Habilitation à diriger des recherches–HDR' from the University of Perpignan Via Domitia (the highest university degree in France), which entitles him to supervise PhD theses. Dr Ríos, who specialises in International Law, has published two monographs and approximately 30 articles. He has also edited two collective works, organised several symposiums and participated in more than 20 symposiums. Moreover, Dr Ríos is a member of the Société française pour le droit international (SFDI) and of the Asociación española de profesores de Derecho Internacional y Relaciones Internacionales (AEPDIRI), and he has also collaborated as an expert with the Agence nationale de la recherche (ANR) in France. His research topics focus on the role of the individual on the international legal order, especially on themes such as international expertise, UN governance, cinematic representation of law, universal jurisdiction in the prosecution of international crimes, human rights and migrations. With regard to this last field, he has participated in projects at the Centre for Studies and Research in International Law and International Relations, The Hague Academy in International Law.

Sara Iglesias Sánchez LLM (Yale Law School), PhD (Universidad Complutense of Madrid) currently holds a position as a lawyer at the European Court of Justice. Prior to this, Dr Iglesias was Lecturer of Public International Law and EU Law at the University of Cádiz Law School, where she also coordinated the Bilingual Master in International Relations and Migration Policies. She has also lectured at the IE University (Instituto de Empresa) and has acted as master's thesis supervisor in the Centre for Constitutional and Political Studies (Madrid). Her research has mainly focused on EU migration law, citizenship and the protection of fundamental rights in the European Union. She has been visiting researcher at the Max Planck Institute for International and Comparative Law, at the Radboud University in the Netherlands, and the Centre of Research and Studies of The Hague Academy of International law, and has been a Schuman Fellow at the legal service of the European Parliament. Dr Iglesias is the author of a book on the status of third country nationals in the EU, and has produced numerous contributions to journals (including the *Common Market Law Review*, the *European Law Journal* and *the European Journal of Migration and Law*) and collective volumes in various languages. Additionally, she actively participates as a researcher in several international and European law-related groups and research projects.

Caroline Sawyer BA (Hons) (Oxon), MA (Brunel), PhD (Bristol) is Senior Lecturer in Law at the Victoria University of Wellington, New Zealand. Caroline was admitted as a Solicitor of the Supreme Court of England and Wales in 1989 and as a Barrister and Solicitor of the High Court of New Zealand in 2012. She practises pro bono in Wellington as well as teaching and researching in the fields of property law and laws of citizenship, migration and refugee status. Caroline was the UK Country Expert for the European University Institute's project on *Acquisition and Loss of Citizenship* (Florence, EUDO, 2009) and conducted the comparative project presented in *Statelessness in the European Union* (Cambridge, Cambridge University Press, 2011) with Brad Blitz. She is currently writing in fields such as succession and deprivation of citizenship.

Krista Nadakavukaren Schefer is Professor of International Law at the University of Basel's Faculty of Law. Previously at the University of Bern and its World Trade Institute, she continues to cooperate with these faculties. She is a member of the research council of the Swiss Network on International Studies (SNIS). Long interested in the intersection of the international economic law regimes and other areas of international law, her recent research has looked at the international regimes of investment and trade law and their interactions with poverty, corruption and human rights. She is also actively pursuing research in the legal implications of obesity and of the commercial uses of drones. A long-time resident of Switzerland, Professor Nadakavukaren is a native of the United States. Having begun undergraduate studies at Wellesley College, she graduated from the University of Chicago. She received her *juris doctor* from Georgetown University Law School, and her doctorate and 'habilitation' from the University of Bern.

Francesco Seatzu, JD (Cagliari), PhD (Nottingham) is a Full Professor of International and European Union Law at the University of Cagliari, Italy. He authored *The UN Committee on Economic, Social and Cultural Rights: The Law, Process and Practice* (with M Odello; Abingdon, Routledge, 2012), *The World Bank Inspection Panel* (Turin, Giappichelli, 2007), *Insurance in Private International Law: A European Perspective* (Oxford, Hart, 2003), and co-edited *Armed Forces and International Jurisdictions* (with M Odello; Antwerp/Cambridge, Intersentia, 2013), *Foreign Investment, International Law and Common Concerns* (with T Treves and S Trevisanut; Abingdon, Routledge, 2013), and *Tradition and Innovation in Private International Law* (with L Pereznieto Castro and T Treves; New York, Juris Publishing, 2005). Professor Seatzu is the author of several articles on public and private international law published in Italy as well as other countries.

Anja Wiesbrock is a Senior Policy Advisor at the Research Council of Norway. She has previously worked as a Researcher at the Department of Private Law, University of Oslo and as an Assistant Professor in European Law at the University of Maastricht. She has also been a Visiting Researcher and Lecturer at several institutions around the world, including Harvard Law School, Jawaharlal Nehru University (New Delhi), Dokuz Eylul University (Izmir), and Universitat Pompeu Fabra (Barcelona). Her main research interests focus on EU free movement law, EU migration law, public procurement, and state aid, and she has published widely in these areas, including her book *Legal Migration to the European Union* (Martinus Nijhoff, 2010) and the edited volume *The Greening of Business under EU Law: Taking Article 11 TFEU Seriously* (Routledge, 2014).

1

Introduction

FRANCESCA IPPOLITO AND SARA IGLESIAS SÁNCHEZ

I. THE NOTION OF VULNERABILITY

VULNERABILITY HAS BEEN described as 'a universal, inevitable, enduring aspect of the human condition'.[1] From this point of view, vulnerability can be considered as an attribute inherent to human nature: individuals are constantly exposed to potential harm (whether intentional or accidental), to the risks of fluctuating circumstances (due to rearrangements in society or merely because of the changes that come with ageing) or to the perspective of being dependent (as a result of innate or acquired disease or disability). Hence vulnerability is a particularly dynamic concept that encompasses, but also transcends, the notions of minority groups.

It is precisely the universality and the different ways in which individuals may be considered vulnerable which make this notion a particularly difficult one to define. Moreover, the fact that a certain level of vulnerability is present in any human life, risks depriving the concept of its utility as an element to which legal consequences can be attached. Therefore, attempts to define vulnerability are often coupled with a narrowing-down of the specific groups of individuals that could be considered 'vulnerable'. As a result, the legal concept of 'vulnerable groups' has emerged, albeit having blurred contours. One of the most successful attempts to provide a comprehensive definition of vulnerable groups is to be found in the Brasilia Regulations Regarding Access to Justice for Vulnerable People:[2]

> Vulnerable people are defined as those who, due to reasons of age, gender, physical or mental state, or due to social, economic, ethnic and/or cultural circumstances, find it especially difficult to fully exercise their rights before the justice system as recognised to them by law. The following may constitute causes of vulnerability: age, disability, belonging to indigenous communities or minorities, victimisation, migration and internal displacement, poverty, gender and deprivation of liberty.

[1] MA Fineman, 'The Vulnerable Subject: Anchoring Equality in the Human Condition' (2008–09) 20 *Yale Journal of Law & Feminism* 1, 8.

[2] 100 Brasilia Regulations Regarding Access to Justice for Vulnerable People, approved by the Plenary Assembly of the Ibero-American Judicial Summit in March 2008, available at: www.osce.org/odihr/68082.

The different aspects and circumstances with regard to which vulnerability can arise that are captured by this definition also find recognition in European law. Indeed, the notion of 'vulnerability' is gradually gaining momentum in the field of fundamental rights protection at the European level, particularly through the case law of the European Court of Human Rights (hereinafter ECtHR) and of the European Social Committee (ESC), and is also present in certain legal instruments of the Council of Europe (CoE) and of the European Union (EU).

In this regard, the clearest manifestation of the notion of vulnerability in European law has taken place in the field of human rights. Taking as the point of departure the fact that vulnerable individuals may find it more difficult to exercise their rights, the CoE has identified, in a number of instruments of a different nature, specific groups of individuals, thereby laying down the foundations for European cooperation in protecting vulnerable groups.[3] In this sense, different documents refer to the vulnerability of certain groups, which comprise irregular migrants,[4] refugees,[5] asylum seekers,[6] environmental migrants and internally displaced persons,[7] children,[8] people experiencing financial problems (such as the unemployed, single-parent families, children, the elderly, as well as Roma, refugees, migrants—especially those in an irregular situation—transgender persons, persons in detention and homeless people),[9] and the socially vulnerable.[10]

[3] See for instance the European Social Charter (revised); the 1995 Framework Convention for the Protection of National Minorities; the 1996 European Convention on the Exercise of Children's Rights; the 2005 Council of Europe Convention on Action against Trafficking in Human Beings; the 2007 Council of Europe Convention on the Protection of Children against Sexual Exploitation and Sexual Abuse; or the 2011 Convention on preventing and combating violence against women and domestic violence. Different monitoring bodies comprise the European Committee of Social Charter; the European Commission against Racism and Intolerance; the Advisory Committee on the Framework Convention for the Protection of National Minorities; the Group of Experts on Action against Trafficking in Human Beings; and the Gender Equality Commission. In the field of rights of the elderly, the works of the 'drafting Group on the Human Rights of Older Persons' can be followed at www.coe.int/t/dghl/standardsetting/hrpolicy/other_committees/cddh-age/default_EN.asp.

[4] Resolution 1509 (2006) Human rights of irregular migrants; Resolution 1918 (2013) Migration and asylum: mounting tensions in the eastern Mediterranean.

[5] Recommendation 1802 (2007) Situation of longstanding refugees and displaced persons in South-Eastern Europe.

[6] Resolution 1637 (2008) Europe's boat people: mixed migration flows by sea into southern Europe.

[7] Recommendation 1862 (2009) Environmentally induced migration and displacement: a 21st-century challenge.

[8] Resolution 1733 (2010) Reinforcing measures against sex offenders; Recommendation 1371 (1998) Abuse and neglect of children.

[9] Resolution 1946 (2013) Equal access to health care.

[10] This last case is particularly salient, since in 2012 the Parliamentary Assembly adopted a resolution on austerity measures, urging the member states of the Council of Europe to 'sign and ratify the revised European Social Charter and the European Convention on Social Security, if this has not yet been done'. In addition, states parties were called upon to 'closely assess current austerity programs from the view-point of their short- and long-term impact on democratic decision-making processes and social rights standards, social security systems and social services to the most vulnerable groups (people with disabilities, migrants, the unemployed, etc)'. Resolution 1884 (2012) Austerity measures—a danger for democracy and social rights §§10.3, 10.6.

The concept of vulnerability is often to be found in the case law of the ECtHR, even if there is still neither a clear-cut definition of vulnerability in the case law, nor an exhaustive determination of the circumstances that give rise to a finding of an element of vulnerability. This notion is present in the case law of the Court with respect to victims of torture,[11] minors,[12] groups that have suffered different treatment on account of their sex,[13] sexual orientation,[14] race or ethnicity,[15] the Roma population,[16] prisoners,[17] applicants for international protection,[18] and people with mental disorders[19] or disabilities.[20] More recently the ECtHR has also recognised the vulnerability of the elderly living in nursing homes,[21] and has taken the applicant's age into account when awarding damages.[22] Furthermore, the Court has also taken into account, when assessing the applicant's suffering, other elements of vulnerability, such as their financial situation, or their possibility of benefiting from medical assistance.[23]

Most significantly, the European Convention on Human Rights (ECHR) has moved beyond the identification of the particular circumstances of vulnerability affecting specific individuals, to recognise the existence of 'particularly vulnerable groups', which entails specific legal consequences, inter alia, in the determination of the margin of appreciation. This collective conception of vulnerability has so far being recognised with regard to Roma, asylum-seekers, people with mental disabilities, and people with HIV.[24] In this regard, the Court has adopted an approach, which takes into account, not only belonging to a minority,[25] but, in particular, the existence of 'a

[11] *Aydin v Turkey* App no 23178/94 (ECtHR, 25 September 1997), para 103.

[12] *V v United Kingdom* App no 24888/94 (ECtHR, 16 December 1999), para 64; *Popov v France* App nos 39472/07 and 39474/07 (ECtHR, 19 January 2012), para 91.

[13] *Abdulaziz, Cabales and Balkandali v United Kingdom* (1985) Series A no 94, paras 70, 78; February, *Burghartz v Switzerland* (1994) Series A no 280-B, para 27.

[14] *Schalk and Kopf v Austria* App no 30141/04 (ECtHR, 22 November 2010), para 97, and *Smith and Grady v United Kingdom* App nos 33985/96 and 33986/96 ECHR 1999–VI, para 90.

[15] *DH and Others v Czech Republic* App no 57325/00 (ECtHR [GC], 13 November 2007), para 182; *Timishev v Russia* App nos 55762/00 and 55974/00 ECHR 2005–XII, para 56.

[16] *DH and others* (n 15), para 176.

[17] *Shamayev and other v Georgia and Russia* App no 36378/02 (ECtHR, 12 April 2005), para 375; *Aswat v United Kingdom* App no 17299/12 (ECtHR, 16 April 2013), para 50; *Zarzycki v Poland* App no 15351/03 (ECtHR, 12 March 2013); *Gülay Çeytin v Turkey* App no 44084/10 (ECtHR, 5 March 2013); *Claes v Belgium* App no 43418/09 (ECtHR, 10 January 2013).

[18] *MSS v Belgium and Greece* App no 30696/09 (ECtHR [GC], 21 January 2011), para 232.

[19] *Keenan v United Kingdom* App no 27229/95 (ECtHR, 3 April 2001), para 111; *Shtukaturov v Russia* App no 44009/05 (ECtHR, 27 March 2008), para 95; *Alajos Kiss v Hungary* App no 38832/06 (ECtHR, 20 May 2010), para 42.

[20] *Glor v Switzerland* App no 13444/04 (ECtHR, 6 November 2009), para 84. *D v United Kingdom* and *N v United Kingdom* App no 26565/05 (ECtHR, 27 May 2008); *Kiyutin against Russia* App no 2700/10 (ECtHR, 10 March 2011), para 74.

[21] *Heinisch v Germany* App no 28274/08 (ECtHR, 21 July 2011), paras 71 and 82.

[22] *Georgel and Georgeta Stoicescu v Romania* App no 9718/03 (ECtHR, 26 July 2011), paras 34 and 61.

[23] ibid, para 80.

[24] See, at length, L Peroni and A Timmer, 'Vulnerable groups: The promise of an emerging concept in European Human Rights Convention law' (2013) 11 *International Journal of Constitutional Law* 1056–85.

[25] See, eg *Chapman v UK* App no 27238/95, ECHR 2000–I, (2001) 33 EHRR 399.

history of prejudice and stigmatisation'. Indeed, the identification of particularly vulnerable groups by the Court relies on a conception of vulnerability that is rooted in a complex interaction of 'broader societal, political, and institutional circumstances'.[26]

In the European Union, the notion of vulnerability appears in various legislative instruments with different consequences, even if there is not an exhaustive determination of the situations which may fall under this notion. In this regard, even though vulnerability as an autonomous and specific notion has only rarely been explicitly framed as a legal criterion in EU law,[27] the notion of vulnerability is implicitly present in many areas of EU competence which directly affect the legal position of individuals. In this regard, from the outset of the European integration project, EU law has enhanced the legal situation of workers, through measures in the field of social policy, has actively protected the rights of EU migrant workers through EU free movement law, and has provided a solid framework for the prohibition of discrimination in different fields. The impact of EU law on the legal situation of vulnerable individuals has been considerably enlarged with the introduction of competences in the area of freedom, security and justice, where the European Union has identified different situations in which vulnerability is taken into account, such as with regard to the victims of crimes,[28] asylum-seekers,[29] trafficked persons[30] and unaccompanied minors.[31] Some of these instruments even provide for a definition of who should be considered to be particularly vulnerable. For example, Directive 2013/33/EU, laying down standards for the reception of applicants for international protection,[32] provides for

[26] See Peroni and Timmer (op cit n 24) 1063.

[27] Eg EU legislation has recognised the particular vulnerability of pregnant women. See Council Directive 92/85/EEC of 19 October 1992 on the introduction of measures to encourage improvements in the safety and health at work of pregnant workers and workers who have recently given birth or are breastfeeding (tenth individual Directive within the meaning of Art 16(1) of Directive 89/391/EEC) [1992] OJ L348/1, which states in its preamble that 'the vulnerability of pregnant workers, workers who have recently given birth or who are breastfeeding makes it necessary for them to be granted the right to maternity leave of at least 14 continuous weeks, allocated before and/or after confinement, and renders necessary the compulsory nature of maternity leave of at least two weeks, allocated before and/or after confinement'.

[28] Case C-105/03 *Pupino* [2005] ECR I-5285 interpreting the Council Framework Decision of 15 March 2001 on the standing of victims in criminal proceedings [2001] OJ L82/1.

[29] See, particularly, the asylum package of 26 June 2013. See also Cases C-411/10 and C-493/10 C-411/10 *NS and others* [2011] ECR I-13905.

[30] Directive 2011/36/EU of the European Parliament and of the Council of 5 April 2011 on preventing and combating trafficking in human beings and protecting its victims, and replacing Council Framework Decision 2002/629/JHA [2011] OJ L101/1–11.

[31] See, inter alia, Council Resolution of 26 June 1997, on unaccompanied minors who are nationals of third countries and the Commission Communication to the European Parliament of 6 May 2010 on the 'Action Plan on Unaccompanied Minors (2010–2014)' COM (2010) 0213. See also Case C-648/11 *MA and others* (judgment of 6 June 2013) EU:C:2013:367, and, as a result of this judgment, the Proposal for a Regulation amending Regulation (EU) 604/2013 as regards determining the member state responsible for examining the application for international protection of unaccompanied minors with no family member, sibling or relative legally present in a member state COM (2014) 382 final.

[32] [2013] OJ L180/96.

a non-exhaustive enumeration, encompassing 'minors, unaccompanied minors, disabled people, elderly people, pregnant women, single parents with minor children, victims of human trafficking, persons with serious illnesses, persons with mental disorders and persons who have been subjected to torture, rape or other serious forms of psychological, physical or sexual violence, such as victims of female genital mutilation'.[33]

Building on this attempt to identify who is regarded as 'vulnerable' under European law, this book covers different groups of individuals and situations which give rise to vulnerability, and looks at how the Council of Europe and the European Union have contributed to the determination of the legal status of 'vulnerable' individuals from different points of view.

II. VULNERABILITY IN EUROPEAN LAW

What is, might be or should be the added value of introducing a perspective of 'vulnerability' into legislation and legal reasoning in the European context? This book analyses both the EU and the Council of Europe approaches to vulnerability, in order to ascertain whether there exists a clear-cut framework or set of criteria to determine which individuals or groups should be considered to be vulnerable and disadvantaged, and what is the impact of such vulnerability on the policy approaches and on the legal reasoning of both organisations. For this purpose, the different methods used to determine the levels of protection afforded by the two systems are analysed with the aim of ascertaining whether the combined actions of the different actors in the framework of the Council of Europe and of the EU enhance the protection of vulnerable groups and expand the protection of their rights in a significant manner, or whether they only tend to fill in relatively minor gaps or the occasional lapses in national rights guarantees.

Our collective effort to examine the European law approaches to the notion of vulnerability has been organised in five different parts, which attempt to provide an account of the progressive 'vulnerabilisation' of European law, relying on the root causes of vulnerability. The first part examines some of the classic groups traditionally regarded as vulnerable, encompassing broad groups whose innate or physical characteristics make them socially perceived as 'inherently' vulnerable. The second part focuses on groups whose vulnerability derives from their status as a minority by reference to the dominant cultural, social, ethnical or sexual orientation positions of their society of reference. The third part considers vulnerability from the point of view of the legal position awarded by states to non-nationals—ranging from those deprived of any nationality and those who cannot avail themselves of the protection of their state of nationality, to those awarded the highest level of protection as citizens of the European Union. The

[33] Art 21 of Directive 2013/33/EU of 26 June 2013 laying down standards for the reception of applicants for international protection (recast).

fourth part covers those situations of vulnerability that arise out of intentional human conduct, turning an individual into a victim (trafficked migrants, victims of crime and victims of terrorism). The fifth part covers three very different groups: prisoners/detainees, irregular immigrants, and socially vulnerable people. Despite the obvious differences among these groups, the reason that brings them together is the fact that their vulnerability is contingent upon circumstantial elements that may well be temporary, and which are often imposed by state-created or social conditions. Additionally, despite their undeniable vulnerability, their need for protection is sometimes countered in the political and legal discourses by the perception that individual choice has somehow contributed to their own position (either because they have committed criminal offences or because they have disregarded the applicable migration rules, or because of failure to achieve social inclusion).

Part I: Inherent Vulnerability

Children, the elderly, the disabled and women are illustrative of individuals who by their innate or physical conditions are socially construed as 'inherently vulnerable'. Children, together with older people, are arguably a group of the population that is distinguished from the rest merely because of their age. The quality of being a 'child' or 'elderly', however, is culturally and geographically relative, and dependent on average life expectancy, life style, etc. In both cases, the vulnerability of age groups is rooted in their disproportionate need of support from family or the state. However, their dependency varies according to their progressive development and autonomy (when reference is made to children), or according to the different phases of ageing (according to what Article 23 of the European Social Charter describes as the specific needs of elderly persons).[34] This distinguishing element, together with the fact that the experience of youth and old age can be very different depending on 'gender, race and class', and the fact that the elderly might also be a particularly powerful group in society, with a larger

[34] Art 23 ESC provides that 'With a view to ensuring the effective exercise of the right of elderly persons to social protection, the Parties undertake to adopt or encourage, either directly or in co-operation with public or private organisations, appropriate measures designed in particular:

- to enable elderly persons to remain full members of society for as long as possible, by means of:
  - a) adequate resources enabling them to lead a decent life and play an active part in public, social and cultural life;
  - b) provision of information about services and facilities available for elderly persons and their opportunities to make use of them;
- to enable elderly persons to choose their life-style freely and to lead independent lives in their familiar surroundings for as long as they wish and are able, by means of:
  - a) provision of housing suited to their needs and their state of health or of adequate support for adapting their housing;
  - b) the health care and the services necessitated by their state;
- to guarantee elderly persons living in institutions appropriate support, while respecting their privacy, and participation in decisions concerning living conditions in the institution.'

share of political power,[35] makes both categories 'internally heterogeneous'. As a conceptual consequence, there is no clear categorisation of both age groups either as vulnerable individuals, or as genuinely vulnerable 'groups' within the context of ECtHR case law.

Within this framework, **Ippolito** deconstructs, in her chapter, the concept of vulnerability when applied to children because of their inherent and intrinsic inability to secure protection of their own rights. She identifies the constitutive elements of the notion of vulnerability as interpreted and constructed in both the Council of Europe and the European Union protection systems. The first element has been recognised in respect of children's financial and care dependency on parents/family, which serves as the basis for derivative rights in European Union (EU) law and for the enlargement of the spectrum of the notion of family life under Article 8 ECHR. This element is combined with the child's limited—but gradated—autonomy, which reflects the distinction between the ownership of rights and the capacity to act, recognising that children have a progressive capacity to exercise their rights as a consequence of their condition as individuals in development. Ippolito's chapter stresses a certain degree of convergence between the EU and the Council of Europe in such legal constructions. This convergence is equally visible as regards the practical effects produced by the conceptualisation of children's vulnerability in European law, being functional to a correction of the model of formal equality, and to the elaboration of special guarantees and positive—procedural and substantial—obligations upon states parties, paying particular attention to those children who 'may be *especially vulnerable* to experiencing disparities in the enjoyment of their rights'.[36]

From a complementary standpoint, **Seatzu** considers in his chapter the vulnerability of the elderly. This chapter focuses mainly on the EU level where, until 2000, when the Charter of Fundamental Rights of the European Union was approved, the rights of the elderly were neglected by the law and policy of the European Union; older persons were not considered specifically relevant to the EU's most fundamental economic and political aims. Rather, policy and legal provisions addressing the elderly have evolved as something of an afterthought: a secondary or an additional product of more non-older-adult-focused EU social law and policy. Nonetheless, the period since 2000 has seen something of a sea change in the elderly's rights at EU level, culminating in 2010 with the publication of the European Charter of the Rights and Responsibilities of Older People in Need of Long-Term Care and Assistance by the EUSTACEA Project, 'A European Strategy to fight elder abuse'. By complementing and supporting the charters and other measures which are already implemented in some countries of the European Union, this Charter sets out an innovative and complex new agenda for the future of EU activity in the field of the elderly's rights, an agenda that would build upon

[35] Gerontocracy has been described as government by the elderly, and there is some truth in the notion that many societies are governed by their most senior members.

[36] Report of the UN Committee of the Rights of the Child, A/57/41 New York 2002, para 41, para 41.

the EU's existing *acquis* across a wide range of areas, and that would aim to incorporate the elderly's rights issues into all aspects of the EU regulatory framework. The idea is to ascertain the extent of the EU's forthcoming duties to comply with international human rights standards (in particular the UN Principles on the Rights of Older Person), and to assess the extent to which this jurisprudence has been (or could be) used to inform judicial interpretations of EU old age law and policy, with the aim of enhancing the EU's ability to boost and uphold the elderly's rights and liberties more efficiently. According to Seatzu the main value of the integration of such standards into the rights of the elderly is to overcome the current problem of the absence of any clear ideological frame of reference in the new-found EU agenda for the rights of the elderly. More specifically, EU old age law and policy lack consistent and persuasive allegiance to the international elderly rights principles as embodied in different international instruments. This, it is maintained, has given rise to conflicting indications on the currency of the rights of the elderly at the EU level and their vulnerability in being overlooked in the face of concurrent economic and political goals.

While, together with the elderly, the disabled and women are socially constructed categories whose disadvantage emanates more from social treatment than from inherent deficiencies or differences, this does not seem to be the approach resulting from both European systems. Indeed, according to the case law of the Court of Justice of the European Union (CJEU), even if the notion of 'handicap' is interpreted by referring to the concept of disability under the UN Convention (covering a limitation which results in particular from physical, mental or psychological impairments and which hinders the participation of the person concerned in professional life),[37] its effects have been confined to the possibility for the person to work or develop a professional activity.[38] In this regard, **Wiesbrock** suggests that the CJEU has sacrificed the interests of persons with disabilities, limiting their protection to the context of market participation and employment. The distinction between the capable 'average' market participant and the 'vulnerable' person with a disability is based on stereotypical categories associated with the emergence of protective policies as a 'spill-over' from the internal market. In this regard, the scenario is not much different when we turn our attention to the Council of Europe where, even though the ECtHR has recognised persons with mental disabilities as a particularly vulnerable group deserving special protection, case law demonstrates deference to national sovereignty and a reluctance to rely specifically on the intellectual disability of the applicant when it comes to finding a violation under the ECHR. As a result, it appears that neither of the two legal regimes succeed in providing successful and adequate means of tackling the special vulnerability of persons with disabilities. Indeed, according to Wiesbrock, although the concept of vulnerability opens up a number of opportunities for enhancing the protection

[37] Joined Cases C-335/11 and C-337/11 *HK Danmark* (CJEU, 11 April 2013) confirmed in Case C-312/11 *Commission v Italy* (CJEU, 4 July 2013).

[38] Case C-363/12 *Z v A Government Department* (CJEU, 18 March 2014).

of persons with disabilities in Europe, a close scrutiny of EU and CoE law reveals that the concept has major inherent difficulties that may in fact exacerbate the marginalisation of such people.

An analogous precarious and still inadequate form of protection through the concept of vulnerability emerges when women are considered. It is clear that the vulnerability of women does not in any way arise out the patriarchal falsehood that they are biologically inferior. Vulnerability here is conceived as 'inherent' on the premise that woman remain particularly exposed to specific violations such as gender-based violence, trafficking and sex discrimination. The series of instruments which have been specifically developed at universal and regional levels for the protection of women, the elimination of discrimination against women and the promotion of equal rights are clear evidence of such forms of gender vulnerability. The Convention on the Elimination of All Forms of Discrimination against Women (CEDAW) and its Optional Protocol, together with the revised European Social Charter and Article 14 ECHR, combat any 'distinction' based, inter alia, on grounds of sex, in relation to the rights protected under the Conventions but also in relation to any right set forth by law (Protocol 12 ECHR). Furthermore, the UN Convention for the Suppression of the Traffic in Persons and of the Exploitation of the Prostitution of Others (1949), as well as the various Conventions of relevance to women concluded within the framework of the ILO[39] and Article 7 of the Rome Statute of the International Criminal Court (1998), aim to protect women from the sexual violence to which they are especially exposed (ie, rape, sexual slavery, enforced prostitution, forced pregnancy, enforced sterilisation and other forms of sexual violence, each considered to be a crime against humanity). **Fines** addresses both these aspects of gender discrimination and gender abuse (physical or psychological, rape, genital mutilation, harassment, sexual exploitation, prostitution, pimping) highlighting a growing and converging involvement of European organisations in that direction. Starting from EU law, Fines traces the historical evolution of European intervention from solely the economic sphere,[40] to the recognition of a fundamental right of equality between women and men enshrined in both CJEU case law and the Charter of Fundamental Rights of the European Union, and to the increasing actions in the fight against violence

[39] ILO 3 (1919) and ILO 103 (revision of ILO 3, 1952) concerning Maternity Protection, providing for 12 weeks' maternity leave during which women shall be entitled to financial benefits and medical care and may not be dismissed; ILO 45 (1935) concerning Underground Work by Women in Mines; ILO 89 (1948) (to which a Protocol was added in 1990) concerning Night Work by Women in Industrial Employment; ILO 100 (1951) concerning Equal Remuneration for Men and Women Workers for Work of Equal Value, which seeks to eliminate forms of discrimination based solely on gender; ILO 102 (1952) concerning Minimum Standards of Social Security, which contains regulations for all areas of social security, including maternity benefits; ILO 111 (1958) concerning Discrimination in Respect of Employment and Occupation, which provides a definition of discrimination; ILO 156 (1981), known as the Workers with Family Responsibilities Convention, on equal opportunities and equal treatment for men and women workers; and ILO 183 (2000) Maternity Protection Convention.

[40] Case C-450/93 *E Kalanke* (ECJ, 17 October 1995); Case C-409/95 *H Marschall* (CJEU, 11 November 1997).

towards women, particularly in developing new legal tools relating to the area of freedom, security and justice. The chapter then looks at the CoE system, examining the recent Convention adopted in 2011 which specifically deals with preventing and combating violence against women and domestic violence, requiring states to promote a series of concrete actions to bring real help to women who are victims of violence; and the ECtHR's judicial practices in successful rape cases, in particular when committed by state agents, or domestic violence against women and the issue of therapeutic abortion.

Part II: Minorities

International law does not provide a uniform definition of the term 'minority'. According to the definition provided in 1977 by the Special Rapporteur of the UN Sub-Commission on the Prevention of Discrimination and Protection of Minorities, a minority is '[a] group numerically inferior to the rest of the population, in a non-dominant position, ... possessing distinct ethnic, religious or linguistic characteristics and showing a sense of solidarity aimed at preserving those characteristics'.[41] Indeed, the international recognition of the need for the protection of minorities emanates not only from their relatively inferior number with regard to the dominant group, but from the fact that there are some characteristics of minoritary communities which deserve protection, preservation and promotion.

In this regard, the protection of minorities in Europe has a long tradition and is often considered a precursor to the emergence of human rights instruments, particularly with the treaties adopted after the First World War.[42] In this regard, the Permanent Court of International Justice stated in 1935 that the underlying idea of the protection of minorities is precisely 'to secure for certain elements incorporated in a State, the population of which differs from them in race, language or religion, the possibility of living peaceably alongside that population and cooperating amicably with it, while at the same time preserving the characteristics which distinguish them from the majority, and satisfying the ensuing special needs'.[43] The consequence of this finding was twofold: the need 'to ensure that nationals belonging to racial, religious or linguistic minorities shall be placed in every respect on a footing of perfect equality with the other nationals of the State' and the need to 'ensure for the minority elements suitable means for the preservation of their racial peculiarities, their traditions and their national characteristics'.[44]

[41] F Capotorti, 'Study on the Rights of Persons Belonging to Ethnic, Religious and Linguistic Minorities', (1977) UN Doc E/CN.4/Sub.2/384/Rev.1: Sales No E.78XIV.1, para 568. Published by the UN in 1991 (New York, United Nations, 1991).

[42] Josef L Kunz, 'The Present Status of the International Law for the Protection of Minorities' (1954) 48 *The American Journal of International Law*, 282–87.

[43] *Minority Schools in Albania*, Advisory Opinion, 6 April 1935, Series A/B, fascicule 60.

[44] ibid.

Nonetheless, the determination of the elements that deserve such protection remains a debated issue nowadays, as the multiple declarations attached to the CoE Framework Convention for the Protection of National Minorities make apparent. The tension between the efforts to protect the culture, traditions and identities of minorities, while at the same time ensuring the equal treatment of all nationals and the territorial integrity of states, is one element that cannot be ignored.

At the European level, the CoE Framework Convention for the Protection of National Minorities (1994) is the most comprehensive international instrument dealing specifically with minority protection. Another instrument in the CoE framework worth mentioning with regard to the protection of minorities is the European Charter for Regional or Minority Languages (1992) whose purpose is to protect languages 'that are traditionally used within a given territory of a State by nationals of that State who form a group numerically smaller than the rest of the State's population; and different from the official languages of that State'.[45] Moreover, although there is no minority rights provision in the ECHR, and the proposal for a new protocol to the Convention providing for these rights was hampered by the lack of consensus among states in 1993, many articles of the ECHR can be resorted to in connection with minority issues, such as: Article 5 (liberty and security of person), Article 8 (privacy and family life), Article 10 (freedom of association), Article 11 (freedom of peaceful assembly and association) and Article 2 First Protocol (education). Furthermore, Article 14, which precludes discrimination in the enforcement of Convention rights and must be read together with other Convention provisions, might represent a legal basis for such claims, together with Article 34 which confers standing to groups, as well as to individuals and NGOs, to submit claims before the Court.

With regard to the European Union, the Treaty of the European Union (TEU), after the reform of Lisbon, situates the 'respect for human rights, including the rights of persons belonging to minorities' as one of the common values to the member states, which are enumerated in Article 2 of the Treaty. Moreover, Article 3 TEU states that the Union 'shall respect its rich cultural and linguistic diversity, and shall ensure that Europe's cultural heritage is safeguarded and enhanced'. Nonetheless, despite this relevant mention in the TEU, the Charter of Fundamental Rights of the EU has failed to explicitly recognise minority rights. Despite this absence, the Charter is undoubtedly a relevant legal instrument, in that it mandates respect for linguistic, cultural and religious diversity, and prohibits discrimination on the grounds of race, social or ethnic origin, language, religion or belief, and membership of a national minority. In any case, the Union has only a limited capacity to act in the field of the protection of minorities within the framework of its enumerated

[45] Art 1.

powers,[46] and often, the attention has to be directed to the several policies that may indirectly affect minorities in different manners.[47]

Against this background, **Dubos and Guset** analyse the framework protection of languages put forward by the unique mechanism of the Charter for Regional Minority Languages. The protection of linguistic minorities in this instrument seems to serve the primary purpose of protecting the languages themselves. Since those can only be protected by protecting their speakers, the prevailing objective approach poses important challenges to determine the territorial and personal scope of application. In the framework of the EU, the relevance of protecting languages emerges at different levels. The protection of official languages has been recognised as an overriding interest of public interest and can be regarded as an element appertaining to the 'constitutional identity', now explicitly recognised by Article 4(2) TEU. Nonetheless, the authors put forward that this approach can also serve as a justification to protect one official language at the expenses of being unfavourable to regional or minority languages. Moreover, the EU plays a modest role in the promotion of regional and minority languages, which is a task mostly entrusted to the states. Finally, the Union has also recognised language rights of speakers, even though the Union's linguistic pluralism induces a situation of unequal treatment between minority languages. All in all, and despite the differences in both systems, the authors identify a common threat: the desire to preserve the cultural diversity that is considered a core value in Europe.

Ahmed focuses her analysis on one of the most visible vulnerable minority groups in Europe—the Roma community. Her chapter explores the European Union's legal and policy measures applicable to improving the prospects of the economic and social protection of Roma in EU member states. In minority rights terms, these goals bring into play, inter alia, the right to non-discrimination, the right to cultural identity, and economic and social integration into society. They highlight that the protection of minorities concerns the goals of both (i) integrating Roma into their states of residence, and (ii) protecting the identity of those Roma to enable them to continue their traditional cultural practices. The chapter then explores how EU law serves these purposes. Anti-discrimination is one of the strongest legal domains of EU law, offering protection against discrimination in various situations, within and outside the employment context. These provisions are explored in depth, together with the fields of cultural and social policy. The recent emphasis on protection of Roma within the EU mirrors the developing ECHR case law on Roma rights, and illustrates that both jurisdictions view belonging to the Roma community as a justification for tailored measures to be aimed at the group. The ECHR case law holds significance for the EU, in light of both the fact that the ECHR is a standard-setter for EU law and the imminent

[46] B de Witte, 'The Constitutional Resources for an EU Minority Protection Policy', in GN von Toggenburg (ed), *Minority Protection and the Enlarged European Union* (Budapest, OSI, 2004) 118–23.

[47] D Kochenov, 'EU Minority Protection: A Modest Case for a Synergetic Approach' (2011) 3 *Amsterdam Law Forum* 33–53.

accession of the EU to the ECHR. Nonetheless, the author remains sceptical as to the accomplishments of both organisations in the actual outcomes, putting forward the need for a better engagement in the domestic arena.

As regards indigenous peoples, **Beqiraj**'s chapter discusses the engagement of the EU and the CoE. Even if both organisations have traditionally dedicated little attention to indigenous human rights issues, these having being considered of lesser social and political concern in comparison with other national, ethnic or linguistic minorities, there is a considerable emergence of indigenous rights as a European issue, particularly, due to the impact of climate change in the Arctic. In this regard, the vulnerability of indigenous peoples is reflected in the lack of legal, social or political mechanisms suitable to effectively assure the full enjoyment of their social, cultural and political rights. The author departs from an analysis of the scope and variety of the instruments and procedures available at the European level, with particular focus on the perspective of the right to cultural identity, which is considered to be a prerequisite for the enjoyment of other relevant rights such as the right to land, the right to access to and use of natural resources, the right to non-discrimination or the right to economic and social developments. EU policy on the Arctic is in the spotlight, and Beqiraj posits the 'seals case' as a paradigmatic example of the challenges in the protection of indigenous rights in Europe, as it sheds light on the substantial and procedural protection gaps for indigenous peoples within both the EU and the ECHR systems.

Howard's chapter focuses on the protection accorded by the EU and the Council of Europe to religious minorities in Europe, highlighting that their vulnerability is compounded by the fact that, due to their tendency to manifest their beliefs more openly and publicly, they are easily identifiable, and are vulnerable to becoming the target of discrimination and of anti-religious, anti-immigrant or anti-foreigner attitudes. This chapter examines the legal protection of EU law and of the ECHR to religious minorities via the guarantees of the right to freedom of religion and via the prohibition of discrimination on the grounds of religion or beliefs. The author concludes from the examination of the case law of the ECtHR that there has been an evolution towards a higher level of protection, which may also prove influential in the EU arena. In this field, the interpretation of Article 4(2) of Directive 2000/78 may prove to be a key aspect, in that it allows room for churches and other organisations to protect their religious ethos.

After conceptualising sexual minorities as a vulnerable group, **Ducouloumbier** presents the legal corpus of protection of sexual minorities by the European Union and the Council of Europe, analysing the different components of the protective legal framework and the specific case law of both European courts. Departing from the recognition of sexual orientation and gender identity as key aspects of one's self, the author focuses on the protective approach afforded to gender minorities through the prism of non-discrimination law. The protection of sexual minorities in the framework of the protection of family rights is also a central theme. In this regard, the chapter explores the approaches of both the CJEU and the ECtHR to unmarried couples, to homosexual marriage and to adoption.

Part III: Non-Nationals

The fact of being present in a state which is not the state of one's own nationality has been openly perceived as an element of vulnerability at the international level. The UN General Assembly highlights in this regard 'the situation of vulnerability in which migrants frequently find themselves, owing, inter alia, to their absence from their State of origin and to the difficulties they encounter because of differences of language, custom and culture'.[48] In the extra-European regional context, the Inter-American Court of Human Rights has advanced in this sense, basing this vulnerability on the fact that non-nationals 'are in an individual situation of absence or difference of power with regard to non-migrants (nationals or residents) … [leading] to the establishment of differences in their access to the public resources administered by the State'.[49] In this scenario, the third part of this book engages with the different approaches to the vulnerability of non-nationals, ranging from those who lack nationality de facto or de jure, asylum-seekers, or climate-displaced persons, to the more privileged group of European citizens.

Whilst citizenship is a fundamental aspect of modern life representing 'the individual's status in organised society,' attribution of citizenship varies amongst countries and some people are born without entitlement to citizenship of any state; others are non-nationals. **Sawyer**'s chapter deals with statelessness in the European context. Most countries attribute citizenship to stateless persons born in their territory, following the Convention on the Reduction of Statelessness, but the phenomenon of statelessness is nonetheless growing with the increasing loss of the *jus soli,* or birthright citizenship. Moreover, there exists the more pressing problem of the de facto stateless—those who have a claim to citizenship, but not of the country in which they live (and maybe only in a country to which they have never been), and of those who have an irregular status in that country. In particular, the author points out that the ECHR does not contain a right to nationality, though recent developments suggest that the right to the development of a private life may extend that far at least in limited circumstances. In any case, the limitations imposed by the ECHR on the deprivation of citizenship are weak. With regard to the situation in the European Union, it is certain that strong rights are afforded to Union citizens: EU citizenship, even if it is not citizenship in the traditional sense, is of the highest value, since it provides for the right to work and to make a life. Nonetheless, the fact that those rights are determined by reference to the citizens of the member states leaves it to each state to exercise its sovereign right to define its members, meaning that the EU itself has no direct control over who its citizens are. In this regard, the author unveils the existence of an 'unexpected precariat'. Reminding us that de jure and de facto statelessness have never left Europe completely, the author

[48] Resolution A/RES/54/166 of 24 February 2000 on 'Protection of migrants'.

[49] Advisory Opinion on Juridical Condition and Rights of the Undocumented Migrants, OC-18/03 (IACrtHR, 17 September 2003) 112.

points to the destructive effect of a hypothetical reshaping of European policy towards free movement and immigration, which could entail that many people with 'well-established European lives outside their country do not necessarily have the stability of status they may believe they have'.

Asylum-seekers who seek protection in a member state of the European Union, for as long as their status is not yet determined, are in a particularly vulnerable position. This goes for their entry into the territory, for the phase until their application is formally declared admissible, and continues during the determination procedure. Moreover, the Reception Conditions Directive, in its recast 2103 version, introduces additional guarantees to the general standards of the EU asylum acquis, with the aim of ensuring the special treatment of particularly vulnerable applicants, in light of the case law of the CJEU. Nonetheless, the definition of which categories of applicants are particularly vulnerable is still vague: according to Article 2(k), applicants with special reception needs are 'vulnerable persons … in need of special guarantees in order to benefit from the rights and comply with the obligations provided for in this Directive'.[50] **Brandl and Czech** analyse such a renewed attention to vulnerable categories of asylum-seekers in EU law with the aim of comparing it with the recently established asylum-seekers' vulnerability as a group-centred concept within the Council of Europe. In particular, the chapter analyses the reasons for the recognition of such vulnerability, and highlights the importance attached to cases where the general vulnerability is aggravated by personal circumstances such as age or ill-health. Additionally, persons in need of international protection often do also belong to another vulnerable group, such as mentally or physically disabled persons, or ethnic minorities, which suffer from stigmatisation and prejudice. The interaction of the two European systems is highlighted as a tool for a higher level of protection for vulnerable individuals seeking protection in Europe.

The same EU asylum protection framework—in its Qualification Directive which introduces forms of subsidiary protection to the refugee status and in the Temporary Protection Directive—also provides a partial response to the special vulnerability of those who are susceptible to, and unable to respond, adapt and cope with, the adverse impacts of climate change. As **Chassin** highlights, though such climate-induced migrants cannot be qualified as refugees according to the 1951 Geneva Convention, the best option at present to provide them with adequate protection is to refer to the international human rights framework. Discarding the proposed option of a dedicated international Convention, which might create more difficulties than solutions, because of the genuine risks of contradicting the existing Human Rights Conventions and aggravating the vulnerability of the affected population, Chassin proposes to use both the ECHR and Directive 2001/55/CE to provide a first solution, even though neither text specifically aims to tackle the situation of such individuals.

[50] Art 21 explicitly refers to the guarantees for these persons.

The last chapter of the third part analyses the situation of the most privileged kind of non-nationals—citizens of the EU—who may still find themselves facing vulnerability despite the generally acknowledged fact that EU citizenship has overcome the division between citizens and aliens. Indeed, the free movement of persons within the European Union is a fundamental right granted to the citizens of the Union directly by the Treaty and fine-tuned by 40 years of case law of the Court of Justice. In this regard, the central element, Directive 2004/38/EC, lays down the administrative formalities that the citizens of the Union have to comply with when they move from one member state to another. This instrument also strikes a fair balance between the right of the individual to enjoy security of residence, and the interests of states to have an exact knowledge of population movements in their territory, to protect public order, public security and public health, and to avoid an unreasonable burden on their social assistance systems. Against this background, the aim of **Lang**'s contribution is to examine the conditions of the free movement of persons who are not 'standard' European Union citizens. For this purpose, the first section of the chapter discusses the right of residence for those who do not fall into the categories provided for by the directive. The second section explores the issue of the security of residence of the 'standard European Union citizens' when they lose their status, for instance because they become unable to work. Particular attention is devoted to third country family members, in the case of divorce, departure, or death of the European Union citizen they depend on. The final and third section is devoted to the issue of how to fill the unavoidable gaps of the directive and to discuss the current status of EU free movement law as an adequate tool to address the situation of vulnerable people.

Part IV: Victims of Illegal Acts

The term 'vulnerable' has often been associated with the category of 'victims', intending to refer to a person 'who is unusually vulnerable due to age, physical or mental condition, or who is otherwise particularly susceptible to criminal conduct'.[51] This marks a strong convergence between the categories encompassed by this group and the ones described as 'inherently vulnerable' persons. Indeed, the analysis relating to the latter often focuses on the particular exposure to abuse and exploitation of children, the elderly, women and the disabled,[52] particularly in times of economic recession and restructuring, armed conflict, episodes of mass violence, major disasters, or even seasonal variation and migration. Article 3 of the

[51] *Sandra Janković v Croatia* App no 38478/05 ECHR 2009; and *X and Y v Netherlands* App no 8978/80 (1985) 8 EHRR 235. See also Judy Pearsall and Patrick Hanks (eds), *New Oxford Dictionary of English* (Oxford, Oxford University Press, 2001).

[52] See in particular how the ECtHR recognised the duty to prosecute people who do abuse vulnerable adults (*AX and Y v The Netherlands* (1985) and *Sandra Jankovic v Croatia* (2009)).

Trafficking Protocol incorporates a consideration of the exposure to exploitation when it provides as part of the definition of trafficking the 'abuse of ... a position of vulnerability',[53] deriving from 'conditions' or factors such as age and gender, together with poverty, social and cultural exclusion, political instability, war and conflicts, and forced displacement without traditional protection mechanisms. In this regard, **Mitsilegas**'s chapter looks at the evolution of European Union legislation on the rights of the victims of crime and examines the synergy between European Union law and European human rights law in this field. The development of the legal framework is examined from both a constitutional and a human rights perspective. From a constitutional perspective, the chapter evaluates the development of substantive standards in light of the evolving and complex constitutional framework on EU criminal law and assesses whether the insertion of a specific legal basis for legislation on victims' rights in the Treaty of Lisbon (Article 82(2) TFEU) has made a substantial impact on the rights of victims of crime. Such an analysis of the impact of European law on the rights of the victims, and also on other actors in the criminal justice system such as the defendants, from a human rights perspective is pivotal in determining whether victims' rights entail a rebalancing of the concept of criminal justice in Europe. In this light, the increased prominence of victims' interests in the criminal justice system has profound implications for the relationship between the individual and the state on the one hand, and the relationship between various categories of individuals in the criminal justice process on the other.

Victims of terrorism, a 'sophisticated form of transnational crime that poses a threat to all nations', constitute a specific category of victims of crimes. Indeed, as **Almqvist** states, their special multidimensional vulnerability stems in part from the mass destruction context in which their victimisation occurs, making it more difficult to attend to the particular needs and interests of each of them in an individualised manner. Another relevant fact is that victims of terrorism are never the real targets of terrorist acts, since the killing and harming of innocent people is instrumental to inducing general fear and to punishing governments for their actions and policies. In this sense, their status as victims of political violence makes them vulnerable to the politicisation of their suffering, transforming it into a political argument about the need to be tough on terrorism, resorting to extrajudicial measures, which infringe fundamental freedoms and liberties. Finally, their vulnerability is also the result of the media attention that the effects of terrorist acts usually receive, which may intrude on their right to privacy. Taking this reality into account, Almqvist scrutinises the European efforts made to remedy the situation, focusing on the CoE 2005 Convention on the Prevention of Terrorism, on the Guidelines on the Protection of Victims of Terrorist Acts adopted by the Committee of Ministers of the CoE, and on its Recommendation

[53] See the note on Art 3 subpara (a) of the Trafficking Protocol in the *travaux préparatoires* (A/55/383/Add 1, para 63).

(2006) 8, on assistance to crime victims, which contains a specific reference to the victims of terrorism. She further analyses both the OSCE responses and the EU approach according to which victims of terrorism are broadly defined as 'victims of crime' in pursuance of the EU Framework Decision of 2001 on the standing of victims in criminal proceedings. Nevertheless, no common EU victim of terrorism policy that overcomes the differences between the national legal systems of victim compensation exists yet; in addition, there is no consensus on how to deal with compensation claims, and most of the initiatives are relegated to *soft law* instruments. Moreover, the European approach to victims of terrorism does not sufficiently consider that criminal justice can fail depending on the nature of the criminal act. The right of legal standing and participation for victims in criminal proceedings becomes next to meaningless in cases where it is especially difficult, if not practically impossible, to bring the actual perpetrators of the crimes to justice. In light of these findings, it is suggested that European law and policy can benefit from the insights of contemporary international policy recommendations related to victims of gross violations of human rights.

Finally, **Ríos Rodríguez** examines the case of victims of trafficking and smuggling in light of the tension existing between the interest of states to control their borders and protect their sovereignty on the one hand, and the international protection of human rights on the other. The author posits that some achievements are common both to the European Union with Directive 2011/36/EU and to the judicial protection afforded by the ECtHR, which goes beyond the formal differences between the offenses of smuggling and trafficking, and tries to adopt a unified approach to both phenomena to better fight them. However, a real willingness of states to properly implement international instruments at their disposal, progressively incorporating the positive obligations coming from international jurisprudence, is still far away from being realised.

Part V: Circumstantial Vulnerability

The fifth and last part of this book explores the legal impact of European law on the situation of those whose vulnerability is determined by particular and even temporary circumstances. The socially vulnerable, prisoners and irregular migrants are groups that possibly cannot be brought together in terms of their situations and root causes of their vulnerability. However, and despite the obvious and striking differences among these groups, there is an additional element that exacerbates their vulnerability: the fact that in the foundation of their vulnerable status there exists a perceived element of individual choice or individual failure leads to an erratic response and a general lack of concern and sensitivity on the part of public authorities towards their situation. Indeed, despite the undeniable vulnerability resulting from their situation, their need for protection is sometimes countered in the political and legal discourses by the perception that individual choice has somehow contributed to their position, either because they have committed criminal offences, because they have disregarded the applicable migration rules, or because of a failure to achieve social inclusion and success in an economic system which is progressively distancing itself from the pre-existing European social model. This entails that states may not only remain inactive towards their vulnerability, but also that their situations of vulnerability may have been created or worsened by state action.

Incarcerated prisoners are particularly vulnerable to violation of their basic rights and human dignity. Indeed, despite their detention being within the law, there may be a general reluctance on behalf of the state and the general public to offer them conditions which care appropriately for their health and well-being. Against this background, **Foster**'s chapter examines the various agencies and instruments responsible for ensuring basic prison conditions. Focusing on the case law of the ECtHR, the chapter analyses how that jurisprudence, and the general protection of detainees from inhuman and degrading prison conditions, can be enhanced by reliance on various judicial and monitoring processes, and by a higher profile for the issue of substandard prison conditions, which it is hoped will be provided by the EU. Nonetheless, the author highlights that the effective judicial challenge to inhuman and degrading conditions in Europe is still inconsistent and limited. Indeed, on the one hand, regulatory schemes are not, directly, at least, legally binding, and are only taken into consideration by judicial bodies to a limited extent. On the other hand, protection through the courts can only be useful with respect to the specific cases brought before them, and therefore, its role on standard-setting and education is limited.

Nadakavukaren Schefer examines poverty—whether absolute or relative, extreme or threatened—propelled by the effects of the recent global financial crisis. Poverty is a cause of, a contributor to, and an effect of most of the other social vulnerabilities found in communities around the world. In this sense, after providing an account of the notions and of the factual reality of poverty and social vulnerability in Europe, the author engages in the analysis of the existing instruments at hand for the protection of individuals with low incomes. In this regard, the author focuses on the potential of the European Union to improve the conditions of social equality through the different available policy instruments. The case law of the ECtHR with regard to poverty, and the consequences of this case law, are further examined. From the analysis of both approaches in European law, the author concludes that an approach centred upon the notion of 'income deprivation', rather than on the concept of 'social exclusion', would avoid the risk of potential denigration assumptions, particularly in the current economic scenario. Indeed, as the author rightly asserts, '[t]oday's income poor may not be undereducated, they may not be untrained, and most importantly, they may not be socially excluded'.

The last chapter, by **Iglesias Sánchez**, is devoted to the legal status of foreign nationals who find themselves undocumented and therefore irregularly present in the country in which they reside. Even though undocumented migrants could be considered from the perspective of vulnerability attached to the lack of *nationality* of the state of residence, the particularity of irregular migrants is precisely the fact that the state is the actor that creates their vulnerability, establishing legal differentiations able to deprive individuals of status and rights on the basis of their administrative situation. Despite this reality, the notion of vulnerability is struggling to make its way in European law as a legal concept with concrete legal ramifications with regard to irregular migrants. In the framework of the CoE, the legal consequences of the vulnerability of irregular migrants in the case law of the ECtHR seem to remain under construction. The most advanced approach towards an autonomous role of irregular status as an element of vulnerability appears in the framework of the European Social Committee, in which it has been used to ensure the relevance of the most fundamental rights of the Charter to immigrants in an irregular situation, overcoming the limitations of scope of application of the ESC. In the framework of the EU, the absolute focus of the EU migration policy continues to be the objective of 'fighting illegal migration', and has so far prevented the emergence of a general and comprehensive EU approach towards the legal status of irregular migrants. This debate seems still to be ongoing in both organisations. In this sense, the inspiration provided by the Council of Europe's approach may indeed overcome the view that the predominant objective of the 'fight' against irregular migration as an undesirable phenomenon prevents any possibility of actively regulating the status of irregular migrants.

I

Inherent Vulnerability

2

(De)Constructing Children's Vulnerability under European Law

FRANCESCA IPPOLITO

I. INTRODUCTION: AGE AS AN 'INHERENT' VULNERABILITY

IF WE CONSIDER the concept of vulnerability as based on its root causes, innate or physical characteristics make some individuals 'inherently' vulnerable.[1] Children are vulnerable due to their youth, their inability to look after themselves, their limited autonomy, their incomplete physical and psychological development, and their emotional and educational immaturity, all of which make them totally or partially dependent. This is precisely the conceptualisation of children's vulnerability acknowledged in the *Dudgeon* judgment of 1981 by the European Court of Human Rights (ECtHR hereinafter). The Court recognised the legitimate necessity in a democratic society for some degree of control over homosexual conduct (even extended to consensual acts committed in private) in order to provide safeguards against the exploitation and corruption of those who are 'especially vulnerable' by reason, for example, of their youth, which makes them 'weak in body or mind, inexperienced, or in a state of special physical, official or economic dependence'.[2] This chapter aims to elucidate the elements contributing to the notion and conceptualisation of vulnerability when related to the age factor—thus, the child's dependency on the family and primary carers and the legal constructs developed for making their gradated autonomy accountable—as considered in both the Council of Europe and the European Union. The focus of the chapter will then shift to the practical effects produced by the conceptualisation of children's vulnerability in European law. This proposes a way to correct the model of formal equality, and elaborates on the notion of positive obligations—both procedural and substantial—arising upon states parties,

[1] M Fienman, 'Cracking the Foundational Myths: Independence, Autonomy, and Self-Sufficiency' (2000) 8 *American University Journal of Gender, Social Policy & the Law* 13–29, 18, 20, qualified dependency as deemed 'inevitable' when applied to biological or developmental stages of life.

[2] *Dudgeon v United Kingdom* App No 7525/76 (ECHR, 22 October 1981), para 49, where the vulnerability of children was functional in the Court's reasoning to theoretically admit the legitimacy of the use of criminal law to protect vulnerable children from homosexual influence.

with particular attention to those children who 'may be *especially vulnerable* to experiencing disparities in the enjoyment of their rights'.[3]

II. CHILDREN'S VULNERABILITY AS DEPENDENCY ON FAMILY: THE CONTOURS OF THE BASIS FOR DERIVATIVE RIGHTS IN EUROPEAN UNION (EU) LAW

The dependency of the child is primarily on the family, and it is related both to the fundamental functions of physical care, protection, and emotional support which take place within it (which is mainly a gender-related caring) and the economic and financial dimension.

The EU recognises the existence of financial dependency when a member of the family of an EU national needs financial assistance from a parent to achieve or maintain a desired standard of living, or when the member of the family could not attain a minimum acceptable standard of living in his country of origin or in his country of usual residence without that financial assistance. In the latter case, such dependence is considered to be proven by factual circumstances, such as those according to which a Union citizen regularly, for a significant period, pays a sum of money to that descendant, which is necessary in order for the descendant to support himself in the state of origin. However, the descendant cannot be required to establish that he has tried without success to find work or obtain subsistence support from the authorities of his country of origin and/or otherwise tried to support himself (also because he might subsequently find employment in the host member state) in order to be regarded as a 'dependant'.[4]

According to the Court of Justice of the European Union (CJEU hereinafter), the parental care element (when combined with financial dependency) has two consequences. First, dependency on the parent has been a conduit through which the primary carer of a disabled child could stake a claim for equal treatment of her/his rights. Hence, in *Coleman*, a disability discrimination was recognised in the context of employment (punishment for arriving late and being refused permission to take time off work) not because of the characteristics of the mother but in relation to the characteristics of those she was 'associated' with (her disabled child), as she was the primary carer.[5] Applying a similar line of reasoning,

[3] Report of the UN Committee of the Rights of the Child, A/57/41 New York 2002, para 41.

[4] Case C-423/12 *Reyes* (CJEU, 16 January 2014). Ms Reyes, a national of the Philippines now 21 years old, at the age of three was left in the care of her grandmother as her mother moved to Germany in order to work and be able to support her family in Philippines (it appears that the mother kept constant contact with her family in the Philippines and supported them economically by sending them money on a monthly basis and paying for the children's tuition). When the mother moved to Sweden and married a Norwegian national living in Sweden, both Ms Reyes and her mother depended on the Norwegian citizen's resources, because her mother stopped working. The CJEU refused to consider that Directive 2004/38 requires the proof that the money transferred to her by her mother and her cohabiting partner was used by the applicant in order to supply her basic needs.

[5] Case C-303/06 *Coleman*, [2008] ECR I-5603.

the national choice of interpreting the notion of 'worker' according to Article 45 TFEU as not covering also a mother who voluntarily left the job market to take care of a newborn child should be considered as amounting to discrimination on the grounds of sex. As recalled by AG Wahl in his Opinion in *Jessy St Prix*,[6] an interpretation of Article 7(3) of the Citizenship Directive, read in light of Article 45 TFEU, would in practice entail offering less protection for women than for men: because only women can become pregnant, this would lead to loss of the status of worker in the case of a temporary absence from work because of the physical effects of late-term pregnancy and the aftermath of childbirth.

On the other hand, the crucial relationship of the child with his parents has been instrumental for the judicial recognition of a quasi-automatic right of entry and residence in the host member state or in the home state of the child for his/her parents (also if they are third country nationals). Using the element of care-giving in order to ensure the practicability of a child's right (first, the right to education, and then the rights of EU citizenship), the Court has conferred such a derivative residence right on the new category of 'primary carers' of a school-going child of a (former) migrant worker[7] (but not of former self-employed persons[8]). The need for the presence and the care of the parent has also been used to further extend the derivative right beyond the child's age of majority,[9] and the satisfaction of the conditions of the parents having sufficient resources and comprehensive sickness insurance.[10]

Though such care-giving in practice is almost always gender-specific (maternal), from the legal standpoint it appears as a gender-neutral legal construct which has been and is able to strengthen a broader notion of family members as potential possessors of such derivative residence rights and parenthood. Its potential has already appeared in *Carpenter*,[11] when the derivative residence rights were recognised (not in the host member state but in the home states of the applicants) for the spouse of a service provider selling advertising space also to

[6] Case C-507/12 *Jessy St Prix* (CJEU, 12 December 2013).

[7] Case C-413/99 *Baumbast and R v Secretary of State for the Home Department* [2002] ECR I-7091 and S Currie, 'EU Migrant Children, their Primary Carers and the European Court of Justice: Access to Education as a Precursor to Residence under Community Law' (2009) *Journal of Social Security Law* 76–105.

[8] Joined Cases C-147/11 and C-148/11 *Czop and Punakova* (CJEU, 6 September 2012).

[9] Case C-480/08 *Teixeira* [2010] ECR I-1107, para 86 with case notes by Elsmore in [2010] *European Law Review* 1160.

[10] Case C-310/08 *Ibrahim* [2010] ECR I-1065, paras 57–58 with case note by Starup in [2010] *European Law Review* 571 and O'Brien in (2011) 48 *Common Market Law Review* 203–25. On the contrary, the simple offer of a definitive job has not been considered possible to evaluate by the national jurisdictions in order to verify if once employed there are sufficient resources for the applicant and his/her child in order to recognise the derivative residence right when the owner of the derivative rights is a third country national (see Case C-86/12 *Alokpa* (CJEU, 10 October 2013) and contrasting Opinion in the same case of AG Mengozzi (CJEU, 21 March 2013)).

[11] Case C-60/00 *Carpenter* [2002] ECR I-6279 with case notes by Acierno in (2003) *European Law Review* 398–407; Jadoul and Vanneste in (2003) *Columbia Journal of European Law* 447–55 and H Toner in (2003) *European Journal of Migration and Law* 163–72.

continental companies: the spouse—Mrs Carpenter—was a stepmother.[12] The CJEU considered decisive for the recognition of a residence right to Mrs Carpenter the childcare of her husband's children by another marriage, together with her homemaking role: in this way she was indirectly assisting and facilitating her husband's exercise of his rights under Article 49 EC, by providing him with economic assistance which permitted him to spend greater time on his business. Although the spectrum of family beneficiaries of the recognition of residence derivative rights has been enlarged through the concept of care-giving, the potential has not yet reached its maximum. Indeed the Court has recently interpreted Article 45 TFEU as conferring on a third-country national who is the family member of a Union citizen a derived right of residence in the member state of which that citizen is a national, where the citizen resides in that member state but regularly travels to another member state as a worker within the meaning of that provision, if the refusal to grant such a right of residence discourages the worker from effectively exercising his rights under Article 45 TFEU. The CJEU leaves such an evaluation to the referring court.[13] However, it has underlined that the desirability of the child's being cared for by the third-country national who is the direct relative in the ascending line of the Union citizen's spouse (grandmother) is not sufficient in itself to be considered as able to discourage[14] the EU citizen from effectively exercising his rights under Article 45 TFEU because of the refusal to grant a right of residence to that third-country national. Therefore, in order to reach a different conclusion the national jurisdictions have to provide evidence of family financial constraints, or the fact that the wife also works and is not available to take care of the child, or perhaps the inadequacy of day-care facilities for the child.[15]

Moving on to the potential of the concept of care-giving and dependency as regards fatherhood, *Ruiz Zambrano*[16] is illustratory. In that case, the neutral legal construct of the care-giving element has precluded a member state from denying residence to the third country national parent (a father) of an EU citizen child, notwithstanding that this EU citizen had yet to exercise his right of free

[12] But since Case C-456/12 *O and B v Minister voor Immigratie, Integratie en Asiel* (CJEU, 12 March 2014) the *Carpenter* ruling extends also to cross-border employees.

[13] Case C-457/12 *S and G v Minister voor Immigratie, Integratie en Asiel* (CJEU, 12 March 2014), para 44.

[14] This argument of discouragement is not new to the reasoning of the CJEU in free movement cases: see case law on the obstacle to the exercise of freedom of movement related to indirect discrimination.

[15] See also *Marx v Belgium* App no 6833/74 (ECtHR, 27 April 1979), para 45, according to which 'family life, within the meaning of Article 8, includes at least the ties between near relatives, for instance those between grandparents and grandchildren, since such relatives may play a considerable part in family life'.

[16] Case C-34/09 *Ruiz Zambrano* (CJEU 8 March 2011). For a detailed discussion of the case, see Hailbronner and Thym, 'Case C-34/09, Gerardo Ruiz Zambrano v. Office national de l'emploi' (2011) *Common Market Law Review* 1253–70; P Mengozzi, 'La sentenza "Zambrano": prodromi e consequenze di una pronuncia inattesa' (2011) 6(3) *Studi sull'integrazione europea* 417–32; D Kochenov, 'The right to have what rights?: EU citizenship in need of clarification' (2013) 19(4) *European Law Journal* 502–16.

movement within the Union, 'in so far as such decisions deprive those children of the genuine enjoyment of the substance of the rights attaching to the status of European Union citizen'. Thus, if the combination of EU citizenship and dependency on the family member(s) shall oblige the child to undergo forced exile not only from the territory of the member state of which he is a national but also that of the European Union as a whole, in order to *accompany both his parents* on whom he depends, national authorities shall have to recognise a right to residence and a permit to work (in order to ensure his/her ability to honour the financial dependency of the child) for the third country national who is the family member.

On the other hand, if the possibility exists for the child to remain with one of his/her parents within the territory of the European Union, though in a different state from that of his European nationality, according to the CJEU the child is not automatically deprived of 'the genuine enjoyment of the substance of the rights attaching to the status of European Union citizen'. The wish to live in his/her family with both parents is not proof in itself that the child will otherwise decide to follow the parent who has to leave European territory when national authorities refuse to issue a residency permit in a member state: it is up to the national authorities to evaluate this consequence and if possible avoid it by according the residence permit to the parent. Such a margin of appreciation recognised for national jurisdictions has to be exercised while upholding the EU Charter of Fundamental Rights when it is necessary to apply both national and EU law according, inter alia, to the Family Reunion Directive.[17] In this type of case Article 7 of the EU Charter should be interpreted in conjunction with the obligation to have regard to the child's best interests, recognised in Article 24(2) of the Charter, and with account being taken of the need for a child to maintain a personal relationship with both parents on a regular basis, as expressed in Article 24(3).[18]

Similar reasoning should also be applied, if necessary, to recognise derivative residence rights for both parents where a relationship has broken down. This will put the EU better in line with the ECtHR case law. Although the ECtHR often sees no reason why the contact should not be maintained through visits (without always verifying whether such visits will be permitted), it has sometimes considered that the situation requires non-nationals to be permitted to remain. This is happening because—according to the ECtHR—when parents are divorced, it is in the best interest of the child to grow up with both parents (or to have regular contact with both parents): the regularisation of the position of the irregular parent derives from the consideration that the divorced partner could not be expected to follow the latter with their children.[19]

[17] Joined Cases C-356/11 and 357/11 *O and S and L* (CJEU, 6 December 2012).

[18] ibid, para 76.

[19] *Udeh v Switzerland* App no 12020/09 (ECtHR, 16 April 2013). See also *Berrehab v The Netherlands* App no 10730/84 (ECtHR, 21 June 1988) and *Beldjoudi v France* App no 12083/86 (ECtHR, 26 March 1992).

In the peculiar context of international protection, the element of care-giving and family dependency has at last led the CJEU to extend not the category of beneficiaries of a right, but the obligations upon member states: the reception conditions obligations upon the state in order to protect the family unit of children and their parents. If member states are not in a position to grant the material reception conditions in kind to asylum-seekers, and they opt instead to grant the material reception conditions in the form of financial allowances, the amount of those allowances, according the Court, should be directed at the family's housing.[20]

III. THE CHILDREN'S FAMILY DEPENDENCY AND THE EUROPEAN COURT OF HUMAN RIGHTS

Within the Council of Europe, ECtHR jurisprudence has developed a conceptualisation of children's vulnerability as comprising both economic and emotional family dependency. The Court has recognised the element of economic dependency when it recalled that although the Convention does not guarantee, as such, the right to a pension,[21] it has not excluded that, in certain circumstances, the refusal to grant social benefits can be problematic in terms of Article 8 of the Convention. For instance, in the case of providing for orphans, such a refusal would effectively make it impossible for the normal development of the private and family life of the minor.[22]

The care-giving element and parental responsibility have been crucial for the ECtHR in order to uphold 'family life' as existing under Article 8 ECHR also in a broader context than in the traditional married nuclear family. Indeed the ECtHR has included an 'illegitimate' family within the notion of Article 8 ECHR, because it was undisputed that the parent (a mother in the specific case) had assumed responsibility for her daughter from the moment of her birth and had continuously cared for her.[23] On the other hand, due to the lack of 'further elements of dependency involving more than the normal emotional ties', the Court did not recognise as a 'family' one composed of an aunt who had looked after her nieces and nephews before their full age.[24] According to the Court, it is necessary for there to be other elements of dependency besides the normal emotional ties for relationships between parents and adult children to enjoy the protection of Article 8.[25]

In the case of foster parents, the Court has affirmed that it is necessary to take a number of factors into account in order to recognise the presence of a family

[20] Case C-79/13 *Saciri* (CJEU, 27 February 2014), para 46.

[21] See *X v Sweden* (1983) 8 EHRR 269.

[22] *Domenech Pardo v Spain* App no 55996/00 (ECtHR, 3 May 2001).

[23] *Marckx v Belgium* App no 6833/74 (ECtHR, 27 April 1979).

[24] *Javeed v the Netherlands* App no 47390/99 (ECtHR, 3 July 2001).

[25] See, mutatis mutandis, *Kwakye-Nti and Dufie v Netherlands* App no 31519/96 (ECtHR, 7 November 2000).

life: the time spent together, the quality of relationships and the role played by the adult to the child—ie if the adult provided for social development of the child—and the strength of the bond established between the applicants and the child.[26] In more detail, foster care of a child for 19 months during the initial important stages of her life was held to fulfil the conditions of 'family life', enabling an application by the carers to adopt the child to go ahead, instead of that of another couple who had sought to adopt her. Also, even when children had never lived with, and had not even met, the prospective adopters, 'family life' in principle existed according to the Court by virtue of the fact that, despite many efforts over a three-year period, the couples had been prevented from proceeding to take the children into their homes.[27]

Even in the absence of custody or guardianship of the children, the mere factual obligation of care for the children might be the sole decisive element for the evaluation of the admissibility of an application before the ECtHR: as the applicant had been entrusted with at least the care of the children, he 'had a valid personal interest in the welfare of the children'.[28]

Moreover, in the context of migration—when evaluating whether refusal of a family reunification constitutes illegitimate interference with the family life of the applicants—the ECtHR considered the child's degree of economic[29] and parental dependency, attributing particular weight if the child is particularly young. When that is the case, coming into the host state has appeared to be 'the most appropriate way to develop family life'[30] and to foster the child's integration into the family unit of the parents able and willing to care for her.[31] Instead, when other family members and relatives *could* give care (irrelevantly, if appropriately, being *effectively willing and able*) to the child left behind, the Court has not found Article 8 ECHR to be breached by the decision of national authorities to deny the

[26] *Moretti and Benedetti v Italy* App no 16318/07 (ECtHR, 27 April 2010).

[27] *Pini and Bertani & Manera and Atripaldi v Romania* App nos 78028/01 and 78030/01 (ECtHR, 22 June 2004). Nonetheless, the ECtHR noted that it was the expressed desire of the girls to remain where they were, and that 'their interests lay in not having imposed upon them against their will new emotional relations with people with whom they had no biological ties and whom they perceived as strangers'. Taking due account of the children's views (they were by then 13 years old), the Court ruled that no violation of 'family life' had taken place.

[28] In *Becker v Denmark* App no 7011/1975 (ECtHR, 3 October 1975).

[29] *Şen v Netherlands* App no 31465/96 (ECtHR, 21 December 2001), para 37. In that case such financial dependency, in terms of a contribution to a child's economic care by parents who had left him behind and sent back money for his support, was not considered to be proven.

[30] Interestingly, the focus of the Court shifted from not interfering with family life, to allowing it to develop. The fact that two further children were born to the applicants in the Netherlands, who had grown up there and had no ties with Turkey other than their official nationality, made it unreasonable, according to the Court, for them to resettle in Turkey (ibid, para 39). This allowed the Court to avoid a break from the earlier jurisprudence (*Gul v Switzerland* App no 23218/94 (ECtHR, 19 February 1996) and *Ahmut v The Netherlands* App no 21702/93 (ECtHR, 28 November 1996)). Judge Türmen's concurring opinion proved this when he expressed regret that the Court had not taken a stronger position which would have found a violation of Art 8 even if the two youngest children had not been born).

[31] ibid, para 40 and, mutatis mutandis, *Johansen v Norway* ECtHR 1996–III 1001–02, para 52, and 1003–04, para 64, and *X, Y and Z v UK* ECtHR 1997–II 632, para 43.

reunification of the children in the host states parties to the Convention. Such a scenario occurs mostly if this is combined with the possibility for the parents who migrated to be relocated in the state of origin.[32]

Likewise, the Court has put the interest of the children first when considering the possible regularisation of the immigration position of the one parent who happens to have custody of the children.[33] In this case the Court was confronted with the daily care of the mother, the fact that emotionally, together with the father, the parents were the most important people in the children's lives, and that the children's ability to visit their parents pending their expulsion—as well as their parents' ability to return—was uncertain.[34] *A contrario*, where the dependency became less intense, for example because family ties exist in the return state, or because the age of the applicant children (17 and 19 years old, respectively) allows for their support at a distance, the ECtHR did not find that the refusal to regularise—on this occasion, the irregular children—amounted to a violation of Article 8 ECHR.[35] Instead, with regard to the parents' regularisation (and in contrast with what was decided in the European Union case in *Ruiz Zambrano)*, the factor of the children's citizenship of the host state has not been considered of particular significance even in situations where the removal of the parents (or of one of them) would have involved the 'constructive exile'[36] of child family members who are citizens *ius soli* or *iure sanguinis* of the contracting state. Hence, to expect children of unlawful overstayers to follow their parents even if they had acquired theoretical rights of abode in the deporting country has been considered compatible with Article 8 ECHR, if they are of an 'adaptable age' (three to four years old) to the change in environment and if the possibility exists for them to return regularly to the state of their nationality.

Anyhow, it still remains to be seen whether this conceptualisation of children's family dependency might lead the Court to use it in order to include children within the category of 'vulnerable groups'. The expression 'vulnerable groups' emphasises that among the victims of Convention Rights violations some deserve a greater degree of attention, as they are historically 'subject to prejudice with

[32] See *Şen v the Netherlands*, para 41 *a contrario*, and the dissenting opinions in *Gul v Switzerland* and *Ahmut v The Netherlands.* When requiring that any family reunification was only to take place in the children's countries of birth, the Court has failed to consider important issues such as parents' wishes to act in the best interests of their children.

[33] *Rodriguez da Silva and Hoogkamer v Netherlands* App no 50435/99 (ECtHR, 31 January 2006).

[34] The applicant had returned to Norway in breach of a two-year-prohibition on re-entry imposed the same year (1996). She had given misleading information about her identity, her previous stay in Norway and her criminal conviction. By having intentionally done so she had obtained residence and work permits, which were renewed a number of times, then a settlement permit, none of which she had been entitled to. She had thus lived and worked in the country unlawfully throughout and the seriousness of her offences does not seem to have diminished with time.

[35] *Berisha v Switzerland* App no 948/12 (ECtHR, 30 July 2013).

[36] *O and O L* App no 11970/86 (ECtHR, 13 July 87); *Jaramillo* App no 24865/94 (ECtHR, 23 October 1995) and *Sorabjee v United Kingdom* App no 23938/94 (ECtHR, 23 October 1995) and *Üner v Netherlands* App no 46410/99 (ECtHR, 18 October 2006 (Grand Chamber)).

lasting consequences, resulting in their social exclusion',[37] whereas hitherto children have been categorised exclusively as 'vulnerable individuals' entitled to state protection owing to their age.[38] The argument in *MSS v Belgium and Greece*, which relies on the situation of *total dependency* in which asylum-seekers find themselves in the host state so as to consider them as a 'vulnerable group',[39] opens an interesting possibility—at least when the child is experiencing special vulnerabilities. I shall return to this in the last paragraph of the chapter.

IV. CHILDREN'S VULNERABILITY AS LIMITED AUTONOMY AND PROGRESSIVE DEVELOPMENT

A person's age is always in a state of transition: the object of solicitude (Locke); a temporality, a series of 'moments' (Hannah Arendt) or 'The seven ages of man', according to Shakespeare.[40] At the normative level, the notion of gradated autonomy, which might be seen as another element of the conceptualisation of children's vulnerability, reflects the distinction between ownership of rights and the capacity to act, recognising that children have a progressive capacity to exercise their rights in response to their condition of people in development.

Starting from when the capacity to exercise the rights conferred on a child by the law is totally, or almost totally, absent, such procedural incapacity does not take away from the child the ownership of these rights because other persons appointed by the operation of law (parents, guardian, representative, legal assistant) will be able to give effect to the child's rights by acting on his or her behalf. European law recognises this concept and provides that children should be entitled to adequate assistance by parents or legal representatives,[41] mandatory

[37] Judge Sajó, in his partly concurring and partly dissenting opinion in *MSS v Belgium and Greece* App No 30696/09 (ECtHR, 21 January 2011).

[38] *A v United Kingdom* App no 25599/94 (ECtHR, 23 September 1998), para 22; and *Đurđević v Croatia* App no 52442/09 (ECtHR, 19 July 2011), para 109.

[39] *MSS v Belgium and Greece*, paras 249–64.

[40] *As You Like It*, Act II, ch vi.

[41] For parental representation see, eg, ECtHR, *X v Sweden*, above; *Hokkanen v Finland* App no 19823/92 (ECtHR, 23 September 1994); *Osman v United Kingdom* (ECtHR, 28 October 1998), para 15 and *Scozzari e Giunta v Italy* App nos 39221/98 and 41963/98 (ECtHR, 13 July 2000), para 250. On the legal representation see *Nielsen v Denmark* App no 10929/84 (ECtHR, 28 November 1988). In *SP, DP, and AT v United Kingdom* App no 23715/94 (ECtHR, 20 May 1996) the Court noted the absence of any adequate alternative sources of representation besides the solicitor appointed to represent the children during domestic proceedings. The only two sources of representation, besides the solicitor, available to the children would have been their mother or the local authority. However, since 'the mother [was] apparently disinterested and the local authority [was] the subject of criticism in the application', the ECtHR decided that the solicitor's actions were neither 'inappropriate nor unnecessary'. It has to be noted that at the EU level, the appointment of a representative does not occur the moment an unaccompanied minor is detected by the authorities, namely before the relevant instruments are triggered, and no common understanding exists on the powers, the qualification or the role of representatives. On the contrary, as a consequence of gradated autonomy, the obligation to appoint a representative can be derogated from where the unaccompanied minor is likely to 'age out', and no mention is made of the best interests of the child in the derogation provision. See, critically, the European Commission in COM (2010) 213 final, 6 May 2010.

access to a lawyer at all stages[42] and to free legal counselling and free legal representation,[43] including for the purpose of claiming compensation (free if they do not have sufficient financial resources).[44]

On the other hand, when children's capacity becomes progressively evident, depending on the stage of their maturity and development, European practice rests between recognising children as active agents in their own lives, entitled to be listened to, respected and granted increasing autonomy in the exercise of rights, while also being 'entitled to protection in accordance with their relative immaturity and youth'.[45] Such considerations have been declined by the ECtHR with respect to special procedural guarantees for the child in both criminal and custody proceedings. In the first hypothesis, when the trial has taken place for criminal offences, such special procedural guarantees imply that: (a) the trial deals with the child in a manner which takes full account of his/her age, level of maturity and intellectual and emotional capacities, and (b) promotes his/her ability to understand and participate in the proceedings[46] (including conducting the hearing in such a way as to reduce as far as possible their feelings of intimidation and inhibition),[47] from the first stages of his/her involvement in a criminal investigation and during any questioning by the police.[48]

At the EU level, measures relating to procedural rights which have already been adopted following the Stockholm Programme[49] provide insufficient guarantees to ensure that vulnerable persons, and children in particular, can effectively exercise their rights if suspected or accused in criminal proceedings (eg, appropriate assessment mechanisms of their vulnerability, mandatory access to a lawyer, medical assistance, specific training for law enforcement authorities and judges). However, in 2013 the new Commission Recommendation on procedural

[42] See at the EU normative level, Arts 14(2), 15(2) and 16 of Directive 2011/36/EU, on preventing and combating trafficking in human beings and protecting its victims [2011] OJ L101/1; and on the assistance of an interpreter or a lawyer, eg *Salduz v Turkey* App no 36391/02 (ECtHR, 27 November 2008) and *Adamkiewicz v Poland* App no 54729/00 (ECtHR, 2 March 2010).

[43] See *Benham v United Kingdom* App no 19380/92 (ECtHR, 10 June 1996); *Perks and Others v United Kingdom* App nos 25277/94, 25279/94, 25280/94, 25282/94, 25285/94, 28048/95, 28192/95, 28456/95 (ECtHR, 12 October 1999); *Shabelnik v Ukraine* App no 16404/03 (ECtHR, 19 February 2009). At the EU level Art 9(6), 24(1) and Art 26(2) of the Reception Conditions Directive recast; Art 9(2) of the Return Directive; Art 10(c) of Directive 2001/558 and Arts 19 and 20 of the Procedure Directive recast.

[44] Art 12 of Directive 2011/36/EU on preventing and combatting trafficking in human beings and protecting its victims, see above n 42 and Arts 13 and 14 of Directive 2012/29/EU of the European Parliament and of the Council of 25 October 2012 establishing minimum standards on the rights, support and protection of victims of crime, and replacing Council Framework Decision 2001/220/JHA, [2012] OJ L315/57. See also Case C-105/03 *Pupino* [2005] ECR I-5285.

[45] G Lansdown, *The Evolving Capacities of the Child* (Florence, UNICEF Innocenti Research Centre and Save the Children Sweden, 2005).

[46] *T v United Kingdom* App no 24724/94 (ECtHR, 16 December 1999) and *V v United Kingdom* App no 24888/94 (ECtHR, 16 December 1999), when the two applicants, 10-year-old boys, were convicted for the abduction and murder of a two-year-old boy.

[47] *SC v United Kingdom* App no 60958/00 (ECtHR, 10 November 2004).

[48] *Panovits v Cyprus* App no 4268/04 (ECtHR, 11 December 2008).

[49] [2010] OJ C115/1.

safeguards for vulnerable persons suspected or accused in criminal proceedings[50] introduced a 'presumption of vulnerability' in particular for persons with serious psychological, intellectual, physical or sensory impairments, or mental illness or cognitive disorders hindering their understanding. The complementary proposal for a Directive to set common minimum standards throughout the European Union on the rights of children who are suspected or accused in criminal proceedings and of children subject to proceedings pursuant to Framework Decision 2002/584/JHA ('European arrest warrant proceedings') has provided a specific set of special procedural rights ranging from the right to information, the right to medical assistance, the right to a lawyer, respect for privacy and, where appropriate, to rights related to pre-trial detention.[51]

In proceedings for custody purposes, the gradated autonomy of the child should emerge in his/her procedural participation, namely, in his/her right to be heard in court. Thus, both the ECtHR and the CJEU case law have refused to impose on domestic courts a general obligation to always hear a child in court on the issue of access to a parent not having custody, as the issue depends on the specific circumstances of each case, and the courts have due regard for the age and maturity of the child.[52] Accordingly, the ECtHR has recognised that there is no reason to call into question the findings of a national jurisdiction that the child had become sufficiently mature for his views to be taken into account in custody proceedings and that access should therefore not be accorded against his own wishes.[53] Similarly, in *Bronda v Italy*,[54] the Court 'attaches special weight to the overriding interest of the child, who, now aged fourteen, has always firmly indicated that she does not wish to leave her foster home'.[55] More generally, the Court imposes this approach when individuals can no longer be reliant on family structures and public institutions of social protection have become determinant having due regard to, inter alia, the age, maturity and ascertained wishes of the child.[56]

On the other hand, the ECtHR has found it plausible that, having regard to the child's age, hearing her would not have served any purpose;[57] and has recognised a violation of Article 8 ECHR in a case where the national jurisdiction 'placed exclusive weight on the views expressed by the children without considering any other factors, in particular the applicant's rights as a father, effectively giving the children, who had both reached the age of 12, an unconditional veto power, and reversing the decisions which had hitherto been in the applicant's favour'.[58]

[50] COM (2013) 8178/2.

[51] COM (2013) 822/2.

[52] *Sahin v Germany* App no 30943/96 (ECtHR, 8 July 2003), para 73.

[53] *Hokkanen v Finland* App no 19823/92 (ECtHR, 23 September 1994).

[54] *Bronda v Italy* App no 40/1997/824/1030 (ECtHR, 9 June 1998).

[55] ibid, para 62.

[56] *YC v United Kingdom* App no 4547/10 (ECtHR, 13 March 2012), para 135 and *KS v United Kingdom* App no 62110/10 (ECtHR, 10 July 2012), para 39.

[57] *Eskinazi and Chelouche v Turkey* App no 14600/05 (ECtHR, 6 December 2005).

[58] *C v Finland* App no 18249/02 (ECtHR, 9 May 2006), para 58.

A similar reasoning was followed by the CJEU when applying the Brussels II Regulation, which imposes an obligation on national courts to hear children's views on matters related to custody, access and return to his/her country of habitual residence.[59] Failure to do so might be used as the basis for the non-recognition and enforcement of parental responsibility decisions.[60] Indeed, when in the case *Aguirre Zarraga*[61] the CJEU had to pronounce on the right of a child to be heard in civil proceedings relating to the custody of that child, it recognised that the Regulation, in conjunction with Article 24 of the EU Charter of Fundamental Rights, created an obligation to hear the views of the competent child, but not an 'absolute obligation': what is required in the best interests of the child must be assessed in each individual case.[62] This appears perfectly consonant with Article 6 of the Dublin III Regulation, which finds the following criteria relevant to determining the child's best interest: the family reunification possibilities; the minor's well-being and social development; safety and security considerations; and the views of the minor, in accordance with his or her age and maturity. Instead, more absolutely, when the EU Trafficking Directive provides that child victims of trafficking should be supported in their physical and psycho-social recovery, it requires such support to be provided after an individual assessment of the special circumstances of each particular child victim, taking due account of the child's views, needs and concerns with a view to finding a durable solution for the child.[63]

The gradated relevance of different ages as a consideration has also arisen in the context of the administrative (not pre-trial)[64] detention of children. In such cases, where the special vulnerability of an alien is combined with the general vulnerability of a child,[65] the Court has used the age to shorten the duration of

[59] Recital 19; Art 11(2).

[60] Art 23(b) and 41(2)(c).

[61] Case C-491/10 PPU *Aguirre Zarraga*, [2010] ECR I-14247.

[62] ibid, para 64.

[63] Arts 14 and 15 of Directive 2011/36 on preventing and combating trafficking in human beings and protecting its victims, see above n 42.

[64] In *Georgiev v Bulgaria* App no 47823/99 (ECtHR, 15 December 2005), although here the ECtHR took the view (but by four votes to three) that the detention conditions of a minor of 17 years old did not attain the minimum level of severity required to fall within the scope of Art 3, particularly since they had lasted a relatively short time; it then revisited its opinion, recognising a breach of the Convention rights of protection of personal freedom for children at the ages of 16, 17 and 18 years old. See *Selcuk v Turkey* App no 21768/02 (ECtHR, 10 January 2006), and *Nart v Turkey* App no 20817/04 (ECtHR, 6 May 2008).

[65] Within the CoE Parliamentary Assembly, which first recognised special aggravated vulnerability for children who are seeking asylum among others. This occurred in its Recommendation 1703 (2005), entitled Protection and assistance for separated children seeking asylum, where the Assembly held that 'Children are vulnerable and among them the most vulnerable group is represented by those who are in a foreign country seeking asylum and separated from their parents or legal or customary primary caregivers'. Similarly, the Committee of Ministers' Recommendation on life projects for unaccompanied minors and the *Council of Europe Strategy for the Rights of the Child (2012–2015)* also affirms the particular vulnerability of unaccompanied children seeking asylum, and provides that states must devote special attention to their needs. See Council of Europe, Committee of Ministers, Recommendation CM/Rec (2007)9 of the Committee of Ministers to member states on life projects for unaccompanied migrant minors, 12 July 2007, para 17, available at: https://wcd.coe.int/ViewDoc.jsp?id=1164769;

the detention required to meet the threshold of Articles 3 and 5 ECHR. Moreover, the Court aims to enhance the minimum standards in detention facilities where such people are held.[66] Conversely, in EU law, where the detention of minors is still permitted—though only in 'exceptional' cases—the legislator has provided that 16-year-olds might be placed with adults.[67]

Lastly, as regards social rights, the EU has clearly acknowledged such a model of gradated autonomy and progressive development of children when it considers social security systems distinguishing between 'young people' (all minors under the age of 18); 'adolescents' (at least of 15 years of age but under 18 who are no longer subject to compulsory full-time schooling) and 'children' (those under the age of 15) if the relevant context is that of employment.[68] Similarly, the Committee of the European Social Charter has imposed on state parties the obligation to grant children specific rights, including the right to shelter,[69] the right to health,[70] the right to education,[71] protection of the family and the right

Committee of Ministers, *Council of Europe Strategy for the Rights of the Child (2012–2015)*, 15 February 2012, available at: www.coe.int/t/dg3/children/MonacoStrategy_en.pdf.

[66] In *Kanagaratnam and others* App no 15297/09 (ECtHR, 13 December 2011), where the period of detention was four months, the minors were 13, 11 and eight years old, while in *Muskhadzhiyeva and others* App no 41442/07 (ECtHR, 12 October 2006), and *Popov* App nos 39472/07, 39474/07 (ECtHR, 19 January 2012) where the length of detention was respectively over one month and 15 days, the minors were aged seven months, three and a half, five and seven years; and five months and three years, respectively. Whilst the length was not excessive per se, it could be perceived by them as never-ending, bearing in mind that the facilities were ill-adapted to their accommodation and age. See more generally on the fact that any form of deprivation of liberty of children should be a measure of last resort, and for the shortest appropriate period of time, the Council of Europe Recommendation of the Committee of Ministers (2008), 11, on European rules for Juvenile Offenders, point 59.1; Guidelines of the Committee of Ministers of the Council of Europe on child-friendly justice, point 19.

[67] Art 24(2). But see Green Paper on 'Strengthening mutual trust in the European judicial area', ch 5 on children, COM (2011) 327 final, and Art 8 of the Council Framework Decision 2009/829/JHA of 23 October 2009 on the application, between member states of the European Union, of the principle of mutual recognition to decisions on supervision measures as an alternative to provisional detention ([2009] OJ L294/20) and more recently Art 12 of the proposal for a Proposal for a Directive on procedural safeguards for children suspected or accused in criminal proceedings (COM(2013) 822/2) which provides that 'In accordance with international standards children should be kept separately from adults in order to take into account their needs and vulnerability. When a detained child reaches the age of 18, the person should have the possibility to continue the separate detention. For that purpose, the individual circumstances of the case should be taken into account. The measures foreseen by this Directive do not require, however, the creation of separate detention facilities or prisons for children.'

[68] EC Regulation 883/2004 on the coordination of social security systems [2004] OJ L200/1 Art 1(i)(2).

[69] Art 31(2) ESC.

[70] Arts 8, 11, 7, 19§2 ESC.

[71] Arts 9, 10, 15, 17, 19(11) and (12) ESC. It has to be noted that the consideration that access to education is crucial for every child's life and development led the Committee, in *Médecins du Monde-International v France*, complaint n° 67/2011 (11 September 2012), to recognise that its denial would exacerbate the vulnerability of an unlawfully present child. The Committee also noted that the personal scope of the Charter needed to be enlarged to cover such a category of children and requires state parties, under Art 17(2) of the Charter, to also ensure the effective access to education to these children unlawfully present in their territory, in keeping with any other child.

to family reunion,[72] protection against danger and abuse,[73] prohibition of child labour under the age of 15,[74] and specific working conditions between 15 and 18,[75] as children are inherently vulnerable individuals because of their 'limited autonomy' and merely enjoy 'potential adulthood' as individual rights holders[76].

Moreover, once children, and especially migrant or unaccompanied children, reach majority, it is recommended that during their transitional status from 18 to 25 they should be ensured 'the most elementary rights, which are a condition sine qua non for autonomy, and successful integration (omissis), by taking policy measures on: welfare assistance and education; access to information on the relevant administrative procedures, extensions of housing assistance until solutions are found; access to health care; and measures to ensure specific training for social workers'.[77]

V. THE EFFECTS OF CHILDREN'S VULNERABILITY: A 'SUBSIDIARY' NOTION FOR TRANSCENDING FORMAL EQUALITY

The conceptualisation of the age-related inherent gradated vulnerability of the child appears to have (and has been used by the European monitoring bodies as having) a particular meaning in the context of the problems he/she has experienced in his/her adequate protection because of age discrimination. This is especially so for 'direct discrimination', which arises when the differentiated treatment between people in the same situation has 'no objective and reasonable justification' because it does not pursue a 'legitimate aim', or when there is not a 'reasonable relationship of proportionality between the means employed and the aim sought to be realized'.

On the one hand, children's vulnerability (as conceptualised above) appears to be the rationale behind the EU's broader range of exceptions to the principle of equal treatment,[78] and the justification of different treatment than is permitted

[72] Arts 16, 27, 19(6) ESC.

[73] Arts 7(1), 17 ESC.

[74] Art 7(1) and (3) ESC.

[75] Art 7 ESC.

[76] ESC, *Defence for Children International (DCI) v Netherlands* Complaint No 47/2008 (20 October 2009), para 25.

[77] Council of Europe, Parliamentary Assembly, Committee on Migration, Refugees and Displaced Persons: Migrant children: what rights at 18?, Draft Resolution adopted unanimously on the 13 March 2014 available at http://website-pace.net/documents/19863/168397/20140313-MigrantRights18-EN.pdf/ea190a6e-1794-4d30-b153-8c18dc95669f.

[78] See EC Council Directive 2000/78/EC of 27 November 2000 establishing a general framework for equal treatment in employment and occupation, [2000] OJ L303/16. Thus, in Case C-229/08 *Wolf v Stadt* [2010] ECR I-1, because according to Directive 2000/78 age can thus constitute an occupational requirement when necessary and appropriate, the then CJEU admitted that in the fire service the need to possess high physical capacities is related to age because some of the tasks of persons in the intermediate career of the fire service, such as fighting fires or rescuing persons, require exceptionally high physical capacities and can be performed only by young officials.

in connection with any other protected characteristic.[79] Differentiating on the grounds of age is socially and economically useful, as children and young people have different levels of wisdom, maturity, physical ability, education, economic power and other means of self-determination. Where children and young people require specific, closely defined protective measures (either collectively or within different age bands) in particular circumstances, the legislation should not only allow for this differential treatment but it should also recognise that such different treatment may be required. The thrust of these exceptions should be to ensure the best interests of the child.[80]

On the other hand, when direct discrimination arises with regard to children, the most difficult task is to determine the 'fixed comparative group' with which to compare the deliberate and unjustifiable less favourable treatment, as the term of comparison is another child: this is not a uniform category owing to the graded autonomy each of them might have achieved. Moreover, the vulnerability of children has strengthened the enhancing of the effectiveness of the prohibition of discrimination through the development of the concept of *indirect* discrimination: a policy or rule which applies to everyone, but which has an inadvertent but nevertheless unfair/disproportionate impact/prejudicial effect on people in a particular group. Differently from the case of direct discrimination, the focus is not on the outward appearance of a measure, but on its (significantly) detrimental effect which might bring to light and also challenge the underlying causes of discrimination, which are often of a structural nature.[81]

This is strongly evident in the Council of Europe. In contrast to the EU Equality Directives, which neglects to include in the definition of indirect discrimination both the failure to treat differently a specific individual or category by providing for an exception to the application of the general rule and disparate impact discrimination (as demonstrated by statistics), the Committee of the European Social Charter promotes a definition of indirect discrimination encompassing the effect of a failure to take due and positive account of all relevant differences. According to the Committee the notion should also embrace the discrimination which arises 'by failing to *take adequate steps* to ensure that the rights and

[79] According to the CJEU in Case C-88/08 *David Hütter* [2009] ECR I-5325, national legislation allowing the exclusion of professional experience acquired before the age of 18 while determining employees' grading is not justified, and constitutes age discrimination; while in Case C-555/07 *Kücükdeveci* [2010] ECR I-365, disadvantaging 'younger workers generally compared to older workers' should be forbidden and precludes any national legislation providing that periods of employment completed before the age of 25 are not to be taken into account while establishing the dismissal notice.

[80] See in this sense also AG Mazak in Case C-388/07 *Age Concern England* [2009] ECR I-1569, Opinion delivered on 23 September 2008.

[81] For instance, caused by prejudices, practices based on the idea of the inferiority or the superiority of particular groups of people, and stereotyped roles. See in that regard, C Tobler, *Indirect Discrimination. A Case Study into the Development of the Legal Concept of Indirect Discrimination under EC Law* (Antwerpen, Intersentia, 2005) and T Loenen, 'Indirect Discrimination: Oscillating between Containment and Revolution' in T Lonen and PR Rodriguez (eds), *Non Discrimination Law Comparative Perpsectives* (The Hague/London/Boston, Kluwer Law International 1999), 195–211, 199.

collective advantages that are open to all are genuinely accessible by and to all'.[82] In the Committee's view, this entails that 'the burden of proof should not rest entirely on the complainant, but should be the subject of an appropriate adjustment'.[83] For instance, admitting statistical data as proving 'unexplained differences' in the education of mentally disabled children in Bulgaria, the Committee considered that it was up to the government to demonstrate that there was no ground for finding discrimination against those children.[84] Likewise, the ECtHR reduced and corrected the burden of proof when it found indirect racial discrimination based on the fact that the percentage of Roma children placed in special schools in the Czech Republic was much higher than that of other children.[85] Moreover, putting together the element of the detrimental impact of the indirect discrimination with 'a general picture' of disadvantage or vulnerability has allowed the ECtHR to shift onto states the onus of proving that the difference in impact has an objective and reasonable justification unrelated to ethnic origin, something that the states have often failed to do.[86]

There is an analogous combination between the presence of measures violating human rights specifically targeting and affecting vulnerable groups and the passive role of public authorities which not only do not take appropriate action against the perpetrators of these violations, but even contribute to such violence.[87] The ESC has therefore identified an 'aggravated violation' of the Charter and enlarged the scope of application *ratione personae* of the Charter to children irregularly present in the territory of state parties. This is because the refusal of the right to shelter and the right to health care by national authorities would have

[82] ESC, *Association internationale Autisme-Europe (AIAE) v France*, Complaint No 13/2002, Merits 4 November 2003, para 54.

[83] ESC, *Mental Disability Advocacy Centre (MDAC) v Bulgaria,* Collective Complaint No 41/2007, Merits 3 June 2008, para 52.

[84] See ESC, *European Roma Rights Centre (ERRC) v Greece*, Complaint No 15/2003, Merits, 8 December 2004; *European Roma Rights Centre (ERRC) v Italy*, Complaint No 27/2004, Merits, 21 December 2005; *European Roma Rights Centre (ERRC) v Bulgaria*, Complaint No 31/2005, Merits, 18 October 2006; *International Helsinki Federation for Human Rights (IHF) v Bulgaria*, Complaint No 44/2007, Merits 14 September 2007; *European Roma Rights Centre (ERRC) v Bulgaria*, Complaint No 46/2007, Merits 3 December 2008; *European Roma Rights Centre (ERRC) v Bulgaria*, Complaint No 48/2008, Decision on admissibility, 2 June 2008; *European Roma Rights Centre (ERRC) v France*, Complaint No 51/2008, Merits 19 October 2009; *Centre on Housing Rights and Evictions (COHRE) v Italy*, Complaint No 58/2009, Merits 25 June 2010; *European Roma Rights Centre (ERRC) v Portugal*, Complaint No 61/2010 Merits 30 June 2011.

[85] *DH and others v Czech Republic* (also called the 'Ostrava case'), App No 57325/00 (ECtHR, 13 November 2007 (Grand Chamber)) para 175.

[86] ibid, paras 190–95.

[87] ESC, *Centre on Housing Rights and Evictions (COHRE) v Italy,* above, para 76; ECSR, *European Roma Rights Center (ERRC) v Italy,* where the Committee notes that 'statements by public actors ... create a discriminatory atmosphere which is the expression of a policy-making based on ethnic disparity instead of on ethnic stability' and that 'the racist misleading propaganda against migrant Roma and Sinti indirectly allowed or directly emanating from the Italian authorities constitutes an aggravated violation of the Revised Charter' (para 139) under Art E in combination with Art 19(1) (the right of migrant workers and their families to protection and assistance) of the Revised Charter.

had an inadmissible and unreasonably detrimental effect or an adverse impact on such children.[88]

VI. THE OTHER SIDE OF VULNERABILITY'S EFFECTS: PROTECTION DUTIES AS POSITIVE OBLIGATIONS

If the legal construct of children as a 'vulnerable group' has been significant in the context of equality in order to realise it in European law at a more substantive level, the same notion has also been functional in European law in order to elaborate the notion of substantial positive obligations upon state parties. Positive obligations (together with positive actions) are two notions which share with the notion of indirect discrimination the idea that the substantive element lies in the focus on the effect of a measure, rather than on its outward appearance. These notions are based on the recognition that equal treatment (ie applying the same rule for all) may lead to an unequal outcome, and that therefore, respectively, preferential or protective treatment is needed. As Tobler has stated, exposing the causes underlying indirect discrimination may help states to identify areas where they should actively adopt a legislative or practical protective regime which goes beyond the effective deterrence of serious violations of personal rights.[89] In an EU constitutional perspective, age as a vulnerability criterion has been recognised as necessitating a special protective regime. This may be seen in: (a) Article 19(2) TFEU, which provides for positive actions to prevent or compensate for disadvantages linked to, inter alia, age; and (b) the structure of the EU Charter of Fundamental Rights Chapter on Equality, which stipulates that special protection is necessary for certain groups, namely, children (Article 24), the elderly (Article 25) and persons with disabilities (Article 26). In so doing, the Charter has explicitly admitted that some people are potentially more vulnerable—in the sense of subject to substantial structural inequality—than others.

On the other hand, when the ECtHR elaborated the concept of 'positive obligations' upon states[90] (including the case where breaches are inflicted by non-state actors[91]), it expressly applied them in order to evaluate the adequateness

[88] ESC, *Defence for Children International (DCI) v The Netherlands* Complaint No 47/2008, Merits 20 October 2009 as to the right to shelter and *International Federation of Human Rights Leagues v France*, Complaint No 14/2003, Merits 8 September 2004, para 32 for the right to health (emergency medical assistance).

[89] C Tobler, *Limits and Potential of the concept of Indirect Discrimination* (Luxembourg, European Communities, 2008).

[90] In general, on positive obligations and the ECHR, see J-P Costa, 'The European Court of Human Rights: Consistency of Its Case Law and Positive Obligations' (2008) 26 *Netherlands Quarterly of Human Rights* 449, 454; A Mowbray, *The Development of Positive Obligations under the European Convention on Human Rights by the European Court of Human Rights* (Oxford, Hart Publishing, 2004) 5; B Conforti, 'Exploring the Strasbourg Case-Law: Reflections on State Responsibility for the Breach of Positive Obligations' in M Fitzmaurice and D Sarooshi (eds), *Issues of State Responsibility Before International Judicial Institutions* (Oxford, Hart Publishing, 2004) 129.

[91] See, mutatis mutandis, *HLR v France* 1997–III, para 40.

of the legislative, administrative and judicial protective regime related to age vulnerability.[92] Hence, national authorities fail to fulfil their positive obligation when they 'knew or ought to have known at the time of the existence of a real and immediate risk of children's rights' and thus they would be expected to provide reasonable measures to prevent that risk. In order to evaluate the fulfilment of positive obligations by state parties the ECtHR has used the foreseeability or causality test.[93] For instance, the Court found that the absence of legislation criminalising sexual advances towards a mentally handicapped adolescent meant that the state had failed to fulfil a positive obligation to protect the Article 8 rights of the victim, and it rejected the government's argument to the effect that the facts were 'exceptional' and that the legislative gap was unforeseeable.[94] The respondent state should have been aware of the risk of sexual abuse of mentally handicapped adolescents in a privately run care home for children and should have legislated for that eventuality. On the other hand, the Court did not find that a causal link had been sufficiently established between the likelihood of the applicant's father having been exposed to dangerous levels of radiation and leukaemia in a child subsequently conceived, with the consequence that the state could not have been expected to act on its own initiative to notify the parents of these matters or to take any other special action in relation to the child.[95]

When the breaches are inflicted by non-state actors, the positive obligation to protect is to be interpreted in such a way as not to impose an excessive burden on the authorities, although the required measures should include reasonable steps to prevent children's ill-treatment of which the authorities had or ought to have had knowledge.[96] A failure to take reasonably available measures which could have had a real prospect of altering the outcome or mitigating the harm is sufficient to engage the responsibility of the state.[97] It has to be seen, if upheld in future

[92] *DG v Ireland* App no 39474/98 (ECtHR, 16 May 2002); *Bouamar v Belgium* App no 9106/80 (ECtHR, 29 February 1988). *A contrario*, for a not deficient and inadequately protective legislation, see *A v United Kingdom*, and ESC, *World Organisation against Torture (OMCT) v Italy* Complaint 19/2003, Merits, 1 August 2003, and *World Organisation against Torture (OMCT) v Portugal* Complaint 20/2003, Merits, 31 July 2003, because Portuguese legislation prohibits corporal punishment against children and in Italy the prohibition of all forms of violence has a legislative basis and a consistent judicial practice. On the contrary, ESC, *World Organisation Against Torture (OMCT) v Belgium* Complaint 21/2003, Merits, 23 September 2003, a violation of Art 17 of the 1961 Social Charter because legislation did not explicitly and effectively prohibit corporal punishment of children by parents and 'other persons'; mutatis mutandis, *Osman v United Kingdom*, above, para 116, and *E and Others v United Kingdom* App no 33218/96 (ECtHR, 26 November 2002), para 88.

[93] On the use by the Court of the causality test in alternative to the one of foreseeability, see B Conforti, 'Exploring the Strasbourg Case-Law: Reflections on State Responsibility for the Breach of Positive Obligations', above, 132.

[94] *X and Y v Netherlands* App no 8978/80 (ECtHR, 26 March 1985).

[95] *LCB v United Kingdom* App no 23413/94 (ECtHR, 9 June 1998).

[96] *X and Y v Netherlands*, above, paras 21–27; *A v United Kingdom* (ECtHR, 23 September 1998), para 22; *Z and Others v United Kingdom* App no 29392/95 (ECtHR, 10 May 2001), paras 74–75; *DP and JC v United Kingdom* App no 38719/97 (ECtHR, 10 October 2002), para 109; and *MC v Bulgaria* App no 39272/98, ECHR 2003-XII, para 149.

[97] *E and Others v United Kingdom*, n 92 above, para 99.

litigation, whether positive obligations that are 'inherent to conventional rights'[98] should be confirmed as inherent to the powers of public authorities, as recently affirmed by the ECtHR (Grand Chamber 11 to 6) in *O'Keeffe v Ireland*. In this case, as primary education is an 'important public service', school authorities are obliged to protect 'young children who are especially vulnerable and are under the exclusive control of those authorities'.[99] Likewise, seeking confirmation is the other novelty introduced by the same recent judgment: will the risk assessment of national awareness persist as a 'real and immediate risk',[100] or will it shift to a more protective 'potential risk' to children's safety in public education[101] when there is no appropriate framework of protection?

VII. POSITIVE OBLIGATIONS DIRECTED AT AGGRAVATED FORMS OF CHILDREN'S VULNERABILITY

Besides such general obligations, both European systems have also engaged in a detailed recognition of positive obligations upon states when children's vulnerability is 'special'. This means that if age is taken as the basis, qualifying factors such as sex (girls, and also teenage mothers), general status (legitimacy), health (children with disabilities or suffering from HIV/AIDS), family background (single-parent families), relocation (voluntary (nomads) as much as involuntary (refugees)), and ethnicity (ethnic minority families) all elevate particular (groups of) already vulnerable children to the status of even more vulnerable. Here below are examples of the cases where age is combined with ethnic origin, and the exploited migratory status will show how the conceptualisation of the vulnerability of the child is made more explicit by both the European orders as qualifying factors for the elaboration of a positive obligation, moving on from procedural towards substantial responsibilities.

As regards the case of the 'special aggravated vulnerability' of Roma children, the ECtHR stressed their qualification 'as members of a disadvantaged group'[102] in order to require active and structured involvement by the relevant social services to take additional steps and safeguards to ensure that the state had sufficient regard to Roma children's special needs. This would require, inter alia, that they should be assisted with any difficulties they encountered following the school

[98] *Marckx v Belgium*, n 23 above, para 31.

[99] *O'Keeffe v Ireland* App no 35810/09 (ECtHR, 28 January 2014 (Grand Chamber)), para 145–46, 150.

[100] See, for instance, *DF v Latvia* App no 11160/07 (ECtHR, 29 October 2013).

[101] *O'Keeffe v Ireland*, n 99 above, para 162, when dealing with victims of sexual assault in schools some 41 years after the initial school incident, applying the positive obligations theory retroactively found that the state, when delegating duties in primary education to private actors, is not absolved from the 'inherent obligation' to protect young children who are especially vulnerable and are under the exclusive control of those authorities.

[102] *Oršuš and Others v Croatia* App no 15766/03 (ECtHR, 16 March 2010 (Grand Chamber)), paras 177 and 183.

curriculum. The classification of Roma children as members of a disadvantaged class led the ECtHR to establish a substantive positive obligation in *Horvath and Kiss v Hungary*, namely to 'undo a history of racial segregation in special schools',[103] in particular to prevent the perpetuation of past discrimination or discriminative practices disguised in allegedly neutral tests.[104] Whether, however, this entails a specific obligation on the state to provide specialised tests for children with a Roma background, and for children from other socially disadvantaged backgrounds, is not entirely clear.

An analogous recognition of specific positive substantial obligations upon states with regard to the Roma community has been established by the European Committee of the Social Charter.[105] According to the Charter, 'the State has failed to meet its positive obligations to ensure that Roma enjoy an adequate access to health care, in particular by failing to take reasonable steps to address the specific problems faced by Roma communities stemming from their often unhealthy living conditions and difficult access to health services'.[106] In the Committee's view, the specific instances of abuse put forward by the ERRC 'cannot be relied on to conclude that there are systematic discrimination practices against Roma in the health care system'; however, 'these specific cases taken together with all other evidence submitted by the complainant serve to reinforce the Committee's overall conclusion that Roma in Bulgaria do not benefit from appropriate responses to their general and specific health care needs'.[107]

At the EU secondary law level, the EU Racial Equality Directive contains no explicit positive duty for member states to ensure equal opportunities for the historic dimensions of disadvantage suffered by racial and ethnic minorities. However, the Directive allows for the adoption of measures that 'compensate for disadvantages' (recital 17), and Article 5 holds out the possibility, 'with a view to ensuring full equality in practice', of maintaining or adopting specific measures 'to prevent or compensate for disadvantages linked to racial or ethnic origin'.[108] Will this allow equal opportunities in relation to minority language needs? On the other hand, the Directive's conceptualisation of educational segregation is that it is direct rather than indirect discrimination, which might also help to understand whether and when the establishment or maintenance of Roma classes or schools reflects segregated residential patterns. This would preclude the possibility of using 'justification defences', such as parental consent, lower educational ability or other commonly used factors also retained by the ECtHR jurisprudence until

[103] *Horvath and Kiss v Hungary* App no 11146/11 (ECtHR, 29 April 2013), para 127.

[104] ibid, para 116.

[105] ESC, *ERRC v Bulgaria,* Collective Complaint No 46/2007, Merits, 3 December 2008.

[106] ibid, para 49.

[107] ibid, para 50.

[108] On this point see C McCrudden, 'National Legal Remedies for Racial Inequality' in S Fredman (ed) *Discrimination and Human Rights: The Case of Racism* (Oxford, Oxford University Press, 2001) 253–59; L Farkas, 'A good way to equality: Roma seeking judicial protection against discrimination in Europe' (2006) 3 *European Antidiscrimination Law Review* 21–30.

very recently. Furthermore, the European Commission's proposal for a wider anti-discrimination directive on equal treatment with regard to religion or belief, disability, age or sexual orientation,[109] which would extend protection to children in the school environment, might significantly enhance the provision already available under Council Directive 2000/43/C.[110] Although, in the Council debate on the proposal it emerged that some delegations oppose the inclusion of social protection and education within the scope of the Directive, such enhancement of the current provision would be possible unless the will of these parties prevails in the on-going negotiation process.[111]

Instead, when age vulnerability is aggravated because of an overlapping exploitation criterion, such as in the case of child victims of trafficking, the ECtHR started recognising procedural positive obligations upon states. States are held to have duties of criminal prosecution and effective investigation[112] that are instrumental in bypassing the sometimes extreme difficulties that minors encounter in order to prove abuse.[113] Moroever, it has been recognised that states have a duty to provide child victims of trafficking with greater protection in on-going compensation proceedings and prescription terms[114] together with the duty of effective inter-state cooperation when the exploitation and trafficking to be investigated are events which occurred outside the applicant's territories.[115]

Subsequently, in *Rantsev*, the Court moved towards considering that the spectrum of safeguards set out in national legislation must be adequate to ensure the practical and effective protection of the rights of victims or potential victims of trafficking. Accordingly, in addition to criminal law measures to punish traffickers, Article 4 requires member states to put in place adequate measures regulating the businesses often used as a cover for human trafficking. Furthermore, a state's immigration rules must address relevant concerns relating to encouragement, facilitation or tolerance of trafficking.[116] Crucially, as a last step, states were recognised as not being permitted to leave a victim of an Article 4 violation unprotected or to return her to a situation of trafficking and exploitation.[117] However, in order for this positive obligation to be made operational, it must be demonstrated that the state authorities were aware, or ought to have been aware, of circumstances giving rise to a credible suspicion that an identified individual had been, or was,

[109] Proposal for a Council Directive on implementing the principle of equal treatment between persons irrespective of religion or belief, disability, age or sexual orientation, COM (2008) 426.

[110] [2000] OJ L 180/22.

[111] 2008/0140(APP)—09/12/2013 Debate in Council (3280).

[112] *MC v Bulgaria*, n 96 above, paras 167, 179 and 184; *M and C v Romania* App no 29032/04 (ECtHR, 27 September 2011), para 112 et seq; *Siliadin v France* App no 73316/01 (ECtHR, 26 July 2005), para 130.

[113] *Assenov and others v Bulgaria* App no 24760/94 (ECtHR, 28 October 1998).

[114] *Okkali v Turkey* App no 52067/99 (ECtHR, 17 October 2006).

[115] *Siliadin v France*, n 112 above, paras 89 and 112.

[116] ibid, para 284.

[117] ibid, para 271.

at real and immediate risk of being trafficked or exploited.[118] Such an obligation should be interpreted in a way that does not impose 'an impossible or disproportionate burden on the authorities',[119] although what might be an impossible or disproportionate burden for one state will not necessarily be so for another. In a similar way to ECtHR jurisprudence as regards direct and indirect refoulement, some possible elements to be considered in assessing the risk of treatment contrary to Article 4 upon return to the country of origin might include the legislative and administrative framework in that country, and whether it affords effective protection against trafficking and exploitation; the capacity, training, and willingness of the authorities to identify and protect victims, to take operational measures and to conduct an effective investigation.

These more substantial positive obligations were recognised, albeit feebly, equally by the Committee of the European Social Charter and by the EU in its 2011 Directive. When the ESC in *Defence for Children International (DCI) v Belgium*[120] enlarged the scope of application of Article 17(1)(b) to trafficked children, the European Committee held that Belgium's persistent failure on reception of such children showed that the government had not taken the necessary and appropriate measures to ensure that the minors in question were given the care and assistance they needed. In addition, the Belgian government had failed to protect against negligence, violence or exploitation, thus seriously jeopardising the children's enjoyment of their fundamental rights such as the right to life, psychophysical integrity and respect for human dignity. Furthermore, in 2006, the European Committee confirmed its Conclusions against Moldova when it stated that according to paragraph 10 of Article 7, states must protect children not only from the risks and forms of exploitation resulting directly or indirectly from their work, but also from exploitation resulting from trafficking and 'the fact that they are on the streets—domestic exploitation, begging, pick pocketing, servitude or the removal of organs, for example—and take measures to prevent and assist street children'.[121] In this specific case, according to the ESC,

> the significant and persistent deficiency in providing housing for foreign minors unlawfully present in the territory demonstrates that the Government has not taken the necessary steps to ensure to these children special protection against physical and moral dangers required by Article 7 (10), and has therefore created a serious risk to the enjoyment of their fundamental rights such as the right to life, psychophysical integrity and respect for human dignity.[122]

Likewise, in the EU the procedural positive obligations of sanctions for crimes, prosecuting the offenders, and prevention of human trafficking were established

[118] ibid, para 286.

[119] ibid, para 287.

[120] ESC, *Defence for Children International (DCI) v Belgium*, Complaint No 69/2011, Merits, 27 June 2011.

[121] ibid, para 94 and ESC Conclusions 2006, Art 7(10), Moldova.

[122] ibid, para 97.

under Council Framework Decision 2002/629/JH. More recently, however, Article 11 of Directive 2011/36/EU[123] has also introduced the national substantial obligation to provide victims of trafficking with assistance, support and protection before, during and after criminal proceedings for an appropriate period of time after their conclusion. This has been emphasised as regards child victims of trafficking, who belong to the only vulnerable group with special provisions (contrasting with the gender perspective that it would be expected to have). Article 14(1) provides that the positive obligation of specific actions to assist and support child victims of trafficking in human beings, in the short and long term, in their physical and psycho-social recovery, are to be undertaken 'following an individual assessment of the special circumstances of each particular child victim, taking due account of the child's views, needs and concerns with a view to finding a durable solution for the child', and providing them with access to education within a reasonable time.

Unfortunately, the temporal limit of children's substantial protection is still present in the corollary norm of Directive 2004/81, which enables third country nationals who are victims of trafficking to be issued with a residence permit. Like the positive obligations under Directive 2011/36, this is still subordinated to the condition of their cooperation with the competent authorities in the identification of the perpetrators of the crime: trafficked children are excluded from its scope.[124] But protection should be commensurate with the victim's needs and should not necessarily be made conditional upon collaboration in every case by the trafficked person. Moreover, short-term assistance and support might not be sufficient for trafficking victims (especially trafficked children) who fear persecution or other serious human rights violations and cannot return home. Such people therefore need durable protection against refoulement, and in many instances also the granting of asylum, subsidiary protection or another protection status. It would therefore have been better for Council and Parliament to insert the provisions requested by the UNHCR for the early identification of child victims of trafficking who are also in need of international protection. These would ensure that any children who give an indication that they could be at risk of persecution are identified and referred to the competent national asylum authorities.

VIII. CLOSING REMARKS

The inherent vulnerability of the child as a particular subject (rather than object) of rights is present in philosophy, psychiatry and anthropology, but it remains rather an implicit notion in the law. This chapter has attempted to break down and examine in all its parts the concept and the notion of vulnerability when

[123] Directive 2011/36 on preventing and combating trafficking in human beings and protecting its victims, n 42 above.

[124] Art 3 Directive 2004/81 [2004] OJ L261/19.

applied to children in European law. The constitutive elements of the inherent vulnerability of the child have been identified and constructed equally, in both systems of protection, as financial and care dependency on the parents/family in combination with the child's limited autonomy. The chapter has stressed a certain degree of convergence between the EU and the Council of Europe in such a legal construction. In the case of the ECtHR these elements have progressively led to a child-based reasoning, with the consequence of reducing states' margin of appreciation even in contexts such as those regarding migration issues where the national space for manoeuvre has traditionally been very broad. Within the EU the centrality of the child has likewise increased in legislative, constitutional and judicial considerations, thanks to its combination with EU citizenship. This has brought about a shift from the child as the object of attention and (as yet incomplete) protection to a veritable subject of rights who may also be a conduit for derivative rights for the family, although in the latter case the positions of the CJEU and the ECtHR diverge as to the regularisation of the parents.

The other side of children's inherent vulnerability, as described in the chapter in terms of their gradated autonomy, determines a certain degree of autonomisation of the child's position as a veritable subject of rights. This has been achieved mainly in the dimension of his/her procedural capacity, with a similar extension in both European legal orders, although it remains more developed in the Council of Europe and especially in the ECtHR jurisprudence.

Also the effect of a conceptualisation of children's vulnerability is convergent on the affirmation of a model of substantive equality. The sanctioning of indirect discrimination and the development of protective procedural and substantial regimes by requiring states to take positive action and by imposing on them positive obligations have been shown not only to effectively ensure the rights of the child, but also to give back to the child his/her childhood. Substantial scope for improvement is nonetheless expected, mainly at the EU level with the entry into force of the Lisbon Treaty. Previously, the absence of any explicit reference to children in the Treaties has meant that, traditionally, 'hard' EU law relating to children has been introduced either indirectly (embedded in more generic legislation relating to the free movement rights of family members or vulnerable immigrant groups), or through EU health and safety legislation with its distinctly protection-focused agenda (such as toy safety or television advertising), or by less formalised means. The inclusion of children's rights in the internal and external objectives of the Union means that children's rights could be mainstreamed into the legislation, policies and programmes for which the EU has a competence.

Moreover, although the Charter could not be seen as extending competence, the CJEU could enhance rights protection in areas where EU law directly or indirectly impacts upon the rights of an individual, such as in the case of extradition and the rights of children. Whilst the framework decision on the European arrest warrant does not mention the rights of the child as a bar to extradition, it has, nevertheless, to be interpreted in accordance with the Charter, one provision of which concerns the best interests of the child. Furthermore, in developing the jurisprudence under the Charter, the CJEU might recognise circumstances, as has the ECtHR, where a positive duty to act to protect the Charter correctly will be required in order for the national law to remain in compliance.[125] So far, the ECtHR has recognised that member states have positive duties, but not that the European Union has: it is necessary to wait for the EU's accession to the ECHR before the latter can become a reality. In that case, the EU itself may be held to account as to how far its action or omission contributed to the eventual breach of children's rights and for the degree to which it should have anticipated such breaches.

[125] See Case C-68/95 *T Port GmbH & Co KG v BLE* [1996] ECR I-6065, paras 37–41.

3

Reshaping EU Old Age Law in the Light of the Normative Standards in International Human Rights Law in Relation to Older Persons

FRANCESCO SEATZU

Old-Age, a second Child, by Nature curs'd.
With more and greater evils than the first,
Weak, sickly, full of pains; in every breath
Railing at life, and yet afraid of death …
'Gotham' Pt 1, Lines 215–18, *The Poetical Works of Charles Churchill*, ed Douglas Grant (Oxford, Clarendon Press, 1956), p 298.

I. INTRODUCTION

ELDERLY PEOPLE ARE often vulnerable for a number of reasons, including limited physical mobility and difficulties when searching for information, decreased information-processing and problem-solving skills due to declining memory capacity and weakened reasoning/evaluation skills,[1] and thus are very much in need of special legal protection. Until 2000, when the Charter of Fundamental Rights of the European Union was adopted,[2] the rights of the elderly were considered an anathema to the law and policy of the European Union; older persons were not considered specifically relevant to the EU's most fundamental economic and political aims. Rather, policy and legal provisions addressing the elderly evolved as something of an afterthought; a secondary or

[1] See EJ Kim, L Geistfeld, *What makes older adults vulnerable to exploitation or abuse?*, http://ncsu.edu/ffci/publications/2008/v13-n1-2008-spring/Kim-Geistfeld.php, who also stress that: 'elder vulnerability is a combination of three factors: health status, cognitive ability, and social support'. See also M Albertson Fineman, '"Elderly" as Vulnerable: Rethinking the Nature of Individual and Societal Responsibility' (2012) 20 *Elderly Law Journal* 73 ff.

[2] The text of the Charter of Fundamental Rights of the European Union was adopted at the Nice Summit in December 2000 ([2000] OJ C364/1).

an additional product of more non-older adult-focused EU social law and policy. This is confirmed by several indicators, including the EU's almost exclusive focus on the OMC ('Open Method of Coordination') that rests on soft law systems such as indicators, benchmarking, guidelines and sharing of best practice to enhance elderly issues of crucial importance such as pensions, social inclusion and health care.[3] That being said, the period since 2000 has seen something of a sea change at EU level in the rights of the elderly, culminating in 2010 with the publication of the European Charter of the Rights and Responsibilities of Older People in Need of Long-Term Care and Assistance ('the Charter') by the EUSTaCEA Project—'A European Strategy to fight elder abuse'.[4] The text covers the major challenges facing older persons, under the following chapters: autonomy and participation; non-discrimination; protection from violence and abuse; social protection and employment; care; and administration of justice. By complementing and supporting the charters and other measures which are already implemented in some countries of the European Union, the Charter sets out an audacious and complex new plan for the future of EU activity in the field of the elderly's rights, a plan that would build upon the EU's existing *acquis* across a wide range of areas, and that would aim to incorporate the elderly's rights issues into all aspects of the EU regulatory framework.

This declaration of the EU's long-term commitment to older persons' rights is of not only symbolic but also legal pertinence. This however, like the UN General Assembly resolution A46/91 of 1991 (the UN Principles for Older Persons),[5] is not legally binding. Nevertheless, the coherence with which the Charter applauds the various EU achievements in the field of the elderly's rights and sets out their plans of action for the future belies what has been, in reality, a chaotic and fragmented journey. There remains a high level of scepticism, therefore, as to whether the new-found elderly's rights plan has the necessary conviction and substance to have a meaningful effect for older persons over a longer period. This scepticism is produced fundamentally by the fact that, until now, the EU elderly's rights measures have been deprived of any clear ideological frame of reference. More specifically, EU old age law and policy lacks a consistent and persuasive allegiance to international elderly's rights and principles as embodied in the 1982 Vienna International Plan of Action on Ageing,[6] the UN Principles for Older Persons,

[3] Amplius DM Trubek and LG Trubek, 'Hard and Soft Law in the Construction of Social Europe: the Role of the Open Method of Co-ordination' (2005) 11 *European Law Journal* 343–64. See also F Vandenbrouke, 'La Coordination ouverte et le vieillissemente: quelle valeur ajoutèe pour l'Europe sociale?' (2001) 9/10 *Europa-Novas Fronteiras* 59–66.

[4] For a good résumé of the Charter see K Leichsenring, J Billings and H Nies (eds), *Long-Term Care in Europe: Improving Policy and Practice* (New York, Palgrave Macmillan, 2013) 123 ff.

[5] A/RES/46/91.

[6] The Vienna International Plan of Action on Ageing, the first international instrument on the subject, was endorsed by the United Nations General Assembly in 1982 (resolution 37/51), having being adopted earlier the same year at the World Assembly on Ageing at Vienna, Austria. The text is available at: www.un.org/ageing/vienna_intlplanofaction.html.

the 2002 Madrid International Plan of Action on Ageing (MIPAA),[7] the CESCR General Comment No 6 to the economic, social and cultural rights of older people,[8] and more recently the Recommendation on the promotion of human rights of older persons ('the Recommendation') by the Council of Europe. Indeed, this is despite the importance both in theory and practice of these rights and principles, since they conceptualise elderly as 'vulnerable'.[9] As a result, it is maintained that two consequences follow: first, that conflicting indications on the currency of the elderly's rights arise at EU level; secondly, that their vulnerability has being overlooked in the face of concurring economic and political goals.[10]

It is the present author's opinion that any future elderly's rights plan, to be effective and feasible, should be cast within a more persuasive and lucid normative framework, and should openly identify the normative standards in international human rights law in relation to older persons as its primary influence in this respect. This is notwithstanding the body of soft law standards adopted by the Council of Europe and the United Nations such as, respectively, the Recommendation on the promotion of human rights of older persons, the Vienna International Plan of Action on Ageing, the UN Principles of Older Persons and the Madrid International Plan of Action of Ageing, all non-binding in nature and unable to substitute legally binding standards. In fact, as has been recently advocated by others (the Office of the High Commissioner for Human Rights), 'these standards are of critical importance to the further realization of the welfare of older persons'.[11] Indeed, the European Commission could usefully refer to these and other standards as tools to scrutinise future EU acts and measures in the field of the elderly's rights. In other words, the normative standards in international human rights law in relation to older persons could have been singled out by the European Commission as the definitive framework within which to elaborate and enforce its future elderly's rights strategy. Again, explicit references to the normative standards in international human rights law in relation to older persons could also inform European Court of Justice (ECJ) interpretations of EU legislation on the elderly.

[7] On the subject, see M Malloch-Brown, *Joint Statement to the Second World Assembly on Ageing*, (Madrid, Tirant Lo Blanch, 2002) 10 ff; A Evrard, *La personne agée dans le droit international et européen des droits de l'homme* (Bruxelles, Bruylant, 2005) 11 ff.

[8] See *Economic, Social and Cultural Rights of Older Persons: General Comment 6*, UN ESCOR, Econ, Soc, & Cultural Rts Comm, 13th Sess, para 1, UN Doc E/C12/1995/16/Rev 1 (1995) (General Comment 6). For a commentary, see F Seatzu, 'The Rights of Older Persons and the International Covenant on Economic, Social and Cultural Rights' (2011) 15 *Mediterranean Human Rights Law Journal* 254 ff.

[9] For a thorough discussion in general terms of the vulnerability of older persons see M Albertson Fineman, above n 1, p 73 ff.

[10] See also H Meenan, 'Reflecting on age discrimination and rights of elderly in the European Union and the Council of Europe' (2007) 14 *Maastricht Journal of European and Comparative Law* 41 ff.

[11] OHCHR, *Human Rights of Older Persons: International Human Rights Principles and Standards, Background Paper: OEWGA (18–21 April 2011)*, available at: http://social.un.org/ageing-working-group/firstsession.shtml.

The aim of this chapter is to critically assess and evaluate the impact that a more explicit integration of the normative standards in international human rights law in relation to older persons in these various EU contexts could have on older persons' rights. In doing so, it will explore how a more pro-vulnerable approach and a more international human rights law sensitive approach to EU law and policy-making might be obtained. The second section that follows this introduction sets the scene for the debate, with a brief résumé of how the elderly's rights have evolved under European law. The third section then considers, respectively, the impact of the normative standards in international human rights law in relation to older persons considered as a vulnerable group at EU institutional level with a view to ascertaining the extent of the EU's forthcoming duties to comply with these standards. The fourth section will discuss how the normative standards in international human rights law in relation to older persons have been integrated into EU legislation, and the consequences of this. The fifth section will assess the extent to which the above-mentioned standards in international human rights law in relation to older persons have been (or could be) used to inform judicial interpretations of EU old age law and policy. The sixth section will conduct a study of the influence of such instruments of soft law on the case law of the European Court of Justice. The seventh section conveys how the above-named standards on the elderly's rights might be more usefully integrated into the EU decision-making process with the aim of enhancing the EU's ability to fight against the vulnerability of older persons more efficaciously. The last section concludes.

II. BRIEF SURVEY OF HOW THE ELDERLY'S RIGHTS HAVE EVOLVED AT THE COUNCIL OF EUROPE AND EU LEVELS

Starting with the evolution of 'the elderly's rights' within the framework of the Council of Europe, we must recall that neither the European Convention on Human Rights (ECHR) nor its Additional Protocols contain a provision such as Article 23 of the Revised Social Charter. This does not signify, however, that the ECHR and its Protocols do not recognise elderly people as subjective rights holders. On the contrary, the European Court of Human Rights (ECtHR) has pronounced a number of judgments relating to violations of human rights that can have a direct impact on older persons. For instance, it has emphasised the obligations of contracting states to take measures which guarantee the full and free enjoyment of the rights recognised in the ECHR to every individual within its jurisdiction. Moreover, when it stressed that the principles of equal entitlement is strengthened by Article 14, that forbids discrimination in the enjoyment of Convention rights and freedoms. Therefore, it is clear that, in theory, there is little to prevent the application of ECHR freedoms and rights to older persons. Furthermore, unsurprisingly but crucially, in practice, the ECtHR has desisted from setting up explicit or general boundaries on the application of the ECHR to the elderly. On the contrary, it has adopted some dynamic interpretative principles that have positive repercussions to the protection that the ECHR grants to older persons. This is confirmed in the numerous decisions of the ECtHR concerning elderly persons, notably in the *Dodov* case, where the Court maintained that the legal system as a whole, faced with an arguable case of negligent acts endangering human life, did not supply a timely and adequate response consonant with the state's procedural duties under Article 2 (right to life).[12] Yet again, this is confirmed in *Runkee and White v United Kingdom*, where the ECtHR ruled in favour of the applicants who claimed a breach of the prohibition of discrimination in conjunction with the right to the protection of property as they, as men, were not allowed to receive benefits equivalent to those available to comparable bereaved women.[13] Nevertheless, the ECHR itself does not provide for elderly people based rights.

Elderly rights are guaranteed in the Revised European Social Charter in Article 23.[14] Although this article does not enshrine a dynamic contributory image of elderly people, and regards the rights of the elderly only as 'rights of progressive implementation',[15] it enshrines the most wide-ranging of protection of the human rights of older persons. Thus, it is clear that Article 23 of the Revised European Social Charter represents significant progress. According to Article 23, states must take 'appropriate measures' to ensure the effective exercise of the right of elderly people to social protection. The Governmental Committee of the European Social Charter indicates that the concept of what is considered to be appropriate in this respect may change over time in line with a changing attitude in society related to ageing, and a progressive notion of what life shall be for elderly people.[16] In any event, under Article 23 states are demanded to make focused and planned provision in accordance with the specific needs of older persons.

Moving to the development of 'the elderly's rights' at EU level over the past 30 years, this has been both random and progressive, characterised by isolated, largely economic and social provisions, with no acknowledged association with

[12] *Dodov v Bulgaria* App no 59548/00 (ECtHR, 17 January 2008) (Fifth Section), paras 97–98.

[13] *Runkee and White v United Kingdom* App nos 42949/98 and 53134/99 (ECtHR, 10 May 2007), para 45.

[14] See European Social Charter (Revised), entered into force 7 Jan 1999, ETS No 163, available at: http://conventions.coe.int/93.

[15] 'Rights of progressive implementation' means that states are not immediately required to fully realise those rights in their jurisdiction, as they are only aims or goals which will be attained to the maximum of the states' available resources. However, even in relation to rights that call for progressive state implementation, states have the duty 'to move as expeditiously and effectively as possible towards the goal' (see CESCR, General Comment No 3: The Nature of States Parties' Obligations (Art 2, para 1, of the Covenant), 14 December 1990, E/1991/23, available at: www.refworld.org/docid/4538838e10.html, para 9.

[16] On this approach, see inter alia P Schoukens, 'Instruments of the Council of Europe and Interpretation Problems', in *International Social Security Standards: Current Views and Interpretation Matters* (Antwerp, Intersentia, 2007) 74 ff; L Jimena Quesada, 'La charte sociale a 50 ans. Réflexions de l'intérieur autour d'un anniversaire accesibil', available at: www.raison-publique.fr/article501.html.

any fundamental rights programme.[17] Measures of relevance to the elderly arose initially in the early 1980s in the context of the equal treatment rulings of the ECJ when the equal treatment principle of men and women was extended to the retirement age with a view to substantially modifying national pension arrangements.[18]

The late 1980s was something of a fallow period for the provision of rights to the EU elderly, but activities gathered pace again towards the beginning of the 1990s with the approval of an important resolution by the European Parliament to improve the protection of the people suffering from Alzheimer's,[19] followed by more comprehensive measures aimed at protecting the elderly s rights such as the communication entitled 'Towards a Europe for all ages—Promoting prosperity and solidarity between the generations' that was adopted by the European Commission on 21 May 1999.[20]

In the following years, the elderly became the indirect beneficiaries of other important measures in the field of employment equality, due to the adoption of the European Council's Directive 2000/78/EC.[21] This body of law (the Employment Equality Directive) was mainly aimed at establishing a general framework for equal treatment in employment and occupation as well as at introducing age among other grounds of differential treatment.[22] The elderly necessarily benefited from such measures, including the prohibition of discrimination on the grounds of age as a result of its ability to enhance active ageing in relation to different aspects, such as fighting premature resigning, making people work beyond pensionable age and facilitating the employment of older workers.

Priorities changed again in the late 2000s when the EU strengthened its competences to legislate on a range of public health issues, and to fight social exclusion. Responding to its renewed competence, the EU then engaged in a flurry of law-making activity in these two areas in particular, with the elderly's rights measures afforded increasing prominence in many of the normative texts.

[17] See A Evrard, C Lacour, 'A European Approach to Developing the Field of Law and Aging', in Israel Doron and Ann M Soden (eds), *Beyond Elder Law: New Directions in Law and Aging* (Heidelberg, Dordrecht, London, Springer, 2012) 149 ff.

[18] References are found in L Woods, J Steiner, P Watson, *Steiner & Woods EU Law* (Oxford, Clarendon, 2012) 605 ff.

[19] European Parliament resolution of 19 January 2011 on a European initiative on Alzheimer's disease and other dementias (2010/2084(INI)). On the issues, see N Delperee, 'European Social Policy for the Elderly', available at: http://users.skynet.be/delperee/NICOLE/European_social_policy.pdf. See also M Bell, 'The right to equality and non-discrimination', in TK Hervey and J Kenner (eds), *Economic and Social Rights Under the EU Charter of Fundamental Rights: a legal perspective* (Oxford, Hart Publishing, 2003) 106 who indicates that: 'Since the early 1990s, there has been a steady growth in the EU's attention to the position of older workers within the internal market'.

[20] *Towards a Europe for all ages—promoting prosperity and intergenerational solidarity* (COM (1999) 221 final, 21.05.1999).

[21] Council Directive 2000/78/EC establishing a general framework for equal treatment in employment and occupation [2000] OJ L303/16.

[22] Amplius A Numhauser-Henning, 'The EU Ban on Age-Discrimination and Elderly Workers–Potentials and Pitfalls', available at: www.upf.edu/gredtiss/_pdf/2013-LLRNConf_Numhauser-Henning.pdf. See also J Brottes, 'L'interdiction des discriminations en raison de l'age en droit de l'Union européene' (2011) VI *Annuaire International des Droits de l'Homme* 711 ff.

Development in the legislative sector tells only part of the story of the provision of rights to the EU elderly, nevertheless; the late 2000s also saw the emergence of a more prominent discourse on Europe's 'elderly' in the context of active citizenship, civil dialogue and strategic investment in the skills and workforce of the future (see the European Charter of rights and responsibilities of older people in need of long-term care and assistance, that aims to complete and support the charters and other measures which are already implemented in some member countries of the EU).[23] This, in turn, prompted the development of an 'EU Elderly Strategy' that continues to invest in projects for elderly people, with a special emphasis on activities that enhance social inclusion. Equally, there has been a surge of EU support for cross-sectorial cooperation programmes aimed at defending and empowering elderly people in the use of online technologies (see inter alia the Lifelong Learning Programme).[24]

This brief and rather basic summary depicts the incremental advancement of the elderly's rights within formal EU law and policy which has witnessed a gradually more explicit recognition of the role of the EU in defending and upholding elderly people's interests with the turn of each decade. Nevertheless, a closer observation of these measures, and in particular of the legislation, shows a rather less positive trend. In the framework of EU social law and policy, the elderly rights in particular the rights of the oldest old who are currently the most rapidly expanding segment of the elderly population, often remain dependent on their relatives or guardians' decisions to exercise those rights.[25] The laws relating to equality and safety in the workplace arguably offer more direct protection but only within the limited contexts in which they operate. In that respect, elderly rights across many of the EU areas summarised above remain highly conditional and restrictive. Furthermore, they are still widely circumscribed to a few measures scattered sparingly across five or so instruments with no ideological thread to link them together.

The extent to which the normative standards in international human rights law in relation to older persons might provide this ideological thread depends on a number of issues: if these instruments have sufficient legal standing at EU level to authorise using them as authoritative sources for the development and interpretation of EU measures; how these instruments can be integrated into EU law and policy in practice; and if more explicit integration of these instruments within official texts will necessarily lead to more elderly-sensitive interpretations of EU

[23] The text of the European Charter of rights and responsibilities of older people in need of long-term care and assistance is available at: www.age-platform.eu/age-policy-work/quality-care-standards-and-elder-abuse/1018-a-european-strategy-for-older-people-in-need-of-long-term-care-and-assistance#sthash.6j3x3odx.dpuf.

[24] Further informations on this programme are available at: http://eacea.ec.europa.eu/llp/index_en.php.

[25] Amplius J Gracia Ibáñez, *El maltrato familiar hacia las personas mayors* (Zaragoza, Prensas Universitarias, 2013) 33 ff; J Herring, *Older People in Law and Society* (Oxford, Oxford University Press, 2009) 13 ff.

measures. It is these questions that the following paragraphs seeks to answer, but only after a brief description of the main normative standards in international human rights law in relation to older persons.

III. THE NORMATIVE STANDARDS IN INTERNATIONAL HUMAN RIGHTS LAW IN RELATION TO OLDER PERSONS

To explore the possibilities of reshaping EU law and policy on the elderly in the light of the normative standards in international human rights law in relation to older persons and in particular in the light of the 2014 Recommendation on the promotion of human rights of older persons, it is useful to consider those standards which have succeeded in clarifying some of the most complex issues on the protection of older persons.

A broad and rather heterogeneous range of international standards on the protection of fundamental rights of elderly persons has existed for the international community since the early 1980s. The historical origins and main features of the standards that are, objectively speaking, the most useful for interpreting and applying EU old age law are briefly outlined below.

The first modern (non-legally binding) international standards for the protection of the rights of the elderly, the Vienna International Plan of Action on Ageing (the Vienna Action Plan, or VIPAA), were adopted by the World Assembly on Ageing held in Vienna in August 1982. According to their drafters, these standards were meant for governments and civil society professionals directly involved in the protection of elderly people. In fact they aim to strengthen the capacities of Governments and civil society to deal effectively with ageing populations and to address the developmental potential and dependency needs of elderly people. As they were founded on previous studies on the subject and on the work of the General Assembly of the United Nations, they were not therefore created *ex nihilo*. The most noteworthy aspect of these standards is their inclusion of over 60 recommendations for action addressing research, data collection and analysis, training and education, as well as the following sectorial areas: health and nutrition, protection of elderly consumers, housing and environment, family, social welfare, income security and employment, and education. These standards are divided into three main parts concerning respectively: a) general principles to preserve the protection of the elderly; b) recommendations for action; and c) recommendations for implementation. Twenty years later, the Madrid International Plan of Action on Ageing (MIPAA) was approved in the form of an updated and widely expanded version at the Second World Assembly on Ageing.[26] The plan indicates more than 30 objectives and formulates more than 200 detailed recommendations

[26] UN, The Madrid International Plan on Ageing, available at: www.un.org/ageing/documents/building_natl_capacity/guiding.pdf.

for action mainly by national governments, concerning all areas of life.[27] It has its primary focus on human rights.

Adopted by the UN General Assembly in 1991, the UN Principles for Older Persons are currently the most comprehensive and perhaps even the most authoritative non-binding rules of international law addressed to national authorities concerning the interpretation of fundamental rights of elderly people (jurisdictional authorities, caregivers, physicians and all those who are involved either professionally or as part of their social involvement in the wellbeing of older persons), but they are not the only ones. As framed, these principles strike a proper balance between the integration of older people into society and the acknowledgment of their special needs. A core provision is paragraph 18, which states that: 'older persons should be treated fairly regardless of age, gender, racial or ethnic background, disability or other status, and be valued independently of their economic contribution'. Perhaps what is most important to stress about these Principles is that they do not restrict their scope of application to a defined category of 'elderly people'. In so doing, the drafters of the UN Principles for Older Persons avoided dealing with the difficulties inherent in any attempt to define 'elderly people' or older persons and therefore, though implicitly, they dismissed either the alternative offered by the WHO's definition of the elderly[28] or even the most obvious criterion of the age at which a person becomes eligible for an old age pension and other 'senior citizen' benefits.[29] However, the fact that the UN Principles do not define elderly affects its scope of application and also undermines its usage by the competent national authorities.

A similar approach may be found in other non-binding international legal instruments that deal with the problems of monitoring violations of human rights of the elderly. Among these are the European Charter of the Rights and Responsibilities of Older People in Need of Long-Term Care and Assistance, which was developed in response to concerns about the violation of individual human rights of people in need of long-term care and assistance; and the 2014 Recommendation on the promotion of human rights of older persons (the Recommendation) by the Committee of Ministers of the Council of Europe, namely the first European instrument dealing specifically with the human rights of older persons and recommending action against age-discrimination in many areas.

[27] See H Meenan, 'The Future of Ageing and the Role of Age Discrimination in the Global Debate' (2005) 1 *Journal of International Aging, Law & Policy*, available at: www.stetson.edu/law/agingjournal/media/journal-of-international-aging-law-and-policy-vol-1.pdf.

[28] WHO, 'Definition of an older or elderly person', available at: www.who.int/healthinfo/survey/ageingdefnolder/en/.

[29] On the latter criterion, see DJ Harris, *The European Social Charter* (Ardsley NY, Transnational Publishers, 2001) 251, who also stresses the main limitation that is inherent in its utilisation of the criterion of the age at which a person becomes eligible for an old age pension and other 'senior citizen' benefits, namely that the age differs between men and women and varies from state to state.

IV. THE STATUS OF THE NORMATIVE STANDARDS IN INTERNATIONAL HUMAN RIGHTS LAW IN RELATION TO OLDER PERSONS AT THE EU CONSTITUTIONAL LEVEL

Notwithstanding the widespread use of 'soft law' standards as instruments that inspire general principles of EU social law and policy,[30] until recently there was nearly no reference to elderly people in any of the main European declarations of fundamental rights or the EU's treaties. On the one hand, this was clearly a consequence of the aims of these instruments to achieve economic development. Nevertheless, it is a standpoint that became less justifiable as the social and rights-based constraints of the EU have increased in importance and a progressively more explicit plan in relation to older persons has evolved.

The overall picture started to change at the beginning of the millennium and, since then, references to issues of the normative standards in international human rights law in relation to elderly people have started to appear in specific constitutional instruments. The Charter of Fundamental Rights of the European Union constitutes the first and most notable reference to these instruments.[31] This was approved in December 2000 and was motivated by the idea that the EU law concerning fundamental rights was set out in a fragmented manner across several primary and secondary law rules and presents a clear statement of the fundamental rights principles to which the EU should comply.[32] One of the most noteworthy innovations of the Charter of Fundamental Rights is that it encompasses an explicit reference to the rights of the elderly, granting them the right to lead a life of dignity and independence and to participate in social and cultural life (Article 25). This innovation is, however, partially undermined by the Explanations to the EU Charter that include Article 25's rights of the elderly (but not children (Article 24)) among the Charter rights that are not justiciable.[33] The Charter also encompasses recent trends towards the suppression of age barriers, since it provides (Article 21) that the non-discrimination clause of the Charter also includes age, and it applies horizontally.[34] Such provision resonates strongly

[30] References are found in David M Trubek and Louise G Trubek, above n 3, p 343 ff.

[31] [2010] OJ C83, Art. 25.

[32] Amplius A Weber, 'The European Charter of Fundamental Rights' (2001) 43 *German Yearbook of International Law* 101–15. See also T Eicke, 'The European Charter of Fundamental Rights: Unique Opportunity or Unwelcome Distraction' (2000) 5 *European Human Rights Law Review* 280–96.

[33] See J Blackstock, 'The EU Charter of Fundamental Rights Scope and Competence', available at: http://eutopialaw.com/2012/04/17/the-eu-charter-of-fundamental-rights-scope-and-competance/ who also stresses that: 'The provisions of this Charter which contain principles may be implemented by legislative and executive acts taken by institutions, bodies, offices and agencies of the Union, and by acts of member states when they are implementing Union law, in the exercise of their respective powers. They shall be judicially cognizable only in the interpretation of such acts and in the ruling on their legality.'

[34] However, notwithstanding the EU Charter, the elimination of age barriers in general is still very much a work in progress; to date, EU law prohibits discrimination on the grounds of age only in the field of employment. On the issue see inter alia M Schmidt, 'The Principle of Non-Discrimination in Respect of Age: Dimensions of the ECJ's Mangold Judgment' (2005) 7 *German Law Journal* 506 ff.

with the general principles of the UN Principles for Older Persons, notably those expressed in Articles 1 to 6.

The most recent, and perhaps most significant, development at EU constitutional level is the entry into force of the Treaty of Lisbon on 1 December 2009.[35] While this instrument does not refer directly to any normative standards in international human rights law in relation to older persons, it carries with it several constitutional amendments that potentially impact upon the status of elderly people's rights at EU level.[36] Specifically, the Treaty specifies the protection of the rights of older persons as one of the stated objectives of the EU (Article 1(a) of the Lisbon Treaty).[37] Nevertheless, unlike in the case of children's rights (Article 3(5) TEU), the same Treaty fails to single out the protection of the rights of the elderly as an essential feature of the EU's external relations policy. Furthermore, it also omits to encompass a provision that allows the Council and the European Parliament to adopt measures specifically addressed at fighting elderly abuse. However a range of more generic Treaty provisions relating to non-discrimination (Article 19 TFEU) and citizenship (Article 20 TFEU) support the enactment of more elderly-sensitive and inclusive EU laws and policies. Similarly, the Lisbon Treaty enhances the status of fundamental rights at the EU level within the amended Treaty on European Union. It grants 'Treaty-level' status to the Charter provisions (Article 6(1) TEU) and clarifies that the EU: 'shall accede to the European Convention for the Protection of Human Rights and Fundamental Freedoms' (Article 6(2) TEU).[38]

The renewed visibility of human rights on the EU constitutional scale as a result of the entry into force of the Lisbon Treaty bodes well for the future adoption of normative standards in international human rights law in relation to elderly people. It attests, quite simply, that measures adopted within the scope of EU competence shall comply with human rights standards. Although, at least in theory, this means a more solid basis for challenges to EU or member state activities that are assumed to be incompatible with international instruments, including soft-law instruments like the European Charter of the Rights and Responsibilities

[35] Treaty of Lisbon amending the Treaty on European Union and the Treaty establishing the European Community [2007] OJ C306.

[36] See also PF Lotito, 'Article 25: The Rights of the Elderly', in WBT Mock and G Demuro (eds), *Human Rights in Europe: Commentary on the Charter of Fundamental Rights of the European Union* (Durham NC, Carolina Academic Press, 2010) 158–64.

[37] Art 1(a) of the Lisbon Treaty makes clear: 'The Union is founded on the values of respect for human dignity, freedom, democracy, equality, the rule of law and respect for human rights, including the rights of persons belonging to minorities. These values are common to the member states in a society in which pluralism, non-discrimination, tolerance, justice, solidarity and equality between women and men prevail.' See also the Case C-555/07 *Kücükdeveci* v *Swedex GmbH & Co KG* (2010), [2010] *IRLR* 346 where the ECJ maintained that non-discrimination on the ground of age was a general principle of law. It is applicable in individual relations, even if it has not been implemented into domestic before the expiry of the transposition period, provided that it falls under the scope of EU law (which means in the area of employment).

[38] On the subject, see recently Paul Gragl, *The Accession of the European Union to the European Convention on Human Rights* (Oxford, Hart Publishing, 2013).

of Older People in Need of Long-Term Care and Assistance, the Recommendation CM/Rec (2011) 5 of the Committee of Ministers on reducing the risk of vulnerability of elderly migrants and improving their welfare and the Council of Europe Recommendation on the promotion of human rights of older persons,[39] it can also provide increased sensitivity to the compatibility of EU acts and measures with the content of the above-named standards at the drafting stage.

V. INTEGRATING THE NORMATIVE STANDARDS IN INTERNATIONAL HUMAN RIGHTS LAW IN RELATION TO OLDER PERSONS INTO EU LEGISLATION

The above analysis of the status of the normative standards in international human rights law in relation to older persons within the EU constitutional order generates some debates on the extent to which the instruments have filtered down to impact on secondary legislation at the EU level.

References to some of the above-named standards, including the European Charter of the rights and responsibilities of older people in need of long-term care and assistance have occasionally featured in EU policy and legislative instruments over the course of the past decade. The most noteworthy examples in this regard are the instruments relating to non-discrimination and the prevention of trafficking of human beings. For instance, European Council Directive 2000/78/EC, which establishes a general framework for equal treatment in employment and occupation (the Employment Equality Directive), protects older workers against age discrimination.[40] The basis of this provision is that it upholds the elderly's rights and covers age among other grounds of differential treatment, age discrimination is permitted in very few circumstances, such as protecting older or younger workers in certain situations, but otherwise discrimination purely on the grounds of age cannot be justified, in accordance with Articles 1, paragraphs 1 and 7 of the International Convention on the Protection of the Rights of All Migrant Workers and Members of Their Families.[41]

Other instruments, while they do not clearly name any normative standards in international human rights law in relation to older persons as their source, directly refer to normative rules and principles that are usually associated with current documents concerning older persons. Most notably, the primacy of

[39] Recommendation CM/Rec (2014) 2 of the Committee of Ministers to member states on the promotion of human rights of older persons (Adopted by the Committee of Ministers on 19 February 2014 at the 1192nd meeting of the Ministers' Deputies). The text of the Recommendation is also available at: https://wcd.coe.int/ViewDoc.jsp?id=2162283&Site=COE&BackColorInternet=C3C3C3&BackColorIntranet=EDB021&BackColorLogged=F5D383.

[40] Council Directive (EC) 2000/78 establishing a general framework for equal treatment in employment and occupation [2000] OJ L303/16.

[41] International Convention on the Protection of the Rights of All Migrant Workers and Members of Their Families, adopted by General Assembly resolution 45/158 of 18 December 1990. The text of the Convention is available at: www2.ohchr.org/english/bodies/cmw/cmw.htm.

the principle according to which elderly people have the same rights as the rest of the population (as enshrined in several binding and non-binding international standards on elderly protection) resonates throughout the relevant non-discrimination instruments. For instance, decisions to grant or withdraw working rights from older adults must be consistent with the principle according to which differences of treatment on the grounds of age shall not constitute discrimination (see Article 6 European Council's Directive 2000/78/EC). Similarly, EU legislation on preventing and combating trafficking in human beings and protecting its victims (paragraph 20 Preamble Directive 2011/36/EU of the European Parliament and of the Council of 5 April 2011 on preventing and combating trafficking in human beings and protecting its victims) demand that assessment of the individual needs of victims of trafficking during criminal investigations and proceedings should, among other circumstances, have regard to their age.[42]

EU healthcare law provision is also inspire by normative principles enshrined, inter alia, in the UN Principles for Older Persons. For example, it demands that proper consideration shall be taken of the need for elderly patients not to be discriminated against due to their condition (paragraph 21 Preamble Directive 2011/24/EU on the application of patients' rights in cross-border healthcare).[43] Such measures clearly resonate with Article 18 of the UN Principles for Older Persons, which provides that elderly people shall be treated fairly regardless of age, gender, racial or ethnic background, disability or other status, and be valued independently of their economic contribution.[44]

The UN Principles for Older Persons' overarching commitment to non-discrimination, that is, to uphold the rights of *all* older persons on an equal basis (as enunciated in Article 18 of the UN Principles for Older Persons), is also reflected in EU social security law. For example, EEC Regulation 1408/71, which aims at ensuring that all European citizens and Third-Country Nationals who legally reside within the European Community have the right to social security benefits when they move to another Member State in order to stay live or work there, states that: 'persons entitled to benefits for … old age … must be able to enjoy all the benefits which have accrued to them in the various Member States' (paragraph 11 Preamble Regulation (EEC) 1408/71 of the Council of 14 June 1971 on the application of social security schemes to employed persons and their families moving within the Community).[45] This instrument further provides that member states in the application of the provisions of the Regulation must be sensitive to the specific needs and limitations of the people who perceive an old age pension (see, eg, Article 28 Regulation (EEC) 1408/71 dealing with pensions payable under the

[42] [2011] OJ L101.

[43] [2011] OJ L88/45.

[44] Accordingly, see also Art 7 of the Council of Europe Recommendation on the promotion of human rights of older persons, stressing that: 'Member States should consider making explicit reference to "age" in their national anti-discrimination legislation'.

[45] [1971] OJ L149.

legislation of one or more states where no right to benefits in kind is enjoyed in the country of residence). The same instruments require member states to adapt their procedures for the payment of pensions to respond to the specific vulnerabilities of old-age pensioners; Article 33 Regulation (EEC) 1408/71, for example, requires member states to ensure that: 'contributions payable by a pensioner to cover benefits in kind, shall be authorised to make such deductions from the pension payable by such institution, calculated in accordance with the legislation concerned, to the extent that the cost of the benefits in kind under Articles 27, 28, 31 and 32 are to be borne by an institution of the said Member State'. Such provisions reflect not only the general principles of Articles 12 and 18 of the UN Principles for Older Persons, but also more substantive provisions such as Article 2 of the UN Principles for Older Persons which provides that older persons must have access to other income-generating opportunities.

It appears then that the EU has embraced the UN Principles for Older Persons, or at least the normative principles it endorses, across a range of key legislative areas, in a way that would have been inconceivable a decade ago. Issues abound, however, as to what mere reference to such principles achieves in practice; do they truly boost the elderly's rights in any tangible way, or are they merely rhetorical? Closer examination of the elderly's rights provisions referred to above mitigate optimism bias: most fall into two categories corresponding to different levels of 'deficiency'.

The first category encompasses those normative tools that, clearly, encompass proper, legally binding provisions for elderly people but whose effectiveness depends largely on how conscientious member states are in their enforcement. Clearly, the same applies to the secondary legislation recalled above because any provisions encompassed by the EU Directives will only be as effective as the domestic implementing measures on which they hang and, indeed, on how rigorous the EU is in enforcing their implementation. The fact remains, however, that regardless of the range of enforcement systems available in the EU, all too often even the most elderly-targeted EU legislation has often been ignored. An example of this is found in legislation, adopted in 2000, to eradicate obstacles to the involvement of people of all ages in employment and training in the context of the European drive for economic growth and employment (Council Directive 2000/78/EC of 27 November 2000). This tool sets out a comprehensive range of duties addressed simultaneously at fighting age discrimination in employment and ensuring older workers can enjoy equal protection across the EU. Indeed, this Directive boosts a strikingly intuitive idea of elderly people's fundamental rights. Subsequent analyses show, however, that only a minority of member states have adopted any steps to implement the rules.[46]

[46] References are found in AGE contribution to the European Commission's assessment of the transposition and application of Employment Equality Directive (2000/78/EC), available at: www.age-platform.eu/images/stories/EN/AGE_response_to_EC_consultation_on_implementation_of_Employment_Directive_FINAL.pdf.

A second, and more common obstacle hampering the impact of the normative standards in international human rights law in relation to older persons-inspired measures, relates to the conditional nature of many EU legislative rules on elderly people. In other terms, they refer to the need to safeguard elderly people's rights but only in accordance with current domestic law or process. Such is the case for some of the most important provisions of Regulation (EEC) 1408/71 referred to above. This instrument may make various references to social security benefits and measures of protection against social risks, nevertheless, it does not endow the EU with any noteworthy competence to establish the content and scope of such measures at the domestic level; they rely instead on appropriate domestic procedures and guidance being in place at the national level to give effect to such rights. For example, Article 43 of this Regulation provides that: 'invalidity benefits shall be converted into old age benefits, where appropriate, under the conditions laid down by the legislation or legislations under which they were granted'. In practice, research has illustrated how this power of conversion has been exercised differently in the member states of the EU. Similarly, although healthcare legislation prescribes that due consideration be given to the needs of elderly patients, the nature and extent of this requirement is notoriously inconsistent across the member states, not to mention across regions within each member state.

These failings are further evidenced through the CJEU's interpretation of EU legislation relating to older persons, an issue to which our consideration focuses below.

VI. THE INEXPERIENCE OF THE EUROPEAN COURT OF JUSTICE IN DEALING WITH THE NORMATIVE STANDARDS IN INTERNATIONAL HUMAN RIGHTS LAW IN RELATION TO OLDER PERSONS

Although the CJEU has a long tradition of upholding and promoting human rights, it nevertheless does not has, as observed above, a long tradition of promoting the human rights of elderly people.

With things being as such, it is clear that the CJEU would benefit from referring to the above-mentioned standards as major (if not indispensable due to the absence of a UN convention on the rights of older persons)[47] resources for their interpretation. In themselves these instruments are not legally binding. Nevertheless, as they contain several clarifications on issues such as the measures of protection of older persons against violence and abuse, the positive obligations to prevent discrimination and eliminate structural patterns of disadvantage, the right to social security and the right to a standard of living adequate for the

[47] On the debates focusing on a UN Convention of the rights of older persons, see among others J Williams, 'An International Convention on the Rights of Older People ?', in M Odello and S Cavandoli (eds), *Emerging Areas of Human Rights in the 21st Century—The Role of the Universal Declaration of Human Rights* (Abingdon, Routledge, 2011) 129 ff.

health and well-being of elderly people and their families, and the measures to prevent discrimination on the grounds of age in employment and occupation and to develop retirement programs, they can provide valuable recommendations to the CJEU to steer the enforcement of the rights of elderly people and members of their families in the EU member states. In particular the Council of Europe Recommendation on the promotion of human rights of older persons which: 'applies to persons whose older age constitutes, alone or in interaction with other factors, including perceptions and attitudes, a barrier to the full enjoyment of their human rights and fundamental freedoms and their full and effective participation in society on an equal basis' can be useful, because it: 'set out a number of principles to be followed and gives examples of good practices that can help governments adopt appropriate measures promoting also respect for the inherent dignity of the aged', as the press communiqué of the Council of Europe observed.[48] Mutatis mutandis, the same conclusion applies to the UN Principles on the Rights of Older Persons, that encompass a wide and useful range of principles to be incorporated into national policies that enhance the independence, participation, care, self-fulfilment and dignity of older persons.

The next question is therefore whether the CJEU in its case law has already referred to the Council of Europe Recommendation on the promotion of human rights of older persons, the UN Principles on the Rights of Older Persons, the European Charter of the Rights and Responsibilities of Older People in Need of Long-Term Care and Assistance, or other normative standards in international human rights law in relation to older persons as interpretative aids to the EU legislation relevant to older people's issues. In other words, in light of these rules and instruments the question is now whether the CJEU has ever scrutinised the compliance of national measures with the fundamental rights of older persons. To answer this it is necessary to investigate the most significant judicial decisions by the CJEU in the field of the rights of the elderly.

In the ground-breaking case of *Mangold v Helm*[49] the then ECJ stated that the principle of non-discrimination on grounds of age is to be regarded as a general principle of EU law.[50] Nevertheless, it did not refer to sources of law outside the EU's normative framework, namely the UN Principles on the Rights of Older Persons to support its decision. Surprisingly though, the 'findings of the ECJ as regards the interpretation of Article 6 of Directive 2000/78/EC *which deals with the justification of differences of treatment on grounds of age* were highly problematic', as Magdalene Schmidt lucidly observed.[51] A similar pattern emerges from

[48] Available at: www.coe.int/t/dghl/standardsetting/hrpolicy/other_committees/cddh-age/default_EN.asp.

[49] Case C-144/04 *Werner Mangold v Rüdiger Helm* (2005) 58 *Neue Juristische Wochenschrift* 3695 (the *Mangold* case).

[50] On the *Mangold* case, see inter alia M Schmidt, above n 34, p 505 ff.

[51] See M Schmidt, above n 34, p 516 (my emphasis) and p 519, stressing that: 'In its decision in *Mangold*, the ECJ did not transfer its established case law concerning the principle of non-discrimination with respect to gender, but argued that a general principle of non-discrimination in respect of age

the case of *Incorporated Trustees of the National Council on Ageing (Age Concern England) v Secretary of State for Business, Enterprise and Regulatory Reform*[52] where the ECJ confirmed the legitimacy of a UK law allowing employers the right to require employees to retire at the age of 65. Moreover, in its decision in *Rosenbladt*,[53] the ECJ did not refer to the above-named standards and principles when it held that clauses on the automatic termination of employment contracts may escape the prohibition on discrimination on the grounds of age, on the ground that the clauses are the reflection of a balance between diverging but legitimate interests. Moreover, the idea that the above-mentioned standards and principles in international human rights law in relation to older persons are not indispensable tools of interpretation of EU legislation can be (implicitly) derived from the decision in *Ingeniørforeningen i Danmark*,[54] where the ECJ refused a severance allowance on the ground that he was entitled to draw an old-age pension. An analogous line of reasoning is also found in the *Commission v Greece*[55] case, which concerns the issue of the provisions of the Greek Civil and Military Pensions Code. Reaffirming the interpretative approach from the *Mangold* case, the ECJ held that: 'because the pension is regarded as pay, it would be contrary to the principle of equal treatment to impose rules that differ on the grounds of the worker's gender'. Furthermore, an analogous line of reasoning and approach is also found in *Femarbel v Commission Communautaire commune de Bruxelles-Capitale*,[56] where the Court held that the exclusion of 'social services' from the scope of the Parliament and Council Directive 2006/123/EC of 12 December 2006 on services in the internal market covered any activity intended to assess, maintain or restore the state of health of patients, where that activity was carried out by healthcare professionals recognised as such by the member state concerned, regardless of the ways in which the facilities where care was provided were organised and financed or whether they were public or private.

Moving to the reasons behind the almost systematic rejection of the normative standards in international human rights law in relation to older persons as interpretative tools of EU legislation applicable to older persons, the case law of the now CJEU as a whole indicates that the Court's aim is always and primarily to avoid the discrimination of older workers and retired people. Even though this

could be found in various international instruments and in the constitutional traditions common to the Member States'.

[52] Case C-388/07 *Incorporated Trustees of the National Council on Ageing (Age Concern England) v Secretary of State for Business, Enterprise and Regulatory Reform* ECJ (Third Chamber), Judgment of 5 March 2009.

[53] Case C-45/09 *Gisela Rosenbladt v Oellerking Gebäudereinigungsges mbH*, ECJ (Grand Chamber), Judgment of 12 October 2010.

[54] Case C-499/08 *Ingeniørforeningen i Danmark v Region Syddanmark*, ECJ (Grand Chamber), Judgment of 12 October 2010.

[55] Case C-559/07 *Commission of the European Communities v Hellenic Republic*, ECJ (Third Chamber), Judgment of 26 March 2009.

[56] Case C-57/12 *Fédération des maisons de repos privées de Belgique (Femarbel) ASBL v Commission communautaire commune de Bruxelles-Capitale* [2013] WLR (D) 278.

aim would certainly not be compromised by the application of these standards, it is also true that, if applied, these standards, since they generally articulate the principle of non-discrimination in broad and abstract terms, would not be of great help to the CJEU in fighting the discrimination of the elderly in the workplace. Secondly, the rejection of such normative standards is suggested by a widespread opinion among scholars as to the limited effectiveness (if not ineffectiveness) of soft law instruments as a framework of legal interpretation at the European and the domestic level. Indeed, as the EU member states, at both the administrative and political level, do not easily endorse non-binding rules or follow the incentives given under soft forms of governance, it is not easy to ascertain how the CJEU may exercise its review power.[57] Undoubtedly in the case law of the CJEU it would be hard, if not impossible, to find something more operative than rather generic statements on the existence of a need for member states not to resist non-binding EU law instruments.[58] Thirdly, the rejection of the above-mentioned standards and principles was most likely inspired by the major difficulties of selecting—from among the various standards and general principles currently existing on the protection of fundamental rights of older people—the most appropriate ones for the interpretation of EU legislation applicable to older persons. Fourth, it was most likely prompted by the fact that the mere existence of soft law is a controversial issue.[59] Fifthly and finally, such rejection was clearly, though only indirectly, influenced by the fact that the CJEU has refused to extend its constructive methods of interpretation to the use of soft law instruments designed to protect the fundamental rights of vulnerable people that it expressly fails to incorporate them within its technique of purposive interpretation.[60]

None of these difficulties must be underestimated, at least as regards the Council of Europe Recommendation on the promotion of human rights of older persons and the UN Principles on the Rights of Older Persons. Nevertheless, this is no justification for the exclusion of these and other corresponding standards and general principles such as the European Charter of the Rights and

[57] Good references are found in Sabine Saurugger, 'Resistance to EU Soft Law: A Typology of Instruments', available at: www.euce.org/eusa/2013/papers/8c_sarugger.pdf. See also F Terpan, 'Does EU Soft Differ from International Soft Law?—Using Soft Law in a Supranational System of Governance—An Agenda for Research', Paper presented at the 53rd International Studies Association Conference, San Diego, 2012.

[58] See Sabine Saurugger, above n 57.

[59] See among others L Blutman, 'In the Trap of a Legal Metaphor: International Soft Law' (2010) 59 *International & Comparative Law Quarterly* 605–24; J d'Aspremont, 'Softness in International Law: A Self-Serving Quest for New Legal Materials' (2008) 19 *European Journal of International Law* 1075–93; M Barelli, 'The Role of Soft Law in the International Legal System: the Case the United Nations Declaration on the Rights of Indigenous Peoples' (2009) 58 *International & Comparative Law Quarterly* 957–83.

[60] Denis Batta, 'Better Regulation and The Improvement Of EU Regulatory Environment', available at: www.pedz.uni-mannheim.de/daten/edz-ma/ep/07/pe378.290-en.pdf, who also stresses that: 'Due to a long-standing tradition of soft law in Community law, however, the ECJ has developed a case law on the nature and legal status of some soft law instruments. Still, an inclusive collection of all soft law instruments that have been used in the Community does not exist.'

Responsibilities of Older People in Need of Long-Term Care and Assistance as interpretative tools of EU legislation applicable to older persons. On the contrary, given in particular the utility of the Council of Europe Recommendation on the promotion of human rights of older persons in clarifying both the meaning and operational character of EU legislation applicable to older persons and thus also in fighting against the vulnerability of this category of individuals, the CJEU's approach to this legislation should be based on a coherent and systematic use of these rules of soft law. Indeed, this is though the consequences of the negative approach of the CJEU towards the aforesaid standards and general principles have not been universally recognised as being particularly relevant in practice. Nevertheless, they have been (implicitly) recognised as such by Israel Doron, who rightly observed that the geriatric-related jurisprudence of the CJEU is not particularly helpful in protecting the rights of older Europeans and in fighting against their vulnerability.[61]

VII. DEVELOPING MORE NORMATIVE STANDARDS IN INTERNATIONAL HUMAN RIGHTS LAW IN RELATION TO THE OLDER PERSONS-BASED APPROACH TO EU LAW AND POLICY-MAKING

The above analysis shows the unstable and uncertain character of the EU's relationship with the normative standards in international human rights law in relation to older persons. Indeed, the instruments now feature more systematically in the jargon of the EU normative process than it once did, though they remain restless companions. These remarks support the point that true allegiance to the normative standards in international human rights law in relation to older persons implies more than making reference to it judicial decisions or normative texts; the whole process, ideology and investment surrounding the normative standards in international human rights law in relation to older persons also need to be embraced. This obligation is well described in the Preamble of the Council of Europe Recommendation on the promotion of human rights of older persons, which provides that: 'the governments of the member States *shall* ensure that the principles set out in the appendix to this recommendation are complied with in national legislation and practice relating to older persons, and evaluate the effectiveness of the measures taken'. This duty is further bolstered by the same Preamble that sets out, in a form appropriate to the recommendatory character of this instrument, reporting tasks of Council of Europe member states on the measures they have enacted to give effect to its provisions.[62] The list of activities

[61] See I Doron, 'Older Europeans and the European Court of Justice' (2013) 42 *Age and Aging* 606 who stresses that: 'the amount of elder rights cases brought before the ECJ is very low, and their overall quantitative weight is minor at best'.

[62] Para 2 of the Preamble which provides that: 'member states *must* ensure, by appropriate means and action—including, where appropriate, translation—a wide dissemination of this recommendation

included within these guidelines is extensive and sheds new light on what genuine allegiance to the normative standards in international human rights law in relation to older persons demands also of the EU: review of existing practices; a comprehensive rights of the elderly-based national strategy; making elderly people visible in the budgets; training, awareness raising; cooperation with civil society; international cooperation and working with elderly people directly.

The European Commission, which is committed to healthy and dignified ageing for Europeans, has already made a good start in identifying many of these issues in its pilot European Innovation Partnership on active and healthy ageing and, by the same token, there has been much talk at the EU level of mainstreaming the elderly's rights into its policies and laws. However, so far, this approach seems to consist primarily of sporadic references to some normative standards in international human rights law in relation to older persons like the UN Principles on the Rights of Older Persons within legislative texts, with little evidence of the more comprehensive approach recently suggested by the Council of Europe Recommendation on the promotion of human rights of older persons. To achieve this, we recommend that the following key issues demand urgent attention.

First of all, in order to move forward with the elderly's rights, the EU must reflect on past and current results or failures in the area. This demands the introduction of a much more effective, tailored monitoring systems to check the impact of EU law and policy on older persons. While a number of systems could be introduced to achieve this, reference to high quality comparative statistical data is essential. At present, nevertheless, there is a worrying and distinct absence of data relating to elderly people at the EU level, making effective monitoring hard if not impossible. Addressing this void is not just an issue of resourcing the acquisition of additional information, a procedure that would be both expensive and time-consuming. Alongside this, additional efforts could be made to disaggregate existing data to identify thc distinct status of elderly people and to expose the position of different groups of the elderly. This might be obtained via detailed consultation with the European Statistical body, EUROSTAT, and with national statistical bodies to enhance a Europe-wide consensus on gathering more elderly-focused data. Such endeavours must be complemented, however, by a more resolute allegiance on the part of the Commission to reverse the findings of such supervisory activities into substantive policy responses.

Besides, it also appears that the abolition of structural obstacles within the European Commission in particular (and more in general within the EU), has to be become a priority task. Currently, the European Commission is badly equipped to deal with the requests of developing the all-embracing elderly's rights strategy is envisages. Most noteworthy, there is still inadequate co-ordination or collaboration between the different departments (DGs—Directorates-General) within

among competent authorities and stakeholders, with a view to raising awareness of the human rights and fundamental freedoms of older persons.'

the Commission; in fact the Elderly's Rights Strategy is mostly connected with and driven by DG Justice (DG JUST), notwithstanding the fact that other DGs have been leading highly innovative and far-reaching activities relating to elderly people for some years now. In addition, the European Commission shall also take into consideration the related activities of the Fundamental Rights Agency, as well as of the related activities of other EU agencies. There are frequent anxieties that this endemical divisiveness between the various EU Commission departments is hindering the joined-up, all-embracing approach that the Elderly's Rights Strategy requires.

Furthermore, a more regular engagement with those dealing with elderly people's rights issues and, where indispensable or appropriate, direct involvement with elderly people themselves would also boost the possibilities of application of the above-named normative standards on an EU scale. An additional reflection has to be made on how this result will be accomplished, though it is clear that it has to bc realised in an entirely different form than that of the broad-brush surveys which have been conducted within the EU to date. Elderly people's direct involvement shall become a constant of each policy and normative development at EU scale, and shall be strengthened at domestic level in the enforcement of EU policy and normative measures. The absence of data and research reflecting the opinions of elderly people is clearly an issue that the EU might face as a priority in itself via increased investment in programmes that boost authentic and advanced participatory techniques with older persons from a different range of backgrounds. Furthermore, information on elderly people and the EU could be made more accessible to older persons, via more interactive and elderly-friendly media, consistent with the Preamble of the Council of Europe Recommendation on the promotion of human rights of older persons.[63] Lastly, additional training and guidelines on how this research, where suitable, may be translated into objective policy recommendations might also be developed in cooperation with international stakeholders and NGOs with a view to obviating tokenism.

VIII. FINAL REMARKS

The above paragraphs have shown that the EU has achieved a broad range of outcomes in the battlefield of elderly people's rights. These activities have touched upon a different and, at points, somewhat disconnected, range of areas. As progress has deepened, especially in the last decade, efforts have been made to insert some appearance of skilfulness to guarantee that these evolutions continue and boost the rights of the elderly in an agreeable and substantive way. Nevertheless,

[63] Some progress has been made towards developing a dedicated website on the elderly's rights issues but this is not readily accessible and there has been limited input of older persons into this process.

in spite of these attempts, the lack of any ideological linchpin inherent in these activities is both impressive and baffling.

There are signs, nevertheless, that the EU institutions are rapidly embracing the above-named standards and principles as an authoritative reference point in EU law and policy processes relating to the elderly. Sporadic legislative provisions progressively reflect the ethos of some of the major normative standards in international human rights law in relation to older persons, especially in the areas of employment, non-discrimination and gender equality, where the core principles of the normative standards in international human rights law in relation to older persons have clearly informed legal measures. However, the ideals adopted by the instruments have yet to pervade the policy, legal and judicial process in a more substantive and all-embracing manner.

Of course, it is crucial to recall that the normative standards in international human rights law in relation to older persons are just some of various instruments at the EU's disposal in its journey toward warring against the vulnerability of elderly people and achieving a more elderly-sensitive approach; elderly rights can arise and be enforced at the EU level even in the absence of a formal and reconciled commitment to the above-named standards. The Council of Europe Recommendation on the promotion of human rights of older persons, for instance, might offer extremely impelling platforms for the improvement of the elderly's rights at this level and thus, indirectly, also for the development of feasible strategies against the vulnerability of older persons.[64]

Indeed, the case law of the CJEU shows that the judiciary is rather more at ease with advancing the elderly's rights within these frameworks rather than through more direct references to the less acquainted framework of the above-mentioned standards. The accomplishment of a more consonant, pro-vulnerable approach to elderly people, nevertheless, demands more emphatic commitment to the unambiguously elderly-focused agenda of the latter. Indeed, with proper counselling on how to use these devices as auditing instruments at different levels of EU activity, many of the actual anomalies and, indeed, breaches of elderly people's rights and underestimations of the vulnerability of older persons currently manifest in EU law, might be reduced. This, of course, requires that the EU's institutions move beyond simple rhetorical commitment to the principles of the above-mentioned standards themselves, towards a more proactive engagement in the whole process surrounding the normative standards in international human rights law in relation to older persons.

[64] See also F Mégret, 'The human rights of older persons: a growing challenge' (2011) 11 *Human Rights Law Review* 37–66, who stresses that the European Convention on Human Rights has been used by older persons seeking to protect their rights with mixed success.

4

Disability as a Form of Vulnerability under EU and CoE Law: Embracing the 'Social Model'?

ANJA WIESBROCK

I. INTRODUCTION

ONE IN SIX people in the European Union (EU) has a mild to severe disability. This means that around 80 million people are affected to some extent by environmental and attitudinal barriers preventing their full participation in society and the economy.[1] People with disabilities[2] are affected by poverty to a much larger extent than other EU citizens, and face limitations in access to employment as well as limited opportunities to enjoy goods and services, such as education, healthcare, transport, housing and technology. Historical discrimination against people with disabilities and their marginalised position means they are particularly vulnerable members of society.

Whilst vulnerability is universal, in that the threat of harm in the form of physical damage from injury or disease affects all human beings to varying degrees at different points of time, it is also particular and experienced uniquely by every person due to differences in the magnitude and potential of vulnerabilities at the individual level.[3] Some members of society are more vulnerable than others due to their specific characteristics. This applies amongst others to people with

[1] European Commission Communication, European Disability Strategy 2010–2020. A Renewed Commitment to a Barrier-Free Europe, COM (2010) 636 final, 15 November 2010, 3.

[2] In an area full of stigmatising words and phrases, I would like to explain the use of terminology throughout the Article. I recognise that the use of the concept 'disabled persons' is problematic in that it perceives people with disabilities as a monolith, or collective noun. This is, however, the terminology used by the Courts and I therefore use the concepts of 'disabled persons' and 'persons with disabilities' interchangeably. Moreover, I adopt a broad notion of the concept of disability, including all persons with some kind of physical or mental impairment. This includes persons with physical, mental, intellectual and sensory impairments as well as persons living with medical conditions such as HIV/AIDS or diabetes.

[3] M Albertson Fineman, 'The Vulnerable Subject and the Responsive State' (2010) 60 *Emory Law Journal* 272.

disabilities, who may be placed at increased risk of harm and human rights abuses due to cognitive, intellectual or physical impairments. Moreover, in a liberal market economy, disabled persons may face particular difficulties in understanding the choices available to them, and may not be aware of their rights and face more problems in enforcing them.

Traditionally, disability has primarily been seen as a medical problem rather than a human rights issue. The international disability law framework has for a long time lagged behind the human rights protection of other vulnerable groups, such as women or children. Until recently there was no United Nations (UN) treaty expressly protecting people with disabilities, and the particular human rights concerns of disabled persons were confined to soft law instruments, such as General Assembly resolutions, declarations and protocols. The last decade has, however, seen a boost in disability-specific human rights protection and a gradual consolidation of the 'social model' of disability in international and regional human rights instruments. Legislators and policy-makers have increasingly adopted legislation addressing the physical, social, attitudinal, legal and other barriers, which prevent disabled persons form participating fully in society.[4] The 'social model of disability',[5] which focuses on the societal obstacles preventing people with physical, sensory, intellectual or other impairments from participating in mainstream society, has gradually turned into the major basis for new legislation in this area.

The 2006 UN Convention on the Rights of Persons with Disabilities (CRPD) marked a watershed moment for the worldwide disability movement and has played an important role in consolidating the social model of disability, promoting the human rights of people with disabilities and fostering the principles of inclusion and participation. It has been considered to provide a paradigm shift in policies towards persons with disabilities, signalling a deeper understanding of equality.[6] The Convention identifies equality, dignity, autonomy, independence, accessibility and inclusion as key principles to ensuring that people with disabilities are able to fully participate in society on an equal basis with others. It aims to promote, protect and ensure the full and equal enjoyment of all human rights and fundamental freedoms by all persons with disabilities.[7] Article 5(3) CRPD obliges state parties to take all appropriate steps to ensure that reasonable accommodation is provided for persons with disabilities in order to promote equality and eliminate discrimination.[8] This means that they must make all necessary and

[4] A Lawson, 'Disability, degradation and dignity: the role of Article 3 of the European Convention on Human Rights' (2005) 56 *Northern Ireland Legal Quarterly* 462.

[5] See amongst others the contributions in C Barnes (ed), *Implementing the Social Model of Disability: Theory and Research* (Leeds, The Disability Press, 2004).

[6] For a comprehensive analysis of the Convention see O Mjöll Arnardóttir and G Quinn (eds), *The UN Convention on The Rights of Persons with Disabilities. European and Scandinavian Perspectives* (The Hague, Martinus Nijhoff Publishers, 2009).

[7] Art 1.

[8] The Convention specifically requires reasonable accommodation in respect to the right to liberty and security of the person (Art 14), the right to education (Art 24), and the right to work and employment (Art 27).

appropriate modifications and adjustments to ensure the enjoyment or exercise on an equal basis with others of all human rights and fundamental freedoms by persons with disabilities. Moreover, Article 12(3) CRPD requires state parties to take all appropriate measures to provide access by persons with disabilities to the support they may require in exercising their legal capacity.

This chapter discusses the special protection awarded to persons with disabilities as a particularly vulnerable group under the European Convention on Human Rights (ECHR) and under European Union law behind the background of the CRPD. As a party to the CRPD,[9] the EU is bound by the Convention, and all EU legislation and policy must be compliant with it. Moreover, EU legislation and policy must implement the relevant provisions of the Convention in areas where it has competence to act.[10] Recent policy and legislative developments in the EU and its member states reflect the paradigm shift marked by the CRPD from a medical to a human rights-based model of disability, and testify to the harmonising effect of the Convention on national legislation. New legislation and policies adopted at the national level following CRPD ratification reflect the potential for the Convention to drive the harmonisation of the rights of persons with disabilities across the EU.[11] Within the Council of Europe (CoE), most state parties have ratified or at least signed the CRPD, and the (draft) Convention has been embraced by the Committee of Ministers in various documents.[12]

Nonetheless, it appears that neither the ECHR nor the EU law framework satisfactorily embrace the 'social model of disabilty'. Neither of the two legal regimes succeeds in providing successful and adequate means of tackling the special vulnerability of persons with disabilities. The Council of Europe upholds the social model in non-binding documents, notably the Disability Action Plan and the Recommendation on the rights to participation in political and public life. Be that as it may, even though the European Court of Human Rights (ECtHR) has recognised persons with mental disabilities as a particularly vulnerable group deserving special protection, its case law reveals that the concept has major inherent difficulties that may in fact exacerbate their marginalisation.

Under EU law, the concept of vulnerability in a disability-context primarily relates to the role of disabled persons as market participants. There is a wide range of EU laws and policies that affect disabled people in varying degrees, including primary and secondary EU legislation as well as soft-law instruments. It is,

[9] Council Decision of 26 November 2009 concerning the conclusion, by the European Community, of the United Nations Convention on the Rights of Persons with Disabilities (2010/48/EC) [2010] OJ L303/16.

[10] For a more detailed insight see L Waddington, 'The European Union and the United Nations Convention on the Rights of Persons with Disabilities: A Story of Exclusive and Shared Competences' (2011) *Maastricht Journal of European and Comparative Law* 431.

[11] European Union Agency for Fundamental Rights (FRA), *Annual Report 2012. Fundamental challenges and achievements in 2012*, 147–50.

[12] See for instance the Disability Action Plan 2006–2015 (Rec(2006)5) and the Recommendation on the right to participation in political and public life (CM/Rec(2011)14).

however, notable that the concept of vulnerability and the explicit identification of disabled persons as a particularly vulnerable group is not part of the standard EU discourse in policy documents or legislation. Disabled persons are identified as particularly vulnerable persons that deserve special protection mainly in EU consumer law. Moreover, even in this area of law, the conceptualisation of vulnerability is inadequate to provide the necessary protection for persons who are disadvantaged on grounds of their disability. It appears that by promoting market integration and by putting emphasis on the capacities of the 'average' market participant, the Court of Justice has sacrificed the interests of particularly vulnerable groups, notably persons with disabilities. The chapter concludes by arguing for a stronger focus on the social model of disability in EU and ECtHR case law and a shift towards an individualistic or situational approach to assessing vulnerability.

II. DISABLED PERSONS AS A VULNERABLE GROUP UNDER THE ECHR

A. The Council of Europe and Disability Rights

The Council of Europe has not adopted any specific human rights instrument on disabled persons, but has paid attention to the rights of disabled persons in the Social Charter and various non-binding documents. In fact, the European Social Charter was the first human rights treaty in which disabled persons were explicitly mentioned as human rights holders. Pursuant to Article 15 of the (revised) European Social Charter, state parties are obliged to take adequate measures for the provision of training facilities for disabled persons, to promote their access to employment and to promote their full social integration and participation in the life of the community. Moreover, Articles 11 and 13 of the Charter are of particular relevance to persons with disabilities, requiring states to provide advisory and educational facilities for the promotion of health as well as social and medical assistance for all persons.

In the case law of the European Committee of Social Rights, the rights of disabled persons have been dealt with in particular within the context of children with disabilities. In *Autism-Europe v France*,[13] the Committee found that, while it is acceptable for a distinction to be made between children with and without disabilities in the application of the right to education (Article 17), the integration of children with disabilities into mainstream schools in which arrangements are made to cater for their special needs should be the norm and teaching in specialised schools must be the exception. In 2008, the Committee concluded that Bulgaria[14] had violated the human rights of children with intellectual disabilities by institutionalising them in settings without equal access to education. The Committee highlighted that in assessing whether states are successfully establishing and

[13] *Autism-Europe v France*, Complaint no 13/2000.

[14] *Mental Disability Advocacy Center v Bulgaria*, Complaint no 41/2007.

maintaining an effective education system in compliance with Article 17 of the Charter, particular attention must be paid to vulnerable groups, such as children with disabilities.

In addition, the Council of Europe has issued a number of non-binding instruments that concern people with disabilities, including a Recommendation on Rehabilitation Policies for the Disabled,[15] a Recommendation on a coherent policy for people with disabilities,[16] a Recommendation towards full social inclusion of people with disabilities,[17] a Disability Action Plan,[18] and a Recommendation on the right of participation in political and public life.[19] In particular the latter two documents pay witness to the social model of disability. The Disability Action Plan addresses participation of disabled persons in political and public life, education, information and communication, employment, accessibility of the built environment and transport. It clearly opts for the social model of disability by emphasising the shift from a medical to a social and human rights-based approach.[20] Moreover, the document pays specific attention to vulnerable groups of people with disabilities who face specific barriers, such as women, children and elderly persons with disabilities, as well as people with disabilities from minorities and migrant communities and those suffering from a particularly severe or complex disability.[21] The 2011 Recommendation on the right of participation in political and public life builds upon the CRPD and aims to safeguards the rights of people with intellectual disabilities who are excluded from political participation in European countries. It contains in its preamble an even more explicit recognition of the social model of disability, focusing on the societal obstacles that prevent persons with physical, sensory, intellectual or other impairments from participating fully in society. The Committee of Ministers acknowledges the change in approach towards disability in international law and emphasises the importance of considering persons with disabilities not as patients, but as subjects of rights and full citizens who, when interacting with social and environmental barriers, may be prevented from participating in the life of society. The shift towards a social model of disability in CoE Recommendations is a welcome development. It is, however, not satisfactorily reflected in the European Convention on Human Rights and the case law of the European Court of Human Rights.

[15] Recommendation 1185 (1992) on rehabilitation policies for the disabled.

[16] Recommendation No R (92) 6 on a coherent policy for people with disabilities.

[17] Recommendation 1592 (2003) towards full social inclusion of people with disabilities.

[18] Recommendation Rec (2006) 5 on the Council of Europe Action Plan to promote the rights and full participation of people with disabilities in society: improving the quality of life of people with disabilities in Europe 2006–2015.

[19] Recommendation CM/Rec (2011)14 on the participation of persons with disabilities in political and public life.

[20] Point 2.2.

[21] Point 1.4.

B. The Rights of People with Disabilities under the ECHR

The European Convention on Human Rights has played an important role in advancing the human rights of people with disabilities in Europe. The Convention contains a number of rights relevant to persons with disabilities, and the European Court of Human Rights has identified disabled persons as a particularly vulnerable group deserving special protection. The situation and treatment of disabled persons raises important issue of substantive human rights law, such as the prohibitions on inhuman and degrading treatment (Article 3 ECHR) and unjustified discrimination (Article 14 ECHR), the right to liberty (Article 5 ECHR) and the right to respect for private and family life (Article 8 ECHR). The ECtHR has embraced a wide notion of the concept of persons with disabilities, including not only physically or mentally impaired people, but also persons with a serious illness, such as diabetes.[22] The concept of disabled persons as a 'particularly vulnerable group' has arisen within the context of the right to vote contained in Article 3 of Protocol 1 to the Convention as well as the prohibition of torture, inhumane and degrading treatment (Article 3 ECHR). After given a short overview of the importance of various Convention rights for disabled persons, the following section focuses on the concept of vulnerability as developed by the ECtHR and its application to persons with disabilities.

Various Convention rights have become relevant for persons with disabilities, mainly in an institutional context. Persons with mental disabilities who are detained or otherwise institutionalised deserve protection of their life, physical integrity and private life. Article 5 ECHR guarantees the right to liberty and the ECtHR has laid down a number of requirements for the detention of a mentally disabled person, or in the wording of the Convention, a 'person of unsound mind'.[23] A true mental disorder must have been established before the competent national authority on the basis of objective medical expertise.[24] The mental disorder must be of a kind or degree warranting compulsory confinement. Finally, the validity of continued confinement must depend upon the persistence of such a disorder. Moreover, the procedures for mentally disordered patients who are to be institutionalised must satisfy the minimum procedural requirements of Article 5 ECHR. The Court has held that the inability of a mentally disabled person placed in a psychiatric hospital to directly access the court for review of the measure taken regarding his legal incapacity constitutes a violation of Articles 5(4) and 5(5) of the ECHR.[25] Guaranteeing that no one is arbitrarily deprived of his/her

[22] *Glor v Switzerland* App no 13444/04 (ECtHR, 30 April 2009).

[23] The principles were first established in *Winterwerp v The Netherlands* (1979) Series A no 33, 2 EHRR 387, para 39.

[24] A medical opinion must be obtained and the assessment of the individual must be based on the actual mental state of the person rather than solely on past events. See *Varbanov v Bulgaria* App no 31365/96 (ECtHR, 5 October 2000).

[25] *Stanev v Bulgaria* App no 36760/06 (ECtHR, 17 January 2012).

liberty, Article 5 is thus of central importance to the compulsory admission and treatment of persons with mental disorders.

Moreover, the state has a duty to protect persons with disabilities from injury and harm so as to comply with the prohibition of torture, inhumane and degrading treatment (Article 3 ECHR).[26] Disabled persons are particularly vulnerable to inhuman or degrading treatment, as certain types of treatments by the state, including prison conditions, interrogation techniques and deportation methods may amount to inhuman or degrading treatment when applied to disabled persons. For instance, the expulsion of a deaf non-national to his/her country of origin may constitute inhuman and degrading treatment if found to inevitably lead to a total sensory isolation of the person concerned.[27] In addition, the higher risk of disabled persons being exposed to inhuman or degrading treatment results in an increased obligation on states to offer protection from such treatment. For example, disabled persons detained in prisons or psychiatric institutions must be provided with certain medical or psychological services to avoid a violation of Article 3 ECHR.

Moreover, institutionalised persons with disabilities have a right to private live, which also comprises to a certain degree the right to establish and develop relationships with other human beings. According to the Court, the right to private life is primarily intended to ensure the development, without outside interference, of the personality of each individual in his relations with other human beings. Even though deciding against the applicant in a case concerning the lack of facilities for disabled people at private beaches,[28] the Court emphasised that a state's positive obligations inherent in Article 8 ECHR might involve the adoption of measures designed to secure respect for private life even in the sphere of the relations of individuals between themselves.

The Convention also provides protection from discrimination on the basis of disability, in spite of the fact that disability is not explicitly mentioned as a ground for discrimination under Article 14 ECHR. The provision does not provide for a self-standing right to non-discrimination, but can be invoked in combination with another Convention article. The Court has for instance found discrimination on the basis of disability violating Article 14 jo 8 ECHR in the case of a person who was deemed medically unfit to perform military service due to his diabetes, but whose disability was not considered severe enough for him to forgo an 'exemption tax'.[29]

[26] See T Degener and Y Koster-Dreese, *Human Rights and Disabled Persons: Essays and Relevant Human Rights Instruments* (The Hague, Martinus Nijhoff Publishers, 1995) 117–30.

[27] Report of the European Commission of Human Rights of 10 March 1994 in the case of *Nasri v France* App no 19465/92 (ECtHR, 13 July 1995). The Court found a violation of Art 8 ECHR and did not consider it necessary to examine the complaint also under Art 3 ECHR.

[28] *Botta v Italy* (1998) Series A no 66, 26 EHRR 241.

[29] *Glor v Switzerland*, n 22 above.

C. The ECtHR's Concept of 'Vulnerability' as Applied to Disabled Persons

In its case law on (amongst others) disabled persons, the ECtHR has relied increasingly on the concept of 'vulnerability'. In the disability cases under Article 3 ECHR, it has called for a heightened intensity of judicial review in cases concerning institutionalised mentally disabled persons. It held in *Herczegfalvy v Austria*[30] that the position of inferiority and powerlessness typical of patients in psychiatric hospitals calls for increased vigilance in ensuring that the Convention has been complied with. Even though the mentally disabled applicant in *Herczegfalvy*, who was forcibly administered food and medication, isolated and attached with handcuffs to a security bed, was not successful in establishing a violation of Article 3 ECHR,[31] the Court emphasised the necessity for increased vigilance because of the increased vulnerability of patients with mental health problems. Moreover, the severe imprisonment conditions of a person with disability can amount to 'degrading treatment' in violation of Article 3 ECHR even if there was no intention to humiliate or debase the applicant. Focusing on the special situation of disabled persons, the Court held in *Price v UK*[32] that detaining a severely disabled person using a wheelchair in conditions where she was dangerously cold, at risk of developing sores because her bed was too hard or unreachable, and was unable to go to the toilet or keep clean without the greatest of difficulty, constituted degrading treatment contrary to Article 3.

Keenan v UK[33] was another case in which the Court used the concept of vulnerability within the context of an Article 3 violation concerning disabled persons. It held that when considering whether the treatment or punishment of people with mentally disability is incompatible with the standards of Article 3, it had to take into consideration the person's vulnerability and their inability, in some cases, to complain coherently or at all about how they are being affected by any particular treatment. The absence of proper medical monitoring and lack of informed psychiatric assessment and treatment in prison of a person suffering from schizophrenia, suicidal feelings and depression, combined with the imposition of seven days' segregation, was held to be incompatible with the standard of treatment required in respect of a mentally ill person.[34] Article 3 ECHR thus bears great potential for safeguarding the dignity of disabled persons who are imprisoned or living in institutional care. The Court so far has, however, failed to

[30] *Herczegfalvy v Austria* (1992) Series A no 244, 15 EHRR 437, para 82.

[31] See also the opinion of the European Commission of Human Rights, which considered that the cumulative use of compulsory medical treatment, artificial feeding and placing of the applicant in an isolation cell constituted a violation of Art 3 ECHR.

[32] *Price v United Kingdom* (2001) 34 EHRR 1285.

[33] *Keenan v United Kingdom* (2001) 33 EHHR 38.

[34] Para 115.

apply the principles of Article 3 to the suffering of persons with disabilities in a non-institutional context.[35]

The categorisation of persons with disabilities as a particularly vulnerable group has also appeared within the context of the right to free elections under Article 3 of Protocol 1 to the Convention. In *Alajos Kiss v Hungary*[36] the Court held that the absolute ban on voting in Hungarian parliamentary elections for people under guardianship violated the applicant's right to free elections. It emphasised that the treatment of those with intellectual or mental disability as a single class was a questionable classification, and that the curtailment of their rights had to be subject to strict scrutiny. The indiscriminate removal of voting rights, without an individualised judicial evaluation and solely based on mental disability necessitating partial guardianship, could not be considered compatible with the legitimate grounds for restricting the right to vote. By calling for strict scrutiny, the Court thus established a high threshold for the restriction of rights of persons with intellectual or mental disabilities. In *Alajos* the Court identified people with mental disabilities as a 'particularly vulnerable group' due to the considerable discrimination they have experienced in the past. It found that since mentally disabled persons have historically been subject to prejudice with lasting consequences, resulting in their social exclusion, they deserve special protection. According to the Court, 'the treatment as a single class of those with intellectual or mental disabilities is a questionable classification, and the curtailment of their rights must be subject to strict scrutiny'.[37]

An evaluation of the Court's case law on disabled persons as a particularly vulnerable group provides a mixed picture. On the one hand the concept of vulnerable groups has allowed the Court to move closer to a 'more robust idea of equality'.[38] Vulnerability considerations have not only allowed the Court to prioritise both in its workload and in its case assessment, they have also led to an extension of rights, in particular via the doctrine of positive obligations.[39] The vulnerability of an applicant with disabilities can be an important factor in establishing positive obligations of the state both in the context of Article 14 ECHR and of other Conventions rights, such as Articles 3 and 8 ECHR. The Court has used the vulnerability reasoning in order to impose positive obligations upon states to pay attention to the specificities of people with a disability and thus to provide them with adequate protection form human rights abuses. The ECtHR requires states to respond to the particular circumstances of a disabled person and, on occasion,

[35] A Lawson, 'Disability, degradation and dignity: the role of Article 3 of the European Convention on Human Rights' (2006) 56 *Northern Ireland Legal Quarterly* 4, 481–85.

[36] *Alajos Kiss v Hungary* App no 38832/06 (ECtHR, 20 May 2010).

[37] Para 44.

[38] L Peroni and A Timmer, 'Vulnerable Groups: The Promise of an Emergent Concept in European Human Rights Convention Law' (2013) 11 *International Journal of Constitutional Law* 1056–85.

[39] A Timmer, 'A Quiet Revolution: Vulnerability in the European Court of Human Rights' in M Fineman and A Grear (eds), *Vulnerability: Reflections on a New Ethical Foundation for Law and Politics* (Farnham, Ashgate, 2013) 147–70.

to treat disabled persons differently from other applicants on account of their vulnerability.

The vulnerability of an applicant may also play a role in the Court's proportionality analysis under Articles 3 or 8 ECHR by increasing the weight of ill-treatment inflicted. This becomes apparent in the Court's case law on asylum-seekers,[40] but the same reasoning can be applied to persons with disabilities who may be more severely affected by certain types of mistreatment, such as harsh detention conditions. Moreover, as disabled persons have suffered considerable discrimination and prejudice in the past, resulting in their social exclusion, a state's margin of appreciation is narrower in disability discrimination cases. States must have very compelling reasons to limit the rights of persons with disabilities, for example in relation to the right to vote or the refusal of a residence permit. The concept of vulnerability has thus helped create a human rights law that is more responsive to the needs of vulnerable people, including persons with disabilities.[41] It has been argued that by focusing on the built environment and negative attitudes towards people with mental impairments, the Court has taken 'the first step towards embracing a social model of disability'.[42]

On the other hand, the Court risks reinforcing the vulnerability of disabled persons by essentialising and stigmatising them.[43] The 'essentialism' of a vulnerable group is problematic in that it does not pay witness to the differences in type and magnitude of the vulnerability of the people belonging to the group. This applies in particular to persons with disabilities, due to the wide range of impairments falling under this concept. For instance, a mentally handicapped person may be vulnerable in a completely different way to a person suffering from diabetes, a difference which is disregarded by placing all disabled persons in the same 'vulnerable group'. Moreover, whilst the Court emphasises the need to rectify the past stigmatisation and discrimination of disabled people, it risks stigmatising them itself by placing the label 'vulnerable' on them. Disabled persons might not like to be categorised as being vulnerable, a term which inevitably carries negative associations. It has been argued that in order to avoid the pitfalls of reasoning based on vulnerability, the Court should strengthen its contextual inquiry and focus on the circumstances under which certain individuals are vulnerable, rather than on which groups are vulnerable.[44] The casuistic case law of the ECtHR lends itself perfectly to an approach which evaluates the vulnerability of a person with a disability in a specific situation. An applicant with visual loss or hearing loss may be vulnerable and in need of special protection in completely different situations than a person confined to a wheelchair or suffering from a mental illness. By focusing on the vulnerability of disabled persons in a specific situation, the Court

[40] *MSS v Belgium and Greece* (2011) 53 EHRR 2.
[41] Timmer, 'A Quiet Revolution', n 39 above, 147–70.
[42] Peroni and Timmer, 'Vulnerable Groups', n 38 above, 1066.
[43] ibid, p 1070.
[44] ibid, p 1073.

could at the same time avoid their stigmatisation/essentialisation and ensure a heightened degree of human rights protection when needed. Such an approach would also be in line with the social conception of vulnerability embraced in recent Council of Europe documents, which focuses on the social context that creates or reinforces the vulnerability of a particularly group of persons.

III. DISABLED PERSONS AS A PARTICULARLY VULNERABLE GROUP UNDER EU LAW

For a long time the EU lacked legal competence in the area of social policy, depriving it of any opportunity to take an active part in the shaping of disability policy in Europe.[45] EU engagement in the area of disability was restrained to soft-law mechanisms, promoting thc exchange of experience, dissemination of innovations, ideas and information to promote good practice in the member states through successive action programmes. In the mid-1990s this cautious approach gave way to a more activist stance on the side of the EU institutions and a desire to play a greater role in the disability field by influencing the policies and practice of the member states. In 1996 the European Commission adopted a Communication on disability[46] (endorsed by the Council later that year[47]), emphasising the significant added value of an EU-level involvement to the efforts of the member states and the importance of identifying and removing the various barriers to equal opportunities and full participation of people with disabilities in all aspects of life.

This Communication came only a few years before the entry into force of the Treaty of Amsterdam in 1999, which signalled an important shift in the area of EU disability policy, granting the EU competence to take measures to combat discrimination on a number of grounds, including disability (ex-Article 13 EC). The 2009 Lisbon Treaty equally gives the EU institutions the power to adopt legislation to address such discrimination (Article 19). In addition, it includes a new provision (Article 10), which requires the Union to combat discrimination based on, inter alia, disability when defining and implementing its policies and activities. The entry into force of the Lisbon Treaty also brought about the legally binding force of the EU Charter on Fundamental Rights, which contains a number of provisions relevant to disabled persons. Article 21 of the Charter prohibits any discrimination on the basis of disability, whilst Article 26 requires the EU to recognise and respect the right of persons with disabilities to benefit from measures

[45] See B Hvinden, 'Nordic Disability Policies in a Changing Europe: Is There Still a Distinct Nordic Model?' (2004) 38 *Social Policy & Administration* 170, 182–84.

[46] European Commission Communication, 'Equality of opportunity for people with disabilities: A New European Community Disability Strategy' COM (96) 406 final.

[47] Resolution of the Council and of the Representatives of the Governments of the member states meeting within the Council of 20 December 1996 on equality of opportunity for people with disabilities [1997] OJ C12.

designed to ensure their independence, social and occupational integration and participation in the life of the Community.

On the basis of ex-Article 13 EC, the first legal instrument of direct relevance to disability was adopted in the year 2000. Directive 2000/78/EC obliges member states to adopt measures to eliminate direct and indirect discrimination, harassment and instructions to discriminate against disabled persons in the area of employment and occupation. It contains an obligation on employers to provide 'reasonable accommodation' in order to meet the needs of persons with disabilities, ie to take appropriate measures to enable a person with a disability to have access to, participate in, advance in employment or undergo training, unless this would imply a disproportionate burden for the employer (Article 5). The Directive also provides for the possibility to adopt measures to compensate for the disadvantages historically experienced by persons with disabilities in the labour market.[48]

Next to the Employment Discrimination Directive, there is a wide range of EU laws and policies that affect disabled people in varying degrees, including primary and secondary EU legislation as well as soft-law instruments. Some instruments are disability-specific, whilst many others are mainstream instruments in different areas of EU law that relate to disability in some way. Relevant areas of EU law range from free movement and competition law to agriculture, transport, taxation, external relations, environment, consumers and health protection, science information, education and culture, law relating to undertakings and the area of freedom, security and justice to economic and monetary, industrial, regional and social policy.[49]

It has long been criticised that neither Directive 2000/78/EC nor any other piece of secondary legislation contains a definition of what 'disability' means for the purpose of EU law. Early on in the case law on Directive 2000/78/EC, in *Chacón Navas*, the Court adopted a narrow concept of disability, defining it as a limitation which, as a result of physical, mental or psychological impairments, hinders the participation of the person in professional life. This definition seems to reflect the medical concept of disability, focusing on the impairment which makes it difficult for the person concerned to adapt or to integrate into the surrounding societal environment. In its recent case law, however, the Court of Justice has had the opportunity to clarify the concept of disability in the light of the UNCRPD. In *HK Danmark*[50] and *Z v A Government Department and the Board of Management of a Community School*[51] it explicitly aligned the EU concept of disability with that of the UN Convention. Acknowledging that disability must be seen

[48] Art 7(2).

[49] For a full overview and discussion of EU laws and policies that affect disabled people see Academic Network of European Disability experts (ANED), *Annotated review of European law and policy with reference to disability* (Brussels, ANED, 2009).

[50] Joined Cases C-335/ 11 and C-337/11 *HK Danmark* [2014] nyr.

[51] Case C-363/12 *Z v A Government Department and the Board of Management of a Community School* [2014] nyr.

as an 'evolving concept', it found that in line with Article 1 UNCRPDD, disability must be understood as the result of the interaction between the individual's impairment and the barriers created by society. As a result of the EU's ratification of the UNCRPD, the EU concept of disability as applicable in various areas of EU law must, thus, be based on the social model of disability.

Yet, in spite of an increasingly comprehensive set of EU legislation addressing directly or indirectly the situation of disabled persons, few pieces of EU secondary legislation identify disabled persons as a *particularly vulnerable* group. The concept of vulnerability under EU law is mainly present with regard to the situation of disabled persons as market participants, more specifically in their role as consumers under EU consumer law.[52]

A. Disabled Persons as Particularly Vulnerable Consumers[53]

Whilst absent from most of EU legislation and policy, the concept of vulnerability is gaining increasing visibility in the area of EU consumer law. As discussed below, EU Consumer Protection law is based on the notion of an 'average consumer', who is reasonably well informed, reasonably observant and circumspect. This formula was developed by the CJEU in its free movement case law and clearly pays witness to an internal market rationale. Be that as it may, references to the need for specific protection of particularly vulnerable persons can be found in a number of EU consumer law instruments, including the Unfair Commercial Practices Directive, the General Product Safety Directive and the Consumer Rights Directive.[54]

The Unfair Commercial Practices Directive 2005/29/EC[55] lays down harmonised rules for the fight against unfair commercial practices. It aims at approximating national standards to prevent market distortions, as well as providing consumers with a high level of protection. According to Article 5(2) of the Directive, commercial practices are considered to be unfair if they fail to comply with the requirement of professional diligence and materially distort the economic behaviour of the *average consumer*. In particular, the Directive identifies

[52] The need for greater levels of protection of particularly vulnerable persons has also been recognised in the area of criminal procedural law, which will not however be discussed in this chapter. The Council Framework Decision 2001/220/JHA of 15 March 2001 on the standing of victims in criminal proceedings requires member states to enable vulnerable victims to give their evidence in a way which protects them from the effects of testifying in open court. Moreover, on 27 November 2013 the European Commission adopted a Recommendation on procedural safeguards for vulnerable persons suspected or accused in criminal proceedings ([2013] OJ C378/8).

[53] Part of this text is based on a report prepared by the author for the Academic Network of European Disability Experts (ANED).

[54] This chapter focuses on 'mainstream' EU consumer law. There are, however, also other sectoral Directives that concern the needs of particularly vulnerable consumers, such as the Gas Market Directive 2009/73/EC and the Universal Services in Electronic Communication Directive 2002/22/EC.

[55] Directive 2005/29/EC of 11 May 2005 concerning unfair business-to-consumer commercial practices in the internal market [2005] OJ L149/22.

as 'unfair' certain commercial practices that can be defined as misleading or aggressive in accordance with Articles 6, 7, 8 or 9.[56] Article 5(3) of Directive 2005/29/EC awards special protection to 'a clearly identifiable group of consumers who are particularly vulnerable' to a certain commercial practice or product.

The other two Directives refer to the concept of 'particularly vulnerable consumers' only in their non-binding preambles. The General Product Safety Directive[57] aims to ensure a high level of product safety for consumer products that are not covered by specific sector legislation (eg toys, cosmetics). Producers and distributors are not only required to comply with the basic requirement to place only safe products on the market. They must also inform consumers of the risks associated with the products they supply and take appropriate measures to prevent such risks and be able to trace dangerous products. The safety of a product is assessed in accordance with European standards, Community technical specifications, codes of good practice and the state of art and the expectation of consumers. The most recent instrument devoted to the protection of consumer rights is the Consumer Rights Directive 2011/83/EU.[58] The Directive lays down standards or harmonised rules for the common aspects of distance and off-premise contracts.[59] By virtue of the Directive, the trader should give the consumer clear and comprehensible information before the consumer is bound by a distance or off-premises contract.

i. The Average vs the Vulnerable Consumer

Even though the EU Consumer Law Directives do not explicitly mention consumers with disabilities, their relevance from a disability-rights perspective springs from the distinction made between 'average' and 'particularly vulnerable' consumers. In order to determine the 'unfairness' of a certain commercial practice, Directive 2005/29/EC operates an objective standard of the *average consumer*, expecting him/her to be reasonably well-informed, reasonably observant and circumspect.[60] The standard test for defining the average consumer is based on the case law of the Court of Justice, which has employed the concept of the 'average consumer' since the late 1980s.[61] Dealing with national restrictions on labelling and marketing designed to protect consumers, the Court has used the standard of an 'average' consumer, who is 'reasonably well informed and reasonably observant

[56] Certain misleading and aggressive practices that are contained in Annex 1 to the Directive are always considered to be unfair (Art 5(5) jo Annex 1 of the Directive).

[57] Directive 2001/95/EC of 3 December 2001 on general product safety [2002] OJ L11/4. The Directive is currently subject to revision, see the Proposal for a Regulation on Consumer product safety and repealing Council Directive 87/357/EECC and Directive 2001/95/EC, COM (2013) 78 final.

[58] Directive 2011/83/EU of 25 October 2011 on consumer rights [2011] OJ L204/46.

[59] These include internet sales, sales made through mail order, telephone or fax, and other contracts negotiated away from business premises.

[60] Recital 18 of the preamble.

[61] The standard test was developed in Case C-210/96 *Gut Springenheide* [1998] ECR I-4657, para 31; see also Case C-470/93 *Mars* [1995] ECR I-1923, para 24.

and circumspect' in order to evaluate whether consumers could be confused or misled by a certain labelling of imported products.[62]

The 'average consumer' test has been criticised in the academic literature for being an overly simplistic concept which requires of consumers an overly demanding standard of rationality and information, without dedicating much attention to the real functioning of individual consumer behaviour. According to Incardona and Poncibò, 'the economists' idealistic paradigm of a rational consumer in an efficient marketplace ... departs from the unpredictable realities of individual human behaviour and is hardly an appropriate standard for legislative or judicial sanctions'.[63] The European Parliament has equally criticised the notion of an 'average consumer' for lacking the flexibility needed to adapt to specific cases and sometimes not corresponding to real-life situations.[64] Even though the Court has distinguished between different types of consumers in establishing the identity and skills of the 'average' consumer, the reasonably well-informed, observant and circumspect person continues to serve as the standard benchmark.

The Court has mitigated the effects of application of the average consumer test by introducing the concept of 'particularly vulnerable consumers', who are entitled to a higher degree of protection. In *Buet*[65] the Court upheld national restrictions to the free movement of goods based on the justification of protecting vulnerable consumers. The case concerned French consumer law, which prohibited canvassing for the purpose of selling educational material to consumers. Even though the measure was considered to constitute a restriction to the free movement of goods, the Court held that it was justified by the need to protect *particularly vulnerable consumers* from the purchase of unsuitable teaching material, which could compromise the consumer's chances of obtaining further training and thus consolidating his position on the labour market.[66]

This distinction between the average, rational market participant and particularly vulnerable consumers is reflected in the Consumer Law Directives referred to above. In addition to guaranteeing a consistent interpretation of the 'average consumer' test throughout the member states, the Unfair Commercial Practices Directive aims at preventing the targeting and exploitation of particularly vulnerable consumers.[67] For the purpose of the Directive, the benchmark of the average consumer is altered in respect of vulnerable consumers. Article 5(3) of Directive 2005/29/EC awards special protection to 'a clearly identifiable group of consumers

[62] Case C-315/92 *Verband Sozialer Wettbewerb, 'Clinique'* [1994] ECR I-317; Case C-99/01 *Linhart and Biffl* [2002] ECR I-9375, para 35.

[63] R Incardona and C Poncibò, 'The average consumer, the unfair commercial practices directive, and the cognitive revolution' (2007) 30 *Journal of Consumer Policy* 35.

[64] European Parliament Resolution of 22 May 2012 on a strategy for strengthening the rights of vulnerable consumers [2013] OJ C264 E/11.

[65] Case 382/87 *Buet* [1989] ECR 1235.

[66] ibid, para 8.

[67] European Commission, Proposal for a Directive concerning unfair business-to-consumer commercial practices in the Internal Market, COM (2003) 356 final.

who are particularly vulnerable' to a certain commercial practice or product. Vulnerability for the purpose of the Directive may arise out of consumers' 'mental or physical infirmity, age or credulity'.[68] Commercial practices which are likely to 'materially distort the economic behaviour' of such specifically vulnerable consumers will be assessed from the perspective of the average member of that group. Yet, the trader must have been 'reasonably expected to foresee' the vulnerability of the consumer. Moreover, the test of the 'vulnerable consumer' does not preclude 'the common and legitimate advertising practice of making exaggerated statements or statements which are not meant to be taken literally'.

Similarly, the Product Safety Directive, though not using the concept of the 'average consumer', takes as its starting point the informed market participant who is able to make rational choices. Safety is to be assessed with regard to the 'reasonable use' of a product, meaning that a product can be considered safe if, under normal or reasonably foreseeable conditions of use, it does not present any risk or only the minimum risks compatible with the product's use, considered to be acceptable and consistent with a high level of protection for the safety and health of persons.[69] In this context, the categories of consumers at risk when using the product must be taken into account. Recital 8 of the preamble specifies that the safety of products should be assessed by taking into account the categories of consumers, which can be particularly vulnerable to the risks posed by the products under consideration, in particular children and the elderly.

Lastly, the Consumer Rights Directive provides that in providing information to the consumer that is about to be bound by a contract or corresponding offer, the trader must take into account the specific needs of consumers who are particularly vulnerable because of their mental, physical or psychological infirmity, age or credulity in a way which the trader could reasonably be expected to foresee. Taking into account such specific needs should, however, not lead to different levels of consumer protection.[70]

ii. The Concept of the 'Vulnerable Consumer' from a Disability Perspective

The question arises as to when a consumer with disabilities must be considered vulnerable for the purpose of EU Consumer Law. The Unfair Commercial Practices Directive[71] as well as the Consumer Rights Directive[72] mention age, 'physical or mental infirmity' and 'credulity' as characteristics which make consumers particularly susceptible to a commercial practice or to the underlying product. According to the European Commission, the reasons for establishing vulnerability are listed

[68] See Art 5(3) as well as recital 19 of the Directive's preamble.
[69] Art 2(b) of the Directive.
[70] Recital 34 of the preamble.
[71] Art 5(3) and Recital 19 of the preamble.
[72] Recital 34 of the preamble.

'indicatively' and cover a wide range of situations.[73] 'Mental or physical infirmity' is the reason most relevant from a disability perspective, as the concept covers all kinds of disabilities, including sensory impairment and limited mobility.[74] Also the concept of 'credulity', which is broadly defined, may be relevant for consumers who have some kind of intellectual impairment or learning disability that cannot strictly be categorised as a 'mental infirmity'. The concept of credulity encompasses all types of consumers who are susceptible to believe in certain claims more readily than others, because of particular individual circumstances. However, it is unclear as to how exactly the concepts of 'mental infirmity' and 'credulity' are to be defined. What is the standard mental capacity of an 'average consumer' against which 'mental infirmity' and 'credulity' are to be assessed? Moreover the vagueness of the concept of 'credulity' is bound to lead to difficulties in determining the 'average member' of that group and in proving the existence of vulnerability.

The Product Safety Directive speaks more generally of particularly vulnerable categories of consumers and merely mentions children and elderly as examples. Even though the Directive only explicitly refers to children and elderly, the provision most certainly also applies to people with disabilities, in particular those with a visual or intellectual impairment, which affects their understanding of how the product should be used. In the draft Regulation on Product Safety that is to replace Directive 2001/95/EC, recital 13 of the preamble stipulates that the safety of products must be assessed by taking into account the vulnerability of the categories of consumers who are likely to use the products, in particular children, the elderly and the *disabled*.[75]

The reference to 'physical or mental infirmity' seems outdated and is out of tune with the UN Disability Convention, which speaks of persons with 'long-term physical, mental, intellectual or sensory impairments'.[76] The CJEU has made clear that, following the ratification by the EU of the UN Convention on Disability, the Convention can be relied upon for the purpose of interpreting Directive 2000/78 and defining the concept of 'disability' contained therein.[77] The same principle must apply to the concept of disability in the Consumer Law Directives, which must be based on the UN Disability Convention. Thus, the concept of 'disabled persons' within the meaning of the Consumer Law Directives must be understood as referring to those who have long-term physical, mental, intellectual or sensory impairments which in interaction with various barriers may hinder their full and effective participation in society on an equal basis with others.

[73] European Commission, Staff Working Document, Guidance on the Implementation of Directive 2005/29/EC on unfair commercial practices, SEC (2009) 1666, pp 29–31.

[74] ibid, p 30.

[75] Proposal for a Regulation on consumer product safety and repealing Council Directive 87/357/EEC and Directive 2001/95/EC, COM(2013) 78 final.

[76] Art 1 CRPD.

[77] Joined Cases C-335/11 and C-337/11 *Jette Ring and HK Danmark* [2013] nyr, paras 37 to 39.

iii. The Social Model of Disability

It appears that the EU instruments fail to take sufficient account of the social model of disability embraced in the UN Convention, which focuses on impairments which *in interaction with various barriers* may hinder full and effective participation in society. Article 2 of the Convention defines 'discrimination on the basis of disability' broadly, comprising 'any distinction, exclusion or restriction on the basis of disability which has the purpose or effect of impairing or nullifying the recognition, enjoyment or exercise, on an equal basis with others, of all human rights and fundamental freedoms in political, economic, social, cultural, civil or any other field'. Moreover, it is recognised in the Convention's preamble that 'disability is an evolving concept and that disability results from the interaction between persons with impairments and attitudinal and environmental barriers that hinders their full and effective participation in society on an equal basis with others'. The Convention's definition of disability clearly reflects the social model of disability, referring to physical, mental or intellectual or sensory impairments which in interaction with various barriers may hinder full and effective participation in society. The Convention thus focuses on societal barriers as opposed to the individual and their perceived limitations. It recognises that disability arises from a failure of the social environment to adapt to and accommodate the needs of people with impairments.[78] Crucially, under the social model embraced by the UNCPRD disability is context-dependent and situational, depending on the surrounding environment and the reaction and organisation of society.[79]

The Directives, to the contrary, treat the vulnerable consumer as a static concept. It has been argued that all consumers can be considered vulnerable in certain situations when transacting with an expert party, in particular in the context of mass or standard form contracts.[80] This is not accounted for in the Directives, which describe vulnerable consumers as a clearly identifiable group on account of their 'mental or physical infirmity', age or 'credulity'. By emphasising that the provision only concerns vulnerable groups that are 'clearly identifiable', it is primarily useful with regard to certain particular groups of consumers, but does not cover 'situational vulnerableness',[81] ie vulnerability that arises from the interaction of a person with a consumption situation, rather than a characteristic intrinsic to certain individuals.

[78] L Waddington, 'The European Union and the United Nations Convention on the Rights of Persons with Disabilities: A Story of Exclusive and Shared Competences' (2011) 4 *Maastricht Journal of European and Comparative Law* 431, 436.

[79] Opinion of AG Wahl in Case C-363/12 *Z v A Government Department and the Board of Management of a Community School* [2014] nyr, para 84.

[80] I Barral-Vinals, 'Freedom of contract, unequal bargaining power and consumer law on unconscionability', in M Kenny, J Devenney and L O'Mahony, *Unconscionability in European Private Financial Transactions* (Cambridge, CUP, 2010) 46–61.

[81] For the use of this term see T Wilhelmsson, 'The Informed Consumer v the Vulnerable Consumer in European Unfair Commercial Practices Law—A Comment' (2007), in G Howells et al (eds), *The Yearbook of Consumer Law 2007* (Farnham, Ashgate, 2007) 218.

Yet, whilst being relevant for the interpretation of the concept of disability and therewith the rights of particularly vulnerable disabled consumers, the UNCPRD cannot be directly relied upon by individuals before the Courts. The CJEU held in *Z v A Government Department and the Board of Management of a Community School*[82] that being of a 'programmatic nature', the provisions of the Convention are not unconditional and sufficiently precise and therefore do not have direct effect in EU law. As a consequence, the UNCRPD cannot be relied upon in order to challenge the validity of EU secondary legislation, such as the Consumer Directives.

The Directives are not only out of tune with the UN Convention, they also lag behind current EU law developments. EU law has slowly moved towards a social concept of disability, a development, which is not yet reflected in the Consumer Law Directives. Recent policy documents indicate a shift away from the 'medical model' of disability, which conceives disability as a state intrinsic to the individual, caused by his/her functional impairment and unrelated to external factors. The EU institutions seem to have embraced a 'social model', which sees disability as a social construct, resulting from the relationship between the impaired individual and society.[83] In its 1996 Communication referred to above,[84] the Commission adopted a rights-based strategy, focusing on the removal of barriers to full participation of disabled people and emphasising the importance of equality and the valuing of human diversity. In 2003, it endorsed more explicitly a 'social approach to disability', which recognises that the circumstances of people with disabilities and the discrimination they face, are socially created phenomena which are not directly related to their impairments per se. The problem results from the structures, practices and attitudes preventing persons with disabilities from exercising their capabilities, rather than from their impairment itself.[85]

In the same vein, the European Parliament has criticised the concept of vulnerable consumers as currently employed under EU law, as it is based on the notion of vulnerability as endogenous, targeting a heterogeneous group comprised of persons who are considered vulnerable on a permanent basis because of their mental, physical or psychological disability.[86] This endogenous notion of vulnerability focuses on vulnerability resulting from temporary or permanent causes that are inherent to the consumer or his or her physical or mental situation. It disregards, however, exogenous causes of vulnerability that are linked to external causes, such as a lack of knowledge of the language, a lack of education or the need

[82] Case C-363/12 *Z v A Government Department and the Board of Management of a Community School* [2014] nyr, para 90.

[83] K Wells, 'The Impact of the Framework Employment Directive on UK Disability Discrimination Law' (2003) 32 *Industrial Law Journal* 253, 257 and 260.

[84] COM (96) 406 final.

[85] European Commission Communication, 'Towards a United Nations Legally Binding Instrument to Promote and Protect the Rights and Dignity of Persons with Disabilities' COM (2003) 16 final.

[86] European Parliament Resolution of 22 May 2012 on a strategy for strengthening the rights of vulnerable consumers [2013] OJ C264 E/11.

to use new technologies with which the consumer is not familiar. This means that consumers who find themselves in a state of temporary powerlessness resulting from a gap between their individual state and characteristics on the one hand, and their external environment on the other hand, are currently not covered by the concept of vulnerability under EU law. Even though disabled consumers are to a certain extent covered by the endogenous concept of vulnerability, a broader reading of this concept, including external factors, would certainly come to their benefit. In particular persons with mental disabilities would benefit from a reading of vulnerability that focuses not only on their static characteristics, but that includes situations where consumers experience difficulties in accessing or assessing the information given to them or from their lack of assertiveness and comprehension of the information they receive or of the options available or from their lack of awareness of the existing complaint and redress schemes.[87]

iv. Internal Market vs Consumer Protection Objectives

The notion of the vulnerable consumer pays tribute to the tension in EU consumer law between the liberal free-market principles governing the single market and the desire to promote a high level of consumer protection. In particular, Directive 2005/29/EC is characterised by its efforts to balance internal market and consumer protection objectives. Also the Consumer Rights Directive aims at striking the right balance between a high level of consumer protection and the competitiveness of enterprises.[88] In recent cases, the Court has emphasised the role of consumers as active agents in the internal market, rather than weak parties needing protection.[89] Similarly, when assessing the situation of particularly vulnerable consumers, the Court has been reluctant to attach much weight to overriding public interests in order to justify a restriction on the free movement of goods or services, as most consumers are presumed to be sufficiently well informed to take care of themselves in the market place.[90] It appears that by promoting market integration and by putting emphasis on the capacities of the 'average' consumer, the Court has sacrificed the interests of particularly vulnerable consumers.[91] The Consumer Law Directives fail to remedy this situation by giving statutory authority to the distinction between average and vulnerable consumers, and by applying a non-individualistic, stereotypical test to the identification of the vulnerable consumer.

[87] L Waddington, *The Protection of Consumers with Disabilities in the European Union: Persons with Disabilities as Active Participants in the Internal Market* (Brussels, ANED, 2012) 20.

[88] See recital 4 of the preamble.

[89] See Case C-362/88 *GB-INNO-BM* [1990] ECR I-0667; Case C-238/89 *Pall Corp* [1990] ECR I-04827; Case C-315/92 *Verband Sozialer Wettbewerb* [1994] ECR I-00317.

[90] S Weatherill, 'Consumer Policy', in P Craig and G de Búrca, *The Evolution of EU Law* (Oxford, OUP, 1999) 700–01.

[91] L Waddington, 'A Disabled Market: Free Movement of Goods and Services in the EU and Disability Accessibility' (2009) 15 *European Law Journal* 575–98.

When applying and interpreting the Directives, the member states, national courts and the Court of Justice should be careful not to compromise the objective of protecting particularly vulnerable consumers to the objective of guaranteeing the smooth functioning of the internal market. National measures aimed at protecting persons with disabilities from unfair commercial practices, unsafe products or lacking/misleading information when concluding a contract should be scrutinised and not discarded too easily as unjustified restrictions on the free movement of goods or services on the basis of the average consumer test. This would require a change of approach in applying the proportionality test. The Court has recently stressed that it will not accept any national legislation which provides for a prohibition of certain commercial practices in principle, without taking account of the specific circumstances of the individual case.[92] A more individualistic approach in assessing vulnerability as suggested above would also mean that national measures could more easily satisfy the requirement of proportionality.

Such a change in approach could possibly be supplemented by disregarding in certain cases the prohibition for member states contained in the Directives of maintaining or adopting more restrictive national measures, even where such measures are designed to ensure a higher level of consumer protection.[93] Exceptions to this prohibition could be permitted in respect of measures intended to protect particularly vulnerable consumers. Such a derogation from internal market principles for the purpose of protecting particularly vulnerable consumers seems to be in line with the UN Disability Convention, which expressly encourages 'necessary and appropriate modification and adjustments … to ensure to persons with disabilities the enjoyment or exercise on an equal basis with others of all human rights and fundamental freedoms'.[94] An obligation to specifically protect persons with disabilities from unfair commercial practices also arises from Article 16 of the UN Disability Convention. Article 16 obliges state parties to 'take all appropriate' measures to protect persons with disabilities from all forms of exploitation and abuse. Even though the article is primarily aimed at physical types of abuse, it must include the exploitation of persons with disabilities for the purpose of commercial practices. State parties also have an obligation on the basis of Article 16(2) of the Convention to provide persons with disabilities with information, in accessible formats, on how to avoid the danger of abusive and exploitative commercial practices.

In addition, a focus on the heightened protection to be granted to disabled persons should be present in EU soft law documents. Currently, the focus in EU consumer as well as disability law continues to be set on the internal market

[92] Case C-304/08 *Plus Warenhandelsgesellschaft* [2010] ECR I-217, para 54; Case C-540/08 *Mediaprint Zeitungs-und Zeitschriftenverlag* [2010] ECR I-10909, para. 36.

[93] See for instance Joined Cases C-261/07 and C-299/07 *VTB-VAB and Galatea* [2009] ECR I-2949, para 63.

[94] Art 5(2) jo Art 3 CRPD.

agenda. The European Consumer Agenda[95] refers amongst others to vulnerable consumers when identifying current problems and future challenges in the context of consumer protection. It also notes that the current context may exacerbate the disadvantaged situation of vulnerable consumers, such as people with disabilities or with reduced mobility, who face difficulties in assessing and understanding information and in finding appropriate services on the market. Yet, in spite of this remark and the occasional reference to the generic category of vulnerable consumers in its action plan, the Agenda does not further mention consumers with disabilities and fails to propose specific strategies to improve their protection.[96] Even the new European Disability Strategy,[97] which sets out the Commission's action plan and policy priorities for the period 2010–20, does not mention the concept of vulnerability and does not identify persons with disabilities as a particularly vulnerable group. Instead, it underlines the importance of ensuring disabled persons' participation in the European economy, notably through the single market.[98]

IV. CONCLUSION

It can be concluded from the discussion in this chapter that neither EU law nor the case law of the European Court of Human Rights succeeds in providing successful and adequate means of tackling the special vulnerability of persons with disabilities. In spite of the emergence of disability issues as a major human rights concern, the disability law framework still 'lags behind' other grounds of discrimination, such as gender and race. Even though the European Court of Human Rights has recognised persons with mental disabilities as a particularly vulnerable group deserving special protection, its case law reveals that the concept has inherent difficulties that may in fact exacerbate their marginalisation. The concept of vulnerability as a means to provide protection to disabled persons is questionable, as it may result in labelling and stigmatisation, running counter to the Court's objective of rectifying the history of prejudice and stigmatisation experienced by persons with disabilities. In addition, the case law fails to take account of the wide range of impairments experienced by persons with disabilities by placing them all in one and the same 'vulnerable group'.

Under EU law, the concept of vulnerability in a disability-context primarily relates to the role of disabled persons as market participants. It is notable that the concept of vulnerability and the explicit identification of disabled persons as a particularly vulnerable group is not part of the standard EU discourse

[95] European Commission Communication, 'A European Consumer Agenda—Boosting confidence and growth' COM (2012) 225 final.

[96] L Waddington, *The Protection of Consumers with Disabilities in the European Union: Persons with Disabilities as Active Participants in the Internal Market* (Brussels, ANED, 2012) 23.

[97] European Commission Communication, 'European Disability Strategy 2010–2020. A Renewed Commitment to a Barrier-Free Europe' COM (2010) 636 final.

[98] ibid, p 4.

in policy documents or legislation. The situation of particularly vulnerable consumers is specifically addressed in EU consumer law, most notably in the Unfair Commercial Practices Directive, the Product Safety Directive and the Consumer Rights Directive. Yet, the conceptualisation of vulnerability under EU consumer law is inadequate to provide the necessary protection for persons who are disadvantaged on grounds of their disability. EU law focuses on protecting the 'average' consumer, who is reasonably well-informed, observant and circumspect. The distinction between the capable 'average' consumer and the 'vulnerable' consumer does not treat consumers as individuals, but is based on stereotypical categories associated with the emergence of consumer policies as a 'spill-over' from the internal market.[99] Even in those cases where provisions provide for specific additional protection to vulnerable consumers, such protection may not hinder the smooth functioning of the internal market. The scope of protection offered to vulnerable consumers can thus be seen as rather limited, and has been labelled a compromise.[100] It appears that by promoting market integration and by putting emphasis on the capacities of the 'average' market participant, the Court of Justice has sacrificed the interests of particularly vulnerable groups, notably persons with disabilities. Moreover, EU legislation and case law lack a specific definition of vulnerability. It is not clear which groups of consumers can be categorised as 'vulnerable' and EU law fails to differentiate between various groups of 'vulnerable' consumers and the kinds of additional protection that they should be granted.[101]

Neither the ECHR nor the EU law framework satisfactorily embraces the 'social model of disability', which focuses on the societal obstacles preventing people with physical, sensory, intellectual or other impairments from participating in mainstream society. The social model pays witness to the fact that disabled people experience disability as a social restriction,[102] resulting from the environmental, built or human barriers that hinder their social participation, such as inaccessibly built environments, prejudices and questionable notions of intelligence. Both the Council of Europe and the EU institutions have adopted the social model of disability in soft-law documents, such as communications and recommendations. This trend is, however, not yet satisfactorily reflected in binding legislation. The ECHR and the EU Directives do not take account of the social model of disability, which goes hand in hand with the concept of situational vulnerability, and are therefore out of tune with the UN Disability Convention. Both legal frameworks fail to take sufficient account of the fact that disability is a socially constructed

[99] JR Davies, 'The European Consumer Citizen: A Coherent, tangible and relevant notion of citizenship?' (Doctoral dissertation, University of Leicester, 2010) 59.

[100] See J Stuyck, 'The Notion of the Empowered and Informed Consumer in Consumer Policy and How to Protect the Vulnerable Under Such a Regime', in G Howells et al (eds), *The Yearbook of Consumer Law 2007* (Farnham, Ashgate, 2007) 178, 179.

[101] L Waddington, 'Reflections on the Protection of 'Vulnerable' Consumers under EU Law' [2013] 2 *Maastricht University Working Papers* 16.

[102] RK Scotch, 'Models of Disability and the Americans with Disabilities Act' (2000) 12 *Berkeley Journal of Employment and Labour Law* 215.

category, and that key disadvantages faced by disabled people emanate from social treatment rather than from deficiencies in their constitution. At the same time, the legislation and case law discussed in this chapter does not recognise that *vulnerability* is socially constructed rather than inherent in our physical or cognitive conditions.

From the perspective of consumers with disabilities it would be desirable to operate an individual rather than a categorical test determining vulnerability. This means that vulnerability should be assessed in each specific situation, in the case of persons with disabilities but also persons who fall outside the categories of 'physical/mental infirmity' or 'credulity' in situations in which they are particularly vulnerable. The focus would thus shift from identifying certain persons with disabilities as particularly vulnerable and in need for special protection to recognising that disabled persons can be placed in a situation which renders them vulnerable. The vulnerability of disabled persons may differ considerably, depending on the type and severity of their impairment as well as with regard to the situation they find themselves in (eg in relation to divergent consumer products). The legal framework should thus identify the situation and factors which render particular groups of consumers vulnerable and provide appropriate measures and remedies.[103] This would be in line with Article 12(3) CRPD which requires state parties to take all appropriate measures to provide access by persons with disabilities to the support they may require in exercising their legal capacity. A person with disability would thus no longer be categorised as particularly vulnerable and requiring special protection, but the legal framework would provide protection to persons in certain situations in which they are particularly vulnerable on grounds of their disability. The abandonment of a static approach, which distinguishes categorically between 'average' and 'vulnerable' persons with disabilities, may also be desirable in light of Article 5 of the UN Disability Convention, which prohibits discrimination on the basis of disability, including the operation of stereotypes.[104]

Such an individualistic approach would impose a greater burden on national courts to assess the vulnerability of consumers with disabilities in each specific case. Yet, it would also do away with the difficulty of determining the 'average' member of a group of disabled persons, and allow for the granting of special protection to all persons in situation in which they are particularly vulnerable. Adopting the 'social model' of disability and taking account of 'situational vulnerability' in EU and ECHR law is certainly not an easy task, as it may create legal uncertainty and imposes a high burden on legislator and judiciary. Be that as it may, it appears to be the only mechanism which recognises the situational causes of vulnerability of disabled persons and meets their individual needs, whilst at the same time avoiding the discrimination and stigmatisation that comes along with labelling certain categories of persons as vulnerable.

[103] See more generally with regard to 'vulnerable' consumers, L Waddington, 'Reflections on the Protection of "Vulnerable" Consumers under EU Law' [2013] 2 *Maastricht University Working Papers* 28.

[104] See Art 8 CRPD.

5

European Protection for Women

FRANCETTE FINES

ACCORDING TO THE European approach, women (who are, in the legal sense, equal to men) are not considered a priori as vulnerable persons. Indeed, vulnerability is quite obviously not inherent to the female condition in general. But then how can European law—which tirelessly asserts the equality between women and men, implying that belonging to a particular sex cannot constitute a determining factor in the place or position of individuals in society[1]—conceive of or apprehend women's vulnerability? The promotion of women's rights, which seeks to recognise or ensure that women enjoy the same universal rights as men, in no way aims to class women in a new category of particularly vulnerable persons. Nevertheless, doctrine has shown that 'a method of enunciation "by category" appears in some cases to be a means of taking account of the vulnerability of certain groups with the aim of guaranteeing the true effectiveness of those rights proclaimed as universal'.[2]

It must be noted, first of all, that the Council of Europe Convention on preventing and combating violence against women does identify persons made vulnerable owing to a particular set of circumstances, specifically

> pregnant women and women with young children, persons with disabilities, including those with mental or cognitive impairments, persons living in rural or remote areas, substance abusers, prostitutes, persons of national or ethnic minority background, migrants—including undocumented migrants and refugees, gay men, lesbian women, bi-sexual and transgender persons as well as HIV-positive persons, homeless persons, children and the elderly.[3]

However, European action is not confined to these particular circumstances, and generally aims to reduce the vulnerability of women brought about by violent or discriminatory behaviour against them, which presents the risk of placing them

[1] F Fines, 'Egalité entre l'homme et la femme', in J Andriantsimbazovina, H Gaudin, J-P Marguénaud, S Rials and F Sudre (eds), *Dictionnaire des Droits de l'Homme* (Paris, PUF, 2008) 353–57.

[2] D Lochak, 'Penser les droits catégoriels dans leur rapport à l'universalité', in séminaire Droit des femmes face à l'essor de l'intérêt de l'enfant. (2013) juin *La Revue des Droits de l'Homme*, http://revdh.files.wordpress.com/2013/06/1secc81minairelochak1.pdf.

[3] Explanatory Report on Art 12.

in a vulnerable situation. For instance, Directive 2012/29/EU of the European Parliament and Council, dated 25 October 2012, establishing minimum standards on the rights, support and protection of victims of crime, is aimed at 'those persons who are particularly vulnerable or who are in situations exposing them to a particularly high risk of prejudice, such as persons suffering repeated acts of domestic violence, persons who are victims of gender-based violence' (point 38). Indeed, on the one hand women are subject to many forms of sexual discrimination and, on the other hand, they are the victims of all sorts of violence (physical or psychological aggression, rape, genital and sexual mutilation, harassment, trafficking for the purposes of sexual exploitation, etc), which risks making them vulnerable.

Consequently, Europe now concerns itself with the treatment of women and girls,[4] with a view to protecting them from such attacks and aggression. It must be added that a large number of charities, NGOs and lobby groups are active and vigilant in this field: the European Women's Lobby (EWL), for instance, or the Women Against Violence Europe network (WAVE). In this respect, Europe shares the UN's preoccupations[5]—for example with the Beijing Declaration and Platform for Action adopted at the Fourth World Conference on Women in 1995—and part of its activities relate to those same preoccupations. European organisations, however, also intend to provide themselves with the means to pursue a much more ambitious policy in this area.

We can therefore class the protection granted to women under European law amongst the values of European democratic society, as is attested by the ECtHR's decision in *Refah Partisi (The Welfare Party) & Others v Turkey*.[6] Since the entry into force of the Treaty of Lisbon, Article 2 TEU[7] must also be cited, the new wording of which does indeed reveal this preoccupation, in that it enshrines a European society characterised by 'equality between women and men', which is placed on the same level as other values such as pluralism. The decision to pick

[4] Under Art 3 of the Council of Europe Convention, '"women" includes girls under the age of 18'.

[5] See the 1993 Declaration on the elimination of violence against women, adopted by the General Assembly of the United Nations (Resolution 48/104 of 20 December 1993).

[6] *Refah Partisi (The Welfare Party) & Others v Turkey* App nos 41340/98, 41342/98 and 41344/98 (ECtHR, 13 February 2003). According to para 123, '[i]t is difficult to declare one's respect for democracy and human rights while at the same time supporting a regime based on sharia, which clearly diverges from Convention values, particularly with regard to its criminal law and criminal procedure, its rules on the legal status of women and the way it intervenes in all spheres of private and public life in accordance with religious precepts'.

According to para 128, 'any other Contracting Party, may legitimately prevent the application within its jurisdiction of private-law rules of religious inspiration prejudicial to public order and the values of democracy for Convention purposes (such as rules permitting discrimination based on the gender of the parties concerned, as in polygamy and privileges for the male sex in matters of divorce and succession)'.

[7] 'The Union is founded on the values of respect for human dignity, freedom, democracy, equality, the rule of law and respect for human rights, including the rights of persons belonging to minorities.

These values are common to the member states in a society in which pluralism, non-discrimination, tolerance, justice, solidarity and equality between women and men prevail.'

out that form of equality at the end of Article 2 TEU, and indeed only that one after the reference to non-discrimination, is quite remarkable in that it will indisputably play a specific role in the development of greater cohesion within the emergent European society.

It is right to question the competence of European bodies (primarily the European Union and the Council of Europe, but also the Organization for Security of Co-operation in Europe (OSCE)). Admittedly, the activities of international co-operation organisations are aimed at reminding states of the need to act in protecting women; they will therefore act with a view to supporting member states in their efforts to prevent and combat discrimination towards women. The issue of the division of powers with member states is raised with respect to the European Union, as EU law can lead to incursions into the field of domestic competence; such an incursion is illustrated by the *Tanja Kreil*[8] decision, in which the now CJEU compared the principle of equality with national constitutional rules relative to the structure of the German Army, insofar as those rules excluded women from jobs in the military; the Court ruled that the European principle prevailed. The European courts have since developed a case law aimed at affording a better protection to women, by attempting to make the most of the written provisions in this area. The Treaty of Amsterdam extended the scope for Community action with the inclusion of a new Article 13 EC, now Article 19 of the Treaty on the Functioning of the European Union. This article must be viewed as an enabling clause, granting the European Council powers to act, and particularly to 'take appropriate action to combat discrimination based on sex'; in this respect, it is notable that sex constitutes the first category targeted by this provision, amongst others that it identifies. However, the action taken by EU institutions has also consisted in activities to support policies led by member states; in this respect, see for example Article 153(1) TFEU.

In seeking to eradicate violence and discrimination against women, the various European institutions (organisations, bodies and courts) have established legal principles, together with internal and external policies, all structured around the fight against those two types of abuse against women. Our study will focus on the actions taken against such abuse: the prevention of violence against women (section I); and the fight against discrimination towards women (section II).

I. THE PREVENTION OF VIOLENCE AGAINST WOMEN

There continues to be a lack of reliable figures on both a European and a comparable national level. Collecting such data is quite difficult, particularly as women, through either fear or shame, can hesitate to report acts of violence of which they are the victims. This is why an instrument such as the Convention on preventing

[8] Case C-285/98 *Tanja Kreil v Bundesrepublik Deutschland* [2000] ECR I-69.

and combating violence against women provides that 'Parties shall undertake to collect disaggregated relevant statistical data at regular intervals on cases of all forms of violence covered by the scope of this Convention' (Article 11(1)(a)). The European Agency for Fundamental Rights also conducted a survey on physical, sexual and psychological violence against women,[9] the results of which were published in March 2014 and surprised many with the disparities that they revealed between the various countries in Europe.

As regards violence, there are several types of measures in the European sphere. They attest to the growing mobilisation in Europe on this issue (section A, below). European organisations have developed a very broad conception of their actions in order to cover all forms of violence against women (section B), and above all to work with a view to enshrining effective legal mechanisms to protect women (section C).

A. The Growing Mobilisation of European Organisations in Addressing the Issue of Violence against Women

Emanating from awareness-raising forums, we must first mention the steps taken by the various bodies within the Council of Europe,[10] be it through the resolutions of the Parliamentary Assembly[11] or the recommendations made by the Committee of Ministers. Of particular note in this respect is Recommendation (2002)5 on the protection of women against violence, which provides for a follow-up on its implementation.[12] The resolutions passed by the European Parliament[13] must also be highlighted. The OSCE, it will be noted, also adopted a decision on the subject in 2005,[14] and published a study in 2009 titled 'Bringing Security Home: Combating Violence against Women in the OSCE Region—A Compilation of Good Practices'.

[9] European Agency for Fundamental Rights, *Violence against women: an EU-wide survey*, available at, http://fra.europa.eu/en/publication/2014/vaw-survey-results-factsheet.

[10] S Reid, *Preventing Violence against Women—a European Perspective* (Strasbourg, Council of Europe Publishing, 2003).

[11] Among the Resolutions and Recommendations adopted, the following are of note: Resolution 1247 (2001) on female genital mutilation; Resolution 1582 (2002) on domestic violence; Resolution 1327 (2003) on so-called 'honour killings'; Recommendation 1723 (2005) on forced marriage and child marriage; Resolution 1654 (2009) on feminicide; Resolution 1691 (2009) on the rape of women, including marital rape.

[12] See the 2013 Analytical Study of the results of the fourth round of monitoring the implementation of Recommendation Rec (2002)5 on the protection of women against violence in Council of Europe member states; document prepared by C Hagemann-White.

[13] The first Resolution of the European Parliament, on violence against women, dates back to 11 June 1986; see also the Resolution of the European Parliament of 26 November 2009 on the elimination of violence against women. The European Parliament is active on this issue, particularly through its commission for women's rights and gender equality (FEMM).

[14] Decision No 15/05, Preventing and combating violence against women.

In 1997, the European Community decided to launch the 'Daphne' Programme, the purpose of which is to prevent and combat all forms of violence against children, young adults and women by encouraging the development of Community policies and actions in favour of victims. Through this programme, now integrated into the 'Rights, equality and citizenship' programme for 2014–20, the European Union funds[15] activities led by NGOs, local authorities and research centres to combat such violence. The Women's Charter adopted by the European Commission in March 2010[16] seeks to 'put in place a comprehensive and effective policy framework to combat gender-based violence'. The EU has also concerned itself with violence towards women and girls in the scope of its co-operation with third party states, and thus has integrated that dimension into the European Instrument for Democracy and Human Rights (EIDHR).[17] On 8 December 2008, the EU's General Affairs Council adopted 'Guidelines on violence against women and girls and combating all forms of discrimination against them', which underscores the political will to make the topic of women's rights, together with the protection of women and girls, a priority in EU foreign policy.

However, the most notable tool on a European level is the recent Convention adopted by the Council of Europe in 2011, which relates precisely to preventing and combating violence against women and domestic violence. On August 2014, the Council of Euorpe Convention entered into force. In devoting a specific instrument to them, the Council of Europe intended to bring out into the open those forms of violence that are all too often hushed up or played down, of which women are the victims. The Istanbul Convention is unique on an international level, and has thus opened the way to other actions (such as the 2013 UN Declaration on violence against women). The principle of responsibility on the part of state authorities lies at the heart of the Convention; under Article 5, states are in effect bound to act with due diligence in preventing, investigating and punishing acts of violence against women. The Convention provides for the creation of a Group of Experts on combating violence against women and domestic violence (known as 'GREVIO'), responsible for monitoring the implementation of the Convention by states.

As regards the European Court of Human Rights, it is worth noting that cases concerning violence against women or the risks of violence faced by women are 'considered a priority'.[18]

[15] While the Daphne III Programme (2007–13) had a budget allocation of €116.85 million, the new programme, with its much wider field of application, totals €439.473 million for the 2014–20 period.

[16] Communication from the Commission of 5 March 2010, 'A Strengthened Commitment to Equality between Women and Men—A Women's Charter' COM(2010) 78 final.

[17] Regulation (EC) 1889/2006 of the European Parliament and Council of 20 December 2006 on establishing a financing instrument for the promotion of democracy and human rights worldwide.

[18] R Toma, 'Panorama de la jurisprudence de la Cour européenne des droits de l'homme sur les obstacles à la justice pour les femmes victimes de violence', Discours pour l'Audience publique du 9 décembre 2013, à Paris Au Ministère des droits des femmes, http://www.coe.int/t/DGHL/STANDARDSETTING/EQUALITY/05conferences/2013ParisHearingAccessJustice/Speeches/Toma_speech_Paris.pdf.

B. The Scope of the Fight against Violence towards Women

It is interesting to note in this regard the interaction and empowerment of the fight against violence in relation to the approach in terms of discrimination. We can begin by emphasising that, unlike international law,[19] there is a separate convention. In reality—and according to the Explanatory Report—the Istanbul Convention 'places the obligation to prevent and combat violence against women within the wider framework of achieving equality between women and men'; moreover, Article 4 of the Convention is devoted to fundamental rights, equality and non-discrimination. Thus the Preamble to the Convention[20] recognises 'that violence against women is a manifestation of historically unequal power relations between women and men, which have led to domination over, and discrimination against, women by men and to the prevention of the full advancement of women'. Equally, the fight against violence constitutes one of the principal themes in the European Union's Strategy for equality between men and women (2010–15). There remain inextricable links between violence and the various forms of discrimination or inequality, as has also been established on an international level by the Committee on the Elimination of Discrimination against Women (CEDAW), in its General Recommendation no 19 (1992). The ECtHR's decision in *Opuz v Turkey*, evokes the general correlation between discrimination and violence against women.[21] It will also be noted that harassment, which is considered to be discrimination under EU law and is therefore tackled in anti-discrimination directives,[22] is also targeted by the Convention on preventing and combating violence against women (under Article 40).

Nevertheless, while they may contain elements that make reference to discrimination, the definitions of violence towards women are separate. Three interesting definitions are contained in Article 3 of the Convention. The term 'violence towards women' designates 'all acts of gender-based violence that result in, or are likely to result in, physical, sexual, psychological or economic harm or suffering to women, including threats of such acts, coercion or arbitrary deprivation of liberty,

[19] See principally the UN International Convention on the elimination of all forms of discrimination towards women.

[20] Art 13 of the 1993 Declaration on Policies for Combating Violence against Women in a Democratic Europe had already analysed violence towards women, including the refusal of the right to free choice of motherhood, 'as a means of controlling women, originating from the unequal power relationship still prevailing between men and women, and is therefore an obstacle to the achievement of genuine equality between women and men'.

[21] *Opuz v Turkey* App no 33401/02 (ECtHR, 9 June 2009), paras 184–91. Furthermore, concerning the Turkish case before it, the European Court declared at para 200: 'Bearing in mind its finding above that the general and discriminatory judicial passivity in Turkey, albeit unintentional, mainly affected women, the Court considers that the violence suffered by the applicant and her mother may be regarded as gender-based violence which is a form of discrimination against women.'

[22] This is a contribution from Directive 2002/73/EC of the European Parliament and Council of 23 September 2002, amending Directive 76/207/EEC cited above ([2002] OJ L269/15).

whether occurring in public or in private life'.[23] The term 'domestic violence' refers to 'all acts of physical, sexual, psychological or economic violence that occur within the family or domestic unit or between former or current spouses or partners, whether or not the perpetrator shares or has shared the same residence with the victim'. We find the same approach in the term 'gender-based violence towards women', which 'shall mean violence that is directed against a woman because she is a woman or that affects women disproportionately'. The Preamble is drafted as follows: '[r]ecognising that violence against women is a manifestation of historically unequal power relations between women and men, which have led to domination over, and discrimination against, women by men and to the prevention of the full advancement of women'.

Many types of violence are listed in the Council of Europe's Convention on violence, which strives to provide the broadest possible enumeration.[24] The Convention thus covers, in its Preamble, 'serious forms of violence such as domestic violence, sexual harassment, rape, forced marriage, crimes committed in the name of so-called "honour" and genital mutilation'; as a result of the definitions mentioned above, the following are targeted: psychological violence (Article 33), physical violence (Article 35) and sexual violence (Article 36). Moreover, according to the Convention, '[p]arties shall ensure that culture, custom, religion, tradition or so-called "honour" shall not be considered as justification for any acts of violence' (Article 12).[25]

The Convention also strives to cover acts of violence committed overseas. Article 44(3) is particularly innovative in this respect, in that it removes the double criminality rule (which requires that the criminal offence committed also be viewed as such in the country where it has taken place) for the most serious offences that are often committed outside the territories of European states, such as forced marriage or female genital mutilation. The Convention also aims to protect migrant women as well as female refugees and asylum-seekers.[26]

The European Court of Human Rights (see below) has also ruled on cases raising the issue of therapeutic abortion,[27] intended (though not exclusively[28]) for women or adolescent girls in vulnerable situations; another case concerned the

[23] This definition broadly reiterates that contained in the abovementioned 2002 Recommendation of the Committee of Ministers of the Council of Europe.

[24] It also refers, in the Preamble, to other Conventions that relate to other forms of violence towards women and girls, such as the Council of Europe Convention Against Human Trafficking (STCE no 197, 2005) and the Council of Europe Convention on the Protection of Children Against Sexual Exploitation and Sexual Abuse (STCE no 201, 2007).

[25] On this subject, see also the recent 2013 UN Declaration on violence against women.

[26] For instance, under the terms of Art 60, member states must take measures to ensure that 'gender-based violence against women may be recognised as a form of persecution within the meaning of Article 1, A (2), of the 1951 Convention relating to the Status of Refugees and as a form of serious harm giving rise to complementary/subsidiary protection'.

[27] J-M Larralde, 'La Cour européenne des Droits de l'Homme et la promotion des droits des femmes. Cour européenne des droits de l'homme (4e section) Tysiac c. Pologne, 20 mars 2007' (2007) 71 *Revue Trimestrielle des Droits de l'Homme* 855–74.

[28] *A, B & C v Ireland* App no 25579/05 (ECtHR, 16 December 2010).

forced sterilisation of Roma women in Slovakia.[29] Moreover, the Court has taken account of marital rape in two decisions in 1995, *SW v United Kingdom*[30] and *CR v United Kingdom,*[31] declaring that

> the abandonment of the unacceptable idea of a husband being immune against prosecution for rape of his wife was in conformity not only with a civilised concept of marriage but also, and above all, with the fundamental objectives of the Convention, the very essence of which is respect for human dignity and human freedom.

C. The Legal Mechanisms Protecting Women against Violence

The case law emanating from the European Court of Human Rights (which one writer[32] did not hesitate in calling 'the European Court of Women's Rights') is audacious, in that the Court has effectively imposed positive obligations on member states. According to consistent case law, and as has already been seen, the ECtHR views as sexual discrimination the lack of protection on the part of state authorities for women against domestic violence, which is prohibited by the Convention.[33] Several articles under the Convention have been invoked by female victims (namely Articles 2, 3, 8), either separately or cumulatively, or even combined with Article 14. The ECtHR has notably found several states to be in breach of the requirement to protect women who are the victims of violence at the hand of their husband or partner;[34] in a number of such cases, the Court took the view that the state authorities in question had been unaware of the positive obligations placed on them, on the basis of Article 2 ECHR which guarantees the right to life.[35] In its decision in *Valiuliene v Lithuania*[36] the Court also found a violation of the ban on inhuman treatment owing to the delay in handling a complaint made by a battered woman, which eventually fell outside the limitation period. It will be noted that many member states have been found to be in breach of their obligations in rape cases and particularly where the offence has been committed by state officials. On the matter of rape, the decision in *MC v Bulgaria* is important: in basing its decision on Articles 3 and 8 of the ECHR, the Court imposed on the state, '[i]n accordance with contemporary standards and trends in that area', a positive obligation to penalise and effectively prosecute before the criminal courts

[29] *VC v Slovakia* Appno 18968/07 (ECtHR, 8 November 2011).
[30] *SW v United Kingdom* App no 20166/92 (ECtHR, 22 November 1995).
[31] *CR v United Kingdom* App no 20190/92 (ECtHR, 22 November 1995).
[32] J-P Marguénaud, 'Quand la Cour de Strasbourg poursuit sa mutation en Cour européenne des droits de la Femme; la question du viol (Cour EDH., 1ère sect., *M.C. c/ Bulgarie*, du 4 décembre 2003)' (2004) avril-juin *Revue Trimestrielle des Droits de l'Homme* 364–65.
[33] See eg *Opuz v Turkey*, n 21 above, para 200; mention must also be made of the decision in *Eremia v Republic of Moldova* App no 3564/11 (ECtHR, 28 May 2013).
[34] Many cases involve spouses or partners suffering from psychiatric problems.
[35] See in particular the decision in *Opuz v Turkey*, n 21 above.
[36] *Valiuliene v Lithuania* App no 33234/07 (ECtHR, 26 March 2013).

'any non-consensual sexual act, including in the absence of physical resistance by the victim'.[37] Moreover, a rape case triggered the recognition of the horizontal effect of Article 8 ECHR, faced with the lack of judicial protection for an underage victim who was also mentally handicapped.[38]

In the case of a court of law established by the UN Security Council, we may also note the judgment on appeal of the International Criminal Tribunal for the former Yugoslavia, which handed down sentences for offences of slavery and rape committed during the armed conflict in the former Yugoslavia.[39]

By means of a restrictive convention, the Council of Europe has sought to afford effective protection against violence, asking member states to promote a series of concrete actions that provide real help to women who find themselves in vulnerable situations as victims of violence; this is to be understood as a 'breach of human rights' under Article 3. As analysts[40] have commented, 'the structure of the new Convention rests on the principle of the three Ps: Prevention, Protection for victims and Prosecution of perpetrators; it also provides for a fourth P, which refers to an integrated Policy', since a sector-based approach appears to be ineffectual. A legal status must therefore be available to women who are victims of violence. Article 29(1) aims to provide victims with civil remedies against perpetrators, while Article 29(2) ensures that they are provided with adequate civil remedies against state authorities that have failed to take the necessary preventive or protective measures. Under Article 45, states are under a duty to draw inferences from the seriousness of such offences by adopting measures that are 'effective, proportionate and dissuasive', which includes prison sentences and may even give rise to extradition. Under Article 48(1), states must prohibit mandatory alternative dispute resolution processes. Article 52 stipulates that, in situations of immediate danger, a perpetrator of acts of domestic violence may be ordered to vacate the residence of the victim and be prohibited from returning thereto.

In building an area without borders, the European Union has adopted restrictive legal acts,[41] aiming to impose a duty on member states to protect women as victims, though the legislation in question is not limited to gender-based violence. For instance: Directive 2012/29/EU establishing minimum standards on the

[37] *MC v Bulgaria* App no 39272/98 (ECtHR, 4 December 2003), para 166. See F Sudre, *J.C.P.*, 2004, ed. G, I 107, 181; see also J-P Marguénaud, ibid.

[38] *X and Y v Netherlands* App no 8978/80 (ECtHR, 26 March 1985).

[39] *The Prosecutor v Dragoljub Kunarac, Radomir Kovač and Zoran Vuković* (ICTY, 12 June 2002).

[40] Maud de Boer-Buquicchio, Deputy Secretary General of the Council of Europe, 'Le principe des 4 P. Prévention, Protection des victimes et Poursuite des auteurs et Politique intégrée', in Actes du colloque de novembre 2010, *Des violences conjugales aux violences intrafamiliales, une affaire à trois: victimes, auteurs, enfants témoins*, www.regain-association.org/files/doc/Acte.pdf.

[41] Joined Cases C-483/09 and C-1/10 *Gueye and Salmerón Sánchez* [2011] ECR I-8263; on the subject of Council Framework Decision of 15 March 2001 2001/220/JHA, on the standing of victims in criminal proceedings (2001 OJ L82/1), the Court declared that 'Articles 2, 3 and 8 of the Framework Decision must be interpreted as not precluding the mandatory imposition of an injunction to stay away for a minimum period, provided for as an ancillary penalty by the criminal law of a Member State, on persons who commit crimes of violence within the family, even when the victims of those crimes oppose the application of such a penalty' (point 70).

rights, support and protection of victims of crime (see above); Directive 2011/99/EU on the European protection order, in criminal matters;[42] Regulation (EU) 606/2013 of the European Parliament and Council of 12 June 2013 on the mutual recognition of protection measures in civil matters.

II. THE FIGHT AGAINST DISCRIMINATION TOWARDS WOMEN

The fight against discrimination towards women, which has become much more widespread (section B, below), is linked to the assertion of legal equality between women and men, which has been enshrined as a fundamental principle (section A, below); this legal equality involves the equal ability to enjoy all rights and freedoms, without experiencing discrimination. But how to conceive of the equality of two beings, man and woman, who are presented as different from the outset? The promotion of physiological, social or psychological differences has often served as a pretext for the subordination, marginalisation or even the treatment of women as inferiors; this is what European organisations seek to combat, by developing their own conception of equality between women and men (section C, below).

A. Enshrining a European Fundamental Principle of Equality Between Women and Men

This concerns a fundamental right, enshrined as much in case law as it is in various European charters including the Charter of Fundamental Rights of the European Union, under which Article 23 is devoted in its entirety to equality between women and men.

The decisions in *Gabrielle Defrenne* (a flight attendant who was made redundant because she had reached the age limit of 40) were an opportunity for the now CJEU to define the status of what appeared to be a principle but was also an objective,[43] a duality that testified to the originality of this equality between the sexes. In the *Defrenne II* decision of 8 April 1976,[44] the now CJEU asserted that

[42] Under Art 1, the objective of the Directive is to establish 'rules allowing a judicial or equivalent authority in a Member State, in which a protection measure has been adopted with a view to protecting a person against a criminal act by another person which may endanger his life, physical or psychological integrity, dignity, personal liberty or sexual integrity, to issue a European protection order enabling a competent authority in another Member State to continue the protection of the person in the territory of that other Member State, following criminal conduct, or alleged criminal conduct, in accordance with the national law of the issuing State'.

[43] Equally, in its decision in Case C-50/96 *Deutsche Bundespost Telekom v Lilli Schröder* [2000] ECR I-743, the ECJ emphasised that the economic aim of Art 141 EC 'is secondary to its social aim' targeted by this provision, 'which constitutes the expression of a fundamental human right not to be discriminated against on grounds of sex'.

[44] Case 43/75 *Defrenne v Sabena* [1976] ECR 455.

equality between the sexes did not relate to a purely economic objective, but also concerned social objectives that the Treaty assigned to the Community. This article thus carries with it a degree of social cohesion; it corresponds to the European social model promoted within the European Union. In the *Defrenne III* decision of 15 June 1978,[45] it was enshrined as a fundamental principle of Community law: 'there can be no doubt that the elimination of discrimination based on sex forms part of those fundamental rights' of each human being. The principle stated must be guaranteed and it is in this regard that the ECJ enshrined the right to an effective legal remedy, in the *Johnson* decision[46] of 15 May 1986. Thus the now EU law imposes a duty on member states to provide legal remedies enabling workers to enforce their rights to equal treatment. It must also be noted that the principle of equality between women and men has been 'a field of innovation for the production of evidence';[47] thus the Directive of 15 December 1997[48] on the burden of proof was adopted by the Council in order to facilitate actions brought by victims of discrimination, in cases of suspected discrimination based on sex.

Just such a conception of equality was also enshrined in the European Social Charter (Article 20), signed in Turin on 18 October 1961 and revised on 3 May 1996; and the Community Charter of Fundamental Social Rights for Workers, adopted in 1989. More recently, the principle of non-discrimination based on sex has been included as such in the Charter of Fundamental Rights of the European Union (Article 21). Following a general Article on equality before the law (Article 20) and another listing prohibited forms of discrimination (beginning with discrimination based on sex), the drafters of the Charter decided to dedicate an article specifically to 'equality between women and men' (Article 23). The decision to set this equality apart, thus establishing it as a fully fledged fundamental right, is noteworthy. Special mention must also be made of the symbolic nature of the reversal in the presentation of the sexes compared with the version contained in the Charter of Fundamental Rights as adopted in December 2000; in the new version, which was redrafted in 2007, women are mentioned first, followed by men.

B. The Widespread Fight against Discrimination between Women and Men

The fight against discrimination towards women is conducted within the Council of Europe and by the European Court of Human Rights; it is to be noted that this fight had been planned since the inception of the European construct, and has been considerably fleshed out ever since.

[45] Case 149/77 *Defrenne v Sabena* [1978] ECR 1365.

[46] Case 222/84 *Johnston v RUC* [1986] ECR 1651.

[47] O Dubos, 'La lutte contre les discriminations entre les femmes et les hommes: modèle et laboratoire?', in F Fines, C Gauthier and M Gautier (eds), *La non-discrimination entre les européens* (Paris, Pedone, 2012) 97–112.

[48] Council Directive 97/80/EC on the burden of proof in cases of discrimination based on sex [1998] OJ L14/6.

The European Court of Human Rights stated with good reason in its judgment in *Abdulaziz, Cabales and Balkandali v United Kingdom*, 'that the advancement of the equality of the sexes is today a major goal in the member States of the Council of Europe'.[49] Indeed, Article 14 of the European Convention on Human Rights offers protection against discrimination based particularly on sex in the enjoyment of rights and freedoms guaranteed by the other provisions of the Convention. This implies, for example, that equal civil rights also be recognised, be it equality between spouses or equality between parents. Thus, under the terms of Article 5 of Protocol 7 to the European Convention on Human Rights, '[s]pouses shall enjoy equality of rights and responsibilities of a private law character between them, and in their relations with their children'. Equality between men and women has also led the Court to find that the duty imposed on a married woman to take her husband's surname constituted a breach of Article 14.[50]

The 1957 Treaty of Rome already contained a provision aimed at guaranteeing equal pay for men and women. Today, this equality between women and men is linked to the aims of the European Union (Article 3(2) TEU). Mention must also be made of Article 8 TFEU, which now features amongst the provisions having general application, and which contains a further innovation from the Treaty of Amsterdam in that it sets a new cross-cutting objective, under the terms of which the Union seeks 'to promote equality between men and women' in all its activities; this, together with the Treaty of Lisbon, concerns those activities relative to the Union's internal and external policies. Article 10, which also features amongst the provisions having general application, states that 'the Union shall aim to combat discrimination based on sex'; this constitutes the first category mentioned ahead of the others, following an identical list under the above-mentioned Article 19 TFEU.

The activities of the European Union have become more diverse, with the involvement of its various bodies and the creation of a specialist institute: EIGE.[51] The Union now tracks direct[52] and indirect[53] discrimination, the latter emerging 'where an apparently neutral provision, criterion or practice would put persons of one sex at a particular disadvantage compared with persons of the other

[49] *Abdulaziz, Cabales and Balkandali v United Kingdom* App nos 9214/80, 9473/81 (ECtHR, 28 May 1985).

[50] *Ünal Tekeli v Turkey* App no 29865/96 (ECtHR, 16 November 2004).

[51] The Institute came into being when the European Parliament and the Council adopted Regulation (EC) 1922/2006 establishing a European Institute for Gender Equality.

[52] The ECJ ruled for instance that national regulations permitting an employer to dismiss a salaried employee who has acquired the right to draw a retirement pension, where this same right is acquired at the age of 60 for women but 65 for men, 'constitutes discrimination based on sex': Case C-356/09 *Pensionsversicherungsanstalt v Christine Kleist* [2010] ECR I-11939.

[53] Case C-243/95 *Hill and Stapleton v Revenue Commissioners and Department of Finance* [1998] ECR I-37399.

sex'.[54] Moreover, relating even more broadly to the world of work (see Directive 2006/54/EC on the implementation of the principle of equal opportunities and equal treatment of men and women in matters of employment and occupation, jointly adopted by the European Parliament and Council on 5 July 2006[55]), and although there remains a great deal to do (as shown by the continued existence of the 'glass ceiling'), European intervention is no longer confined solely to the economic sphere, though this remains a priority field. The Council therefore adopted Directive 2004/113/EC, implementing equal treatment of men and women, in the access to goods and services and in the provision of goods and services.[56]

The ECJ has given a very broad interpretation of the provisions contained in the Treaty and the various Directives. In this way, the rule relating to equal pay under the former Article 141 EC also targets company pensions.[57] However, it must also be noted that this rule may also manifest itself as a form of discrimination against men; given that the setting of a different retirement age would be contrary to the principle of equal pay, the ECJ, in its decision in *Barber*,[58] prohibited the alignment of benefits with the national statutory social security scheme setting a different retirement age depending on sex. The Court has since gone further and found some retirement schemes (the Italian civil service one, for instance[59]) to be in breach where these have set different retirement ages for men and women.[60]

C. The European Concept of Equality between Women and Men

It must be noted that, on a general level, this concept begins with a neutral principle: equal treatment for all; more generally, it is a matter of combating gender stereotypes;[61] in its decision in *Stoeckel*,[62] the ECJ found French legislation prohibiting night work for women to be in breach. As regards content, the now

[54] According to the definition contained in the recast Directive 2006/54/EC of the European Parliament and Council on the implementation of the principle of equal opportunities and equal treatment of men and women in matters of employment and occupation.

[55] [2006] OJ L204/23.

[56] [2004] OJ L373/37.

[57] Case 170/84 *Bilka-Kaufhaus GmbH v Weber von Hartz* [1986] ECR 1607.

[58] Case C-262/88 *Douglas Harvey Barber v Guardian Royal Exchange Assurance Group* [1990] ECR 1889.

[59] Case C-46/07 *Commission v Italy* [2008] ECR I-151.

[60] According to the Court, 'the determination of a retirement age that differs according to sex is not by its nature likely to compensate for the disadvantages to which the careers of female civil servants are exposed by helping these women in their professional lives and by remedying those problems that they may encounter during their professional careers' (point 58).

[61] See, eg, *Konstantin Markin v Russia* App no 30078/06 (ECtHR, 22 March 2012). It may also be a matter of combating a national law that 'is liable to perpetuate a traditional distribution of the roles of men and women by keeping men in a role subsidiary to that of women in relation to the exercise of their parental duties': Case C-104/09 *Pedro Manuel Roca Álvarez v Sesa Start España ETT SA* [2010] ECR I-8661.

[62] Case C-345/89 *Criminal proceedings against Alfred Stoeckel* [1991] ECR I-4047.

EU legislators have developed a broad notion, including harassment and sexual harassment, since the above-mentioned 2002 Directive.[63]

However, equal treatment does not always suffice in eliminating the various forms of inequality that affect men and women in society. This does not, however, preclude distinctions that may be made between them. These may result in particular in the taking into account of specificities linked to sex and, for instance, in the greater vulnerability in the workplace of pregnant or breastfeeding women, or those women who have recently given birth.[64] In identifying such women as constituting a specific at-risk group, these measures therefore aim to guarantee protection for the biological condition of women as well as the particular relationship between a woman and her child during the period following birth. The measures permit, even compel, member states to create specific rights, such as the prohibition of night work for pregnant women, the prohibition of the dismissal of pregnant women,[65] or the granting of maternity leave; in this way, pregnant workers must benefit from a scheme that is distinct from that of their male colleagues,[66] owing to their specific situation.[67] However, the CJEU has not recognised a right to maternity leave for commissioning mothers who have had a child through a surrogacy agreement.[68]

Differentiation may also arise from the acceptance of positive discrimination in favour of women. It is worth noting the convergence between the approaches adopted by the European courts,[69] illustrated by the CJEU's decision in

[63] Directive 2002/73/EC of the European Parliament and Council.

[64] Council Directive 92/85/EEC on the introduction of measures to encourage improvements in the safety and health at work of pregnant workers and workers who have recently given birth or are breastfeeding (tenth individual Directive within the meaning of Article 16(1) of Directive 89/391/EEC) [1992] OJ L348/1.

[65] This prohibition also relates to a member of a Board of Directors of a capital company: Case C-232/09 *Dita Danosa* [2010] ECR I-11405; the Court asserted that '[w]hichever directive applies, it is important to ensure, for the person concerned, the protection granted under EU law to pregnant women in cases where the legal relationship linking her to another person has been severed on account of her pregnancy' (point 70), which conclusion is, in the view of the Court, 'supported, moreover, by the principle of equality between men and women enshrined in Article 23 of the Charter of Fundamental Rights of the European Union, in accordance with which that equality must be ensured in all areas, including employment, work and pay' (point 71).

[66] Case C-394/96 *Mary Brown v Rentokil Ltd* [1998] ECR I-4185: 'the situation of a pregnant worker who is unfit for work as a result of disorders associated with her pregnancy cannot be considered to be the same as that of a male worker who is ill and absent through incapacity for work for the same length of time'.

[67] Case C-191/03 *North Western Health Board v Margaret McKenna* [2005] ECR I-7631: 'It does not necessarily follow from the finding that pregnancy-related illnesses are sui generis that a female worker who is absent by reason of a pregnancy-related illness is entitled to maintenance of full pay, whereas a worker absent by reason of an illness unrelated to pregnancy does not have such a right … as it stands at present, Community law does not require the maintenance of full pay for a female worker who is absent during her pregnancy by reason of an illness related to that pregnancy.'

[68] Case C-167/12 *CD v ST* (CJEU, Grand Chamber, 18 March 2014); Case C-363/12 *Z v A Government department, The Board of management of a community school* (CJEU, Grand Chamber, 18 March 2014).

[69] D Martin, 'Strasbourg, Luxembourg et la discrimination: influences croisées ou jurisprudences sous influence?' (2007) 69 *Revue Trimestrielle des Droits de l'Homme* 107–34.

Hepple[70] and the ECtHR's decision in *Stec*[71] concerning a service that included different age conditions based on sex, linked to the statutory retirement age. Furthermore, beyond the approach based on a comparison of legal schemes applied to men and women, equal opportunities have also been proclaimed. In this respect, it is noteworthy that the Community Directive 2006/54/EC[72] should relate specifically to the implementation of the principles of equal opportunities and equal treatment of men and women in matters of employment and occupation. Equal opportunities[73] are also the result of the new Article 157(3) TFEU, concerning the activities undertaken by the Union's institutions. However, while the law has now agreed to take them into account, such equal opportunities remain quite difficult to define. Their aim is to offer everyone the possibility of accessing the assets of society. In theory, such equal opportunities ought to be offered at the very outset of social competition; men and women ought to start in a position offering them the same chance of success, without sex constituting a basis for discrimination. As this is far from being the case, measures intended to correct this initial inequality for the future have been adopted. It is a matter of re-establishing equal opportunities, to begin with, through the implementation of corrective measures to the benefit of the disadvantaged sex.

Above all, in some cases, the specific advantages consist in preference given to the benefit of one sex and intervening symmetrically to the detriment of the members of the group that is excluded; this has led to cases invoking positive discrimination, given concrete expression by equality in the results thereof. Nevertheless, such results may only be obtained through a process that separates the sexes, which is usually prohibited. Faced with this tension, the courts have to decide whether to content themselves with the implementation of such means from the beginning, or whether such equal results may be sought at the end, assuming that women are under-represented in a given sector of activity. In its decision in *Kalanke*,[74] the ECJ initially found the automatic preferential rights guaranteeing one sex 'absolute and unconditional priority' for an appointment or promotion to be in breach; however, in its subsequent *Marschall* decision,[75] the

[70] Case C-196/98 *Regina Virginia Hepple v Adjudication Officer and Adjudication Officer v Anna Stec* [2000] ECR I-3701.

[71] *Stec and others v United Kingdom* App nos 65731/01 and 65900/01 (ECtHR (GC), 12 April 2006).

[72] [2006] OJ L204/23.

[73] Under the previous wording of Art 2(4) of the 1976 Directive, the now EU law admits or does not prohibit 'measures to promote equal opportunity for men and women, in particular by removing existing inequalities which affect women's opportunities'. Further to the introduction of a new wording in 2002, the reference to women's opportunities has been omitted from the new Art 2(8).

[74] Case C-450/93 *Kalanke v Freie Hansestadt Bremen* [1995] ECR I-3051. In the view of Advocate General Tesauro, in his above-mentioned Opinion, equal opportunities can only be such with respect to starting points, not with respect to points of arrival; they therefore cannot be analysed in numerical terms. This decision has been highly controversial in Europe, in that it is allegedly too closely linked to the formal type of non-discrimination.

[75] C-409/95 *Marschall v Land Nordrhein Westfalen* [1997] ECR I-6363. Helmutt Marschall, a teacher, was a candidate for promotion; the administration subsequently informed him that a rival female candidate would be appointed, in accordance with Land Nordrhein Westfalen legislation which

Court adopted a more favourable position, where domestic legislation contained an opening clause stating that the examination of applications made by both sexes had to be subject to an objective assessment. The purpose is then to ensure full equality in practice, as provided under Article 157(4) TFEU;[76] according to the ECJ this exception 'is specifically and exclusively designed to allow measures which, although discriminatory in appearance, are in fact intended to eliminate or reduce actual instances of inequality which may exist in the reality of social life'.[77] A further issue arose as to whether the principle of parity would be retained on a European level; in this respect, although faced with calls from a number of feminist groups in particular, and the choice of a number of member states in the field of political elections, it must be mentioned that the drafters of the Treaties and the Charter did not go so far as to enshrine the principle explicitly in European legislative texts. The European Commission, however, has tackled the subject by proposing a minimum of 40 per cent female members on the boards of directors of companies listed on the stock exchange.[78] This ambitious proposal has yet to reach fruition.

In conclusion, mention must be made of the growing and converging involvement of European organisations (essentially the Council of Europe and the European Union) in favour of the protection of women and girls, together with growth in the field of their activities. While the European Community had initially set out to develop a policy of non-discrimination, the European Union is also increasingly active today in the fight against violence towards women, particularly in developing new legal tools relating to the area of freedom, security and justice. The Council of Europe, which seeks to promote a European model of protection for women across the European continent, and which has long been particularly active in the fight against violence, has increasingly explored the various options available in the fight against discrimination. The construction of the law relating to women's rights also involves the two European courts; the case law of each broadly concurs with the other, even though the ECtHR has developed, in

provided that, where equally qualified, priority would in theory be given to women in those fields where they were in the minority. The ECJ recognised the legitimacy of such a rule, insofar as it could contribute to counterbalancing the prejudicial effects that resulted from 'prejudices and stereotypes concerning the role and capacities of women in working life'.

[76] Art 157(4) TFEU: 'With a view to ensuring full equality in practice between men and women in working life, the principle of equal treatment shall not prevent any Member State from maintaining or adopting measures providing for specific advantages in order to make it easier for the underrepresented sex to pursue a vocational activity or to prevent or compensate for disadvantages in professional careers.'

[77] Case 312/86 *Commission v France* [1988] ECR 6315.

[78] Proposal for a Directive of the European Parliament and Council on improving the gender balance among non-executive directors of companies listed on stock exchanges and related measures, COM (2012) 614 final.

particular, innovative case law in the fight against violence, while the CJEU has been more active in litigation relating to non-discrimination.

Finally, it must be stressed that this model, which plays an active role in the fight against both violence and discrimination, and which is representative of European values to which the two European organisations contribute, is disseminated beyond the boundaries of the European continent, particularly though the Union's international activities.

II

Minorities

6

European Law and Regional or Minority Languages: Cultural Diversity and the Fight against Linguistic Vulnerability[*]

OLIVIER DUBOS AND VICTOR GUSET

IN HIS RENOWNED lecture, 'Qu'est-ce qu'une nation?' ('What is a nation?'), delivered at the Sorbonne on 11 March 1882, Ernest Renan asserted that 'what constitutes a nation is not the fact of speaking the same language, or belonging to the same ethnographic group; it is the fact of having achieved great things together in the past and wanting to do the same in the future'; nevertheless, France under the Third Republic[1] enthusiastically devoted herself to eradicating regional languages. More generally, we cannot ignore the fact that the vast majority of European states have enshrined the existence of an official language in their respective constitutions. Moreover, at least until recently, a national language and the genius attributed to it have remained constitutive aspects of a nation-state's collective imagination. For a long time, it was felt that the preservation of regional or minority languages went against the nation state and, therefore, indirectly against the very principle of democracy—a belief that is still held in some countries. The history of political ideas is particularly edifying in this respect. Until the early twentieth century, the defence of regional languages and regionalism was (at least in France) an integral part of the wave of nostalgia for the *Ancien Régime*, a more or less counter-revolutionary feeling in favour of organic communities. However, from the 1950s onwards, regionalism and the protection of regional languages became an integral part of some progressive schools of thought, challenging the standardisation and the repressive nature of the monolithism inherent to the French conception of the nation-state. The nation—initially a progressive concept—became a conservative idea in the twentieth century, whereas the notion of regionalism moved in the opposite direction.

* All our thanks to Rachael Singh, Lawyer Linguist, University of Bordeaux, for the translation of this chapter.

[1] 1870–1940.

The protection of regional or minority languages therefore involves a conception of the nation-state in line with a model that is not entirely monolithic and in which unity and plurality can work together.[2] Each state—depending on its history and its linguistic realities—may thus implement various mechanisms,[3] whilst bearing in mind that a lack of voluntaristic public policies in favour of regional or minority languages will, in today's world, lead inexorably to their extinction. The concept of minority largely merges here with that of vulnerability.

On an international level, two approaches may be envisaged in order to preserve regional or minority languages: protecting speakers, falling within the framework of the protection of minorities; or protecting languages, falling within the framework of the protection of cultural diversity. The former option may appear to be the most coherent: there is no language without speakers; if we want to preserve a language, let us protect its speakers. This semblance of good sense comes up against a number of objections. First, a language is a collective, cultural phenomenon that transcends its speakers as a whole and which has, in a sense, a life of its own. Consequently, effective public policy on languages must not focus solely on speakers but should concern itself first of all with the language itself. Secondly, the protection afforded to minorities remains a divisive issue for EU member states. Thirdly, the notion of 'minority' has proven difficult, for some even impossible, to define.[4] The term can cover a variety of situations and take on a number of meanings. It may relate to those minorities that François Rigaux calls 'quantitative' or 'qualitative':[5] the former qualification refers to an inferiority in terms of numbers, the latter to an inferiority in terms of 'economic, social or political status'.[6] The lack of any clear delimitation of this notion elicits 'the fear … that a "wrong" definition would excessively broaden the field of those to whom particular protection, which derogates from common law, is due'.[7] Fourthly, we cannot ignore the persistent and bitter memories of the Covenant of the League of Nations, which also ended in failure in this area.[8] The protection afforded to minorities in international legal instruments was therefore consigned to the shadows after the Second World War. Nonetheless, nor can we ignore the Framework Convention for the Protection of Minorities, adopted by the Council of Europe,

[2] The French Constitutional Council's decision concerning the Charter is a clear demonstration of that conception of the state. See Decision 99-412 DC, 15 June 1992. An opposing view had been upheld the year before in a report to the Prime Minister by G Carcassonne, www.ladocumentationfrancaise.fr/rapports-publics/984001697/.

[3] On this issue, see V Bertile, *Langues régionales ou minoritaires et Constitution. France, Espagne, Italie* (Bruxelles, Bruylant, 2009).

[4] F Rigaux, '*Mission impossible: la définition de la minorité*' (1997) *Revue Trimestrielle des Droits de l'Homme* 155.

[5] ibid.

[6] ibid.

[7] J Verhoeven, *Les principales étapes de la protection internationale des minorités* (1997) *Revue Trimestrielle des Droits de l'Homme* 177.

[8] ibid 185.

which contains a number of provisions on language rights.[9] By integrating the right to express oneself in one's own language into the right to freedom of expression, the Framework Convention constitutes the core of the protection afforded to regional and minority languages.[10]

On the other hand, the mechanism established by the European Charter for Regional or Minority Languages, adopted by the Council of Europe,[11] 'sets out to protect and promote regional or minority languages, not linguistic minorities',[12] but relies nonetheless on the fundamental right that is the freedom of expression of linguistic minorities. This mechanism, which is unique in international law, puts in place measures designed to achieve ambitious objectives without clashing head-on with member states. This search for balance can be found in the very structure of the Charter and in its monitoring mechanism. The Charter is divided into three parts. Aside from the first, which is devoted to 'General Provisions', it contains two separate parts that allow undertakings on the part of member states to be modulated. Part II is binding in full on those member states that have ratified it and in respect of all regional or minority languages present within their territories. However, as regards Part III, the member states can choose not only which languages they undertake to protect, but also those preservation measures from which the selected languages will benefit. The monitoring mechanism is itself a collaborative one: member states must submit a report every three years, which is examined by a committee of independent experts. As has been pointed out by Jean-Marie Woehrling,

> the view that the Committee has of its mission is less dominated by the notion of review in the traditional sense than by that of a mission of assistance and co-operation that is closer to what is sometimes called 'compliance management' in international law, and based on the premise that any State may face problems in complying with the Charter and may be given constructive assistance in finding a way to solve its problems. The Committee's reports are not so much aimed at sanctioning failures in this difficult field as they are at encouraging progress.[13]

In the European Union, a meta-national political entity within which 24 languages have been granted the status of official language, the same question arises in very different terms. First of all, a regional or minority language on a state level may not hold the same status on a European Union level. Such is the case for a regional or minority language in one member state, within the meaning of Article 1 of the Charter, which is an official language in another member state. Thus German is a minority language in Italy and Romania, whilst being the official language of two member states, Germany and Austria; from the perspective of the number

[9] This Convention was signed on 1 February 1995 and came into force on 1 February 1998.

[10] See Arts 9(1) and 10(1). See also Art 30 of the UN Convention of the Rights of the Child.

[11] This Convention was signed on 5 November 1992 and came into force on 1 March 1998.

[12] Explanatory Report (1993) §11.

[13] J-M Woehrling, *La Charte européenne des langues régionales ou minoritaires. Un commentaire analytique*, (Strasbourg, Conseil de l'Europe, 2005) 273.

of speakers, it is a majority language in the Union. Conversely, Catalan, a purely regional language, has more speakers than eight of the 24 official languages of the European Union.[14] It is therefore apparent that the languages spoken within the European Union, be they official, regional or minority languages, are ultimately all minority languages from a quantitative point of view.

The European Union could not, however, remain completely isolated from the issue of minority languages. The accession of Central and Eastern European States forced the Union to concern itself with minority rights. The scale of the issue of minorities in those states resulted in the Copenhagen European Council conclusions of 21–22 June 1993 insisting on the 'respect for and protection of minorities'[15] as a condition for accession. While that condition has featured in association agreements since 1993,[16] it did not feature in the Treaties. The former Article 49 EU imposed an obligation on a candidate country to respect the principles stated under Article 6(1) EU, according to which 'the Union is founded on the principles of liberty, democracy, respect for human rights and fundamental freedoms, and the rule of law, principles which are common to the Member States'. The new Article 49 EU is drafted slightly differently as it imposes not only an obligation to respect the values of the Union, but the candidate state is also 'committed to promoting them'. Above all, Article 2 EU—which states the Union's values and to which Article 49 refers—is drafted in a slightly different way to Article 6(1): it explicitly includes 'the rights of persons belonging to minorities' in the obligation to respect human rights. The right to speak one's own language is clearly one of the fundamental aspects of the protection of minorities.[17] Furthermore, Article 21 of the Charter of Fundamental Rights of the European Union prohibits discrimination based on 'language' and above all, under Article 22, 'the Union shall respect cultural, religious and linguistic diversity'.

The very nature of the European Union's powers—and particularly free movement, which both forms the basis of the economic area constituted by the internal market and falls within the civic area constituted by citizenship of the Union—means that, willingly or unwillingly, the Union finds itself facing issues that, a priori, escape its grasp before catching up with it by chance through domestic regulations and matters brought before the Court of Justice. Even those powers

[14] There are more than six million Catalan speakers, a figure greater than the numbers of Danish, Finnish, Slovak, Lithuanian, Latvian, Estonian and Maltese speakers. See A Milian-Massana, 'Le régime juridique du multilinguisme dans l'Union européenne. Le mythe ou la réalité du principe d'égalité des langues' (2004) *Thèmis*, 211, 259–60.

[15] Conclusions of the Presidency, p 25, www.consilium.europa.eu/ueDocs/cms_Data/docs/pressData/en/ec/72921.pdf. It may also be considered that the 'old' member states have adopted a 'do as I say, not as I do' attitude in this matter: the issue of minorities is perhaps not as pressing as in 'new' member states, but they do not appear to be especially eager to address those same issues. While all the 'new' member states have ratified the Council of Europe's Framework Convention for the Protection of National Minorities, neither Belgium, France, Greece, Italy nor Luxembourg has ratified it.

[16] S Ridel, 'Minorités nationales et protection des droits de l'Homme en Europe: un enjeu pour l'élargissement' (2002) 3 *Politique étrangère* 647, 648.

[17] Cf notably, Art 5(1) of the Framework Convention for the Protection of National Minorities.

reserved for member states, which include issues of language, must be exercised in accordance with the laws of the Union. Some national public policies concerning language matters may come into conflict with European Union principles.

Furthermore, it cannot be envisaged that the European Union, as a political power, will settle the language issue once and for all by means of the apparently ecumenical solution of having the same official languages as those of its member states. It cannot be ignored that some official languages hold an enviable status as the working languages of the Union's institutions; this is the case for English, French and German at the European Commission, and French at the Court of Justice. This existence of languages that are more official than others has also crystallised Italian and Spanish opposition to the language arrangements for the Community patent, which may only be filed in English, German or French.[18] On the other hand, is it possible for the EU to ignore regional or minority languages completely, on the pretext that these are not the official languages of a member state?

European law (be it Council of Europe or European Union) is now indisputably concerned with regional or minority languages, which are no longer the preserve of national law. While the paths taken by the latter are many and varied, they appear to be guided by a common goal: the desire to preserve cultural identity. A first step along this path consists in qualifying a language as either a regional or a minority language. Therein lays an initial difficulty specific to the European Charter on Regional or Minority Languages: that of defining its field of application. It will not necessarily be found in the Union, which has not implemented any systematic protective measures and remains, in this respect, indirectly dependent on state definitions (section I). The second aspect leads to a closer examination of the methods adopted under European law to protect regional or minority languages; there is no choice but to accept that several strategies work together here (section II).

I. DIFFICULTIES IN DEFINING THE FIELD OF APPLICATION: LANGUAGES AND LANGUAGE SPEAKERS

Defining the Charter's field of application could only ever be a delicate task owing, first of all, to the sociologically moving phenomenon that is a language,

[18] Italian and Spanish opposition was only overcome by the implementation of greater co-operation, which resulted in two regulations (Regulation (EU) 1257/2012 of the European Parliament and of the Council implementing enhanced cooperation in the area of the creation of unitary patent protection; Council Regulation (EU) 1260/2012 implementing enhanced cooperation in the area of the creation of unitary patent protection with regard to the applicable translation arrangements). Moreover, the Court of Justice rejected the action for annulment brought against the Council decision authorising enhanced co-operation (Joined Cases C-274/11 and C-295/11 *Kingdom of Spain and Italian Republic v Council of the European Union* [2013] ECR 00000. See O Tambou, 'Le brevet européen à effet unitaire: un brevet tant attendu' (2013) avril, étude n°4 *Europe*.

especially when it is not official. Next, the desire to leave member states room for manoeuvre was not such that it would simplify matters. Finally, while the Charter is concerned first and foremost with languages in themselves, and not with linguistic minorities, it is not possible to protect a language without taking an interest—even indirectly—in its speakers. The Charter therefore defines not only what a regional or minority language is (section A), but also the range of language users who will benefit from the provisions of the Charter (section B).

A. In Search of Regional or Minority Languages

Under Article 1(a) of the Charter,

> 'regional or minority languages' means languages that are: i. traditionally used within a given territory of a State by nationals of that State who form a group numerically smaller than the rest of the State's population; and ii. different from the official language(s) of that State; it does not include either dialects of the official language(s) of the State or the languages of migrants.

Some languages are therefore explicitly excluded, while the definition of protected languages remains particularly fraught.

i. Excluded Languages

Some languages are explicitly excluded from the Charter's field of application by the terms of Article 1. Firstly and quite logically, it concerns official languages. The language's 'official' status is meant to guarantee it sufficient protection. The aim is to distinguish regional or minority languages from languages spoken by the majority or a large part of the population with which the member state identifies itself.[19] Where national law, and quite often the Constitution itself, provides for the existence of an official language, exclusion is automatic. For those member states that have not legally instituted the official status of a particular language, the committee of experts will identify those languages that enjoy de facto official status. The Charter does not, however, exclude all languages that enjoy official status. It thus stipulates that states may qualify 'other official languages which are less widely used' as 'regional or minority languages'.[20] This Article takes account 'of the position in certain member states whereby a national language which has the status of an official language of the state, either on the whole or on part of its territory, may in other respects be in a comparable situation to regional or minority languages as defined in Article 1'.[21] It may therefore be considered 'that

[19] Woehrling, *La Charte européenne*, n 13 above, 53.
[20] Charter, Art 3(2).
[21] Explanatory Report (1993), §51.

the determining factor is not that of its official nature, but that of the actual use and vitality of the language'.[22]

Article 1 also excludes the languages of migrants. The exclusion of the languages of migrants is founded, according to Jean-Marie Woehrling,[23] on a difference in legitimacy between the two categories of language, or even in the inclusion of the populations in question. Thus the regional or minority languages that benefit from protection under the Charter are allegedly linked to the culture, geography and history of the territory in question. This exclusion may be connected to those provisions of the Charter that make direct reference to the 'historical' nature of the regional or minority languages that the Charter seeks to protect. The Preamble to the Charter refers to 'the historical regional or minority languages of Europe'. Consequently, the 'historicity'[24] of a given language must be a factor in allowing its protection. The 'traditionality' factor present in Article 1 of the Charter also manifests itself here. The Charter appears to exclude the languages of migrants insofar as the 'traditional' use of the language is lacking and the migrants are not nationals of the member state in question. Should the migrants speaking the language take the nationality of the state in question, they become nationals thereof. However, their language cannot be qualified as a 'regional or minority language' until such time as the traditional use of that language can be proved. The question then arises as to the point at which the use of a language may be called 'traditional'.[25] The Explanatory Report states that 'the charter covers only historical languages, that is to say languages which have been spoken over a long period in the state in question'. The view may be taken that the issue is more one of the 'European-ness' of the language than it is one of 'traditional' use. The concept of 'European-ness' nevertheless runs the risk of creating further problems in terms of interpretation.

ii. Protected Languages

Member states play a considerable role in determining which languages will be protected, given that they are responsible 'as authorities for the application of the charter, for deciding whether the form of expression used in a particular area of their territory or by a particular group of their nationals constitutes a regional or minority language within the meaning of the charter'.[26] This would appear to indicate 'that there is some objective leeway as regards linguistic realities and a

[22] A Viaut, *La Charte européenne des langues régionales ou minoritaires : particularités sociolinguistiques et configuration française*, Mercator Working Papers, 29–30.

[23] Woehrling, *La Charte européenne*, n 13 above, 50.

[24] A Viaut, *Les langues « historiques de l'Europe » et la Charte européenne des langues régionales ou minoritaires* (2006), n°59, Lengas—Revue de sociolinguistique, p 77.

[25] Explanatory Report (1993) § 31.

[26] ibid § 40.

degree of subjective leeway in their definition'.[27] The Committee of Experts does try nevertheless to limit the margin of discretion enjoyed by member states. It takes the view that this margin of discretion is limited to the choice of regional or minority languages that the states intend to protect on the basis of Part III of the Charter. Thus, 'the fact that a regional or minority language corresponding to the Charter's definition is not explicitly mentioned in the declaration(s) of a State Party does not preclude the application of Part II of the Charter to that language'.[28] The margin of discretion can manifest itself in relation to the distinction between languages and dialects. 'Dialect' status excludes a language from the protection that the Charter is intended to confer. The difference between language and dialect is as much a political issue as a genuinely linguistic question.[29] Indeed, for linguists, anything spoken that performs a role in communication constitutes a language. The Committee of Experts does not appear to take a structured approach concerning the criteria relative to the existence of languages. In some instances, the Committee itself proceeds with the assessment of the various criteria, thus concluding that there exists a regional or minority language within the meaning of the Charter.[30] In other instances, however, it appears to give states a greater margin of discretion in assessing the criteria relative to the existence of the relevant language.[31]

Amongst the criteria for defining regional or minority languages, as set down under Article 1 of the Charter, the language area is probably the most fundamental. This may be defined as 'that where a regional or minority language is spoken to a significant extent, even if only by a minority, and which corresponds to its historical base'.[32] The language area must then be identified by the member state. The most straightforward way to proceed is to refer to existing national law, which may itself already provide such protection. Nonetheless, such an approach in law runs the risk of excluding some languages from the Charter's material field of application, thus depriving them of the protection that the latter is intended to afford. Sociological factors may therefore prove useful in identifying a language's territorial base. Censuses, surveys, historical data connected to the language in question may then be called upon. Moreover, the respective legal and sociological approaches can be combined.

Where a language has no territorial base, it cannot be qualified as a 'regional or minority language' within the meaning of Article 1 of the Charter. Indeed, '"[n]on-territorial languages" are excluded from the category of regional or

[27] EJ Ruiz-Viejtez, 'Article 1. Definitions', in Libarona (IU), Lopez (AN), Ruiz Viejtez (EJ) (eds), *Shaping language rights—Commentary on the European Charter for Regional or Minority languages in light of the Committee of Experts' Evaluation* (Strasbourg, Council of Europe Publishing, 2012) 46.

[28] Council of Europe Report on Slovenia (2007), §15.

[29] EJ Ruiz-Viejtez, 'Article 1. Definitions', n 27 above, n°48, p 46.

[30] As to the Serbian and Croatian languages in Slovenia.

[31] As to the Elfdalian language in Sweden.

[32] Explanatory Report (1993) §34.

minority languages because they lack a territorial base'.[33] However, the absence of a territorial base does not lead automatically to a language's exclusion from the Charter's material field of application, even if 'only a limited part of the charter can be applied to these languages'.[34] Thus the absence of a language area does not, in theory, imply the exclusion of these languages from the material field of application. It will prevent such languages from being qualified as 'regional or minority languages' but this does not appear to have particularly significant consequences in practice.[35] Such 'non-territorial languages' are generally protected under Part II of the Charter.[36] The member states must nevertheless apply the provisions under Part II in a flexible manner whilst 'respecting the traditions and characteristics, of the groups which use the languages concerned'. Member states may, however, accept a certain number of obligations on the basis of Part III without this resulting in the inclusion of the language(s) in question within the category of protected languages provided under that part of the Charter. The qualification of 'non-territorial languages' applies mainly to Romany and Yiddish.

The fundamental 'territorial base' criterion is supplemented by two additional factors. Article 1 of the Charter states that the language must be 'traditionally used' within a given territory of a state. This 'traditionality' element also serves to identify languages that may fall within the Charter's material field of application. The Committee of Experts therefore checks for this criterion in its reports. A further requirement under Article 1 is that the language be used by a minimum number of speakers. This is assessed in a particularly flexible way. Thus Cornish, which is protected by the Charter, is only spoken and understood by some 300 persons.[37]

B. In Search of Speakers

The objective approach adopted by the Charter must not conceal the issue of the identification of the persons to benefit from its protection—that is, the speakers of a given language. This issue carries with it both a spatial and a personal dimension.

i. The Spatial Dimension

The Explanatory Report states that '[t]he reason why the charter is mainly concerned with languages which have a territorial base is that most of the measures which it advocates necessitate the definition of a geographical field of application

[33] ibid §36.
[34] ibid §37.
[35] EJ Ruiz-Viejtez, 'Article 1. Definitions', n 27 above, p 72.
[36] See Art 7(5).
[37] Council of Europe Report on the United Kingdom (2004) §31.

other than the state as a whole'.[38] The applicability of the majority of the Charter's provisions supposes the identification of a geographical field of application. For instance, Article 7(1) stipulates that 'In respect of regional or minority languages, within the territories in which such languages are used …, the Parties shall base their policies, legislation and practice' on a number of principles. Equally, Article 10(2) states that '[i]n respect of the local and regional authorities on whose territory the number of residents who are users of regional or minority languages', member states undertake to implement a number of measures. The reinforced presence of the notion of language area within the text of the Charter explains the care taken in defining it.

The Charter[39] stipulates that the '"territory in which the regional or minority language is used" means the geographical area in which the said language is the mode of expression of a number of people justifying the adoption of the various protective and promotional measures provided for in this Charter'. The Explanatory Report nonetheless adds that '[s]ince the terms used in the charter in this respect are inevitably fairly flexible, it is up to each state to define more precisely, in the spirit of the charter, the notion of regional or minority languages' territory'.[40] However, the identification of the language area as the Charter's spatial field of application does not carry the same finality as the identification of the language area as the Charter's material field of application. In the latter case, the language area allows a language to be qualified as a 'regional or minority language'; the language in question may thus be protected under the Charter. As the spatial field of application, a language area plays no part in qualifying a language as a 'regional or minority language'; it is identified with the geographical area in which specific measures designed to protect the 'regional or minority language' are destined to be applied. In other words, the language area has different parts to play within the respective scopes of the material and spatial fields of application. Here too, states combine legal and sociological factors in order to determine the language area, but the Committee of Experts prefers the sociological method.[41]

ii. The Personal Dimension

The identification of the spatial field of application of the Charter's provisions determines the geographical area in which measures for promoting and protecting regional or minority languages are destined to be applied. This reference to the spatial field of application is not to be found solely in the definition put forward

[38] Explanatory Report (1993) §33.

[39] Charter Art 1(b).

[40] Explanatory Report (1993) §34.

[41] It assesses the application of the Charter 'in the territories of the different languages according to realities on the ground and without regard to the constraints of domestic legislation' (EJ Ruiz-Viejtez, 'Article 1. Definitions', n 27 above, p 67).

by Article 1(b) of the Charter.[42] For instance, Article 10(1) states that '[w]ithin the administrative districts of the State in which the number of residents who are users of regional or minority languages justifies the measures specified below and according to the situation of each language, the Parties undertake' to implement the undertakings that they have made.

A link can be made between the recognition of the language users' language rights and their residence in the language area as identified as the spatial field of application. In other words, the language area thus serves to identify the holders of linguistic rights. For example, an Italian speaker in Slovenia would have language rights only if he resided in the 'ethnically mixed areas' defined as the spatial field of application of the Charter's measures for the protection and promotion of regional or minority languages. However, the residence of speakers of a regional or minority language appears to have a greater influence on the identification of the spatial field of application than on the personal field of application. The content of the various protection and promotion measures does not appear to create territorial ties by imposing a residence condition. Thus Article 9 of the Charter[43] provides that, in civil proceedings, the parties undertake 'to allow, whenever a litigant has to appear in person before a court, that he or she may use his or her regional or minority language without thereby incurring additional expense'. Equally, Article 10 states that the parties undertake to allow and/or encourage 'the possibility for users of regional or minority languages to submit oral or written applications in these languages'.

Furthermore, the text of the Charter does not define the concept of 'user of a regional or minority language'. Consequently, it could appear that the quality of 'user' would alone suffice for a person to be granted language rights. However, this lack of a definition may be explained by the wide variety of approaches adopted by states. While some do not appear to have implemented personal factors, other states base their approach on membership of a national minority in order to identify the holders of language rights.

One might very well wonder whether an approach based on personal factors, such as membership of a national minority, tallies with the Charter's objectives. An approach that consists of reserving the language rights resulting from obligations under the Charter for members of a national minority may have a number of consequences. On the one hand, language speakers who do not belong to a national minority would be excluded from the personal field of application of the Charter's provisions. On the other hand, non-speakers of the regional or minority language in question may be deterred from learning it, even though Article 7 of the Charter[44] provides that the parties are under a duty to provide the facilities

[42] Charter Art 1(b): '"territory in which the regional or minority language is used" means the geographical area in which the said language is the mode of expression of a number of people justifying the adoption of the various protective and promotional measures provided for in this Charter'.

[43] Charter Art 9(b)(ii).

[44] Charter Art 7(1)(g).

'enabling non-speakers of a regional or minority language living in the area where it is used to learn it if they so desire'. However, the Committee of Experts does not call these approaches into question in their monitoring reports.

The Charter's objective approach, focused on the preservation of regional and minority languages such as they are, goes some way to explain the difficulties encountered in delineating its field of application. The intention is to move away from a subjective approach based on the protection of language minorities or their members in order to focus to a greater extent on the protection of regional or minority languages as components of cultural diversity. The methods adopted under European law to preserve these languages testify to the same approach.

II. A RANGE OF PROTECTIVE MEASURES: DEROGATION, PROMOTION, PROTECTION

A number of strategies have been implemented in order to protect regional or minority languages. Within the framework of the European Union, the derogation technique is used, otherwise national protection provisions could simply be considered as being contrary to EU law (section A). Public policies may also be put in place to promote regional or minority languages; this is a duty imposed on parties to the Charter, and the European Union plays a modest role in that movement (section B). Finally, there may be protective measures that lead to the recognition of the language rights of language speakers (section C).

A. Derogation

Within the scope of its case law concerning free movement, the European Court of Justice takes a particularly broad approach to the notion of obstacles. Thus national legislation aimed at protecting an official language may be considered as constituting an obstacle to free movement. In a Spanish case where a challenge was brought against national legislation imposing, in particular, a duty on television broadcasters to devote 5 per cent of their annual revenue to financing European film-making, but also to retain 60 per cent of that finance for films made in one of the official languages of the Kingdom of Spain,[45] the Court held

[45] It will be recalled that under Art 3 of the Spanish Constitution, '1. Castilian is the official Spanish language of the State. All Spaniards have the duty to know it and the right to use it. 2. The other Spanish languages shall also be official in the respective Self-governing Communities in accordance with their Statutes. 3. The wealth of the different linguistic forms of Spain is a cultural heritage which shall be especially respected and protected.' The 'other Spanish languages' under para 2 are Basque, Catalan and Galician.

Finally, it must be noted that Aranes became a co-official language of the Autonomous Region of Catalonia with the passing of the Statute of Autonomy on 19 July 2006. Bearing in mind Spain's ratification of the Charter, any co-official language (though these are not explicitly mentioned in the

that there existed 'a restriction on several fundamental freedoms, that is to say on the freedom to provide services, freedom of establishment, the free movement of capital and freedom of movement for workers'.[46] This solution may therefore jeopardise some national public policies that aim to protect official languages as well as regional or minority languages. However, the Court is of the view that such legislation can be justified on grounds of the protection of linguistic identity or linguistic diversity.

i. Linguistic Identity

The *Groener* case centred on Irish regulations that imposed command of Gaelic as a condition for obtaining a permanent teaching position at an arts college in Ireland. A Dutch national who spoke fluent English, the other official language of the Republic of Ireland, had been refused employment on the grounds that she did not speak Gaelic.[47] The Court held that 'the EEC Treaty does not prohibit the adoption of a policy for the protection and promotion of a language of a Member State which is both the national language and the first official language'.[48]

In *UTECA*, the Court took the view that 'the objective, pursued by a Member State, of defending and promoting one or several of its official languages constitutes an overriding reason in the public interest'.[49] This overriding requirement is ultimately based on respect for constitutional identity, as it is a matter of promoting official languages in line with domestic law. Although the Treaty of Lisbon was not yet in force at the time of the Court's decision, there is probably some influence—latent, at the very least—on the new Article 4(2). Indeed, under Article 3 of the Spanish Constitution, linguistic plurality is an aspect of Spanish constitutional identity; it is, in effect, included in a part of the Constitution that can only be amended in accordance with the procedure provided under Article 167. Nonetheless, this is a specificity of the Spanish Constitution. In principle, all languages of an official nature may also benefit from the *UTECA* decision—not by virtue of the Constitution, but rather by virtue of the law or even the European Charter on Regional and Minority Languages where a member state has ratified it. The notion of 'official language' does, however, remain relatively ambiguous. Indeed, some constitutions may make provision for the existence of a language labelled 'official' while simultaneously allowing the use of other languages in communications with the government. Be that as it may, for those regional or

ratification instrument) is protected under Part III of the Charter, and not solely under Part II, which applies to all languages.

[46] Case C-222/07 *Unión de Televisiones Comerciales Asociadas (UTECA) v Administración General del Estado* [2009] ECR I-1407, ground 24.

[47] Case C-379/87 *Anita Groener v Minister for Education and the City of Dublin Vocational Educational Committee* [1989] ECR 3967.

[48] Ground 19.

[49] Ground 27.

minority languages that do not have official language status, the solution derived by the Court of Justice in the *UTECA* decision is not particularly helpful. The justification for restrictions based on the protection of a state's official language or languages may even be unfavourable to regional or minority languages. This constant arises from the Court of Justice's decision in *Runevič-Vardyn.*[50]

At issue in this case was the Lithuanian law relating to civil status, which requires that first names and surnames be written in accordance with the spelling rules in Lithuanian. Thus, under Lithuanian law, the surname of the applicant, a Lithuanian national and a member of the Polish minority there, should be spelt 'Runevič', and not 'Runiewicz' as it would be in Polish. The applicant, now residing in Brussels, is married to a Polish national named 'Łukasz Paweł Wardyn'. Under Lithuanian law, her husband's name is spelled 'Lukasz Pawel Vardyn[51] in application of national rules. The Court of Justice held firstly that the refusal on the part of the authorities to transcribe the applicant's maiden name into Polish did not constitute a restriction. The same applied to the refusal to change the spelling of the second's applicant first name, using the diacritical 'Ł', because

> diacritical marks are often omitted in many daily actions for technical reasons, for example because of the objective constraints inherent in some computer systems. Also, for people who are unfamiliar with a foreign language the significance of diacritical marks is often misunderstood and they will not even notice them.[52]

However, the refusal to change the surname shared by the applicants, pursuant to national regulations, was considered likely to lead to serious inconvenience at administrative, professional and private levels, as there might be doubt relating to the authenticity of the documents presented by the applicants.

Going into the possible justifications for the restriction, the Court recalled that

> according to the fourth subparagraph of Article 3(3) EU and Article 22 of the Charter of Fundamental Rights of the European Union, the Union must respect its rich cultural and linguistic diversity. Article 4(2) EU provides that the Union must also respect the national identity of its Member States, which includes protection of a State's official national language. It follows that the objective pursued by national rules such as those at issue in the main proceedings, designed to protect the official national language by imposing the rules which govern the spelling of that language, constitutes, in principle, a legitimate objective capable of justifying restrictions on the rights of freedom of movement and residence provided for in Article 21 TFEU and may be taken into account when legitimate interests are weighed against the rights conferred by European Union law.[53]

[50] Case C-391/09 *Malgožata Runevič-Vardyn and Łukasz Paweł Wardyn v Vilniaus miesto savivaldybės administracija and Others* [2011] ECR I-03787.

[51] Lithuanian does not use the diacritical symbol Ł and replaces the Polish W with a V.

[52] Ground 81.

[53] Grounds 86 and 87.
The Court adds to these justifications with considerations drawn from the right to a name as a component of the right to respect for private and family life resulting from Art 7 of the Charter on Fundamental Rights and Art 8 ECHR.

This reasoning seems particularly expeditious as it implies that respect for linguistic diversity and respect for national identity are similar in nature. On a European Union level, it is likely that a member state, in protecting its official language, will claim to be adhering to respect for linguistic diversity as well as for national identity. However, on a member state level—as the *Runevič-Vardyn* case shows—respect for linguistic diversity and respect for national identity can be antagonistic principles. Under European Union law, a member state must therefore also respect linguistic diversity, which is a human right.

ii. Linguistic Diversity

The Court of Justice has (at least once) been sensitive to considerations connected to linguistic diversity understood as a fundamental right. The central issue in the *United Pan-Europe* case was Belgian legislation that required cable operators to broadcast programmes transmitted by certain private broadcasters designated by the government. The aim of this legislation—particularly in the Brussels-Capital region, which is bilingual—was to allow Flemish speakers to access programmes in Flemish and French speakers to access programmes in French.[54] The Court's reasoning was not based directly on grounds of language; it ruled that a 'cultural policy may constitute an overriding requirement relating to the general interest which justifies a restriction on the freedom to provide services', as 'the maintenance of the pluralism which that policy seeks to safeguard is connected with freedom of expression'.[55] It added that this legislation

> seeks to preserve the pluralist nature of the range of television programmes available in the bilingual region of Brussels-Capital and thus forms part of a cultural policy the aim of which is to safeguard, in the audiovisual sector, the freedom of expression of the different social, cultural, religious, philosophical or linguistic components which exist in that region.[56]

Here, the overriding reason in the public interest is cultural diversity as a component of freedom of expression.

Additionally in the *UTECA* case, when reviewing the proportionality of the domestic measure, the Court of Justice made mention of the UNESCO Convention on the Protection and Promotion of the Diversity of Cultural Expressions adopted on 20 October 2005, to which the European Union and its member states are party. The Convention allowed the Court to dismiss the argument put forward by the Commission that only those productions marked 'cultural' ought to have enjoyed the protection offered under Spanish legislation. It therefore adopts the notion that linguistic diversity is an aspect of cultural

[54] Case C-250/06 *United Pan-Europe Communications Belgium SA and Others v Belgian State* [2007] ECR I-11135.

[55] Ground 41.

[56] Ground 42.

diversity, with no other qualification. It is true that the legal definition of what is or is not cultural may prove to be highly dangerous insofar as it involves qualitative, and therefore highly subjective, assessments. Significantly, neither intellectual property law (to define the scope of the protection required) nor human rights law (to establish the scope of freedom of expression) takes qualitative elements into account. Be that as it may, the Court of Justice does indeed—at least indirectly—attach this overriding reason in the public interest to linguistic diversity as the latter arises from the UNESCO Convention on cultural diversity. Is it possible to go further?

Linguistic diversity still has to be handled with care by the Court of Justice, owing to its own ambivalence. First, linguistic diversity can come into play as a justification for restrictions on free movement. The Charter has been compulsory since the Treaty of Lisbon came into force, and Article 3 EU now provides in particular that the Union 'shall respect its rich cultural and linguistic diversity, and shall ensure that Europe's cultural heritage is safeguarded and enhanced'.[57] Moreover, pursuant to Article 167(4) TFEU, the respect for and promotion of cultural diversity constitutes a transversal competence for the Union.

However, in order to achieve genuine respect for linguistic diversity on the part of the European Union, it would be appropriate for the Court of Justice to apply the reasoning adopted in the *Schmidberger* case[58] to this particular area. In this case, the Court had agreed to weigh up the freedoms of the internal market in light of the right to freedom of expression. Human rights were not simply a derogation to the principles of free movement, but rather appeared to have the same force as the economic freedoms of the internal market. This reasoning has not, however, subsequently been taken up by the Court of Justice. Furthermore, with regard to language rights, there is no great weight of case law from the European Court of Human Rights as there is with regard to freedom of expression in the usual sense. In a ruling on admissibility, the Court thus considered that the Convention did not enshrine the right to linguistic freedom.[59] It would likely be more appropriate to link the right to speak one's own language to Articles 11, 21 and 22 of the Charter of Fundamental Rights of the European Union.

The fact that the Court is not inclined to promote linguistic diversity is understandable: respect for it can be turned against the member states themselves. In the *Runevič-Vardyn* decision, when examining proportionality, the Court logically put forward various arguments drawn from the rationale underpinning Lithuanian legislation.[60] It would have been equally possible to argue, in accordance with

[57] Equally significantly, with regard to common trade policy in which the qualified majority prevails, Art 207(4) TFEU provides that the Council shall act by qualified majority 'in the field of trade in cultural and audiovisual services, where these agreements risk prejudicing the Union's cultural and linguistic diversity'.

[58] Case C-112/00 *Eugen Schmidberger, Internationale Transporte und Planzüge v Republik Österreich* [2003] ECR I-05659.

[59] *Birk-Levy v France* (dec) App no 39426/06 (ECtHR, 21 September 2010).

[60] See grounds 92 and 93.

well-established case law, that within the framework of restrictions on European Union law, member states are bound to respect fundamental rights. Now, if linguistic diversity were really considered to be a fundamental right, in one context (such as the *Runevič-Vardyn* case), it would not legitimise domestic legislation but rather add weight to the disproportionate nature of that legislation. The Court of Justice thus took into account the rights of native speakers in a case centring on Flemish legislation that required employment contracts to be drafted in Dutch, otherwise they would be null and void. The Court held that

> parties to a cross-border employment contract do not necessarily have knowledge of the official language of the Member State concerned. In such a situation, the establishment of free and informed consent between the parties requires those parties to be able to draft their contract in a language other than the official language of that Member State.[61]

This solution simply requires that the employment contract be drafted in a language understood by the parties, which does not necessarily imply that their respective language rights will be taken into account. In the above case, the contract was drafted in English.

This malleability in the concept of linguistic diversity depending on the level (EU/member state) or the context (depending on the member state) into which it fits is indisputably a manifestation of the European Union's federal nature: whilst being binding on the member states, it must also work with them and, in particular, take into account their respective political, social and cultural structures. That being the case, the European Union as a political power cannot ignore the language rights of native speakers of regional or minority languages insofar as it concerns a constitutive political and social fact in member states—or at least a number of them.

B. Promotion

While the part played by the European Union remains relatively modest, the provisions under the Council of Europe's Charter cannot be ignored.

i. The Modest Part Played by the European Union

The Union's powers with respect to language matters remain quite limited and do not specifically relate to regional or minority languages in any sphere, though this does not exclude them. The Union does, however, have powers in the field of education.[62] First and foremost, under Article 167(1) TFEU, 'the Union shall contribute to the flowering of the cultures of the Member States, while respecting their national and regional diversity and at the same time bringing the common

[61] Case C-202/11 *Anton Las v PSA Antwerp NV* [2013] ECR—nyr, ground 31.

[62] See Art 165 FEU.

cultural heritage to the fore'. Above all, under paragraph (4), 'the Union shall take cultural aspects into account in its action under other provisions of the Treaties, in particular in order to respect and to promote the diversity of its cultures', thus echoing Article 3 EU. Cultural policy, therefore, takes on a lateral dimension and will probably allow the extensive application of a power that has been devolved to the Union. Finally, within the scope of external powers, we cannot overlook trade policy which, owing to Article 207 TFEU, now unambiguously includes cultural services and, therefore, cultural products. It cannot be ignored that in the sphere of cultural and audiovisual services, where these agreements impact upon cultural and linguistic diversity, the Council must act unanimously.

The Union's powers with respect to language matters are therefore limited; member states intend to remain masters of their own language affairs. Education and culture fall within the remit of the supporting, coordinating or complementary powers under Article 6 TFEU. Any future public policies on the Union's part in regional or minority language matters therefore rest on relatively fragile foundations. In addition to a number of resolutions passed by the European Parliament,[63] the Union's actions with respect to regional and minority language matters is led by the European Commission, within the Directorate General for Education and Culture.[64] The support provided by the European Commission is primarily financial support for organisations whose purpose is to promote regional and minority languages.

The Union's concrete actions in favour of regional and minority languages thus remains particularly modest, owing both to the narrow scope of its powers in that field and also what are likely to be limited budgetary resources. Any active public policy on the part of the Union would in any case be highly dangerous as this is an area in which the member states remain divided, as is demonstrated by their attitudes towards the Council of Europe's Charter. Nonetheless, in light of the crisis, the European Union is decidedly more preoccupied with its official multilingualism than it is with regional and minority languages.

ii. Part II of the Charter

Article 7 of the Charter, which makes up Part II, enshrines a range of objectives together with the principles that serve to achieve them. Article 7 does not directly confer any subjective rights on language users, with the exception perhaps of paragraph 2 which prohibits unjustified discrimination against regional and minority languages. This is echoed in Article 5(1) of the Framework Convention for the Protection of National Minorities.

[63] European Parliament Resolution of 13 December 2001 on Regional and Lesser-Used Languages, B5-0770; European Parliament Resolution of 4 September 2003, with recommendations to the Commission on European regional and lesser-used languages—the languages of minorities in the EU—in the context of enlargement and cultural diversity (2003/2057(INI)).

[64] http://ec.europa.eu/education/languages/languages-of-europe/doc139_fr.htm.

First of all, it implies the 'recognition' of regional or minority languages. This first obligation is fundamental as it means that the Charter involves a formal enshrinement, be it legislative or constitutional, of those languages. It would appear, however, that the Committee of Experts is not particularly demanding as it is of the view that the identification of a regional language in the ratification instrument will suffice for the purposes of meeting the requirements under Article 7(1).[65] However, such recognition in no way constitutes a subjective right to the benefit of minorities: it is in their capacity as an 'expression of cultural wealth' that such languages must be recognised. That said, on an anthropological level, the Charter plays a symbolic part in the state's recognition of the speakers of a regional or minority language. Their language behaviour is no longer simply a purely private social practice; it is thereby legitimised by the state, which furthermore undertakes to implement a range of public policies in favour of these languages.

These objectives are listed under sub-paragraphs d) to i) of Article 7(1):

- d) the facilitation and/or encouragement of the use of regional or minority languages, in speech and writing, in public and private life;
- e) the maintenance and development of links, in the fields covered by this Charter, between groups using a regional or minority language and other groups in the State employing a language used in identical or similar form, as well as the establishment of cultural relations with other groups in the State using different languages;
- f) the provision of appropriate forms and means for the teaching and study of regional or minority languages at all appropriate stages;
- g) the provision of facilities enabling non-speakers of a regional or minority language living in the area where it is used to learn it if they so desire;
- h) the promotion of study and research on regional or minority languages at universities or equivalent institutions;
- i) the promotion of appropriate types of transnational exchanges, in the fields covered by this Charter, for regional or minority languages used in identical or similar form in two or more States.

The protection of regional or minority languages is therefore founded on educational and cultural public policies intended to act as a counterweight to the effects of the linguistic dominance induced by the existence of an official language.[66] It is a matter of mobilising the state—and particularly its financial resources—to curb the decline in the use of regional or minority languages. The state's commitments consist more in implementing public policies than in recognising the subjective rights of individuals. It is indeed in this respect that the Charter is first and foremost an instrument at the service of cultural diversity before being a mechanism for the protection of minorities. It is under Part III, which puts actual protective

[65] Woehrling, *La Charte européenne*, n 13 above, 104.

[66] S May, 'Language rights: moving the debate forward' (2005) 9(3) *Journal of Sociolinguistics* 319; P Bourdieu, 'L'identité et la representation. Eléments pour une réfléxion critique sur l'idée de region' (1980) *Actes de la recherche en sciences sociales* 63.

measures in place, that the question of the subjective rights of language speakers inevitably emerges. A true mechanism for the protection of a language entails the acknowledgement of the rights of its speakers. The provisions put forward by the European Union are also a testament to that fact.

C. Protection

Part III of the Charter puts in place a highly original mechanism for the protection of regional or minority languages within states. As for the European Union, its capacity as a political entity has led to it conferring certain language rights on its citizens.

i. Part III of the Charter

Under Article 2 (2) of the Charter,

> [i]n respect of each language specified at the time of ratification, acceptance or approval, in accordance with Article 3, each Party undertakes to apply a minimum of thirty-five paragraphs or sub-paragraphs chosen from among the provisions of Part III of the Charter, including at least three chosen from each of the Articles 8 and 12 and one from each of the Articles 9, 10, 11 and 13.

This is an original 'à la carte' system that combines ambition and protection with the states' room for manoeuvre.

The ambition manifests itself first of all in the variety of rights concerned. Classic measures can be found, such as teaching (Article 8), justice (Article 9) and administration (Article 10). As regards teaching, it is not simply a matter, as it is under Part II, of providing language classes, but rather that teaching be provided, whatever the level, in whole or in part in a regional or minority language. As for justice and administration, it is a question of ensuring that the official language is no longer the sole language in which they operate. This at the very least allows the parties concerned to communicate with the government in a regional or minority language or, better still, the government may find itself under a duty to use a regional or minority language with the said users, or even in the enactment of their legislative provisions. There are even more innovative measures concerning the media (Article 11), and cultural activities (Article 12). Member states must encourage and support the various players in those sectors to provide information or creative projects in a regional or minority language. The link to cultural diversity is obvious here. Barring any conflict with the Charter, it is understandable that the Court of Justice should have held that such measures, which may indeed constitute obstacles to free movement, are justified on grounds of linguistic and cultural diversity.[67] Finally, the Charter also concerns itself with economic and social activities (Article 13). With the latter, it is not merely a question of

[67] *Cf* above under 'Linguistic Diversity'.

acknowledging the rights of speakers of regional languages that are enforceable against the government alone, but also against private individuals. Thus Article 13 provides that states may

> prohibit the insertion in internal regulations of companies and private documents of any clauses excluding or restricting the use of regional or minority languages, at least between users of the same language [paragraph 1(b)]

or even

> include in their financial and banking regulations provisions which allow, by means of procedures compatible with commercial practice, the use of regional or minority languages in drawing up payment orders (cheques, drafts, etc.) or other financial documents, or, where appropriate, to ensure the implementation of such provisions [paragraph 2(a)].

A great number of these rights can be found in the Framework Convention for the Protection of National Minorities. Article 10(2) and (3) provide that:

> 2. In areas inhabited by persons belonging to national minorities traditionally or in substantial numbers, if those persons so request and where such a request corresponds to a real need, the Parties shall endeavour to ensure, as far as possible, the conditions which would make it possible to use the minority language in relations between those persons and the administrative authorities.
> 3. The Parties undertake to guarantee the right of every person belonging to a national minority to be informed promptly, in a language which he or she understands, of the reasons for his or her arrest, and of the nature and cause of any accusation against him or her, and to defend himself or herself in this language, if necessary with the free assistance of an interpreter.

In the same way, Article 14(1) and (2) provide that:

> 1. The Parties undertake to recognise that every person belonging to a national minority has the right to learn his or her minority language.
> 2. In areas inhabited by persons belonging to national minorities traditionally or in substantial numbers, if there is sufficient demand, the Parties shall endeavour to ensure, as far as possible and within the framework of their education systems, that persons belonging to those minorities have adequate opportunities for being taught the minority language or for receiving instruction in this language.

However, the Framework Convention does occasionally go further than the Charter, thus testifying to the limits of an approach that centres on language and not on language speakers. Article 11(1) thus provides that

> [t]he Parties undertake to recognise that every person belonging to a national minority has the right to use his or her surname (patronym) and first names in the minority language and the right to official recognition of them, according to modalities provided for in their legal system.

This is the right to a name, enshrined by the European Court of Human Rights on the basis of Article 8 ECHR.[68]

[68] *Burghartz v Switzerland* (dec) App no 16213/90 (ECtHR, 22 February 1994).

Unlike Part II, member states may decide that the obligations imposed under Part III will not benefit all the regional or minority languages spoken within their respective territories. While this choice is discretionary, it must not be arbitrary; according to the Explanatory Report, 'clearly, however, the reasons which prompt a state to exclude a recognised regional or minority language completely from the benefit of Part III must be reasons compatible with the spirit, objectives and principles of the Charter'. Obviously, it must not be discriminatory. According to Jean-Marie Woehrling, 'it is mainly those languages that are little used, to the point where the provisions under Part III are not adapted to their situation, that should not fall under this part'.[69]

The main aspect of the 'à la carte' nature of Part III of the Charter is the duty to choose 35 of the 61 options put forward by Articles 8 to 13 of the Charter.[70] More specifically, it falls to the states to select at least three undertakings out of eight under Article 8 (teaching); one out of six under Article 9 (justice); one out of 15 under Article 10 (administrative authorities and public services); one out of nine under Article 11 (media); three out of 10 under Article 12 (cultural activities and facilities); and one out of nine under Article 13 (economic and social life). For Article 14 (transfrontier exchanges), no minimum selection is provided.

Lacking the necessary powers, the European Union could not make provision for such an ambitious mechanism, but it was always able to foresee that the same mechanism could be used against the Union in relation to regional or minority languages.

ii. Language Rights in the European Union

Under Article 24 FEU,

> every citizen of the Union may write to any of the institutions or bodies referred to in this Article or in Article 13 of the Treaty on European Union in one of the languages mentioned in Article 55(1) of the Treaty on European Union and have an answer in the same language.

Regional or minority languages are therefore not included in the European Union—except those that are minority languages in a given member state and also enjoy official status in another.[71] The Union's linguistic pluralism is therefore an opportunity for some regional or minority languages within the meaning of the Charter, but also induces a form of unequal treatment between them.

[69] Woehrling, *La Charte européenne*, n 13 above, 141.

[70] According to Jean-Marie Woehrling (*La Charte européenne*, n 13 above, 69–70), there are 65 paragraphs or subparagraphs that are formally identified under these Articles, 'but there are not sixty-five alternatives; in effect, the States must undertake to apply at least thirty-five of those paragraphs or sub-paragraphs, whilst also ensuring that they select undertakings that are indeed distinct, i.e. where one does not include another; this leads to the exclusion of the various subdivisions of Articles 9.2 and 10.3 which are connected by the word "or"'.

[71] This is the case, for instance, for German in Italy or Romania.

The notion of 'languages of the Treaties' only includes those languages that come under Article 55(1). Indeed, the Treaty can only be deemed authentic in those languages mentioned under that provision.

This situation may be viewed as a step backwards for democracy in those member states where these languages may be used in exchanges with the government, and even as an indirect violation of the aims of the Charter itself. Indeed, insofar as the Union may pre-empt some of the member states' powers, if citizens may no longer communicate on such matters with the European government in the language that they usually used in their communication with their national government, the European construct induces a watering-down of their language rights. Moreover, this phenomenon is quite similar to the Union's impact on the powers held by federal bodies in those member states that have a federal system.

Basque and Catalan speakers in particular quickly became aware of this perverse effect of the European construct. Thus, in December 2005, the Commission concluded an administrative agreement with the Spanish government on the use of Basque, Catalan and Galician in the Commission's exchanges of correspondence.[72] The Kingdom of Spain has also entrusted a specific body with the task of translating documents from Spanish into the three languages mentioned above and vice versa. This solution is the direct result of the status of these languages in the Spanish Constitution. In July 2009, the United Kingdom concluded a similar agreement for the benefit of the Welsh language.[73]

These solutions were extended by the Treaty of Lisbon. Article 55 EU on the official languages of the Union now contains a paragraph (2) under which

> this Treaty may also be translated into any other languages as determined by Member States among those which, in accordance with their constitutional order, enjoy official status in all or part of their territory. A certified copy of such translations shall be provided by the Member States concerned to be deposited in the archives of the Council.

In practice, however, only Basque, Catalan and Galician fulfil the conditions to benefit from this provision[74]—as Welsh and Scots likely do, though the notion of constitutional order in the context of the United Kingdom is quite flexible. Turkish ought also to be added, by virtue of Article 3 of the Cypriot Constitution. Some member states have several official languages under the terms of their respective constitutions, but these are always languages that are official languages in another member state of the European Union. Thus, in Ireland and in Malta, English is also an official language;[75] in Finland, Swedish is also a national language;[76] in

[72] [2006] OJ C73/14.

[73] This agreement has not been published.

[74] A Milian-Massana, 'L'émergence du nouveau droit linguistique dans l'Union européenne' [2006] 31 *The Supreme Court Law Review* 29, 47.

[75] Art 8 of the Constitution of Ireland of 1 July 1937: Art 5 of the Constitution of Malta of 21 September 1964.

[76] Art 17 of the Constitution of Finland of 1 March 2000.

Slovenia, Italian and Hungarian are also official languages 'in those municipalities where Italian or Hungarian national communities reside'.[77]

The Estonian Constitution contains a relatively ambiguous provision for the application of Article 55 EU. Its Article 51, subparagraph 2 provides that 'in localities where at least one-half of the permanent residents belong to a national minority, everyone has the right to also receive responses from state agencies, local governments, and their officials in the language of the national minority'. However, it is not possible to consider these to be official languages, because Article 6 of the Constitution also provides that 'the official language of Estonia is Estonian'. A similar ambiguity may be found in the Slovak Constitution, Article 6 of which stipulates that: '(1) Slovak is the state language on the territory of the Slovak Republic. (2) The use of other languages in dealings with the authorities will be regulated by law', but Article 34 adds that '[i]n addition to the right to master the state language, citizens belonging to national minorities or ethnic groups also have, under conditions defined by law, a guaranteed … right to use their language in dealings with the authorities'. The Czech Constitution is equally interesting. It does not stipulate that Czech is the official language of the Republic, but Article 25(2) of the Czech Charter of Human Rights and Fundamental Freedoms (which is included in the Constitution) provides that 'citizens belonging to national and ethnic minority groups are also guaranteed, under the conditions set down by law: … the right to use their own language in their relations with officials'.

It could therefore be thought that all regional or minority languages enjoying protection either under domestic law or under the European Charter for Regional and Minority Languages (where ratified by the relevant member state) would fall outside the remit of Article 55(2) EU. It is not so in practice. Indeed, nearly a year after the Treaty of Lisbon came into force, only the Kingdom of the Netherlands had availed itself of the possibility offered by Article 55(2); and yet the status of Frisian has not even been legally codified.[78]

Contrary to what Article 55(2) may lead us to believe, the translation of the Treaty does not depend on a constitutional acknowledgement on the part of a member state. The reality—at least as emerges from the position of the Netherlands—is ultimately not so different from the reasoning of the Court of Justice in the *UTECA* case, which bases the overriding reason on the protection of an official language without stipulating a priori whether it is an official language within the meaning of the Constitution. Be that as it may, the recognition of language rights within the European Union is not direct: it has to pass through state channels. What is true is that Article 55(2) is ultimately of symbolic value only, and in no way challenges the monopoly of official languages as the means of communication between citizens and the Union.

[77] Art 11 of the Constitution of Slovenia of 23 December 1991.
[78] www.uoc.edu/euromosaic/web/document/friso/fr/i1/i1.html#2.4.

In their own ways, the laws passed by the Council of Europe and those of the European Union strive to protect regional or minority languages. In spite of the relative heterogeneity of their respective approaches, a common thread emerges: the desire to preserve the cultural diversity that thus appears as a core value of European rights. These European rights thus stand alongside the universal international mechanisms adopted within the framework of UNESCO, such as the Convention for Safeguarding Intangible Cultural Heritage[79] or the Convention on the Protection and Promotion of the Diversity of Cultural Expressions.[80] The purpose of all of these provisions is not so much directly to protect minorities as it is to combat cultural dominance and standardisation. By concerning themselves with practices rather than people, these mechanisms are decidedly more ecumenical, as they avoid often dogmatic discussions on minorities, but they are not neutral in this respect. In grasping the nettle of a pre-existing social reality, such as a language, the law not only protects but also reconfigures it, as it must define that reality and at least partly determine the scope of its uses. Any form of protection by law is inextricably linked to a relative alienation. The dominance-disappearance/protection-alienation alternative is what is so tragic about any situation of vulnerability.

[79] See Art 2(2).
[80] See Art 6(2)(b).

7

The Many Vulnerabilities of the Roma and the European Legal Framework

TAWHIDA AHMED

I. INTRODUCTION

THIS CHAPTER PROVIDES a brief overview analysis of the protection amongst European institutions of one of Europe's most vulnerable minority groups—the Roma community.[1] The rights of Roma found their way onto European agendas on the premise that peace and security in Europe[2] was in jeopardy, with the growing discrimination against Roma and the position of Roma in Europe as an impoverished minority group.

The chapter argues that Roma face challenges in European states both in terms of protection of their identity as a minority group and in terms of their social exclusion from society, which results from their position as a vulnerable minority group. Overcoming these challenges requires support for the protection of Roma minority identity, as well as the securing of the economic, social and political development of the group. There is required, therefore, a holistic approach to overcoming the vulnerabilities that Roma face in Europe, both in terms of protection of minority rights and protection from social exclusion.

[1] See generally on Roma in Europe: Yana Kavrokova, 'The Roma Issue in the European Multilevel System: Ideas, Interests and Institutions behind the Failure of Inclusion Policies' (2011) 10 *European Yearbook of Minority Issues* 359–80; European Commission, 'The Situation of Roma in an Enlarged Europe' (Luxembourg, European Commission, 2004); G Toggenburg and K McLaughlin, 'The European Union and Minorities in 2011' (2011) 10 *European Yearbook of Minority Issues* 503–21; A Xanthaki, 'Protection of a Specific Minority: the Case of Roma/Gypsies', in P Thornberry and Martin Amor Estebanez (eds), *Minority Rights in Europe* (Strasbourg, Council of Europe, 2004), 169–194; K Henrard 'The Council of Europe and the Rescue of Roma as a Paradigmatic Case of Failed Integration? Abstract Principles versus Protection in Concreto' (2011) 10 *European Yearbook of Minority Issues* 271–316; Mark Dawson and Elise Muir, 'Individual, Institutional and Collective Vigilance in Protecting Fundamental Rights in the EU: Lessons from the Roma' (2011) 48 *Common Market Law Review* 751–75; Helen O'Nions, *Minority Rights Protection in International Law: The Roma of Europe* (Aldershot, Ashgate, 2007); Robert Dunbar, *Comparative Study of the Working Methods and Conclusions of the Committee of Experts of the European Charter for Regional or Minority Languages and the Advisory Committee of the Framework Convention for the Protection of National Minorities* (Strasburg, Council of Europe, 2005).

[2] Kavrokova (n 1 above) 361–63.

This chapter first sets out the position of Roma in Europe and the multi-faceted vulnerabilities of the group, and identifies the human rights frameworks of action necessary to address these concerns (section I). The chapter then analyses the extent to which the Council of Europe (CoE) and the European Union (EU) address these frameworks, in terms of identity preservation (section II) and social exclusion (section III).

II. WHO ARE THE ROMA? AND IN WHAT WAYS ARE THEY 'VULNERABLE' IN EUROPE?

This chapter adopts the term 'Roma' (meaning 'men' in the Romani language)[3] as an umbrella for what is in fact a variety of groups with a multiplicity of identities. The Roma have an intriguing (and, still to some extent, unearthed) history. Roma are present not only in Europe, but also in the United States of America, Australia and the countries of Latin America and Asia. They are thought to have migrated to Europe from northern India[4] between the ninth and fourteenth centuries. There are up to 12 million Roma in Europe.[5] Roma are present all over Europe, but the majority are found in Central and Eastern Europe and the Balkans.

There is much by way of stereotyped perceptions of who members of the Roma group are and what their traditional lifestyles entail, which makes them part of a minority group that differs from majority populations in European countries.[6] In reality, however, very little can be said about Roma culture with any certainty, partly due to inadequate information on Roma culture, and partly also because Roma are not a singular group with a singular culture. In cultural terms, Roma can be typically presented as both nomadic[7] (usually in Western Europe)

[3] Singular 'Rom'. On terminology, see GD Kwiek, 'Afterword: Rom, Roma, Romani, Kale, Gypsies, Travellers, and Sinti … Pick a name and stick with it, already!', in D Le Bas and T Acton (eds), *All Change! Romani Studies through Romani eyes* (Hatfield, University of Hertfordshire Press, 2010) 79–83; Roma Center for Social Intervention and Studies from Romania, 'Roma and the Council of Europe's Framework Convention for the Protection of National Minorities', www.romanicriss.org/Roma%20and%20the%20Framework%20Convention%20for%20the%20Protection%20of%20National%20Minorities%20ENG.pdf, 9; Yaron Matras, 'Scholarship and the Politics of Roma Identity: Strategic and Conceptual Issues' (2011) 10 *European Yearbook of Minority Issues* 211–47.

[4] As illustrated by the links found between the language of the Roma (Romani) and the Sanskrit script of other Indian languages. See the Patrin Web Journal 'A Brief History of the Roma', www.reocities.com/Paris/5121/history.htm.

[5] European Commission, 'EU and Roma', http://ec.europa.eu/justice/discrimination/roma/index_en.htm; Council of Europe Special Representative of the Secretary General of the Council of Europe for Roma Issues, 'Estimates and Official Numbers of Roma in Europe' http://hub.coe.int/c/document_library/get_file?uuid=3f6c4a82–0ca7–4b80–93c1–fef14f56fdf8&groupId=10227.

[6] See a critical analysis of the European Court of Human Rights's 'stereotyped' jurisprudence on this: Doris Farget, 'Defining Roma Identity in the European Court of Human Rights' (2012) *International Journal on Minority and Group Rights* 291–316.

[7] Travelling communities.

and sedentary (more common in Central and Eastern Europe);[8] as having tight family and community bonds; using a traditional language;[9] undertaking traditional activities and occupations such as metalwork or woodwork; and practising traditional music, dancing and folklore. In one Council of Europe report of a roundtable discussion, the fact that such perceptions of Roma are stereotypes is confronted.[10] The roundtable discussed issues such as inadequate knowledge of Roma culture, as well as the false assumption that Roma culture is singular. Moreover, it raised the issue of whether, for the purposes of identifying Roma as a minority group, characteristics currently attributed to Roma reflect the traditional culture of Roma? The question is important because it is difficult to identify which of the characteristics of Roma lifestyle is part of their cultural heritage and which have developed over time in Europe, as a means of necessity. For example, the idea that nomadism is a firm part of Roma cultural lifestyle is challengeable when we take into account that Roma have historically used travelling in Europe as a means of economic and physical survival and as an escape from political oppression—implying therefore that this is not a traditional cultural trait per se. Relatedly, is it part of Roma cultural identity to prefer to live in travelling sites, or has this equally developed as an adaptation response to the discriminatory and poverty-stricken conditions Roma faced in Europe? Whilst some commentators challenge the certainty of these characteristics as traditional to Roma, there are others who argue that, irrespective of the root of the tradition, Roma culture can now legitimately be described as encompassing these traits, as it is a culture of survival and adjustment.[11]

Given the lack of clarity over what is or is not Roma culture, this chapter favours a default position of self-identification, and one of plurality. Thus, the question of what Roma culture is, is ultimately one that can only be defined by members of the Roma community themselves. It is also something which is likely to differ from country to country and within different Roma groupings themselves. However, whatever the precise nature of Roma cultural traits—which is for members of the Roma themselves to agree upon—it can be broadly agreed that there are differences between the Roma and the majority populations in European states in respect of cultural traditions,[12] language and ethnicity, and also the desire that Roma indicate in preserving their unique identity, and these differences make the Roma a 'minority' group within Europe.[13] The Roma are a 'minority'

[8] Roma are presented as both nomadic and sedentary groups in the ECtHR's jurisprudence: see Farget (n 6 above) 302.

[9] Many Roma still speak Romani, eg Vlach Roma in Romania and Hungary.

[10] Alexander Raykova 'Report of the Seminar Cultural Identities of Roma, Gypsies, Travellers, and Related Groups in Europe', 15–16 September 2003, www.coe.int/T/DG3/RomaTravellers/archive/documentation/culture/repseminaronCulturalIdentities_en.asp, accessed on 28/5/2014.

[11] ibid.

[12] Such as solidarity, respect, purity and honour: ibid.

[13] A minority is defined as 'a group numerically inferior to the rest of a population of a State, in a non-dominant position, whose members—being nationals of the State—possess ethnic, religious or linguistic characteristics differing from those of the rest of the population and show, if only implicitly,

in whichever European country they reside in.[14] The Roma are not a 'majority' in any European state, and have no European kin state.

Despite a long presence in Europe, Roma have failed to integrate or find acceptance in European society. They suffer misunderstanding, discrimination, rejection and even persecution. Roma are a vulnerable minority group in Europe in several ways. One aspect of vulnerability for Roma as a minority group is the inadequate framework in European states for respect for the preservation of their minority identity. The traditional languages, travelling nature and lifestyles of Roma are not supported by the law and policy of European states. For instance, the teaching of Roma languages, provision for alternative schooling arrangements for children of travelling Roma families, access to caravan sites, and the general celebration of Roma cultural identity are not found in strong measure in European states. Instead, situations in European countries have contributed to breaking down Roma cultural identity. Indeed membership of the Roma minority has been a positive cause for discrimination. Many Roma do not declare their identity as Roma,[15] and Romani is not taught adequately in schools, nor is it a language of instruction.[16] France, Italy and other countries have expelled Roma from travelling sites without providing alternative sites, thus presenting obstacles to the travelling lifestyle of Roma.[17] Amnesty reports that French politicians have been expressly negative about Roma identity:

> Some French politicians have said Roma live a 'peculiar lifestyle' and are 'unwilling to integrate'. In September 2013, in an interview with Radio France International, Manuel Valls, the Minister of Interior said: 'Those people [Roma migrants] have lifestyles that are extremely different from ours. For this reason, they should return to Romania or Bulgaria.'[18]

a sense of solidarity, directed towards preserving their culture, traditions, religion or language': F Capotorti, *Study on the Rights of Persons Belonging to Ethnic, Religious and Linguistic Minorities* (Geneva, UN, 1991). See also J Deschenes, *Proposal Concerning a Definition of the Term 'Minority'* (1985) UN Doc E/CN4/Sub2/1985/31).

[14] They are resident in most European countries—see Council of Europe, Special Representative of the Secretary General of the Council of Europe for Roma Issues, 'Estimates and Official Numbers of Roma in Europe' http://hub.coe.int/c/document_library/get_file?uuid=3f6c4a82–0ca7–4b80–93c1–fef14f56fdf8&groupId=10227.

[15] ERRC, Written Comments of the European Roma Rights Centre, PRAXIS and Other Partner Organisations, Concerning Serbia, for Consideration by the Committee on Economic, Social and Cultural Rights at the 52nd Session (28 April to 23 May 2014), www.errc.org/cms/upload/file/serbia-cescr-20–march-2014.pdf.

[16] See eg Sigrid Lipott, 'The Roma as Protected Minority? Policies and Best Practices in the EU' (2012) 12(4) *Romanian Journal of European Affairs* 78, 87.

[17] See eg ERRC, 'Written Comments by the European Roma Rights Centre, Concerning Italy, to the Human Rights Council, within its Universal Periodic Review, for consideration at the 20th session (27 October to 7 November 2014)', www.errc.org/cms/upload/file/italy-un-upr-submission-20-march-2014.pdf; ERRC, 'On the Eve of the EU Roma Summit, Respect for the Human Rights of Roma is an unfulfilled Promise', www.errc.org/article/on-the-eve-of-the-eu-roma-summit-respect-for-the-human-rights-of-roma-is-an-unfulfilled-promise/4265; Rob Kushen 'Scapegoating will not solve 'Roma Problem', *The Guardian* www.theguardian.com/commentisfree/libertycentral/2010/aug/03/scapegoating-roma-problem-europe.

[18] Amnesty International, 'France; They said they would have killed us if we stayed', 8 April 2014, www.amnesty.org/en/news/france-they-said-they-would-have-killed-us-if-we-stayed-2014–04–08.

Another aspect of vulnerability is that Roma are an impoverished minority group, and in general this has resulted in their social exclusion from the societies in which they live. As a socially excluded group, Roma are marginalised from the rights, opportunities and resources that are available in society. These rights include, but are not limited to economic, social and political participation in society. Each of these will now be discussed in turn. Each has a preservation of minority identity component, in that economic, social and political participation in society can either further or must take into account Roma identity.

Roma are one of the most economically deprived groups in Europe. For Roma as a vulnerable minority group in Europe, there are two concerns with respect to employment: one concern is access to traditional Roma employment for those Roma who still desire it, and the other concern is access to (mainstream) employment. Some Roma engage in, or wish to engage in traditional employment. These traditional occupations allow Roma to travel freely. Examples of this are horse trading, metalwork, brick-making, wood carving and other crafts, door-to-door selling, involvement in arts, music, dance and fortune telling, seasonal labour, fairground operators and other small-scale trading. However, securing employment in traditional fields is not easy, due to the demise and relevance of these occupations in the modern world and the insufficient income that they are likely to, in any case, produce. Consequently, access for Roma to the mainstream labour market is vital to overcoming their economic vulnerability.

However, Roma face ongoing obstacles to accessing mainstream employment because of discrimination from majority populations and also because state policies and actions are poorly designed to encourage and guarantee Roma employment. In addition, problems in accessing mainstream employment result not only from the attitudes of the majority population and weak government practices: Roma also display reluctance to engage in mainstream employment. This may be due to self-protection tendencies aimed at preserving the identity of the group, or reluctance amongst Roma to integrate into mainstream society.

Roma also face concerns regarding their access to other social rights in society. In this context, issues concern adequate access to housing, health care and education, amongst others. The concerns encompass access to these goods within a mainstream structure, but issues also arise as to how to combine access to these goods with identity preservation. For instance, this may include the teaching of Roma languages, history and culture, within mainstream education systems.

Finally, Roma lack political empowerment in Europe—and this is important in terms of the capacity of the Roma to improve their situation in European states. Not only are Roma underrepresented in the political systems of the states in which they live, public authorities neglect Roma concerns at best, and actively persecute Roma at worst. The active participation of Roma is needed to address these concerns.

> Policies and laws aimed at improving the situation of Roma will no doubt fall without the active participation of Roma in the identification and elaboration of programs and

> projects, and ultimately, their implementation. This means that … Roma must enjoy some form of effective participation in political decision making processes.[19]

From the discussion undertaken in this section, it can be seen that the Roma are a vulnerable minority group in many ways, without the conditions in Europe necessary for for the support of their traditional lifestyles. However, the vulnerabilities of Roma go beyond the framework of preserving their traditional lifestyles, and are intertwined with their general social exclusion from society, including adequate participation in the economic, social and political life of European states.

Addressing these forms of vulnerabilities requires a minority rights and human rights framework to be adopted towards the Roma, enabling policies to focus on the preservation of Roma identity, as well as on increasing the presence of Roma in economic, social and political European society.

Gergely identifies the dual fundamental rights and minority rights concerns of the Roma:

> More than any other group, Roma face immediate and pressing problems of systematic exclusion from the societies in which they live, including discrimination in access to education, employment, health care and goods and services, for which legal redress is rarely forthcoming. Yet Roma are targeted in part because they form a separate community—a community which has been historically marginalized and prevented from developing according to its own interests.[20]

And Mirga and Gheorghe identify that dealing with this is not only a question for the majority society and the public authorities. The Roma themselves have decisions to make and a role to play in determining the course of their future:

> The desire of the Roma to maintain their identity and to be different is a basic human right. The problem, however, is how to maintain a traditional identity and culture while facing the challenges of modernity … The Roma face the basic dilemma of either maintaining traditional differences, which contribute to their different and unequal treatment, or accepting the need for change and modernization, which may help them gain equality but may also alter their identity.[21]

There are thus compromises to be made in addressing Roma concerns in Europe, and these compromises require a balance to be struck between the goals of human rights protection for Roma and integration (including, but not limited to economic, social and political participation in society), and support for the preservation of Roma identity. The next sections examine the role of European international institutions—namely the Council of Europe and the

[19] OSCE High Commissioner on National Minorities, Report on the Situation of Roma and Sinti (2000), p 128.

[20] Roma Center for Social Intervention and Studies from Romania, 'Roma and the Council of Europe's Framework Convention for the Protection of National Minorities', www.romanicriss.org/Roma%20and%20the%20Framework%20Convention%20for%20the%20Protection%20of%20National%20Minorities%20ENG.pdf, p 7.

[21] A Mirga and N Gheorghe, 'The Roma in the Twenty-First Century: A Policy Paper', Project on Ethnic Relations, www.per-usa.org/1997–2007/21st_c.htm, p 23.

European Union—in achieving these goals. Section II begins with examining the preservation of Roma identity and section III analyses social inclusion strategies.

III. THE PRESERVATION OF ROMA IDENTITY

A. The Council of Europe

The Council of Europe's primary vehicle for human rights protection is the European Convention on Human Rights (ECHR). The Convention does not, however, contain a provision on minority identity protection. It has therefore been unable to adequately or explicitly secure minority identity preservation (although there is some related case law, discussed below). Nonetheless, as an expression of the importance that the Council of Europe gives to minority identity protection, in 1995 it adopted the Framework Convention for the Protection of National Minorities (FCNM).[22]

The Advisory Committee to the FCNM firmly extends the scope of the FCNM to Roma by actively addressing Roma issues within its jurisdiction,[23] and many states willingly accept Roma as falling within the minorities protected by the instrument.[24] The FCNM has a number of provisions explicitly concerning the preservation of identity and the Advisory Committee to the FCNM has also placed pressure on states to ensure that due regard is given to the wishes of Roma to maintain their cultural identity. Under Article 3, members of national minority groups are permitted the right to freely choose to be treated or not to be treated as such and under Article 5 states are required to undertake to promote the conditions necessary for the maintenance and development of cultural identity, and to avoid measures of assimilation against the will of the minority. Other provisions pertain to, for instance, freedom of religion (Article 8); language preservation (Articles 9, 10, 11, 14); minority education institutions (Article 13).

The Advisory Committee also addresses explicitly the issue of identity preservation of Roma. For instance, in its Opinion on Romania's first State Report, it asks Romania to 'emphasise the cultural identity of the Roma, particularly in the

[22] Generally on the FCNM, see Charlotte Altenhoener, 'Review of the Monitoring Process of the Council of Europe Framework Convention for the Protection of National Minorities' (2011) 10 *European Yearbook of Minority Issues* 461–68.

[23] See for example, Advisory Committee on the Framework Convention for the Protection of National Minorities, Commentary on Education under the Framework Convention for the Protection of National Minorities, Strasbourg, 2 March 2006, ACFC/25DOC(2006)002; Advisory Committee on the Framework Convention for the Protection of National Minorities, Commentary on the Effective Participation of Persons Belonging to National Minorities in Cultural, Social and Economic Life and in Public Affairs, Adopted on 27 February 2008, ACFC/31DOC(2008)001, Strasbourg 5 May 2008. See also Roma Center for Social Intervention and Studies from Romania (n 20 above).

[24] Eg, UK, Hungary, Czech, Slovakia, Moldova. See Roma Center for Social Intervention and Studies from Romania (n 20 above).

educational field, and support their traditional crafts'[25] and asks the government to devise new initiatives for the promotion of inter-cultural dialogue (paragraph 33). The Committee praises a law which permits use of a minority language in dealings with local authorities in areas where more than 20 per cent of the population constitute a minority group (paragraph 49) but notes that there is no provision in the education system for instruction in Romani, despite the size of the Roma population in Romania (paragraph 63). In its Opinion on Italy's first State Report,[26] the Advisory Committee raises concerns about the shortcomings of the existing statutory provisions in Italy for safeguarding the identity and culture of Roma[27] and takes particular care to ensure that Roma ought to come within the confines of the FCNM, despite having no association with a given territory in Italy (paragraph 16). It highlights the lack of broadcasting in Romani (paragraph 47) and the need to accentuate the language and culture of Roma in the education system (paragraph 55).[28]

The importance of discussing explicitly the need for identity preservation should not be underestimated. The Opinions of the Advisory Committee are supported by the mechanism of state visits that the Committee undertakes when drafting its Opinion. Dunbar notes that the Advisory Committee has been particularly proactive in its role.[29] However, at the same time, the FCNM lacks a strong judicial enforcement mechanism to place any real pressure on states.

The European Charter for the Protection of Regional and Minority Languages (ECRML) is another relevant instrument falling within the bracket of 'specific identity preservation' tools. Examples of relevant provisions of the Charter concern the promotion of the use, maintenance and development of minority languages (Article 7), eg through use of the language in education (Article 8), before the judiciary (Article 9), before public authorities and in other public services (Article 10) and the creation or functioning of media outlets in the language (Article 11), as well as facilitating the language in cultural activities and facilities, such as libraries (Article 13), and not limiting the use of the language in economic and social life (Article 13) and finally to promoting the language in transfrontier exchanges (Article 14).

The Romani language falls within the parameters of the Charter, as it is a language which has been spoken over a long period of time in European states,[30] but having no territorial base, only some parts of the Charter (not connected to

[25] Advisory Committee Opinion on Romania, Adopted on 6 April 2001, para 31.

[26] Advisory Committee Opinion on Italy, Adopted on 14 September 2001.

[27] Executive summary, p 2.

[28] See further on comments made by the Advisory Committee: Roma Center for Social Intervention and Studies from Romania (n 20 above).

[29] Robert Dunbar, *Comparative Study of the Working Methods and Conclusions of the Committee of Experts of the European Charter for Regional or Minority Languages and the Advisory Committee of the Framework Convention for the Protection of National Minorities* (Strasbourg, Council of Europe, 2005).

[30] It thus corresponds to the explanations given to the Charter, Explanations to the Charter, para 31.

a territorial base) will be relevant to it.[31] On top of this, it is not clear what the content of the protection for the Romani language will be, because although states parties are bound by Part II of the Charter, they select which of the obligations in Part III they wish to commit to. Romania for example applies Part II obligations only to Romani.[32] Dunbar highlights the shortcomings of the ECRML in this respect, where the focus of Part II measures has been the elimination of discrimination, and not the preservation of a language per se[33] and moreover, the protection of Roma extended only to those Roma who spoke a language protected by Part II of the Charter.[34]

Thus, measures aimed at preserving languages are the focal point of the Charter, and hence it is a targeted instrument for identity preservation for Roma. Examples of this focus in the Romania report include the Committee noting the existence of the National Centre for the Culture of the Roma, which has a central objective of preserving and promoting the Roma culture and language (paragraph 46); noting the use of Romani language in administration and the police (paragraph 58) and in education (paragraph 77) and requests that Romania provides further information on how they promote Romani in economic and social life, and to what extent Romani can be used before judicial authorities. All of these points are identity preservation points.[35]

Outside of the system of the FCNM and ECRML, the Council of Europe undertakes little in terms of activities specifically targeting Roma identity preservation. The case of *Munoz Dias* does directly concern the preservation of an aspect of Roma identity. In *Munoz Diaz v Spain*[36] the Court held that not granting a survivor's pension to the spouse of a Roma man, where their marriage was valid within their own traditions (although there was no marriage according to Spanish law) was a breach of Article 14 ECHR together with Article 1 of Protocol 1 concerning the right to possession. This case relates to identity preservation in that it recognises a particular aspect of Roma identity—marriage according to Roma cultural traditions.

Aside from this, a greater proportion of CoE jurisprudence and activities is actually geared towards the social inclusion of Roma and thus will be addressed in section III below.

[31] Explanations to the Charter, paras 36–37.

[32] Application of the Charter in Romania, 1st Monitoring Cycle, Report of the Committee of Experts on the Charter, 19 June 2012, ECRML (2012) 3, para 7.

[33] See for eg in relation to Hungary, Dunbar, *Comparative Study* (n 29 above), 27.

[34] Dunbar quotes that this was the case for only 30 per cent of the Roma community in Hungary: Dunbar, *Comparative Study* (n 29 above), 28.

[35] For more detailed analysis of the ECRML and the Romani language, see Vesna Crnic-Grotic, 'Developments in the Field of the European Charter for Regional or Minority Languages in 2011' (2011) 10 *European Yearbook of Minority Issues* 469–85.

[36] *Munoz Diaz v Spain* (1982) Series A no 44, 4 EHRR 34.

B. The European Union

Preservation of minority identity in the EU is, by comparison with the CoE, more limited. The EU is the more disadvantaged institution because it has no minority identity protection instrument and no power which provides it with the competence to act in the field.

The most significant provision relating to minority protection in the EU is Article 2 TEU. According to this provision, the EU is declared to be founded on 'respect for … the rights of persons belonging to minorities'. Although this is not a competence provision, it acknowledges the fundamental and distinguished role of minority protection in EU identity, according to it the status of a founding value. A breach of Article 2 values by EU member states may lead to the potential investigation of an EU member state's actions under Article 7 TEU and may, inter alia, lead to the suspension of that state from the Union (in reality, Article 7 TEU will rarely be invoked). Article 2 TEU is also supported by new Article 49 TEU, which for the first time moves the achievement of minority protection as a condition of accession to the EU from a political to a legal obligation. Thus, Article 2 TEU, with its supporting provisions, arguably demonstrates the explicit importance given to minority protection as a key aspect of the EU project. Nonetheless, as a declaration of a value, it does not provide the EU with the authority to act for the preservation of Roma identity.

A limited form of competence is found in the field of EU cultural diversity. Article 166 TEU enables the EU to support and supplement the actions of the member states in the field of education, whilst respecting their cultural and linguistic diversity. Article 167 TEU enables the EU to contribute to the flowering of the cultures of the member states. Article 22 EUCFR also proclaims that 'The Union shall respect cultural, religious and linguistic diversity'. The competences within the Treaty provide the basis for the EU's funding programmes which supported cultural and linguistic diversity in the EU, including Culture 2000 and Culture 2007–13,[37] and an Intercultural Dialogue since 2007,[38] which are programmes which fund projects on the ground of promoting cultural diversity and cultural dialogue in the EU. These schemes have conducted some activities which can contribute to the preservation of Roma identity. For instance, the Khamoro Festival is an annual week-long festival in Prague which celebrates Roma culture;[39] another project sought to revive the interest of young Roma in

[37] European Parliament and Council (2000) Decision 508/2000/EC establishing the Culture 2000 programme, [2000] OJ L63/1; European Parliament and Council (2008) Decision 1352/2008/EC amending Decision 1855/2006/EC establishing the Culture Programme (2007 to 2013) [2008] OJ L348/128.

[38] European Commission, 'Creative Europe', http://ec.europa.eu/culture/policy/strategic-framework/intercultural-dialogue_en.htm. Promotion of intercultural dialogue is also a key priority of the European agenda on culture (COM (2007) 242).

[39] See further www.khamoro.cz; European Commission, *EU Projects in Favour of the Roma Community*, Exhibition Catalogue (Brussels, European Commission, 2010) 20.

their own traditions and cultures;[40] and RomFashion trained Romani women to design, sew and market traditional Roma clothing.[41] In recent years, the EU has developed a European Summit and Roma platform for addressing the EU-wide hardship Roma face, with a focus on Roma inclusion and integration.[42] However, in this section of the chapter, it is important to note that the Platform is not intended to focus on issues of preservation of Roma identity.

IV. SOCIAL EXCLUSION OF ROMA

A. The Council of Europe

The ECHR does not include provisions relating to rights to economic participation in society. The Council of Europe's European Social Charter 1961 (ESC), which was revised in 1996, however, concerns, amongst others, employment rights in Europe, in the majority of provisions from Articles 1 to 31. It also harbours a general provision on non-discrimination on grounds of, inter alia, race, colour, national extraction or social origin, and association with a national minority.[43] Whilst the ECHR does not mention employment explicitly, the ESC provides quite detailed employment rights such as the right to work (Article 1); just conditions of work (Article 2); safe and healthy work conditions (Article 3); fair remuneration (Article 4); vocational training (Article 10); social security (Article 12); and rights relating to migrant workers (Articles 18 and 19).

The ESC also provides social rights, such as the right to health, social security, social and medical assistance, social welfare services, the social legal and economic protection of the family and children and young persons, protection against poverty and social exclusion, and housing.[44] Adding to this, the ECHR provides protection for the private, home and family life of individuals (Article 8 ECHR) and Article 3 prohibits inhumane and degrading treatment. Political rights are covered both by the ECHR (Article 10 on freedom of expression, Article 11 on freedom of association and assembly) and its Protocol 3, Article 1 on the right to vote.

Between the provisions of the ECHR, ESC and Protocol 3, the CoE therefore covers the rights to economic, social and political participation in society. With respect to the Roma, it has been most active in the field of social participation and this has taken place mainly through the ESC, with limited coverage through the ECHR. The ESC, which operates a collective complaints mechanism, has enabled activist groups to bring several complaints on behalf of Roma. The ESC has taken

[40] 'Cultural Heritage from People to a United Europe', in ibid 26–27.

[41] In ibid 34.

[42] Started in 2008: European Commission, 'Roma Summits', http://ec.europa.eu/justice/discrimination/roma/roma-summits/index_en.htm and European Commission, 'Roma Platform', http://ec.europa.eu/justice/discrimination/roma/roma-platform/index_en.htm.

[43] Art E.

[44] Arts 11–17; 30–31.

a favourable approach to Roma, finding violations of the ESC in almost all cases, concerning issues such as expulsion of Roma from France, inadequacy of Roma traveller sites, unacceptable living conditions on these sites, inadequate access to housing and other social benefits, inadequate access to education for Roma children and access to healthcare, and use of racist propaganda which contributes to the social exclusion of Roma.[45]

Despite these successes, the ESC does not have access to the strong judicial enforcement mechanism of the ECHR. Nonetheless, there have been some cases under the ECHR which have helped Roma by requiring that the implementation of ECHR rights take into account the vulnerability of Roma as a minority group in Europe. In *Connors*, the ECtHR held that in enforcing policies on the use of travelling sites, the state must take into account the needs and different lifestyles of Roma as a minority group.[46] In addition, deplorable living conditions that Roma were forced to endure following the burning of their villages, was held to amount to degrading treatment.[47] In *Nachova v Bulgaria*, the Court held that allegations of discrimination by the police needed to be investigated where the Roma are concerned.[48] In *DH and Others v Czech Republic*, the Court recognised indirect discrimination as a concept and applied this to Roma children who were automatically placed in schools for low achievers.[49] The Court found that the number of Roma in these schools raised a concern of indirect discrimination. The *Oršuš* case[50] built on this, when it held that Roma children who had been placed in Roma-only classes had been discriminated against, because the state failed to take into account the background of the children as Roma. In this regard, the state was at fault in not providing language support, and in relying on parents' consent to separate classrooms, where Roma parents were generally unable to weigh up all the relevant factors before giving their consent. The same concern was also applied in *Mižigárová*[51] to criticise the permanent sterilisation of a Roma women who was in labour—the Court took into account that there are shortcomings in

[45] Complaint No 64/2011 *European and Travellers Forum v France*, Decision on merits 24/1/2012; Complaint No 62/2010 *International Federation of Human Rights (FIDH) v Belgium*, Decision on Merits 21/3/2012; Complaint No 67/2011 *Médecins du Monde-International v France*, Decision on Merits 11/9/2012; Complaint No 46/2007 *ERRC v Bulgaria*, Decision on Merits 3/12/2008; Complaint No 58/2009 *Centre for Housing Rights and Evictions (COHRE) v Croatia*, Decision on Merits 25/6/2010; Complaint No 63/2010 *European Council of Police Trade Unions (ESP) v COHRE (Portugal)*, Decision on Merits 28/6/2011; Complaint No 61/2010 *ERRC v Portugal*, Decision on Merits 23/4/2010.

[46] *Connors v United Kingdom* (2005) 40 EHRR 189. For analysis, see Farget (n 6 above).

[47] *Moldovan et al and others v Romania* (2005) 44 EHRR 16.

[48] *Nachova and Others v Bulgaria* (2006) 42 EHRR 43. See also *Cobzaru v Romania* (2005) 47 EHRR 10. In *Nachova* and *Cobzaru*, previous incidents indicating anti-Roma attitudes by state officials were sufficient to trigger this investigation duty. However, in subsequent cases, the Court narrowed its protection by requiring that incidents related to the specific case at hand, *Soare et al and others v Romania* App no 24329/02 (ECtHR, 22 February 2011); *Carabulea v Romania* App no 45661/99 (ECtHR, 13 July 2010); *Mižigárová v Slovakia* App no 74832/01 (ECtHR, 14 December 2010).

[49] *DH and Others v Czech Republic* (2008) 47 EHRR 3.

[50] *Oršuš and Others v Croatia* (2011) 52 EHRR 7, ECtHR (Grand Chamber).

[51] *Mižigárová v Slovakia* App no 74832/01 (ECtHR, 14 December 2010).

relation to sterilisation legislation and that Roma as a vulnerable group are liable to be particularly affected.[52] In *Aksu v Turkey*, the Court recognises negative stereotyping as a human rights issue (although ultimately finding no breach of the ECHR).[53]

A final strand of the CoE contribution to tackling the social exclusion of Roma—adding to ESC and ECHR jurisprudence—is the CoE's activities. The Committee of Experts on Roma and Travellers was appointed in 1995 as the first CoE body to review the situation of Roma in Europe and to assist the CoE member states in this respect. There is also a Special Representative of the Secretary General for Roma issues, which was created in 2011. Through these and other mechanisms, the CoE, inter alia, celebrates international Roma day (8 April); runs the ROMED programme, which trains Roma to act as mediators between the Roma and public authorities); holds an international Roma Women's day conference; and runs ROMACT which helps governments—through peer learning, guidance, coaching and mentoring—to develop policies towards Roma inclusion.

With respect to political participation, the CoE has had less of an impact than it has in respect of economic and social participation, although it has also been active in this field. In particular, it supports organisations which seek to promote or represent Roma. This includes the European Roma and Travellers Forum (ERTF) which was set up in 2004 and brings together national Roma federations and international Roma organisations to promote Roma rights and monitor respect for them; the Forum for European Roma Young People (Feryp) which is an international NGO supporting the representation of Roma young people; and the International Roma Women's Network (IRWN), set up in 2003 to tackle specific concerns of Roma women.[54] The CoE has been less involved in adjudicating on Roma political rights. The ECtHR has adjudicated one case relating to the political rights of Roma. In this case, the Roma applicant successfully contested a rule in Bosnia and Herzegovina which only entitled ethnic Bosniaks, Serbs and Croats to be elected members of the Presidency and House of Peoples of Bosnia and Herzegovina.[55] Finally, the FCNM has issued a commentary on political participation of minorities.[56]

[52] For further discussion of many of these cases, see Bill Bowring, 'Protecting Minority Rights through an Individual Rights Mechanism: The Strasbourg Court and some Significant Developments to June 2012', (2011) 9 *European Yearbook of Minority Issues* 437–60 and K Henrard, 'The Council of Europe and the Rescue of Roma as a Paradigmatic Case of Failed Integration? Abstract Principles versus Protection in Concreto' (2011) 10 *European Yearbook of Minority Issues* 271–316.

[53] *Aksu v Turkey* App nos 4149/04, 41029/04 (ECtHR, 15 March 2012).

[54] The Council of Europe: Protecting the rights of Roma, file:///G:/RESEARCH/EU%20Roma%20chapter/CoE/roms_en.pdf.

[55] *Sejdic and Finci v Bosnia and Herzegovina* (2009) ECHR 2122, ECtHR (Grand Chamber).

[56] Advisory Committee on the Framework Convention for the Protection of National Minorities, Commentary on the Effective Participation of Persons Belonging to National Minorities in Cultural, Social and Economic life and in Public Affairs, SCFC/31DOC(2008)001.

B. The European Union

Just as the CoE has prioritised economic participation through the ESC, the EU first and foremost also acts in the field of economic participation, given the internal market focus of the EU project. Under EU law, every EU citizen has the right to work in another EU member state without facing discrimination on grounds of nationality. This includes members of Roma who are EU citizens.[57] The EU strengthens this provision by requiring that such persons may also not be denied opportunities because of their race or ethnic origin (Race Directive)[58] or because of their membership of a national minority group (Article 21 EU Charter of Fundamental Rights (CFR)). Under the Race Directive, Roma may not be discriminated against in relation to conditions for access to employment, vocational training, employment and working conditions or membership of work-related organisations.[59] These legally binding sources of law provide a robust form of protection for Roma in seeking employment opportunities. The Race Directive and the CFR also apply to Roma who seek work within their own member states, and thus Roma need not move between EU member states in order to obtain these benefits.

The EU complements these provisions with strategies to promote the employment opportunities of Roma. Articles 145–50 TFEU govern the EU's activities in the promotion of employment. On the authority of these articles, the EU may, in various ways, support the member states in achieving high employment rates domestically and therefore across the EU. The legal basis (establishing a non-harmonising coordinating role for the EU) led to the development of the European Employment Strategy[60] and endorses a soft law mechanism that takes the best practices of the various member states and uses them as benchmarks in order to enhance the performance of all member states in reaching certain goals (the open method of coordination). This method does not impose legal obligations on member states.[61] However, where Roma are concerned, it combines usefully with the EU's goals in the field of non-discrimination In this regard, the EU has placed significant emphasis on the Roma. Evident of this is the dedicated programmes and funding for Roma, which is not the case with other vulnerable groups in Europe. The strategy consists of both policy guidance and funding for national bodies involved in increasing employment levels in their country.[62]

[57] Art 45 TFEU; Directive 2004/38 EU Citizens Directive.

[58] Directive 2000/43/EC.

[59] Art 3 Race Directive.

[60] There are four features of the European Employment Strategy, as found in Art 128 ECT: 1) The employment guidelines outline a general set of objectives for all the member states. 2) National Action Plans are formulated for each member state. Funding is provided to assist in meeting those aims. 3) The Joint Employment Report of the EU and each member state is issued. 4) The Council may issue country-specific recommendations, as additional guidelines.

[61] Lisbon European Council, 23/24 March 2000.

[62] European Commission, Report on the Implementation of National Roma Integration Strategies, SWD (2014) 121 final p 5.

On the policy guidance side, in 2011, the European Commission adopted an EU Framework for National Roma Integration Strategies,[63] focusing on four key areas: education, employment, housing and healthcare. The policy requires member states to outline how each state intends to progress in the four areas up to 2020. National contact points have been set up in each country and the Commission oversees member states' strategies and overall progress in the key areas. In its 2014 report on the implementation of the strategy, the Commission assessed all four areas and provided its recommendations for further progress. In relation to employment, the Commission was quite critical, noting that the expected outcomes were not reached from the initiatives implemented to date and that there still lacked systematic national measures in place to tackle Roma employment difficulties.

As well as policy guidance, the European Commission provides financial assistance to the member states in order to enable them to accomplish the aims of EU employment policy. Examples include TRAVELCOM, which provided skills to Roma to enter the employment market; a project to promote the vocational training of Roma; Youngbusiness.net, which offers business support to young Roma; and Acceder, which links Roma jobseekers directly with employment service providers.[64]

Due to the generally poor economic situation of minorities like the Roma, the possibilities within EU law for inclusion of Roma within the mainstream labour market are extremely important. Any EU action which offers Roma the chance of economic participation, contributes towards that right. The proviso is that, where Roma wish to preserve their identities, EU action on economic participation is conducted within a framework which allows for such. In this latter regard, the EU does not fare so well. Despite the regard it shows for minority protection in Article 2 TEU, it does very little to promote traditional Roma occupations in the field of employment.[65] Thus, Roma vulnerability in employment is addressed by the EU, but Roma vulnerabilities with regard to their identity preservation in employment is not.

Participation for Roma in the social life of society has also been emphasised within the EU's policies and activities. The EU's Race Directive requires that Roma are not discriminated against on grounds of race or ethnic origin, in relation to social protection, including social security and healthcare; social advantages; education; and access to and supply of goods and services which are available to the public, including housing.[66] In addition to the context of non-discrimination,

[63] COM (2011) 173 final [2011] OJ L76/68; followed by Council Recommendation of 9 December 2013 on effective Roma integration measures in the member states [2013] OJ C378/01.

[64] See European Commission, *EU Projects in Favour of the Roma Community* (n 39 above); and European Commission, Report on the Implementation of National Roma Integration Strategies, SWD (2014) 121 final.

[65] Nonetheless it has done so on ad-hoc occasions, such as a project teaching Roma women how to sew traditional Roma clothing. Above, n 32.

[66] Art 3 Race Directive.

the Treaty provides the EU with competence on social policy per se, including to combat social exclusion.[67] The EU's employment strategy is thus now complemented by the social inclusion strategy. Originally a feature of the European employment strategy, the latter strategy has developed in its own right. The areas of education, housing and healthcare feature within the Roma-specific strands of EU policy, namely within the European Commission's 2011 framework on Roma integration, noted earlier.[68] In 2014, the Commission reported that member states' initiatives on the ground had led to an improvement in access to early childhood education for Roma, but calls for education systems to be more inclusive and tailored to the needs of Roma, to tackle segregated schooling and reduce the number of Roma early school leavers.[69] The Commission highlights that very little progress has been made in the area of health,[70] and that housing interventions have often been the weakest area of member states' national integration strategies.[71] Where discriminatory treatment is not being sufficiently reduced, the Commission has opined that this is due to lack of implementation of legislation and policy, rather than gaps in legislation.[72] The Commission accordingly calls for better implementation.

In terms of improvement in the situation of the political participation of Roma in society, the EU, like the CoE, is again weakest in this field. EU law guarantees EU citizens political rights when they move to other member states.[73] However, what Roma require is political representation. There is no defined EU law and policy in this field, and just like the CoE, the EU has promoted this field to a minimum degree. It does however, recognise the need for the political mobility of Roma by acknowledging that effective impact of policies on Roma depends upon Roma involvement at all stages of the process.[74]

V. CONCLUSION

This chapter has analysed the engagement of the European international legal framework with the position of Roma as a vulnerable minority group on the European territory. It has been seen that Roma face challenges both in terms of requiring minority-specific identity preservation, and also measures to tackle their economic, social and political exclusion from European society. In summary, although framing Roma as a 'minority group' in relevant documents and policies,

[67] Art 153(1)(j) TFEU.

[68] European Commission, *EU Projects in Favour of the Roma Community* (n 39 above).

[69] European Commission, Report on the implementation of the EU Framework for National Roma Integration Strategies COM (2014) 2009 final p 3.

[70] ibid p 6.

[71] ibid p 8.

[72] ibid p 9.

[73] Eg the right to vote and stand in elections, Arts 20 and 22 TFEU.

[74] European Commission (n 1 above), p 47.

both the CoE and the EU have sought to tackle the social exclusion of Roma within an inclusion, human rights or discrimination framework, rather than a preservation of identity framework. Policies or activities relating to the preservation of identity have been established, but these have not been the predominant focus of these European organisations.

As a result, neither of the European organisations analysed here have adequate frameworks for the protection of Roma identity. The CoE is the most developed in standard-setting, through the FCNM and the ECRML. Both of the monitoring mechanisms of these instruments have addressed Roma identity, although these mechanisms remain generally weak forms of enforcement. The EU fares less well in standard-setting, but has been more active in project funding relating to the celebration and promotion of Roma cultural identity. It may therefore be viewed as complementing the standard-setting activities of the CoE. However, even if one takes the activities of these two organisations together, the European framework for identity preservation for Roma is inadequate. Both organisations are more active in attempts to integrate the Roma into society, by tackling social exclusion. This was the focus of section III.

Section III indicated that activities for 'inclusion' of Roma are more numerous in the CoE and the EU than activities for Roma identity preservation. Both the CoE and the EU focus first and foremost on the field of economic integration of Roma. Much activity has been conducted, and reports drafted on the employability of Roma. In addition, both organisations have been vocal in condemning, and attempting to cater for, the exclusion of Roma in education, housing, and other social areas. In this regard, the CoE has generally provided better access to judicial enforcement mechanisms for many of these cases, through the European Court of Human Rights (ECHR) and the collective complaints mechanism of the European Social Charter. The EU has been less active in terms of adjudication, although it has legally binding rules which prohibit discrimination, most pertinently in the EU Race Directive. The area of protection with the least progress in terms of legislation, activity and progress on the ground is that of the political inclusion of Roma in European societies. Both the CoE and the EU have neglected this field, when compared to the fields of economic and social participation.

Having said this, for over a decade, the Roma problem has been a targeted feature of the CoE agenda and has received dedicated support in the EU for a number of years too. This is encouraging and was a much anticipated and required action. However, despite the dedication amongst both of the European institutions, Roma remain as vulnerable as ever, with commentators remarking on 'The discrepancy between Europe-wide multilevel efforts for Roma inclusion and the entirely inadequate results of these initiatives.'[75]

[75] Kavrokova (n 1 above).

It is argued that greater improvements require better engagement by states in the domestic arena,[76] because European international measures—no matter how targeted they attempt to be—are insufficient to drive through significant reforms on the ground at national level.

[76] ibid, 377; and Lilla Farkas 'A Good Way to Equality: Roma seeking judicial protection against discrimination in Europe' (2006) 3 *European Anti-Discrimination Law Review* 21–29 (in relation to the EU Race Directive).

8

Indigenous Peoples' Cultural Identity under EU Law and the ECHR: A Non-trade Interest or a Human Right?

JULINDA BEQIRAJ*

I. INTRODUCTION

In recent years the international community has devoted special attention to the human rights conditions of indigenous peoples. This process has prompted significant progress in international thinking and action concerning indigenous issues and rights, in particular, through the adoption of international standards and guidelines, and through the establishment of institutions and bodies that specifically target indigenous peoples' concerns. The ILO (International Labour Organization) Indigenous and Tribal Peoples Convention of 1989 (ILO C169),[1] the UN Declaration on the Rights of Indigenous Peoples (UNDRIP) of 2007[2] and among others, three UN-related mechanisms, notably the Permanent Forum on Indigenous Issues (UNPFII),[3] the Expert Mechanism on the Rights of Indigenous Peoples[4] and the Special Rapporteur on the rights of indigenous peoples[5] constitute ground-breaking developments in this sector. The rights of indigenous peoples are further promoted by organisations and human rights mechanisms

* The author would like to thank Kristin Hausler, Associate Senior Research Fellow at BIICL for her thoughtful comments on earlier drafts of this chapter.

[1] International Labour Organisation Convention no 169 Concerning Indigenous and Tribal Peoples in Independent Countries, 27 June 1989, 1650 UNTS 383.

[2] United Nations Declaration on the Rights of Indigenous Peoples, GA Res 61/295, UN DOC A/RES/61/295 (2 October 2007).

[3] The United Nations Permanent Forum on Indigenous Issues is an advisory body to the Economic and Social Council (ECOSOC), with a mandate to discuss indigenous issues related to economic and social development, culture, the environment, education, health and human rights.

[4] The Expert Mechanism on the Rights of Indigenous Peoples was established by the Human Rights Council in 2007 as a subsidiary advisory body of the Council (Resolution 6/36, A/HRC/RES/6/36) on issues concerning the rights of Indigenous peoples.

[5] The Special Rapporteur on the rights of indigenous peoples is an independent human rights expert appointed by the Human Rights Council with the mandate to report and advise on the human rights of indigenous peoples and to receive communications on alleged violations of indigenous peoples' rights. See also below section II.

operating at the regional level, and this has occurred in particular in the context of the African and Inter-American human rights systems.[6]

By contrast, the European regional human rights system, consisting of the European Convention on Human Rights (ECHR) and several Protocols, and their complaints mechanism—namely the European Court of Human Rights (ECtHR) and formerly the European Commission of Human Rights—have dedicated little attention to indigenous human rights issues and have attached even less importance to the collective dimension of the rights of these groups.[7] Indigenous peoples' rights at the European level have traditionally been of lesser social and political concern, in comparison with the issue of the protection of the rights of individuals belonging to national, ethnic, or linguistic minorities—as demonstrated by the adoption of human rights standards specifically targeting minorities in the context of the Council of Europe (CoE) and by the special emphasis historically placed on minority protection by the Organization for Security and Co-operation in Europe (OSCE).[8]

However, even if mostly 'dormant' in recent years—especially at the level of (supranational) European litigation—indigenous rights issues are rapidly emerging as a European issue in general and as a European Union (EU) concern in

[6] F Coomans, 'The Ogoni Case Before the African Commission on Human and Peoples' Rights' (2003) 52 *International and Comparative Law Quarterly* 749–60; J Anaya, *International Human Rights and Indigenous Peoples* (New York, Wolters Kluwer, 2009); P Thornberry, *Indigenous Peoples and Human Rights* (Manchester, Manchester University Press, 2002); A Xanthaki, *Indigenous Rights and United Nations Standards: Self-determination, Culture and Land* (Cambridge, Cambridge University Press, 2007); J Anaya and MS Campbell, 'Gaining Legal Recognition of Indigenous Land Rights: the Story of the Awas Tingni Case in Nicaragua' in D Hurwitz and ML Satterthwaite (eds), *Human Rights Advocacy Stories* (London, Thomson Foundation Press, 2009); EC Olivares Alanís, 'Indigenous Peoples' Rights and the Extractive Industry: Jurisprudence From the Inter-American System of Human Rights' (2013) 5 *Goettingen Journal of International Law* 187–214; D Shelton, 'Water Rights of Indigenous Peoples and Local Communities' in L Boisson de Chazournes, C Leb and M Tignino (eds), *International Law and Freshwater: the Multiple Challenges* (Cheltenham, Edward Elgar Publishing, 2013); M Fitzmaurice, 'The Question of Indigenous Peoples' Rights: a Time for Reappraisal?' in D French (ed), *Statehood and Self-Determination: Reconciling Tradition and Modernity in International Law* (Cambridge, Cambridge University Press, 2013).

[7] For a complete analysis of the evolution of the ECtHR's jurisprudence over the years, see T Koivurova, 'Jurisprudence of the European Court of Human Rights Regarding Indigenous Peoples: Retrospect and Prospects' (2011) 18 *International Journal on Minority and Group Rights* 1–37. See also G Pentassuglia, 'Protecting Minority Groups Through Human Rights Courts: The Interpretive Role of the European and Inter-American Jurisprudence' in A Vrdoljak (ed), *The Cultural Dimension of Human Rights* (Oxford, Oxford University Press, 2013) 73–116.

[8] See eg, K Drzewicki, 'Framework Convention as a Pan-European Instrument: a Perspective of the OSCE High Commissioner on National Minorities' in A Verstichel et al (eds), *The Framework Convention for the Protection of National Minorities: a Useful Pan-European Instrument?* (Antwerp, Intersentia, 2008); RM Letschert, *The Impact of Minority Rights Mechanisms: The OSCE High Commissioner on National Minorities, the UN Working Group on Minorities and the CoE Advisory Committee on Minorities* (The Hague, TMC Asser Press, 2005); J Packer, 'The OSCE High Commissioner on National Minorities' in G Alfredsson et al (eds), *International Human Rights Monitoring Mechanisms: Essays in Honour of Jakob Th Möller* (The Hague, Martinus Nijhoff, 2001); WA Kemp, *Quiet diplomacy in action: the OSCE High Commissioner on National Minorities* (The Hague, Kluwer Law International, 2001).

particular.[9] The impact of climate change on the Arctic marine and terrestrial environment has been increasingly affecting the indigenous peoples and communities of the north of Europe—the Inuit living in Greenland (part of the Kingdom of Denmark), the Saami people living in Norway, Finland, Sweden and Russia, and other indigenous peoples living in the Russian Federation—threatening their traditional livelihoods and the survival of their cultural identity.[10] Climate change is an additional (yet probably the most pervasive) source of vulnerability for the indigenous peoples of the Arctic; it adds to traditional patterns of discrimination and assimilation, and to the risks that economic globalisation poses to indigenous peoples' natural environment and well-being by reason of a wider demand for the exploitation of natural resources available in high quantities in their territories. Increasing reliance by governments on extraction of such resources, either for export or through authorisation of foreign investments—frequently without the free prior and informed consent of the indigenous people inhabiting the areas involved—has a negative impact on the survival of the indigenous language, culture and traditions. In the light of these factors, indigenous peoples are subject to particularly accelerated change, but they have little or no control over the processes causing this transition and affecting their lives and territories. In this sense, indigenous peoples are 'vulnerable' groups in need of 'empowerment' to regain or to maintain control over their territories, natural resources and their culture. Their vulnerability is reflected in the lack of legal, social or political mechanisms guaranteeing full compliance with their social cultural and political rights, including through the establishment of effective remedies and sanctions in case of violation of their rights.

In the light of these considerations, the chapter aims to carry out an analysis of the scope and variety of the instruments and procedures available at the European level—within both the EU and the CoE—for the protection of the rights of indigenous peoples living in this region and of the main barriers to access to remedies and fair procedures for the enforcement of indigenous peoples' rights. More specifically, these issues are addressed from the perspective of the right to cultural identity, which is inherent in the self-determination and self-conception of indigenous peoples and which represents an essential component and a prerequisite of the effective enjoyment of other indigenous peoples' rights, such as

[9] See below section IV.

[10] Arctic areas are inhabited by approximately four million people and the proportion of indigenous people is estimated to be about 10 and 12 per cent of this population. However, the number of indigenous people is not accurate because of the definition of indigenousness. The Arctic region is divided between eight Arctic countries, namely Canada, United States, Russia, Finland, Sweden, Norway, Iceland and Denmark (including Greenland). Arctic indigenous peoples include for example Saami in circumpolar areas of Finland, Sweden, Norway and Northwest Russia, Nenets, Khanty, Evenk and Chukchi in Russia, Aleut, Yupik and Inuit (Iñupiat) in Alaska, Inuit (Inuvialuit) in Canada and Inuit (Kalaallit) in Greenland. See www.arcticcentre.org/InEnglish/SCIENCE-COMMUNICATIONS/Arctic-region/Arctic-Indigenous-Peoples. See also Commission Communication of 20 November 2008 on the European Union and the Arctic Region (COM (2008) 0763).

the right to land, the right to access to and use of natural resources, the right to non-discrimination, and the right to economic and social development.[11]

In addition to providing an overview of the EU and CoE (mainly ECHR) legal framework for the protection of indigenous peoples' cultural identity—by tracing the relevant legal framework and case law—the chapter discusses a recent case brought before the EU General Court by the Inuit indigenous communities that may help to clarify some of the limits to the effective enjoyment and enforcement of their rights in practice. The case of *Inuit Tapiriit Kanatami and Others* and the facts at its basis provide a paradigmatic example of the level of complexity and interrelatedness of the issues that affect the enjoyment of the right to cultural identity by indigenous peoples in Northern Europe.

II. INDIGENOUS PEOPLES' RIGHT TO CULTURAL IDENTITY AND INTERNATIONAL INSTRUMENTS OF PROTECTION

At the international level, the only binding instrument that specifically provides for the protection of the rights of indigenous peoples is the ILO Indigenous and Tribal Peoples Convention of 1989 (ILO C169).[12] However, only four European states—Denmark, the Netherlands, Norway, and Spain—have ratified the Convention, and its relevance for the indigenous peoples and communities of northern Europe is even more limited if one considers that the Spanish and the Dutch governments have indicated that there are no indigenous or tribal peoples within the meaning of the Convention in their territories.[13] A more recent, broader but non-binding instrument, the landmark Declaration on the Rights of Indigenous Peoples (UNDRIP), was adopted by the UN General Assembly in 2007.[14]

These instruments generally establish, first, that states shall recognise, respect, protect and promote the 'full realization of the social, economic and cultural rights of [indigenous] peoples with respect for their social and cultural identity, their

[11] The right to internal self-determination of indigenous peoples, is well established within international law, including the UN Charter and the ICCPR and the ICESCR (Common Art 1) and has also been defined by the ICJ in the West-Saharan case (*Western Sahara*, Advisory Opinion, 16 October 1975, ICJ Reports 1975, p 12, paras 54–59). See R Stavenhagen, Special Rapporteur on the situation of human rights and fundamental freedoms of indigenous people, First report on the activities carried out during the period 10 August 2001–10 August 2004, presented to the UN General Assembly, 59th session, 12 August 2004, UN Doc A/59/2582004, paras 46–49. See also Human Rights Committee, General Comment no 23, The Rights of Minorities (art 27), Doc CCPR/C/21/Rev 1/Add 5 (4 August 1994) para 7.

[12] See ILO C169, above n 1.

[13] See for instance Direct Request (CEACR) to the Netherlands—adopted in 2013, published on 103rd ILC session (2014); Direct Request (CEACR) to Spain—adopted in 2010, published on 100th ILC session (2011).

[14] See UNDRIP, above n 2.

customs and traditions and their institutions'.[15] They clearly establish indigenous peoples' 'right to practice and revitalize their cultural traditions and customs' including through 'the right to maintain, protect and develop the past, present and future manifestations of their cultures'.[16] Additionally, indigenous peoples have the right 'to be secure in the enjoyment of their own means of subsistence and development, and to engage freely in all their traditional and other economic activities'[17] as well as the right to the enjoyment of the highest attainable standard of physical and mental health, in relation to which 'States shall take the necessary steps with a view to achieving progressively the full realization of this right'.[18] Secondly, the UN Declaration and the ILO Convention make clear that indigenous peoples have the right to participate anad to be consulted in relation to decision-making in matters which would affect their rights.[19] Thirdly, the right to effective remedies and to an effective legal protection of the individual and collective rights of indigenous peoples is a common thread to these two instruments.[20]

Among the mechanisms and procedures for the promotion and protection of the rights of this group, the Special Rapporteur on the rights of indigenous peoples, appointed initially in 2001 by the Commission on Human Rights (now replaced by the Human Rights Council)[21] plays a fundamental role in communicating and liaising with the concerned governments on specific cases of alleged violations of human rights notified by indigenous peoples and their organisations (the so-called 'communications procedure') and in promoting good practices in the implementation of international standards concerning the rights of indigenous peoples. The lack of strict formal requirements for submitting a case to the Special Rapporteur—eg, no exhaustion of domestic remedies, or a detailed legal argument, or a particular relationship with the victim(s) of the alleged violation is required—represents a strong advantage of the procedure that makes it highly accessible to everyone as well as an efficient instrument in cases of imminent danger of violations of the rights of indigenous individuals and peoples.

[15] ILO C169, above n 1, at Arts 2, 4, 5 and Arts 24, 31, 41. It should be noted that ILO C169 replaces C107, which talked about assimilation and therefore is now obsolete. However, this old treaty is still in force for those states that have not denounced it or have not ratified the new C169.

[16] UNDRIP, above n 2, Art 11. Similarly, ILO C169, above n 1, Art 8.2 states that 'These peoples shall have the right to retain their own customs and institutions, where these are not incompatible with fundamental rights defined by the national legal system and with internationally recognized human rights.'

[17] UNDRIP, above n 2, Art 20. Similarly, Art 23 of ILO C169 stipulates that 'Handicrafts, rural and community based industries and subsistence economy and traditional activities of the peoples concerned, such as hunting, fishing, trapping and gathering, shall be recognized as important factors in the maintenance of their cultures and in their economic self-reliance and development. Governments shall ensure that these activities are strengthened and promoted.'

[18] UNDRIP, above n 2, Art 24.

[19] ibid, Arts 18–19; ILO C169, above n 1, Arts 6, 7.

[20] UNDRIP, above n 2, Art 40; ILO C169, above n 1, Art 12.

[21] Commission on Human Rights, resolution 2001/57, of 24 April 2001, UN Doc E/CN 4/RES/2001/57. The mandate was later renewed by the Human Rights Council by resolution A/HRC/RES/6/12 of 28 September 2007.

The Special Rapporteur has intervened in several cases in response to alleged violations of the rights of indigenous peoples living in northern Europe addressing issues, such as: interference of mining activities authorised by the Norwegian government with the Saami culture and reindeer management, absence of free prior and informed consent and failure to provide benefit-sharing to the concerned Saami communities;[22] effective participation of the Saami people in the consultation process concerning the possible expansion of mining activities and the potential effects on traditional reindeer herding activities and way of life of indigenous Saami communities in Sweden;[23] failure to take into consideration Saami reindeer herding methods in land use planning in Finland, resulting in the risk of imminent slaughter of reindeer belonging to a Saami cooperative;[24] interference with the indigenous peoples' rights to freedom of association and freedom of expression following the suspension of the Russian Association of Indigenous Peoples of the North by government authorities.[25]

Besides the communications procedure of the Special Rapporteur on the situation of indigenous people, the UN mechanisms operating in the context of general or thematic human rights treaties may also be relevant for the protection of the rights of indigenous peoples, especially in cases involving violations of individual rights.[26] Indeed, indigenous peoples living in northern Europe have resorted to such mechanisms for the protection of their rights, from time to time, in particular to the Human Rights Committee (HRC),[27] which has addressed indigenous peoples' rights under the International Covenant on Civil and Political Rights (ICCPR) in the context of minorities' right to enjoy their own culture

[22] Report by the Special Rapporteur on the situation of human rights and fundamental freedoms of indigenous people, James Anaya, Addendum, Summary of communications transmitted and replies received, A/HRC/12/34/Add 1, 18 September 2009, paras 330–38.

[23] ibid, paras 399–403. See also Special Rapporteur on the situation of human rights and fundamental freedoms of indigenous people, James Anaya, Situation of Sami people in the Sápmi region spanning Norway, Sweden and Finland, A/HRC/15/37/Add 6, 7 July 2010; A/HRC/18/35/Add.2, 6 June 2011.

[24] Report of the Special Rapporteur on the rights of indigenous peoples, James Anaya, Addendum, Communications sent, replies received, and follow-up, A/HRC/21/47/Add 3, 7 September 2012, paras 47–48. In general see also M Fitzmaurice, 'The UN Declaration on the Rights of Indigenous Peoples: Recent Developments regarding the Saami Peoples of the North' in S Allen and A Xanthaki (eds), *Reflections on the UN Declaration on the Rights of Indigenous Peoples* (Oxford, Hart Publishing, 2011).

[25] Report of the Special Rapporteur on the rights of indigenous peoples, James Anaya, Addendum, Communications sent, replies received and observations, A/HRC/24/41/Add 4, 2 September 2013, paras 140–42. See also Special Rapporteur on the situation of human rights and fundamental freedoms of indigenous people, James Anaya, Situation of indigenous peoples in the Russian Federation, A/HRC/15/37/Add 5, 23 June 2010.

[26] For further references on the relevant jurisprudence see the doctrine cited above in n 6.

[27] The first Optional Protocol to the International Covenant on Civil and Political Rights vests the Committee with the competence to receive and consider individual complaints concerning alleged violation of state obligations under the Covenant; with the exception of the UK, all EU member states have ratified the Optional Protocol. See Optional Protocol to the International Covenant on Civil and Political Rights, GA Res 2200A (XXI), UN GAOR, 21st Session, Supplement no 16, UN Doc A/6316.

(Article 27),[28] and more recently to the Committee on the Elimination of Racial Discrimination (CERD) in the context of the 'early warning and urgent action procedure' which may be activated directly by indigenous peoples and is aimed at preventing serious and irremovable violations of the Convention.[29] Additionally, indigenous peoples' issues are often considered by the HRC, the CERD and the Committee on Economic Social and Cultural Rights (CESCR) in the context of general recommendations and concluding observations on state reports.[30]

By comparison to international human rights supervisory mechanisms and procedures, regional human rights judicial bodies are generally endowed with broader and more penetrating powers as to the legal impact of their decisions on states. Their rulings and judgments are mostly legally binding for the state party specifically concerned, and the execution of the final judgment may be subject to further supervision under political and/or quasi-judicial procedures. This begs the question of why indigenous peoples did not resort to the European instruments, organisms and procedures for the protection of their rights in the cases mentioned above or in other cases. Assuming that forum choice is a strategic decision based on an analysis of the costs and opportunities related to one procedure or the other, it is important to delineate and discuss, as a result: first, the normative framework for the protection of indigenous peoples' rights in Europe; second, the extent to which the existing judicial review mechanisms and procedures are

[28] UN Human Rights Committee, *Kitok v Sweden*, UN Doc CCPR/C/33/D/197/1985 (1988); *Länsman v Finland*, UN Doc CCPR/C/52/D/511/1992 (1994); *Länsman v Finland*, UN Doc CCPR/C/58/D/671/1995 (1996); *Länsman v Finland*, UN Doc CCPR/C/83/D/1023/2001 (2005). The way the Committee envisages the protection of indigenous rights within the context of minority rights is clarified in General Comment no 23, The Rights of Minorities (Art 27), UN Doc CCPR/C/21/Rev 1/Add 5 (4 August 1994).

[29] The mechanism has been developed by the CERD itself to respond to problems requiring immediate attention and to prevent or limit the scale or number of serious violations of the Convention. See Report of the Committee on the Elimination of Racial Discrimination, 42nd Session, 1–19 March 1993, 43rd Session, 2–20 August 1993, annex III, UN Doc A/48/18; GAOR, 48th Session, Supplement no 18 (1993). See letters to the Russian Federation dated 11 March 2011 and 2 September 2011 expressing concern over the indigenous people from the Nanai District (Far East Russia) in relation to the new draft law on traditional fishing activities, which would reportedly negatively affect traditional economic activities by preventing them from selling fish for their livelihood. See Report of the Committee on the Elimination of Racial Discrimination, 78th Session, 14 February–11 March 2011, 79th Session, 8 August–2 September 2011, p 10, para 28, UN Doc A/66/18; GAOR, 66th Session, Supplement no 18 (2011). The letters are available at http://www.ohchr.org/EN/HRBodies/CERD/Pages/EarlyWarningProcedure.aspx.

[30] See Report of the Committee on the Elimination of Racial Discrimination, 62nd Session, 3–21 March 2003, 63rd Session, 4–22 August 2003, para 405, UN Doc A/58/18; GAOR, 58th Session, Supplement no 18 (2003) (concluding observations on Finland); Report of the Committee on the Elimination of Racial Discrimination, 48th Session, 26 February–15 March 1996, 49th Session, 5–23 August 1996, paras 139, 148, UN Doc A/51/18; GAOR, 51st Session, Supplement no 18 (1996) (concluding observations on Russian Federation); ibid paras 177, 189 (concluding observations on Finland); CESCR, E/2012/22, E/C 12/2011/3, Consideration of reports submitted by States parties (Russian Federation), para 153. See also L Pineschi, 'Cultural Diversity as a Human Right? General Comment No 21 of the Committee on Economic, Social and Cultural Rights' in S Borelli and F Lenzerini (eds), *Cultural Heritage, Cultural Rights, Cultural Diversity, New Developments in International Law* (Leiden, Brill Nijhoff, 2012) 27–53.

effectively accessible in practice; third, the extent to which the legal, institutional and jurisprudential framework has changed through the years and whether it currently provides an adequate level of protection.

III. ACCOMMODATING INDIGENOUS PEOPLES' RIGHTS WITHIN THE EUROPEAN CONVENTION OF HUMAN RIGHTS

The Council of Europe represents the main institutional context for the protection of human rights in Europe, including the rights of indigenous peoples. As part of it, the ECHR and its judicial review mechanism, the ECtHR, together with the Committee of Ministers that supervises the execution of judgments of the Court, concretely provide for the protection of such rights. The ECHR binds all the states of northern Europe in which indigenous peoples live—ie Norway, Denmark (including Greenland), Finland, Sweden and Russia—as well as all the EU member states in general. It follows that the European Court of Human Rights (ECtHR) would be in principle the competent regional court to deal with cases of alleged violations of indigenous peoples' human rights. However, as earlier anticipated, indigenous peoples' rights have not traditionally been on the agenda of the Council of Europe—the latter being more concerned with the rights of national, ethnic, or linguistic minorities—and this is reflected to a certain extent in both the quantity and the content of the jurisprudence of the ECtHR.

In a number of cases involving indigenous peoples, the ECtHR and (until its abolition in 1998) the European Commission of Human Rights, have addressed the situation of the Saami and Inuit indigenous populations and have examined the issue of alleged state interference with their natural resources and cultural heritage—mainly in relation to traditional hunting, reindeer herding and fishing rights—under the perspective of: the length of proceedings (ie under ECHR, Article 6); the right to peaceful enjoyment of possessions (ECHR Protocol I, Article 1); and the right to respect for private and family life (ECHR Article 8).[31] Even though the majority of these applications was declared inadmissible, the considerations made by the Court and the Commission elucidate the main contours of the extent to which indigenous peoples and their members are protected under the ECHR.

Firstly, ECtHR jurisprudence clarifies the locus standi criteria for submitting an application to the judicial organisms operating under the Convention in cases involving alleged violations of indigenous peoples' rights. This procedural aspect is particularly relevant in cases concerning indigenous peoples because of the

[31] *Handölsdalen v Sweden* App no 39013/04 (ECtHR, 30 March 2010) (violation of Art 6, length of proceedings); *Johtti Sapmelaccat Ry v Finland* App no 42969/98 (ECtHR, 18 January 2005) (inadmissible); *Könkämä v Sweden* App no 27033/95 (ECtHR, 25 November 1996) (inadmissible); *OB and Others v Norway* App no 15997/90 (ECtHR, 8 January 1993); *Östergren and Others v Sweden* App no 13572/88 (ECtHR, 1 March 1991) (inadmissible); *Hingitaq 53 and Others v Denmark* App no 18584/04 (ECtHR, 12 January 2006) (inadmissible).

strong relationship and frequent overlap between individual and collective rights. In two comparable cases brought by Saami against Sweden and Finland, the Commission and the Court, respectively, were called to decide on whether a government's decision to extend to the general public hunting and/or fishing rights in an area traditionally used by the Saami indigenous communities amounted to an unacceptable interference with their right to property in the form of immemorial land and water usage rights (ie rights established by custom). From the procedural perspective, the first case, *Könkämä and other 38 Saami villages v Sweden*, posed the issue of whether the Saami villages could correctly stand as applicants in the dispute.[32] The Commission acknowledged the responsibilities of the village as a legal person for the herding activities within the respective areas and that Saami individuals could exercise herding rights only as members of the village; it accordingly concluded that villages could correctly claim to be 'victims'—as 'non-governmental organisations' within the meaning of Article 34 of the Convention—of the violation of property rights.[33] In the more recent case, *Johtti Sapmelaccat RY and Others v Finland* while confirming the *Könkämä* ruling, the ECtHR missed the opportunity to give a broader interpretation of the locus standi requirement in the case of non-governmental organisations.[34] The Court denied victim status to Johtti Sapmelaccat RY, an association promoting Saami culture, of which all the other applicants of the case were members, arguing that the association was not responsible as such for fishing within its respective area and that fishing rights, as designated under Finnish law, could be exercised by a Saami only as a private individual. The Court thus confirmed the individual dimension of the human rights infringements in the context of the ECHR, at least from the procedural perspective: while indigenous peoples' organisations may in principle lodge applications on alleged violations of the rights of the Convention before the Court, this is only possible if the right specifically belongs to the organisation in question but not if the latter generally represents the rights and interests of indigenous peoples.

Secondly, as regards the material scope of protection, the Commission has clarified since the beginning that, although the Convention does not guarantee specific rights to members of indigenous minorities, such rights can nevertheless come within the scope of one of its provisions.[35] Accordingly, in the case of *G and*

[32] The European Commission of Human Rights, *Könkämä* case (decision on the admissibility of the application) above n 31.

[33] Art 34 stipulates that 'The Court may receive Applications from any person, nongovernmental organisation or group of individuals claiming to be the victim of a violation by one of the High Contracting Parties of the rights set forth in the Convention or the Protocols thereto'. More generally on land claims see G Otis and A Laurent, 'Indigenous land claims in Europe: The European Court of Human Rights and the decolonization of property' (2013) 4 *Arctic Review on Law and Politics* 156–80.

[34] ECtHR (Fourth Section), *Johtti Sapmelaccat* case (decision on the admissibility of the application) above n 31.

[35] *G and E v Norway* App nos 9278/81 & 9415/81 (ECtHR, 3 October 1983) (decision on the admissibility of the applications). The Commission however finally declared the application inadmissible, augmenting that any interference with the rights of the Lapps was proportionally small and was justified as being necessary for the economic well-being of the country.

E v Norway, the Commission addressed the detrimental effects of the erection of a hydroelectric power station in the Alta valley, on the traditional reindeer herding and fishing activities of two Norwegian Lapps (Saami people), as an issue of interference with their private life under Article 8 of the Convention. The extension of the concept of 'private and family life', under ECHR Article 8, to the right to cultural identity for indigenous peoples and their members, is a key element of the protection of their rights in Europe because, as earlier highlighted, all the other rights of this group rest on and are strongly related to the protection of cultural identity.

The importance of the link made by the Commission between the right to private life and indigenous peoples' rights grounded in their cultural tradition—although in an embryonic version—becomes even more evident in light of the fact that the ECHR enshrines mainly civil and political rights and that it contains no specific recognition of the rights of indigenous peoples or of cultural rights. It also needs to be stressed that the protective impact deriving from such interpretative finding is quite strong, especially if the scope and content of 'cultural tradition' is construed by analogy to the Court's case law concerning minority rights. For instance, in the *Chapman* case, the Grand Chamber had to examine the issue raised by a Gypsy applicant under Article 8 of the Convention,[36] namely, that measures interfering with her occupation of her land in caravans affected not only her home and property but also her 'private and family life as a Gypsy with a traditional lifestyle of living in mobile homes which allow travelling'.[37] Despite finding no effective violation in the concrete case, the ECtHR recognised that ECHR Article 8 protects the right to maintain a minority identity and to lead one's private and family life in accordance with the traditions forming an integral part of such identity.[38] Even more importantly, the Court acknowledged an emerging international consensus amongst the CoE members in recognising 'the special needs of minorities and an obligation to protect their security, identity and lifestyle … not only for the purpose of safeguarding the interests of the minorities themselves but to preserve a cultural diversity of value to the whole community'[39] and implicitly accredited the applicants' suggestion of a reduced margin of appreciation for states in these cases. The ECtHR also recognised that Article 8 entails positive obligations for the state 'to facilitate' minorities' way of life, especially as concerns 'vulnerable minorities'.[40]

[36] ECHR Art 8 states: '(1) Everyone has the right to respect for his private and family life, his home and his correspondence. (2) There shall be no interference by a public authority with the exercise of this right except such as is in accordance with the law and is necessary in a democratic society in the interests of national security, public safety or the economic well-being of the country, for the prevention of disorder or crime, for the protection of health or morals, or for the protection of the rights and freedoms of others.'

[37] *Chapman v United Kingdom* App no 27238/95 (ECtHR, 18 January 2001) (no violation).

[38] ibid, para 73.

[39] ibid para 93.

[40] ibid para 96.

In other cases concerning indigenous peoples the Commission and the Court have regarded immemorial hunting and fishing rights as a possession within the scope of the right to property under Article 1 of Protocol No 1 of the ECHR.[41] In particular, in *Handölsdalen Sami Village* concerning the restriction—as a result of a domestic court's judgment—of the applicants' right to use land for winter grazing, the Court not only reiterated that the right to reindeer grazing, as such, may constitute 'existing possession' within the meaning of ECHR Protocol No 1 but it additionally underlined that the scope of protection of the right to property also includes claims and 'legitimate expectations' of obtaining effective enjoyment of a property right.[42] An additional case considered by the Court under the perspective of the right to peaceful enjoyment of possessions (ECHR Protocol No 1 Article 1) concerned the application lodged by members of the Inuit community of the Thule district in Denmark, complaining that they had been deprived of their natural resources and cultural heritage as a consequence of an agreement between Denmark and the United States after WWII for the establishment of a US air base which had forced them to relocate.[43]

It should however be noted that despite the inclusion of indigenous rights issues (eg, protection of natural heritage and resources or rights of time immemorial) within the general protection coverage of the Convention, the ECtHR has almost always failed to identify a concrete breach by the state party concerned—either by denying the applicants' locus standi as victims, or by interpreting broadly the margin of appreciation of states in cases of interference with the rights established in the Convention or, in other cases, by strictly relying on the findings of the national courts. The ECHR system has thus not yet spread its full potential for the protection of the rights of indigenous peoples of Northern Europe. Yet, the Court has always found room to accommodate new societal concerns in its application of the Convention by insisting that the ECHR is a 'living instrument'.[44] It has done so, in particular, when new international instruments have developed on a certain subject and when the values behind them they are generally shared among the contracting regardless of whether such international instruments are binding or whether most CoE member states have ratified them.[45] Looking

[41] See for instance the *Könkämä* and *Johtti Sapmelaccat* cases, above n 31. On the concept of 'time immemorial' as a legal fiction in of 'antiquity' and 'legal memory' in relation to land titles in English law, and repurposed in indigenous rights cases in Canada see L Weir, '"Time Immemorial" and Indigenous Rights: A Genealogy and Three Case Studies (Calder, Van der Peet, Tsilhqot'in) from British Columbia' (2013) 26 *Journal of Historical Sociology* 383.

[42] *Handölsdalen* case, above n 31, paras 48, 51–52.

[43] *Hingitaq 53* case, above n 31.

[44] Among the first cases to employ this concept see *Tyrer v United Kingdom* App no 5856/72 (ECtHR, 25 April 1978) and *Van Der Mussele v Belgium* (Plenary) App no 8919/80 (ECtHR, 23 November 1983).

[45] See for instance *Russian Conservative Party of v Russia* App nos 55066/00 and 55638/00 (ECtHR, 11 January 2007), in which the Court referred to the reports of the 'Venice Commission'; *Bekos and Koutropoulos v Greece* App no 15250/02 (ECtHR, 13 December 2005), in which the Court referred to the reports of the European Commission Against Racism; *Christine Goodwin v United Kingdom*

forward, this is certainly the case of indigenous peoples' rights, as earlier noted, considering the adoption of international standards and guidelines, as well as the establishment within the UN system of institutions and bodies that specifically target indigenous peoples' concerns.

IV. THE PLACE OF INDIGENOUS PEOPLES' RIGHTS WITHIN THE EU FRAMEWORK

Indigenous peoples' issues have been on the EC/EU agenda since 1997, when the Council of Ministers invited the European Commission to present a document on the relation between indigenous peoples and the development process. Although the Commission's working document did not specifically address the internal (European) dimension of the phenomenon of indigenous peoples, it nevertheless underlined as a general point 'the weakness of the existing human rights framework, which does not account for the social, cultural and political rights claimed by indigenous peoples'.[46] However, Arctic indigenous peoples concerns, in particular as regards hunting and fishing rights, are protected by special provisions included by the interested member states in their act of accession to the EC/EU.[47]

The Treaty of Lisbon, currently in force, in several instances puts strong emphasis on the protection of the different cultural identities and traditions in Europe; however, the issue is approached in terms of the integration of non-trade interests among the trade objectives of the Union, rather than in terms of genuine respect and protection of human rights. The need to balance the objective of European integration with the respect of the multiple cultural traditions clearly emerges in the Preamble[48] of the Treaty on the European Union (TEU) and is reiterated in its Article 3(3), which pronounces, on the one hand, the objective of the establishment of the internal market and, on the other, the Union's commitment to 'respect its [of the Union] rich cultural and linguistic diversity' and to 'ensure that Europe's cultural heritage is safeguarded and enhanced'. Even more specifically, Article 167(1) of the Treaty on the Functioning of the European Union (TFEU) clarifies the scope of Union's involvement in the protection of cultural identities and heritage; it affirms that 'The Union shall contribute to the flowering of the cultures of the member states, while respecting their national and regional diversity and at the same time bringing the common cultural heritage to the fore'.

App no 28957/95 (ECtHR, 11 July 2002), in which the Court referred to the EU Charter of Fundamental Rights.

46 Working Document of the Commission of May 1998 on support for indigenous peoples in the development co-operation of the Community and the member states, p 6, http://eeas.europa.eu/human_rights/ip/docs/index_en.htm.

47 See Protocol 3 to the Act of Accession of Sweden, Finland and Norway (although the latter did not eventually accede because the membership issue was rejected in the national referendum).

48 The 6th consideration of the Preamble reads: 'Desiring to deepen the solidarity between their peoples while respecting their history, their culture and their traditions'.

It should however be noted that the responsibility for the protection and promotion of cultural identities and heritage rests primarily with each member state, while the Union's competence consists in supporting, coordinating and supplementing states' action in this area (competence ex-Art 6 TFEU).[49] At a minimum, this type of competence implies that Union legislation and activities should not negatively affect the right to cultural identity, including that of indigenous peoples living in the EU. This is implicitly recognised in Article 167(4) TFEU, which clarifies that 'The Union shall take cultural aspects into account in its action under other provisions of the Treaties, in particular in order to respect and to promote the diversity of its cultures.'[50]

The reference to 'cultural diversity' or to 'heritage' in these provisions of the treaties is very broad, and they certainly include indigenous peoples' culture and traditions (despite the absence of a specific allusion thereto) as it becomes evident in light of the EU policy on indigenous peoples and of the EU Arctic policy. Both policies are developed in the framework of the EU External Action; however, as earlier mentioned, some of the Arctic states in which indigenous peoples live are already member states of the EU—namely Finland, Sweden, Denmark (including Greenland)—and have included specific provisions on the protection of indigenous peoples living in their territories at the moment of accession.

In the context of the policy on indigenous peoples, the EU specifically supports the protection of the rights of indigenous peoples—in particular the full participation and free, prior and informed consent of indigenous peoples—trying to integrate such issues into the framework of its external policies and relations with third countries and regional organisations.[51] The EU Policy on the Arctic recognises the growing strategic importance of the Arctic area and the multiple implications of EU policies and legislation for Arctic stakeholders, and accordingly aims to collaboratively address common challenges;[52] it is the product of the EU's efforts to develop an integrated policy aimed at coordinating the activities of EU institutions and the different policies that may have an impact on this area. Among its strategic objectives it comprises the protection and preservation

[49] See Art 6(c) TFEU and Art 167(2), (5).

[50] Similarly, Art 107 TFEU allows state aid that promotes culture and heritage conservation in so far as it 'does not affect trading conditions and competition in the Union to an extent that is contrary to the common interest'.

[51] Joint statement by the Council and the representatives of the governments of the member states meeting within the Council, the European Parliament and the Commission on European Union Development Policy: 'The European Consensus' (2006/C 46/01), 24 February 2006, para 103.

[52] See especially European Parliament Resolution of 9 October 2008 on Arctic governance; Commission Communication of 20 November 2008 on the European Union and the Arctic Region (COM (2008) 0763). See also Council Conclusions on the European Union and the Arctic region of 8 December 2008; Council Conclusions on Arctic issues of 8 December 2009; European Parliament resolution of 20 January 2011 on a sustainable EU policy for the High North (2009/2214 (INI)); European Commission and High Representative of the European Union for Foreign Affairs and Security, Joint Communication to the European Parliament and the Council, Developing a European Union Policy towards the Arctic Region: progress since 2008 and next steps, JOIN(2012) 19 final, Brussels, 26 June 2012.

of the Arctic 'in unison with its population' and places great attention on issues relevant to indigenous peoples living in the region.[53] The EU policy on the Arctic also emphasises the importance of international cooperation that the EU tries to pursue through its engagement with the Arctic Council and its members. The Arctic Council represents an important forum for international cooperation in the region among the eight states facing the Arctic area—Canada, Denmark (including Greenland and the Faroe Islands), Finland, Iceland, Norway, Russian Federation, Sweden, and the United States of America—and the indigenous communities, whose representative organisations enjoy the status of permanent participants.[54] Additionally the Arctic Council grants to states, intergovernmental organisations and NGOs observer status allowing them to attend the meetings of the Arctic Council. During the 8th Ministerial Meeting of the Arctic Council in May 2013, in which Canada took the chairmanship until 2015, quite interestingly, the decision on the application of the EU for observer status was deferred until the issue of the EU Regulation on trade in seal products that has impeded EU-Canada relations for several years has been positively resolved.[55]

A. The EU Charter of Fundamental Rights

The Lisbon Treaty grants binding effects to the Charter of Fundamental Rights of the European Union[56] and affirms that it has the same status as the EU treaties.[57] Despite the absence of a specific reference to indigenous peoples in the EU Charter, its Preamble affirms that the Union respects 'the diversity of the cultures and traditions of the peoples of Europe', and Article 22 of the Charter reiterates

[53] Commission Communication of 20 November 2008 on the European Union and the Arctic Region (COM (2008) 0763).

[54] The Permanent Participants of the Arctic Council include organisations of indigenous peoples either representing a single people resident in more than one Arctic state, or more than one Arctic Indigenous people resident in a single Arctic state. They are: the Arctic Athabaskan Council (AAC), the Aleut International Association (AIA), the Gwich'in Council International (GCI), the Inuit Circumpolar Council (ICC), the Russian Association of Indigenous Peoples of the North (RAIPON) and the Saami Council (SC).

[55] See below on the jurisprudential developments of the controversy. See also Joint Statement by EU High Representative Catherine Ashton and EU Commissioner Maria Damanaki regarding Arctic Council decision on EU's observer status, A 255/13, Brussels, 15 May 2013, which states that 'the EU will now work expeditiously with them [the Canadian authorities] to address the outstanding issue of their concern'.

[56] The Charter of Fundamental Rights of the European Union was initially signed and proclaimed by the Presidents of the European Parliament, the Council and the Commission at the European Council meeting in Nice on 7 December 2000 [2000] OJ C364. On the drafting process of the Charter see G de Búrca, 'The drafting of the European Union charter of fundamental rights' (2001) 26 *European Law Review* 126–38; J Schönlau, *Drafting the EU Charter: Rights, Legitimacy and Process* (Hampshire, Palgrave Macmillan, 2005).

[57] Art 6.1 TEU stipulates that 'The Union recognizes the rights, freedoms and principles set out in the Charter of Fundamental Rights of the European Union of 7 December 2000, as adapted at Strasbourg, on 12 December 2007, which shall have the same legal value as the Treaties'.

that '[t]he Union shall respect cultural, religious and linguistic diversity'. But how and to what extent does the EU Charter affect the protection of the rights of indigenous peoples in Europe?

First, in order to avoid inconsistencies between international and EU obligations during the application of Union law, Article 52.3 establishes that

> [i]n so far as this Charter contains rights which correspond to rights guaranteed by the Convention for the Protection of Human Rights and Fundamental Freedoms, the meaning and scope of those rights shall be the same as those laid down by the said Convention …;

nevertheless, higher protection may be granted under Union law. The right to respect for private and family life and the right to property enshrined in the Charter[58] have a specific equivalent, respectively, in Article 8 ECHR and Article 1, Protocol 1 of the ECHR. Quite importantly, the Explanations relating to the Charter clarify that the reference to the ECHR covers both the Convention and its Protocols, and that the scope of the rights should be determined having regard to both the text of the Articles and the case law of the European Court of Human Rights (ECtHR) and of the European Court of Justice (ECJ).[59] It follows that the ECtHR jurisprudence on these rights will potentially inform the application of the provisions of the Charter in cases concerning indigenous peoples.

Second, even though the Charter enshrines a comprehensive binding catalogue of human rights, the peculiar character of the EU Charter as an instrument of Union law needs to be emphasised. The Preamble of the Charter stipulates that it is the Union that recognises the rights, freedoms and principles set out in that instrument, not the member states in their own right. Indeed, the scope of application of the provisions of the Charter is circumscribed to the areas of state activity ruled by Union law. In this regard, Article 51 of the Charter emphasises that 'The provisions of th[e] Charter are addressed to the institutions and bodies of the Union … and to the member states only when they are implementing Union law.' Accordingly, in the case of EU institutions, compliance with the Charter is a requirement for the validity and legality of EU secondary legislation.[60]

Third, from a substantial perspective, the Explanations relating to the Charter of Fundamental Rights clarify that Article 22 of the Charter is based on the above-mentioned Article 167(1) and (4) TFEU, which establishes an obligation for the Union to respect and to promote the diversity of its cultures by taking cultural aspects into account in its action under other provisions of the Treaties.[61] Given the different approach of the two provisions, namely, human rights protection on the one hand and balancing trade concerns and non-trade interests on the

[58] Respectively, in Arts 7 and 17 of the Charter.

[59] Explanations relating to the Charter of Fundamental Rights [2007] OJ C303/20, 23.

[60] As regards EU member states, instead, the Charter adds to the existing human rights obligations but does not modify them; member states remain nevertheless responsible (for instance under the ECHR or other human rights instruments) for potential violations of human rights, irrespective of whether they are implementing Union law or not.

[61] Explanations relating to the Charter of Fundamental Rights [2007] OJ C303/25.

other, how does the relationship between them translate in terms of obligations for the Union? When applied in relation to indigenous peoples, the expression 'taking cultural aspects into account' and the commitment to respect cultural diversity may, at a minimum, imply an obligation on the Union not to interfere in a detrimental way with the cultural and economic interests and rights of indigenous peoples when formulating and implementing its policies in fields, such as, agriculture, fisheries, transport, internal market, research and technological development defence etc; they may also entail a requirement to consult the interested communities before the adoption of EU action or legislation in the context of such policies. The provision of Article 22 TFEU, however, also needs to be read together with Article 7 TFEU, which establishes that the 'Union shall ensure consistency between its policies and activities, taking all of its objectives into account' and Article 13 TFEU which stipulates that the Union will 'pay full regard to the welfare requirements of animals' in its policies 'while respecting the legislative or administrative provisions and customs of the member states relating in particular to religious rites, cultural traditions and regional heritage'.

Against the background of the forthcoming accession to the ECHR the European Union is faced with the important challenge of finding the right balance between trade promotion, integration of non-trade interests in its policies and protection of human rights, including indigenous peoples' rights. To what extent and under what conditions can the Union interfere with the rights of indigenous peoples for the purpose of 'preventing the disturbance of the internal market' or for the protection and promotion of other non-economic values, such as animal welfare? The Union was recently faced with such complex questions in a recent case concerning seal hunting and involving the Arctic Inuit indigenous community.

B. The Case of *Inuit Tapiriit Kanatami and Others v Parliament and Council*

Following the adoption and enforcement of an EU Regulation introducing a controversial ban on the placement of seal products in the EU market,[62] a group of private applicants—including Inuit seal hunters and trappers' associations, organisations representing the interests of Inuit and individuals in another ways engaged in activities related to the processing of seal products—brought a case against the EU institutions before the EU Court of Justice.[63] Seal hunting represents a

[62] Regulation (EC) 1007/2009 of the European Parliament and of the Council on trade in seal products [2009] OJ L286/36. The Commission later adopted also an implementing regulation related to the ban: Commission Regulation (EU) 737/2010 laying down detailed rules for the implementation of Regulation (EC) 1007/2009 of the European Parliament and of the Council on trade in seal products [2010] OJ L216/1.

[63] The case is at the basis of different actions before the EU judicial system and involves two actions for annulment before the General Court concerning each of the two regulations: Case T-18/10 *Inuit Tapiriit Kanatami and Others v Parliament and Council*, action brought on 11 January 2010 and Case

traditional practice carried out for the purpose of personal consumption of seal meat, as well as for commercial trade of related by-products by the indigenous communities (mainly Inuit) living in the Arctic Circle. Although the ban enforced by the EU explicitly excludes from its scope of application traditional sealing by Inuit communities, it was (and it still is) expected that the overall demand on seal products will fall as a consequence of the impact of the ban on trading chains directed to Europe and this will likely adversely affect the fundamental economic and social interests of the indigenous communities engaged in sealing as a means to ensure their subsistence.

Accordingly, from a substantive point of view, the applicants contested that the Regulation introduced undue limits to their subsistence possibilities.[64] They claimed that the EU institutions failed to weigh the surviving interests of the Arctic Inuit people against the moral convictions of some citizens in the Union concerning animal welfare, thereby violating Article 1 of Protocol I ECHR on the right to property and the right to private and family life under Article 8 ECHR read in light of the freedom of thought, conscience and religion (ECHR Article 9) and the freedom of expression (Article 10) and the fundamental right to be heard.[65] These are challenging questions that address the core issue of the extent to which interference with the rights enshrined in the EU Charter and corresponding to ECHR rights can be tolerated in order to pursue trade interests or non-trade related objectives. The Court however sidestepped the analysis of the merits of these issues by declaring the application inadmissible for lack of locus standi, in particular, for lack of 'direct and individual concern' under Art 263(4) TFEU. Nevertheless some of the Court's considerations and observations deserve some short comments here.

First, the Court's restrictive interpretation of the conditions upon which natural or legal persons may contest EU acts, although justifiable to some extent, has an important impact on the substantial protection of their rights and raises the important issue of the extent to which the EU judicial system is compatible with the right to effective access to judicial remedies stipulated in both the ECHR and the EU Charter of Fundamental Rights. Indeed, the right of access to an effective

T-526/10 *Inuit Tapiriit Kanatami and Others v Commission*, action brought on 11 November 2011. In relation to the first action for annulment, an appeal was lodged before the EU Court of Justice, Case C-583/11 P *Inuit Tapiriit Kanatami and Others v European Parliament, Council of the European Union, Kingdom of the Netherlands, European Commission*, Appeal brought on 23 November 2011 by Inuit Tapiriit Kanatami et al against the Order of the General Court (Seventh Chamber, Extended Composition) delivered on 6 September 2011 in Case T-18/10 [2011] EUR II-05599. In relation to the first action for annulment, the applicants also submitted to the President of the GC two requests for provisional suspension of the application of the disputed Regulations until the decision on annulment had been rendered: Case T-18/10 R *Inuit Tapiriit Kanatami and Others v Parliament and Council*, Application of 11 February 2010; Case T-18/10 R II, *Inuit Tapiriit Kanatami and Others v Parliament and Council*, Application of 28 July 2010. See generally J Beqiraj, 'The Delicate Equilibrium of EU Trade Measures: The Seals Case' (2013) 14 *German Law Journal* 279–320.

[64] Case T-18/10 *Inuit Tapiriit Kanatami and Others v Parliament and Council* [2010] OJ C100/64.
[65] ibid.

remedy is guaranteed today under Article 47 of the EU Charter of Fundamental Rights,[66] and the right to effective judicial protection was along ago recognised by the ECJ as a general principle of community law stemming from the constitutional traditions common to member states.[67]

Secondly, in relation to the type of interest that the applicants must have for bringing a case, the Court took the view that the responsibility for protecting general economic, social and cultural interests rests with states or local intra-state bodies; but since no entity of this kind was among the applicants, the latter could not rely on the general interests of the Inuit population in the proceedings for interim measures.[68] The suggestion that group rights—in the case at issue, indigenous peoples' rights—can only be voiced through states or intra-state bodies, and that non-governmental organisations or associations set up for the purpose of promoting and strengthening the rights of such groups have no power in this regard points out the problematic issue of the scope and purpose of EU judicial review: to what extent does it also include the protection of diffuse public interests against legislative or administrative abuse?[69] By overlooking the important presence among the applicants of the Inuit Circumpolar Council (ICC) Greenland, and by requiring that each of the applicants, taken individually, should have adduced pertinent evidence to show that the Regulation would have caused him personally serious and irreparable harm if no suspension was granted,[70] the Court obviously dismisses the collective argument of the harm produced by the

[66] Art 47 of the EU Charter reads: 'Everyone whose rights and freedoms guaranteed by the law of the Union are violated has the right to an effective remedy before a tribunal in compliance with the conditions laid down in this Article'.

[67] Case C-222/84 *Johnston v Chief Constable of the Royal Ulster Constabulary* [1986] ECR 1651, para 18.

[68] Case T-18/10 R II, Order of the President of the General Court, 25 October 2010, para 52.

[69] Individual and group standing to challenge EU measures directly before the EU Court(s) is, and has been, extremely restrictive. By definition the 'individual concern' test is hardly satisfied by groups or associations representing public interests: Case T-447–9/93 *AITEC v Commission*; Case C-358/89 *Extramet Industrie SA v Council of the European Communities* [1991] ERC I-2501; Case C-309/89 *Codorníu v Council* [1994] ECR I-1853; Case T-38/98 *Associazione Nazionale Bieticltori v Council* [1998] ECR II-4191, paras 25–29. However, in relation to applicants claiming non-purely economic interests, the ECJ has constantly denied locus standi: Case T-585/93 *Greenpeace and Others v Commission* [1995] ECR II-2205, paras 59–62; Joined cases T-236/04 and T-241/04 *European Environmental Bureau (EEB) and Stichting Natuur en Milieu v Commission* [2005] ECR II-04945; Case T-91/07 *WWF–UK Ltd v Council* [2008] ECR II-81. On the doctrinal debate see JM Cortés Martín, 'Ubi ius, Ibi Remedium?: Locus Standi of Private Applicants under Article 230 (4) EC at a European Constitutional Crossroads' (2004) 11 *Maastricht Journal of European and Comparative Law* 233; A Cygan, 'Protecting the Interests of Civil Society in Community Decision-making: The limits of Article 230 EC' (2003) 52 *The International and Comparative Law Quarterly* 995; C Harlow, 'Access to justice as a human right' in P Alston (ed), *The EU and Human Rights* (Oxford, Oxford University Press, 1999) 187, 194; D Chalmers, G Davies and G Monti, *European Union Law* (Cambridge, Cambridge University Press, 2010) 425.

[70] Case T-18/10 R II, Order of the President of the General Court, 25 October 2010, para 54.

Regulation to the surviving interests of the Arctic Inuit Community in general and thus rejects a broader reading of the purposes of EU judicial review.[71]

The EU measures triggered a strong reaction, not only from indigenous people living in the Arctic region, but also from neighbouring states, in particular Canada and Norway, who raised a dispute before the WTO dispute resolution mechanisms.[72] In its very recent report, the WTO Appellate Body declared the EU Regulation incompatible with the WTO rules, but it is worth underlining here that the approach to the disputed issue in the WTO application is fundamentally different from the EU dispute approach. To begin with, it is dispute between WTO members, ie governments and/or intergovernmental organisations. Under WTO rules, individuals and groups, including both indigenous communities and firms operating in the seal products industry, do not have the right to be heard or the right to participate in the proceedings, except for the limited possibility that written briefs are accepted to be considered by the panels or the Appellate Body, which is at their discretion.[73] Moreover, the WTO approaches the disputed issue from the perspective of the restrictions on trade and the problem of the impact of the EU measure on indigenous peoples' rights is only incidentally and indirectly addressed.

The seals case is a paradigmatic example of the complexity and interrelatedness of different sectors and subject areas of international law, which inevitably have a bearing on the ability of States (and of the Union) to freely pursue policy choices based on ethical, social, or environmental concerns while being compliant with human rights obligations. The intersectional nature of the seals case, additionally, signals an important procedural gap in the access to justice remedies for indigenous peoples which ultimately affects how their rights are judicially enforced and redressed in practice.

The general unsuitability of the WTO dispute settlement system for dealing with indigenous peoples concerns was already underlined. In the seals case, the

[71] ICC Greenland is a member of the Inuit Circumpolar Council, an Indigenous Peoples' NGO representing approximately 160,000 Inuit living in the Arctic regions of Alaska, Canada, Greenland and Chukotka, Russia. The ICC holds consultative status to the United Nations Economic and Social Council (ECOSOC).

[72] Request for the establishment of a Panel by Canada, WT/DS400/4, 14 February 2011; Request for the establishment of a Panel by Norway, WT/DS401/5, 15 March 2011. Argentina, China, Colombia, Ecuador, Iceland, Japan, Mexico, Norway and the United States joined as third parties. At its meeting on 25 March 2011, the DSB established a panel. China, Colombia, Iceland, Japan, Mexico, Norway and the United States and subsequently Argentina, Ecuador and the Russian Federation reserved their third party rights. The two requests were addressed by a single panel. The Report of the panel was circulated on 25 November 2013 and the Appellate Body report was circulated to the Members on 22 May 2014.

[73] The issue of the admissibility of *amicus curiae* submissions in WTO dispute settlement proceedings is highly contentious. However, the Appellate Body has confirmed the panels' discretion as well as its own authority to accept or reject information and advice from interested entities, which are neither parties nor third parties to the dispute: *US—Import Prohibition of Certain Shrimp and Shrimp Products*, WT/DS58/AB/R, 6 November 1998, paras 105–08; *US—Imposition of Countervailing Duties on Certain Hot-Rolled Lead and Bismuth Carbon Steel Products Originating in the United Kingdom*, WT/DS138/AB/R, 7 June 2000, para 43.

fact that the measure originated at the EU level also rendered potentially unsuitable and incomplete the procedure before the ECHR from a human rights protection perspective. First, this is because—as earlier discussed—the ECHR lacks a well-established case law that strongly and extensively protects the cultural, social and economic values of the members belonging to minorities and indigenous peoples. Second, the procedure would have in any case addressed only the situation in single states, not the overall effects of the EU Regulations because the EU has not yet acceded to the ECHR. Moreover, applicants can bring claims in relation to violations occurred under the jurisdiction of one of the member states, and this would have left out part of the applicants in the *Inuit Tapiriit Kanatami and Others* case, such as the Inuit indigenous communities of Canada. This consideration is very important and sheds light on the problem of the protection of the rights of indigenous peoples that live in the territories of more states: failure to recognise a collective dimension of their rights strongly affects the enjoyment of their rights in practice. Finally, it should be recalled that individual applications to the ECtHR are admissible upon previous exhaustion of effective domestic remedies and this requirement is quite burdensome for individual applicants by reason of often unreasonably protracted national procedures.

V. CONCLUSIONS

In the Preamble and in different Articles of the EU Treaties (Article 3 TEU, Articles 13, 167 TFEU) respect for cultural diversity is recognised as a relevant EU value that needs to be promoted and mainstreamed into EU action and policies. The EU policy on the Arctic comprises among its strategic objectives the protection and preservation of the Arctic 'in unison with its population' and places great attention on issues relevant to indigenous peoples living in the region. From a human rights perspective, notwithstanding the absence of a specific reference to indigenous peoples in the ECHR, cases of alleged violations of their members' rights (in particular cultural identity considered under the right to property or the right to private and family life) have been every now and then brought before the ECtHR. Additional principles drawn from the case law on minorities can be applied to them by analogy. Nevertheless, whether indigenous peoples' interests are considered in the context of the promotion of non-trade interests such as cultural diversity or in the framework of the protection of human rights under the EU Charter of Fundamental Rights and the ECHR, states and the European Union are called upon to reconcile multiple interests and concerns as it becomes apparent in the Union's efforts to develop an integrated policy for the Arctic aimed at coordinating the activities of EU institutions and the different policies that may have an impact on this area. As the analysis of the seals case shows, while the Union has embarked upon a very narrow path leading to a difficult and delicate reconciliation between the demands for animal welfare, protection of indigenous peoples' rights and measures directed at the elimination of barriers to trade in the internal market, access to mechanisms of judicial review of such decisions is of crucial importance in this process. The seals case is a paradigmatic example of these challenges because it sheds light on the substantial and procedural protection gaps for indigenous peoples within the EU, the ECHR, and the WTO—particularly as regards the important weaknesses of the review procedure taking place before the ECJ related to the requirements for individual standing, the failure to take into adequate consideration the collective dimension of the human rights of indigenous peoples at both EU and ECHR levels and the 'self-contained' character of the WTO system and overemphasis on trade interests. Because of its multi-sector impact, the seals case also raises the problem of how to reconcile the conflicting interests pursued by state policies with different but contextually applicable obligations under international law. The general picture that currently emerges is a fragmented one, in which different systems operate on the basis of their own rules with occasional consideration of external sources. Finally, the proliferation of judicial courts and bodies as a consequence of the expansion of international law and the lack of circulation of legal solutions across sectors intensify the internal weaknesses that characterise each system. Different outcomes are to be expected depending on the focus of each system, which in turn stimulates considerations of opportunity and forum shopping logics and increases the unpredictability of disputes' final outcome. However, whether a non-trade interest to be mainstreamed in EU's economic policies or a human right protected under the ECHR and the EU Charter, the main challenge to the protection and promotion of indigenous peoples' cultural identity in Europe is a procedural one related to their access to effective remedies.

9

The Protection of Religious Minorities in Europe: Strengths and Weaknesses

ERICA HOWARD

I. INTRODUCTION

OVER THE LAST 50 years, many European countries have seen an influx of migrants from many different parts of the world. These migrants have often been from different religions to the dominantly Christian population of these countries. Whereas the European countries have become more secularised in terms of traditional religious practices, with many Christians seeing religion as a private rather than a public issue, the incoming migrants often practise and promote their religion in a much more public manner. This has led to debates about whether the newcomers, with their different religions, should be able to manifest their religion without interference in areas such as employment and education and in public spaces. For example, issues have arisen when considering whether such religious migrants should be given time off work to attend to religious duties or to make pilgrimage, or whether they can wear their religious attire, like turbans and head scarves, to work or to school. Similar requests are also sometimes made by Christian people, but it must not be forgotten that many European countries are based on Christian values and follow a Christian calendar, with Sundays, the day of Christian worship, a traditional day of rest and many Christian festivals, such as Christmas and Easter, official holidays. Because the holy days of religious minorities fall on different days and at different times of the year, religious minorities are more vulnerable to restrictions on the manifestations of their beliefs by their employers or by service providers. This vulnerability is compounded by the fact that, because these groups manifest their religious belief in much more open and public ways, they are easily identifiable as religious minorities. As they are also often part of an ethnic minority, they are even more vulnerable to becoming the target of discrimination and of anti-religious and anti-immigrant or anti-foreigner attitudes.

This chapter contains an examination of the legal protection given by EU law, both through the EU Charter of Fundamental Rights (EUCFR) and the EU anti-discrimination measures, and by the Council of Europe's European Convention for the Protection of Human Rights and Fundamental Freedoms (ECHR) to people from religious minorities who are restricted, by the state or by their public or private employer or by any other public or private organisation, in practising their religion in a public way, either alone or in community with others. This legal protection in EU law and in the ECHR is mainly provided under two different headings: via guarantees of the right to freedom of religion; and, via the prohibition of discrimination on the ground of a person's religion or belief. The legal measures and the way they have been interpreted in the case law of the relevant courts will be discussed and their effectiveness in protecting religious minorities will be analysed.

Before doing this, some attention needs to be given to the definitions of the terms 'religious minority', and 'religion' and 'belief'. The term 'religious minority' is not used in the ECHR or in the EU legal instruments providing protection of the freedom of religion and against religious discrimination, discussed here. For example, the only mention of minorities in the ECHR is found in Article 14, the article that prohibits discrimination on a number of grounds, which include 'association with a national minority', while the EUCFR only mentions 'membership of a national minority' in Article 21, which also contains a prohibition of discrimination on a large number of grounds. Even in other human rights instruments, a formal legal definition of both the terms 'minority' and 'religious minority' is absent, as Henrard[1] notes. She continues that, despite this absence, 'it is broadly acknowledged that it concerns non-dominant groups with a distinct religious identity, that are a numerical minority within a given territory, and that wish to hold on to that identity'.[2] In the following, the term 'religious minority' will be understood in this way.

The definitions of 'religion' and 'belief', the terms used in the EUCFR, in EU anti-discrimination law and in Article 9 ECHR also need to be discussed. There is no definition of what constitutes 'religion or belief' in any of these instruments, but the European Commission of Human Rights (ECnHR) and the European Court of Human Rights (ECtHR)[3] have given a wide interpretation to the term. All traditional religions and beliefs are covered, but also beliefs such as druidism, the Church of Scientology, pacifism, veganism and atheism.[4]

In *Campbell and Cosans v United Kingdom*,[5] the ECtHR explained that, to qualify for protection, a religious or philosophical conviction or belief must attain

[1] K Henrard, 'Minority Specific Rights: A Protection of Religious Minorities Going Beyond the Freedom of Religion' (2009) 8 *European Yearbook of Minority Issues* 5, 7.

[2] ibid.

[3] The ECnHR existed until 1998. Protocol 11 ECHR, which came into force in 1998, abolished the ECnHR, enlarged the ECtHR and allowed individuals to take cases directly to the Court.

[4] Druidism: *Chappell v United Kingdom* (1990) 12 EHRR 1; Church of Scientology: *X and Church of Scientology v Sweden* (1979) 16 DR 68; Pacifism: *Arrowsmith v United Kingdom* (1981) 3 EHRR 218; Veganism: *W v United Kingdom* (1995) 19 EHRR CD 60; Atheism: *Angeleni v Sweden* (1988) 10 EHRR CD 123.

[5] *Campbell and Cosans v United Kingdom* (1982) 4 EHRR 293.

a certain level of cogency, seriousness, cohesion and importance; must be worthy of respect in a democratic society; must not be incompatible with human dignity; and must relate to a weighty and substantial aspect of human life and behaviour. The wide interpretation of the terms 'religion' and 'belief' is likely to be followed by the EU and the Court of Justice of the EU (CJEU), as will be explained in the next part.

However, the above raises the question: who determines whether a belief is seriously held and attains a level of cogency, seriousness, cohesion and importance, and thus attracts protection under human rights and anti-discrimination laws? Is a person's religion or belief not very personal and subjective? What is the task of a court in relation to this? The ECtHR has held, in both *Manoussakis v Greece* and in *Hasan and Chaush v Bulgaria,* that 'the right to freedom of religion as guaranteed under the Convention excludes any discretion on the part of the State to determine whether religious beliefs or the means used to express such beliefs are legitimate'.[6] This suggests that courts should only be concerned with making sure that an assertion of religious belief is made in good faith, but they should not assess the validity or correctness of a belief.

One more issue will have to be pointed out: not only do the European instruments discussed here not use the term 'religious minority', the rights provided are mainly framed as rights of individuals, or, as Bowring writes about the protection given by the ECHR, 'it protects the rights of individuals, physical and legal, and of groups of individuals, but not of groups as such'.[7] The same can be said for the protection provided by the EUCFR and the EU anti-discrimination measures. Therefore, all these instruments have a clear focus on individual rights, although there are important group aspects of these rights which are also protected, as will be made clear in the following.

II. RELIGIOUS MINORITIES AND THE EU

A. Protection of Religious Minorities under the EU Charter of Fundamental Rights

Under EU law, religious minorities enjoy protection in different ways. Their right to freedom of religion is guaranteed by Article 10 of the EUCFR, while Article 21 EUCFR contains a prohibition of discrimination on a large number of grounds, including religion or belief. The EUCFR has been given legally binding force

[6] *Manoussakis and Others v Greece* (1997) 23 EHRR 387, para 47 and *Hasan and Chaush v Bulgaria* (2002) 34 EHRR 55, para 78.

[7] B Bowring, 'Protecting Minority Rights Through an Individual Rights Mechanism: the Strasbourg Court and Some Significant Developments to June 2012' (2011) 10 *European Yearbook of Minority Issues*, www.academia.edu/1890245/Protecting_minority_rights_through_an_individual_rights_mechanism_the_Strasbourg_Court_and_some_significant_developments_to_June_2012.

by Article 6 TEU. EU law also contains a prohibition of discrimination on the grounds of religion or belief in Directive 2000/78/EC.[8]

Article 10(1) EUCFR, which corresponds to Article 9 ECHR, states that everyone has the right to freedom of thought, conscience and religion, including the freedom to change religion or belief and the freedom, either alone or in community with others, and in public or in private, to manifest one's religion or belief, in worship, teaching, practice and observance. Article 52(3) EUCFR determines that, if rights in the Charter correspond to rights guaranteed in the ECHR, the meaning and scope of those rights shall be the same as those in the Convention. The Explanations make it clear that this includes limitations and that the reference to the ECHR includes the text and the Protocols as well as the case law of the ECtHR and the CJEU.[9] This is why the EU is likely to follow the interpretation of the terms 'religion' and 'belief' of the ECtHR.

As mentioned, Article 21 EUCFR prohibits discrimination on the ground of religion and belief, among an extensive list of grounds. However, neither Article 10 nor Article 21 gives any indication as to whether restrictions on these rights are allowed, but Article 52(1) EUCFR determines that any limitation on the exercise of the rights and freedoms in the Charter must be: 'provided for by law and respect the essence of those rights and freedoms'; and 'subject to the principle of proportionality'. Furthermore, they 'may be made only if they are necessary and genuinely meet objectives of general interest recognised by the Union or the need to protect the rights and freedoms of others'. According to the Explanations to the Charter,[10] this is based on the case law of the CJEU which held, in *Karlsson and Others*,[11] that restrictions may be imposed on the exercise of fundamental rights provided that those restrictions 'do not constitute, with regard to the aim pursued, disproportionate and unreasonable interference undermining the very substance of those rights'. This is what is often referred to as an objective justification test: the restriction must have a legitimate aim and the means used to achieve that aim must be proportionate and necessary. A similar test can also be found in EU anti-discrimination law and in the ECHR as interpreted by the ECtHR, as will become clear in the following.

B. Protection of Religious Minorities under EU Anti-Discrimination Law

Apart from the protection provided in Articles 10 and 21 EUCFR, in Directive 2000/78/EC the EU also prohibits discrimination on the ground of religion or belief. However, this Directive is only applicable in the area of employment and

[8] Directive 2000/78/EC establishing a general framework for equal treatment in employment and occupation [2000] OJ L303/16.

[9] Explanations relating to the Charter of Fundamental Rights [2007] OJ C 303/33.

[10] ibid.

[11] Case C-292/97 *Karlsson and Others* [2000] ECR I-2737, para 45.

occupation, including vocational training.[12] Thus, EU law does not protect members of religious minorities against discrimination on the basis of their religion or belief outside these areas, although many EU member states have gone beyond the minimum requirements of the Directive and have extended the protection provided by their national laws against religious discrimination beyond these fields.

Article 2 of the Directive prohibits both direct and indirect discrimination. Direct discrimination shall be taken to occur where one person is treated less favourably than another is, has been or would be treated in a comparable situation, on the ground of their religion or belief. Indirect discrimination shall be taken to occur where an apparently neutral provision, criterion or practice would put persons of a particular religion or belief at a particular disadvantage compared with other persons unless that provision, criterion or practice is objectively justified by a legitimate aim and the means of achieving that aim are appropriate and necessary. An example would be a workplace rule that nobody could take Fridays off because this is the busiest day of the week. This would be a neutral rule applicable equally to all employees, but Muslim employees, who wanted to attend prayers at the mosque, would be put at a particular disadvantage. It will be clear that indirect discrimination gives more attention to the group aspect of the protected minority groups.

However, people belonging to religious minorities are also often from a non-Western ethnic origin, and thus discrimination against them could well amount to indirect racial or ethnic origin discrimination. Directive 2000/43/EC[13] provides protection against direct and indirect discrimination on the grounds of racial and ethnic origin and has a much wider material scope than Directive 2000/78/EC, as, apart from employment and occupation, it also covers social protection, including social security and health care, social advantages, education and access to and supply of goods and services.

Religious minorities are thus protected against both direct and indirect discrimination. The protection given against direct religious discrimination in Directive 2000/78/EC is strong, because direct discrimination cannot be justified unless expressly provided for in the Directive (Article 4(1) and (2) allow for genuine and determining occupational requirements and Article 7 allows for certain forms of positive action, both of which will be discussed below). It is submitted that the protection of people belonging to religious minorities against indirect discrimination is also strong because, although indirect discrimination, as will be clear from the definition given, can be objectively justified, it can be argued

[12] The Directive prohibits discrimination on the grounds of religion and belief, disability, age and sexual orientation. COM (2008) 426, Proposal for a Council Directive implementing the principle of equal treatment between persons irrespective of religion or belief, disability, age or sexual orientation extends the material scope of Directive 2000/78/EC beyond the area of employment, but this proposal has not been adopted to date.

[13] Directive 2000/43/EC implementing the principle of equal treatment between persons irrespective of racial or ethnic origin [2000] OJ L180/22.

that this test includes a duty to consider whether religious or other practices can be accommodated. In *Bilka Kaufhaus*,[14] the CJEU held, in relation to indirect sex discrimination, that this test consists of three parts: the means chosen must correspond to a real need, they must be appropriate with a view to achieving the objective pursued, and they must be necessary to that end. This includes a consideration of the question whether there is an alternative, less far-reaching and less discriminatory way of achieving the aim pursued.[15] This clearly means that the interests of the individual applicant must be taken into account and weighed in the balance and, if there is an alternative which affects the individual less, then that should be chosen. This comes close to considering whether reasonable accommodation for people from (religious) minorities should be made.[16] As the CJEU generally aims at a uniform application of EU law, it is likely to hold that the same standard of justification should be applied to all grounds of discrimination, including religion and belief.

Article 4(1) Directive 2000/78/EC contains an exception for occupational requirements in situations where being of a particular religion or belief (or having any of the other characteristics covered by the Directive),[17] is a genuine and determining occupational requirement of a job due to the nature of the particular occupational activities concerned or of the context in which they are carried out. In such cases, provided that the objective is legitimate and the requirement proportionate, there is no discrimination. So this provision is also subject to an objective justification test.

However, there is a further exception in Article 4(2) Directive 2000/78/EC which only applies to religion and belief. There are two parts to Article 4(2). The first covers occupational activities within churches and other public or private organisations with an ethos based on religion or belief. In this case, a difference in treatment based on a person's religion or belief will not be discriminatory where, by reason of the nature of these activities or of the context in which they are carried out, a person's religion or belief constitutes a genuine, legitimate and justified occupational requirement, having regard to the organisation's ethos. This difference of treatment should not justify discrimination on another ground. This suggests that, for example, an Islamic school could require a teacher who is involved in leading worship or teaching religion to be of the Islamic faith but it could not require cleaners to be of the Islamic faith, as the nature and context of their activities do not require this.[18]

[14] Case C-170/84, *Bilka Kaufhaus GMBH v Karin Weber von Hartz* [1986] ECR 1607, para 36.

[15] D Schiek, 'Indirect Discrimination', in D Schiek, L Waddington and M Bell (eds), *Cases, Materials and Text on National, Supernational and International Non-Discrimination Law* (Oxford, Hart Publishing, 2007) 357.

[16] See: E Howard, 'Reasonable Accommodation of Religion and Other Discrimination Grounds in EU Law' (2013) 38, 3 *European Law Review* 360–75.

[17] Art 4 Directive 2000/43/EC contains the same exception.

[18] See: M Bell, 'Direct Discrimination', in Schiek, Waddington and Bell above n 15, 308–09.

The second part of Article 4(2) determines that churches and other organisations with an ethos based on religion or belief can require individuals working for them to act in good faith and with loyalty to the organisation's ethos, provided that the Directive's provisions are otherwise complied with. So, they can impose requirements on employees in relation to their behaviour and conduct.

Therefore, Article 4(1) and (2) provide churches and other religious organisations with some freedom in relation to whom they can employ or appoint, and a way of protecting their religious ethos. However, this freedom is not unlimited, and both paragraphs contain limitations. Article 4(1) contains an objective justification test, while both parts of Article 4(2) contain the proviso that there should be no discrimination on any other ground protected under EU anti-discrimination measures. This suggests that an organisation with a religious ethos would not be able to refuse to employ someone because they are homosexual, as this would mean discrimination on another prohibited ground.

Article 7 Directive 2000/78/EC and Article 5 Directive 2000/43/EC, under the heading 'positive action' determine that, '*with a view of ensuring full equality in practice*, the principle of equal treatment shall not prevent any Member State from maintaining or adopting specific measures to prevent or compensate for disadvantages linked to' the grounds protected by the two Directives, including religion or belief and racial or ethnic origin [emphasis added]. Both Directives mention in their Preambles that such measures may permit the existence of organisations of persons of a particular religion or belief or of a particular racial or ethnic origin where their main object is the promotion of the special needs of those persons.

So, both Directives allow for positive action measures—special measures aimed at compensating for the social inequalities and disadvantages suffered by certain minority groups. Positive action thus has a clear group aspect. The articles mention 'ensuring full equality in practice', and this is important for religious minorities. Equality before the law or formal equal treatment (or equality of consistency) consists of treating like alike, treating people in similar situations in the same way. But this ignores the fact that treating people in the same way might not lead to full equality in practice. Treating everyone in the same way, for example, applying the same rule to every employee in a company, ignores the fact that some employees might not be able to comply with this rule because of their religion or belief. Therefore, people who are not in the same situation should be treated differently, something that is recognised within the concept of indirect discrimination and, to an even greater extent, in the concept of positive action.[19]

Prohibitions of indirect discrimination, especially if these are interpreted as including a duty of reasonable accommodation of minorities, and positive action measures recognise that some people belonging to particular minority groups are unable to enjoy true equality in access to employment or services and are unable

[19] See also: K Henrard, *Equal Rights v Special Rights? Minority Protection and the Prohibition of Discrimination* (Luxembourg, Office for Official Publications of the European Communities, 2007).

to participate fully in society. In order to create full equality in practice, these groups should be treated differently according to their needs and states should take special legislative and administrative measures to prevent or correct situations of inequality.

This could be a very strong aspect of the protection provided for religious minorities by EU anti-discrimination law. However, a number of issues could limit this provision. First, the Directives allow member states to take positive action measures, but they do not require them to do so. Second, much will also depend on the interpretation of these provisions by the CJEU and there is as yet no case law on this, except in relation to positive action in relation to gender. If the CJEU interprets these provisions in the same way it has interpreted Article 2(4) Directive 76/207/EEC[20] and Article 157 TFEU concerning positive action in relation to gender, then it will exclude programmes which involve automatic preferential treatment at the point of selection for employment, although it does seem to accept a wide range of measures prior to that point.[21] A third issue that could limit this provision is that the CJEU has always held that restrictions and limitations to individual rights in EU law, including the right not to be discriminated against, should be interpreted strictly.[22] Positive action is seen as a derogation of the right to equal treatment, as it involves more favourable treatment of people belonging to a certain group, and thus it should be interpreted strictly.

Article 2(5) Directive 2000/78/EC also contains a general clause which appears to allow exceptions to its provisions. This article reads:

> This Directive shall be without prejudice to measures laid down by national law which, in a democratic society, are necessary for public security, for the maintenance of public order and the prevention of criminal offences, for the protection of health and for the protection of the rights and freedoms of others.

This exception is similar to the exception found in Article 9(2) ECHR and 'necessary in a democratic society', in that the article has been interpreted by the ECtHR as meaning that the interference complained of must correspond to a pressing

[20] Directive 76/207/EEC on the implementation of the principle of equal treatment for men and women as regards access to employment, vocational training and promotion, and working conditions [1976] OJ L39/40. This Directive has been replaced by Directive 2006/54/EC on the implementation of the principle of equal opportunities and equal treatment of men and women in matters of employment and occupation (recast) [2006] OJ L204/23. The positive action provision can be found in Art 3 of the latter Directive and this refers to Art 141(4) EC, which is now Art 157 TFEU.

[21] See: Case C-450/931 *Kalanke v Freie Hansestadt Bremen* [1995] ECR I-3051; Case C-409/95 *Marschall v Land Nordrhein-Westfalen* [1997] I-6363; Case C-158/1997 *Badeck's Application* [2000] ECR I-1875; Case C-407/98 *Abrahamsson and Anderson v Fogelqvist* [2000] ECR I-5539; Case C-476/99 *Lommers v Ministerie van Landbouw, Natuurbeheer en Visserij* [2002] ECR I-2891; and, Case C-319/03 *Briheche v Ministre de l'Interieur, Minstre de l'Education Nationale and Ministre de la Justice* [2004] ECR I-8807.

[22] See: Case C-222/83 *Johnston v Chief Constable of the Royal Ulster Constabulary* [1986] ECR 1651, para 36. Repeated recently in relation to Directive 2000/78/EC in: Case 341/08 *Petersen v Berufungsausschuss für Zahnärzte für den Bezirk Westfalen-Lippe* [2010] IRLR 254, para 60; and Case C-447/09 *Prigge and Others v Deutsche Lufthansa AG* [2011] ECR I-8003, paras 56 and 72.

social need, must be proportionate to the legitimate aim pursued and be justified by relevant and sufficient reasons.[23] Therefore, here too, an objective justification test is used, with the legitimate aims laid down in the article itself.

C. Conclusion on the Protection of Religious Minorities under EU Law

To date, the CJEU has not been asked to decide on any cases under Articles 10 or 21 EUCFR or on cases of religious discrimination under Directive 2000/78/EC. However, there are a number of points that can be made here. There are some signs that the CJEU when called upon to decide on the objective justification tests under Articles 10 and 21 EUCFR and under Articles 2(b), 2(5) and 4(1) Directive 2000/78/EC will apply a strict test. It is submitted that a stricter application of this test is desirable for people belonging to religious minorities, because it means that the court will perform a rigorous balancing of all the interests involved and will give weight to the right of the individual to freedom of religion and to non-discrimination and the importance of these rights for the individual concerned. Two reasons have already been given for this. The first is the strict interpretation of this test for gender discrimination in *Bilka Kaufhaus*.[24] And, secondly, the CJEU has consistently held that restrictions and limitations to individual rights in EU law, including the right not to be discriminated against, should be interpreted strictly.[25]

A third issue that would support a strict application of the objective justification test can be found in the fact that Directive 2000/78/EC, in Article 6(1), allows for justification of direct age discrimination: such discrimination shall not constitute discrimination if the difference in treatment is objectively and reasonably justified by a legitimate aim and if the means to achieve that aim are appropriate and necessary. The CJEU appears to require a high standard of proof before it finds that a measure which directly discriminates on the grounds of age is objectively justified.[26] It can be argued that, if a high standard of proof is required for justifications of direct age discrimination, where Directive 2000/78/EC allows for a fairly wide range of justifications, the CJEU will very likely require a high standard of proof for justifications of indirect discrimination on other grounds provided

[23] *Handyside v United Kingdom* (1979–1980) 1 EHRR 737, paras 48–50. This case concerned a claim under Art 10(2) ECHR (freedom of expression), but the test has been held to apply to Art 9(2) as well: *Dahlab v Switzerland* App no 42393/98 (ECtHR, 15 February 2001) 12.

[24] *Bilka Kaufhaus*, above n 14.

[25] See the cases, above n 22.

[26] Case C-144/04 *Mangold v Helm* [2005] ECR I-9981; Case C-411/05 *Felix Palacios de la Villa v Cortefiel Servicios* [2007] ECR I-8531; Case C-555–07 *Kücükdeveci v Swedex GmbH & Co KG* [2010] ECR I-365; and Case C-388/07 *R on behalf of the Incorporated Trustees of the National Council on Ageing (Age Concern England) v Secretary of State for Business, Enterprise and Regulatory Reform* [2009] ECR I-1569. For a more extensive discussion of this argument: E Howard, 'EU Equality Law: Three Recent Developments' (2011) 17(6) *European Law Journal* 785–803.

for in the anti-discrimination directives.[27] Moreover, the CJEU has also required a high standard of proof for the justification of genuine occupational requirements in relation to age[28] and for the justification under Article 2(5).[29]

How the CJEU will interpret Article 4(2) Directive 2000/78/EC is not clear yet. This paragraph does allow room for churches and other organisations to protect their religious ethos, but only if this does not lead to discrimination on another prohibited ground. The CJEU could very well consider this article a restriction of the right not to be discriminated against, and then interpret this strictly and thus scrutinise the exceptions made rigorously. For example, recently an Islamic school in Britain advertised for a science teacher but made it clear in the advert that women need not apply. The agency through which the advert was placed argued that this was allowed under British equality law as it was an occupational requirement. But the advert was withdrawn after a warning from the Department for Education over the need to comply with equality law.[30] It is submitted that the advert could well be seen as a breach of Article 4(2) Directive 2000/78/EC as it was discriminatory on another prohibited ground, namely gender.

III. RELIGIOUS MINORITIES AND THE COUNCIL OF EUROPE

A. Protection of Religious Minorities under Article 9 ECHR

Religious minorities also enjoy protection under different articles of the ECHR. Article 9 (freedom of religion) and Article 14 (right not to be discriminated against) are the most important articles here, but Article 10 (freedom of expression) and Article 11 (freedom of assembly and association) have also been invoked by religious individuals or groups applying to the ECtHR. This part of the chapter will concentrate on Articles 9 and 14.

Like Article 10 EUCFR, Article 9(1) ECHR guarantees the freedom of thought, conscience and religion, which includes the freedom to change one's religion or belief and the freedom, either alone or in community with others and in public or in private, to manifest one's religion or belief, in worship, teaching, practice and observance. However, Article 9 has a second paragraph, which determines that the freedom to manifest one's religion or belief can be restricted but only if the restriction is prescribed by law and is necessary in a democratic society for the protection of public safety, public health or morals or for the protection of the rights and freedoms of others. Therefore, the right to freedom of conscience,

[27] S Haverkort-Speekenbrink, *European Non-discrimination Law A Comparison of EU Law and the ECHR in the Field of Non-Discrimination and Freedom of Religion in Public Employment with an Emphasis on the Islamic Headscarf Issue* (Cambridge, Intersentia, 2012) 230.

[28] Case C-229/08 *Wolf v Stadt Frankfurt am Main* [2010] ECR I-1; and, *Prigge*, above n 22.

[29] *Petersen* and *Prigge*, both above n 22.

[30] See: www.telegraph.co.uk/news/religion/10666129/Muslim-boys-school-bans-women-from-applying-for-job-as-science-teacher.html.

thought and religion cannot be restricted by a state, but the manifestation of religion or belief can be restricted under Article 9(2). In *Kokkinakis v Greece*, the ECtHR stated that Article 9(2):

> [R]ecognises that in democratic societies, in which several religions coexist within one and the same population, it may be necessary to place restrictions on this freedom in order to reconcile the interests of the various groups and ensure that everyone's beliefs are respected.[31]

So restrictions on a person's religion or belief can be justified under certain conditions. The first condition is that a restriction must be prescribed by law. This means that the law must be accessible and sufficiently precise to make its effects foreseeable. In *Kervanci and Dogru v France*, two French girls were excluded from school because they did not want to take off their Muslim headscarves during sports lessons. The ECtHR held that, according to its settled case law, 'the concept of "law" must be understood in its "substantive" sense, not its "formal" one. It therefore includes everything that goes to make up the written law, including enactments of lower ranks than statutes'.[32]

The second condition is that the restriction on the freedom to manifest one's religion or belief must pursue a legitimate aim, and these aims are summed up in Article 9(2) ECHR: the interests of public safety, the protection of public order, health and morals, and the protection of the rights and freedoms of others. And the third condition is that the restriction is 'necessary in a democratic society'. The interpretation given to this by the ECtHR has already been discussed: it has been interpreted to mean that the interference complained of must correspond to a pressing social need and be proportionate to the legitimate aim pursued and be justified by relevant and sufficient reasons.[33] It is thus an objective justification test similar to the tests under the EUCFR and EU anti-discrimination law.

In *Handyside v United Kingdom*, the ECtHR explained that, because the national authorities are considered to be better placed to assess what is necessary in a democratic society, states enjoy a certain margin of appreciation to make the initial assessment of the reality of the pressing social need implied by the notion of 'necessity', but this margin is not unlimited and the ECtHR is empowered to give the final ruling.[34] In other words, the domestic margin of appreciation goes hand in hand with European supervision. However, the ECtHR appears to allow states a wider margin of appreciation in relation to Article 9 ECHR than it does in relation to other articles like Articles 8 (right to respect for private and family life), 10 and 11, which all contain the same term 'necessary in a democratic society'. The level of consensus or the existence or absence of a common standard on the issue in Europe appears to be the most important factor for the ECtHR

[31] *Kokkinakis v Greece* (1994) 17 EHRR 397, para 33.

[32] *Kervanci and Dogru v France* App nos 31645/04 and 27058/05 (ECtHR, 4 December 2008), para 62.

[33] *Handyside v United Kingdom* and *Dahlab v Switzerland*, both above n 23.

[34] *Handyside v United Kingdom*, above n 23, paras 48–49.

when it determines the width of the margin of appreciation. In *Otto-Preminger-Institute v Austria*, the ECtHR held that 'it is not possible to discern throughout Europe a uniform conception of the significance of religion in society … even within a single country such conceptions may vary'.[35] Because of this absence of a common European consensus, the ECtHR leaves states a wide margin of appreciation in relation to restrictions on the Article 9 right to manifest one's religion or belief and this means that restrictions are likely to be easily accepted as being justified. The ECtHR thus appears not to apply a very strict justification test for interferences with a person's Article 9 right and, as mentioned, this is not a positive interpretation for religious minorities as it would mean that the ECtHR will not perform a rigorous balancing of all the interests involved, including those of the religious person.

On the other hand, there are also positive aspects for religious minorities to be found in the case law of the ECtHR and these can assist them in claiming a violation of their Article 9 ECHR right. The ECtHR has held that 'pluralism, tolerance and broadmindedness are hallmarks of a "democratic society"'.[36] And that:

> [A]lthough individual interests must on occasion be subordinated to those of a group, democracy does not simply mean that the views of a majority must always prevail: a balance must be achieved which ensures the fair and proper treatment of minorities and avoids any abuse of a dominant position.[37]

This might, very tentatively, suggest that the ECtHR would allow for special measures (or positive action) for minorities to 'ensure fair and proper treatment'.

The ECtHR has also repeatedly stressed the important of the right to freedom of religion for a democratic society. For example, in *Kokkinakis v Greece*, the ECtHR held:

> As enshrined in Article 9 … freedom of thought, conscience and religion is one of the foundations of a 'democratic society' within the meaning of the Convention. It is, in its religious dimension, one of the most vital elements that go to make up the identity of believers and their conception of life, but it is also a precious asset for atheists, agnostics, sceptics and the unconcerned. The pluralism indissociable from a democratic society, which has been dearly won over the centuries, depends on it.[38]

The ECtHR has also pointed out that 'in its relations with various religions, denominations and beliefs, the State has a duty to remain neutral and impartial';[39] that 'the autonomous existence of religious communities was indispensable for

[35] *Otto-Preminger-Institute v Austria* (1995) 19 EHRR 34, para 50.

[36] *Handyside v United Kingdom*, above n 23, para 49.

[37] *Young, James and Webster v United Kingdom* (1982) 4 EHRR 20, para 63; repeated in *Valsamis v Greece* (1997) 24 EHRR 294, para 27.

[38] *Kokkinakis v Greece*, above n 31, para 31. See also: *Buscarini and Others v San Marino* (2000) 30 EHRR 208, para 34; and *97 Members of the Gldani Congregation of Jehovah's Witnesses and 4 Others v Georgia* (2008) 46 EHRR 30, para 130.

[39] *Manoussakis and Others v Greece*, para 47 and *Hasan and Chaush v Bulgaria*, para 78, both above n 6. See also: *Metropolitan Church of Bessarabia v Moldova* (2002) 35 EHRR 13, para 123.

pluralism in a democratic society'; and that 'the role of the authorities where there was conflict between religious groups was not to remove the cause of tension by eliminating pluralism, but rather to ensure that competing groups tolerated each other'.[40] Encouraging pluralism and tolerance might be seen as moving towards more equality in practice for (religious) minorities.

There are two specific areas where the ECtHR has, in the past, been rather reluctant to find an interference with the right to manifest one's religion or, if it did find an interference, to find that this was not justified, but where recent case law might have brought some change which could be positive for religious minorities. These areas are bans on the wearing of religious symbols and the manifestation of religion or belief in the workplace

In relation to the wearing of religious symbols, the ECtHR's case law has developed and it is now generally held that the wearing of such symbols is a manifestation of religion or belief and that bans are a restriction on that manifestation.[41] The ECtHR then examines whether such bans are justified under Article 9(2) ECHR. Two cases in particular set the precedent which was followed in further cases. The first of these cases is *Dahlab v Switzerland,* where Dahlab, a primary school teacher, was directed to stop wearing an Islamic headscarf because this was seen as going against the religious neutrality of the school. The ECtHR held that the interference with her religious manifestation was justified under Article 9(2) and was proportionate to the stated aim of protecting the rights and freedoms of others, namely the rights of the children in the school. The ECtHR considered that the wearing of the headscarf might have some proselytising effect and was hard to square with the principles of tolerance and respect for others and of gender equality.[42]

In the second case, *Sahin v Turkey,* a medical student was not allowed to take her exams, because she refused to remove her headscarf. Both Chamber (C) and Grand Chamber (GC) of the ECtHR considered that the interference with Sahin's right to manifest her religion by wearing a headscarf was justified because it had a legal basis and pursued the legitimate aims of protecting the rights and freedoms of others and of protecting public order. The restriction was seeking to achieve constitutional principles—secularism and equality—and thus it was held to be necessary in a democratic society and to meet a pressing social need (paragraphs 107–09 (C), paragraph 115 (GC)). The ECtHR considered that there was a diversity of approaches taken by the national authorities on the wearing of religious symbols in educational institutions and thus that the state in this case

[40] *Supreme Holy Council of the Muslim Community of Bulgaria* (2005) 41 EHRR 3, para 93.

[41] See, for example, *Dahlab v Switzerland,* above n 23; *Sahin v Turkey* (2005) 41 EHRR 8 (Chamber) and (2007) 44 EHRR 5 (Grand Chamber); *Kervanci and Dogru v France,* above n 32; and, *Eweida and Others v United Kingdom* (2010) 57 EHRR 8. But see: *Karaduman and Bulut v Turkey* (1993) 74 DR 93, where the ECnHR held that wearing a headscarf is not a manifestation of religion or belief.

[42] *Dahlab v Switzerland,* above n 23, 13.

should be given a wide margin of appreciation (paragraph 102 (C), paragraph 109 (GC)).

Both cases have been criticised for leaving a very wide margin of appreciation to the state concerned and for not giving any weight to the interests of the applicants themselves. In neither case was there any evidence that the applicants were pursuing a political agenda or were trying to convert their pupils/fellow students, and the ECtHR thus did not appear to undertake any justification test.[43] Even the dissenting judge in *Sahin v Turkey*, Judge Tulkens, criticised the majority because the European supervision that must accompany the margin of appreciation 'seems quite simply to be absent from the judgment' and this European supervision cannot 'be escaped simply by evoking the margin of appreciation'.[44]

Despite the criticism, the ECtHR continued to allow states a wide margin of appreciation in relation to bans on the wearing of religious symbols, including headscarves and turbans, and has generally held these to be justified in the interest of public order and/or the protection of the rights and freedoms of others or public safety.[45]

But in two recent cases, the ECtHR might have moved away from this by applying a more rigorous justification test. The first of these cases is *Ahmet Arslan and Others v Turkey*,[46] where 127 members of a religious group were convicted for touring the streets of Ankara while wearing turbans and distinctive trousers and tunics, a dress code based on their religious beliefs. The ECtHR held that the Turkish government had not made out that the restriction was necessary in a democratic society and thus it found a violation of Article 9(2) (paragraph 52). The ECtHR stressed that there was a distinction between wearing religious dress in public spaces open to all and doing so in schools and other public establishments, where religious neutrality might take precedence over the right to manifest one's religion or belief (para 49). This suggests that the ECtHR saw this case as different from the earlier cases, and this could explain the different conclusion. However, the ECtHR applied a more rigorous justification test because it considered that there was no evidence that the members of the religious group had represented a threat to public order or that they had tried to put inappropriate pressure on passers-by (paragraph 50). This case thus seems to show a greater willingness on the part of the ECtHR to balance the interest of applicants in

[43] See for this criticism: E Howard, *Law and the Wearing of Religious Symbols* (London and New York, Routledge, 2012) 59–62, and the authors referred to there.

[44] *Sahin v Turkey*, above n 41 (GC), Judge Tulkens, dissenting opinion, para 3.

[45] See: *Phull v France* App no 35753/03 (ECtHR, 11 January 2005) (turban); *Kōse and 93 Others v Turkey* (2006) ECHR 1175 (headscarf); *Kurtulmus v Turkey* (2006) ECHR 1169 (headscarf); *Kervanci and Dogru v France*, above n 32 (headscarves); *El Morsli v France* App no 15585/06 (ECtHR, 4 March 2008) (veil); *Aktas, Bayrak, Gamaleddyn, Ghazal, J Singh and R Singh v France* (2009) ECHR 1142 (headscarves and under-turbans); *El Morsli v France* App no 15585/06 (ECtHR, 4 March 2008 (veil); and, *Mann Singh v France* (2008) ECHR 1523.

[46] *Ahmet Arslan and Others v Turkey* (2010) ECHR 2260.

their freedom to manifest their religion or belief with the interests of the state in restricting this freedom.

The second case in which this willingness can be found is *Eweida and Others v United Kingdom*.[47] These cases concerned four practising Christians. Eweida, who worked for British Airways as check-in staff, and Chaplin, who worked as a nurse, both wanted to wear a cross in a visible way with their uniforms. Ladele, a registrar of births, deaths and marriages, and McFarlane, a relationship and psycho-sexual counsellor, both believed that homosexual relationships are contrary to God's law and complained that they had been dismissed for refusing to carry out certain parts of their duties which they considered condoned homosexuality. Eweida, Chaplin and McFarlane all claimed a violation of Articles 9 and 14 ECHR, but Ladele only claimed a breach of Article 14 in conjunction with Article 9. The ECtHR accepted, in relation to all four applicants, that there was a manifestation of their belief (paragraphs 89, 97, 103 and 108). In relation to Eweida and Chaplin, the ECtHR accepted that there was an interference and considered whether this was justified under Article 9(2) ECHR. The ECtHR appeared to be applying a stricter justification test by taking the importance of the right to freely manifest their religion for the applicants themselves into account, as it considered that 'on one side of the scales was Eweida's desire to manifest her religious belief' and that 'as in Eweida's case, the importance for the second applicant [Chaplin] of being permitted to manifest her religion by wearing her cross visibly must weigh heavily in the balance' (paragraphs 94 and 99). The ECtHR concluded that a fair balance had not been struck between Eweida's right to freely manifest her religion and her employer's wish to protect its corporate image and that the domestic courts had given too much weight to the latter (paragraph 94). But, in Chaplin's case, the balance between the interests involved was held to have been struck in the right way because the reason for asking Chaplin to remove her cross was the protection of health and safety on a hospital ward, and this was inherently of much greater importance than that which applied in respect of Eweida (paragraph 99).

These two cases can thus be seen as a significant and positive development for people belonging to religious minorities who want to manifest their religion or belief through the wearing of religious symbols because, in contrast to the earlier cases of *Dahlab v Switzerland*[48] and *Sahin v Turkey*[49] and the cases following these, the ECtHR applied a stricter justification test and gave more attention to the importance of the freedom to manifest one's religion for the applicants.

Eweida and Others v United Kingdom[50] is also important in relation to the manifestation of religion in the workplace because, here too, there appeared to be a positive departure from previous case law. The ECnHR had consistently held that where an individual complains of a restriction on his or her freedom of religion in

[47] *Eweida and Others v United Kingdom*, above n 41.
[48] *Dahlab v Switzerland*, above n 23.
[49] *Sahin v Turkey*, above n 41.
[50] *Eweida and Others v United Kingdom*, above n 41.

the workplace, the possibility of changing jobs and changing employment meant that there was no interference with the employee's religious freedom.[51] In relation to the four applicants in *Eweida and Others v United Kingdom*, this would have meant that no interference would have been found because all four could have resigned and taken another job where they could manifest their religion openly. However, the ECtHR stated that the better approach would be to weigh this possibility in the overall balance when considering whether or not the restriction is proportionate (paragraph 83). And, in relation to McFarlane, the ECtHR, when considering whether a fair balance was struck between the competing interests at stake, took into account that, on the one hand, the loss of his job was a severe sanction with grave consequences for the applicant. But, on the other hand, the applicant had voluntarily enrolled on his employer's post-graduate training programme in psycho-sexual counselling, knowing that it operated an Equal Opportunities Policy and that filtering of clients on the ground of sexual orientation would not be possible (paragraph 109).

For people from religious minorities who want to manifest their religion at work, this is a welcome departure from previous case law. It recognises that for many people, choosing between their religious principles and their job is not as simple as was previously made out, and that resigning is often not a realistic option.

B. Protection of Religious Minorities under Article 14 ECHR

Article 14 ECHR provides protection against discrimination on a large number of grounds, including religion or belief. However, Article 14 does not provide a freestanding right to non-discrimination as it only prohibits discrimination in the enjoyment of the rights in the ECHR. Therefore, Article 14 can only be invoked in conjunction with one of the other rights or freedoms. Protocol 12 to the ECHR was adopted to provide a free-standing right to non-discrimination, but this Protocol has only been signed and ratified by 18 (of which eight are also EU member states) out of the 47 member states of the Council of Europe. In *Sejdic and Finci v Bosnia Herzegovina*, the ECtHR held that Protocol 12 should be interpreted in the same way as Article 14.[52] So the following applies to Protocol 12 as well.

In *Thlimmenos v Greece*, the ECtHR considered that the right under Article 14 not to be discriminated against is violated not only 'when States treat differently persons in analogous situations without providing an objective and reasonable justification', but also 'when States without an objective and reasonable

[51] *Ahmad v United Kingdom* (1982) 4 EHRR 126, para 15; *Kontinnen v Finland* (1996) 87 DR 68, under 'The Law', point 1; and *Stedman v United Kingdom* (1997) 23 EHRR CD 168, under 'The Law', point 1.

[52] *Sejdic and Finci v Bosnia Herzegovina* (2009) ECHR 2122, para 55.

justification fail to treat differently persons whose situations are significantly different'.[53] This indicates not only that both direct and indirect discrimination are covered, but also that neither form of discrimination violates Article 14 if it is objectively and reasonably justified. The ECtHR has held that, to be justified, a difference in treatment must not only pursue a legitimate aim, there must also be a reasonable relationship of proportionality between the means employed and the aim sought to be realised. This test is thus very similar to the justification test of Article 9(2) ECHR, especially as, here again, 'the Contracting States enjoy a certain margin of appreciation in assessing whether and to what extent differences in otherwise similar situations justify a different treatment'.[54]

This same case could also, tentatively, be used to support an argument that the ECtHR sees a duty of reasonable accommodation as part of the justification test under Articles 9(2) and 14. The ECtHR considered that Greece failed to introduce appropriate exceptions to the rule in question for people in Thlimmenos's circumstances.[55] This would suggest that, if no attempt is made to accommodate a religious manifestation, the means used to achieve a legitimate aim cannot be considered appropriate and the duty of reasonable accommodation can thus be seen as part of the objective justification test. However, whether the ECtHR will continue to interpret the test in this way is unclear. *Jakobski v Poland* and *Kovalkovs v Latvia* appear to support this interpretation but, in *Sessa v Italy*, the majority (four judges) of the ECtHR did not follow this, although the three dissenting judges appear to have done so.[56]

In *DH and Others v the Czech Republic*, the ECtHR considered that

> Article 14 does not prohibit a member State from treating groups differently in order to correct 'factual inequalities' between them; indeed in certain circumstances a failure to attempt to correct inequality through different treatment may in itself give rise to a breach of the Article.[57]

This suggests that the ECtHR would allow positive action measures.

Because Article 14 can only be invoked in conjunction with one or more other articles of the ECHR, the ECtHR often does not find it necessary to consider whether there is a breach of Article 14 or it will find that no separate question arises under Article 14. For example, in relation to the Article 14 claims of Eweida, Chaplin and McFarlane in *Eweida v United Kingdom*, the ECtHR seems to have

[53] *Thlimmenos v Greece* (2001) 31 EHRR 15, para 44.

[54] *Case Relating to Certain Aspects of the Laws on the Use of Languages in Education in Belgium v Belgium* (1979–1980) 1 EHRR 252, under THE LAW, B, para 10.

[55] *Thlimmenos v Greece*, above n 53, para 48.

[56] *Jakobski v Poland* (2010) ECHR 1974, paras 46–47; *Kovalkovs v Latvia* (2012) ECHR 280, para 64; *Francesco Sessa v Italy* App no 28790/08 (ECtHR, 3 April 2012). See further for this argument: Howard, above n 16.

[57] *DH and Others v Czech Republic* (2006) ECHR 113, para 175.

dismissed these rather perfunctorily by holding that there was no need to examine these claims separately.[58]

However, the ECtHR does, sometimes examine the Article 14 claim in more detail and then it applies the objective justification test described above. For example, in both *Canea Catholic Church v Greece* and *97 Members of the Gldani Congregation of Jehovah's Witnesses and 4 Others v Georgia*, the ECtHR held that the state did not bring forward an objective and reasonable justification for the difference in treatment on the ground of religion and thus it found a violation of Article 14.[59] The ECtHR also applied this test to Ladele's claim under Article 14 in conjunction with Article 9 in *Eweida v United Kingdom.* It took into account that the consequences for the applicant were serious because she ultimately lost her job and that she was already in the job when civil partnerships between same-sex couples were introduced by legislation. On the other hand, the local authority's policy aimed to secure the rights of others which are also protected under the Convention.[60] So in this case, the ECtHR applied a more rigorous justification test and took Ladele's interests into account.

C. Conclusion on the Protection of Religious Minorities under the ECHR

Religious minorities can find protection in Article 9 ECHR, but this protection has its strengths and weaknesses. On the one hand, the ECtHR stresses the importance of the freedom of religion for a democratic and plural society and points out the state's duty to remain neutral and impartial in its relations with various religions and to create tolerance amongst different religious groups. On the other hand, the ECtHR appears to leave states a wide margin of appreciation in deciding whether a measure restricting a person's or a group's manifestation of their religion or belief is necessary in a democratic society. This would suggest that the ECtHR will not apply a very rigorous justification test, and many cases indicate that this has indeed been the outcome. However, there are some grounds for optimism because there are signs that the ECtHR is moving towards a more rigorous test, in two more recent cases: *Ahmet Arslan v Turkey*[61] and *Eweida and Others v United Kingdom.*[62] In both cases, the ECtHR considered the question of justification in more detail and gave greater weight to the importance of the manifestation for the applicants themselves. This is a significant development for people belonging to religious minorities, and it is to be hoped that the ECtHR will continue

[58] *Eweida v United Kingdom*, above n 41, paras 95, 101 and 110. See also: *Metropolitan Church of Bessarabia v Moldova*, above n 39, para 134; and, *Kimlya and Others v Russia* (2009) ECHR 1424, para 104.

[59] *Canea Catholic Church v Greece* (1999) 27 EHRR 521, para 47 and *97 Members of the Gldani Congregation of Jehovah's Witnesses and 4 Others v Georgia*, above n 38, para 140.

[60] *Eweida v the United Kingdom*, above n 41, para 106.

[61] *Ahmet Arslan v Turkey*, above n 46.

[62] *Eweida and Others v United Kingdom*, above n 41.

along these lines and apply the justification test in this way in future cases, both under Article 9 and under Article 14 ECHR, as this ensures that the interests of the religious individual or group are weighed in the balance in the decisions. The ECtHR will have a chance to follow these cases in its decision in *SAS v France*, which concerns a challenge to the French ban on all face covering clothing in public places.[63]

Another very positive departure from previous case law is the abandoning of the opinion that the possibility of changing employment negates any interference with the right to freedom of religion in the workplace. As the ECtHR itself stated *in Eweida and Others v United Kingdom*, 'the better approach would be to weigh this possibility in the overall balance when considering whether or not the restriction is proportionate' (paragraph 83).

In relation to the protection against discrimination given by Article 14, the inclusion of indirect discrimination and, tentatively, positive action, can be seen as enhancing the protection of persons belonging to religious minorities. The possible inclusion of a duty to consider reasonable accommodation of religious practices in the justification tests under Articles 9(2) and 14 would further enhance the protection, although it is uncertain if the ECtHR will follow this route.

So the ECtHR has taken a number of positive steps towards better protection of religious people against interference with their right to manifest their religion or belief and to non-discrimination on the grounds of their religion and it is hoped that the ECtHR will continue along this path.

IV. CONCLUSION

There are a number of ways in which vulnerable religious minorities are protected under both EU law and under the ECHR. The case law of the ECtHR has mostly developed towards more protection and there are signs that the CJEU case law will also interpret the EU provisions in a way that affords more protection to religious minorities. It is submitted that it is very important to ensure equality in practice for religious minorities and the prohibition of indirect discrimination, with the possible inclusion of a duty to consider accommodation, and the possibility of positive action measures can contribute to this. Another contribution can be made by the application of a strict objective justification test under all measures analysed here, as this would ensure that, in the balancing between the interests of the state or of employers to restrict a person's religious manifestation and the interests of the person who wants to manifest their religion, proper weight is given to the latter. It is therefore submitted that both the CJEU, in relation to justification under the EUCFR and under anti-discrimination law, and

[63] *S.A.S. v France* 43835/11. In its judgment of 1 July 2014, the Grand Chamber did indeed pay more attention to the importance of the religious manifestation for the individual applicant, although they did find the interference justified.

the ECtHR, in relation to Articles 9 and 14, should apply the justification tests strictly. There is, therefore, quite an array of protection for people belonging to religious minorities, although there are also limits to the protection and both legal systems recognise that this is so. Whether this protection is enough to change the vulnerable status to the satisfaction of religious minorities remains to be seen, but a strict application of the justification test should at least ensure that all interests are weighed into the balance.

As mentioned in the introduction, the instruments discussed here provide rights that are mainly framed as rights of individuals and groups of individuals and not as rights of groups as such. However, not only are there clear group aspects in the legal provisions discussed, especially the provisions against indirect discrimination and for positive action, but there also appears to be growing attention for disadvantaged and vulnerable minorities in Europe. The ECtHR in particular seems to have started using the substantive provisions of the ECHR in support of minority protection, especially in relation to Roma,[64] although there is no specific move towards protection of religious minorities as yet. This is another positive development which would complement and enhance the individual protection discussed in this chapter.

[64] See Bowring, above n 7; and, A van Bossuyt, 'Fit for Purpose or Faulty Design? Analysis of the Jurisprudence of the European Court of Human Rights and the European Court of Justice on the legal Protection of Minorities' (2007) 1 *Journal on Ethnopolitics and Minority issues in Europe,* www.isn.ethz.ch/Digital-Library/Publications/Detail/?ots591=0c54e3b3-1e9c-be1e-2c24-a6a8c7060233&lng=en&id=115556.

10

The Protection of Sexual Minorities in European Law

PEGGY DUCOULOMBIER

I. INTRODUCTION

> Sexual orientation is understood to refer to each person's capacity for profound emotional, affectional and sexual attraction to, and intimate and sexual relations with, individuals of a different gender or the same gender or more than one gender … gender identity is understood to refer to each person's deeply felt internal and individual experience of gender, which may or may not correspond with the sex assigned at birth.[1]

This chapter seeks to explore the scope of the protection afforded by European law[2] to sexual minorities,[3] who face human rights violations, in particular in the form of discrimination based on sexual orientation or gender identity.

The chapter begins by conceptualising sexual minorities as a vulnerable group, then moves to present the European protective legal framework, and continues

[1] *The Yogyakarta Principles*, 2007, Introduction, available at www.yogyakartaprinciples.org.

[2] European law comprises European Union (EU) law and European Convention on Human Rights (ECHR) law. Within the Council of Europe (CoE), the Parliamentary Assembly (PACE), the Commissioner for Human Rights and the Committee of Ministers contribute to the protection of sexual minorities (see among recent instruments adopted by the PACE, Resolution 1728 (2010) and Recommendation 1915 (2010) on Discrimination on the basis of sexual orientation and gender identity, and for the Committee of Ministers, see Recommendation CM/Rec (2010)5 on Measures to combat discrimination on grounds of sexual orientation or gender identity). Within the EU, the European Parliament has adopted several resolutions (see, eg, Resolution on the EU Roadmap against homophobia and discrimination on grounds of sexual orientation and gender identity, 4 February 2014). In addition, European institutions regularly condemn human rights violations against lesbian, gay, bisexual and transgender—LGBT—persons outside the EU (see, eg guidelines adopted by the European Council to help officials from EU institutions and Member States to Promote and Protect the Enjoyment of all Human Rights by Lesbian, Gay, Bisexual, Transgender and Intersex (LGBTI) Persons within its external relation, 24 June 2013). However, space precludes a comprehensive analysis of these instruments.

[3] This category refers to LGBT persons. It must be noted that homosexual and transgender persons are the main focus of the European Court of Human Rights (ECtHR) and of the Court of Justice of the European Union (CJ; this acronym is used to encompass the former Court of Justice of the European Communities and the new Court of Justice of the European Union).

with an analysis of the case law of the European courts in different areas[4] in order to identify achievements, shortcomings and prospects in the protection of sexual minorities.

II. SEXUAL MINORITIES AS A VULNERABLE GROUP

Sexual minorities may be considered as a vulnerable group as they are more likely than the general population to experience human rights violations, both from domestic authorities and individuals. They may be threatened in their bodily and moral integrity by physical and verbal abuse; their freedom to live according to their identity and to publicly express this identity may be limited by law and public morality; their economic situation may be weakened by employment discrimination or discrimination in accessing benefits otherwise allocated to heterosexual couples. Identifying specific groups as vulnerable may be criticised, as it carries with it the risk of further stigmatisation and victimisation of these groups. Moreover, it may be argued with Fineman that vulnerability is 'universal and constant, inherent in the human condition'.[5] We are all, as human beings, vulnerable, since we are all susceptible to harm. This universal approach is particularly interesting,[6] as it avoids the risk of reinforcing stigmatisation of particular groups, as we should remember that their vulnerable status is linked to a long-term process of exclusion by which they were cast out as different. In this latter sense, vulnerability is a divisive rather than an inclusive notion. However, if one may regret the undertones of stigmatisation that the 'vulnerable label' may carry, this notion, even understood in a non-universal sense, allows the recognition of the social and institutional discrimination suffered by particular groups and, as a result, may be used to impose on states specific and stricter obligations of protection. The concept of vulnerability should thus be seen as an opportunity to expand the protection offered to sexual minorities.

Despite the fact that this concept has never been used in relation to sexual minorities in its case law,[7] the ECtHR has been the main source of protection for LGBT persons. Peroni and Timmer stress that vulnerability, applied to groups,

[4] The recognition of sexual orientation and gender identity as key aspects of one's self, discrimination in the work place and the protection afforded to same-sex couples.

[5] M Albertson Fineman, 'The Vulnerable Subject: Anchoring Equality in the Human Condition' (2008–2009) *Yale Journal of Law and Feminism* 1, 1.

[6] Fineman questions the manner in which the state may unfairly privilege certain individuals by refusing to some access to the protective social and legal institutions that help us cope with our inherent vulnerability; an approach which may be very fruitful to address subjects such as same-sex marriage. See Fineman (n 5 above), 19–23.

[7] On this subject, see L Peroni and A Timmer, 'Vulnerable groups: The promise of an emerging concept in European Human Rights Convention Law' (2013) *International Journal of Constitutional Law* 1056.

has only been used by the ECtHR in relation to Roma people,[8] asylum-seekers[9] and persons suffering from HIV[10] or mental disability.[11] The ECtHR also uses this notion in relation to prisoners[12] and children,[13] although Peroni and Timmer note that the vulnerability element is not attached to groups but rather to individuals.[14] The difference between vulnerable groups and individuals was stressed by Judge Sajó, in his partly concurring and partly dissenting opinion in *MSS v Belgium and Greece*, to challenge the categorisation of asylum-seekers as a vulnerable group on the basis that they had not historically been 'subject to prejudice with lasting consequences, resulting in their social exclusion'. The criteria used to consider that a group is particularly vulnerable are not yet fixed and comprise historical prejudice leading to discrimination and exclusion, but also poverty. Indeed, in *MSS*, the ECtHR relied on the situation of total dependency in which asylum-seekers found themselves in Greece to consider them as a vulnerable group.[15] The boundaries of the category are thus not immutable and may evolve to include other groups. The criteria used by the Court, in particular stigmatisation and exclusion, lead us to consider that sexual minorities could legitimately be included in the 'vulnerable groups' category.[16] Moreover, without expressly considering sexual minorities as a vulnerable group, the ECtHR has often used interpretative tools identical to those present in the case law related to vulnerable groups, such as a narrow margin of appreciation and a strict proportionality test.[17]

The leading role of the ECtHR can be easily explained by the very purpose of the ECHR, dedicated to the protection of civil and political rights and the prohibition of discrimination in the enjoyment of these rights, while the purpose of the European Economic Community (EEC) was, at least in its inception, mainly an economic one. However, recent amendments to EU law have allowed EU institutions to contribute to the protection of LGBT persons in a meaningful manner. Although it may be difficult for the CJ to play as important a role as the ECtHR in that field, the primacy and direct effect of EU law are powerful tools in the protection of sexual minorities. However, if steps have already been taken, allowing the CJ to deliver important rulings, progress remains slow. It is hoped that the protection afforded by the two jurisdictions should complement each other, as

[8] See, for an early case, *Chapman v UK* (2001) 33 EHRR 18, para 96. See also, eg *DH and Others v Czech Republic* (2008) 47 EHRR 3, para 182, *Horváth and Kiss* (2013) 57 EHRR 31, para 102.

[9] See *MSS v Belgium and Greece* (2011) 53 EHRR 2, para 251.

[10] See *Kiyutin v Russia* (2011) 53 EHRR 26, para 64, *IB v Greece* App no 552/10 (ECtHR, 3 October 2013), para 81.

[11] See *Alajos Kiss v Hungary* (2013) 56 EHRR 38, para 42.

[12] See *Semikhvostov v Russia* App no 2689/12 (ECtHR, 6 February 2014), para 84, in relation to prisoners with physical disabilities.

[13] See, eg *O'Keeffe v Ireland* 35 BHRC 601, paras 144–46, *Söderman v Sweden* App no 5786/08 (ECtHR, Grand Chamber, 12 November 2013), para 81.

[14] See Peroni and Timmer, 1057.

[15] At paras 249–64.

[16] See also Peroni and Timmer, 1070.

[17] On the legal consequences deriving from the ECtHR's recognition that a group is 'particularly vulnerable', see Peroni and Timmer, 1074–82.

EU law extends to fields which are not expressly covered by the ECHR. However, for the time being, the ECtHR remains the most advanced forum in which sexual minorities can seek redress for the human rights violations they experience.

III. THE PROTECTIVE LEGAL FRAMEWORK

The protection of sexual minorities is often studied through the prism of discrimination, although substantive provisions of the ECHR alone can be the source of protection.[18] In EU law, anti-discrimination provisions are the main vehicle for protecting LGBT persons. The principle of non-discrimination is thus enshrined in EU law, albeit in a different manner than in the ECHR, the latter being more generous than the former at its inception. While the principle of non-discrimination on the grounds of nationality is the founding principle of the EEC, and the principle of equal pay for equal work for men and women has been protected from the Rome Treaty onwards,[19] the ECHR conceives non-discrimination, embodied in Article 14, in a more extensive manner. First, the grounds listed in Article 14 extend beyond sex and nationality to include eg religion, race, age and 'other status', signalling that the list is open-ended. Then, although falling short of being a general anti-discrimination clause,[20] Article 14 can be invoked in conjunction with the wide range of rights guaranteed by the ECHR,[21] while the protection offered by the EEC was limited to economic matters. The legal bases available to the EEC institutions to tackle discrimination were limited, while the ECtHR could potentially fight violations of human rights in a wide number of areas of life.[22] The EEC Treaty and its resulting secondary legislation could, however, be seen as complementing the ECHR, as the Convention does not include the right to work. However, both instruments shared a common silence on the issue of discrimination on the grounds of sexual orientation and gender identity.

[18] Although Art 14 had been regularly invoked by early applicants, it was not until 1999, in *Salgueiro da Silva Mouta v Portugal* (2001) 31 EHRR 47, that the Court found a violation of Art 14 in conjunction with Art 8 with respect to discrimination on the grounds of sexual orientation. Prior to this case, when the Court found a violation of Art 8, it generally decided that no separate issue arose under Art 14, ignoring the discriminatory aspect of the application.

[19] See ex-Art 141 TEC, now Art 157 TFEU.

[20] Art 14 must be invoked in conjunction with a right guaranteed by the ECHR. For a general anti-discrimination clause, see Art 1.1 of Protocol No 12 to the ECHR which prohibits discrimination in the enjoyment of 'any right set forth by law'.

[21] Moreover, the ECtHR is willing to analyse discrimination claims as long as the facts of the case 'fall within the ambit' of an ECHR provision. For instance, applications alleging discrimination in adoption procedures are admissible, despite the fact that the Court persistently refuses to include a right to adopt in Art 8. See, eg *Fretté v France* (2004) 38 EHRR 21; *EB v France* (2008) 47 EHRR 21.

[22] However, it could be propounded that EU law is more effective than ECHR law, as EU law allows justification only in relation to indirect discrimination while such a distinction is not made by ECHR law. See E Ellis and P Watson, *EU Anti-Discrimination Law*, Oxford EU Library, 2nd edn (Oxford, Oxford University Press, 2012) 108–09. This, rather than proving that ECHR law is less effective, illustrates the differences in the reasoning of the courts, the ECtHR generally spending little time, unless forced by the facts of the case, considering the nature of discrimination.

This silence has been more complex to deal with for the EU institutions than for the ECtHR. Deprived of an express legal basis to fight discrimination on the grounds of sexual orientation, the CJ was, at first, more protective of transgender persons than of homosexuals. In *Grant v South-West Trains Ltd*,[23] the CJ refused to entertain a discrimination claim in relation to travel expenses afforded to employees' spouses and heterosexual partners while denied to homosexual partners, by recalling that discrimination based on sexual orientation could not be equated with discrimination based on sex and was, at the time, not prohibited by an express provision of EC law. However, this was no obstacle to the protection of transsexuals, for whom the prohibition of sex discrimination could be relied on, thanks to the CJ's dynamic interpretation,[24] creating a form of hierarchy within the category of sexual minorities, which also transpires from the case law of the ECtHR.[25]

The European Commission on Human Rights (EComHR) considered homosexuality through sexual activity as part of private life, accepting claims that the criminalisation of homosexuality could engage Article 8.[26] Then, Convention bodies relied on the non-exhaustive nature of Article 14 to include sexual orientation in the 'other status' category, opening the way for discrimination claims lodged by homosexuals.[27] As far as claims based on transsexual status are concerned, the ECtHR recognised that failing to fully recognise one's gender identity was in breach of Article 8,[28] before considering that discrimination on this ground, albeit different from discrimination based on sexual orientation, was nonetheless covered by Article 14.[29]

Anti-discrimination tools in European law have evolved since the 1950s. The Amsterdam Treaty provided the first major change in EU law. Thanks to Article 13 TEC (now Article 19 TFEU), the European institutions gained a legal basis on which to enact secondary legislation to fight discrimination on a wider range of grounds, including sexual orientation. On the basis of this provision, an

[23] Case C-249/96 *Grant v South-West Trains Ltd* [1998] ECR I-621.

[24] See, eg Case C-13/94 *P v S and Cornwall County Council* [1996] ECR I-2143; Case C-117/01 *KB v NHS Pensions Agency* [2004] ECR I-541; Case C-423/04 *Sarah Margaret Richards v Secretary of State for Work and Pensions* [2006] ECR I-3585. Provisions of primary and secondary law prohibiting gender discrimination were interpreted to include discrimination arising from gender reassignment.

[25] See, eg the recognition of a right to marry for transsexuals stemming from Art 12, in *Christine Goodwin v UK* (2002) 35 EHRR 18, still denied to homosexuals, or the recognition of a family life based on de facto links created by a female-to-male transsexual with her partner and her son in *X, Y and Z v UK* (1997) 24 EHRR 143, while it was not until *Schalk and Kopf v Austria* (2011) 53 EHRR 20, that a stable homosexual relationship could qualify as a family.

[26] However, applications made on this basis were declared inadmissible. For an extensive study of the case law of the EComHR, see P Johnson, *Homosexuality and the European Court of Human Rights* (Abingdon, Routledge, 2013) 19–40.

[27] See *Salgueiro da Silva Mouta v Portugal* (n 18 above) para 28. In *Sutherland v UK* (1997) 24 EHRR CD22, para 51, the EComHR declined to rule on whether discrimination based on sexual orientation should be considered as discrimination based on sex or on other status, since it was in any case covered by Art 14.

[28] See *Christine Goodwin v UK* (n 25 above).

[29] See *PV v Spain* App no 35159/09 (ECtHR, 30 November 2010), para 30.

important directive was enacted to preclude discrimination on the grounds of race, religion, disability, age and sexual orientation in the field of employment.[30] In 2008, a proposal was made to extend the principle of non-discrimination on the aforementioned grounds, with the exception of race, to other fields. This proposal is still under consideration; however the enactment of the 'Horizontal Directive' is not yet in sight.[31] Unfortunately, this confines the prohibition of discrimination on the grounds of sexual orientation to the employment field, while non-discrimination on the grounds of race or sex is more developed thanks to the enactment of the Racial Equality Directive,[32] covering access to social security, the welfare system, goods and services, and the Gender Goods and Services Directive,[33] complementing the Recast Directive[34] by expanding the prohibition of discrimination based on sex to the access to and supply of goods and services. Finally, with the ratification of the Lisbon Treaty, the Charter of Fundamental Rights (CFR) was given binding force and acceded to the rank of primary law. Consequently, it must be complied with by the EU institutions and by Member States when implementing EU law, providing a new source of protection thanks to Article 21.1 which prohibits discrimination on an extensive list of grounds, including sexual orientation.

The evolution in ECHR law has mainly taken place through dynamic judicial interpretation, as will be demonstrated below.[35] Moreover, Protocol No 12 was added to the ECHR, thereby introducing a general non-discrimination clause in relation to rights recognised by domestic law,[36] although it is unsure whether it will have a noticeable impact. Only 18 states have ratified the protocol thus far and due to the wide scope of Article 14, it is unlikely that the Court will often need to rely on it, on the basis that the right engaged would only be guaranteed at the national level and not by the Convention.

From the outset, the ECtHR was hence in a better position to deal with claims from LGBT persons and, despite major changes to the EU Treaties, it is unlikely that the CJ will regain ground any time soon, even if it wanted to.[37] This explains why this study, although discussing the case law of the CJ when relevant, is mainly

[30] Directive 2000/78/EC establishing a general framework for equal treatment in employment and occupation [2000] OJ L303/16.

[31] Proposal for a Council Directive on implementing the principle of equal treatment between persons irrespective of religion or belief, disability, age or sexual orientation, COM (2008) 426 final.

[32] Directive 2000/43/EC implementing the principle of equal treatment between persons irrespective of racial or ethnic origin [2000] OJ L180/22.

[33] Directive 2004/113/EC implementing the principle of equal treatment between men and women in the access to and supply of goods and services [2004] OJ L373/37.

[34] Directive 2006/54/EC implementing the principle of equal opportunities and equal treatment of men and women in matters of employment and occupation (recast) [2006] OJ L204/23.

[35] Soft law enacted by the PACE or the Committee of Ministers of the CoE is also used by the ECtHR when relying on the method of global interpretation in its reasoning.

[36] Protocol No 12 replicates the list of grounds contained in Art 14 to avoid extrapolations that omitted grounds, such as sexual orientation, had been voluntarily excluded from Art 14.

[37] Discrimination cases are mostly brought to the CJ by way of a preliminary reference, a procedure which is not at the discretion of the applicants. Moreover, in *Ullens de Schooten and Rezabek v Belgium*

dedicated to the case law of the ECtHR. One could at least hope for an increased dialogue between the two courts on these issues, in light of the forthcoming accession of the EU to the ECHR. However, recent cases seem to indicate that the CJ may no longer be willing to rely extensively on the Convention and ECtHR's case law.

The protection offered by the ECtHR to sexual minorities has been gradual. This is due to the interpretation methods used by the Court, namely the margin of appreciation, the search for a European consensus and dynamic interpretation. It could be considered that the margin of appreciation and consensus analysis are illegitimate tools of interpretation, as they leave minorities vulnerable to the predominant moral views of the majority.[38] However, these techniques are also used by the Court to protect its legitimacy and authority as an international court, which is now strongly disputed by certain states. Whatever position one may take concerning the ECtHR's interpretation methods, the difficulty lies within the very functioning of these techniques, in particular the margin of appreciation as contradictory factors are at play in the case law on sexual minorities. Due to the particular intimate aspect of sexual orientation or gender identity, the scope of the margin of appreciation should be limited and any differential treatment based on compelling arguments, calling for an exacting standard of review from the Court.[39] However, in matters such as same-sex marriage, the Court often relies on the lack of consensus to widen the margin of appreciation and to limit its control of the proportionality of the interference or of the justification of any difference in treatment. There are no clear criteria to decide which of the relevant factors should weigh more in the reasoning of the Court, neither is there any set method to identify a consensus among states. Thus, the Court is left with an important margin of manoeuvre and depending on the result it wants to achieve, it will insist on chosen aspects of the case, revealing how interpretative tools are used as legitimising tools of subjective moral positions.[40]

Despite the criticisms that can be voiced against the consistency of its reasoning or the substance of its rulings, the ECtHR has been instrumental in protecting sexual minorities. The substantive analysis will begin with the basis upon which the rest of the case law is founded, namely the recognition of sexual orientation and gender identity as key aspects of one's self. Then, the chapter will analyse the case law on discrimination in relation to employment, where it could be expected that the CJ would play a leading role. Finally, questions related to the protection of couples will be examined as this part of the ECtHR's case law exemplifies the

App nos 3989/07 and 38353/07 (ECtHR, 20 September 2011), the ECtHR ruled that a duly motivated refusal to refer a preliminary question to the CJ did not breach Art 6.

[38] See G Letsas, *A theory of interpretation of the European Convention on Human Rights* (Oxford, Oxford University Press, 2007) esp 120–30.

[39] This is also consistent with the legal framework related to the emerging category of 'vulnerable groups' in the ECtHR's case law. See Peroni and Timmer, 1080–82.

[40] See Johnson, 65–89.

progress made but also raises questions as to the differential treatments of transsexuals and homosexuals, and ultimately reveals the gaps left in the protection of LGBT persons.

IV. BACK TO BASICS: THE RECOGNITION OF SEXUAL ORIENTATION AND GENDER IDENTITY AS A KEY ASPECT OF AN INDIVIDUAL'S SELF

ECHR case law was instrumental in recognising sexual orientation, and particularly homosexual orientation, as a key aspect of a person's identity. Article 8 was the vehicle via which successful claims were brought.[41] This comes as no surprise in light of the flexibility of the notion of 'private life'. However, if the EComHR admitted at an early stage that legislation criminalising homosexual relations fell within the ambit of Article 8, it also considered that states were free to control homosexual activities, on the basis of the protection of morals and the rights of others. As demonstrated by Johnson in his illuminating study of ECHR case law on homosexuality, the EComHR first adhered to the national authorities' view that society, and in particular its most vulnerable members—male teenagers unsure of their sexuality—had to be protected from homosexuals. It is not until *Dudgeon v UK*[42] that the position of the Convention bodies began to evolve to follow the applicants' discourse on homosexuality, in particular the argument that sexuality was innate and therefore could not be altered to adapt to a hostile social and cultural context.[43] In *Dudgeon*, the Court chose to give more weight to the idea that sexual orientation represents a most intimate aspect of private life, an essentially private manifestation of human personality,[44] and decided to limit the scope of the margin of appreciation, while the legitimate aim pursued by the criminalisation of homosexual relations—the protection of morals—called for a wider margin of appreciation. The Court relied on the evolution of mentality and legal developments in European societies, to rule that

> Although members of the public who regard homosexuality as immoral may be shocked, offended or disturbed by the commission by others of private homosexual acts, this cannot on its own warrant the application of penal sanctions when it is consenting adults alone who are involved.[45]

Nevertheless, as rightly stressed by Johnson, the early case law contained the idea that homosexuality was to be protected as part of *private* life and it was, at first,

[41] See Johnson, 93.

[42] *Dudgeon v UK* (1982) Series A no 45, 4 EHRR 149. See also *Norris v Ireland* (1991) Series A no 142, 13 EHRR 186; *Modinos v Cyprus* (1993) Series A no 259, 16 EHRR 485.

[43] See Johnson, 46–49. In favour of a non-essentialist approach to the protection of homosexuals, see M Grigolo, 'Sexualities and the ECHR: Introducing the Universal Sexual Legal Subject' (2003) 14 *European Journal of International Law* 1023.

[44] Paras 52 and 60.

[45] Para 60.

doubtful whether that protection extended beyond the walls of one's bedroom.[46] However, the visibility in the public sphere of sexual minorities is now clearly protected by the Court. Since it is no longer possible for European politicians to seriously defend the criminalisation of homosexuality,[47] interference with sexual minorities' rights unfortunately takes the route of hindering the public expression of LGBT persons and associations, based on the same principles that, in the past, justified the criminalisation of homosexual relationships, namely the protection of morals and of the rights of others, including the protection of religious beliefs. The Court fights such arguments and has found violations of Article 11 against several contracting parties for the prohibition of demonstrations.[48] Moreover, in the face of the increasing tendency in certain states to abuse freedom of expression to attack and insult sexual minorities, while hate speech may lead to hate crime, *Vejdeland and Others v Sweden*,[49] in which a conviction for homophobic leaflets distributed in a school was considered not to infringe Article 10, is a milestone in the fight against homophobic hate speech, despite the caveats expressed by several judges.[50]

The difference in the age of consent between homosexual and heterosexual relationships, and sometimes within the category of same-sex relationships—between gay and lesbian couples—is another example of the persistence of

[46] Johnson, 103–12. Johnson considers that the ECtHR maintains an ambiguous position towards what he calls the 'public/private binary'.

[47] See however the communicated case *HÇ v Turkey* App no 6428/12 (ECtHR, 14 February 2013) on provisions criminalising homosexual activities in the 'Turkish Republic of Northern Cyprus'.

[48] *Bączkowski and Others v Poland* (2009) 48 EHRR 19; *Alekseyev v Russia* App nos 4916/07, 25924/08 and 14599/09 (ECtHR, 21 October 2010); *Genderdoc-M v Moldova* App no 9106/06 (ECtHR, 12 June 2012). On the refusal to register an association defending LGBT rights, see the communicated case *Zhdanov and Rainbow House v Russia* App no 12200/08 (ECtHR, 11 March 2011). On allegations of ill-treatment and the illegal search of LGBT activists during a police raid at the association office, see the communicated case *Aghdgomelashvili and Japaridze v Georgia* App no 7224/11 (ECtHR, 3 December 2013), and the communicated case *Identoba and Others v Georgia* App no 73235/12 (ECtHR, 18 December 2013), on allegations of ill-treatment by counter-demonstrators.

[49] *Vejdeland and Others v Sweden* (2014) 58 EHRR 15. At para 55, the ECtHR states that discrimination based on sexual orientation is as serious as discrimination based on race, origin or colour. See also *Mladina DD Ljubljana v Slovenia* App no 20981/10 (ECtHR, 17 April 2014), in which the Court considered that the domestic court's order to a publisher to pay damages to a parliamentarian for an article in which he was insulted, while the article was a response to his negative remarks, ridicule and offensive portrayal of homosexuals during the debates on same-sex civil partnerships, breached Art 10.

[50] It appears that the fact that the leaflets were distributed in a school was instrumental in finding a violation for several judges (see the concurring opinion of Judge Spielmann joined by Judge Nussberger, and the concurring opinion of Judge Zupančič). This may mitigate the importance of the first application to homophobic statements of the Court's reasoning on hate speech (see the concurring opinion of Judge Yudkivska joined by Judge Villiger, who regret that 'the Court missed an opportunity to "consolidate an approach to hate speech" against homosexuals').

stereotypes about homosexuals as 'sexual predators'.[51] It was not before 2003[52] that the ECtHR[53] had the opportunity to rule on this issue. The finding of a violation was not surprising as the difference was clearly based on no objective justification whatsoever.[54] It is worth noting that, in this case, the Court does not rely on the notion of consensus—and therefore the margin of appreciation plays no role—as this would only have been necessary had the government provided compelling justification for the difference in treatment in the first place. It is regrettable that this very firm and laudable position is not followed in other cases where differences in treatment are justified by less than convincing arguments.[55]

In addition to protecting the sexual life of minorities, ECHR law protects gender identity as part of private life. Similarly to its evolution regarding homosexuality, the ECtHR finally adhered to the manner in which applicants perceived their gender identity. Overruling its precedents,[56] in *Christine Goodwin v UK*, the Court considered that the situation in which the applicant found herself, due to the discrepancy between her social reality and the law preventing the full recognition of her new gender, was a disproportionate interference with Article 8. Due to an emerging trend in the international community on a better acceptance and legal recognition of transsexuals, the United Kingdom could no longer rely on a period of transition necessary for its legal system to adapt, in particular in light of the existing precedents which could be considered as warning signals that the state needed to amend its legislation. The margin of appreciation that could be relied on was therefore limited to the means used to give effect to the state's positive obligation to fully recognise the applicant's new gender and did not extend to the existence of the positive obligation itself.

Despite its positive record in protecting the ability of sexual minorities to live in accordance with their gender identity and sexual orientation, the ECtHR could be criticised for the manner in which it treats migrants fighting their deportation on the basis of the risks faced if sent back to a country where homosexuality is still a criminal activity. In this area, the case law seems contradictory. For instance, in one case the application was dismissed on the basis that discreet homosexual

[51] See Johnson, 101, relying on *Dudgeon* at para 62, where the Court stressed that it was necessary to impose 'some degree of control over homosexual conduct notably in order to provide safeguards against the exploitation and corruption of those who are specially vulnerable by reason, for example, of their youth…'.

[52] *L and V v Austria* (2003) 36 EHRR 55.

[53] See also EComHR, *Sutherland v UK*.

[54] This case has been complemented by *EB and Others v Austria* App nos 31913/07, 38357/07, 48098/07 and others (ECtHR, 7 November 2013), in which the applicants denounced the refusal to amend the record of their conviction, on the basis of Art 209 of the criminal code—which was the subject of the *L and V* case—repealed for being unconstitutional and unconventional. The Court unanimously found a violation of Art 14 in conjunction with Art 8.

[55] See, eg the joint dissenting opinion of Judges Rozakis, Spielmann and Jebens in *Schalk and Kopf v Austria* at para 8. It must be noted that judge Rozakis chaired the chamber in *L and V v Austria*.

[56] *Rees v UK* (1987) Series A no 106, 9 EHRR 56; *Sheffield and Horsham v UK* (1999) 27 EHRR 163.

activities were not prosecuted in Iran.[57] In another case, the discretion of the applicant played against him in the assessment of the risk he faced if sent back to Iraq.[58] In the former case, the Court indicated that as long as the applicant kept his sexual orientation to himself he would be safe at home; in the latter case concerning a married man who intended to maintain his family life as it was, the Court doubted the veracity of the applicant's claim to have had a homosexual relationship in Iraq, the discovery of which had allegedly led to the death of his sexual partner. The findings in these cases could be explained by the high burden of proof[59] and the fact that the Court limits itself to preventing deportation only if there is a serious risk of violation of Articles 2, 3 and 6 in the event of a flagrant denial of a fair trial.[60] However, the Court does not seem particularly sympathetic to the difficulty for migrants to be forthcoming about their sexual orientation, where such orientation is considered to be a crime in their home countries. This position also illustrates that the ECtHR seems to follow the idea—the myth, according to Fineman[61]—that applicants are rationalistic legal subjects, rather than vulnerable individuals who may not be able to defend their rights as expected. Moreover, the ECtHR does not pay attention to the dual vulnerable status of those applicants, as members of vulnerable groups, namely sexual minorities and asylum-seekers. It was doubtful whether, in interpreting Directive 2004/83/EC,[62] the CJ would be more open to the predicament of asylum-seekers. Nevertheless, the cases *Minister voor Immigratie en Asiel v X, Y* and *Z v Minister voor Immigratie en Asiel*[63] are, on one specific point, more advanced than the case law of the ECtHR. The CJ recognises that homosexuals may be considered as a 'social group',[64] on the basis that they meet the two criteria laid down by Article 10.1(d) of the Directive, namely that 'a person's sexual orientation is a characteristic so fundamental to his identity that he should not be forced to renounce it', and that 'the group whose members share the same sexual orientation

[57] *F v UK*, dec App no 17341/03 (ECtHR, 22 June 2004). Evidence relied on by the Court indicated that the burden of proof in Islamic law was so high that a conviction for homosexuality seemed implausible. However, public transgression of Islamic morals, through declarations defending homosexuality, would undoubtedly be harshly condemned. See also *IIN v the Netherlands* App no 2035/04 (ECtHR, 9 December 2004).

[58] *MKN v Sweden* App no 72413/10 (ECtHR, 27 June 2013). Moreover, the fact that the applicant, being Christian, belonged to a 'vulnerable minority' did not help his case.

[59] The applications were considered as lacking in credibility, or insufficiently substantiated.

[60] The Court often recalls that 'it cannot be required that an expelling Contracting State only return an alien to a country which is in full and effective enforcement of all the rights and freedoms set out in the Convention', see *F v UK*, at para 2.

[61] Fineman, 10–11. See also M Albertson Fineman, 'The Vulnerable subject and the responsive State' (2010–2011) *Emory Law Journal* 251, 262–64, and Peroni and Timmer, 1061.

[62] Directive 2004/83/EC on minimum standards for the qualification and status of third-country nationals or Stateless persons as refugees or as persons who otherwise need international protection and the content of the protection granted [2004] OJ L304/12.

[63] Joined Cases C-199/12 to C-201/12 *Minister voor Immigratie en Asiel v X, Y* and *Z v Minister voor Immigratie en Asiel* (CJEU, 7 November 2013).

[64] Persecution for 'membership of a particular social group' is one of the conditions laid down by the 1951 Geneva Convention and the Directive to grant refugee status.

has a distinct identity because it is perceived by the surrounding society as being different'—the existence of legislation criminalising homosexuality demonstrating the manner in which, through this stigmatisation, homosexuals are perceived as different.[65] However, on the negative side, the mere fact that the home country criminalises homosexuality is not considered, per se, as persecution. Only incarceration for homosexuality qualifies as an act of persecution, being a disproportionate and discriminatory punishment within the meaning of the Directive. So far, the CJ is in line with the restrictive case law of the ECtHR, as both courts are reluctant to export European standards on the criminalisation of homosexuality to third countries. However, the CJ departs from the *F* case by making it clear that

> requiring members of a social group sharing the same sexual orientation to conceal that orientation is incompatible with the recognition of a characteristic so fundamental to a person's identity that the persons concerned cannot be required to renounce it. Therefore, an applicant for asylum cannot be expected to conceal his homosexuality in his country of origin in order to avoid persecution.[66]

This assertion seems to indicate that the fact that the threat would remain theoretical as long as homosexuality is kept private will not impede the applicant's claim, if it can be demonstrated that public expression of homosexual orientation will lead to time in jail. However, the principle according to which the criminalisation of homosexuality is a necessary but insufficient condition to meet the definition of persecution is problematic, as it ignores the fact that persecution against homosexuals takes various forms.

V. DISCRIMINATION AT WORK: AN OPPORTUNITY FOR THE CJ TO TAKE THE LEAD IN THE PROTECTION OF SEXUAL MINORITIES

Work is an important part of an individual's life, but is also a place where discrimination may unfortunately thrive. Surprisingly, the case law in this area is underdeveloped. As far as the ECHR is concerned, protection could have been hindered by the fact that there is no express provision in the Convention protecting the right to work. Moreover, the Court can only tackle discrimination by a private employer if national authorities can be considered responsible on the international plane because of their actions or omissions in dealing with the claim.[67] In *Smith and Grady* and *Lustig-Prean and Beckett v UK*,[68] the leading cases on this matter, the applicants had been dismissed from the army because of their sexual

[65] See paras 45–49.

[66] Paras 70–71.

[67] However the public/private divide is not as serious an obstacle as one may think. National authorities may become liable through the courts reviewing the private dispute or if the discrimination is directly or indirectly facilitated by the law.

[68] *Smith and Grady v UK* (2000) 29 EHRR 493 and *Lustig-Prean and Beckett v UK* (2000) 29 EHRR 548.

orientation. Although the ECHR does not protect the right to work, Article 8's flexibility allowed the Court to consider that the impact of the investigations of the military police into their homosexuality and their consequent discharge from the army interfered with the applicants' private life. The Court drew a comparison with discrimination on the grounds of race to dismiss the Government's justification of the policy as based on 'a predisposed bias on the part of a heterosexual majority against a homosexual minority'. The case contains one of the strongest statements of the Court in defence of sexual minorities:

> these negative attitudes cannot, of themselves, be considered ... to amount to sufficient justification for the interferences with the applicants' rights outlined above any more than similar negative attitudes towards those of a different race, origin or colour.[69]

Recent cases of discrimination against sexual minorities have reached the Court, albeit indirectly, as the applications were lodged by individuals sanctioned by their employer due to their discriminatory behaviour towards sexual minorities.[70] The problem was rendered more sensitive, as the applicants relied on their religious beliefs to justify their refusal to deal with homosexual partners in the course of their work, thus creating a conflict of rights. The majority of the Court[71] rightly, but summarily,[72] concluded that the applicants' religious beliefs were not sufficient to counter the legitimate aim of promoting equality pursued by the national authorities.

Although prohibition of discrimination in the work place was included in the Founding Treaties, it was, at first, limited to sex discrimination. The CJ's case law expressly excluded discrimination based on sexual orientation from the interpretation of the notion of 'sex' in Directive 76/207/EEC on Equal Treatment for men and women, while accepting that discrimination in the form of dismissal due to gender reassignment could be included, as condoning such discrimination 'would be tantamount ... to a failure to respect the dignity and liberty' of the individual concerned. This daring interpretation was made in *P v S and Cornwall County Council*,[73] under the influence of Advocate General Tesauro, who pleaded for the CJ to depart from its traditional reasoning, according to which there was no discrimination if male and female transsexuals were treated equally badly, while the real issue was to sanction discrimination faced by individuals by reason of their

[69] *Smith and Grady*, para 97 and *Lustig-Prean and Beckett*, para 90.

[70] See *Eweida and Others v UK* (2013) 57 EHRR 8, esp the applications of Ladele and McFarlane. Ladele worked for a local council and refused to register civil partnerships; McFarlane, a counsellor working for a private organisation, refused to provide guidance to same-sex couples.

[71] While the ruling was unanimous with respect to McFarlane, Judges Vučinič and De Gaetano argued that it was Ladele who had suffered discrimination on the ground of her religious beliefs.

[72] The Court relied on the wide margin of appreciation afforded to states in cases involving conflicting Convention Rights. On this subject, see P Ducoulombier, 'Conflicts between Fundamental Rights and the European Court of Human Rights: an Overview' in E Brems (ed) *Conflicts between Fundamental Rights* (Antwerp, Intersentia, 2008) 217–47.

[73] Esp para 22.

gender.[74] The opportunity to continue this extensive interpretation was missed in *Grant v South-West Trains Ltd* as the CJ was not prepared to extend the definition of sex to cover sexual orientation. Reverting to its traditional reasoning, the Court considered that the refusal of travel concessions to the lesbian partner of a female employee, while afforded to employees' heterosexual partners, was not discrimination directly based on sex, as the concession would have been denied to the gay partner of a male employee.[75] This case demonstrates how the choice of the comparator can frame the conclusion of the Court. In *Grant*, the CJ also relied on the new legal basis provided by the Amsterdam Treaty to combat discrimination on the grounds of sexual orientation to support its findings.[76] Indeed, it is thanks to the enactment of the 'Framework Directive' that discrimination on the grounds of sexual orientation could be tackled. The case law remains nonetheless limited, illustrating the sensitivity of the issue.[77] Sexual orientation is a characteristic that is not apparent to the eye and which is likely to remain hidden if individuals have reasons to fear discrimination. Moreover, discrimination from an employer may be difficult to prove without risking infringing upon an employee's right to privacy. Therefore, when hostile statements are publicly made by employers, they must be appropriately sanctioned, as confirmed by the CJ in *Asociaţia ACCEPT*.[78] In an interview about the potential transfer of a player portrayed by a journalist as homosexual, the shareholder of a football club made an aggressive statement that the club would never hire homosexual players. The association lodged a complaint with the national body responsible for handling discrimination allegations. This body decided that the statements were discriminatory and imposed a warning, the sole penalty available in accordance with the law. In addition, it ruled that the case did not fall within the scope of a possible employment relationship, as the shareholder did not have the legal capacity to determine the recruitment policy of the club. The association sought an annulment of the decision, and the domestic court asked the CJ for clarification of the interpretation of Directive 2000/78/EC. The CJ answered that the public perception of the role played by the shareholder was a relevant criterion in the overall assessment of the situation. The football club, as an employer, could not

> deny the existence of facts from which it may be inferred that it has a discriminatory recruitment policy merely by asserting that statements suggestive of the existence of a homophobic recruitment policy come from a person who, while claiming and appearing

[74] Opinion of Advocate General Tesauro, 14 December 1995, esp paras 17–18.

[75] Paras 27–28.

[76] Para 48.

[77] See also Cases C-267/06 *Maruko v Versorgungsanstalt der Deutschen Buhnen* [2008] ECR I-1757 and C-147/08 *Römer v Freie und Hansestadt Hamburg* [2011] ECR I-3591. As these cases concern the financial situation of the surviving partner of a same-sex relationship, they will be analysed under the subheading 'protection of couples'.

[78] Case C-81/12 *Asociaţia ACCEPT v Consiliul Naţional pentru Combaterea Discriminării* (CJEU, 25 April 2013).

to play an important role in the management of that employer, is not legally capable of binding it in recruitment matters.[79]

The burden of proof shifting then to the employer, the Court rightly added that, in order to prove that the football club did not have a discriminatory recruitment policy, it was not necessary to rely on the fact that persons of a particular sexual orientation had been recruited in the past, as this could infringe upon these persons' right to respect for private life.[80] Finally, the Court implied[81] that warnings, being symbolic penalties, were not sufficient to deter and sanction discrimination on the grounds of sexual orientation, while Article 17 of the Directive requires 'effective, proportional and dissuasive' sanctions,[82] transposing its reasoning on race discrimination.[83]

VI. PROTECTION OF COUPLES: A MARRIAGE IN ANYTHING BUT NAME?

A. From Private to Family Life

In ECHR case law, the protection of family life was difficult to achieve for sexual minorities, with the exception of rights related to pre-existing families. In that respect, the ECtHR had no trouble finding a violation of Article 14 in conjunction with Article 8 in a case where a father was denied his parental rights on the sole ground of his sexual orientation.[84] The principle was extended to discrimination based on gender identity, although in the particular circumstances of the case, no violation was found as the change in the applicant's rights was temporary and justified by the emotional disorder created by the gender reassignment operation.[85]

It was however more difficult for the Court to accept that sexual minorities could enjoy a family life as heterosexuals do. In that respect, a hierarchy first appeared in the case law, as the Court admitted that transsexuals could enjoy a family life,[86] while applications brought by homosexuals were channelled through the other limbs of Article 8.[87] However, this did not prevent the Court

[79] Para 49.

[80] Para 57.

[81] The Court asserts that it is for national authorities to ascertain whether warnings are appropriate while at the same time giving a strong indication that such sanctions are not commensurate to the seriousness of the breach of the principle of equal treatment (paras 69–70).

[82] Para 61.

[83] See Case C-54/07 *Centrum voor gelijkheid van kansen en voor racismebestrijding v Firma Feryn NV* [2008] ECR I-5187, concerning statements made by an employer that he would not hire immigrants. The CJ concluded that this was direct discrimination, for which effective sanctions were required, although there was no identifiable victim.

[84] See *Salgueiro da Silva Mouta v Portugal.*

[85] See *PV v Spain.*

[86] See *X, Y, and Z v UK.*

[87] See, eg *Kozak v Poland* (2010) 51 EHRR 16, para 83, for the use of the 'private life' limb of Art 8. In *Karner v Austria* (2004) 38 EHRR 24, para 33, the Court avoided the problematic issue by relying on the protection of one's home, also used in *Kozak*, para 84.

from defending the right of same-sex partners to be treated like unmarried heterosexual partners, in respect of social and economic benefits. The Court refused to accept that the protection of the traditional family[88] could justify differences of treatment in the allocation of rights to the surviving partner of a same-sex relationship.[89] However, the Court still maintains that states are free to differentiate between married and unmarried couples. Thus, granting rights to married couples while denying them to unmarried couples, both homosexual and heterosexual, does not constitute discrimination based on sexual orientation, even when marriage is not available to same-sex couples.[90] The CJ case law is in line with that of the ECtHR, as demonstrated by the case of *Maruko* confirmed by *Römer*. When assessing the compliance of domestic legislation with the Framework Directive, the CJ relied on the fact that surviving partners of registered partnerships were in situations comparable to those of married couples with respect to pension rights under national law.[91] Denying the benefit of rights afforded to married couples constituted, therefore, direct discrimination. These cases resemble those of the ECtHR. Both bodies of case law reject the argument of indirect discrimination based on the fact that marriage is not available to same-sex partners, preventing them from accessing the most protective legal regime. The CJ's case law may seem more advanced, as by insisting on the comparability of the situations of registered and married partners—registered partnership not being available to heterosexual couples—the CJ seems to reject the idea that the mere fact of being married is sufficient to consider that couples are in different situations. The ECtHR, on the other hand, has, thus far, focused on the comparability of situations within the category of unmarried couples.[92] However, it could be argued from *Burden v UK* that when a state offers same-sex couples a legal status similar to marriage, discrimination against registered partners will be difficult to justify by relying on the argument that the state is entitled to treat married couples in a more favourable manner.[93] Nevertheless, the two courts are closer than initially thought, as the

[88] Depending on whether the disputed right is allocated to married couples only or also benefits stable heterosexual relationships, the 'traditional family' defended by the state oscillates between married couples and de facto heterosexual couples.

[89] See, eg *Kozak v Poland* and *Karner v Austria* on the right to succeed to a tenancy.

[90] See, eg *Manenc v France*, dec App no 66686/09 (ECtHR, 21 September 2010).

[91] Discrimination in relation to pay is extensively understood by the CJ to cover occupational pensions.

[92] See, eg *Karner* and *Kozak*. It was not necessary to expand on the comparability of the situations of same-sex and married couples, as same-sex partners were denied rights granted to both de facto heterosexual partners and married couples. On the contrary, see *Manenc*, where the 'marriage excuse' could be used by the government as the issue concerned a right afforded to married couples but denied to civil partners, whether heterosexuals or homosexuals. The Court considered that civil partners and married couples were not in similar situations, as the legal regime of the civil partnership is too different from that of marriage. The Court could therefore easily dismiss the application, as homosexuals were treated equally as badly as unmarried heterosexuals. However, the Court ignored the fact that, at the time, homosexuals, as opposed to heterosexuals, did not have access to marriage.

[93] *Burden v UK* (2008) 47 EHRR 38, esp paras 64–66. The Court insisted on the difference between the situation of sisters living together and that of married and registered couples. It stressed that civil partnership was designed to correspond, as much as possible, to marriage.

CJ's position is the result of the fact that German law put married and registered couples in the same situation with respect to pension rights.[94] Had it not been the case, the case law seems to infer that EU law would not impose equal treatment of married and registered couples, in light of the lack of consensus among Member States on the 'assimilation of marriage and other forms of statutory union'.[95] Therefore, both the CJ and ECtHR admit that states remain free to maintain a more favourable regime for married couples and fall short of imposing on states an obligation to create a civil partnership regime mirroring the rights and obligations of marriage, a marriage in anything but name.[96] Moreover, the CJ's solution is only applicable where a system of registered partnership exists alongside marriage. It offers no assistance to applicants living in a country where there is no legal recognition for homosexual couples. Similarly, if the ECtHR recently found a violation of Article 14 in conjunction with Article 8 as regards Greek legislation opening civil partnership to heterosexual couples only, it was cautious to limit the question under consideration so as to exclude the key issue of whether states were compelled to provide for a form of legal recognition of homosexual unions.[97]

It was not until *Schalk and Kopf v Austria* that the Court finally considered it 'artificial to maintain the view that, in contrast to a different-sex couple, a same-sex couple cannot enjoy "family life" for the purposes of Article 8'.[98] However, this welcome step would not translate immediately into the recognition of new rights, as will be shown below. It is propounded that the 'sexual alterity element', missing in same-sex relationships, explained the Court's reluctance to admit the existence of a family life, despite the evolution of this notion since the Convention entered into force. Although the Court has finally included stable homosexual relationships in de facto family ties worthy of protection, family has remained for a very long time a heterosexual institution.[99] The same is true of marriage.

[94] This is a question which, under EU law, is to be decided by domestic courts. It is, therefore, possible for a higher court to differ from the interpretation of the referring court on the comparability of the situations. This also demonstrates that national authorities remain free to maintain different legal regimes for marriage and civil partnership. In countries where civil partnership offers a regime identical to that of marriage, denial of a pension benefit would certainly be considered as direct discrimination while in countries where the two regimes are different with respect to financial rights and obligations, it is unlikely that domestic courts would find direct discrimination, the situations of married and registered couples being insufficiently comparable, in line with the decision of the ECtHR in *Manenc v France*.

[95] See joined Cases C-122/99P and C-125/99P *D and Sweden v Council* [2001] ECR I-4319, para 50.

[96] See, eg *Manenc v France*, *Burden v UK*, para 63, *Schalk and Kopf v Austria*, para 108: 'States enjoy a certain margin of appreciation as regards the exact status conferred by alternative means of recognition'.

[97] See *Vallianatos and Others v Greece* App nos 29381/09 and 32684/09 (ECtHR, Grand Chamber, 7 November 2013) para 75.

[98] Para 94.

[99] For certain judges, family should remain as such. See the dissenting opinion of Judge Loucaides in *EB v France*, in which he considered that the circumstances of the case—the applicant applied for an agreement to adopt as a single person but was cohabiting with her partner—presented 'a real risk that the model and image of a family in the context of which the child would have to live and develop his/her personality would be distorted'.

B. Access to an Official Protective Status: the Resistance of the States' Margin of Appreciation

Marriage remains a traditional institution in which the Court is no longer willing to interfere. The Court now asserts that the evolution undergone by marriage in several states, leading it to become available to same-sex couples, reflects their own particular perception of the institution and does not derive from Article 12. Therefore, the daring ruling of *Christine Goodwin* cannot be transposed to homosexuals. In *Goodwin*, the Court, after deciding that the United Kingdom had failed to fulfil its positive obligation under Article 8, went further by stating that the situation breached Article 12. Being unable to have her birth certificate amended to reflect her gender reassignment, the applicant could not marry her partner. Relying on the wording of the CFR that no longer used the terms 'man' and 'woman' in relation to marriage, on the evolution of society and medical progress, the Court considered that the particular wording of Article 12 could not prevent dynamic interpretation of the Convention, entailing that gender was no longer to be determined solely by biological criteria. Therefore, despite the margin of appreciation afforded to the state in that field, there was no reason justifying that transsexuals should be deprived of their right to marry.

However, sexual alterity remains central in the case law of the ECtHR, and marriage is still between a man and a woman, hindering progress in sexual minorities' rights.[100] In *Schalk and Kopf*, the Court relied exceptionally on historical interpretation,[101] and less unusually on holistic interpretation[102] as well as on the lack of consensus in Europe,[103] to prevent an evolutive interpretation of Article 12 requiring states to grant same-sex couples access to marriage. Global interpretation was of no avail, as the Court relied on the explanations relating to the CFR to confirm its own interpretation that the decision to provide same-sex couples access to marriage was to be left to the discretion of the states.[104]

[100] See *Schalk and Kopf*, para 59, distinguished from *Christine Goodwin*: '*Christine Goodwin* is concerned with marriage of partners who are of different gender…'.

[101] Para 55: 'regard must be had to the historical context in which the Convention was adopted. In the 1950s marriage was clearly understood in the traditional sense of being a union between partners of different sex.'

[102] ibid: 'looked at in isolation, the wording of Article 12 might be interpreted so as not to exclude the marriage between two men or two women. However, in contrast, all other substantive Articles of the Convention grant rights and freedoms to "everyone" or state that "no one" is to be subjected to certain types of prohibited treatment. The choice of wording in Article 12 must thus be regarded as deliberate.'

[103] Para 58. At the time of the ruling, only six states out of 47 allowed same-sex marriage.

[104] Paras 60–61.

Cases related to transsexuals confirm the importance of sexual alterity. In *Hämälaïnen v Finland*,[105] the ECtHR found no violation of Article 8 with respect to Finnish legislation compelling married transsexuals to end their marriage in order to have their gender reassignment fully recognised. The applicant, a male-to-female transsexual, was married and had a family. The couple refused to trade their marriage for a civil partnership as required by law,[106] mainly for religious reasons. The Court refused to extend its reasoning in *Goodwin*, and relied rather on its findings in *Schalk and Kopf*. It considered that it was not possible to accept the applicant's claim, as this would impose on Finland recognition of same-sex marriage, and it was not possible to obtain under Article 8 what the Court refused to grant under Article 12.

However, since *Schalk and Kopf*, the Court has made some progress on the issue of access to an official status for same-sex couples. In *Schalk and Kopf*, the Court found no violation of Article 8 with respect to the state's failure to provide for a civil partnership regime before 2010. Although the Court acknowledged the existence of an emerging consensus, it was recent and still evolving. On this basis, the Court concluded that Austria could not be considered at fault for not having introduced the Registered Partnership Act at an earlier date. With the passing of time and increasing recognition in Europe of civil marital status for homosexuals, it will become more difficult for states to justify their inaction in that field.[107] However, three years after the *Schalk and Kopf* ruling, the Court is still reluctant to take a strong stance on the obligation for states to offer homosexual couples access to some sort of official status. *Vallianatos and Others v Greece* confirms this impression. In 2008, Greece enacted an unprecedented law, providing for civil unions to be registered alongside marriages. However, civil unions were open only to different-sex couples. The Court first decided that heterosexual and homosexual couples were in a similar situation, on the basis of the general assertion taken from *Schalk and Kopf* that they share the same need for legal recognition and protection of their relationships. The Court then departed from *Schalk and Kopf* by finding a violation of Article 14 in conjunction with Article 8, as the authorities did not provide the strong justification required when a difference in treatment is based on sexual orientation. First, the Court rejected the government's argument according to which it was not necessary to open civil unions to same-sex couples as a similar degree of protection could be achieved by other means, such as contracts. Even if the argument were true, the Court rightly emphasised the intrinsic

[105] *Hämälaïnen v Finland* App no 37359/09 (ECtHR, Grand Chamber, 16 July 2014). See also *Parry v UK* and *R and F v UK*, dec App nos 42971/05 and 35748/05 (ECtHR, 28 November 2006).

[106] It was necessary to have the consent of the spouse to end the marriage, which would be automatically changed into a civil partnership.

[107] However, it could be argued in light of *A, B and C v Ireland* (2011) 53 EHRR 13 that, in this area, the moral values of a country could prevail over an opposite consensus. See also *Vallianatos*, para 92: 'The fact that, at the end of a gradual evolution, a country finds itself in an isolated position as regards one aspect of its legislation does not necessarily imply that that aspect conflicts with the Convention.'

symbolic value of attaining an official status, irrespective of its legal effects.[108] Paying lip service to the government's second argument, according to which the exclusion of same-sex partners pursued the legitimate aim of protecting the traditional family, the Court added that the Convention being a living instrument, the state needed to take into consideration the evolution of society and 'the fact that there is not just one way or one choice when it comes to leading one's family or private life'.[109] In addition, as the government strongly insisted on the protection of children born out of wedlock, it was easy for the Court to stress the inanity of the argument, as civil unions were open to heterosexual couples whether they had children or not. If the *Vallianatos* case is one step further in the right direction, the Court was cautious to warn that it was not called to rule on the issue of whether states were obliged to provide same-sex couples some sort of legal recognition, framing the question as strictly one of discrimination.[110] Therefore, states are still free, in light of the insufficient consensus in Europe and despite the emerging trend stressed by the Court in *Vallianatos*,[111] to deny same-sex couples any official status, although same-sex partners are increasingly protected with respect to the material consequences of their union.

C. Adoption

Applications related to adoption were first brought by single individuals, alleging discrimination on the basis of their sexual orientation. The leading case on this issue is *Fretté v France*. Under French law, single individuals are entitled to adopt, but need to apply for prior authorisation. During the course of the social services' inquiry, Fretté revealed that he was homosexual. He was then denied the authorisation on the basis that it was not in the best interest of a child to be adopted by a homosexual, regardless of his personal and educational qualities. The Court, by four votes to three, found no violation. The Court admitted the legitimacy of the aim pursued by the authorities, namely the protection of the health and rights of children. It then recognised a wide margin of appreciation, due to the lack of consensus among European countries on the issue of adoption by homosexuals, while ignoring the factor limiting the scope of the margin, namely that discrimination based on sexual orientation requires particularly strong and compelling justification. The Court finally concluded that the interest of the child should prevail over the right of the applicant. The dissenting judges regretted that the Court had analysed the case in an abstract manner, condoning the fact that the adoption agreement had been refused on the sole basis of sexual

[108] Para 81.
[109] Para 84.
[110] Para 75.
[111] The Court stressed that Greece was, with Lithuania, one of only two states to exclude same-sex couples from civil partnerships.

orientation, which is normally incompatible with the Convention, and that no concrete evidence had been brought forward to exemplify how the interest of an orphan would be endangered by the sexual orientation of the applicant. As would be reiterated in other cases by dissenting judges,[112] when it comes to discrimination on the grounds of sexual orientation, the margin of appreciation should only play a role once the Government has presented solid justification for the difference in treatment, which was not the case in this instance.

However, in *EB v France*, the Grand Chamber overruled this precedent. In *EB*, the domestic authorities had cautiously avoided any reference to the applicant's sexual orientation by relying on two grounds to deny the necessary authorisation: the lack of a referent of the other sex, and EB's partner's ambivalent attitude towards the adoption. While the second ground is a legitimate concern, since the environment in which the child is welcomed is important, the Court considered that the first ground was problematic, as it could render ineffective the right for single individuals to adopt. The Court added that the government had been unable to provide statistics demonstrating that the argument was not used in a discriminatory manner. The Court finally decided that the potentially discriminatory nature of the first ground contaminated the whole decision, which led to a violation of Article 14 in conjunction with Article 8, by a majority of 10 votes. The case of *EB* represents progress in the rights of homosexuals, although it had been stressed that the Court chose an inadequate case to set important principles.[113] However, those who criticise the Court's reasoning in *EB* seem to minimise the covert influence of the applicant's sexual orientation in the authorities' decision.

The Court was also confronted with the problem of second-parental adoption, when a member of a same-sex couple sought to adopt the other partner's child. In *Gas and Dubois v France*,[114] the Court relied on the lack of comparability between the applicants and married couples to rule that the impossibility for the female partner of a same-sex couple to adopt her partner's child was not discriminatory, as this would lead to the child losing her filial ties with her biological mother. Second-parental adoption was indeed unavailable to all unmarried couples, reducing the chances of success of a discriminatory claim, since the 'right' comparator would be the category of heterosexual unmarried couples. However, one may question the choice of this comparator and wonder why unmarried stable couples, whether heterosexual or homosexual, should be considered to be in a different situation from married couples when it comes to second-parental adoption,[115] despite the fact that the rights and obligations of civil partnership are different from those attached to marriage. However, the majority of the Court maintains the principle according to which states remain free to give more rights to married couples. Moreover, the Court again overlooks the argument according

[112] See, eg the joint dissenting opinion of Judges Rozakis, Spielmann and Jebens in *Schalk and Kopf*.
[113] See the dissenting opinion of Judge Costa joined by Judges Türmen, Ugrekhelidze and Jočienė.
[114] *Gas and Dubois v France* App no 25951/07 (ECtHR, 15 March 2012).
[115] See the concurring opinion of Judge Spielmann joined by Judge Berro-Lefèvre.

to which, at the time of the case, marriage was not open to homosexuals, on the basis that the Convention does not impose an obligation to offer access to this institution to same-sex couples.

In light of *Gas and Dubois*, *X and Others v Austria* may come as a surprise.[116] However, the Court was particularly cautious to prevent any extensive interpretation of its findings by limiting the scope of the question to be determined. In the latter case, the applicants disputed the domestic courts' refusal to approve an adoption agreement seeking to replace, as a second parent, the father of a child by the mother's female partner, against the father's will. However, the courts refused to investigate whether it was in the best interest of the child to overrule the father's opposition, a procedure which can be pursued when heterosexual couples are involved, as according to Austrian law, adoption by the parent's homosexual partner was prohibited. The applicants, instructed by *Gas and Dubois*, knew that it was hopeless to claim discrimination vis-à-vis married couples and, instead, insisted that they were claiming a right afforded to unmarried heterosexual couples. This crucial difference allowed the Court to depart from the *Gas and Dubois* precedent. The Court considered that unmarried heterosexual couples and homosexual couples were in comparable situations. It could be then foreseen that it would be difficult for the government to justify a difference in treatment based on sexual orientation only, in particular as the Court narrowed the margin of appreciation, using in a arguable manner the European consensus.[117] Indeed, if the relevant provisions of the civil code were drafted in a prima facie neutral manner, it appeared from the domestic courts' interpretation that homosexual couples were excluded from second-parental adoption. The Court relied on the fact that the applicants' claim was not reviewed by the courts because of their sexual orientation while, had it been a heterosexual couple, it would have been necessary to analyse in concreto whether the adoption agreement was in the best interest of the child. Thus, the majority's reasoning insisted on the procedural nature of the violation, while the minority emphasised that the real question was to know whether the domestic courts' refusal was illegitimate, in light of the father's opposition and the best interest of the child to maintain ties with his father. Despite the potential criticism of the Court's reasoning, *X and Others* is a new step forward in achieving equality for homosexual couples.

[116] *X and Others v Austria* (2013) 57 EHRR 14.

[117] As the minority stressed, it seems that a consensus against second-parental adoption exists. However, the Court considered that no conclusion can be drawn from the comparative analysis. This shows, once again, the lack of coherence of the consensus analysis. As noted by Judge Rozakis, in case of discrimination on the grounds of sexual orientation, the margin of appreciation and the consensus analysis should not be relied on, unless the government presents solid justification for the difference in treatment. It would have been better for the Court to avoid this issue, despite having been invited to answer the government's argument on this point.

VII. CONCLUSION

Over recent decades, sexual minorities' rights have been strengthened by the CoE, in particular thanks to the ECtHR, and the EU, and have become a major issue in the field of human rights law, demonstrating the importance of achieving equality for this vulnerable group. However, even if Europe remains one of the most advanced continents in the protection of sexual minorities, the situation is far from being perfect. The legal situation has undoubtedly improved as battles have been fought and won and legislation has been enacted at the European and domestic levels to improve sexual minorities' rights; however, equality is yet to be achieved, as the issue of same-sex marriage illustrates. Nevertheless, social acceptance of sexual minorities is not as widespread as might have been expected, and a divide seems to have emerged between the west and the east of the continent, which may translate into the enactment of homophobic laws and an increase in hate crimes. If the social situation seems to worsen the further east we go, the surprising and rather worrying demonstrations and debates in Parliament in France during the passing of the Bill on same-sex marriage demonstrate that societies remain divided on sexual minorities' rights. Traditional values and institutions as well as religious beliefs are used to deny equality to sexual minorities and are accepted as legitimate aims for restrictions to Convention Rights by the ECtHR. Even if the weight of these arguments is gradually reduced in the Court's analysis, it is hoped that, in the near future, the Court will question the very legitimacy of such arguments to deny human beings their basic right to equality.

III

Non-Nationals

11

The Unexpected Precariat

CAROLINE SAWYER

I. STATELESSNESS AND THE PRECARIAT IN MODERN EUROPE

UNTIL RECENTLY, STATELESSNESS and its attendant miseries attracted little interest amongst European legal academics. The political and social ravages of the mid-twentieth century left many people de jure stateless and without a country, but international law and the United Nations were able to regularise most of them, especially through the systems set up for resettling refugees, and Europe in particular had established a commitment to human rights and the institutional structures to enforce them.[1] During the Cold War, perhaps the most noticeable nationality issues in Europe were the competing claims for populations—the claim of West Germany that East Germans were theirs, in order to support the claim for reuniting Germany, or the claim of the Republic of Ireland to all of those born on the whole island of Ireland, along with the territory itself. The end of the Cold War and the rise of liberal democracy, and then the fragility of the national and global economies, have changed the debate. First of all, within the enlarging European Union, covering almost all the continent, European nationals have become citizens with rights valid across the continent.[2] The focus of concern, if any, became the non-Europeans who had made lives in Europe without obtaining formal immigration status—the de facto stateless, or status-less, populations arising usually from clandestine immigration of those unwilling or perhaps unable to return.[3] The spirit of the European outlook

[1] The panoply of relevant United Nations documents began with the Universal Declaration of Human Rights 1948 and included the Convention on the Status of Refugees of 1951. These treaties generally set up principles but leave the mechanics of the implementation to the national states. Later instruments that might be relevant in principle here, such as the Declaration on the Protection of the Rights of All Migrant Workers and Their Families, or the Declaration on the Human Rights of Individuals who are Not Nationals of the Countries in Which They Live, but they attract little support in migrant-receiving European countries and do not bind them to give any rights to those without status.

[2] Art 20(1) TFEU: 'Citizenship of the Union is hereby established. Every person holding the nationality of a Member State shall be a citizen of the Union. Citizenship of the Union shall be additional to and not replace national citizenship.'

[3] Manuel Angel Castillo and James C Hathaway, 'Temporary Protection' in James C Hathaway (ed), *Reconceiving International Refugee Law* (Leiden, Martinus Nijhoff, 1997).

however then changed, at least with the global financial crisis in 2008, followed by debt issues across the continent which are not yet resolved: more protectionist and nationalistic policies are in the air, including the irony of the number of anti-European Union members being elected to the European Parliament in the spring of 2014. In the economic aftermath of both the financial and economic crisis, and the widespread liberation from state regulation that preceded it, there is now a new group whose position may appear unexpectedly insecure: the internal migrant.

There has been recent discussion of the concept of 'precariats'—classes or groups of people whose basic rights are fragile, and whose lives are consequently built on precarious foundations. The author of a recent widely publicised work, *Dangerous Precariats*, Guy Standing, has suggested that those in short-term, low-paid jobs, though they fall into various subgroups, have in common that their place in society is that of 'denizens' rather than full citizens: they have, in effect, insufficient social, cultural, political and economic rights to make a secure life.[4] The similarities between statelessness, at least the de facto kind, and precariats is clear—it is the lack of assurance of the basic wherewithal to make a life. That wherewithal can be practical, as when jobs and social welfare are unavailable to anyone because society itself is not prospering, or legal—when a person lacks the rights to establish a life, such as the right to work. The two may combine where economies are weak and societies seek to protect some groups at the expense of others. Especially where the issue is employment, those disfavoured politically are often foreigners. It will be suggested here that the European endeavour has created a new precariat, and one that does not immediately look like previous such groups, though its legal conditions are similar. It is a group that appears to have the sort of substance that makes life solid and prosperous—education, money, desirable skills and often high-status employment—but whose members have an unexpectedly precarious status in the country in which they lead their lives. There are many settled internal migrants in the Union, including professionals working across both the public and the private sectors, who must glimpse the risk of insecurity in the changing political conditions. Changes to free movement rights, even if they are primarily aimed at the unskilled (or a myth of the unskilled), will affect skilled workers too, and perhaps more, since they often embed themselves thoroughly in a host country, making social and professional networks and investing in property. Removing their civic status would render them in a similar position in their host country to nationals deprived of citizenship. Nevertheless that is the

[4] The term 'denizens' has recently resurfaced, especially in sociological discussion of the de facto stateless, to mean the inhabitants of a place, either without reference to their status or with reference to those who do not have formal status. It is however properly a mediaeval term for the status taken by aliens who wished in particular to be able to purchase or inherit land, which was at that time restricted. The process of denization, by letters patent, was akin to modern naturalisation, with an oath of allegiance, but it did not amount to naturalisation. Denization operated from the thirteenth century until naturalisation became available in the nineteenth. 'Denizens' in Standing's work generally do not lack formal citizenship, but are economically dispossessed and disenfranchised.

implication of many anti-European ideas that are now politically mainstream across Europe, and it is not a foregone conclusion that those ideas will retreat and disappear.

A. Constructing Precariats in Europe

The legal construction of the lives of Europe's new precariat owes more to ideas of state sovereignty than to the endeavours of international law or human rights; the twentieth century saw the latter concepts meeting the challenges of events, but within the framework of the former. The legacy of legal statelessness was substantial. In the aftermath of the Russian Revolution of 1917, thousands of people left or were expelled by the new Soviet government; more people fled into Europe from the Armenian genocides. The outcome of the First World War left many people across Europe in civil limbo. In the rise of nationalism that led into the catastrophe of the fascist era, there were exchanges of peoples between Greece and Turkey in the 1920s. The 1930s and 1940s found individuals and peoples across Europe losing citizenship status anywhere. Amidst rising disorder amongst people and nations, stateless and unprotected people were impoverished, excluded, persecuted and murdered.

A person without a country was fundamentally devoid of any form of legal protection—if citizenship was, as Hannah Arendt famously said, 'the right to have rights', then statelessness meant abject vulnerability. The international legal structures that deal with statelessness came out of Europe's heritage of competing systems of nationality attribution and its disastrous history of genocide. The focus of international law measures was to deal with the practical position of the stateless—the consequences of statuslessness—by assuring everyone of a status by ensuring everyone had a state. International and domestic laws requiring the attribution of citizenship to stateless persons therefore relate to the de jure stateless—those with no legal nationality at all. De jure statelessness is however very difficult to show, and in any case states are unwilling to sign up to such a potential infringement of their basic right to choose their own nationals.

The de facto stateless, who include precariats such as domestic communities of foreign heritage to whom the relevant state will not grant status, are more akin legally to immigrants. They are often not de jure stateless but are the nationals of some place they do not know or will not or cannot return to, or where they have never been. The assumption is often that they nevertheless have the bottom-line protection of a universalist human rights law, again based in the post-war European endeavour which aimed to settle the debts of man's inhumanity to man and provide a foundation for both peace and the recognition and enforcement of human rights. Notwithstanding its origins, the law and practice of human rights does not, however, deal with citizenship or immigration status, or the fundamental problem of those who have made their lives in a country that does not want them. The strongest practical rights in Europe are those in the ECHR, which are primarily 'negative' rights, or the right to keep the state from interfering with one's life; those can be enforced by individuals before the court at Strasbourg as well as domestically, and damages claims lie for breach.[5] The sort of 'positive' rights that go to make up a life, such as the right to work, arise if at all from international obligations under less enforceable treaties, and are in effect a matter for the state to decide on in the individual case. But they do not prevent denial or withdrawal of immigration status or citizenship.

Twentieth-century attempts to deal with nationality issues had focused on ending not only statelessness but also, for example, its gender-related elements, or the perceived problem of dual nationality,[6] but some voices spoke of the fundamentally destructive nature of statelessness. Anna Aszkanazy, writing in 1930, the year of the Hague Convention on Nationality, spoke of how in the inter-war years, countries rejected sections of society so that 'human lives are trifled with in the worst manner of the Middle Ages'. Save perhaps for the expectation of some basic right to subsistence, her characterisation of the problems of statelessness is little different from today's:

> We must grasp clearly all that is involved in lack of nationality: it means that the stateless person can do no work without permission of the authorities. And how can the authorities give permission when hundreds of thousands of their own citizens are out of work? Statelessness therefore means starvation, for the stateless gets no unemployment relief, he can get no public assistance, his children have to pay for their schooling as foreigners, generally two or three times more than other people, and finally he can get no passport or visum. Moreover, at any moment he can be deported for no given reason.[7]

The seeds of future confusion in discussing statelessness can already be seen, however: a truly stateless person, who has no nationality at all, would have nowhere to be deported to. Perhaps a more accurate word for those Aszkanazy is discussing would be 'statusless'—without any 'effective nationality' or rights to work and carry on a life in the country they live in; the phenomenon also called de facto statelessness.

B. Legal Obligations of States Towards Precarious Groups

After the Second World War came international Conventions to deal with refugees, who were often stateless, and, eventually, stateless people who were not refugees.

[5] Since Joined Cases C-6/90 and C-9/90 and C-9/90 *Andrea Francovich and Others v Italian Republic* [1991] ECR I-5357, states are liable to compensate individuals for breaches of rights where they have failed to implement Directives which would have secured their protection.

[6] The United Nations Convention on the Nationality of Married Women 1958, providing that marriage and divorce should not automatically affect women's nationality, and giving special privileges for wives; European Convention on Reduction of Cases of Multiple Nationality and Military Obligations in Cases of Multiple Nationality 1963.

[7] Anna Aszkanazy, *The Problem of Statelessness* (Geneva, Women's International League for Peace and Freedom, 1930).

The non-refugee stateless were relatively neglected in legal principle, often because of the substantial numbers whose status overlapped.[8] Whilst all the European states signed up to the limited but effective tidying-up operation for refugees, the subsequent statelessness Conventions were received very differently. Relatively few states signed up to the Convention relating to the Status of Stateless Persons of 1954, which in effect requires stateless people to be given similar rights in their host country as the 1951 Convention required to be given to refugees; and even fewer signed up to the Convention on the Reduction of Statelessness 1961, which requires in effect a commitment to giving status to stateless persons born in their territory, though in practice states often incorporated equivalent provisions in their laws.[9] Moreover, the definition of statelessness used in the Conventions, and still used by the United Nations in its discussions and statistics as well as by individual states, is the de jure definition, which means those with no citizenship at all. That is difficult to prove even where it is capable of being asserted, since citizenship rights may bc inherited, and a country may regard a person as a citizen of somewhere they could obtain recognition from even if they have not done so. The combination of these factors with the confusion with the status of refugees led to a lack of clear debate around statelessness, or de facto statelessness, as well as de jure statelessness, as pressing issues in the later twentieth century, and the issue was seen as one of immigration, which in the context of the 'Fortress Europe', meant non-Europeans.[10]

The political stumbling-block with the statelessness conventions was partly their requirement that states sign away part of the most inviolable aspect of state sovereignty—the right of a country to choose its own members—but there was also a perception that statelessness in Europe was a problem of the past. Paul Weis, the father of literature on statelessness and of those international Conventions to do away with it, was optimistic that statelessness was withering away.[11] Post-war Europe was mindful of man's capacity for inhumanity to man, and the rise of anti-racism and the rhetoric of tolerance and diversity in the 1970s fed into a distaste for exclusion. The relative quiet of Europe in the decades following the war tended to mean the question of what the Conventions could really do rarely arose: the

[8] The 1951 Convention was drafted to deal very specifically with existing, known populations of displaced people; it originally referred specifically only to those displaced in Europe by the Second World War, covering subsequent refugees only from the later 1960s onwards (Convention on the Status of Refugees 1951: Preamble and Arts 1A(b) and 1B; Protocol Relating to the Status of Refugees 1967). The definition of a Convention refugee requires however an element of state persecution in one's country of nationality or habitual residence that may however be lacking in the case of a person who is merely stateless (Art 1A).

[9] There are currently 23 signatories and 80 parties to the Convention on the Status of Stateless person 1954, and five signatories and 55 accessions to the Convention on the Reduction of Statelessness 1961.

[10] Andrew Geddes, *Immigration and Integration: Towards Fortress Europe?* (Manchester, Manchester University Press, 2000).

[11] Paul Weis, 'The Convention relating to the Status of Stateless Persons' (1961) *International and Comparative Law Quarterly* 255

post-war settlement gave almost everyone a nationality; multiple nationality became more acceptable (multiple obligation for military service being the main concern); and, for decades, the sort of political changes and break-ups that rendered people de jure stateless were avoided. The strengthening and enlargement of Europe went hand in hand with economic improvements—strong industrial economies bringing forward the weaker ones—and statelessness in Europe, at least in the de jure sense, offered no obvious academic or political concern.

II. THE RISE OF DE FACTO CITIZENSHIP IN EUROPE

The biting problem of statelessness was not the theoretical lack of citizenship, but the inability to make a life—statuslessness, or the lack of the rights of a citizen, especially the right to work. But clearly for European citizens, and also (albeit in a less clear and more fractured way) their predecessors in the European Economic Community, statuslessness is and was not a practical or political problem: free movement and the right to work in other member states vastly pre-date the Union.[12] The gradual transformation of the Coal and Steel Community via the European Economic Community and into the European Union not only aligned ever more individual rights across the borders, but made them portable—and often apparently more widely available than merely to citizens of the European states.[13] The close connection between citizenship and rights, and statelessness and lack of rights, together with the apparent universality of basic human rights in the post-war European settlement, gives the impression that indeed there is a basic right to rights. Accession to the Council of Europe's European Convention on Human Rights and Fundamental Freedoms of 1950 became part of the *acquis communautaire* or institutions obligatory for all actual and aspiring European Union nations. Many more countries than merely the members of the European Economic Community, later the European Union, have subjected themselves to its regime—a particularly strong one, since the right of individual petition to Strasbourg that was included almost incidentally makes it very enforceable and powerful, and the Article that guarantees freedom from discrimination adds to the impression of universality. The language and rhetoric of human rights spread eastwards after the fall of the Berlin Wall and the collapse of the former Eastern bloc. By the time of the triumph of liberalism and the alleged 'end of history', it seemed that access to rights was no longer a contested issue in Europe, even if

[12] The free movement of workers was one of the four basic aims of the Treaty of Rome 1957, the original founding document of what later, in 1993, became the European Union.

[13] See for example the 1963 Ankara Accession Agreement, under which Turkish nationals obtained favourable rights which, under the treaty, could not be reduced. The Euro-Mediterranean Association Agreements concluded between 1998 and 2005 with Algeria, Egypt, Jordan, Israel, Morocco and Tunisia are more focused on trade liberalisation and social and cultural co-operation.

sometimes it might be difficult to realise those rights in practice.[14] Statuslessness was therefore largely a non-issue too, and appeared likely to remain so.

Rights under the ECHR are broadly negative—the right to keep the state away from interference with your life. The ECHR does not, however, deal with citizenship or immigration status. Though the origins of the ECHR are bound up with the underlying deprivation and statelessness issues that had made so many people's lives difficult or impossible, in reality the ECHR still protects only those with status. Even Article 14, prohibiting discrimination, relates only to discrimination in relation to the rights and freedoms set out elsewhere in the ECHR, none of which require the granting of status or of the substantive rights that come with it. The ECHR cannot be brought to bear on the withdrawal of practical positive rights, such as the right to work or receive state welfare, and not even easily on the disastrous results of such policies for individuals.[15] By the mid-1980s, much as the ECHR was often directly enforceable by individuals within their own jurisdictions, and indeed it was of the essence of the Convention that a breach would usually be committed against an individual by their own country, it had been established that the ECHR did not apply to admission and expulsion.[16] For practical purposes, human rights are not universalist in construction. If a person claims ECHR rights that a country does not want to give, they can be expelled.

Other international treaties, such as the International Covenant on Civil and Political Rights, provide strong, positive rights. Those are unfortunately often not easily enforceable, and therefore are of relatively little immediate practical use. European Union law, however, provides a framework of rules which are to be enforced by governments on behalf not only of their own citizens but of citizens of other Union countries. Indeed, the prohibition on discrimination as

[14] Francis Fukuyama famously wrote of the *The End of History and the Last Man* (London, Penguin, 1992): during the summer of 1989, when the Berlin Wall had fallen, it seemed that Europe had finally become a united and successful liberal market economy, upholding human rights and democratic values.

[15] See for example the English case of *Adam, Limbuela and Tesema v SSHD* [2005] UKHL 66: this was an attempt to establish a breach of Art 3 (the right not to be subject to torture or inhuman and degrading treatment) where persons without status were left without shelter or support. It was held that this condition was capable of breaching Art 3, but not where the people in question were, in practice, supported by organised or individual charity. The deprivation of status and entitlement itself was not enough.

[16] R Beddard, 'The Status of the European Convention of Human Rights in Domestic Law' (1967) *International and Comparative Law Quarterly* 255; *Abdulaziz, Cabales and Balkandali v UK* (1985) 7 EHRR 471. The implication of this principle—that European human rights are not enforceably universalist in their practical structure, even if the persons claiming them are within the territory of a member state—is rarely stated in this way. More common is the debate over extra-territoriality—whether a member state is liable for breaches that do or will occur outside its own territory, both of which have been established: in the first case where government agents have such control over a person that the person is effectively within the state's jurisdiction (see for example *Banković and Others v Belgium and Others* [2001] ECHR 890 or the English cases in the *Al-Skeini* series following *R (on the application of Al-Skeini and others) v Secretary of State for Defence* [2004] EWHC 2911 (Admin)), and in the second where the state is expelling someone into a situation where they will suffer from a breach, or at least who will suffer a breach from the process of expulsion (for example *Soering v UK* (1989) 11 EHRR 439 or *N v UK* [2008] ECHR 453).

to nationality has spawned the phenomenon of 'reverse discrimination', by which a foreign EU citizen may even have more rights than a national.[17] For example, a country may restrict its own nationals from bringing in foreign national partners, but it cannot restrict EU citizens from coming and doing the same under EU law, because the latter are exercising European free movement rights.[18] At the legal level, this has led to the development of attempts by nationals to bring themselves within the definition of persons exercising free movement, where they have previously established a life in another member state, and of a corresponding jurisprudence.[19] At the level of popular perception, it has strengthened the perception of EU citizenship as a potentially stronger status than national citizenship, again making the rights-holder feel less like a 'migrant worker' and more like a 'citizen', with full claims to rights in general.

It is here that the unexpected precariat has its roots. Though the roots of the European Union lie in a hope that the interlinking of trade would make another consuming war in Europe impossible, amongst its major developments are broad rights for 'European citizens' to cross internal borders and to work and make a life in other member countries. As European Union law has also developed strong rights for third-country nationals, perhaps counter-intuitively, given the origins of the institution, on the practical basis that European citizens cannot realistically move without their families, EU law is thus a greater source of the sort of fundamental human-life rights that are the incidents of citizenship—the rights to remain, to work, to establish a family—than is the ECHR.[20]

III. EUROPEAN UNION CITIZENSHIP AND THE BASES OF ENTITLEMENT

A system that gives the rights incident to citizenship to foreign nationals is however in effect a law for migrants, even if its availability is dependent on another

[17] See for example Alina Tryfonidou, *Reverse discrimination in EC law* (Alphen aan den Rijn, Kluwer Law International, 2009).

[18] Case C-370/90 *The Queen v Immigration Appeal Tribunal and Surinder Singh, ex parte Secretary of State for the Home Department* [1992] ECR I-04265 established the principle that, although a British person did not have a right to bring in a spouse, a British person returning from abroad was able to benefit from the European free movement rules, under which they did have such a right. See also Directives 2004/38/EC (free movement) and 2008/34 (right to reside), and the resulting case law. Since then, Case C-256/11 *Dereci v Austria* [2011] EUECJ has confirmed that the right to be accompanied by a partner is a free movement right and not available to nationals who remain within their own country, and Case C-434/09 *McCarthy v United Kingdom* [2011] ECR I-3375 has confirmed that dual nationals living within a country of their nationality likewise do not benefit from the family rights attendant to the right of free movement if they do not in fact move countries.

[19] The *Surinder Singh* route to bringing a foreign national spouse into the UK under EU rules was amended as from 1 January 2014 (Immigration (European Economic Area) (Amendment) (No 2) Regulations 2013 (SI 2013/3032), amending reg 9 of the Immigration (EEA) Regulations). It now must be shown that the British person had transferred the centre of their life to an EU country where they worked or were self-employed.

[20] As well as supporting the impression that EU citizenship really is a 'citizenship' of the host country through the strength of the institution of reverse discrimination, some of those rights may be seen to accrue to the third-country nationals themselves, including the right to remain: see for example *Zhu and Chen v UK* [2004] ECR I-9925 (third-country national allowed to be in Europe with her European citizen child).

formal citizenship and it is itself called a 'citizenship'. But where the rights are given as a matter of the person's own status elsewhere, rather than decided upon by the host country on the person's merits, this lessens the distinction between migrants and citizens—a blurring only furthered by the institution being named 'EU citizenship'. The main direct beneficiaries of EU citizens' free movement rights in their developed form are tourists and travellers, who escape the expense and trouble of visas, and migrant workers, who gain the entitlement to work and live across the Union. The broader family and third-country-national rights follow from those. Nationality law itself remains comparatively untouched in any direct way by the formal institutions of the European endeavour, though EU citizenship is entirely dependent on citizenship of a member state, and, though there have been some changes across the continent nevertheless.

The Council of Europe promulgated a Convention on Nationality in 1997, which aimed to harmonise the attribution of citizenship across its member states.[21] The attribution of nationality however has harmonised across the continent more probably for other reasons. The archetype of *jus sanguinis* (bloodlines, or citizenship by descent) systems, by which citizenship is attributed by heritage and parental status, was the German one, under which dual citizenship was also not generally permitted. Under that system, the descendants of eighteenth-century émigrés who had not been in Germany in generations, could claim German nationality, whereas the native-born resident communities of Turkish descent remained forever foreigners. This was changed in 2000, so that where the parents were lawful long-term residents, a child born in Germany would be a German national at birth, and naturalisation was made easier.[22] Since they were then deprived of their German nationality and the process of naturalisation then had to begin again, in effect for them the changes meant a temporary but debilitating de jure statelessness. Moving in the opposite direction, Britain ceased to operate the pure *jus soli* (citizenship by right of birth in the territory, typical of the traditional common law) in 1983, requiring that for citizenship by birth a child had to have a parent with settled status. By the end of the century, these two systems, which had long represented the extremes of citizenship attribution, had approached very close together and contributed to the consolidation of a basic system under which migrant communities could attain citizenship status, but only with the active oversight and permission of the state. The native-born children of those with long-term status would be recognised as citizens, but irregular migrants, temporary workers or new residents without permanent status (such as refugees) would not be able to give their children the nationality of the host country simply by giving birth there. The overall effect of the broad harmonisation of

[21] This now has eight signatories and 20 ratifications.

[22] Staatsangehőrigkeitgesetz 1999. The process of change, however, involved a compensatory crackdown on surreptitious (and previously tolerated) dual nationality achieved by those who had given up their Turkish nationality of birth in order to naturalise, and then regained their Turkish documentation.

European citizenship attribution has been to give greater control of the lawful, member population of Europe to the European governments—not in the sense of each country having the power to regulate its own membership, because that was always the case, but in the sense of closing the membership of Europe itself from within. The phenomenon of 'Fortress Europe' has attracted much discussion, focusing principally on the increasingly efficient and sometimes ruthless exclusion of non-Europeans, but the framework of European-ness remains. Any restrictions to free movement rights that a country can carry off without leaving the EU altogether are likely to be reciprocal. A country that leaves the EU will take with it the free movement and establishment rights of its citizens, or their 'EU citizenship'. Its members that live elsewhere in the Union on the basis of EU rights may be left in limbo.

The idea that the European framework itself might alter has not been much countenanced in the relevant academic legal discussion. Politically, it now appears possible or even likely that there will at least be some attenuation of free movement rights. The aftermath of the global financial crisis and the long-term inability to resolve the ensuing debt problems across Europe is feeding—or being fed—into an increasingly xenophobic approach to migrant workers. Even if the European Union is structurally unaffected by the current trajectory of public opinion, and the irony of the 2014 election of so many anti-EU MEPs, does not result in any fundamental dismantling of the institution itself, there is certainly a possibility that free movement and establishment rights will be restricted. Previous cases of resiling from commitment towards free movement have concerned groups that have been in a precarious position historically, such as disadvantaged ethnic groups or would-be refugees: in recent years, France for example has pursued a harsh policy of expelling Roma from Eastern Europe who do not establish a settled life, and has had a well-publicised tussle with Italy over the latter's granting of visas to unsought arrivals from the troubled regions of North Africa, who then sought to cross into France under the open-borders Schengen agreement.[23] The poor too know that life is precarious, and unskilled workers may more easily appreciate the precarity of their position: they are also more likely to attract antipathy of the 'taking our jobs' variety. Skilled and professional migrant workers however not only may have an aura of solidity, confidence and stability, but may also consider they are in a different category of status. Their employers will probably have more invested in their continuing in their employment; they are more likely to have influential contacts; and they are more likely to invest in housing, with its feeling of permanence. They may feel that they would be granted visas even outside the EU regime. They are, nevertheless, equally holding one of the most valuable and difficult-to-obtain rights of citizenship—the right to work.

[23] This occurred after some 25,000 such migrants were granted visas by Italy http://www.bbc.com/news/world-europe-13189682.

If that right is attenuated, their position is undermined. In that sense, EU citizenship is of the highest value—it gives migrants the right to work and make a life—even if it is not really citizenship as it was traditionally understood.

IV. ALTERNATIVE STRUCTURES OF CITIZENSHIP RIGHTS: CITIZENS, MIGRANTS AND THE PRECARIAT

During the decades of economic prosperity after the Second World War, not only were there increasing European free movement rights but also increasingly accessible transport links and a growing willingness to employ migrants and to work abroad. Many migrants took up opportunities across the European Union and established settled lives in their new host countries. The citizenship entitlements of the children born in the host countries have been the subject of legal discussion and development, but since those children would otherwise almost invariably be citizens of their parents' countries, they would in any case have rights to live and work in the host countries. Naturalising in the new country is unlikely to be the norm: as well as the process being expensive and sometimes administratively extremely difficult, it might sometimes involve relinquishing the previous citizenship if the relevant country does not permit multiple nationality. The countries of the European Union have thus become host not only to the sort of migrant workers usually thought of as vulnerable—the unskilled and low-paid, often living in very poor conditions and now eligible to be considered as part of Standing's 'precariat'—but also to numbers of professional and middle-class people, some native-born but without citizenship in the host state, often property-owning and living very comfortably, but who are, however, dependent on their personal status in European law for their continuing lifestyle.

The rights to enter and to live and work in a country are the basic everyday rights of citizenship, along with rights to educate one's children in any state school system or to claim welfare benefits as necessary if they exist. The right to work abroad comes with 'EU citizenship', but the legal implications of not being formally a citizen of the country one lives in are further obscured by the various other groups, other than member-state citizens, who have similar rights by virtue of their personal status. Rights have also been extended to the nationals of some non-European states, on the basis that the states were coming into Europe, or had sufficient strong connection for such rights to be appropriate.[24] And, despite the formal lack of status, the substantial populations of de jure stateless people who do live in Europe, in the Baltic states in particular, are not necessarily disadvantaged day to day. There, the breakdown of the Soviet Union left ethnic Russian

[24] A number of non-EU countries have concluded Association Agreements with the European Union under Art 217 TFEU. Particularly notable in terms of migrants' rights is the Agreement concluded with Turkey in 1963, which contains strong rights that cannot be abrogated. The Mediterranean Accession Agreements which allow North Africans working rights are also notably used.

populations stranded outside Russia, in newly independent states that considered them part of a metaphorically defeated former occupying power. Naturalisation depends particularly on fluency in the local language, and was often beyond the capacity—and to an extent the inclination—of many. But there was no real need to naturalise; the stateless populations had the status of permanent residents and all the everyday rights of citizens.[25] The position of permanent residents was aligned with that of citizens domestically by the development of the 'grey passports' system, and EU free movement rights were gradually accorded to permanent residents, further eroding any perception that formal domestic citizenship was important.[26] As with migrant workers' rights, the attribution of rights traditionally associated with citizenship had become dissociated from the need for national citizenship itself.

Alongside the acknowledgement of the position of de jure stateless permanent residents, there developed the idea of domestic residence rights for those who had taken, rather than been given long de facto residence; this was certainly the subject of academic discussion as well as the jurisprudence of the European courts and institutions.[27] The development of the right to respect for family and private life under Article 8 established foreigners' qualified rights to come to Europe or remain there based on private relationships; Articles 3 (the absolute right not to be subject to torture or inhuman and degrading treatment) and 8 in particular enabled many to resist removal and even to resist deportation after criminal offending. In order to establish the engagement of an ECHR right, the claimant would have to establish that they were 'within the jurisdiction' of the ECHR member state and to establish EU rights; the non-EU claimant would have to establish that they were entitled through a relationship with an EU citizen. The original focus was on 'bogus asylum-seekers', considered to be disguised unwanted economic migrants, though the potential for also catching genuine refugees did not appear to cause undue concern. There was however some slippage here. The right not to be expelled is not the same as a positive right to have status. This is a problem not fully addressed even in the Refugee Convention, which on a proper reading requires a state party only to refrain from expelling a refugee to the frontiers of the country of persecution;[28] all other promised rights depend on the immigration

[25] See Raivo Vetik, 'The Statelessness Issue in Estonia' (esp 236–39), and Brad Blitz and Caroline Sawyer 'Analysis: the practial and legal realities of statelessness in the European Union' (esp 287–288) in Sawyer and Blitz (eds), *Statelessness in the European Union* (Cambridge, Cambridge University Press, 2011). The European Court of Human Rights was also ready to oblige the granting of resident status: see for example *Shevanova* and *Kaftailova v Latvia* App nos 58822/00 and 59643/00 (ECtHR, 2006).

[26] See eg, Council Directive 2003/109/EC.

[27] See eg, *Boultif v Switzerland* [2001] ECHR 497; compare *Üner v Netherlands* [2006] ECHR 873.

[28] The perception that the Refugee Convention is a fully humanitarian document, designed to give succour to the needy, is not borne out by the terms of its Articles. The only right that a refugee necessarily has under the Convention is that of non-refoulement (Art 33); certain dangerous refugees may still be sent back (Art 33(2)). It does not of itself require any status to be given to a person found to be a refugee. Moreover, some commentators and even judges have erroneously asserted that a person is not a refugee until they have been found to be so, which has itself had considerable

status of the particular refugee.[29] Within the European Union, the granting of temporary status to those who could not reasonably be returned was accompanied by stronger practices of expulsion for the rest.[30] Rights accruing through long residence could be avoided by preventing arrival in the first place, or by prompt and forceful expulsions should unwanted arrival happen: the latter especially would prevent Article 8 rights from accruing. By the time of the global financial crisis, the battle lines for rights of residence in Europe were drawn there.[31]

Thus regional European law was not merely attributing rights to the citizens chosen by the member states, but indeed beginning to make people into something close to citizens, by attributing the rights of citizenship to foreigners, including those the member states preferred to expel, whilst popular politics especially after the economic downturn of 2008 onwards was headed in the opposite direction. At the academic level, ideas of inclusion and diversity fed on the one hand into a rising academic political philosophy of 'cosmopolitanism' reflecting ideas about universal legal human rights.[32] At the level of popular politics, it fed into populist fears that the borders of the individual countries were being breached and that European law was eroding national sovereignty.

V. FROM STRENGTH TO VULNERABILITY: THE FAULT LINES OF FREE MOVEMENT RIGHTS

So far as the third-country-national migration rights that came from the EU and ECHR (or were perceived as doing so) were concerned, the view of much public rhetoric tends to be that they are too strong. European migrant workers from

practical legal implications: see for example the judgment of the English House of Lords in *Szoma v DWP* [2005] UKHL 64.

[29] The Refugee Convention distinguishes between those lawfully present and lawfully residing; most rights under the Convention depend on the refugee having one of these statuses.

[30] The history of the 'Dublin Convention' is salutary here: the original Convention, requiring asylum-seekers to be sent to the first European country they entered, never worked well. 'Dublin II', in fact made in Brussels by the Council of Ministers, worked better, largely because of its computer links with international fingerprinting processes. However, the numbers of asylum-seekers who were accordingly sent to Greece caused practical problems regarding their treatment there, and with the collapse of the Greek economy 'Dublin III' not only allowed exceptions, for example for those seeking reunion with family in other countries, but also provided a more humanitarian regime for children and a temporary ban on returns to Greece.

[31] The fate of expulsion practices foundered however not only on clashes with individual human rights under the ECHR (such as the right to family life) but also on the effects of economic and social decline in Europe: the operation of the Dublin Convention 1990 (in force 1997) and its successor regulation 'Dublin II' (Regulation 2003/343/CE), designed to discourage asylum-seeking and 'asylum-shopping' (seeking refugee status in an amenable country) by sending all claimants back to the country of entry led to conditions in a collapsing Greece that necessitated the more generous treatment of 'Dublin III' (Regulation 604/2013) to prevent a humanitarian disaster within the Union.

[32] See for example Sayla Benhabib, *The Rights of Others: Aliens, Residents and Citizens* (Cambridge, Cambridge University Press, 2004) or Yasmin Soysal, *The Limits of Membership: Migrants and Postnational Membership in Europe* (Chicago, University of Chicago Press, 1994).

the East took the same place in the popular anti-migrant rhetoric surrounding the progressive enlargements of the EU as did irregular migrants from Africa and Asia. Their legal position, however, was very different. Even if the rights for migrants from some new EU countries were delayed in coming into force,[33] they were established lawful rights. The legislative structures supported and entrenched their rights to live and work across the EU, rather than providing a way for the host state to decide on their presence or expellability. If Hannah Arendt had famously said, in 'The Decline of the Nation-State and the End of the Rights of Man', that citizenship was 'the right to have rights', in the context of the EU, EU 'citizenship' was not just the border-crossing right of free movement but the right to have the most important substantive rights—the right to work and to make a life—in all the countries of the Union.[34] Whilst on a proper analysis the rights of EU 'citizenship' may be rights of border-crossing and establishment—immigration rather than citizenship—their removal would have the same effect as the deprivation of citizenship, which itself has strengthened across the Union during the same timeframe, reflecting a general nervousness of foreigners fattened on concerns about terrorism and enemies within.

The idea that statelessness in its destructive form might once again haunt Europe may seem particularly improbable to the European, or perhaps at least to the western European. But neither de jure and de facto statelessness has ever left Europe completely: the de jure stateless populations of the Baltic countries—Latvia, Lithuania and Estonia—whose day-to-day needs are met by alternative domestic status, are not the only groups to know legal statelessness in the European region. The collapse of Yugoslavia after the death of President Tito unleashed the Balkan wars of the 1990s and led to a formal Council of Europe Convention on the avoidance of statelessness in relation to State Succession. Made in 2006, this provides that everyone made stateless as a result of state succession[35] has the right to a nationality in one of the states concerned. Again, as with the international statelessness Conventions, this deals with de jure statelessness. It would not prevent the removal or exchange, forced or constructive, of individuals and populations.[36] Moreover the same break-up produced de facto stateless populations,

[33] EU law generally allows a maximum of seven years' delay in acceding rights after accession. There was widespread imposition of such delay on the working rights of Romanians and Bulgarians after accession in 2007, which had only just expired at the time of writing.

[34] Hannah Arendt, *The Origins of Totalitarianism* (first published 1951; New York, Harcourt Brace Jovanovich, 1968).

[35] Where country borders move or countries disappear or are created, so that a people living in one state find, without moving themselves, that they are now living in a different country, their country of nationality possibly having ceased to be.

[36] Indeed, a similar exchange of populations, but in that case Gypsy populations, took place within Europe between Slovakia and the Czech Republic. The United Nations High Commission for Refugees had expressed concern at the position of the Czech Roma, saying their conditions meant they were entitled to refugee status, but the response at least from the more attractive destinations in Europe was to close the borders (see eg *R v Immigration Officer at Prague Airport, ex parte European Roma Rights Centre* [2004] UKHL 55).

and these are more difficult legally. Under the former Yugoslavia, the citizenship of the various constituent states was relatively unimportant compared to the overarching citizenship of Yugoslavia itself. But when Yugoslavia fell, the individual states became the operative institutions, and could choose their own members. Many individuals and families found themselves at odds with what they considered to be their home state as to whether or not they belonged there. In Slovenia, for example, established middle-class people with settled lives and jobs lost their homes and even families—not when or because they were found to be foreigners (having been formally Yugoslavs who considered themselves Slovene, they discovered after the demise of Yugoslavia that Slovenia considered them Serbs, or Croatian) but because they were removed or 'erased' from the register of permanent residents.[37] Though they were not generally de jure stateless, and moreover had not changed anything in their everyday life, their position became, overnight, that of undocumented, unwanted immigrants.[38] Political changes around them brought the problems of de facto statelessness or statuslessness: disentitlement from the means of everyday life—the right to work, their pensions, their documented life and their very presence. It was not something they saw coming, even as a consequence of the higher-level political turmoil; the reactions of their neighbours and sometimes their families were unexpected; often they became outcasts overnight.[39] Whilst it is certainly to be hoped that no such disasters will befall western Europe, the reshaping of European institutions to accord with recent shifts in political attitudes, especially towards immigration, certainly suggests that many people with well-established European lives outside their home country do not necessarily have the stability of status they may believe they have. Insofar as the political possibility is real, that status is in jeopardy, and some of the most prosperous and successful professionals in Europe are at the same time amongst the new precariats.

VI. PROSPECTS FOR THE FUTURE

Effectiveness statelessness of the native-born in Europe is not a thing of the past. There are existing de jure and de facto stateless populations that have reached legal accommodations with the European Union and its member states; other such populations of non-European origin are subject to increasingly efficient expulsion.

[37] See Jelka Zorn, 'Non-citizens in Slovenia: erasure from the register of permanent residents' in Sawyer and Blitz (eds) *Statelessness in the European Union* (Cambridge, Cambridge University Press, 2011) 195–229.

[38] Although the case eventually brought by this population in the European Court of Human Rights is often referred to as concerning statelessness, in fact only a tiny number of those involved were de jure stateless (*Kurić and Others v Slovenia* App no 26828/06 (ECtHR, 2012)). Some limited redress was obtained in relation to the loss of practical rights.

[39] Jelka Zorn, n 37 above. This chapter has numerous examples throughout of the loss of dignity and rights of the people interviewed.

The right of a state to decide on its own membership remains fundamental not only in international law but also in European law: there is no real prospect of making states take on people as citizens merely because they have established a life in the country; the political trajectory is towards greater enforcement of removals and deportations. Citizenship, though currently more fragile than it has been for decades, is still the most solid form of guarantee of rights, but the current political tendency is towards the closing of borders and even increasingly naked nationalism, rather than inclusivity, especially any inclusivity imposed from outside the country in question.

The status of permanent residence, which brings with it all the everyday rights of citizenship, is perhaps not particularly vulnerable. Since it is generally less inheritable than citizenship, it is more within the control of the individual country to grant: permanent residents have been chosen, perhaps for their economic value. Nor is it likely that the rights that attach to permanent residence will change: permanent residents are usually desirable people, rather than potential burdens, who are perhaps on their way to citizenship. It might be that the status will however become more difficult in practice to obtain, since it usually depends on first obtaining more limited rights, such as a work visa, and then expanding them, or on exercising European free movement rights for a certain period of time before formalising them at the domestic level. It may also become more fragile, with increasingly effective laws or more widely-used practices of cancellation of status. But permanent residence rights are domestic rights, not European ones, and therefore although they are less vulnerable to European-level change, they are also more vulnerable to a national change of heart.

It looks at least plausible that there will be restrictions on rights of free movement across Europe. The political impulse for such limitations arises from several connected sources: populist movements against immigrants and foreigners feed into resentment against employed workers in a time of unemployment; at a higher political level, these combine into calls for greater national sovereignty on border control. Family rights are strong in the EU; they include rights for non-EU family members and unmarried de facto partners, whom some perceive as being less legitimate than married spouses (though it is surely more difficult to establish the fact of a cohabiting relationship than to go through a marriage ceremony); family members once established also become difficult to remove. European rights then become representable as a threat not only to national sovereignty within Europe but also to Europe's own borders.

There are many targets for the political rhetoric protesting against European intrusions into national sovereignty, but those relating to migration and establishment rights touch the fundamental legal institutions.[40] The place where the

[40] There will no doubt continue to be argument, when it is alleged that European human rights are an unnecessary and foreign intrusion, as to how far they are merely a unified expression of rights that already existed in domestic laws, or would have developed there regardless. The British, for example, have often claimed that the ECHR is a product of common law jurisprudence—a claim often used to support its validity in the UK: G Marston 'The United Kingdom's Part in the Preparation

major rights that can be used to found a right to bring family, or a right not to be expelled, is Europe: by definition, these are the rights that are most vulnerable in the current political climate. There is little international law that restricts state sovereignty in those areas. European human rights law asserts that it does not affect state rights in relation to admission or expulsion; where it has been developed so as to increase migrants' rights against expulsion, that development has itself been under attack, as the perception that the ECHR (or often just 'Europe') requires countries to retain and even sustain dangerous foreigners whom they would prefer to expel. Whilst it is EU law that asserts most strongly the positive rights to bring family, and thus the rights to work and to establishment across the Union, the increased intertwining of the ECHR and EU jurisdictions gives credence to the popular perception that it is Europe that is to blame, and that the ending of European powers is the way to deal with contemporary disorders.

The nuances of which European rights have what effect are often lost on the voting public, and there is then always a risk that policy will follow. Dutch or Danish voters may find the idea of ending the right of eastern Europeans to come and work in their countries appealing, and may not consider that bringing the reciprocity of free movement arrangements to an end would matter, or they might expect eastern Europe to welcome them in any event. Many people imagine that owning residential property in a country gives them some right to claim a visa in order to live in it: the settled and prosperous may feel invulnerable, as they surely did in Slovenia. Those under 40 or perhaps 50 may not remember, or imagine, the parameters of travelling in Europe if visas are needed: the casual weekend in Paris, business trip to Milan or family holiday that is common today would become as difficult administratively as it was in the 1960s, but with the added frustration of knowing that much better transport systems make travel otherwise much easier. The pitfalls of the loss of European rights may be far from obvious or believable, especially to those who are hunkering down against economic recession. The political scene is currently relatively open, for the first time, to the structural restriction of the European right to work and even to travel across the Union.

The curtailment or withdrawal of free movement rights would mean, for some, inconvenience. But for others, it would mean the end of a job and a life plan. It would have the same effect for migrant workers as if their country withdrew from the EU, and in several countries that, like the restriction of free movement rights, appears less unthinkable than it did only a few years ago. Even with transitional provisions, the effects would be much more sudden and obvious than would changes to agreed rules on human rights or trade issues or even welfare benefits, which are less directly affected by European rules and have often become part of the internal laws. Whilst arrangements between countries may also be subject to

of the European Convention on Human Rights, 1950' (1993) 42 *International and Comparative Law Quarterly* 796.

bilateral agreements, those can be complex to put in place: if the broad principles of free movement work rights is restricted, many people's current lives will have to change.

It is usually easier to survive upheavals if you are a member of the professional classes. You have portable and transferable skills, and can in effect buy advantage. The difference where status is concerned is that it is less easily obtained that way, since bigger issues of politics and national sovereignty come into play, and without it, all other advantages may be useless. Michael Walzer wrote that amongst things that operate outside the market is membership of the community: it may be possible to obtain a work visa or more, on the basis of offering economically viable skills or just money, but there is a considerable difference between the opportunity to seek a job—or even a country-specific visa—and the right to work and live in a country as one chooses, subject only to the same laws and rules as others.[41] The former is the immigrant life; the latter is membership. At a time of economic strain, solidity often evaporates: Marshall Berman said, adapting Marx and Engels' famous statement of what was to come from the *Communist Manifesto* of 1848, the 'year of revolution', for the postmodern uncertainties of the later twentieth century, that 'all that is solid melts into air', and the same uncertainty applies to Europe's immediate future now.[42] The immigrant life is precarious, and what makes it so is the fundamental lack of a right to claim rights by virtue of personal status; the control of rights is very directly in the hands of the host state. As those states resile from the free movement endeavour, so those rights become precarious.

National reaction to European structures may only add to the problems of Europe's unexpected precariat. For the migrant worker who has to return, conditions in the 'home state' may have changed as a result of attempts to restrict rights to immigrants within a framework that prohibits discrimination against persons from other European countries, so that returning professional middle-class expatriates may be equated with more classic job-seeking foreign immigrants. In Britain, for example, the right to National Health Service treatment, long based on residence in practice, now formally and actively requires actual and lawful residence to be shown.[43] And the admission of third-country national partners is increasingly subject to extra requirements, such as a substantial capital sum or an established income by the British partner, which can be difficult for even a

[41] Michael Walzer, *Spheres of Justice* (New York, Basic Books, 1983).

[42] Marshall Berman, *All that Is Solid Melts Into Air* (New York, Verso, 1983).

[43] For example, in Britain the right to National Health Service treatment has been made dependent on showing habitual residence, disqualifying even British nationals (or there would have been discrimination contrary to EU rules). If EU rights are removed, and the British person has partnered abroad, they will be bound by any requirements to show income or capital to support the partner, who will no longer be able to enter in their own right.

professional returning expatriate to establish.[44] These new provisions are already making foreigners of those with native identities; their rights echo the difficulties bemoaned by Aszkanazy in 1930. The prospect of change to EU citizenship status or the reversal of free movement policies makes a precariat of the middle classes, but one whose vulnerability was not expected in the good years. It is to be hoped that the bad years will pass without incident, but the precariousness is already with us.

[44] Sums required for sponsors of partners were increased from the social security level on 9 July 2012 to a level which excludes 47 per cent of British workers, including everyone on the minimum wage. The High Court in *MM, R (On the Application Of) v The Secretary of State for the Home Department* [2013] EWHC 1900 (Admin) held that the rules were not unlawful, but that the £18,600 minimum income threshold (for partners; more if there are children) could amount to a disproportionate interference with family life under Art 8 ECHR in combination with another requirement in the rules. Applications that fail for the sole reason of British income are being processed while the government appeals against this judgment.

12

General and Specific Vulnerability of Protection-Seekers in the EU: Is there an Adequate Response to their Needs?

ULRIKE BRANDL AND PHILIP CZECH[1]

I. INTRODUCTION

PERSONS WHO APPLY for international protection[2] in a member state of the European Union have certain rights contained in international law obligations of that state, in municipal law and also in the legislation establishing the Common European Asylum System (CEAS).[3] These rights are based on the assessment that applicants for protection are vulnerable. This vulnerability is generated by the fact that these persons are outside their country of origin, that they have lost the protection of that country and thus are in need of a surrogate for this protection, namely international protection. Additionally there are special

[1] Philip Czech wrote section II, Vulnerable Applicants for International Protection in the Jurisprudence of the ECtHR; Ulrike Brandl wrote section III, Treatment of Protection-Seekers in the European Union.

[2] Application for international protection is defined in Art 2(g) of the Qualification Directive as 'a request made by a third-country national or a stateless person for protection from a Member State, who can be understood to seek refugee status or subsidiary protection status'. Directive 2011/95/EU on standards for the qualification of third-country nationals or stateless persons as beneficiaries of international protection, for a uniform status for refugees or for persons eligible for subsidiary protection, and for the content of the protection granted (recast) [2011] OJ L337/9.

[3] The main legal acts establishing the Common European Asylum System are the Dublin III Regulation, the Qualification Directive, the Procedures Directive and the Reception Conditions Directive. There are also implementing acts and a Directive on Temporary Protection, they are however not dealt with in this section. Dublin III Regulation, Regulation (EU) 604/2013 of the European Parliament and of the Council establishing the criteria and mechanisms for determining the member state responsible for examining an application for international protection lodged in one of the member states by a third-country national or a stateless person [2013] OJ L180/31; Qualification Directive, n 2; Procedures Directive: Directive 2013/32/EU on common procedures for granting and withdrawing international protection (recast) [2013] OJ L180/60; Reception Conditions Directive: Directive 2013/33/EU laying down standards for the reception of applicants for international protection (recast) [2013] OJ L180/96.

rights and guarantees for applicants, who are particularly vulnerable, eg because of their health, age, mental or physical condition, or for another reason.[4]

II. VULNERABLE APPLICANTS FOR INTERNATIONAL PROTECTION IN THE JURISPRUDENCE OF THE ECTHR

The European Convention on Human Rights (ECHR) neither grants a right to asylum nor does it guarantee social rights. There is, however, quite a comprehensive and significant jurisprudence of the ECtHR concerning the vulnerability of applicants with regard to detention conditions and also with regard to the transferal of asylum-seekers under the Dublin Regulation. As all the member states of the EU are members of the ECHR, they are bound by the obligations arising out of this jurisprudence. The following section will analyse the case law on the vulnerability of asylum-seekers. Two main questions shall be answered: first, why are asylum-seekers regarded as vulnerable, and does this concept apply to all persons seeking international protection? Second, what consequences arise from their vulnerability under the ECHR?

A. Why are Asylum-Seekers Vulnerable?

In the judgment *MSS v Belgium and Greece,* the Court for the first time applied the concept of vulnerability in the context of international protection.[5] The case concerned, inter alia, the reception conditions for asylum-seekers in Greece. It was brought forward by an Afghan national who had asked for international protection in Belgium in early 2009 after having spent several months in Greece. The Belgian authorities transferred him back to Greece under the Dublin Regulation after a 'hit' in the *Eurodac* database had revealed his illegal border crossing into that country. Immediately upon arrival in Greece, the applicant was placed in detention in a building next to the airport for four days. After his release from detention he lived in a park in central Athens as he found himself without any means of subsistence. In July 2009 the Court indicated to the Greek government under Rule 39 not to have the applicant deported pending the outcome of the proceedings before the Court. In his application to the ECtHR the applicant claimed a violation of Articles 2, 3 and 13 of the ECHR, alleging that the conditions of detention as well as the state of extreme poverty in which he had lived in Greece amounted to inhuman and degrading treatment and that he did not have access to an effective

[4] See Art 21 Reception Conditions Directive, n 3. This article refers to the special vulnerability of minors, unaccompanied minors, disabled people, elderly people, pregnant women, single parents with minor children, victims of human trafficking, persons with serious illnesses, persons with mental disorders and persons who have been subjected to torture, rape or other serious forms of psychological, physical or sexual violence, such as victims of female genital mutilation.

[5] *MSS v Belgium and Greece* ECHR 2011-I, 53 EHRR 2.

asylum procedure in Greece. According to the applicant, the Belgian authorities were responsible for exposing him to this treatment because they had been aware of the deficits in the Greek asylum system.

In assessing the applicant's claims regarding the degrading and inhuman character of the treatment he had been exposed to, the ECtHR took into account his vulnerability. The consequences this statement had for the outcome of the case will be presented later. What shall be discussed first are the reasons for applying the concept of vulnerability to asylum-seekers and the conditions a person has to fulfil to be regarded as vulnerable.

i. Vulnerability as a Group-Centred Concept

The judgment's wording is quite unambiguous. According to the Court, the applicant's vulnerability was 'inherent in his situation as an asylum-seeker'.[6] The ECtHR did not make much effort to give reasons for these findings, but rather seemed to consider them as self-evident. Only in one paragraph is an explanation given, when the Court holds that the applicant, as an asylum-seeker, 'was particularly vulnerable because of everything he had been through during his migration and the traumatic experiences he was likely to have endured previously'.[7] Although this statement seems to imply that the vulnerability depends on personal experiences, it should not be understood in this way, as the Court in another paragraph of its judgment clearly states that the applicant as an asylum-seeker was 'as such, a member of a particularly underprivileged and vulnerable population group in need of special protection'.[8] This statement elucidates that every asylum-seeker, irrespective of his or her personal circumstances, must be regarded as vulnerable. The vulnerability is inherent in the situation of being an asylum-seeker and therefore it is an attribute of the entire class of people.[9]

The ECtHR applies vulnerability to asylum-seekers as a group-centred concept. Vulnerability is not derived from an applicant's individual personal circumstances, but from his or her affiliation to a group with special needs. This approach is in accordance with the case law regarding other groups found to be vulnerable, such as Gypsies,[10] members of the Roma minority,[11] people with mental disabilities[12] or people living with HIV.[13] In these cases the Court relied on the 'history of prejudice and stigmatisation' the respective group had suffered when asserting

[6] ibid, para 233.

[7] ibid, para 232.

[8] ibid, para 252.

[9] L Peroni and A Timmer, '*Vulnerable Groups*: The Promise of an Emerging Concept in European Human Rights Convention Law' (2013) 11 *International Journal of Constitutional Law* 1056, 1068.

[10] *Chapman v United Kingdom* ECHR 2001-I, para 96.

[11] *DH and Others v Czech Republic* ECHR 2007-IV, para 182; *Oršuš and Others v Croatia* ECHR 2010-II, para 147; *Horváth and Kiss v Hungary* App no 11146/11 (ECtHR, 29 January 2013), paras 102, 110.

[12] *Alajos Kiss v Hungary* App no 38832/06 (ECtHR, 20 May 2010), para 42.

[13] *Kiyutin v Russia* ECHR 2011-II, para 64.

its vulnerability.[14] Therefore, it is not relevant whether a person applying for international protection is in an especially difficult situation compared to other asylum-seekers. The vulnerability arises from the mere fact of affiliation to this group. In contrast to its preceding judgments, where the Court based its findings on the negative attitudes prevailing in society against the relevant group, in *MSS* it relied on the trauma and negative experiences asylum-seekers have generally gone through. This approach was criticised in Judge Sajó's separate opinion. According to him, vulnerability of a group resulted from historically being 'subjected to prejudice with lasting consequences'. This would not apply to asylum-seekers, who furthermore would not even constitute a homogenous 'class'.[15]

ii. Reasons Leading to Vulnerability

The majority's approach shows the open-endedness of the concept.[16] Vulnerability may not only arise from prejudice and stigmatisation suffered by a certain class of people in the past, but also from other factors. In *MSS*, two different elements seem to coincide: on the one hand the vulnerability of asylum-seekers arises from their painful experiences that made them leave their home country and on the other hand it is derived from the difficult situation they find themselves confronted with while awaiting the outcome of proceedings on their application for international protection. While the first aspect is based on the assumption that the personal distress asylum-seekers have suffered before coming to the host country causes an increased sensitivity that deserves attention, the second aspect relates to the specific problems asylum-seekers face in their struggle to make a living while awaiting the decision on their request for international protection. These two aspects differ in respect of the harm's perpetrator. A direct responsibility of the Convention state can only be assumed regarding the living conditions, as asylum-seekers are generally dependent on state support. In this respect, the vulnerability results directly from actions or omissions of the state. In other words, the asylum-seeker does not only come to the host country in a state of vulnerability, but he or she is made vulnerable by that state. We will come back to this issue when discussing the consequences of the status of vulnerability. The traumatic experiences refugees were exposed to in their home country, in contrast, cannot be attributed to the host state. Nevertheless, they influence the state's obligations towards the person concerned under the Convention, as they increase a refugee's need for support and protection.

iii. Are all Asylum-Seekers Vulnerable?

The question remains to be answered whether or not all asylum-seekers must be considered as vulnerable, and whether there are different degrees of vulnerability.

[14] Eg *Kiyutin v Russia*, para 64.
[15] *MSS v Belgium and Greece*, separate opinion of Judge Sajó.
[16] Peroni and Timmer, 'Vulnerable Groups', 1069.

Some member states reacted to the Greek asylum system's shortcomings with moratoria stopping expulsions, but only regarding *vulnerable* asylum-seekers.[17] Such an approach of course makes sense only if not every asylum-seeker is classed as vulnerable with respect to his or her possible transferal under the Dublin Regulation. The *MSS* judgment seems to imply that every asylum-seeker is to be regarded as vulnerable, and subsequent case law confirms this approach.[18] Therefore, it is inconsistent with Convention standards if a state considers some asylum-seekers as vulnerable and others as not. However, it lies within the state's discretion to determine which asylum-seekers are even more vulnerable than others.

Vulnerability cannot be defined with clear dividing lines. Whether a given person is vulnerable or not can usually not be answered with a clear yes or no. Rather, it involves an element of relativity. As Martha Fineman has elaborated, vulnerability can be understood as arising from the human embodiment as such, so every person can be in a situation where he or she has special needs that make him or her more vulnerable.[19] The application of the concept by the ECtHR leaves open the possibility to differentiate within the group of asylum-seekers according to their personal state of vulnerability. As long as the vulnerability is not negated, there is little to be said against acknowledging that some asylum-seekers are more vulnerable than others and have special needs that other members of this groups do not have. To sum up, the ECtHR regards every asylum-seeker as vulnerable because of his or her affiliation to a vulnerable class of people, but this concept allows one to distinguish various grades of vulnerability derived from the personal circumstances of the individual concerned, so long as the general state of vulnerability is sufficiently respected. The following section will further explain what this demands.

iv. Compound Vulnerability

The vulnerability resulting from the status of asylum-seeker can be aggravated by personal circumstances such as minor age or a state of illness and persons in need of international protection often also belong to another vulnerable group such as mentally or physically disabled persons or ethnic minorities which suffered from stigmatisation and prejudice. In such cases the ECtHR attaches even more importance to the 'compounded vulnerability'.[20] As the consequences of the applicant's

[17] *Cf Sharifi v Austria* App no 60104/08 (ECtHR, 5 December 2013), para 36.

[18] *Samsam Mohammed Hussein and Others v the Netherlands and Italy* App no 27725/10 (ECtHR, 2 April 2013), para 76; *Elkhan Chiragov and Others v Armenia* App no 13216/05 (ECtHR, 14 December 2011), para 146; *Aden Ahmed v Malta* App no 55352/12 (ECtHR, 23 July 2013), para 97.

[19] MA Fineman, 'The Vulnerable Subject: Anchoring Equality in the Human Condition' (2008) 20 *Yale Journal of Law and Feminism* 1, 8–9.

[20] A Timmer, 'A Quiet Revolution: Vulnerability in the European Court of Human Rights' in MA Fineman and A Grear (eds), *Vulnerability. Reflections on a New Ethical Foundation for Law and Politics* (Farnham, Ashgate, 2013), 161.

vulnerability depend on the reasons on which it is based, the most important categories of vulnerable asylum-seekers shall be described here.

a. Children

Children are considered to be inherently and constantly vulnerable.[21] The vulnerability results from their state of dependency, as they are reliant on care and support. Whether minor asylum-seekers are vulnerable does not depend on whether they are unaccompanied or travel together with their parents or other relatives who take care of them. The ECtHR in both cases has found that child asylum-seekers are in a state of particular vulnerability,[22] although the vulnerability can be increased when they are unaccompanied.[23] Whether a minor is accompanied or not plays a role in determining the state's obligations to take into account his or her special state of vulnerability, as will be demonstrated below.

The Court's consideration of children's special needs is owed not least to the UN Convention on the Rights of the Child (CRC). If minor asylum-seekers are concerned, the ECtHR regularly refers to this convention, stressing that it obliges states to take into account the best interests of the child (Article 3 CRC), to respect the needs of children when they are deprived of their liberty (Article 37 CRC), and to take appropriate measures to ensure that a child who is seeking refugee status shall, whether unaccompanied or accompanied, receive appropriate protection and humanitarian assistance (Article 22 CRC).[24] This referral to the CRC is not to be understood as lip service but does indeed influence the Court's decisions if children are involved.

b. Asylum-Seekers in a Fragile State of Health

An asylum-seeker's vulnerability can be increased by a fragile state of physical or mental health. In *Aden Ahmed v Malta* the ECtHR derived the applicant's vulnerability not only from the fact that she was an irregular migrant, but also from her fragile health, as she suffered from insomnia, recurrent physical pain and episodes of depression.[25] Also in *Sufi and Elmi v the United Kingdom* one of the applicants, who suffered from a post-traumatic stress disorder, was considered particularly vulnerable because of his psychiatric illness.[26] In further cases the Court required the authorities to consider the applicants' mental state of health in the context of

[21] Timmer, 'A Quiet Revolution', 152.

[22] *Mubilanzila Mayeka and Kaniki Mitunga v Belgium* ECHR 2006-XI, 46 EHRR 23, para 55; *Muskhadzhiyeva and Others v Belgium* App no 41442/07 (ECtHR, 19 January 2010), para 74.

[23] *Rahimi v Greece* App no 8687/08 (ECtHR, 5 April 2011), para 86.

[24] *Muskhadzhiyeva and Others v Belgium*, para 62; *Popov v France* App nos 39472/07 and 39474/07 (ECtHR, 19 January 2012), para 91.

[25] *Aden Ahmed v Malta*, para 97.

[26] *Sufi and Elmi v United Kingdom* App nos 8319/07 and 11449/07 (ECtHR, 28 June 2011), para 303.

transferrals under the Dublin Regulation.[27] In *SJ v Belgium* the applicant's vulnerability resulted from the fact that she was HIV-positive.[28] In the case of HIV, the Court seems to derive vulnerability not just from the need for medical treatment, but also from the history of prejudice and stigmatisation people infected with this disease have suffered.[29] Nevertheless, the approach adopted by the Court regarding asylum-seekers with mental health problems should also apply in a case of physical illness.[30]

c. Asylum-Seekers with Mental or Physical Disabilities

As the ECtHR has repeatedly held, individuals can also be vulnerable because of their mental or physical disabilities.[31] While this case law thus far has only dealt with the deprivation of liberty of mentally disabled persons, it seems quite obvious that this approach also applies to disabled asylum-seekers.

B. Consequences of Vulnerability

The consequences of the finding that an applicant has to be considered as vulnerable vary, depending on the circumstances of the case and the Convention guarantee invoked. What appears from the Court's judgments is that this finding does not create any new obligations but reinforces and specifies given duties under the Convention.

i. Lowering the Threshold of Article 3

The issue of vulnerability first of all plays a role in cases alleging treatment that violates Article 3 of the Convention. According to established case law, the assessment of whether a given treatment (or omission, respectively) reaches the minimum level of severity required to fall within the scope of Article 3 is relative and depends on all the circumstances of the case, 'such as the duration of the treatment, its physical or mental effects and, in some cases, the sex, age and state of health of the victim'.[32] Also, a given vulnerability of the applicant has to be taken into account in this assessment and, as the latest judgments show, can influence the outcome substantially.

[27] *Cf Nasib Halimi v Austria and Italy* App no 53852/11 (ECtHR, 18 June 2013), para 72; *Mohammed Abubeker v Austria* App no 73874/11 (ECtHR, 18 June 2013), para 71.

[28] *SJ v Belgium* App no 70055/10 (ECtHR, 27 February 2014), para 125.

[29] *Kiyutin v Russia*, para 64.

[30] *Cf Popov v France*, dissenting opinion of Judge Power-Forde.

[31] *Storck v Germany* ECHR 2005-V, para 105; *Stanev v Bulgaria* ECHR 2012-I, para 141.

[32] *Ireland v United Kingdom* Series A no 25, para 162; *Hilal v United Kingdom* ECHR 2001-II, para 60.

a. Conditions of Detention

In *MSS v Belgium and Greece* the alleged violation of Article 3 concerned two different aspects: the conditions of detention at Athens international airport, and the living conditions the applicant found himself confronted with during the examination of his application for international protection by the Greek authorities. In both respects the ECtHR relied on the applicant's vulnerability to assess whether the treatment had reached the minimum level of severity for Article 3 of the Convention to be applicable. Regarding the conditions of detention, the Court referred to preceding judgments where the conditions in several detention centres in Greece had been found to amount to degrading treatment.[33] In *MSS* the Greek government had argued that the threshold for applying Article 3 had not been reached, due to the short duration of the applicant's detention as he had been held for only four days in June 2009 and for a week in August 2009. The Strasbourg judges were not convinced by this argument. They took into account that 'the applicant, being an asylum-seeker, was particularly vulnerable because of everything he had been through during his migration and the traumatic experiences he was likely to have endured previously'.[34] The distress suffered by the applicant due to the appalling conditions at the holding centre 'was accentuated by the vulnerability inherent in his situation as an asylum-seeker'.[35]

The same approach was applied in *Rahimi v Greece*. In this case the applicant was an unaccompanied minor who had left his native Afghanistan and come to Greece in 2007 where he was arrested and placed in detention for two days. Again the ECtHR found that the conditions of detention (the applicant had been placed together with adults in an overcrowded detention centre with inadequate hygienic facilities) reached the threshold required for Article 3 to apply. The government's argument pertaining to the short duration of the detention was rejected by the Strasbourg judges holding that the applicant, due to his age and his personal situation, was in an extremely vulnerable situation. As the authorities had not taken into account his vulnerability, his detention gave rise to a violation of Article 3.[36] A comparison of these judgments with the preceding case law illustrates that the Court has lowered the threshold for applying Article 3 to cases of asylum-seekers' detention.[37]

As further judgments illustrate, the special needs of detained persons can not only shorten the minimum duration otherwise required to make Article 3

[33] *Cf SD v Greece* App no 53541/07 (ECtHR, 11 June 2009), paras 49–54; *Tabesh v Greece* App no 8256/07 (ECtHR, 26 November 2009), paras 38–44; *AA v Greece* App no 12186/08 (ECtHR, 22 July 2010), paras 57–65.

[34] *MSS v Belgium and Greece*, para 232.

[35] ibid, para 233.

[36] *Rahimi v Greece*, para 86.

[37] M Bossuyt, 'Belgium Condemned for Inhuman or Degrading Treatment Due to Violations by Greece of EU Asylum Law: *M.S.S. v Belgium and Greece*, Grand Chamber, European Court of Human Rights, January 21, 2011' (2011) *European Human Rights Law Review* 582, 590.

applicable, but also enhance the minimum standards in detention facilities where such people are held. In several cases the ECtHR found a violation of the Convention because minors were detained under conditions that were not per se inhuman or degrading, but inappropriate with respect to children. *Mubilanzila Mayeka and Kaniki Mitunga v Belgium* concerned the detention of an unaccompanied five-year-old girl in a transit centre near Brussels airport for two months. The girl arrived in Brussels accompanied by her uncle who had been asked to take her to Canada, where the girl's mother was living as a refugee. As he did not have the necessary travel papers for his niece, the Belgian authorities refused entry and decided to remove her to the Democratic Republic of Congo. Her uncle returned to the Netherlands and the girl was detained in a transit centre. The Court stressed that the applicant was in an extremely vulnerable situation that obliged the authorities to take appropriate measures for her protection. Holding her in a transit centre that was not accommodating to the needs of young children therefore amounted to inhuman treatment.[38] A similar issue was raised in the case of *Muskhadzhiyeva and Others v Belgium*. Again, Belgium was held responsible for violating Article 3 because of the detention of children in the same transit centre. Although in this case the minors were accompanied by their mother, the Court qualified the detention as inhuman again, taking into account the children's very young age (the youngest child being only seven months old) and their alarming state of health.[39]

The consequences of a state of vulnerability in the context of immigration detention were explained in greater detail by the ECtHR in *Popov v France*. The French authorities had detained a family with two children aged five months and three years respectively for 15 days in a detention centre at Rouen-Oissel. The atmosphere at the detention centre was described as stressful and distressing, it was not equipped with the basic facilities for young children and there was neither any real leisure nor learning area nor an appropriate outdoor zone. The Court found that the conditions in which the children were held were not adapted to their age and would inevitably place them in a 'situation of stress and anxiety, with particularly traumatic consequences'.[40] The judges also referred to the interaction between the length and condition of detention, stating that even a period of 15 days 'could be perceived … as never-ending' by children when the facilities are not adapted to their special needs.[41]

As these judgments show, when children are placed in immigration detention, a state must take into account their age and any special needs arising from their particular vulnerability. The authorities are not only required to limit detention to

[38] *Mubilanzila Mayeka and Kaniki Mitunga v Belgium*, para 55–58; but see M Bossuyt, 'Judges on Thin Ice: The European Court of Human Rights and the Treatment of Asylum Seekers' (2010) 3 *Inter-American and European Human Rights Journal* 3, 24ff.

[39] *Muskhadzhiyeva and Others v Belgium*, para 59.

[40] *Popov v France*, para 102.

[41] ibid, para 100.

the absolute minimum length, but also to furnish detention facilities according to the needs of children. Children's vulnerability leads to a particularly low threshold of applicability of Article 3.

As regards all detained asylum-seekers, vulnerability acts as a 'magnifying glass'.[42] The effects of detention are intensified by the state of vulnerability, and therefore conditions of detention which would be acceptable for other persons reach the threshold to apply Article 3, if the person concerned is vulnerable.

b. Living Conditions in the Receiving Convention State

While the application of Article 3 on conditions of detention is based on a solid basis in the Strasbourg case law, the applicants' vulnerability in some cases gave rise to the finding of a violation of this provision also in a new context, namely asylum-seekers' standard of living in a Convention state.

The case of *MSS* brought up the question of whether a state of extreme material poverty can raise an issue under Article 3. While awaiting the determination of his asylum application, the applicant had been in a precarious situation. Being homeless and without any means of subsistence he had been living in a public park in the middle of Athens for several months. Also the issuing of a 'pink card', which in theory entitled him to work, vocational training, accommodation and medical care, had no practical effect on his situation.

According to established case law, the Convention neither obliges member states to provide everyone within their jurisdiction with a home,[43] nor does it entail any general obligation to guarantee asylum-seekers a minimum standard of living.[44] The reason why the ECtHR nevertheless engaged in an assessment of this part of the application lay in the national Greek law. Transposing the Reception Conditions Directive, the positive law obliged the Greek authorities to provide impoverished asylum-seekers with accommodation and decent material conditions.[45] It was quite clear to the Court that the applicant had found himself in a particularly serious situation, as he had spent months living on the street, unable to cater for his most basic needs.[46] As the applicant as an asylum-seeker was 'a member of a particularly underprivileged and vulnerable population group in need of special protection',[47] his situation could be regarded as reaching the threshold to bring into play Article 3. The crucial question was whether the Greek authorities could be held responsible for the situation of the applicant. The Court referred to the fact that the applicant was 'wholly dependent on State support', as he was as an asylum-seeker unable to make a living on his own because he had

[42] Peroni and Timmer, 'Vulnerable Groups', 1079.
[43] *Chapman v United Kingdom*, para 99.
[44] *Müslim v Turkey* App no 53566/99 (ECtHR, 26 April 2005), para 85.
[45] *MSS v Belgium and Greece*, para 250.
[46] ibid, para 254.
[47] ibid, para 251.

practically no access to the labour market. This approach corresponds to other cases regarding the authorities' responsibility to take care of the needs of persons who are dependent on the state and therefore particularly vulnerable.[48]

A further reason for assuming the authorities' responsibility was their failure to examine his application for international protection in due time. Had they decided earlier, they would have 'substantially alleviated his suffering'.[49] The findings were corroborated by the fact that the situation of the applicant existed on a large scale. This pointed to a general failure of Greece to comply with its obligations under the Reception Conditions Directive.[50] Therefore, the Court held Greece responsible for a violation of Article 3 because of the inactivity of its authorities that had not taken into account the applicant's particular vulnerability.

The authorities' inactivity led to another judgment against Greece concerning similar facts. In *Rahimi v Greece* the applicant was an unaccompanied minor who was left without any support after his release from detention. The ECtHR again noted that the authorities would have been under a positive obligation to protect the applicant as he was a member of one of the most vulnerable groups of society.[51] As the authorities neither appointed a guardian for the applicant nor provided him with accommodation, the Court found a violation of Article 3. Again the applicant's vulnerability as an asylum-seeker, this time even increased by his minority and the fact that he was unaccompanied, proved crucial for qualifying the authorities' omissions as amounting to degrading treatment.

The transformation of the prohibition of inhuman and degrading treatment into a positive obligation to provide asylum-seekers with a minimum living standard has given rise to criticism. Judge Sajó in his separate opinion reproached his colleagues for going too far in deriving social rights from the Convention. The critic voiced by Marc Bossuyt, President of the Belgium Constitutional Court, points in the same direction when he stresses that the Convention parties did not extend the Court's jurisdiction to social rights and therefore the Strasbourg judges should not derive such rights from the Convention. [52] While there is some strength in this critique it should not be overlooked that the ECtHR can base its findings on the state's responsibility for the situation of the applicants. This accountability arises both from the undue length of asylum proceedings and from the national legislation hindering asylum-seekers' access to the labour market. In addition, it must be kept in mind that the respondent state has assumed the obligation to provide minimum reception conditions under EU law.

That the element of state responsibility circumscribes state obligations to provide social living standards is corroborated by the case of *Sufi and Elmi v the*

[48] Eg *Denis Vasilev v Russia*, App no 32704/04 (ECtHR, 17 December 2009), para 105 with further references; *cf* Peroni and Timmer, 'Vulnerable Groups', 1069.

[49] *MSS v Belgium and Greece*, para 262.

[50] ibid, para 259.

[51] *Rahimi v Greece*, para 87.

[52] Bossuyt, 'Belgium Condemned for Inhuman or Degrading Treatment', 592.

United Kingdom. In this judgment, the ECtHR held that the dire humanitarian conditions in refugee camps in Somalia would give rise to a violation if the applicants were to be deported and end up in such a camp. Applying the approach delivered in *MSS*, the Court had regard to the applicants' ability to cater for their most basic needs; such as food, hygiene and shelter, their vulnerability to ill-treatment, and the prospect of their situation improving within a reasonable time-frame.[53] The reasons for applying this approach had their basis in the degree of responsibility for the appalling humanitarian situation. The Court held that the crisis was 'predominantly due to the direct and indirect actions of the parties to the conflict' and therefore had to be distinguished from cases where the dire humanitarian situation was attributable to the state's lack of resources to deal with a naturally occurring phenomenon, such as illness, or natural disaster, like a drought.[54]

c. Expulsion of Vulnerable Persons to Third Countries

While the concept of vulnerability has a significant impact in cases regarding the dealings with asylum-seekers in Convention States, especially in connection with transferrals under the Dublin Regulation, its relevance is far less unambiguous in classic cases of refoulement, where the question to be assessed by the ECtHR is whether the expulsion to a third country, which is not a member of the Convention, would expose the applicant to inhuman or degrading treatment. Besides cases where a risk of persecution in the country of origin is claimed, Article 3 can also come into play when the applicant argues that he or she would be exposed to significantly reduced material and social living conditions following the expulsion. Although such cases show significant parallels with the judgments in *MSS* and *Rahimi*, the Court applies quite a different approach, even when the persons threatened by deportation are acknowledged as vulnerable.

The first category of cases to be mentioned in this context concerns the removal of seriously ill persons to states where they risk being exposed to suffering due to a lack of appropriate medical care. In such a case the ECtHR holds that the deportation only gives rise to a violation of Article 3 in very exceptional circumstances, where the humanitarian grounds against the removal are compelling. The mere fact that the applicant's circumstances, including his or her life expectancy, would be significantly reduced in the case of removal to a country where medical treatment is not available on the same level as in the host country is not sufficient in itself.[55] The strict adherence to this approach is illustrated by the fact that so far, the Court has only held in one such case that the removal would contravene

[53] *Sufi and Elmi v United Kingdom*, para 282.
[54] ibid, para 281.
[55] *N v United Kingdom* ECHR 2008-III, para 42.

Article 3 of the Convention.[56] In *D v United Kingdom* the applicant was in the final stages of AIDS and would have been at risk of dying under the most distressing circumstances if he was removed to the island of St Kitts, where neither medical nor social assistance would have been available and where he did not have any relatives to support him.[57] In contrast to this case, in *N v United Kingdom* the ECtHR accepted the expulsion of an HIV-positive woman to Uganda, although she would not have been able to continue the antiviral treatment she had received in the UK. The Court argued that even the application of Article 3 demanded a balancing between the general interests of society and the protection of the individual's fundamental rights.[58] It would place too great a burden on a Convention state if it was required to provide asylum-seekers with health care and to allow them to stay within its territory to continue their treatment.[59]

While the Court did not explicitly mention the element of vulnerability in its judgment in *N v United Kingdom*, it did so in subsequent decisions, but this did not have a significant impact on the outcome of the cases. *SJ v Belgium* for example once again concerned the removal of an HIV-positive woman to an African state. The applicant argued that her deportation would expose her to the risk of dying, as in Nigeria, her country of origin, the required medication was not available. Therefore, her very young children (all three were born in Belgium) would run the risk of becoming orphans in a country where they did not have any roots and where nobody would take care of them. The Court acknowledged that the applicant was in a vulnerable position but this fact was not apt to alter the finding that the removal would not violate Article 3. Applying the approach delivered in *N v United Kingdom*, the judges reiterated that a removal would be unacceptable only under compelling humanitarian reasons.[60]

d. Reasons Distinguishing the Two Approaches

The application of different approaches in *MSS*, *Rahimi* and *Sufi and Elmi*, on the one hand, where the Court held that the living conditions of asylum-seekers in the receiving country would reach the threshold to apply Article 3, and *N v United Kingdom*, on the other hand, where very exceptional humanitarian reasons were required for the removal of vulnerable persons to be stopped by the Court, calls

[56] *Cf* CW Wouters, *International Legal Standards for the Protection from Refoulement* (Antwerp, Intersentia, 2009) 245 with references to numerous applications declared inadmissible.

[57] *D v United Kingdom* ECHR 1997-III.

[58] This must not be mistaken for a proportionality test as the one applied under Art 8 of the Convention. The ECtHR still adheres to the absolute prohibition of torture and ill-treatment under Art 3 also in the context of expulsion. However, the definition of the minimum threshold for the application of this provision necessarily involves a certain degree of relativity and for the Court this allows the receiving state's limited resources to be taken into account.

[59] *N v United Kingdom*, para 44; see also *Yoh-Ekale Mwanje v Belgium* App no 10486/10 (ECtHR, 20 December 2011).

[60] *SJ v Belgium*, para 125–26.

for an explanation. The factual differences and legal considerations justifying this distinction are made clear by the judgment in *SHH v United Kingdom*.[61]

This application was raised by an Afghan national who had left his home country for the United Kingdom after he had lost his lower right leg in a rocket attack. Before the Strasbourg Court he claimed that disabled persons would be particularly vulnerable in Afghanistan because they were faced with discrimination and ignorance. As he could not rely on any family support after his return, he would be forced to live on the street without any means to provide for his essential needs. The situation in which the applicant would have found himself after deportation was very similar to that of the applicant in *MSS*. Nevertheless, the Court did not apply the *MSS* approach, but adopted the approach of *N v United Kingdom* and asked for compelling humanitarian reasons that could hinder deportation. The Strasbourg judges were unable to accept that the applicant would find himself confronted with a total lack of support in Afghanistan, since he still had some family members there. More importantly the applicant had remained in his home country for four years after he received his injuries and apparently had enjoyed medical treatment there. Therefore, the Court did not see exceptional circumstances that would render Article 3 applicable in the event of removal.

The Court's reasoning reveals two main factors distinguishing this case from *MSS*. The first difference is the degree of responsibility of the receiving state for the situation of the applicant. The distinguishing feature is whether the future harm would emanate from a lack of sufficient resources to provide medical or social support or rather from intentional acts or omissions of the authorities of the receiving state.[62] The second crucial difference lies in the degree of the receiving state's obligations towards asylum-seekers. While in the classical refoulement scenario the Convention cannot oblige member states to guarantee living standards in the country of return, the situation is quite different in the Dublin scenario. The Convention in general does not guarantee a certain standard of social support or medical treatment. Holding a member state responsible for exposing an asylum-seeker to appalling living conditions resulting from a paucity of resources in the receiving state would mean imposing such a guarantee through the backdoor, and therefore the Court applies Article 3 only in the most exceptional cases when the effects of the shortcomings are so grave that they impair the enjoyment of civil and political rights.[63] The situation is quite different if the asylum-seeker is to be removed to another European Union member state. Here the receiving state is obliged by EU law (ie the Reception Conditions Directive) to secure a certain minimum standard of living and the returning state can be held responsible if its authorities know or should have known that the receiving state will not comply with its obligations.

[61] *SHH v United Kingdom* App no 60367/10 (ECtHR, 29 January 2013).

[62] ibid, para 89.

[63] *Cf* E Nykänen, *Fragmented State Power and Forced Migration: A Study on Non-State Actors in Refugee Law* (Leiden, Nijhoff, 2012) 257.

The Strasbourg case law also allows a political reading as it accepts economics-based considerations regarding the danger of overloading the health care systems.[64] The Court strives not to overstretch member states' patience and willingness to cooperate, and is cautious to impose new duties on them that are not explicitly contained in the Convention.[65] This can explain the adherence to a high threshold for the application of Article 3 in classical cases of refoulement to third countries even if vulnerable people are concerned, while at the same time the Court lowers this threshold as soon as the receiving state itself has engaged in obligations to provide asylum-seekers with certain social support. If this is the case, the Court can assess whether or not the state complies with its positive obligations under both national and European legislation without provoking the reproach that it derives duties from the Convention the state parties never wanted to engage in.

Under the specific aspect of vulnerability, there is one further difference between removals to third countries and transferrals under the Dublin system. When an application for international protection has been rejected and the applicant is deported to a third country, he or she can no longer be regarded as an asylum-seeker and is just as vulnerable as any other person living in the country of origin. In Dublin cases, in contrast, the deportee remains an asylum-seeker, as it has not yet been decided on the application for international protection on the merits. In such a case the applicant will also be dependent on the state in the receiving country and therefore more vulnerable compared to the citizens of that state.

ii. Lawfulness of Detention

If asylum-seekers are held in detention, the right to personal liberty under Article 5 can come into play as well as Article 3. While Article 3 is relevant with respect to the conditions of detention, Article 5 guarantees a right not to be deprived of liberty without sufficient reasons. To be compatible with Article 5, detention must comply with national law, it must be carried out in good faith and it must not be arbitrary.[66] In *Rahimi* the ECtHR interpreted Article 5 in light of the UN Convention on the Rights of the Child, demanding the authorities take into account the special situation of unaccompanied minor asylum-seekers. The Court reiterated that the best interests of the child shall be a primary consideration in all actions taken by public authorities concerning children,[67] and also mentioned the Reception Conditions Directive that transposes this provision in Article 18(1). In addition, the ECtHR also referred to Article 37 CRC and stressed that children

[64] E Webster, 'Medical-Related Expulsion and Interpretation of Article 3 of the European Convention on Human Rights' (2013) 6 *Inter-American and European Human Rights Journal* 36, 43.

[65] *Cf* Bossuyt, 'Judges on Thin Ice', 41f.

[66] *Saadi v United Kingdom* ECHR 2008-I, para 74.

[67] *Nunez v Norway* App no 55597/09 (ECtHR, 28 June 2011), para 84; *Neulinger and Shuruk v Switzerland* ECHR 2010-V, para 135.

may be detained only as a measure of last resort.[68] In contrast to this requirement, the Greek authorities, when deciding on the applicant's detention, neither took into account the best interests of the child nor considered less severe alternative measures. Therefore, the ECtHR was not convinced of their good faith and found a violation of Article 5(1)(f) of the Convention.

Although the Court does not explicitly mention the element of vulnerability in its findings on Article 5, it had a major impact on the outcome of the case. The reason for taking into account the special situation of unaccompanied minor asylum-seekers lies in their particular vulnerable situation. Therefore, the judgment makes clear that a person's vulnerability also influences the lawfulness of a deprivation of liberty irrespective of the conditions of detention.

III. TREATMENT OF PROTECTION-SEEKERS IN THE EUROPEAN UNION

The section on the treatment of protection-seekers in the EU is divided into two parts. The first part addresses the standards contained in the legal acts and the rights granted to applicants for international protection regarding their treatment in general and especially regarding the question of whether there are sufficient guarantees for especially vulnerable applicants. The second part analyses the jurisprudence of the CJEU concerning the interpretation of the legal acts establishing the CEAS regarding general or special vulnerability of protection-seekers. As has been shown in section II, the ECtHR also frequently refers to the legal acts establishing the CEAS.

A. General Standards for all Applicants Forming a Vulnerable Group of Persons

Initially it has to be stated that the European legislator treats protection-seekers in general as a vulnerable group. This conclusion can be based on different facts and arguments, especially on the fact that a set of rights is contained in the relevant legislative acts. These rights take into account that the claimants are applying for international protection stating that they are in need of protection because they are threatened by persecution or serious harm in their country of origin. This special situation requires states to grant certain rights to them. The conclusion is also inherent to the concept established by the Dublin II[69] and Dublin III Regulations.[70] Responsibility for dealing with an asylum claim, respectively a

[68] *Rahimi v Greece*, para 108.

[69] Council Regulation (EC) 343/2003 establishing the criteria and mechanisms for determining the member state responsible for examining an asylum application lodged in one of the member states by a third-country national, [2003] OJ L50/1.

[70] See n 3 above.

claim for international protection, is determined by these Regulations, which allocate the responsibility to a single member state. It implies that the member states rely on the fact that all other states participating in the Dublin system fulfil their international obligations and the obligations contained in the Regulations and Directives building the CEAS, and guarantee a certain level of treatment.

The second generation of legal acts, the recasts of the Directives, guarantee a higher standard compared to the earlier legislation. The extended guarantees concern all applicants and improve the protection of particularly vulnerable applicants. Practice will show whether the additional guarantees are sufficient, or if gaps still exist. So far, the jurisprudence of the CJEU has revealed some deficiencies with regard to general treatment and also with regard to the special needs of particularly vulnerable applicants.[71] Not all of them were fully taken into account when the new legislation was adopted.

The following paragraphs only show some examples regarding the rights of protection-seekers to exemplify the conclusion that applicants are considered to be generally vulnerable.

The recast of the Dublin Regulation contains extended procedural guarantees for all applicants, especially the right to information and the right to a personal hearing.[72] A fully fledged appeal against a transfer decision has to be granted as well.[73] These rights should ensure that applicants for protection, who are in an early stage of their procedure and who are vulnerable because they do not know their rights, do not have sufficient language knowledge and are mostly in need of basics for their daily life, are adequately protected.

During the determination procedure, including the Dublin procedure and until the transfer to another Dublin state takes place, the member states have to guarantee certain conditions for the reception of applicants.[74] These conditions comprise housing, material reception conditions, medical care, education and access to the labour market after six months, and upon the fulfilment of certain other conditions. These rights and guarantees are available to all applicants if they fulfil the criteria. These reception guarantees take into account that applicants

[71] See below section III.B.

[72] Art 4 obliges the authorities to inform the applicant that the Regulation applies and in particular about the objectives of this Regulation and the consequences of making another application in a different member state as well as the consequences of moving from one member state to another during the phases in which the member state responsible under this Regulation is being determined and the application for international protection is being examined. Art 5 contains the right to a personal interview.

[73] Art 27 Remedies: '(1) The applicant or another person as referred to in Article 18(1)(c) or (d) shall have the right to an effective remedy, in the form of an appeal or a review, in fact and in law, against a transfer decision, before a court or tribunal.'

[74] Case C-179/11 *Cimade and GISTI v Ministre de l'Intérieur*, Judgment of 27 September 2012, para 61 'Accordingly, the answer to the second question is that the obligation … ceases when that same applicant is **actually transferred** by the requesting Member State, and the financial burden of granting those minimum conditions is to be assumed by that requesting Member State, which is subject to that obligation' (emphasis added).

are usually not able to take care of themselves because of their irregular situation which makes them vulnerable.

The Procedures Directive provides for a right to information for persons held in detention and persons present at border crossing points about the possibility to file a request for protection. Article 8 of the Procedures Directive guarantees that persons in need of protection also have the possibility to file an application when they are in precarious situations. Article 12 contains a number of guarantees for all applicants.

B. Standards for the Treatment of Particularly Vulnerable Applicants

In addition to the general standards, guarantees have been included into the legal acts which should ensure a special treatment of particularly vulnerable applicants. There is, however, no general definition in the legal acts comprising the CEAS, explaining which categories of applicants are particularly vulnerable. Only the Reception Conditions Directive contains a definition of vulnerable applicants. Article 2(k) of the Reception Conditions Directive (recast 2013) defines applicants with special reception needs as 'vulnerable persons … in need of special guarantees in order to benefit from the rights and comply with the obligations provided for in this Directive'. Article 21 explicitly refers to the guarantees for these persons.

The Preambles of the recasts of the legal acts refer to the necessity to guarantee additional rights to particularly vulnerable applicants. Recital 13 of the Preamble of the Dublin III Regulations, for example, refers to the fact that specific procedural guarantees for unaccompanied minors should be laid down on account of their particular vulnerability.[75]

The Dublin system allows exceptions and grants the possibility for member states to assume responsibility based on the assessment that they are obliged to do so because their international obligations or their constitutional law require them to assume responsibility or that the special situation of applicants, including their particular vulnerability, leads to the consequence that they have to assume responsibility. This decision may be based on the discretionary clauses contained in Article 17 of the Dublin III Regulation. According to these clauses, member states may deal with an application even though they are not responsible. Furthermore, member states are obliged to abstain from a transfer to another Dublin state when their international obligations require not sending persons to this state. This obligation has been codified in the Dublin III Regulation following judgments of the ECtHR and the CJEU,[76] where a transfer was classified as a violation of the

[75] Recital 13 of the Preamble of the Dublin III Regulations (n 3 above) shows the intention: 'In addition, specific procedural guarantees for unaccompanied minors should be laid down on account of their particular vulnerability.'

[76] See below section III.C and above section II.A.

non-refoulement obligation contained in Article 3 of the ECHR and in Article 4 of the Charter of Fundamental Rights. Under Article 3(2) of the Dublin III Regulation a transfer is impossible where 'there are substantial grounds for believing that there are systemic flaws in the asylum procedure and in the reception conditions for applicants in that Member State, resulting in a risk of inhuman or degrading treatment within the meaning of Article 4 of the Charter of Fundamental Rights of the European Union …'. The provision classifies such a transfer, though factually possible, as violating international law, thus this transfer is not legally permissible. This should have been clearly stated in the Regulation. It is also noteworthy that the non-refoulement obligations contained in various treaties require states to abstain from a transfer.

To sum up, the Dublin system allows exceptions, which open the possibility to pay attention to the special needs of vulnerable applicants and also oblige states not to transfer applicants when the non-refoulement obligation would be violated.

There are also special guarantees for minors, provisions on tracing family members of these minors for families and persons dependent on certain family members. The definition of a family member in the Dublin III Regulation has been slightly widened and there is also an additional definition of a relative. The category of relative has been created in order to supplement the definition of a family member. 'Relative' means the applicant's adult aunt or uncle or grandparent who is present in the territory of a member state.[77] The clauses on the allocation of the responsibility of unaccompanied minors also provide for the unification with relatives if no family members are present.

Article 16 of the Dublin III Regulation provides for the reunification of dependent persons with family members taking care of them.[78] Persons who are dependent on certain family members due to pregnancy, a newborn child, serious illness, severe disability or old age shall normally be kept or brought together. Article 16 is a compulsory norm and thus family members have to be united and a separation would require their consent and special justifications.

The Reception Conditions and the Procedures Directive also contain special guarantees for particularly vulnerable applicants. These are, inter alia, the rules regarding the treatment of minors and unaccompanied minors, persons with disabilities and persons who suffer from trauma or mental disorders. In order to guarantee that these rights are granted in practice, states have to make sure that the persons who need additional assistance are identified during the procedure, preferably at the beginning of or at a very early stage of the procedure. There are, however, only rudimentary provisions in the Directives serving that purpose.

[77] Art 1(h) of the Dublin III-Regulation.

[78] Above n 3. Art 16 concerns dependent persons.

Already the Reception Conditions Directive from 2003 (Chapter IV) granted certain additional rights to especially vulnerable persons.[79] Article 17 obliges member states to take into account 'the specific situation of vulnerable persons such as minors, unaccompanied minors, disabled people, elderly people, pregnant women, single parents with minor children and persons who have been subjected to torture, rape or other serious forms of psychological, physical or sexual violence, in the national legislation implementing the provisions of Chapter II relating to material reception conditions and health care'. There are also articles containing rights for minors and unaccompanied minors.

As already mentioned, Article 2(k) of the Reception Conditions Directive (recast 2013) defines applicants with special reception needs as vulnerable persons. According to Article 21, especially minors, unaccompanied minors, disabled people, elderly people, pregnant women, single parents with minor children, victims of human trafficking, persons with serious illnesses, persons with mental disorders and persons who have been subjected to torture, rape or other serious forms of psychological, physical or sexual violence, such as victims of female genital mutilation, are classified as particularly vulnerable persons. With regard to material reception conditions, member states have to take into consideration that there are gender- and age-specific concerns and they have to take the situation of vulnerable persons into account in relation to applicants within the premises and accommodation centers.

Article 11 contains positive obligations of member states with respect to the detention of vulnerable applicants. As provisions on detention were not contained in the previous Reception Conditions Directive this is a new area and member states have to transpose the provisions into their national law unless the guarantees required are already in place. Article 11 of the Reception Conditions Directive contains rights of vulnerable persons and applicants with special reception needs when they are detained.[80]

Article 24 of the Procedures Directive provides for special guarantees for applicants in need of such procedural guarantees.

C. Jurisprudence of the CJEU Regarding Vulnerable Applicants

The jurisprudence of the CJEU gives us an insight into the opinion of the Court concerning which standards have to be applied in general and which groups of applicants are especially vulnerable. Concerning additional vulnerability the Court had to express its opinion regarding the allocation of responsibility to deal with a claim made by unaccompanied minors, for family unity with dependent family members in the Dublin allocation procedure and the reception conditions for families with minor children.

[79] Council Directive 2003/9/EC laying down minimum standards for the reception of asylum-seekers [2003] OJ L31/18.

[80] Art 11 of the Reception Conditions Directive (recast), fn 3.

In the case *MA, BT, DA*[81] the Court had to interpret Article 6 of the Dublin II Regulation. Unaccompanied minors with no family members legally present in the territory of a member state had lodged asylum applications in more than one member state. The Court decided that the member state where the minors were present was responsible. The judgment explicitly referred to the vulnerability of unaccompanied minors.[82] As the wording of the provisions and especially the wording of Article 6 of the Dublin II Regulation provide no answer and do not solve the problem, the Court based the interpretation on the object and purpose of the Regulation and came to the conclusion that the procedures should be as short as possible, because the best interest of the children has to be taken into account. This is also guaranteed in Article 24(2) of the Fundamental Rights Charter[83] and requires that, for states, the child's best interests must be a primary consideration in all actions relating to children. Thus lengthy allocation proceedings have to be avoided. The Court explicitly referred to the vulnerability of unaccompanied minors.[84] Article 8(4) of the Dublin III-Regulation aimed to codify the content of the mentioned judgment. In June 2014, the Commission published a proposal for an amendment in order to include additional guarantees for unaccompanied minors and to make sure that unaccompanied minors are not transferred to another member state.[85]

In another judgment, the Court dealt with family unity criteria in the humanitarian clause in Article 15(2) of the Dublin II Regulation. In the case *K v Bundesasylamt*,[86] the Court decided that a member state which is not responsible becomes responsible when Article 15(2) of the Dublin II Regulation is fulfilled, and that this member state has to assume all the relevant obligations. Article 15(2) of the Dublin II Regulation states that in cases in which the person concerned is dependent on the assistance of another, on account of pregnancy or a newborn child, serious illness, severe handicap or old age, member states shall normally keep or bring together the asylum-seeker with another relative present in the territory of one of the member states, provided that family ties existed in the country of origin. In this case, the daughter-in-law of the asylum-seeker was dependent on the asylum-seeker's assistance because she had a newborn baby and suffered from a serious illness and handicap. The Court concluded that in such special

[81] Case C-648/11 *The Queen, on the application of MA, BT, DA v Secretary of State for the Home Department*, Judgment of 6 June 2013.

[82] ibid, para 55: 'Since **unaccompanied minors form a category of particularly vulnerable persons**, it is important not to prolong more than is strictly necessary the procedure for determining the Member State responsible, which means that, as a rule, unaccompanied minors should not be transferred to another Member State' (emphasis added).

[83] Charter of Fundamental Rights of the European Union [2010] OJ C83/391, Art 24(2): 'In all actions relating to children, whether taken by public authorities or private institutions, the child's best interests must be a primary consideration.'

[84] Case C-648/11, n 81, para 55.

[85] European Commission, IP/14/723, Press Release, 'Clearer EU rules for unaccompanied minors seeking international protection', Brussels, 26 June 2014.

[86] Case C-245/11 *K v Bundesasylamt*, Judgment of 6 November 2012.

circumstances the member state had to assume responsibility. According to the judgment, it did not matter that mother or daughter-in-law were not covered by the definition of a family member in Article 2(i) of the Dublin II Regulation. This interpretation is not dependent on whether the other state made a request. That interpretation is, according to the judgment, in conformity with the objective of Article 15, which seeks to bring 'family members' together for humanitarian reasons. The Court does not explicitly refer to vulnerability as the provision uses the definition humanitarian reasons. The interpretation refers to the appraisal of the situation, where the Court acknowledges the particularly vulnerable situation of the dependent family member.

Interestingly enough, Article 15 has been reformulated and is now contained in Article 17 of the Dublin III Regulation, and the provisions on dependent persons (now Article 16) do not cover this special situation. Thus, such a situation would, again, not fall under the special clause for dependent persons. Situations like this or of a similar kind, however, often happen in practice. In this judgment, the opinion of the Court clearly showed the obligation to take humanitarian concerns into account, even if the persons concerned do not fulfil all the criteria laid down in the humanitarian clause.

In the *Saciri* case[87] the Court had to answer questions regarding reception conditions, especially the accommodation of applicants. The request was made in proceedings in the Netherlands, where the authorities refused to grant social assistance to a family of asylum-seekers with minor children because it was not possible to ensure their placement in a reception centre for asylum-seekers. The Court decided that the state has to ensure that financial allowances are paid from the time the application for asylum is made, and that the member state must ensure a dignified standard of living, adequate for the health of applicants and capable of ensuring their subsistence. The financial allowances must enable them in particular to find housing, having regard to the preservation of the interests of persons with specific needs. The amount must be sufficient to enable minor children to be housed with their parents, so that the family unity of the asylum-seekers can be maintained.

The CJEU decided joined cases,[88] where the national Court asked questions with respect to the detention of persons prior to their removal based on the Return Directive.[89] According to the Opinion of the Advocate General[90] Article 16 (1) Return Directive requires the separation of persons in pre-removal detention from ordinary prisoners. States have to grant material conditions appropriate to the legal status of the detained persons and 'capable of meeting their specific needs, in particular

[87] Case C-79/13 *Federaal agentschap voor de opvang van asielzoeker v Selver Saciri et al*, Judgment of 27 February 2014.

[88] Joined Cases C-473/13 and C-514/13 *Adala Bero v Regierungspräsidium Kassel* and *Ettayebi Bouzalmate, v Kreisverwaltung Kleve*, Judgment of 17 July 2014.

[89] Directive 2008/115/EC on common standards and procedures in Member States for returning illegally staying third-country nationals, L 348, 24.12.2008, 98.

[90] Joined Cases C-473/13 and C-514/13 *Adala Bero v Regierungspräsidium Kassel* and *Ettayebi Bouzalmate, v Kreisverwaltung Kleve*, Opinion of Advocate General Bot delivered on 30 April 2014.

those of the most vulnerable'.[91] The Court did not refer to the vulnerability of the applicants. The Court however decided that national authorities must be able to detain third-country nationals in specialised detention facilities, even if the Member State has a federal structure and the federated state competent to decide upon and carry out such detention under national law does not have such a detention facility.[92]

The CJEU had to decide cases based on a similar factual situation as in the judgment of the ECtHR in the case *MSS v Belgium and Greece*.[93] The ECtHR examined the situation of applicants transferred to Greece under the Dublin II Regulation with regard to the standards for the treatment and the status of the applicants taking their special vulnerable status into account. In a slightly later case, *NS*,[94] the CJEU answered questions about the legality of a transfer to Greece with regard to the general situation in that country. The CJEU decided that Article 4 of the Charter of Fundamental Rights must be interpreted in a way that asylum-seekers are not transferred to the state responsible where the authorities of the transferring state cannot be

> unaware that systemic deficiencies in the asylum procedure and in the reception conditions of asylum seekers in that Member State amount to substantial grounds for believing that the asylum seeker would face a real risk of being subjected to inhuman or degrading treatment within the meaning of that provision.[95]

The jurisprudence of the CJEU shows that member states have to pay attention to the special needs of applicants and that they have to take vulnerability into account, eg when they decide on the allocation of responsibility under the Dublin system or when they decide on reception conditions, especially material reception conditions and housing or the detention of vulnerable persons. The judgments clearly indicate that the ECJ interprets provisions of the Regulations and Directives building the CEAS in a way which takes the vulnerable situation of applicants, in general, into account and also considers the factors causing additional vulnerability.

IV. CONCLUSIONS

The concept of vulnerability has become an integral part of European asylum law. This goes for the different legal acts of the CEAS as well as for the jurisprudence of the CJEU and the ECtHR. The advancing entanglement of European Union law and the ECHR can also be observed in the treatment of vulnerable persons seeking international protection. Both legal systems regard asylum-seekers, in general, as members of a vulnerable group and further differentiate due to special

[91] Supra, § 95.

[92] Fn 88, para 32.

[93] Above, section II.A.

[94] Joined Cases C-411/10 and C-493/10 *NS v Secretary of State for the Home Department and ME and Others v Refugee Applications Commissioner and Minister for Justice, Equality and Law Reform*, Judgment of 21 December 2011, para 94.

[95] ibid, para 94.

factors leading to an increased vulnerability. While at the European Union level the relevant obligations are laid down in principal in the different Directives and Regulations, in the system of the Convention they wholly depend on the case law of the ECtHR that has elaborated the concept in a number of judgments. In principle, under the ECHR as well as under the CEAS, every asylum-seeker is deemed to be vulnerable due to the special needs of this group of persons. However, there are gradations of vulnerability within this group and further personal factors, as well as the affiliation to another vulnerable group, may give rise to an increased vulnerability. This applies especially for children and persons with mental or physical health problems.

The exact consequences of a person's vulnerability always depend on the circumstances of the case. Essentially, the states are required to take into account the special needs of persons deemed to be vulnerable. Especially when the vulnerability arises from the person's dependency on state support, the authorities are obliged to take care of that person's needs.

The Convention and the CEAS interact strongly, especially with respect to the application of the Dublin system. As the European Union, meanwhile, has adapted its legal acts to the demands of the ECHR, there is enough room for the member states to obey their obligations arising both from the ECHR and the CEAS. Also, the jurisprudence of the CJEU and the ECtHR are not in conflict with each other, as is shown especially by a comparison of the two judgments, *MSS* and *NS*. Both courts demand that member states refrain from a transfer as long as a situation of systemic deficiencies in the asylum procedure and in the reception conditions of asylum-seekers in another member state exists. The judgments, however, show the different jurisdiction of the courts. The CJEU had to answer questions regarding the legality of a transfer to Greece raised in preliminary proceedings. Thus the CJEU had to decide whether a transfer is allowed or would violate fundamental rights and the Court also had to answer questions about the consequences if a transfer is not allowed. The ECtHR by contrast had to examine upon an individual application, if Belgium and Greece violated the rights of the applicant in a concrete situation, where the transfer had already taken place. This shows that the two systems of protection complete each other and, taken together, guarantee a high level of protection for vulnerable individuals-seeking protection in Europe.

The legal acts establishing the second phase of the CEAS improve the rights of applicants and contain provisions for particularly vulnerable applicants. There are, however, still deficiencies. There is, for example, no guarantee that especially vulnerable applicants are identified at an early stage of the procedure and that they will receive special treatment. The Dublin system contains an early warning mechanism, but no general suspension of transfers in cases of systematic deficiencies in another state. The new provisions on the detention of applicants in the Reception Conditions Directive contain some legal guarantees for detained persons and for particularly vulnerable applicants and oblige States to establish alternatives to detention. The future will show if the practice of member states fulfils the legal requirements contained in the human rights treaties and in the Directive itself.

13

Dealing with International Vulnerability: European Law and Climate-Induced Migrants

CATHERINE-AMÉLIE CHASSIN

I. INTRODUCTION

MIGRATION IS A key topic in contemporary International legal literature. It includes all kinds of migration: migration induced by war, domestic violence, labour, or family ties. The topic of this chapter will be migration caused by the climate. Such climate-induced migrants might appear to be a new topic; however, there is not a month, nor a week that goes by without an article on the subject being published in the news. Such migration is 'fashionable'[1]—probably because climate change is likely to have an ever-greater importance in influencing migration. The UN High Commissioner for Refugees, Mr Guterres, put it clearly:

> Population growth. Urbanisation. Water scarcity. Food and energy insecurity. And volatile commodity prices. As we look into the future, it seems certain that these trends will increasingly interact with each other, creating the potential for increased competition and conflict over scarce natural resources. As a result, we are also likely to see growing numbers of people being displaced from one community, country and continent to another.[2]

However, words mean very little: the notion of climate-induced migration lacks conceptualisation. Due to this shortcoming, climate-induced migrants present, at first sight, a particular vulnerability: no definition, no legal rules. However, this is a mere caricature; reality cannot be so simple.

[1] See M-P Lanfranchi, 'Migrations environnementales et droit international public. Quelques observations', in H Gherari, R Mehdi (eds), *La société internationale face aux défis migratoires* (Paris, Pédone, 2012) 179–94, 179. For a recent global publication on climate-induced migration, see: E Piguet and F Laczko (eds), *People on the move in a changing climate* (Dordrecht, Springer, 2014) 253; GJ Hugo, *Migration and climate change* (Cheltenham, Edward Elgar, 2013) 931.

[2] A Guterres, Statement to the Nansen Conference on Climate Change and Displacement, 6 June 2011, online: www.unhcr.org/4def7ffb9.html.

The present chapter will try to highlight the legal situation of climate-induced migrants, and seek to identify legal instruments for them. It will not take a position on the existence of climate change. The focus will be on European legal rules applicable to these people fleeing climatic or environmental phenomena[3]—which means that first we will have to conceptualise what climate-induced migrants are.

Climatic migration presents two main characteristics. First, it concerns all states, rich and poor alike. At first glance, the economic status of a state has no bearing on the climate: sea levels rise at the same inexorable pace in Port-au-Prince as in New Orleans. Economic development will have an impact on the responses of the state, but not on the causes of the disaster. Second, climate-induced migration is nothing new in human history.[4] Noah's Ark, after all, was the story of a natural disaster and climatic migration. Nomadism is explained by climatic necessities. Migration is one of the oldest strategies for dealing with a degradation of environmental conditions. Moreover, the destruction of the environment is probably as old as the birth of *homo sapiens* on Earth.[5] The twenty-first century has seen the phenomenon accentuated by two factors: climate change, of course, but also people settling in exposed areas (for example, estuaries). This risky combination exists everywhere, in all states. This is a 'new challenge for the twenty-first century'.[6]

International and European law address international migration. The Refugee Law is the result of this preoccupation. However, due to climatic migration, the rules are unclear. The disarray of legal experts—but also of politicians and migrants themselves—comes from the lack of a precise definition of climate-induced migration. This chapter will try to contribute to a legal definition (section II), and will examine the application of European regulations (section III).

II. THE EXISTENCE OF VULNERABILITY: CONTRIBUTION TO THE CONCEPTUALISATION OF CLIMATE-INDUCED MIGRANTS

International and European law, together with legal literature, ignore the concept of climatic migration. The UN Framework Convention on climate change[7] does not even mention it. However, the December 2010 Cancún Adaptation Framework recognised that adaptation to climate change will take the form

[3] The climatic cause refers to an environmental change due to a non-human activity: the climate. The climate-induced migrant is the person who had to flee exclusively because of the climate. The environmental migrant is the person who had to flee because of an environmental change due to a natural cause (climate) or a human cause (for example the construction of a dam). Therefore, a climate-induced migrant is a more restrictive notion than an environmental migrant.

[4] This has been pointed out by J Bustamente, *Report of the Special Rapporteur on the Human Rights of migrants,* 21 March 2011, A/HRC/17/33, para 48.

[5] JN Saxena, 'Environmental degradation and refugees' (1996) 36 (2) *Indian Journal of International Law* 72.

[6] Council of Europe, Parliamentary Assembly, Resolution 1655 (2009), para 1.

[7] UN Framework Convention on climate change, New York, 9 May 1992, 1771 UNTS 107.

of human mobility, including migration. Nevertheless, the Conference simply 'invites all Parties to enhance action on adaptation under the Cancun Adaptation Framework, taking measures to enhance understanding, coordination and cooperation with regard to climate change induced displacement, migration and planned relocation, where appropriate, at the national, regional and international levels'[8]. There is no attempt to characterise such migration. Its vulnerability does exist and is recognised per se, but there is no conceptualisation.

Despite the absence of an international legal definition, some elements are recognised. Climatic migration is probably a forced migration, meaning that the individual has crossed an international frontier and that this departure was not a free decision. Though, what causes this coercion remains unknown.

However, there are some leads, and the legal framework may provide some kind of barometer. We will define what climatic migration is not (section A), and what it may be (section B).

A. What Climate-Induced Migration Is Not

A first glance at legal literature shows the recurrence of the expressions 'climatic refugees' or 'environmental refugees'. The terms were first used in 1985 by Mr El-Hinnawi, in an international Report,[9] and have been used ever since on a regular basis. In 2005, the first Limoges framework for a project of convention focused on 'ecological and environmental refugees'. In 2011, a study entitled 'Climate Refugees'[10] was produced by the European Parliament. Papers on this broad expression usually target both migrants (international field) and displaced persons (domestic field).

We genuinely think that the expression 'climatic refugees'—or whatever it may be—is nonsense from a legal point of view, a misunderstanding of the notion. The international protection based on the 1951 Convention relating to refugees can hardly be applied to climate-induced migrants. The main handbooks on refugee law do not even mention the expression,[11] considering that it is not a *termini technici.*[12] The statement is true: the notion of 'refugees' implies some conditions

[8] Framework Convention on Climate Change, Report of the Conference of the Parties on its 16th session, held in Cancún from 29 November to 10 December 2010, decision 1/CP 16, para 14(c). This statement was renewed during the 18th session held in Doha in 2012, Decision 3/CP 18, para 7a(vi). However, it was not mentioned in the decisions of the 19th session, held in Warsaw in 2013.

[9] E El-Hinnawi, *Environmental refugees* (Nairobi, UNEP, 1985) 41.

[10] See: European Parliament, Directorate for internal policies, *Climate refugees. Legal and policy responses to environmentally induced migration*, 2011, PE 462.422, online: www.europarl.europa.eu/studies.

[11] See G Goodwin-Gill, J McAdam, *The Refugee in International Law*, 3rd edn (Oxford, Oxford University Press, 2007) 848; J Hattaway, *The rights of refugees under International Law* (Cambridge, Cambridge University Press, 2005) 1285.

[12] A Zimmerman (ed), *The 1951 Convention relative to the status of refugees and its 1967 Protocol: a commentary* (Oxford, Oxford University Press, 2011) 438–43, 439. Over almost 1,800 pages, the *Commentary* mentions environmental refugees on only five pages, and states that the concept is not a legal one.

that do not exist in the perspective of climatic migration. Such migrants do not satisfy the international definition of refugees based on the Geneva Convention.

i. There is no Persecution

There is no universal definition of what persecution may or may not be. Moreover, according to the Geneva Convention, there is no universal definition of a well-founded fear of persecution. The practical handbook of the United Nations High Commissioner for Refugees (UNHCR) is perfectly clear on that point.[13] Consequently, it could be difficult to know precisely what persecution is. Nevertheless, there are some pointers to better understanding it.

First, relative to climatic migration, the personal dimension is not taken into account. The individualisation of a well-founded fear of persecution is a central point of the Geneva Convention. The 1951 Convention is characterised by a universalist concept of refugees. Unlike the previous texts,[14] the Geneva Convention may apply to all people fleeing persecution, whatever their country of origin. This universalist approach is balanced by the necessity to individualise the fear. The refugee is the one personally exposed.

The key is: climatic events do not choose and do not target a specific person or a specific group. At a given location and point in time, all people will be exposed to the same climatic phenomenon, no matter their age, religion, skin colour, political opinions, and so on. In essence, climatic migration is a collective migration.

Hence, this argument is not sufficient in itself. The African Convention of 1969 concerning refugees[15] accepts the idea of a mass influx of refugees, but with no individualisation in special circumstances. However, the text is applicable only for Africa, and not for the whole world. Therefore, the objection still stands.

The second objection is invincible: there is no persecution because there is no *dolus specialis*, meaning that there is no intent to hurt. Persecution is the violation of the most fundamental rights; it implies a special intent. When it comes to climatic migration, since there is no persecutor, there is no particular intent; no wilful act from anyone concerning race, religion, or any type of persecution stated in Article 1A2 of the Geneva Convention. This does not mean that climatic migrants could not be refugees under the Convention; but they will have to prove that something unusual and specific is exposing them to a real fear of persecution. The mere climatic event is not sufficient to require international protection.

[13] UNHCR, *Handbook on procedures and criteria for determining Refugee Status under the 1951 Convention and the 1967 Protocol* (Geneva, UNHCR, 1992) para 37.

[14] The Conventions adopted prior to the Second World War dealt with specific nationalities. They targeted Russians, Armenians or Germans, for example. It was a sort of ad hoc definition. See G Melander, 'Les réfugiés et les droits de l'homme' (1990) *Revue du droit public* 1327.

[15] Organisation of African Unity, Convention governing the specific aspects of refugee problems in Africa, Addis Ababa, 10 September 1969.

The same solution applies to European subsidiary protection granted under the 2004 'Qualification' Directive.[16] European protection can be granted in case of serious harm, in particular when there is a risk of torture or inhuman or degrading treatment or punishment of an applicant in the country of origin. This necessarily implies a *dolus specialis*. Therefore, the objection to international refugee status (climatic events have no special intent) is maintained with respect to European protection.

ii. There is State Protection

The second impediment to eligibility for refugee status and international protection concerns the issue of protection by the state. Article 1A2 of the Geneva Convention requires the refugee to be 'unable or, owing to such fear … unwilling to avail himself of the protection of that country'.

During a climatic crisis, most people will be hosted somewhere within their own country. More importantly, most of them will be helped and protected by domestic authorities. If these authorities may be unable to help them, nevertheless they are not persecuting them either. The refusal of international and/or foreign aid by the Republic of Myanmar after the death and destruction caused by Cyclone Nargis (May 2008) was an isolated incident.[17] Usually, states try to help their own people. The problem is not the intention, but the capacity to do so: as noted by Mr Chope in a European opinion in 2009,

> the effects of environmental degradation on peoples' lives are not experienced uniformly. It is well known that the burden of providing for migrants and displaced persons will be borne by the poorest countries that are heavily dependent on agriculture, lacking resources and possibilities to prevent further environmental crisis.[18]

A good example of that may be shown in two situations taking place in two different states: Bangladesh and the Netherlands. Both states face the danger of

[16] Directive 2004/83/EC on minimum standards for the qualification and status of third country nationals or stateless persons as refugees or as persons who otherwise need international protection and the content of the protection granted, [2004] OJ L304/12; amended by Directive 2011/95/EU of the European Parliament and of the Council on standards for the qualification of third-country nationals or stateless persons as beneficiaries of international protection, for a uniform status for refugees or for persons eligible for subsidiary protection, and for the content of the protection granted, [2011] OJ L337/9.

[17] Cyclone Nargis devastated Burma on 8 May 2008. On 12 May, during a Press Conference in New York, the UN General Secretary Ban Ki-Moon said: 'I want to register my deep concern—and immense frustration—at the unacceptably slow response to this grave humanitarian crisis … Unless more aid gets into the country—very quickly—we face an outbreak of infectious diseases that could dwarf today's crisis … I therefore call, in the most strenuous terms, on the Government of Myanmar to put its people's lives first. It must do all that it can to prevent the disaster from becoming even more serious'. See, online: www.un.org/apps/news/.

[18] C Chope, *The challenges posed by climate change*, Council of Europe Parliamentary Assembly, 29 September 2009, Document 12040, para 11.

flooding, with a significant part of their lands below sea level; both have to deal with the same dangers and risks. However, in each state, the answers are quite different.

The Netherlands has developed an elaborate dyke system, which is very accurately maintained and monitored: the Delta Plan. Obviously, this plan cannot withstand all risks: during the night of 1 February 1953, an exceptional storm combined with strong winds overtopped the defences, which resulted in about 1,800 deaths. In January 2012, a breach alert was activated in The Hague and around 800 people were evacuated for 36 hours. Clearly, even though the risk of a flood exists, it is under control and there is no fear within the population. No one believes that they will be forced to leave anytime soon.

Bangladesh has a similar problem.[19] The Ganges Delta and Brahmaputra, two of the largest rivers in the word, cover most of its land. Despite a regular pattern of monsoons, due to a lack of resources there is no accurate response. Year after year, people have to survive by themselves. In 1998 for example, the rainfall was responsible for more than 1,000 deaths. Still, during crises, there are no material and human resources, and no communication channels. The state can neither protect nor help anyone. People are tempted to go elsewhere, to leave Bangladesh. Even if the main reason is, of course, poverty, it is also deeply linked to climatic considerations. The migrant will try to escape flooding.

That is why the state's criteria cannot be used. There is protection, but this protection is not always enough. Therefore, one thing remains: climate-induced migrants are forced migrants; they are not refugees.

B. What a Climate-Induced Migration May Be

The second question is simple: if these people are not refugees, what are they? Both the legal status and the rights of these persons are unclear. Walter Kälin,[20] the former UN Special Rapporteur on internally displaced persons, has recently undertaken an important task, theorising several scenarios for climate-induced migration.

i. Scenarios

According to Mr Kälin's proposals, a distinction must be drawn between five cases. We think that they could be summarised in four different points.

[19] See J MacAdam, B Saul, 'Displacement with dignity: International Law and policy responses to climate change migration and security in Bangladesh' (2010) 53 *Jahrbuch für Internationales Recht* 233–87.

[20] W Kälin, 'Conceptualizing climate-induced displacement', in J MacAdam (ed), *Climate change and displacement*, (Oxford, Hart Publishing, 2010) 81–103.

First, Mr Kälin mentions slow-onset environmental degradation, inducing a growing scarcity of fresh water and, therefore, a loss of biological diversity. This situation ultimately produces a deadlock—desertification and the forced migration of inhabitants. Somalia corresponds to this first scenario: during autumn 2011, hunger forced around 300,000 people to leave the country.

Second, rising sea levels are a real threat for several states, such as the Netherlands or Bangladesh. In 2005, the inhabitants of the Carteret atoll in Papua New Guinea had to flee their homes without any hope of return. Obviously, it was not a global worldwide cataclysm. It affected only a few families (less than a hundred people) in low islands where the average level of the land was about 1.5 metres above the sea. Nevertheless, they left their land because of environmental and climatic facts. The rise in sea level had overwhelmed the only source of clean water, forcing people to leave. Their island was 'just' sinking.[21] Other important crowded territories are nearly at sea level. The Peace Palace of The Hague, seat of the International Court of Justice, is only at six metres above sea level, and Jericho, one of the oldest city of the world, is almost 250 metres below it.

The third scenario described by Mr Kälin makes reference to the increase of extreme climatic events: storms, heat waves, cyclones and monsoons. Each year, if not more often, there is media coverage of floods, typhoons or other events that are forcing thousands of people to flee their homes. In the Philippines, we could mention Typhoon Bopha in December 2012, but principally Typhoon Haiyan in November 2013, which left more than 8,000 people dead or missing, 28,000 wounded and more than four million displaced.[22] The violence of these climatic events was obviously the cause of such movement.

The last scenario is, in fact, the consequence of the others. It has to do with the scarcity of natural resources—water, wood and minerals, for example. This scarcity is a cause of migration. However, migration is also motivated by the conflicts induced by it—conflicts between people, ethnic groups or states. In this last case, weapons enter the picture and add a second cause of migration. Peter Gleick pointed out this very scenario in 1989.[23] The origin of climatic migration may have several causes, but it has the same destination: a secure land. In this new land, the mass influx puts pressure on natural resources, creating a sort of trigger for underlying conflicts.

[21] On the International questions raised by this phenomenon, see J Jeanneney, 'L'Atlantide. Remarques sur la submersion de l'intégralité du territoire d'un Etat' (2014) *Revue générale de droit international public* 95–129; J MacAdam, 'Disappearing States, Statelessness and the Boundaries of International Law', in J MacAdam (ed), *Climate change and displacement*, mentioned above, pp 105–30. It is noteworthy that the first studies on climate-induced migrants were focused on statelessness: see UNHCR, *Climate Change and Statelessness: an Overview*, 15 May 2009, online: www.refworld.org.

[22] Official data reported by the National Disaster Risk Reduction and Management Council, Republic of the Philippines, Report of situation n 92, 14 January 2014: See on www.ndrrmc.gov.ph.

[23] PH Gleick, 'The implication of global climatic changes for International security' (1989) 15 *Climatic Change* 309–25.

These scenarios are helpful because they contribute to a conceptualisation of what climate-induced migration is. However, between one-off or permanent settlement, they cannot help to define the true nature of such migration. Our conception is that climate-induced migration cannot apply to sporadic migration, since the perspective is to return shortly. For example, the earthquake in Haiti in January 2010 or the tsunami in Japan in March 2011 did not create climate-induced migration, even though hundreds of thousands people were impacted and had to flee. However, these are one-time events. A typhoon is not a sea level rise. In the second case, the possibility of returning does not exist. We believe that a climatic migration imposes a long-term upheaval. People who flee a sporadic monsoon are not climate-induced migrants per se since within a few weeks, they will be able to return and rebuild their house. However, if they cannot return, they become migrants—for example if their land does not exist anymore, due to a sea level rise or to erosion. Mr Kälin's proposals relate to the latter.

Nevertheless, this is a theoretical construction. In the real word, migration is not so unequivocal—absolutely not. In 2012, the UN Special Rapporteur on human rights and migration, Mr Crépeau, said 'environmental migration, like every kind of migration, is essentially a complex, multicausal phenomenon which may be driven by a multiplicity of push-and-pull factors'.[24] Climate-induced migration is a polymorphous event, with a wide-range of causes. It is exacerbating trends, tensions and instabilities which has already had an influence on migration patterns. A good example of that is Somalia: desertification, hunger, violence, all of these explained the migration. In such situations, for the lawyer, the question is not to discover if the migration is forced, but to determine what the nature of this coercion is. From a legal point of view, it may be difficult to establish straightforward links between migration and environmental degradation.

ii. Attempt at a European Definition

There is no international or European definition of climate-induced migration. To this day, a definition can only be sketched out in legal literature—and we must confess that academic communities are confused about it, even if most of them agree on the existence of a vulnerability of such migrants.

Two elements are certain: the existence of a migration, which means the crossing of an international border, and the existence of coercion.[25] Concerning the second element, some authors have had thoughts about it, arguing that the transition from will to coercion cannot be determined. For example, is it still coercion when the migrant, anticipating a rise in sea level or a drought, is allowed to organise his

[24] F Crépeau, *Report of the Special Rapporteur on the Human Rights of migrants*, transmitted to the UN General Assembly, document A/67/299, 13 August, 2012, paras 32 et seq.

[25] See D Keane, 'The environmental causes and consequences of migration: a search for the meaning of environmental refugees' (2004) 16 *Georgetown International Environmental Law* 209–23, 214.

departure and sometimes even choose his receiving state?[26] In such a case, we may think that the migration will not be a problem. The usual economic or family ties will come into play, and the migration will be an ordinary one. The problem of climate-induced migration emerges when it cannot be prepared for or organised because of shortage of time or money.

In fact, the main problem is the very notion of what is 'climate-induced'. In his 1985 Report, Mr El-Hinnawi referred to three cumulative elements:[27] the departure from the usual location, the existence of a climatic breach (due to natural or human causes, slow or not), and the threat to human life, or at least a serious perturbation of normal living conditions. It is on this basis that the University of Limoges worked to provide a conceptual definition. The International Centre of Comparative Environmental Law proposed a first Draft Convention in 2005, which was corrected in 2010: a Draft of a Convention on the international status of environmentally displaced persons—a Convention that may be applied, by law, to displaced persons but also to migrants according to the Preamble: 'this status should encompass individuals, families and populations forced to move either within or away from their State of residence'.[28]

The Draft Convention refers to the three elements present in the 1985 Report. Nevertheless, the Limoges text corrects a few points. It mentions the definitive alteration of the living conditions, which was not so clear in the 1985 Report. It also adds something essential: the idea of an irresistible event, an invincible coercion. Article 2 refers to 'a sudden or gradual environmental disaster that inexorably impacts their living conditions'. This idea was probably in Mr El-Hinnawi's notion, but it was not mentioned in his Report. It is important to underline it. In the same way, both the 1985 Report and the 2010 Draft Convention of Limoges consider that climate-induced migration may be temporary or definitive, and that it may have been caused by a sudden or a gradual environmental disaster.

This three-part definition is a positive asset. Yet, there are still some suspicious minds, and other definitions have been proposed. However, we think that these other definitions are less accurate—as an example, it is far too broad a definition to be helpful that climate-induced migration occurs every time a person cannot stay in their home due to an habitual climatic event.[29] We think this proposal is too wide to be useful.

At this point, we may have a first notion of who such migrants are: people forced to leave their home (or their usual location) because of a sudden or gradual irresistible climatic disaster that impacts their normal living conditions. This

[26] See P Gonin, V Lassailly-Jacob, 'Les réfugiés de l'environnement. Une nouvelle catégorie de migrants forcés?' [2002] 18(2) *Revue européenne des migrations internationales.*

[27] E El-Hinnawi, *Environmental Refugees* (Nairobi, UNEP, 1985) 41 (mentioned above).

[28] Draft Convention on the international status of environmentally-displaced persons, 2nd version, May 2010, online: www.cidce.org.

[29] See N Myers, J Kent, *Environmental exodus: an emergent crisis in the global arena* (Washington DC, Climate Institute, 1995) 246, online: www.climate.org.

definition is a first step. The second step will focus on European law: how to deal with climate-induced migrants?

III. THE PARTIAL RESPONSES PROVIDED BY EUROPEAN LAW

As for refugees, it is possible that climate-induced migration will not concern Europe at first. This was highlighted by a European Commission working document in 2013:

> Existing evidence clearly suggests that where environmental change impacts in migration, its effects will be felt primarily in the developing world, with migrants moving either internally or to countries in the same region. New large-scale international population movements to developed regions such as the European Union are therefore unlikely to occur.[30]

We do not think it could justify the absence of any protection. Actually, climate-induced migrants already have protection, as human beings and as migrants. Some authors caution us against an excessive compartmentalisation of the rules on migration,[31] which is a factor of excessive fragmentation of the law.[32] They are not wrong: despite migration, despite climatic events, we are still talking about human beings protected by the International human rights Instruments such as the 1966 International Covenants, or the 1950 European Convention on Human Rights.[33] The fact that a person has been forced to cross borders and/or oceans is certainly disturbing, but it does not consitute dehumanisation (section A). Moreover, Europe has some specific rules that may apply to climate-induced migrants, even if these rules have not been thought of in this respect (section B).

A. The Lack of Special Rules is Not a Lack of Rules

The resilience of the rules of international law is obvious and does not deserve further development. International human rights law persists, even (and mainly) during a crisis such as forced migration.

[30] Commission staff working document, *Climate change, environmental degradation and migration*, Brussels, 16 April 2013, SWD (2013) 138 final, pp 11 and 34, online: http://ec.europa.eu/clima/policies/adaptation/what.

[31] R Mehdi, 'Conclusions générales', in H Gherari and R Mehdi (eds), *La société internationale face aux défis migratoires* (Paris, Pédone, 2012) 215; also C-A Chassin, 'L'appréhension juridique des migrations climatiques' in C-A Chassin, *Les migrations contraintes* (Paris, Pédone, 2014) 117–38.

[32] See S Trevisanut, 'La fragmentation des droits protégés des migrants dans l'Union européenne: entre différenciation nécessaire et besoins d'harmonisation', in A-S Millet-Devalle (ed), *L'Union européenne et la protection des migrants et des réfugiés* (Paris, Pédone, 2010) 169–86.

[33] See T Duong, 'When Islands drown: the plight of climate change refugees and recourse to International Human Rights Law' (2010) 31(4) *Journal of International Law*, University of Pennsylvania 1239–66, 1254: 'The Human Rights approach to Climate change provides a framework wherein obligations to protect Human Rights are enforceable against Governments'.

In this respect, the 'Nansen Initiative', proposed in 2011 by Norway and Switzerland with the support of UNHCR, is an interesting proposition.[34] The 10 Nansen Principles, while not formally adopted, reflect the outcome of the Nansen Conference on 'Climate Change and Displacement in the Twenty-first-Century', hosted by the government of Norway in Oslo in June 2011. This is conceived as a state-owned consultative process, outside the UN, to build consensus—in a bottom-up way—among interested states about how best to address cross-border displacement in the context of sudden and slow-onset disasters. It goes beyond the Cancún Outcome Agreement insofar as it looks not only at climate-related but also at geophysical disasters—which is an extension of the concept of climate-induced migrants. The Nansen Initiative, although having an international perspective, is still a European initiative that points out that humanity does not disappear during the migration, whatever the cause of the migration may be.

i. Resilience of Fundamental Rights

The UN Special Rapporteur Mr Crépeau says it loud and clear: the actual law on human rights offers some answers to the needs and the rights of migrants.[35] In a Resolution adopted in December 2013, the UN General Assembly confirmed this position. The General Assembly 'calls upon States to promote and protect effectively the human rights and fundamental freedoms of all migrants, regardless of their migration status'.[36] It is pretty clear: above all, climate-induced migrants are migrants, and as migrants, they have some rights. There is no legal framework specifically addressing climate-induced migrants; nevertheless, human rights law applies to them, as to all other persons. Wherever they are located, migrants benefit from all International instruments. They belong to the particular conception of humanity that was so dear to Michel Virally: when it comes to human rights, the rules must be governed by two principles, unity and timelessness.[37] International human rights law is, here, an overflow of domestic rules and national interests; it is a common value, representing an 'international new *ethos*'.[38]

With such a concept, states are the first actors in supporting climatic migrants, not only when their own people are fleeing a major event, but also when they receive migrants. According to an ancient and common principle of international

[34] The Nansen Principles contain a broad set of recommendations 'to guide responses to some of the urgent and complex challenges raised by displacement in the context of climate change and other environmental hazards' (Preamble). See W Kälin, 'From the Nansen Principles to the Nansen Initiative' (2012) 41 *Forced migrations review*.

[35] F Crépeau, *Report of the Special Rapporteur on the Human Rights of migrants*, transmitted to the UN General Assembly, document A/67/299, 13 August, 2012, para 54.

[36] UNGA, Resolution 68/179 adopted on 18 December 2013: *Protection of migrants*, para 1; UNGA had previously adopted a similar position: see Resolution 67/172, 20 December 2012, *Protection of migrants*, para 1.

[37] M Virally, 'Droits de l'homme et théorie générale du droit international', in *Mélanges René Cassin*, vol IV: *Méthodologie des droits de l'homme* (Paris, Pédone, 1969) 323.

[38] A Cassese, *Human rights in a Changing World*, 2nd edn (Cambridge, Polity Press, 1994) 159.

law, states control their borders, meaning the entry and the sojourn of foreigners in their territory. Protocol no 4 of the European Convention on Human Rights recalled it in 1963 (Article 2, paragraph 3), and the European Court of Justice said it several times, notably in the *Van Duyn* Case in 1974.[39] Confronted with climate-induced migrants, states will do the same thing and will control their borders, in line with their international obligations. For European states, it means the full respect of the entire European legislation on migrants coming from a non-European state. It also means that they will not have less rights than other migrants.

Some states have adopted specific norms towards climatic migrants, making the entrance and the sojourn easier. The reasoning is similar to the one used for asylum granted on humanitarian grounds. In the United States for instance, the Immigration Act of 1990 permits the arrival of migrants when the migration is caused by earthquake, drought or natural disaster.[40] Sweden and Finland have similar laws.[41] The United States and Sweden, however, limit application of this provision to aliens already settled in the country. This legal experience is still isolated and limited, but interesting. It is the official acknowledgement that some people have to flee because of climatic events, and consequently have to be protected by their host state.

ii. Need for a Specific Rule

Some authors, considering that a domestic answer is not sufficient (and we think they are absolutely right), believe that international human rights law is not sufficient either, and are calling for a specific international convention. They claim that the actual norms will not be enough.[42] In fact, this is the explanation of the Draft Convention of Limoges—again, an interesting European initiative. International law already provides conventions on specific types of migration, such as the 1951

[39] See Case C-41/74 *Van Duyn* (ECJ, 4 December 1974), para 22; also more recently, Case C-456/12 *Mr O* and the Dutch Minister voor Immigratie, Integratie en Asiel* (ECJ, 12 March 2014).

[40] US Immigration and Nationality Act 1952 (L 82–414): see s 244(b)(1)(B)(i): the Act, modified by the Immigration Act 1990 (L 101–649) is explicit.

[41] For Sweden: Aliens Act 2005, see c 4 s 2 para 3 (definition) and c 5 s 1 (residence permit); for Finland: Aliens Act 1991, amended by 537/1999 passed 22 April 1999, c 5 s 31.

[42] See, beyond the Call of Limoges (2005) and the following Draft Convention (2005, amended 2010): G McCue, 'Environmental refugees : applying International environmental Law to involuntary migration' (1993) 6 *Georgetown International Environmental Law Review* 151–90, 177 ; D Zartner Falstrom, 'Stemming the flow of environmental displacement : creating a Convention to protect persons and preserve the environment' (2002) 13 *Colorado Journal of International, Environmental Law and Policy* 5–21; C Cournil, 'Les réfugiés écologiques : quelles(s) protection(s), quel(s) droit(s)?' (2006) *Revue du droit public* 1035–66, 1060; V Kilmannskog and L Trebbi, 'Climate change, natural disasters and displacement : a multi-track approach do filling the protection gaps' (2010) 92(879) *International Review of the Red Cross* 713–30, 721 ; A Epiney, 'Réfugiés écologiques et droit international', in C Tomuschat, E Lagrange and S Oeter (eds), *The right to life* (Leiden, Brill, 2010) 371–402, 395; SM Christiansen, *Environmental refugees: a legal perspective* (Nijmegen, Wolf Legal Publishers, 2010) 68; B Mayer, 'The international legal challenges of climate-induced migration: proposal for an International legal framework' (2011) 22(3) *Colorado Journal of International environmental Law and Policy* 357–416.

Geneva Convention on refugees[43] or the 1990 Convention on migrant workers.[44] The Council of Europe, through its Parliamentary Assembly, also called for the adoption of a dedicated convention for climate-induced migrants. The Council of Europe admits the existence of a large body of well-established International and regional legal instruments, but notes that many gaps remain in the existing protection framework:

> Particularly for those considered to have moved due to gradual environmental degradation, there may be normative and operational protection gaps, nationally and internationally ... the Assembly observes that there is no legal framework or defined policy that would cover the full scope of environmentally induced migration in the widest sense of the term. It therefore calls upon international organisations active in this field to consider the elaboration of a specific framework for the recognition and protection of environmental migrants, either in a separate convention or as part of multilateral environmental treaties, or both.[45]

The Parliamentary Assembly even proposed, on 30 January 2009,[46] the adoption of a new Protocol to the European Convention on Human Rights. However, this new Protocol was not about migrants: it was actually concerning the right to a healthy and safe environment. Such a protocol 'would reflect the way the concept of Human Rights has evolved since the Convention was drafted'—an evolution which was made by the European Court a long time ago: since the *Tyrer* case, the Court recalls on a regular basis that 'the Convention is a living instrument which, as the Commission rightly stressed, must be interpreted in the light of present-day conditions'.[47] Ultimately, this new Protocol has never emerged—others have been proposed, but not dealing with migration and climate change.

Nevertheless, we think that the relevance of a dedicated convention on climate-induced migration is questionable, even if the issue is a valid one.[48] Clearly we have to deal with it,[49] however, a new convention may not be the best way to do so.

The existence of such a convention may be appealing from an intellectual and theoretical point of view, but on the practical side, it may not be such a good idea. We saw that the climatic migrant is still a human being, therefore, the recipient of fundamental rights. Moreover, we must point here that no convention can be provided as long as we have no clear definition of what climate-induced migrants are.

[43] Convention relating to the Status of Refugees, Geneva, 28 July 1951, 189 UNTS 137; on 1 April 2014, the Convention had 145 States Parties.

[44] International Convention on the Protection of the Rights of all migrant workers and members of their families, New York, 18 December 1990, 2220 UNTS 3. On 1 April 2014, the Convention had 47 States Parties.

[45] Council of Europe, Parliamentary Assembly, Resolution 1655 (2009), paras 16–17. See also Resolution 1862 (2009), para 4.

[46] Council of Europe, Parliamentary Assembly, Resolution 1862 (2009), paras 6–3.

[47] *Tyrer v United Kingdom* App no 5856/72 (ECtHR, 25 April 1978) para 31.

[48] See J Bustamente, *Report on the Human Rights of migrants*, 21 March 2011, A/HRC/17/33, para 58. For a larger picture, V Magniny, 'Les réfugiés de l'environnement: hypothèse juridique à propos d'une menace écologique', PhD thesis, Paris I Panthéon-Sorbonne University, 1999, p 461 et seq.

[49] On this point, see, amongst others, S Maier, Les réfugiés dans le monde', in C-A Chassin (ed), *Les migrations contraintes* (Paris, Pédone, 2014) 17–42, esp 35–38.

We saw that some proposals do exist. However, we do not yet have a precise and definitive concept. Some questions still remain, such as the possibility of a return, or the prospect of a sudden or gradual environmental disaster that would cause the migration. We believe that if we do not know exactly who will be protected, it is unreasonable to consider international protection. States will not accept being part of a convention if they cannot anticipate the scale of the arrivals of migrants. It was the problem that surfaced during the negotiations of the 1951 Geneva Convention.[50] We may assume that most states have not changed their mind. As the Italian plenipotentiary minister indicated during the Geneva negotiations, 'trying to help everybody, we could end up helping nobody'.[51]

Moreover, the adoption of a new convention raises several questions that have no answers. The risk of conflict with pre-existing conventions must be considered. As an example we can mention the idea of family reunification introduced in the Draft Convention of Limoges (Article 11 paragraph 7). Is this notion similar to the principle of unity of the family in Refugee Law (1951 Convention, Final Act, paragraph B), or is it similar to the right to family life based on Article 8 of the European Convention on human rights? The two notions are not the same. If the Principle of unity of the family is quite restrictive, the right to family life is wide, since it includes ascendants or fiancés.[52] The confusion between these two notions about family may sometimes be maintained by some instruments,[53] but the two concepts cannot be confused. The Draft Convention of Limoges mentions 'the right not to be separated from family members and the right to the reunification of the family when the members are dispersed by an environmental disaster'. However, the problem is that we do not know who is in this family.[54] There is no mention of the recognition (or not) of polygamous marriages, gay marriages, children born out of wedlock, and so on. Due to this absence of precision, we have no idea about the outlines of the family. A new convention would add an unnecessary complexity.

[50] See, amongst others, the objection of French minister, R Bousquet, *Archives du Quai d'Orsay*, serie Nations-Unies, June 1946, n 294: 'la définition du terme de réfugié est loin de présenter un intérêt purement académique. On s'est aperçu rapidement que suivant celle qui serait adoptée, le nombre de réfugiés appelés à bénéficier de la protection et de l'assistance internationale pourrait varier entre 200.000 et un million.' According to the definition, the commitment of the state would be from one to five.

[51] Report of the Geneva Convention, July 1951, document A/CONF2/SR21, p 4.

[52] See amongst others: *Marckx v Belgium* App no 6833/74 (ECtHR, 13 June 1979), para 45 (family includes grandparents and natural children); *Olsson v Sweden* App no 10465/83 (ECtHR, 24 March 1988) (family life between brothers and sisters); *Keegan v Ireland* App no 16969/90 (ECtHR, 26 May 1994) (family life without marriage); *Schalk and Kopf v Austria* App no 30141/04 (ECtHR, 24 June 2010) (family life between gay partners).

[53] See for example Parliament Assembly of the Council of Europe, Resolution 1686 (2004): *Human mobility and the right to family reunion* ; also from Parliament Assembly of the Council of Europe, *Right to family life for migrants and refugees*, Document 9195, 10 September 2001.

[54] The question was raised by D Vanheule, 'Family reunification of migrants: toleration or right to stay?', in H Bauer, P Cruz Villalón and J Iliopoulos-Strangas (eds), *Les nouveaux Européens Migration et intégration en Europe* (Brussels, Bruylant, Societas Iuris Publici Europaei (SIPE), 2009) 451–76, 457.

This lack of definition is probably the main objection to a dedicated convention. The Draft Convention of Limoges offered a possibility, with the foundation of a new treaty body: the World Agency for Environmentally-Displaced Persons (WAEP) (Article 6). However, this Agency would not determinate status; it would only provide guidelines to states parties (Article 13). The Draft mentions the procedure needed to grant international status in accordance with the WAEP, a procedure that must be adopted by states (Article 16, paragraph 1). The decision to grant the status would come from a National Commission after an adversarial and public hearing (paragraph 4), and all decisions would be appealed by the WAEP (paragraph 2).

This proposal of Limoges is enticing. However, we cannot forget the lessons of the past: in 1946 the International Refugee Organisation (IRO) was created.[55] However, the IRO collapsed in 1951, a victim of the Cold War, but also a victim of mistrust and accusations.[56] The foundation of a new World Agency for climatic migrants, in direct link with domestic jurisdictions, able to judge appeal procedures, would be exposed to the same mistrust and, probably, renewed accusations.

If international law cannot provide a specific answer to climate-induced migrants, we must remember that, due to its sovereignty, any state has the possibility to do so. It is normal to look at sovereignty as being an obstacle to the protection of human rights,[57] but sometimes, sovereignty may be a protection for fundamental rights. As Professor Pellet noted, fundamental rights are, in the first place, the responsibility of states themselves.[58] They have the possibility to provide protection, and can choose to do so.

However, it would be wise to point out that an international response would be better. Nowadays, it obviously does not exist, even though the situation may be evolving thanks to international security—as stated by some papers mentioning that climate-induced migration has a direct link with some armed conflicts in

[55] Constitution of the International Refugee Organization, adopted by the UN General Assembly, 15 December 1946, Resolution 62(I). The very idea of the IRO appeared during the San Francisco Conference (May 1945) to discuss the following United Nations Charter. See L Holborn, *The International Refugee Organisation: a specialised Agency of the United Nations. Its history and work, 1946–1952* (London, Oxford University Press, 1955) 35.

[56] The IRO was accused of leniency towards Republican refugees from Spain, and accused of being an object of imperialism in the hands of the United States. The United States, Belgium and the United Kingdom were in control of the Executive Secretary of IRO. Amongst others, France protested against what she thought was a 'systematical exclusion': on that point, see G Noiriel, *La tyrannie du national* (Paris, Calmann-Lévy, 1991) 144.

[57] See amongst others, L Henkin, 'That "S" word: Sovereignty and globalization, and Human Rights, et ceterae', (1999) LXVIII (1) *Fordham Law Review* 1–14; WJ Aceves, 'Relative normativity: challenging the Sovereignty norm through Human Rights litigation' (2001) 25 *Hastings International and Comparative Law Review* 261–78.

[58] A Pellet, 'La mise en œuvre des normes relatives aux droits de l'homme: souveraineté du droit contre souveraineté de l'Etat ?', in *Droit international et droits de l'homme* (Paris, Montchrestien, Cahiers du CEDIN, 1990) 101–29.

the world.[59] However, it is an ongoing debate focused on the evolution of international law. Still, European law offers some interesting resources in that respect.

B. A First Response? Temporary Protection

Africa may be the first continent that has provided legal protection for climatic migrants. In the 1969 OAU Convention on refugees, Article 1 refers to 'events seriously disturbing public order in either part or the whole of his country of origin'.[60] This definition allows for the inclusion of a mass influx of refugees (in opposition to the 1951 Geneva Convention) and, more importantly for us at this point, for migrants fleeing climatic events, since these events seriously disturb public order. We have here an interesting possibility. The same remark may apply to the Declaration of Cartagena (1984) for Latin America.[61]

Europe chose a different route. In 2001, a Directive on temporary protection was adopted,[62] dedicated to the support of a mass influx of refugees drawing on the facilities of European host countries. The text organises a European response, helping member states whose borders are overloaded. It allows temporary asylum 'in the event of a mass influx of displaced persons from third countries who are unable to return to their country of origin' (Article 1). The genesis of this thought emerged in 1992 with the Yugoslavian war. The crisis in Kosovo in 1999 highlighted the inefficiency of Europe when confronted with a mass influx. The 2001 Directive provides European states with a dedicated procedure for hosting thousands of migrants fleeing their own country in time of emergency. The objective is to divide the weight of support between the 28 European countries, thereby helping the member state who primarily faces the influx. The 2001 Directive promotes 'a balance of effort between member states in receiving and bearing the consequences of receiving such persons' (Article 1).

We will see that this disposition may be an interesting answer for climate-induced migrants, even if, for now, it does not really offer a response to anything.

[59] See J Barnett, WN Adger, 'Climate change, Human Security and violent conflict' (2007) 26(6) *Political Geography* 639–55. See also J Barnett, *Security and climate change* (Canterbury, Tyndal Centre for climate change Research, 2001) online: wwwtyndallacuk.

[60] Organisation of African Unity, Convention governing the specific aspects of refugee problems in Africa, Addis Ababa, 10 September, 1969

[61] Cartagena Declaration on Refugees, 19–22 November 1984, paragraph III, 3°); also San Jose Declaration on Refugees and displaced persons, Colloquium on the 10th anniversary of the Cartagena Declaration, 7 December 1994, paragraph II, conclusion no 2.

[62] Council Directive 2001/55/EC on minimum standards for giving temporary protection in the event of a mass influx of displaced persons and on measures promoting a balance of efforts between member states in receiving such persons and bearing the consequences thereof [2001] OJ L212/12.

i. Conditions

Obviously, the Directive was thought of in the context of an armed conflict. The Preamble says that 'cases of mass influx of displaced persons who cannot return to their country of origin have become more substantial in Europe in recent years', which is, clearly, a reference to the Yugoslav crisis (see Preamble, paragraphs 2 and 3).

However, the text does not explicitly mention this precise circumstance: Article 2, paragraph a refers to

> a procedure of exceptional character to provide, in the event of a mass influx or imminent mass influx of displaced persons from third countries who are unable to return to their country of origin, immediate and temporary protection to such persons, in particular if there is also a risk that the asylum system will be unable to process this influx without adverse effects for its efficient operation, in the interests of the persons concerned and other persons requesting protection.

According to Article 2, paragraph c:

> 'displaced persons' means third-country nationals or stateless persons who have had to leave their country or region of origin, or have been evacuated, in particular in response to an appeal by international organisations, and are unable to return in safe and durable conditions because of the situation prevailing in that country, who may fall within the scope of Article 1 § A of the Geneva Convention or other international or national instruments giving international protection, in particular:
>
> (i) persons who have fled areas of armed conflict or endemic violence
> (ii) persons at serious risk of, or who have been the victims of, systematic or generalised violations of their human rights.

That is all the text says. The use of 'in particular' is an open door for interpretation. The recipients of temporary protection should obviously have fled violence and persecution, but the formulation of the sentence cannot exclude the provision of the same protection in other circumstances—such as climate-induced migration. The only important thing in this context is the existence of a 'mass influx' (Article 1) and that the migrants are 'unable to return in safe and durable conditions because of the situation prevailing in that country' (Article 2). Climate-induced migrants are, indeed, unable to return, and they are, presumably, part of a mass influx. It is the same old song: climatic change does not target a particular person per se. All people living in the same area will be impacted by the necessity of moving to survive. Climatic migration cannot involve some individuals and not the others; it involves all people settled in the same area.

That is why this 2001 Directive is essential, because it leaves a great deal of room for manoeuvre. It provides major potential for protecting this particular kind of migrant. However, enthusiasm may be challenged by reality.

First of all, according to the logic of the text, the protection cannot be applied to slow migration. There must be a mass influx, which means a climatic rupture in the country of origin. The very idea of mass influx means that people had to flee within a short period of time. We are talking about a population forced to leave because of a brutal event.

Secondly, Europe does not seem to be thrilled by the mere idea of temporary protection.

ii. Application

The implementation of temporary protection is subordinated to a decision of the European Council (Article 6). The member state facing the mass influx and seeking help to deal with the migrants has to contact the European Commission. Then, the Commission has to submit the implementation of the European protection to the Council. The proposal of the Commission must include a description of the groups of migrants to whom the temporary protection will be granted, and an estimation of the scale of the migration. The Council decision will be based on several criteria such as the potential for emergency aid and action on the ground or the inadequacy of such measures, but also information received from any member state, the Commission, the UNHCR and any relevant international organisation. The duration of temporary protection shall be one year, with the possibility a further one-year extension (Article 5).

In fact, the problem may be found elsewhere, probably within the European Council. During the 'Arab Spring' in 2011, a majority could not be reached to implement temporary protection. Despite the urgency and immediacy of the situation, Italy's submission was denied.[63] Under pressure, Italy had to adopt a decree on temporary protection for citizens of North Africa who had arrived between 1 January and 5 April 2011.[64] This reluctance at a sensitive time shows that the European Council would probably not accept the application of the 2001 Directive to climatic migrants—even if temporary protection offers an answer.

[63] European Council refused, on 12 April 2011, to implement the 2001 Directive, despite the request of Italy, a member state then facing a large part of the influx. It is noteworthy that two days later, the Parliamentary Assembly of the Council of Europe was encouraging the European Union to apply the temporary protection, observing that 'thousands continue to flee Libya each day'. See Resolution 1805 (2011). However, the same Parliamentary Assembly later underlined, without any nuance, that Italy 'has, unfortunately shown itself, once again, ill prepared for what appears to be a new surge of mixed migration flows, and appears to have learnt few, if any, lessons from its experiences in 2011': see C Chope, *The arrival of mixed migratory flows to Italian coastal areas*, Report of the Committee on Migration, Refugees and Displaced Persons, Strasbourg, 31 October 2013, Document 13348.

[64] Decree of the President of the Council of Ministers of 5 April 2011: Temporary Protection Measures for the Influx of Foreign Citizens from North Africa (Decreto del Presidente del Consiglio dei ministri, 5 aprile 2011, relativo alla durata dei permessi di soggiorno rilasciati per motivi umanitari). The decree was extended for six months by a Decree of 6 October 2011 (Decreto del Presidente del Consiglio dei ministri, 6 ottobre 2011, Proroga dei permessi di soggiorno rilasciati per motivi umanitari, 11A13231, GU n 235 del 8 ott 2011) and again for six months by a Decree of May 2012 (Decreto del Presidente del Consiglio dei ministri, 15 maggio 2012, Proroga dei permessi di soggiorno per motivi umanitari a favore di cittadini nordafricani, 12A05792, GU n 117 del 21 mag 2012).

Considering the genesis of the Directive (connected to armed conflicts) and the response during the Arab Spring, it is hard to envisage a positive reaction of the European Council towards migrants fleeing a climatic event. As a matter of fact, temporary protection is exactly what it is: an exceptional response for exceptional situations. Nevertheless, it may be a pragmatic and temporary solution for forced migrants, no matter the cause of the mass influx—including climate-induced migrants.

IV. CONCLUSION

The conclusion of this chapter cannot truly be optimistic. It is safe to assume that over the coming century, climatic migration will become an increasing reality. This cannot be good news for anyone, neither states nor the people. However, considering that these migrants are not ignored by the actual International law, we think that the picture cannot be completely dark. Moreover, today's European law offers some signs of incoming protection. For instance, member states do not see the need to apply any protection, included towards people fleeing North Africa. However, small steps are taken, and some states have agreed to extend the protection of the 1951 Geneva Convention. In 2014, with the help of the UNHCR, some European states agreed to the relocation of Syrian refugees out of the common procedures for refugees. We are only talking about a few hundreds of people in a context of civil war, but it is still a precedent. Facing a mass influx of climatic migrants, we cannot imagine Europe shutting its eyes and ignoring its international responsibility. Even if it is not an actual reality, the 2001 Directive on temporary protection still exists. It is a path, a tool for helping climate-induced migrants. More importantly, it is an immediately usable tool: the text exists, its implementation only depends on a political decision of the European Council. Obviously, the European Union offers a greater protection than the Council of Europe: except for the 2009 Resolutions, we cannot say the Council of Europe has a strategy or offers a safety net for climate-induced migrants. The only exploitable instrument here is the European Convention on Human Rights, which does not specifically address them.

The truth is: despite the lack of political will in Europe (both European Union and Council of Europe), we cannot ignore the potential dangers of climate-induced migration. The link between such migration and International security has been recognised by legal literature,[65] and more recently by the UN

[65] See, amongst others : LM Elliott, 'Climate migration and climate migrants: what threat, whose security', in J MacAdam, *Climate change and displacement* (Oxford, Hart Publishing, 2010) 175–90; M Beniston, 'Climate change and its impact: growing stress factors for Human societies' (2010) 92 (879) *International Review of the Red Cross* 557–68; R McLeman, *Climate change, migration and critical international security considerations*, IOM Migration Research Series, no 42 (2011) esp 25 et seq; G White, *Climate change and migration: security and borders in a warming world* (Oxford, Oxford University Press, 2011).

General Secretary[66] and the UN Security Council.[67] If Europe does not adopt any dispositions of its own, the UN will adopt some linked with International security. It may be efficient, but we think a European approach, based on human rights and not on security considerations, would be better for climate-induced migrants.

In 1928, the Greek Diplomat Nicolas Politis said:

> The so-called international law cannot be anything other than a set of rules that governs relationships between human beings belonging to various national groups. Whatever the social environment is where it is applied, Law has the same foundation, because it always has the same purpose: it aims at Human Being, and only Human Being. It is so obvious that it would not even need to be mentioned if the fog of sovereignty had not obscured the most elementary truths.[68]

It may be questionable whether this conception of international law is utopian, forgetting the very nature of international law and the weight of states. It may be true. However, European law is, in this point of view, an important evolution in the relationship between states. Where the existence of an international community may still be discussed by both states and academics, the recognition of a European community of interest is a reality. Therefore, European law is (and must be) the laboratory for proposals towards the protection of human rights. The European Union could improve research on all aspects of environmentally induced migration—that is the request of the Commission working document of April 2013.[69] That is obvious. Yet, some tools do exist, we just underlined them. It may be time to test them for real.

[66] *Climate change and its possible security implications*, Report of the Secretary-General addressed to the General Assembly, 11 September 2009, A/64/350. The document highlights our vulnerability (climate change threatens food security and human health, and increases human exposure to extreme events) and the fact that there may be implications for international cooperation from climate change's impact on shared or undemarcated international resources.

[67] Statement by the President of the Security Council, 20 July 2011, S/PRST/2011/1: 'The Security Council expresses its concern that possible adverse effects of climate change may, in the long run, aggravate certain existing threats to international peace and security' and 'notes that in matters relating to the maintenance of international peace and security under its consideration, conflict analysis and contextual information on, inter alia, possible security implications of climate change is important, when such issues are drivers of conflict, represent a challenge to the implementation of Council mandates or endanger the process of consolidation of peace'.

[68] N Politis, *Les nouvelles tendances du droit international* (Paris, Hachette, 1927) 78–79: 'Ce qu'on appelle le droit international ne saurait être autre chose que l'ensemble des règles qui régissent les rapports des hommes appartenant à divers groupements nationaux … Quel que soit le milieu social où il s'applique, le droit a le même fondement, parce qu'il a toujours la même fin: il vise partout l'homme, et rien que l'homme. C'était tellement évident qu'il serait inutile d'y insister si les brumes de la souveraineté n'avaient pas obscurci les vérités les plus élémentaires.'

[69] Commission staff working document, *Climate change, environmental degradation and migration*, 16 April 2013, above mentioned, Conclusions, p 35.

14

The Protection of Vulnerable People and the Free Movement of Persons within the European Union: Two Worlds Apart?

ALESSANDRA LANG

I. THE CITIZENS OF THE EUROPEAN UNION AS ALIENS

FOR AN ALIEN, security of residence in the host country is of paramount importance, for his or her positive integration into society.[1] Aliens' residence depends on the host state legislation. International law places significant limits to the power of the host state to expel foreigners, but it still leaves a wide discretion in setting the condition for admittance and enduring presence.[2] In other words, aliens can reside in the host country as far as they satisfy the conditions laid down by national legislation. The state can put an end to the alien's residence if he or she ceases to satisfy the prescribed conditions. It may happen that an alien ceases to satisfy these conditions for reasons outside his or her control. Therefore, aliens are vulnerable to all the events that make them cease to satisfy the condition for residence: loss of employment, lack of resources, illness, divorce, are dramatic events for everybody, but can also entail the end of residence for an alien. For aliens, any legislation, be it national, regional, or international, limiting the impact of these events on residence is of paramount importance. The present chapter will analyse the European Union legislation on the freedom of movement for citizens of the Union, in order to ascertain the extent to which their security of residence is protected, in case of events that can put their residence under threat.

In the context of the European Union, aliens will be subject to two alternative regimes, depending on their nationality. In the case of European Union nationals

[1] E Guild and P Minderhoud (eds), *Security of Residence and Expulsion: Protection of Aliens in Europe* (The Hague, Kluwer Law International, 2001).

[2] K Hailbronner and J Gogolin, 'Aliens' (2009) *Max Planck Encyclopedia of Public International Law*. *Cf* also International Law Commission, Eighth Report of the Special Rapporteur, Maurice Kamto, on Expulsion of aliens, A/CN 4/L 792, 24 May 2012.

(and their family members), provisions relating to the free movement of persons will apply. On the contrary, if they are non-EU nationals or stateless, they will come within the scope of application of legislations regarding asylum, international protection or immigration. Insofar as not covered by EU law, the status of foreigners (whether EU or third countries nationals) is governed by national legislation.

Free movement of persons is a special law, which governs the conditions for entry, residence and expulsion of nationals of one member state in another member state of the European Union. Directive 2004/38/EC is the principal piece of legislation in this field.[3] It replaces and updates a legislation drawn up between the end of the 1960s and the beginning of the 1990s in implementation of the Treaty establishing the European Economic Community.[4] The objective of this legislation was to facilitate employment mobility and the exercise of economic activities by individuals. While non-economic considerations were not excluded from its scope, they only occupied a marginal position. For example, family reunification was permitted from the start, and equal treatment with the host country's workers was required in all aspects relating to the employment relationship. Such provisions had a dual objective: on the one hand, to avoid worker exploitation, while on the other, to promote his or her integration in the host country. The effect of EC legislation was to reduce the vulnerability of migrant workers, ensuring their residence was more secure than it would have been if based solely on national law. The host country's power to terminate residence was, indeed, circumscribed.

The removal of the adjective 'Economic' from the European Community, the introduction of European Union citizenship (both due to the Treaty of Maastricht) and the raising of the right to free movement to a right enshrined in the European Union's Charter of Fundamental Rights, lead to the rethinking of

[3] Directive 2004/38 [2004] OJ L229/35. A Iliopoulou, 'Le nouveau droit de séjour des citoyens de l'Union et des membres de leur famille: la directive 2004/38/CE' (2004) *Revue du droit de l'Union européenne* 523; M Candela Soriano, 'Libre circulation et séjour dans l'UE: la directive 2004/38 au regard des droits de l'homme' (2005) *Journal des tribunaux. Droit européen* 193; P De Bruycker, 'La libre circulation des citoyens européens entre codification et réforme. Présentation générale de la directive 2004/38', in J-Y Carlier and E Guild (eds), *L'avenir de la libre circulation des personne dans l'UE* (Bruxelles, Bruylant, 2006) 21; J-Y Carlier, 'Le devenir de la libre circulation des personne dans l'Union européenne: regard sur la directive 2004/38' (2006) *Cahiers de droit européen* 13; C Barnard, *The Substantive Law of the EU. The Four Freedoms,* 3rd edn (Oxford, Oxford University Press, 2010) 424; C Morviducci, *I diritti dei cittadini europei* (Torino, Giappichelli, 2010) 117; N Nic Shuibhne, 'The Third Age of EU Citizenship. Directive 2004/38 in the Case Law of the Court of Justice', in P Syrpis (ed), *The Judiciary, the Legislature and the EU Internal Market* (Cambridge, Cambridge University Press, 2012) 331.

[4] F Burrows, *Free Movement in European Community Law* (Oxford, Clarendon Press, 1987); E Guild, 'Free Movement of Workers: From Third Country National to Citizen of the Union', in P Minderhoud and N Trimikliniotis (eds), *Rethinking the Free Movement of Workers: the European Challenges Ahead* (Nijmegen, Wolf, 2009) 25.

free movement as it had been conceived up to that time.[5] Directive 2004/38 puts this development into effect.

Under current law, any citizen of the European Union can move freely within EU countries. For the first three months, the only required formality is the possession of an identity document (Article 6, Directive 2004/38). The European Union citizen does not however have the right to request social benefits from the host country (Article 24). It follows from the above that any person wishing to exercise the right to free movement must be economically self-sufficient, even though no provision has been made for specific checks on this point. In case of residence for more than three months, the right is only conferred on those in employment (either as employee or self-employed) and on those possessing sufficient resources to maintain themselves and who are able to prove it to the public authorities (Article 7). As far as expulsion is concerned, the host country will only be able to expel a European Union citizen if he or she does not meet residence conditions (Article 14) or if his or her personal conduct represents a genuine and actual threat for public order or public security (Article 27). When deciding whether to issue an expulsion order, the country must take account of the degree of integration of the person concerned, the ties developed in that country, and those retained in the country of origin (Article 28). Any automatic procedures are forbidden. It is not thus possible to conclude, merely from the absence of residence conditions, that a person constitutes a danger to public order or public security. While there is extensive and wide-ranging case law on expulsion for public order and public security, the Court has been rather unwilling to recognise that the host country is entitled to expel a European Union citizen without resources. Where the point has been raised, the Court has in fact held that, in the circumstances of the specific case, expulsion was not a proportionate measure.

The main novelty of Directive 2004/38 consists in the permanent right of residence, acquired after five years of regular residence based on the Directive (Article 16). Once the permanent right of residence has been acquired, the European Union citizen has the right to reside without having to demonstrate he or she is in employment or economically self-sufficient, enjoy full equal treatment with nationals of the host country (Article 24), and obtain even stronger protection against expulsion (Article 28(3)).

European Union citizens' family members also benefit from free movement, irrespective of their nationality. Right of entry is subject to possession of an identity document. A right of residence for more than three months will depend on whether the European Union citizen has the right to residence: thus if he or she

[5] On the effect of the citizenship of the Union on the Court of Justice jurisprudence on free movement of persons, *cf* S O'Leary, *The Evolving Concept of Community Citizenship: from the Free Movement of Persons to Union Citizenship* (The Hague, Kluwer Law International, 1996); S Currie, 'The transformation of Union citizenship', in M Dougan and S Currie (eds), *50 Years of the European Treaties: Looking Back and Thinking Forward* (Oxford, Hart Publishing, 2009) 365; F Wollenschläger, 'The Judiciary, the Legislature and the Evolution of Union Citizenship', in P Syrpis (ed), *The Judiciary, the Legislature and the EU Internal Market* (Cambridge, Cambridge University Press, 2012) 302.

has this right because in employment or self-sufficient in the terms indicated, his or her family members will have the same right. The family members enjoy the same protection from expulsion as that laid down by the Directive for European Union citizens and enjoy access to work on the same conditions as those applying to citizens of the host country (Article 23). If the person concerned is a third country family member of a European Union citizen, he or she will not be covered by the legislation which would otherwise apply in the absence of the family ties, but will benefit of the generally more favourable rules applying to the European Union citizen.

II. FREE MOVEMENT FOR MANY, BUT NOT FOR ALL

Directive 2004/38 has a wide scope of application because any European Union citizen is in principle able to benefit from it. Even so, it is not difficult to imagine problematic cases, difficult to fit within the Directive's provisions.

A first group of cases involves those who are unable to demonstrate that they have stable resources but who at the same time, do not request social benefits from the state. On the one hand, they do not have the right to reside there but, on the other, they may succeed in avoiding the relevant checks. Roma are paradigmatic in this context. If they hold EU citizenship, they have the right to free movement, which in fact many have exercised, often to seek a way out of poverty in their country of origin; they nonetheless frequently encounter difficulties in meeting the conditions laid down by the Directive, because they are discriminated against in gaining access to accommodation, education and employment. There have been attempts, most dramatically in France and Italy, but also in other member states, to enforce collective expulsions, using the pretext of the existence of reasons of public order and public security, without adducing evidence that each person represents a real and actual threat to society at large.[6] The Council, in its Recommendation on effective Roma integration measures in the member states, notes:

> In the context of intra-Union mobility, it is necessary to respect the right to free movement of the citizens of the Union and the conditions for its exercise, including the possession of sufficient resources and of a comprehensive sickness insurance cover, in accordance with Directive 2004/38/EC of the European Parliament and of the Council, while also seeking to improve the living conditions of Roma and pursuing measures to promote their economic and social integration in their Member States of origin as well as their Member States of residence.[7]

[6] H O'Nions, 'Roma Expulsion and Discrimination: The Elephant in Brussels' (2011) 13 *European Journal of Migration and Law* 361.

[7] [2013] OJ C378/1.

The words of the Council reflect the great difficulty of finding a balance between the requirements imposed by Directive 2004/38 and the need to provide help and assistance to the Roma. As already mentioned above, while the Directive is clear in excluding all automatic triggers, it is equally unclear in the definition of the state's margin of intervention in the event that a person does not satisfy residence conditions but also does not represent a burden for the country's social welfare system.

A second group of cases, which is difficult to fit into Directive 2004/38, encompasses those wishing to stay in another member state for more than three months but not in a stable or permanent way. Indeed, the Directive only (or at least, mainly) appears to regulate the case of someone who wishes to remain for a short time (less than three months) or permanently. As already mentioned it allows countries to require registration of residence after three months from entry (Article 8). Therefore, any country imposing the obligation of registration after three months will not be in breach of European Union law. A student coming within the Erasmus programme, a person carrying out training for six months, or a patient following a rehabilitation programme of some duration are all hypotheses, certainly not academic in nature, in which mobility is exercised for more than three months but which do not fit easily within the Directive's regime. The European Union encourages mobility,[8] but the conditions, under which it is to be carried out, have been paradoxically left to the decisions of individual states.

III. FREE MOVEMENT VS INTERNATIONAL PROTECTION

The reasons behind a European Union citizen's decision to leave one member state in order to move to another are not taken into consideration by legislation. Free movement fits within the framework of Directive 2004/38, irrespective of the reasons for it. The individual states have sought to deal with European Union citizens fleeing from their country of origin, because of persecution or fear of persecution, into the framework of free movement of persons, excluding, or at least restricting, the application of 1951 Geneva Convention on refugees to European Union citizens.

Protocol 24 on asylum for nationals of member states of the European Union, annexed to the Treaties, states that any application for asylum submitted by a national of a member state should be examined on the presupposition that the

[8] The Erasmus programme was entirely conceived by the European Union. As far as trainees are concerned, the Council of the European Union promotes training courses which, if of sufficient quality, represent a valid means of access to employment. The various recommendations aimed at member states includes that it shall 'Facilitate the cross-border mobility of trainees in the European Union inter alia, by clarifying the national legal framework for traineeships and establishing clear rules on hosting trainees from, and the sending of trainees to, other Member States and by reducing administrative formalities' (Council Recommendation on a Quality Framework for Traineeships, [2014] OJ C88/1). The free movement of patients stems from the right to receive services and is partially regulated by Directive 2012/24. While receiving health services will normally not entail a lengthy stay, it cannot be excluded that the patient may stay for a while in the host state, in order to be treated.

country of origin is safe. According to the concept of safe country of origin, the application can be considered inadmissible or unfounded. There are a number of justifications cited in the Protocol preamble supporting this solution. The first is based on the assertion that member states respect fundamental human rights and are subject to different mechanism of control laid down by European Union law. The second relates to European Union citizenship itself, a status that grants particular protection in member states other than that of origin. The third concerns the intention 'to prevent the institution of asylum being resorted to for purposes alien to those for which it is intended'.

To fully understand the reasons behind, and the scope of, the Protocol, it is necessary to provide a brief account of its genesis.

The Protocol was adopted under the Treaty of Amsterdam, on a Dutch proposal in response to a Spanish proposal to introduce a provision into the Treaty equating European Union citizenship to that of the host country with regard to the grant of the refugee status and the right to asylum. This would have meant that member states could not examine applications for asylum or for the grant of refugee status submitted by nationals of other member states.[9] The Spanish proposal was intended to avoid the repetition of disputes such as the one, which opposed it to Belgium, in relation to the latter's refusal to extradite terrorist suspects who had made applications for asylum. The case giving rise to the question involved two Spanish citizens, Basque separatists, who were in Belgium.[10] Spain requested their extradition in order to try them for terrorism. Belgium did not accede to the request, in the first instance because the two had made an application for asylum and, then, following the rejection of the application, because the offence for which the extradition was requested was of a political nature. Spain considered Belgium's conduct to be unfriendly.

The letter of the Protocol is less straightforward than the Spanish proposal. It does not prevent member states from taking applications for asylum into consideration, when made by European Union citizens, but requires them to consider the applicants as originating from a safe country and to examine the application only if the member state of origin relies on Article 15 of the European Convention on Human Rights, or if the procedure laid down by Article 7(1) TEU has been initiated or if the European Council has adopted a decision pursuant to Article 7(2) or 7(3) TEU—all cases in which objective elements overcome the presumption that the state of origin respects fundamental rights. The fourth hypothesis, in which the member state receiving an application for asylum may examine it, is

[9] For the text of the proposal, *cf* E Bribosia and A Weyembergh, 'Extradition et asile: vers un espace judiciare européen?' (1997) *Revue belge de droit international* 69. The reaction of the European Council was positive, and in its Conclusions of 13–14 December 1996 it asked 'the Conference to develop the important proposal to amend the Treaties to establish it as a clear principle that no citizen of a Member State of the Union may apply for asylum in another Member State, taking into account international treaties'.

[10] Bribosia and Weyembergh, 'Extradition et asile', 72 ff; I Boccardi, *Europe and Refugees. Towards an EU Asylum Policy* (The Hague, Kluwer Law International, 2002) 140 ff.

when it decides to do so itself. In any case, the protocol is clear in its desire to exclude that the status of a European Union citizen is regulated according to the Geneva Convention on Refugees, in favour of free movement of persons.

The historical reasons justifying the adoption of the protocol make it clear how the primary intention was to avoid abuse of the right of asylum, that is, the presentation of an application for asylum in order to impede the execution of an extradition request. At the time of the dispute which gave rise to Protocol 24, there were no EU legislation governing extradition. Today, however, the matter is governed by Council Framework Decision 2002/584/JHA on the European arrest warrant, which would have meant that the dispute between Belgium and Spain would have been assessed and resolved differently.[11] The Framework Decision includes terrorism as one of the offences to which the arrest warrant applies and thus prevents the requested state from considering it as a political offence in order to refuse its execution. It also allows countries to refuse delivery of the person concerned if he or she risks suffering treatment prohibited by the non-refoulement principle or discriminations in the requesting state.

The presumption that member states respect fundamental rights and cannot produce refugees has (as might be expected) been criticised by legal scholars by reference to the fact that the Strasbourg Court has identified breaches (including serious breaches) of fundamental rights by all member states of the Union. The Protocol has also been criticised because it introduces a discrimination among asylum-seekers based on the country of origin, prohibited by the 1951 Geneva Convention.[12] The counter-argument raised by scholars more familiar with European Union law is mainly based on the fact that a European Union citizen, unlike a foreigner, has the right of residence in all countries of the Union.[13] In other words, his or her position is less at risk than that of any non-EU national requesting asylum.

If a comparison is made of the conditions for the right of residence as governed by European Union law on the one hand, and by the Geneva Convention on the other, a number of differences emerge. While, in general, European Union law is more favourable because it establishes the right not to suffer discrimination on the grounds of nationality and protects against expulsion in broader terms than the Geneva Convention, the latter nonetheless appears to be more favourable in

[11] S Peers, *EU Justice and Home Affairs Law*, 2nd edn (Oxford, Oxford University Press, 2006) 317.

[12] H Labayle, 'Un espace de liberté, de sécurité et de justice' (1997) *Revue trimestrielle de droit européen* 813; E Bribosia, 'Le Protocole sur le droit d'asile pour les ressortissants des États membres de l'Union européenne', in Y Lejeune (ed), *Le traité d'Amsterdam. Espoirs et déceptions* (Bruxelles, Bruylant, 1998) 192; S Da Lomba, *The Right to Seek Refugee Status in the European Union* (Antwerp, Intersentia, 2004) 101; G Gilbert, 'Is Europe Living up to its Obligations to Refugees?' (2004) 6 *European Journal of Migration and Law* 975; O Ferguson Sidorenko, *The Common European Asylum System* (The Hague, TMC Asser Press, 2007) 26.

[13] J-Y Carlier, 'Le développement d'une politique commune en matière d'asile', in C Dias Urbano De Sousa and P De Bruycker (eds), *The Emergence of a European Asylum Policy* (Bruxelles, Bruylant, 2004) 7 ff, states that European Union citizenship means that a person cannot be held to be 'outside the country of his nationality', pursuant to Art 1(A)(2) of the Geneva Convention.

some cases. In the first place, this is because the residence is not subject to the status of worker or the availability of resources. In the second place, it is more favourable because, when deciding on the expulsion of the European Union citizen under Directive 2004/38, the host country is not required to take the risks to which the person would be exposed in his or her country of origin into consideration. In reality, the principle of non-refoulement, established by Article 33 of the Geneva Convention, is an integral part of the European Union legal system because contained, inter alia, in Article 19 of the Charter of Fundamental Rights. In the third place, the Geneva Convention provides that account should be taken of the fact that refugees are unable to rely on the protection of their country of origin and cannot thus obtain the documents, which they require whether they be identity cards or other kinds of documents. Directive 2004/38 does not contain analogous provisions. Indeed, the Directive states expressly that the European Union citizens have the right to stay provided they hold an identity card. Case law has however offered a different understanding of the provision. Since the only function of an identity document is that of proof of citizenship, any other means fulfilling this function must be accepted.[14]

In conclusion, if the Geneva Convention is more favourable because it allows account to be taken of the vulnerability of the person in his or her country of origin, EU law offers access to employment, a more solid and long-lasting ground for residence.

IV. SECURITY OF THE WORKER'S RESIDENCE

Workers are the main beneficiaries of the free movement of persons. Residing as a worker is more advantageous than residing as a person who is economically self-sufficient. The reasons are manifold: non-discrimination of workers on the grounds of nationality operates without limits; the person concerned does not have to demonstrate possession of resources for self-maintenance, since it is assumed these can be obtained from the employment; the loss of employment does not result in the loss of the right of residence, at least for a time. In the following pages, we will analyse Directive 2004/38 to establish the extent of the security of workers' residence and, conversely, what is the effect of the absence, or loss, of employment.

The concept of worker has an EU meaning. Thus it must not be taken from national law, but rather from the definition provided by the European Court of Justice. According to *Lawrie-Blum*,[15] representing the leading case in this field, 'the essential feature of an employment relationship … is that for a certain period of

[14] Case C-215/03 *Oulane* [2005] ECR I-1215, para 25. However the Court offers no guidelines to assess the adequacy of other forms of evidence.

[15] Case 66/85 [1986] ECR I-2121. The decision has also been relied on recently—see, for example, Case C-46/12 *LN* [2013] ECLI:EU:C:2013:97.

time a person performs services for and under the direction of another person in return for which he receives remuneration'.

In addition to the three constituting elements of the concept—namely: subordination, duration, and remuneration—the Court also considered it necessary that the activity pursued is effective and genuine.[16]

The broad interpretation of the concept of worker has followed a number of lines.[17] In the first place, the juridical qualification of the relationship has been considered not to be relevant.[18] In the second place, remuneration is required but it may be of limited amount and indeed, even insufficient to ensure the maintenance of the worker concerned.[19] In the third place, working time may be limited.[20] The essential element is that the activities carried out are effective and genuine. If this is not the case, the person does not acquire the status of worker, even if it is possible to identify a relationship of subordination, and even if the work is performed over a particular time in exchange for remuneration.

The extent to which an activity is effective and genuine remains to some extent uncertain. In the *Bettray* case,[21] the dispute centred on whether it was possible to recognise the appellant in the main proceeding as a worker, carrying out activities in the context of a social programme whose purpose was to assist people who were not able to work because of their condition (as drug addicts) to recover work habits. The re-educational purposes of the activities carried out and the fact that the person concerned was unable to hold down a job were considered pre-eminent with respect to the presence of the other elements constituting the concept of worker under European Union law. The decision however, is not of general application because it is based on the particular aspects of the case concerned, as the Court itself stated in the subsequent *Birden* case.[22] More recent judgments of the Court have stressed the connection between the concepts of 'effective and genuine activity' and activities 'forming part of the normal labour market'.[23]

A jobseeker is treated as a worker at least for a limited period. Indeed, although the obligation to satisfy the conditions for prolonged stay arise after three months from entry, the Directive states that a European Union citizen, who is looking for work and has a good chance of finding it, may not be expelled.[24] The gap in the

[16] Case 53/81 *Levin* [1982] ECR 1035.

[17] C Barnard, *The Substantive Law of the EU*, 266 ff; N Rogers, R Scannell, and J Walsh, *Free Movement of Persons in the Enlarged European Union*, 2nd edn (London, Sweet and Maxwell, 2012) 89 ff.

[18] Case 344/87 *Bettray* [1989] ECR 1621. In Case C-94/07 *Raccanelli* [2008] ECR I-5939, the Court admitted that a person could be considered a worker, providing the constituent elements existed, even where the contract excludes the existence of an employment relationship.

[19] Case 139/85 *Kempf* [1986] ECR 1741.

[20] Case C-3/90 *Bernini* [1992] ECR I-1071.

[21] Case 344/87 [1989] ECR 1621.

[22] Case C-1/97 [1998] ECR I-7747, paras 30–32.

[23] Case C-456/02 *Trojani* [2004] ECR I-7573, para 24.

[24] Art 14(4)(b), Directive 2004/38. Case C-292/89 *Antonissen* [1991] ECR 745; Case C-171/91 *Tsiotras* [1993] ECR I-2925.

provisions relating to residence conditions remains though: the person cannot be expelled, nor may he or she claim social benefits (even though there is a right to obtain a benefit of a financial nature intended to facilitate access to employment in the labour market, because persons seeking employment are treated the same as workers).[25] If the state has laid down the obligation of residence registration after the three months from entry, but has not regulated the case involving the residence registration of a jobseeker, it remains uncertain whether the person concerned is able to demonstrate a right of residence as a worker, or whether he or she must demonstrate economic self-sufficiency.

From the point of view of the protection of vulnerable people, some considerations may be made in relation to the concept of worker.

In the first place, the jurisprudence of the Court of Justice ensures security of residence to workers in the informal, black market, when working without a contract or working under contractual conditions worse than those laid down by the law. This conclusion stems from the Court of Justice's statement that 'the national authorities are not authorized to penalize non-compliance with social legislation by refusing to issue a residence permit to a Community national to whom the rules on freedom of movement for persons apply'.[26] It can be deduced from the above that even if the worker is not formally employed or his or her position regularised, the right to stay remains intact.[27]

In the second place, trainees can also be considered as workers on condition that they receive at least a limited amount of money as consideration for the activities carried out.[28] Trainees represent another category vulnerable to exploitation.

As already mentioned, the loss of work does not result in the loss of the right of residence as a worker if the case comes within one of the four hypotheses provided for under Article 7(3) of Directive 2004/38. The first relates to temporary inability to work following illness or accident. No minimum prior period of work is required, nor are limits imposed on the retention of the status—so long as the inability remains, the status of worker remains. Once the inability has terminated the person concerned will be able to present him or herself on the employment market again. The inability referred to by the Directive depends on the illness of a worker. A case where it is impossible to work because of the need to care for a sick or disabled family member does not come within the definition.[29]

The second and third hypothesis where the status of worker is maintained concern involuntary unemployment. In both cases, the person concerned will be required to register with the unemployment office. If he or she has worked

[25] Case C-258/04 *Ioannidis* [2005] ECR I-8275; joined Cases C-22/08 and C-23/08 *Vatsouras and Koupatantze* [2009] ECR I-4585.

[26] Case C-363/89 *Roux* [1991] ECR I-286, para 27.

[27] Even though it might be difficulty for a European Union citizen to prove his or her status as a worker, where there is no employment contract.

[28] Case C-313/01 *Morgenbesser* [2003] ECR I-13467.

[29] C O'Brien, 'Social Blind Spots and Monocular Policy Making: the ECJ's Migrant Worker Model' (2009) 46 *Common Market Law Review* 1107, 1118 ff.

for more than one year before becoming unemployed, the status of worker will be maintained without time limits. On the other hand, if the employment has lasted for less than one year, the status of worker will be maintained for at least six months. The fourth hypothesis envisaged by the Directive relates to a case where the person concerned follows a vocational training course after the termination of employment. If he or she is involuntarily unemployed because of dismissal or the expiry of a fixed-term employment contract without it being renewed, the status of worker will be retained irrespective of the course of training that is followed. In the case of voluntary unemployment, for the status to be maintained it will be necessary to establish a connection between the employment activities carried out and the training course undertaken.[30] The above rules protect the worker from the adverse effects of dismissal or loss of employment during residence.

Practice has however shown that the Directive does not provide sufficient protection, at least in some cases. One such example would be that of a female worker who lost her job because of pregnancy. She could find it difficult to meet the requirements laid down by the Directive because her opportunities of finding new employment are reduced by the very law which protects maternity, or by the unfortunate practice of not appointing pregnant women. The Court of Justice has stated that a woman, who has not been available on the employment market during the last months of her pregnancy and the first months after her child's birth, can still be considered as a worker, provided she returns to work or finds a new job within a reasonable period.[31] Even if the Directive is silent on this point, according to the Court, its interpretation stems from the Treaty itself. The judgment is quite brief and the reasoning obscure, but it can nevertheless be welcome as an indication of a favourable attitude toward pregnant women.

The Directive does not protect workers in the case of voluntary unemployment. Nonetheless, it must be recalled that a European Union citizen has the right to change work, no particular formality being required. Therefore, at least if he or she has found another job, the European Union citizen being subject to exploitation or bullying at work will in any case be able to resign, ending his or her situation of weakness without the fear of losing the right of residence.

The Directive also regulates the case where a worker who has lost his or her job obtains the right to permanent residence even if residing for less than five years (Article 17 of Directive 2004/38). The legislation takes situations giving rise to vulnerability into account in its provisions. The first case where it is possible to obtain permanent rights of residence early relates to a worker leaving employment for reasons of age. If the termination of employment results in early retirement, the worker must have been resident for three years and have worked at least during the 12 months prior to retirement. The second case is where the termination of employment results from subsequent permanent incapacity. The worker must have carried

[30] In certain cases the connection between previous activities and training is not always required: Case C-413/01 *Ninni-Orasche* [2003] ECR I-13187, para 35.

[31] Case C-507/12 *Saint Prix* [2014], ECLI:EU:C:2014:2007 para 41.

out the activity for at least two years, a condition not required if the incapacity is caused by accident at work or occupational disease giving rise to the right to receive benefit from an institution of the host country.

V. SECURITY OF THE LONE PARENT'S RESIDENCE

As already mentioned above, the right of residence extends to the family members of a European Union citizen irrespective of their nationality. Such a right is not autonomous but connected to that of the European Union citizen. It may be invoked in the country in which the European Union citizen resides or intends to reside.[32] The beneficiaries of this right are close family members: the spouse or partner,[33] dependent descendants or descendants under the age of 21, and dependent ascendants. Since what is involved here is a derived right, for the benefit of persons who, if nationals of third countries, might not enjoy an autonomous right of residence, Articles 12 and 13 take on particular importance. These regulate the effects of the death or departure of the European Union citizen or of the dissolution of the marriage or registered partnership, on the family member's right of residence.

The provisions of Article 12 envisage three cases. The first is a case where the family includes children enrolled at an educational establishment, for the purpose of studying there. The death or departure of the European Union citizen will have no effect on the right of residence of the children or the parent having their custody. This right of residence is not subject to any other condition. The second and third cases envisaged by the Article are of residual character with respect to the first.

The second case applies where the European Union citizen dies: the family members have a right of residence but must personally satisfy the conditions laid down by Article 7, that is, they must be workers or economically self-sufficient. Under Article 23 of the Directive, the family members of the European Union citizen have the right to access to work irrespective of their own nationality. If the family members are third country nationals, there is a further condition according to which they must have stayed in the host country for at least one year prior to the death of the European Union citizen. Furthermore, the rights of family members do not extend to others, for example, to a new spouse. The third case is concerned with what happens if the European Union citizen leaves. Only family members who are nationals of a member state will retain the right to reside if they satisfy the conditions of Article 7 of the Directive.

[32] The right of residence based on the status of family member cannot be relied on in a country other than that in which the European Union citizen lives: Case C-40/11 *Iida* [2012] ECLI:EU:C:2012:691 para 64.

[33] The partner has a right of residence if the host country considers a registered partnership to be equivalent to a marriage. If this condition is not met, the partner will not have a right of residence, but only a right to a careful examination of his or her application for entry and residence.

If the deceased worker had resided for two years or if death follows an accident at work or occupational disease, any family member residing with the worker will acquire the right to permanent residence directly (Article 17(4)).

Family members are not treated in the same way, and third country nationals are more vulnerable than European Union citizens. Indeed, the departure of the European Union citizen does not permit the maintenance of a right to residence (save in the presence of children attending school), and death will give rise to such a right only if the family member has resided for at least one year. If a spouse dies leaving very small children, the surviving spouse who has not lived in the country for at least one year is in a position of particular vulnerability, a situation not directly taken into consideration by the Directive. It is indirectly however, because when reaching a decision on expulsion the host state is requested to take account of existing family ties.

Article 13 lays down rules regarding the effects of the termination of marriage (or registered partnership) on the right of residence. This situation is also of particular importance because the spouse might be faced with a difficult alternative: to separate and have to deal with the vulnerability connected with insecurity of residence, or to remain in the marriage even in circumstances where he or she would like to bring it to an end. The situation differs according to the spouse's nationality. If the spouse is a European Union citizen, he or she will retain the right of residence so long as he or she is working or self-sufficient. As far as resources are concerned, divorce maintenance payments could be considered adequate for not being a burden on the state purse. If he or she is a non-EU national, in addition to the conditions applying to the spouse having European Union citizenship, one of the four cases identified by Article 13(2) must occur.

The elements allowing the spouse to maintain a right of residence can be summarised as follows: 1) the duration of the marriage (three years, of which one in the host member state on the date when the procedure for termination of the marriage begins), 2) custody of the children, based on agreed or judicial decisions, 3) the grant of a right to access to a minor child, if it has been established that access must be in the host state, as long as it is considered necessary, or 4) difficult situations, such as having suffered domestic violence during the marriage, justifying the maintenance of the right to residence. Here too, as seen in the case of the European Union citizen's death, the right of residence is not transferred to a new spouse.

With reference to vulnerability, the most significant case is the maintenance of the right to stay, in the event of maltreatment if the competent authorities consider it necessary. The decision of the competent authorities is entirely discretionary.

As already indicated, Directive 2004/38 does not exhaust the right of residence of the European Union citizen. The Court of Justice has identified a wide range of cases in which EU law confers a right of residence to a European Union citizen or his or her family members. A significant number of cases relate to lone parents, often national of a third country.

In a first group of decisions, the Court of Justice has stated that the parent of the child of a migrant worker following a course of study will have a right of residence if the parent has custody of the child or if the child needs the parent in order to be able to continue studying. The foundation of the right of residence has been attributed to Article 12 of Regulation1612/68/EEC, now Article 10 of Regulation 492/2011/EU.

A brief digression at this point might assist in giving a better understanding of the scope of the case law. Article 12 of Regulation 1612/68 (now Article 10 of Regulation 492/2011) grants the child of the migrant worker a right of access to study facilities.[34] The Court of Justice has interpreted this to mean that a child of a migrant worker has a right to reside in the member state where he or she is attending studies, even when the migrant worker parent no longer lives in that member state.[35] The further step taken by the Court was to recognise the right of residence of the parent with custody of the child.

The parent's right of residence has been constructed as a corollary of the migrant worker's children's right to complete their studies in the host country, interpreting Article 12 (Article 10) in the light of the right to the protection of family life set out under Article 8 ECHR. The Court detailed the terms of the right in four judgments relating to five disputes (*Baumbast and R*, *Ibrahim*, *Teixeira*, *Alarape*),[36] all deriving from preliminary references by British courts. The factual bases of the disputes shared a number of common elements, which are worthy of mention. The parents with custody whose rights of residence were in dispute were not migrant workers, which had represented the prerequisite for application of the Regulation.[37] Four cases were concerned with lone parents (mothers) who were separated or divorced.[38] In four cases the parent with custody was a third country national.[39] The nationality of the parents did not seem to have the slightest relevance: suffice it to say that the Court's decisions were identical and the rules relied on were the same. In three cases the parent worked or was in any

[34] A child of a self-employed worker will not enjoy this right because Regulation 1612/68/EEC (and Regulation 492/2011/EU) only applies to employed workers and has been adopted on the basis of Art 48 TEEC (now Art 49 TFEU): see joined Cases C-147/11 and C-148/11 *Czop and Punakova* [2012] ECLI:EU:C:2012:538 para 30.

[35] Joined Cases 389/87 and 390/87 *Echternach and Moritz* [1989] ECR 723.

[36] Case C-413/99 *Baumbast and R* [2002] ECR I-7091; Case C-310/08 *Ibrahim* [2010] ECR I-1065; Case C-480/08 *Teixeira* [2010] ECR I-1107; Case C-529/11 *Alarape* [2013] ECLI:EU:C:2013:290.

[37] There might be some doubt on this point with regard to the *Teixeira* case. The appellant in the main proceedings had worked in the host country even though only on an occasional basis, but it is not clear from the text of the decision whether the migrant worker was the appellant or her husband.

[38] The exception was Mrs Baumbast. She was not separated from her husband, who indeed was responsible for care of their children but worked outside the European Union. The position of Mr Baumbast was examined in the light of Art 18 TEC (now Art 21 TFEU). In other words, while the mother had a right of residence deriving from her children's right to study, the father's right of residence was based directly on the Treaty. The way in which the applications were formulated may have led to this result.

[39] Mrs Baumbast was Colombian, Mrs R American, Mrs Ibrahim Somali, Mrs Alarape Nigerian. Mrs Teixeira, however, was Portuguese.

case economically self-sufficient.[40] In two cases the dispute had arisen following a claim for state benefit by the parent who had neither work nor resources. In the *Ibrahim* and *Teixeira* cases this fact had induced the national court to ask whether the parent's right of residence should be subject to the possession of resources and medical insurance, conditions which Directive 2004/38/EC imposes on inactive migrants. The Court rejected this interpretation, stating instead that Article 12 of the Regulation did not make the residence subject to any requirement.

The parent's right of residence, to the extent that it is functional to the full enjoyment of the child's right to study, is strictly connected to that of the child and arises the moment when the child begins to attend school.[41] The duration of the parent's right of residence was in dispute in the *Teixeira* case because, unlike the cases decided up to that time in which the children had been minors, the daughter had been adolescent and in the mean time had come of age. The problem which had thus arisen was whether the daughter's coming of age had brought the parent's right of residence to an end. The Court adopted a pragmatic approach: since the child's right extended beyond coming of age up to completion of his or her studies, it was necessary to establish on a case-by-case basis whether the child needed the parent to be able to continue with the related study. It might be presumed that, on coming of age, the child was capable of fending for him or herself, but this was a rebuttable presumption. It was for the child to show that he or she still needed his or her parent. The factual criterion prevailed over the juridical one deriving from the power of custody.[42] The *Alarape* case followed the same line of reasoning. It was a question of fact whether the child, a 22-year-old doctoral candidate, needed the presence and care of the mother to be able to continue with the course of study and bring it to completion.[43]

In all the above-mentioned judgments the Court recognised the right of residence of the parent with custody. It has not, however, provided with details of the extent of the connected rights. Does the parent with custody have the right to receive any benefit provided by the host state? What kind of protection against expulsion does he or she enjoy? As matters stand at present, these questions remain open.

[40] Mrs Baumbast was supported by her husband, Mrs R was self-employed and Mrs Alarape worked part-time.

[41] If the child does not go to school because it is not old enough, its parents will not be able to rely on a right of residence pursuant to Art 12: Case C-45/12 *Hadj Ahmed* [2013] ECLI:EU:C:2013:390 para 52.

[42] *Teixeira*, para 86.

[43] *Alarape*, para 30.

A second line of decisions derives from the *Chen* case.[44] The European Union citizen was an Irish newborn child residing in the United Kingdom.[45] The mother of the baby was a third country national. After having stated, recalling the *Baumbast* decision, that the right of residence was connected with European Union citizenship, the Court noted that under Directive 90/364/EEC, applicable at that time, the person concerned should dispose of medical insurance and sufficient resources, without requiring that they should be possessed personally by the EU citizen. In this case, the resources had been made available to the baby by her mother, thus satisfying the Directive's conditions. The mother's position, however, could not be regulated by the same Directive because, according to its provisions, ascendants only have a right to residence if dependent on the beneficiary, while in this case there was no dispute that the daughter was dependent on her mother. The Court did not stop there and added that if a right of residence was not granted to the mother, the daughter would not be able to reside in the host member state, given that the resources representing the conditions for her residence would come to an end. This meant that the mother's right of residence was a prerequisite for the European Union citizen to be able to exercise the right of residence. To deny the mother's right of residence would render the European Union citizen's right of residence useless (paragraph 45). In support of this reasoning, the Court referred once again to *Baumbast*, in the part relating to the parent's right to reside with her student son, considering the two cases to be governed by the same principle.

The principle expressed in the *Chen* case was repeated by the Court, after the entry into force of Directive 2004/38. In the *Alokpa* case, the Court confirmed that the parent of a European Union citizen of tender years, living in a different country to that of origin, had the right of residence if providing the resources; that is, if the children satisfied the conditions laid down by Article 7 of the Directive because of the mother's resources.[46] It remains an open question whether the parent making the resources available to a European Union citizen has to own them or can obtain them from work. In the *Chen* case, the mother had her own resources, but in the *Alokpa* case, the mother did not have resources but she had received an offer of work, which would have allowed her a source of income. The Court did not deal with the issue directly, but according to the Advocate General,

[44] Case C-200/02 *Chen* [2004] ECR I-9925. *Cf* J-Y Carlier (2005) 42 *Common Market Law Review* 1121; B Hofstötter, 'A cascade of rights, or who shall care for little Catherine? Some reflections on the Chen case' (2005) 30 *European Law Rev* 548; A Tryfonidou, 'Further Cracks in the "Great Wall" of the European Union?' (2005) 11 *European Public Law* 527; E Bergamini, 'Il difficile equilibrio fra riconoscimento del diritto alla libera circolazione, rispetto della vita familiare e abuso del diritto' (2006) *Diritto dell'Unione europea* 347; B Kunoy, 'A Union of National Citizens: the Origins of the Court's Lack of Avant-Gardisme in the Chen Case' (2006) 43 *Common Market Law Review* 179.

[45] In this case the baby was born in Northern Ireland and was an Irish national pursuant to Irish law then in force, which granted Irish nationality to anyone born in the island even in that part pertaining to the United Kingdom of Great Britain and Northern Ireland. Ireland subsequently amended this law.

[46] Case C-86/12 *Alokpa* [2013] ECLI:EU:C:2013:645. The mother was a national of Togo and her children, born in Luxemburg, were French citizens because they had been recognised by their father who lived in France but did not contribute to the family.

the concrete prospect of obtaining future work was capable of satisfying the requirements of the Directive (paragraph 28).

Reasoning similar to that followed by the Court in *Chen* could also be relied on in a situation where the European Union citizen is disabled and unable to support him or herself. The case law, however, does not clarify whether only one or both parents have the right of residence. A favourable response could be based on respect for family life.

A third line of case law relating to third country national parents' right of residence can be traced to the *Ruiz Zambrano* case,[47] but it is only applicable where the parent's right of residence is invoked in the country of origin of the European Union citizen, who has never exercised the right to free movement. In other terms it is worthy of mention for its undoubted interest in the field even though it does not represent a precedent of use in founding the parent's right of residence when remaining alone in the country where he or she moved with the European Union citizen in the exercise of the right of free movement.

In the *Ruiz Zambrano* case the Court was asked to assess the refusal of a residence and work permit, submitted by the non-EU parents of two Belgian minors, born and having always lived in Belgium. The case had unusual facts. Suffice it to say that the father worked regularly, although he was illegally in the country because he had made an application for asylum which had been refused without granting him any kind of residence permit. Although at first sight no element in the dispute appeared to represent an actual or potential connection with EU law, the Court decided it was within the scope of application of the treaty because of the nationality of the children. Since they were European Union citizens, they were entitled to the effective enjoyment of the essential core of rights connected with the status of citizens. Any national laws, which had the effect of depriving such citizens of the enjoyment of such core of rights, were in breach of Article 20

[47] Case C-34/09 *Ruiz Zambrano* [2011] ECR I-1177. *Cf* A Adinolfi, 'Diritto di soggiorno di cittadini di Stati terzi per rendere effettivo il diritto di soggiorno di cittadini dell'Unione nel loro Stato di cittadinanza' (2011) *Rivista di diritto internazionale* 467; H van Eijken and SA de Vries, 'A New Route into the Promised Land? Being a European Citizen after Ruiz Zambrano' (2011) 36 *European Law Review* 704; K Hailbronner and D Thym (2011) 48 *Common Market Law Review* 1253; L Montanari, 'Una nuova tappa nella definizione della portata della cittadinanza europea: alcune riflessioni sulle sentenze Ruiz Zambrano e McCarthy' (2011) *La Comunità internazionale* 467; L Manigrassi, 'Vers une citoyenneté européenne fédérale? Quelques réflexions sur l'arrêt «Zambrano»' (2011) *Revue du droit de l'Union européenne* 411; P Mengozzi, 'La sentenza Zambrano: prodromi e conseguenze di una pronuncia inattesa' (2011) *Studi sull'integrazione europea* 417; I Ottaviano, 'La Corte di giustizia riconosce all'art. 20 un'autonoma portata attributiva di diritti al cittadino europeo' (2011) *Europa e diritto privato* 797; R Palladino, 'Il diritto di soggiorno nel "proprio" Stato membro quale (nuovo) corollario della cittadinanza europea' (2011) *Studi sull'integrazione europea* 331; GF Aiello and S Lamonaca, 'Diritto di soggiorno dei familiari del cittadino europeo: erosione del limite delle situazioni puramente interne e delimitazione del nucleo essenziale del diritto di cittadinanza' (2012) *Rivista italiana di diritto pubblico comunitario* 321; S Platon, 'Le champ d'application des droits du citoyen européen après les arrêts Zambrano, McCarthy et Dereci. De la boîte de Pandore au labyrinthe du Minotaure' (2012) *Revue trimestrielle de droit européen* 2.

TFEU.[48] Provisions of the kind under examination in this case which deny residence and work permits to parents and thus oblige them to leave the country, are in breach of Article 20 because their children, European Union citizens, would be forced to leave the territory of the Union (paragraph 44).

The same reasoning has also been applied, although with a different outcome, in the subsequent *Dereci* case.[49] In this case, the mother had the same nationality as the children, being that of their country of residence, while the father was a third country national. The Court followed *McCarthy*,[50] which had ruled out that the *Ruiz Zambrano* case could found the right of residence of a third country national, husband of a citizen of the United Kingdom and Ireland, who has always lived in the United Kingdom. Therefore, it answered the *Dereci* case by stating that in the case before it the right of residence of the mother and children in the European Union was not under threat.

After having cited paragraph 42 of the *Ruiz Zambrano* decision, the Court went on to state:

> the criterion relating to the denial of the genuine enjoyment of the substance of the rights conferred by virtue of European Union citizen status refers to situations in which the Union citizen has, in fact, to leave not only the territory of the Member State of which he is a national but also the territory of the Union as a whole. That criterion is specific in character inasmuch as it relates to situations in which, although subordinate legislation on the right of residence of third country nationals is not applicable, a right of residence may not, exceptionally, be refused to a third country national, who is a family member of a Member State national, as the effectiveness of Union citizenship enjoyed by that national would otherwise be undermined. Consequently, the mere fact that it might appear desirable to a national of a Member State, for economic reasons or in order to keep his family together in the territory of the Union, for the members of his family who do not have the nationality of a Member State to be able to reside with him in the territory of the Union, is not sufficient in itself to support the view that the Union citizen will be forced to leave Union territory if such a right is not granted.[51]

The Court seems willing to circumscribe the effect of the *Ruiz Zambrano* case to its own facts, that is where the European Union citizen is a minor,[52] since a

[48] With regard to the originality of the reasoning adopted by the Court with respect to preceding case law *cf* L Manigrassi, 'Vers une citoyenneté européenne fédérale? Quelques réflexions sur l'arrêt «Zambrano»' (2011) *Revue du droit de l'Union européenne* 411, 420. S Platon, 'Le champ d'application des droits du citoyen européen après les arrêts Zambrano, McCarthy et Dereci. De la boîte de Pandore au labyrinthe du Minotaure' (2012) *Revue trimestrielle de droit européen* 2, 37 ff, was particularly critical of the lack of logical rigour in the Court's reasoning.

[49] Case C-256/11 *Dereci* [2011] ECR I-11315. *Cf* S Adam and P Van Elsuwege, 'Citizenship Rights and the Federal Balance between the European Union and its Member States: Comment on Dereci' (2012) 37 *European Law Review* 176.

[50] Case C-434/09 *McCarthy* [2011] ECR I-3375. *Cf* A Wiesbrock, 'Disentangling the "Union Citizenship Puzzle"? The McCarthy Case' (2011) 36 *European Law Review* 861.

[51] *Dereci*, n 49 above, paras 66–68.

[52] The Court has always excluded reliance on the *Ruiz Zambrano* case if the European Union citizen is of full age: in addition to the *McCarthy* and *Dereci* cases already cited previously, *cf* Case C-87/12 *Ymeraga* [2013]. Legal scholars have wondered whether it would be possible to apply the

European Union citizen of full age can either continue to live in his or her country or move to another member state. This is the critical difference between the *Ruiz Zambrano* and *Dereci* cases. Mrs Dereci, as a person of full age, was able to decide where to locate her and her children's residence, whether in her country of origin or in another member state, where, inter alia, as a result of the *Metock* case, her third country national spouse would have the right to reside pursuant to Directive 2004/38/EC.[53] In contrast, the *Ruiz Zambrano* children would not have been able to live alone in Belgium because of their age, or move to another member state. Although it is true that, in the *Chen* case, the Court recognised that a European Union citizen, who is a minor, has the right of residence in the host country even when the economic resources are ensured by the mother, the *Ruiz Zambrano* parents had to obtain economic resources from employment and it was not certain whether they would have had the right to work.

There is still some doubt as the identification of the person who will have the right of residence to ensure the full enjoyment of the citizenship rights of a European Union citizen. In the *O and S* case, indeed, the Court stated that it is the dependency of a European Union citizen on a third country national in a situation where the refusal of residence to the latter is liable to put in question the effectiveness of the European Union citizenship in practice.[54] There is no doubt as to the dependency of the minor on his or her parents, but the wide formula used by Court leaves open the possibility that any other adult, with whom the minor has some unspecified relationship of dependency, may be able to rely on a right of residence on the basis of the *Ruiz Zambrano* case law.

A further reason for considering the current case law in this area to be unsatisfactory derives from the fact that, particularly in the *Dereci* case, the Court provides very few guidelines to national courts, substantially leaving them without effective principles applicable to the specific cases before them. But even in *Ruiz Zambrano*, in which the Court offers greater guidance to national courts, the question of which regime was to be applied to the father's work and residence

Ruiz Zambrano case to other cases and a variety of hypotheses have been put forward. The more convincing mention school-age children (Ottaviano, 'La Corte di giustizia riconosce all'art. 20 un'autonoma portata attributiva di diritti al cittadino europeo' (2011) *Europa e diritto privato* 797, 806 f), a disabled adult unable to care for him or herself (P Mengozzi, 'La sentenza Zambrano: prodromi e conseguenze di una pronuncia inattesa' (2011) *Studi sull'integrazione europea* 417, 431), or the spouse unable to look after him or herself for reasons of health (A Wiesbrock, 'Disentangling the "Union Citizenship Puzzle"? The McCarthy Case' (2011) 36 *European Law Review* 861, 868). S Adam and P Van Elsuwege, 'Citizenship Rights and the Federal Balance between the European Union and its Member States: Comment on Dereci' (2012) 37 *European Law Review* 176, 181, highlight the fact that a connection of economic dependency must exist between the European Union citizen and the family member because the dependence deriving from the family connection is not enough.

[53] Case C-127/08 *Metock* [2008] ECR I-6241. The Court stated that Directive 2004/38 did not allow member states to deny the right of residence to the European Union citizen's spouse in circumstances where the former is not legally resident.

[54] Joined Cases C-356/11 and C-357/11 *O and S* [2012] ECLI:EU:C:2012:776 para 56. This case involves a discussion of the right of residence of the European Union citizen's mother's new husband.

permits was left open, both with reference to administrative formalities and to their duration and connected rights.[55] It could be the regime laid down by the Directive 2004/38/EC adapted to take account of the special nature of the case, that set up by national law,[56] or a different one drawn up on an ad hoc basis.

VI. CONCLUDING REMARKS

EU law encourages European Union citizens having employment or sufficient economic resources for their maintenance to take advantages of the freedom of movement. The goal of making the residence of the European Union more secure means that some of the events making a foreigner vulnerable have to be taken into account and made ineffective. Under EU law, loss of employment, sickness and divorce might not have any effects on the right of residence. Nonetheless, there are undoubtedly still gaps left, which can be filled by the national law of the host country, at the expense of the uniformity of status that EU law aims to establish.

[55] P Mengozzi, 'La sentenza Zambrano: prodromi e conseguenze di una pronuncia inattesa' (2011) *Studi sull'integrazione europea* 417, 429, and H van Eijken and SA de Vries, 'A New Route into the Promised Land? Being a European Citizen after Ruiz Zambrano' (2011) 36 *European Law Review* 704, 714, consider that no formality or condition can be derived from the case law.

[56] According to K Hailbronner and D Thym (2011) 48 *Common Market Law Review* 1253, 1266, the condition of Mr Ruiz Zambrano was governed by the national law on immigration, a matter not yet governed by European law but which must be applied by member states in such a way as to comply with the European Union law which has been enacted in the field.

IV

Victims of Illegal Acts

15

The Place of the Victim in Europe's Area of Criminal Justice

VALSAMIS MITSILEGAS

I. INTRODUCTION

THE PAST 15 years have witnessed the transformation of the European Union into an Area of Freedom, Security and Justice, marked by the evolution of the EU constitutional framework in the field via the entry into force of the Treaties of Amsterdam and Lisbon, as well as by significant growth in secondary EU legislation in the field. The development of European integration in criminal matters has been a key part of this process, leading to the gradual configuration of a European area of criminal justice. The establishment of such an area faces a number of challenges, which are inextricably linked with the special place that criminal law occupies in the legal and political systems of EU member states. Any attempt towards further European integration in the field of criminal justice has to inevitably address questions regarding the impact of EU action in the field on state sovereignty with regard to the exercise of state power in criminal matters. These sovereignty questions are accompanied by questions related to the impact of Europeanisation on national legal diversity, bearing in mind that domestic criminal justice systems reflect diverse and long-standing national legal traditions and concepts of justice. These questions have led to a number of complex solutions to accompany the supranationalisation of EU criminal law post-Lisbon, both as regards the extent of Union competence to legislate in the field and as regards the means and principles underlying EU legislative intervention. The impact of EU criminal law on state sovereignty, national legal diversity and national concepts of justice remains thus contested. This is the case in particular with regard to the place of the victim in the criminal justice system. When examined at a purely national level, calls to strengthen the position of the victim in criminal procedure have been accompanied by a series of questions and concerns with regard to the impact that victims' rights could have on the balance of interests in the criminal justice process, and in particular with regard to the potentially negative impact on the rights of the defendant in criminal proceedings. Different legal systems in Europe have provided different answers to these questions, leading to a considerable diversity in the protection of the victim and the content and extent of victims' rights in the domestic criminal justice system. It is in the context of this debate on the rights of victims in criminal procedure and their impact on criminal justice and the rights of the defendant in a landscape of considerable legal diversity among EU member states that EU intervention with respect to victims' rights has taken place. Informed by these factors, the aim of this chapter is to provide a legal analysis of the place of the victim in EU criminal law and the EU are of criminal justice more generally. The chapter will begin by putting forward a typology of victims' rights in EU criminal law, by analysing the three different levels within which EU law addresses the position of the victim in the criminal justice process. This typology will be followed by a discussion of the three key challenges facing the evolution of EU criminal law on victims: first, the chapter will address the constitutional challenge, which is related to the extent to which the European Union has used its powers to legislate appropriately in the context of legislation on victims' rights; secondly, the chapter will deal with the challenge on national legal diversity, which involves an analysis of the extent to which EU victims' law has had or can have an impact on the domestic criminal justice systems of EU member states, and of the extent to which EU harmonisation in the field can challenge national diversity; thirdly, the chapter will address the broader question of the challenge that EU criminal law on the victim poses on concepts of criminal justice in the EU member states and in the European Union itself. The analysis will focus on the actual and potential impact of EU victims' law on the rights of the defence and on the balance of interests in the criminal justice process.

II. VICTIMS' RIGHTS IN EU CRIMINAL LAW—A TYPOLOGY

Victims' rights stem from multiple sources (including both legislation and case law) and have been put forward in various stages of European integration, with preoccupation with victims' rights dating before the attribution to the European Union of an express Treaty competence to legislate in criminal matters. EU law has established victims' rights related to the criminal justice process in three main ways. The first way has been to limit the power of member states with regard to the national choices made in the field of criminal justice in order to ensure the protection of the rights of the victim who is an EU citizen—state sovereignty in criminal matters is limited by the need to ensure free movement and to respect fundamental principles of EU law. The second avenue for establishing victims' rights at EU level has been to ensure the extraterritorial reach of national decisions granting rights to victims and their enforcement by authorities in other EU member states by applying the principle of mutual recognition in criminal matters[1]—the aim here being

[1] On the principle of mutual recognition see V Mitsilegas, 'The Constitutional Implications of Mutual Recognition in Criminal Matters in the EU' [2006] 43 *Common Market Law Review* 1277–1311.

again to ensure the free movement of the victim in a borderless Area of Freedom, Security and Justice. The third, and more direct, avenue of victim protection has been the adoption of specific EU legislation setting out a series of rights for the victim in criminal proceedings—such EU harmonisation measures have evolved over time, with the Treaty of Lisbon (Treaty on the Functioning of the European Union—TFEU) granting an express competence to the Union to adopt minimum standards on the rights of the victim. The rationale for EU intervention here goes beyond the justification of the other avenues for victim protection: the perceived need for the adoption of EU legislation establishing minimum standards on the rights of victims is not limited only to the achievement of the effective enjoyment of free movement in the European Union, but is linked more broadly to the need to ensure the effectiveness of the application of the principle of mutual recognition in criminal matters in the European Union (Article 82(2) TFEU). In addition to these three general avenues of ensuring the protection of the rights of victims in the criminal justice process by European Union law, a number of further EU law measures related to the victim have been adopted ranging from specific measures on victims' rights in the context of terrorism,[2] trafficking in human beings[3] and sexual exploitation legislation[4] to legislation on victims' compensation[5] and the mutual recognition of civil protection orders.[6] These measures may be linked on occasion with the development of the EU criminal justice *acquis*, but will not be analysed in detail by this chapter which aims to focus on the general EU framework for the protection of victims in the criminal justice process.

A. Victims' Rights as Free Movement Rights

The first intervention with regard to ensuring the rights of the victim in the criminal process came by the Court of Justice in the 1980s. In an era when the (then) European Community did not possess express competence to legislate in criminal matters, the Court, in a series of rulings, found nevertheless that Community law did have an impact on criminal law in placing limits on national criminal law in cases where the latter was found to be contrary to fundamental principles of Community law such as free movement.[7] The application of this line of judgments in the case of victims of crime led the Court to find that national legislation restricting compensation to victims who were nationals of an EU member state or

[2] Council Framework Decision 2002/475/JHA on combating terrorism [2002] OJ L164/3.

[3] Directive 2011/36/EU of the European Parliament and of the Council on preventing and combating trafficking in human beings and protecting its victims [2011] OJ L101/1.

[4] Directive 2011/93/EU of the European Parliament and of the Council on combating the sexual abuse and sexual exploitation of children and child pornography [2011] OJ L335/1.

[5] Council Directive 2004/80/EC relating to compensation to crime victims [2004] OJ L261/15.

[6] Regulation (EU) 606/2013 of the European Parliament and of the Council on mutual recognition of protection measures in civil matters [2013] OJ L181/4.

[7] See V Mitsilegas, *EU Criminal Law* (Oxford, Hart Publishing, 2009), ch 2.

holders of a residence permit was contrary to Community law. In the well-known *Cowan* ruling,[8] the Court found that the prohibition of discrimination

> must be interpreted as meaning that in respect of persons whose freedom to travel to a Member State, in particular as recipients of services, is guaranteed by Community law that State may not make the award of State compensation for harm caused in that State to the victim of an assault resulting in physical injury subject to the condition that he hold a residence permit or be a national of a country which has entered into a reciprocal agreement with that Member State.[9]

The Court reiterated its earlier case law on the impact of Community law on national criminal law[10] to state that although in principle criminal legislation and the rules of criminal procedure, among which the national provision is to be found, are matters for which the member states are responsible, the Court has consistently held that Community law sets certain limits to their power. In the present case such legislative provisions may not discriminate against persons to whom Community law gives the right to equal treatment or restrict the fundamental freedoms guaranteed by Community law.[11] By treating tourists as recipients of services and limiting national legislative choices as regards compensation of the victims of crime in order to ensure the effectiveness of Community law, the Court of Justice in *Cowan* provided the first major avenue for the protection of victims' rights when exercising free movement rights. Unlike in other cases, where the result of the Court's interference to national criminal justice choices has been to limit national criminalisation or punishment which was deemed to be disproportionate to the achievement of the effectiveness of Community law and thus enhance the rights of the defendant,[12] in *Cowan* the need to respect Community law has been to extend the scope of the rights of the victim in the criminal process.

B. Mutual Recognition

More than 20 years after the Court's ruling in *Cowan*, European integration in criminal matters has made spectacular steps forward from the EC Treaty in the 1980s, which did not contain an express Community competence to legislate in criminal matters to the entry into force of the Lisbon Treaty in 2009 which has largely 'supranationalised' EU criminal law, via the 'half-way house' Maastricht, Amsterdam and Nice Treaties. Yet the passage of time and the ensuing constitutional developments at EU level do not seem to have altered the fundamental aim of granting rights to victims in order to ensure their freedom of movement, this time in a borderless Area of Freedom, Security and Justice. Rather than relying

[8] Case 186/87 *Cowan v Trésor Public* [1989] ECR 195.
[9] ibid, para 20.
[10] See in particular Case 203/80 *Casati* [1981] ECR 2595.
[11] Case 186/87 *Cowan*, para 19.
[12] See eg Case C-193/94 *Skanavi and Chryssanthakopoulos* [1996] ECR I-929.

exclusively on the case law of the Court of Justice, the EU legislator has opted for the adoption of a specific post-Lisbon legislative instrument to ensure the protection of victims when they exercise free movement rights in the European Union. The measure in question is Directive 2011/99/EU on the European Protection Order.[13] The Directive, which was adopted under a legal basis related to judicial cooperation in criminal matters,[14] aims to apply the principle of mutual recognition in criminal matters to orders issued to protect victims in one member state when these victims find themselves in other EU member states—in other words, it is intended that the recognition of a European Protection Order by the authority in the executing member state will mean that the protection will 'follow' the victim to the member state they have moved to. A European Protection Order is defined as a decision, taken by a judicial or equivalent authority of a member state in relation to a protection measure, on the basis of which a judicial or equivalent authority of another member state takes any appropriate measure or measures under its own national law with a view to continuing the protection of the protected person. [15] It may only be issued when a protection measure has been previously adopted in the issuing state, imposing on the person causing danger one or more of the following prohibitions or restrictions: a prohibition from entering certain localities, places or defined areas where the protected person resides or visits; a prohibition or regulation of contact, in any form, with the protected person, including by phone, electronic or ordinary mail, fax or any other means; or a prohibition or regulation on approaching the protected person closer than a prescribed distance.[16]

The objective of the European Protection Order Directive is to set out rules allowing a judicial or equivalent authority in a member state, in which a protection measure has been adopted with a view to protecting a person against a criminal act by another person which may endanger his life, physical or psychological integrity, dignity, personal liberty or sexual integrity, to issue a European protection order enabling a competent authority in another member state to continue the protection of the person in the territory of that other member state, following criminal conduct, or alleged criminal conduct, in accordance with the national law of the issuing state.[17] Upon receipt of a European Protection Order the competent authority of the executing state must, without undue delay, recognise that order and take a decision adopting any measure that would be available under its national law in a similar case in order to ensure the protection of the protected person.[18] The executing authority is granted limited grounds for non-recognition.[19] The Directive also puts forward the principle of assimilation,

[13] Directive 2011/99/EU of the European Parliament and of the Council of 13 December 2011 on the European Protection Order [2011] OJ L338/2.

[14] Art 82(1)(a) and (d) TFEU.

[15] Art 2(1).

[16] Art 5.

[17] Art 1.

[18] Art 9(1).

[19] Art 10.

by stating that a European Protection Order must be recognised with the same priority which would be applicable *in a similar national case*, taking into consideration any specific circumstances of the case, including the urgency of the matter, the date foreseen for the arrival of the protected person on the territory of the executing state and, where possible, the degree of risk for the protected person.[20] The free movement rationale of the Directive is evident in the Preamble, where it is stated that in a common area of justice without internal borders, it is necessary to ensure that the protection provided to a natural person in one member state is maintained and continued in any other member state to which the person moves or has moved and that it should also be ensured that the legitimate exercise by citizens of the Union of their right to move and reside freely within the territory of member states, in accordance with Article 3(2) of the TEU and Article 21 TFEU does not result in a loss of their protection.[21]

C. Harmonisation

The process of harmonisation of national systems with regard to the rights of the victims in criminal procedure began in the era of the third pillar, with the adoption, under Articles 31 and 34(2)(b) TEU, of the Framework Decision on the standing of victims in criminal proceedings.[22] The Framework Decision introduced a number of provisions on the place of the victim in the criminal process.[23] It opens with a rather general provision on 'respect and recognition', calling upon member states to ensure that victims have a real and appropriate role in their criminal justice systems and to continue to make every effort to ensure that victims are treated with due respect for the dignity of the individual during proceedings and to recognise the rights and legitimate interests of the victims with particular reference to criminal proceedings.[24] Specific provisions in the Framework Decision call upon member states to safeguard the possibility for victims to be heard during proceedings and to supply evidence,[25] and establish a right to receive information,[26] a series of communication safeguards[27] and details on specific assistance to the victim.[28] Member states must further afford victims who have the status of parties or witnesses the possibility of reimbursement of

[20] Art 15.
[21] Preamble, recital 6.
[22] Council Framework Decision 2001/220/JHA on the standing of victims in criminal proceedings [2001] OJ L82/1.
[23] For an overview of the Framework Decision, see S de Biolley and A Weyembergh, 'L'Espace Pénal Européen et les Droits des Victimes' [2005] 31 *Revue de la Faculté de Droit, Université Libre de Bruxelles* 93–122.
[24] Art 2(1).
[25] Art 3, first indent.
[26] Art 4.
[27] Art 5.
[28] Art 6.

expenses incurred as a result of their legitimate participation in criminal proceedings[29] with victims also being entitled to obtain a decision within reasonable time on compensation by the offender in criminal proceedings.[30] Member states will seek to promote mediation in criminal cases.[31] Most importantly, in the context of criminal procedure, the Framework Decision provides with a 'right to protection' which includes a duty for member states to ensure that, where there is a need to protect victims, particularly those most vulnerable, from the effects of giving evidence in open court, victims may, by a decision taken by a court, be entitled to testify in a manner which will enable this objective to be achieved, by any appropriate means compatible with their basic legal principles.[32] The Framework Decision thus aims in general to enhance the position of the victim in criminal procedure across the European Union—as is noted in its Preamble, member states should approximate their laws and regulations to the extent necessary to attain the objective of affording victims of crime a high level of protection, irrespective of the member state in which they are present.[33] However, its provisions are drafted in rather general terms and do not provide a high standard of legal certainty. This may be explained by the considerable diversity as regards the position of the victim in the national criminal justice systems of member states, the decision-making limits placed by unanimity in third pillar law, and member states' concerns with regard to the impact that the Framework Decision could have on their criminal justice systems—with the Preamble attempting to ensure minimum interference by stating that its provisions do not impose an obligation on member states to ensure that victims will be treated in a manner equivalent to that of a party to proceedings.[34] Although as seen below the Framework Decision on the rights of victims in criminal procedure has now been replaced by a post-Lisbon Directive, it remains significant in that its provisions have formed the basis for the development of the case law of the Court of Justice in the field.[35] The Framework Decision also forms an important benchmark in relation to which post-Lisbon developments can be assessed.

The entry into force of the Lisbon Treaty led to the adoption of a new Directive on the rights of the victims of crime.[36] A deliverable under the so-called Budapest Roadmap on the rights of victims in criminal proceedings,[37] the Directive was adopted under Article 82(2) TFEU which confers upon the European Union

[29] Art 7.
[30] Art 9.
[31] Art 10(1).
[32] Art 8(4).
[33] Preamble, recital 4.
[34] Preamble, recital 9.
[35] See section IV below.
[36] Directive 2012/29/EU of the European Parliament and of the Council establishing minimum standards on the rights, support and protection of victims of crime, and replacing Council Framework Decision 2001/220/JHA [2012] OJ L315/57.
[37] Council Resolution on a roadmap for strengthening the rights and protection of victims, in particular in criminal proceedings [2011] OJ C187/1.

competence to establish minimum rules on the rights of the victims of crime to the extent necessary to facilitate mutual recognition of judgments and judicial decisions and police and judicial cooperation in criminal matters having a cross-border dimension. According to Article 82(2), such minimum rules must take into account the differences between the legal traditions and systems of the member states. The Directive thus constitutes an attempt to establish minimum rules on the rights of victims in the face of the considerable diversity in national criminal justice systems as regards the position and rights of the victim. The Preamble to the Directive reflects this diversity by recognising that the role of victims in the criminal justice system and whether they can participate actively in criminal proceedings vary across member states, depending on their national system, and is determined by one or more of the following criteria: whether the national system provides for a legal status as a party to criminal proceedings; whether the victim is under a legal requirement or is requested to participate actively in criminal proceedings, for example as a witness; and/or whether the victim has a legal entitlement under national law to participate actively in criminal proceedings and is seeking to do so, where the national system does not provide that victims have the legal status of a party to the criminal proceedings.[38] As will be seen below,[39] national legal diversity is further reflected in the text of the Directive by the inclusion of a number of references to national procedural rules as regards the enforcement of the rights set out in the Directive. According to the Preamble, member states should determine which of the criteria mentioned above apply to determine the scope of rights set out in this Directive where there are references to the role of the victim in the relevant criminal justice system.[40] A notable exception to the definition of rights by reference to national systems constitutes the adoption of a 'European' definition of the victim which is, according to the Directive, a natural person who has suffered harm, including physical, mental or emotional harm or economic loss which was directly caused by a criminal offence; and family members of a person whose death was directly caused by a criminal offence and who have suffered harm as a result of that person's death.[41] The Directive also contains a definition of family members[42] but further allows for the limitation and prioritisation of family members by member states.[43]

As regards the content of the rights, the Directive introduces a multi-level system of protection of the victim. According to Article 1(1), its purpose is to ensure that victims of crime receive appropriate information, support and protection and are able to participate in criminal proceedings. The rights of the victims are structured into three broad categories. The first category involves the provision

[38] Preamble, recital 20.
[39] See section IV below.
[40] Preamble, recital 20.
[41] Art 2(1)(a).
[42] Art 2(1)(b).
[43] Art 2(2).

of information and support to the victim.[44] This includes the right of the victim to understand and be understood;[45] the right to receive information from the first contact with a competent authority;[46] the right of the victim when making a complaint;[47] the right of the victim to receive information about their case;[48] the right to interpretation and translation;[49] the right to access victim support services;[50] and the establishment of minimum rules on support from victim support services.[51] Another category of provisions involves the protection of victims and recognition of victims with specific protection needs.[52] These include the right to protection, under which member states must ensure that measures are available to protect victims and their family members from secondary and repeat victimisation[53] and the right to avoid contact between victim and offender,[54] both of which could be seen as overlapping with the provisions of the Directive on to European Protection Order; the right to protection of victims during criminal investigations;[55] the right to protection of privacy;[56] provisions on the individual assessment of victims to identify specific protection needs;[57] and provisions on the right to protection of victims with specific protection needs during criminal proceedings[58] and the right to protection of child victims during criminal proceedings.[59] A number of the Directive's provisions on the right to protection of the victim may have a significant impact on the rights of the defendant in criminal proceedings, and the drafters of the Directive have been careful to state that a number of these rights are without prejudice to the rights of defence and in accordance with rules of judicial discretion.[60]

The most significant impact on the position of the defendant in criminal proceedings in relation to the victims may arise from the third category of rights set out in the Directive, namely rights related to participation in criminal proceedings. The Directive grants the victim the right to be heard during criminal proceedings, [61] rights in the event of the decision not to prosecute,[62] the right to

[44] Ch 2 of the Directive.
[45] Art 3.
[46] Art 4.
[47] Art 5.
[48] Art 6.
[49] Art 7.
[50] Art 8.
[51] Art 9.
[52] Ch 4 of the Directive.
[53] Art 18.
[54] Art 19.
[55] Art 20.
[56] Art 21.
[57] Art 22.
[58] Art 23.
[59] Art 24.
[60] Arts 20 and 23. See also Art 18 on the right to protection which is without prejudice to the rights of defence.
[61] Art 10.
[62] Art 11.

safeguards in the context of restorative justice services,[63] a right to legal aid,[64] and rights to reimbursement of expenses,[65] to the return of property[66] and to a decision on compensation from the offender in the course of criminal proceedings.[67] The Directive also contains a provision on the rights of victims resident in another member state.[68] However, these rights are largely dependent on national law, with the Directive attempting again to achieve a compromise between the introduction of EU minimum standards and the respect of national diversity in the field. Hence the Directive provides repeatedly that the procedural rules governing the exercise of a number of key rights including the right to be heard, the right to legal aid, the right of reimbursement of expenses, the right of return of property and the rights of the victims in the event of a decision not to prosecute will be determined by national law.[69] Moreover, the Directive grants considerable discretion to member states as regards the content of certain rights: as regards the right to be heard, member states must ensure that victims *may* be heard during criminal proceedings and may provide evidence;[70] member states must ensure the right of the victim to review a decision not to prosecute *in accordance with the victim's role in the relevant criminal justice system.*[71] In addition to these limitations and references to national legal systems, a number of rights are not set out in detail in the text of the Directive, but greater detail on their scope is provided in the Preamble. The Preamble of the Directive contains no less than 72 recitals and a number of them are detailed and serve to explain and, as demonstrated in the case of the right to reimbursement of expenses, limit the rights set out in the text of the Directive.[72] The use of extensive Preambular provisions has been explained as a means of addressing member states' concerns with regard to the perceived lack of legal certainty in the Commission's original proposal, with the recitals acting as an aid to interpreting the operative Articles of the Directive when they are perceived as ambiguous, but also as a means of enabling the Council and the European Parliament to reach agreement on the Directive with recitals being

63 Art 12.
64 Art 13.
65 Art 14.
66 Art 15.
67 Art 16.
68 Art 17.
69 Arts 10(2), 13, 14, 15 and 11(1) and (2) respectively.
70 Art 10(1).
71 Art 11(1).
72 According to recital 47, victims should not be expected to incur expenses in relation to their participation in criminal proceedings. Member states should be required to reimburse only necessary expenses of victims in relation to their participation in criminal proceedings and should not be required to reimburse victims' legal fees: The right to reimbursement of expenses in criminal proceedings should not arise in a situation where a victim makes a statement on a criminal offence. Expenses should only be covered to the extent that the victim is obliged or requested by the competent authorities to be present and actively participate in the criminal proceedings.

used to mention issues where the legislators could not agree real obligations in the operative text.[73]

III. THE PLACE OF THE VICTIM IN EUROPE'S AREA OF CRIMINAL JUSTICE: CONSTITUTIONAL IMPLICATIONS

The adoption of measures on victim' rights at EU level does not always sit easily with the limits of EU competence to legislate in criminal matters. Questions of the legality of both pre-Lisbon and post-Lisbon victims' rights instruments arise, in particular as regards the appropriateness of the legal basis used for their adoption. On the one hand, the extent to which measures on the rights of the victim in criminal procedure can be adopted on the basis of EU competence to legislate in criminal matters is not always clear. On the other hand, national legal diversity concerning means of protecting the victim (and the use of civil and not criminal law in this context) raises the question of whether a criminal law legal basis is appropriate and/or sufficient for the Union to legislate in this context. The latter question has arisen prominently with regard to the adoption of the Directive on the European Protection Order. The Preamble to the Directive clarifies that the latter applies to protection measures adopted in criminal matters and does not therefore cover protection measures adopted in civil matters. It adds however that

> For a protection order to be executable in accordance with this Directive, it is not necessary for a criminal offence to have been established by a final decision. Nor is the criminal, administrative or civil nature of the authority adopting a protection measure relevant. This Directive does not oblige Member States to amend their national law to enable them to adopt protection measures in the context of criminal proceedings.[74]

This flexibility as regards the nature of the authority issuing a European Protection Order and the nature of the protection measure undertaken in the executing state is maintained in the operative part of the Directive. While a protection measure is defined as a decision 'in criminal matters' adopted in the issuing member state,[75] a European Protection Order is defined as a decision, taken by a judicial *or equivalent* authority of a member state in relation to a protection measure, on the basis of which a judicial *or equivalent* authority of another member state takes any appropriate measure or measures under its own national law with a view to continuing the protection of the protected person.[76] However, the Directive does not require these authorities to be part of member states' criminal justice systems, with the Directive not excluding the possibility that such authorities are administrative or civil bodies. According to the Preamble, the Directive takes into

[73] See H Nowell-Smith, 'Behind the Scenes in the Negotiation of EU Criminal Justice Legislation' [2012] 3 *New Journal of European Criminal Law* 381–93, 384.

[74] Preamble, recital 10.

[75] Art 2(2) of the Directive.

[76] Art 2(1).

account the fact that effective protection can be provided by means of protection orders issued by an authority other than a criminal court.[77] Flexibility is retained also with regard to the nature of the European Protection Order. In executing the European Protection Order, the executing state may apply, in accordance with its national law, *criminal, administrative, or civil measures*.[78] The Directive thus allows the transformation of what is a decision in criminal matters in the issuing state to its execution as an administrative or a civil law measure in the executing state. While such flexibility may reflect the considerable diversity in national legal systems in the field,[79] as well as the need to reassure member states that the adoption of the Directive will not alter their domestic criminal justice systems,[80] it is questionable whether Article 82(1) TFEU on judicial cooperation in criminal matters is sufficient as a sole legal basis for this instrument. A joint legal basis of Article 82 and Article 81 TFEU (on judicial cooperation in civil matters) would reflect more accurately the content and the cooperation mechanism set out in the Directive.[81] The adoption of the European Protection Order Directive under multiple legal bases could further serve to focus the mind of the EU legislators on the potential overlap of a number of the Directive provisions with other EU law instruments which may affect the position of the victim in similar circumstances, including mutual recognition instruments in both the civil and criminal law sphere.[82]

Legality questions have also arisen with regard to the adoption of EU legislation aiming to harmonise national laws on the rights of the victims of crime. The third pillar Framework Decision on the standing of victims in criminal proceedings was adopted under the general legal basis of Article 31 TEU on common action on judicial cooperation in criminal matters without specifying further which sub-section of this provision applies. Article 31 TEU was thus used in a flexible manner in order to translate the political will of member states to be seen to be taking action in favour of victims of crime into legal reality. Yet the link between the Framework Decision and the facilitation of judicial cooperation in criminal matters, which is the main objective of Article 31 TEU, has not been demonstrated and remains questionable. Indeed, approximation under the Framework Decision has been justified as necessary to attain the objective of affording victims of crime a high level of protection, irrespective of the member state in which

[77] Preamble, recital 8.

[78] Art 9(1).

[79] See also Preamble, recital 20.

[80] According to the Preamble to the Directive, the latter does not create obligations to modify national systems for adopting protection measures nor does it create obligations to introduce or amend a criminal law system for executing a European protection order.

[81] See S van der Aa and J Ouwerkerk, 'The European Protection Order: No Time to Waste or a Waste of Time?' (2011) 19 in *European Journal of Crime, Criminal Law and Criminal Justice* 267–87, 280.

[82] The Preamble to the Directive contains detailed references on the relationship between the various EU law measures which may be of relevance—see recitals 16 and 33 and 34 for criminal law and civil law measures respectively.

they are present.[83] This approach reflects the need to achieve primarily a free movement objective, rather than an objective geared towards the facilitation of judicial cooperation in criminal matters. Notwithstanding the introduction of an express legal basis by the Lisbon Treaty conferring upon the European Union competence to adopt legislation on the rights of victims under Article 82(2) TFEU, the new Directive on the rights of the victims of crime is not devoid of similar legality shortcomings. Article 82(2) TFEU confers upon the European Union competence to establish minimum rules on the rights of the victims of crime to the extent necessary to facilitate mutual recognition of judgments and judicial decisions and police and judicial cooperation in criminal matters having a cross-border dimension. However, it is questionable whether the Directive on the rights of the victims of crime meets the legality criteria set out by Article 82(2) TFEU. It has not been demonstrated in particular how the Directive will serve to facilitate mutual recognition or judicial cooperation in criminal matters having a cross-border dimension. In the Explanatory Memorandum to its original draft Directive, the Commission attempted to substantiate a link between the rights of victims of crime and the facilitation of mutual recognition as follows:

> Mutual recognition can only operate in a spirit of confidence, whereby not only judicial authorities but all those involved in the criminal justice process and others who have a legitimate interest in it can trust in the adequacy of the rules of each Member State and trust that those rules are correctly applied. Where victims of crime are not subject to the same minimum standards throughout the EU, such trust can be reduced due to concerns over the treatment of victims or due to differences in procedural rules.
>
> Common minimum rules should thus lead to increased confidence in the criminal justice system of all Member States, which in turn should lead to more efficient judicial cooperation in a climate of mutual trust as well as to the promotion of a fundamental rights culture in the European Union. They should also contribute to reducing obstacles to the free movement of citizens since such common minimum rules should apply to all victims of crime.[84]

However, as I have noted elsewhere in the context of the justification by the Commission of the adoption of EU minimum rules on the rights of the defendant in criminal proceedings,[85] the use of mutual trust as an element justifying the adoption of EU measures in the field of criminal procedure is problematic in two respects: it fails to provide a direct and clear link between the rights proposed and their necessity for the operation of mutual recognition; and it is based on a concept (of mutual trust) which is too subjective for it to meet the criteria set out

[83] Preamble, recital 4.

[84] COM (2011) 275 final, Brussels, 2–3.

[85] V Mitsilegas, 'Trust-building Measures in the European Judicial Area in Criminal Matters: Issues of Competence, Legitimacy and Inter-institutional Balance' in S Carrera and T Balzacq (eds), *Security versus Freedom? A Challenge for Europe's Future* (Aldershot, Ashgate, 2006) 279–89. The argument has been developed further in V Mitsilegas, 'The Limits of Mutual Trust in Europe's Area of Freedom, Security and Justice. From Automatic Inter-state Cooperation to the Slow Emergence of the Individual' (201)] 31 *Yearbook of European Law* 319–72.

by the Court of Justice when ascertaining the legality of EU instruments, namely that the choice of legal basis must be based on objective factors which are amenable to judicial review.[86] Compared with EU legislation in the field of the rights of the defendant, where minimum EU rules can be justified on specific human rights grounds and where EU standards can be linked directly with the operation of specific mutual recognition instruments such as the Framework Decision on the European Arrest Warrant,[87] the link between EU minimum rules on the victims of crime and the facilitation of mutual recognition and judicial cooperation in criminal matters is much less direct. It is perhaps no coincidence that the Commission's statement attempting to link the adoption of EU-wide minimum standards on victims of crime with the facilitation of mutual recognition has not been replicated in the finally adopted text of the Directive. However, in this way the EU legislators have not provided with any detailed or specific explanation of the link between the Directive and the criteria set out by its legal basis, namely Article 82(2) TFEU. The political will to legislate on victims' rights post-Lisbon has resulted into a rather flexible use of the Treaty provisions enabling EU action on the harmonisation of national laws of criminal procedure.

IV. THE IMPACT OF EU LAW ON VICTIMS' RIGHTS ON NATIONAL CRIMINAL JUSTICE SYSTEMS

As seen above, one of the key challenges in developing EU criminal law on victims has been how to adopt EU-wide standards in the face of considerable diversity in terms of the legal position of the victim in domestic criminal justice systems. Throughout the development of EU criminal law on victims, the European Union institutions have been called upon to address the tension between the perceived need to create an EU-level playing field as regards the rights of victims and the need to maintain a degree of flexibility and breathing space of national systems in the light of the considerable differences in national criminal laws on victims. The challenge of adopting EU-wide standards on the rights of victims while taking into account national legal diversity has emerged in different ways, but forcefully, at all levels of EU legislative action in the field: from establishing victims' rights via the use of the principle of mutual recognition in criminal matters to legislative efforts to harmonise member states' national law on victims' rights. The evolution of EU harmonisation measures from the largely intergovernmental third pillar to the post-Lisbon more supranational reality has not put an end to these challenges.

[86] See inter alia Case C-300/89 *Commission v Council* [1991] ECR I-2867 (Titanium Dioxide).
[87] Mitsilegas, *The Limits of Mutual Trust.*

A. Mutual Recognition

One of the ways in which EU law has addressed the need to respect national legal diversity has been via the use of mutual recognition as a method of advancing victims' rights, with the prima facie advantage of mutual recognition in this context being that, unlike harmonisation instruments, member states may not be required to introduce immediate and specific changes to their domestic criminal law and procedure as a result of implementing EU law in the field.[88] In the field of victims' rights, the Directive on the European Protection Order aims to achieve the protection of the victim by putting forward a system of interaction of national legal orders resulting in the recognition and execution of a national protection decision by the authorities of another member state. Yet, even in this context of mutual recognition, the European Protection Order contains a number of further provisions aimed at managing the high degree of flexibility in national legal orders. The Preamble sets out a general flexibility clause stating that the Directive takes account of the different legal traditions of the member states as well as the fact that effective protection can be provided by means of protection orders issued by an authority other than a criminal court. It adds at the same time however that the Directive does not create obligations to modify national systems for adopting protection measures nor does it create obligations to introduce or amend a criminal law system for executing a European protection order.[89] The tension between ensuring the effectiveness of the Directive in ensuring maximum flexibility while respecting national legal diversity and not challenging national sovereignty in criminal matters is evident in the wording of this provision.

In addition to this general flexibility provision, the Directive contains a number of provisions aiming to ensure flexibility in how the mutual recognition system established therein will work. In the first place, the Directive aims at ensuring flexibility with regard to the *authorities* which will be competent to operate the mutual recognition system regarding European Protection Orders. This need for flexibility is confirmed in the Preamble, according to which

> since, in the Member States, different kinds of authorities (civil, criminal or administrative) are competent to adopt and enforce protection measures, it is appropriate to provide a high degree of flexibility in the cooperation mechanism between the Member States under this Directive.[90]

The text of the Directive attempts to capture national legal diversity by allowing the issuing of a European Protection Order by *judicial or equivalent* authorities in accordance with the national law of the issuing state.[91] The designation of the judicial or equivalent authorities responsible for issuing and recognising

[88] See Mitsilegas, *The Constitutional Implications of Mutual Recognition.*
[89] Recital 8.
[90] Preamble, recital 20.
[91] Art 1.

European Protection Orders is left to member states.[92] There are two questions in relation to the determination of the authorities competent to act within the framework of the Directive. The first question is whether the use of non-criminal judicial authorities is compatible with the legal basis of the Directive, which focuses on judicial cooperation *in criminal matters*.[93] The second question is whether the use of 'equivalent' authorities is allowed by a legal basis which focuses on *judicial* cooperation. Not only do the answers to these questions have considerable legality implications, but they also have a considerable impact on the protection of fundamental rights. In the context of the implementation of another mutual recognition measure, the Framework Decision on the European Arrest Warrant, serious doubts have been raised by national courts on the extent to which non-judicial authorities are sufficiently independent to provide appropriate human rights safeguards.[94] While the European Protection Order Directive follows the example of other mutual recognition instruments and aims to ensure flexibility by leaving the designation of competent authorities to member states, national courts have expressed doubts as to whether such designation plays a definitive role regarding the assessment of whether an authority is sufficiently independent to be considered a judicial authority for the purposes of these instruments.[95] The discretion given to member states by the European Protection Order to designate authorities combined with the potentially extensive scope and diverse nature of these authorities is likely to prove counter-productive to speedy mutual recognition, as executing authorities are likely to undertake to assess themselves the independence of the issuing authority, especially in cases where the legal systems of the issuing and the executing member states are markedly different. More concrete answers are likely to be provided by the Court of Justice, with the definition of judicial or equivalent authority for the purposes of the European Protection Order constituting an autonomous concept of EU law. The Court of Justice has already found that the meaning of 'court having jurisdiction in particular in criminal matters' for the purposes of the Framework Decision on the mutual recognition of financial penalties cannot be left to the discretion of each member state but constitutes an autonomous concept in EU law.[96]

The need to accommodate national diversity with regard to the protection of victims is also reflected in efforts to achieve flexibility with regard to *the measures of protection* which will follow the recognition of a European Protection Order. Thus, the competent authority in the executing state is not required in all cases to take the same protection measure as those which were adopted in the issuing state, and has a degree of discretion to adopt any measure which it deems adequate and appropriate under its national law in a similar case in order to provide continued

[92] Art 3.
[93] *Bucnys v Ministry of Justice, Lithuania* [2013] UKSC 71. See Lord Mance, para 23.
[94] See *Assange v The Swedish Prosecution Authority* [2012] UKSC 22.
[95] In the context of the European Arrest Warrant, see the ruling of Lord Mance in *Bucnys* above, para 22.
[96] Case C-60/12 *Baláz* (CJEU, 14 November 2013) paras 25–26.

protection to the protected person in the light of the protection measure adopted in the issuing state as described in the European Protection Order.[97] The executing state may apply, in accordance with its national law, criminal, administrative, or civil measures.[98] These and subsequent measures must, to the highest degree possible, correspond to the protection measure adopted in the issuing member state.[99] However, as mentioned above member states are not obliged to change their law to introduce new protection measures.[100] As is recognised in the Preamble, in view of the different legal traditions of the member states, where no protection measure would be available in the executing state in a case similar to the factual situation described in the European Protection Order, the competent authority of the executing state should report any breach of the protection measure described in the Order of which it is aware to the competent authority of the issuing state.[101] The Directive also includes a number of provisions clarifying applicable law and the respective areas of responsibility between the issuing and the executing state in the aftermath of the recognition of the European Protection Order. The law of the executing state will govern the adoption and enforcement of the Order and the consequences of its breach[102] while the issuing state will remain competent for the renewal, review, modification, revocation and withdrawal of the protection measure as well as for the imposition of custodial measure as a consequence of revocation.[103] The executing authority further has the power to discontinue a European Protection Order in a number of cases,[104] including where, according to its national law, the maximum term of duration of the measures adopted in execution of the Order has expired.[105] The Directive thus attempts to establish a system of mutual recognition which will ensure continuous protection while respecting to the extent possible the legal system of the executing member state.

B. Harmonisation

The challenge of ensuring EU-wide protection of victims while at the same time respecting national legal diversity has arisen with greater prominence in EU harmonisation efforts in the field. Both the Framework Decision and its successor Directive on the rights of victims have attempted to strike a balance between Europeanisation and the respect of national diversity by including on the one hand a number of broadly drafted provisions on victims' rights while on the other hand leaving considerable discretion to member states as regards

97 Preamble, recital 20.
98 Art 9(1).
99 Art 9(2).
100 See Preamble, recital 8.
101 Preamble, recital 27.
102 Art 11.
103 Art 13.
104 Art 14.
105 Art 14(1)(b).

implementation. In the case of the Framework Decision, the specificities in the legal effects of third pillar measures would mean that its reach in national legal orders could remain limited. The tension between Europeanisation and the respect of national legal diversity, and its impact on enforcement and legal certainty as regards the Framework Decision on the rights of victims have now been tested before the Court of Justice. The first—and now landmark—ruling of the Court in this context has been its judgment in the case of *Pupino.*[106] In *Pupino,* the Court was asked to interpret the broad provisions of the Framework Decision, and in particular Article 8 on the right to protection in court proceedings, in the light of their applicability to a specific domestic situation. The case arose after a reference by an Italian court asking to what extent the Italian Code of Criminal Procedure could be interpreted, in the light of the Framework Decision, as allowing children allegedly having suffered a number of forms of abuse by their teacher to testify under a special procedure, and not in normal court proceedings, against the defendant. The Italian Code of Criminal Procedure allowed for this possibility for children under 16 only in cases of sexual offences or offences with a sexual background. In a landmark ruling, the Court established that third pillar Framework Decisions, while lacking direct effect, had indirect effect: in other words the national judge was under the duty to interpret domestic law in conformity with Framework Decisions. Having established the principle of indirect effect and its limits, the Court went on to examine the specific case.[107] It confirmed that the achievement of the aims of the Framework Decision on the rights of victims in criminal proceedings require that a national court should be able, in respect of particularly vulnerable victims, to use a special procedure, such as the one provided for already in Italian law.[108] However, in the light of the concerns raised regarding the potential impact of such an interpretation on the rights of the defendant, the Court added two caveats: that, in the light of the Framework Decision, the adopted conditions for giving evidence must be compatible with the basic legal principles of the member state;[109] and that the national court must ensure that the application of those measures is not likely to make the criminal proceedings against the defendant considered as a whole, unfair within the meaning of Article 6 of the ECHR, as interpreted by the European Court of Human Rights.[110]

The Court's priority in *Pupino* appears to have been the clarification of the constitutional position of third pillar measures in EU law by affirming the binding legal effect of Framework Decisions and ensuring their enforcement in national legal orders via the application of the principle of indirect effect.[111] However, the

[106] Case C-105/03 *Maria Pupino* [2005] ECR I-5285.

[107] Paras 50–61.

[108] Para 56.

[109] Para 57. The Court referred in particular to Art 8(4) of the Framework Decision.

[110] Para 60.

[111] V Mitsilegas, 'Constitutional Principles of the European Community and European Criminal Law' (2006) 8 *European Journal of Law Reform* 301–24.

impact of the application of the interpretative obligation to the national judge is significant. In *Pupino,* the Luxembourg Court has in reality rewritten the Italian Code of Criminal Procedure. Following the Court's guidance the Italian judge had little choice but to allow minors in this case to take advantage of the Code's protective provisions, although minors were not originally covered by the legislation. This interpetation raises important questions regarding the impact of the application of the principle of indirect effect on the internal coherence of national criminal justice systems, whose balance may be disturbed by piecemeal attempts of national judges to accommodate Union law demands in specific cases. Judges themselves may be faced with difficult balancing exercises, especially in cases where Union law itself—like in the case of the Framework Decision in question—is drafted in broad terms, having to take into account all complex parameters and interests involved in a criminal trial.

While *Pupino* should be seen within this specific constitutional context, where the Court of Justice has attempted to ensure the enforceability of third pillar law at a time when Treaty reform no longer appeared imminent, the Court has since developed a substantial body of case law resulting from a number of references for preliminary rulings by national courts seeking clarification of various aspects of the Framework Decision and its application in national law.[112] In all these cases, the Court was faced with the challenge of interpreting the provisions of the Framework Decision—a number of which were drafted in a broad, if not aspirational manner—in a way which would achieve the key objectives of the Framework Decision while respecting national legal diversity. The Court has attempted to accommodate national diversity and to address concerns with regard to the potentially negative impact of EU victims' law on state sovereignty and established criminal policy choices made at national level in a number of ways. First of all, the Court emphasised that the Framework Decision does not have an impact on domestic legislative choices with regard to criminalisation and the choice, form and level of penalties imposed under national criminal law.[113] The Court found that this is the case even when upholding national law would result in an outcome which is contrary to the wishes of the victim, as

> it must be borne in mind that where a Member State in the exercise of its powers to enforce the law ensures that the criminal law offers protection against acts of domestic

[112] For an overview of early case law from the perspective of the dialogue between national courts and the Court of Justice in this context, see R Parizot, 'Les Interactions en Procédure Pénale: La Victime, Vecteur Symbolique de la Circulation du Jurisprudence' in G Giudicelli-Delage and S Manacorda (eds), *Cour de Justice et Justice Pénale en Europe* (Paris, Société de Législation Comparée, 2010) 177–202.

[113] Joined Cases C-483/09 and C-1/10 *Gueye* and *Sanchez* [2011] ECR I-8263. According to the Court, the Framework Decision contains no indication that the EU legislature, within the limits of the powers conferred on it by the EU Treaty, intended to harmonise or at least approximate the legislation of member states in respect of the forms and levels of criminal penalties (para 51). Moreover, Art 8 of the Framework Decision cannot be interpreted in such a way that it restricts the choice by member states of the criminal penalties they establish in their domestic legal systems (para 68).

violence, the objective is not only to protect the interests of the victim as he or she perceives them but also other more general interests of society.[114]

The Court has further declined to extend the scope of the Framework Decision and influence thus domestic legislative choices by defining the concept of a victim broadly to include within its scope legal persons.[115] This does not mean that the Framework Decision precludes member states from enacting legislation treating legal persons as victims: since the Framework Decision does not undertake a complete harmonisation of the field in question, a decision that its provisions are also to be applicable where the victim is a legal person is one that member states are neither prevented by the Framework Decision from taking nor obliged to take.[116] On the other hand, the Court has ruled that the Framework Decision contains no indication that the European Union legislature intended to oblige member states to provide that legal persons are to be liable in criminal law.[117] Last, but not least, the Court of Justice has emphasised on a number of occasions that the Framework Decision grants a considerable degree of discretion to member states as regards its implementation.[118] The tension between member states' discretion and the need to ensure the effectiveness of the Framework Decision has been clearly reflected in the case of *Katz*, where the Court of Justice was asked whether a victim who can act as private prosecutor under national law can also be a witness in criminal proceedings instituted in this context. In a fine balancing act, the Court attempted to find a middle ground by ruling as follows:

> It must therefore be concluded that the Framework Decision, while requiring member states, first, to ensure that victims enjoy a high level of protection and have a real and appropriate role in their criminal justice system and, second, to recognise victims' rights and legitimate interests and ensure that they can be heard and supply evidence, leaves to the national authorities a large measure of discretion with regard to the specific means by which they implement those objectives.
>
> However, in order not to deprive the first paragraph of Article 3 of the Framework Decision of much of its practical effect or to infringe the obligations stated in Article 2(1) of the Framework Decision, those provisions imply, in any event, that the victim is to be able to give testimony in the course of the criminal proceedings which can be taken into account as evidence.[119]

[114] See *Gueye*, para 61. According to the Court, the procedural right to be heard under the first paragraph of Art 3 of the Framework Decision does not confer on victims any rights in respect of the choice of form of penalties to be imposed on the offenders in accordance with the rules of the national criminal law nor in respect of the level of those penalties (para 60).

[115] Case C-467/05 *Dell'Orto* [2007] ECR I-5557. According to the Court, there is no indication in any other provision of the Framework Decision that the European Union legislature intended to extend the concept of the victim for the purposes of the application of the Framework Decision to legal persons. The converse is in fact the case, as several provisions in the Framework Decision confirm that the legislature's objective was to limit its scope exclusively to natural persons who are victims of harm resulting from a criminal act (para 55).

[116] Case C-205/09 *Eredics* [2010] ECR I-10231, para 29.

[117] Case C-79/11 *Giovanardi* (CJEU, 12 July 2012), para 45.

[118] See *Gueye* para 58; *Eredics* para 38.

[119] Case C-404/07 *Katz* [2008] ECR I-07607, paras 46–47.

In *Katz*, the Court was faced with the considerable challenge of interpreting the broadly drafted provisions of the Framework Decision in a manner which would ensure the latter's effectiveness while at the same time adjusting and recognising a very specific policy choice by a national criminal justice system. This challenge is compounded by the fact that any answer that the Court would give would have an impact on the balance of power between the parties in the domestic criminal proceedings and ultimately on the delivery of criminal justice.[120] The Framework Decision has now been replaced by a post-Lisbon Directive, which is a significant development both from a substantive and from a constitutional perspective. In terms of substance, the Directive contains a more extensive list of provisions on victims' rights. From a constitutional perspective, the Directive is in principle a more supranational instrument than the Framework Decision and is subject to the full scrutiny of EU institutions. However, a number of questions concerning legal certainty and the development of EU standards on the rights of victims while respecting national diversity remain. First of all, as per the Directive's legal basis of Article 82(2) TFEU, EU law can currently only provide with minimum standards on victims' rights. Secondly, as seen above the Directive maintains throughout its text—and very prominently as regards the rights of the victims related to criminal procedure and the trial itself—a high degree of discretion for national authorities.[121] It can be said that in this context the *existence* of these rights is provided by EU law, while their *exercise* is largely regulated by national law. This legislative choice means that it is highly unlikely that autonomous EU concepts will be developed in relation to the exercise of victims' rights in criminal procedure and that the Court of Justice will face similar interpretative challenges to those it has faced when called to interpret the Framework Decision on victims. Thirdly, while the Directive is 'Lisbonised', key provisions with regard to victims' rights in criminal procedure—and in particular the right to be heard[122]—do not fulfil the requirements which would grant them direct effect. A key enforcement avenue with regard to these rights at national level is thus lost. Having said that, national judges are still under a duty of consistent interpretation, and domestic criminal law must be interpreted to the extent possible in conformity with the key objectives of the Directive. Reconciling the Directive's objectives with national legal diversity will thus remain a challenge for national and European courts.

[120] By quoting *Pupino*, the Court in *Katz* payed lip-service to the need to protect fundamental rights, and in particular the right to fair trial, and delegated this task to the national court—paras 48–49.

[121] For a criticism of the extensive discretion left to member states, see R Letschert and C Rijken, 'Rights of Victims of Crime: Tensions Between an Integrated Approach and a Limited Legal Basis for Harmonisation' (2013) 4 *New Journal of European Criminal Law* 226–55. They argue that the procedural autonomy that member states have with regard to several provisions needs to be monitored (pp 247 and 255).

[122] See Art 10(1) of the Directive, according to which 'Member States shall ensure that victims *may* be heard during criminal proceedings and may provide evidence' (emphasis added).

V. THE IMPACT OF VICTIMS' RIGHTS ON JUSTICE IN EUROPE

Questions on the impact of EU criminal law on victims' rights on national legal diversity and the internal coherence of the criminal justice systems of member states cannot be considered independently from the fundamental question of the impact of the proliferation of victims' rights on the rights of the defendant and, more broadly, of the impact of the strengthening of the position of the victim on criminal justice at national and EU level. The strengthening of the position of the victim in the criminal justice process reflects what I have characterised elsewhere as 'the individualisation of security' whereby the security needs of the individual take centre stage in justifying the expansion of state power: in addition to protecting the state from a number of perceived security threats, the individual is to be protected too.[123] Conferring rights upon victims is a key part of this process. Garland has called this 'the return of the victim' explaining that

> the new political imperative is that victims must be protected, their voices must be heard, their memory honoured, their anger expressed, their fears addressed. The rhetoric of penal debate routinely invokes the figure of the victim—typically as a child or a woman or a grieving family member—as a righteous figure whose suffering must be expressed and whose security must henceforth be guaranteed.[124]

However, taking into account of the interests of the victim in the criminal justice system changes fundamentally the balance of power and interests in the criminal justice process and ultimately the relationship between the individual and the state. The need to protect the individual as defendant in criminal proceedings from the power of the state is watered down by the perceived need to protect the interests of another category of individual, the victim. Commentators have noted in this context the juxtaposition of the interests of offenders and victims in a zero-sum game[125] and the government rhetoric, in particular in the UK, of 'rebalancing the criminal justice system in favour of the law—abiding majority *and the* victim'.[126] In this kind of discourse, the focus on the protection of collective security (of the security of the law-abiding majority) is coupled with the individualisation of security as expressed in the protection of the rights of the victim.

In this light, the increased prominence of victims' interests in the criminal justice system has profound implications for the relationship between the individual and the state on the one hand, and the relationship between various categories

[123] V Mitsilegas, 'Security versus Justice: The Individualisation of Security and the Erosion of Citizenship and Fundamental Rights' in S Ugelvik and B Hudson (eds), *Justice and Security in the 21st Century. Risks, Rights and the Rule of Law* (Abingdon, Routledge, 2012) 199–216.

[124] D Garland, *The Culture of Control. Crime and Social Order in Contemporary Society* (Oxford, Oxford University Press 2001) 11.

[125] M Matravers, 'The Victim, the State and Civil Society' in A Bottoms and JV Roberts (eds), *Hearing the Victim. Adversarial Justice, Crime Victims and the State* (Cullompton, Willan, 2010) 1–16, 3.

[126] M Tonry, '"Rebalancing the Criminal Justice System in favour of the Victim": the Costly Consequences of Populist Rhetoric' in A Bottoms and JV Roberts (eds), *Hearing the Victim. Adversarial Justice, Crime Victims and the State* (Cullompton, Willan, 2010) 72–103, 73. Emphasis added.

of individuals in the criminal justice process on the other. A number of questions need to be answered in this context: What is criminal process for? What is justice in this context? Whose interests are to be protected? Individualising security via calls to protect victims in the criminal justice system, especially at the pre-trial and trial stage, presents profound challenges to fundamental rights, in particular the presumption of innocence. At the same time, the individualisation of security serves as a justification for the increase of state power vis-à-vis the defendant by introducing exceptions to rules of criminal procedure aimed at protecting the defendant and to ensure a balance of power between the prosecution and the defence. The individualisation of security thus has profound justice implications: by placing one category of individual (the victim) against another category of individual (the defendant and alleged offender), the prioritisation of victims' claims may serve to redistribute justice by weakening procedural safeguards in criminal proceedings.[127]

The potential reconfiguration of the relationship between the individual and the state by individualising security via privileging the interests of the victim is apparent in a number of EU policy documents. The protection of the interests of the victim is central in both the Stockholm Programme[128] and in the EU Internal Security Strategy.[129] In its Communication accompanying a package of proposals on the rights of victims, the European Commission outlined its vision on criminal justice focusing on the rights of the victim in greater detail.[130] According to the Commission, with this package the EU 'will contribute to making crime *victims' needs a central part of the justice systems, alongside catching and punishing the offenders*'.[131] The Commission also notes that:

> One of the European Union's objectives is to offer its citizens an area of freedom, security and justice in which their freedom of movement is ensured. However, without effective EU-wide application of a minimum level of rights for victims, mutual trust is not possible. This means that judicial systems should have full faith in each other's standards of fairness and justice, and citizens should have confidence that the same level of minimum rules will be applied when they travel or live abroad … Member States need to raise standards on victims' rights and the EU must ensure that victims benefit from a level playing field. A certain minimum level of safeguards and standards that are applied in all

[127] Mitsilegas, *The Individualisation of Security.*

[128] Point 2.3.4 of the Stockholm Programme on victims of crime, including terrorism reads as follows: 'Those who are most vulnerable or who find themselves in particularly exposed situations, such as persons subjected to repeated violence in close relationships, victims of gender based violence, or persons who fall victim to other types of crimes in a Member State of which they are not nationals or residents, are in need of special support and legal protection. Victims of terrorism also need special attention, support and social recognition.'

[129] Council doc. 5842/2/10 REV 2, Brussels, 23 February 2010. The Internal Security Strategy is aimed at 'protection of all citizens, especially the most vulnerable, with the focus on *victims of crime* such as trafficking in human beings or gender violence, including *victims of terrorism* who also need special attention, support and social recognition' (emphasis added).

[130] Commission Communication, *Strengthening victims' rights in the EU*, COM (2011) 274, Brussels.

[131] ibid p 2, emphasis added.

> Member States will facilitate judicial cooperation and increase the quality of justice *and also improve people's confidence in the very notion of 'justice'*.[132]

The Commission thus puts forward a vision of European criminal justice whereby the interests of the victim are central. Minimum standards on victims' rights are viewed as essential to create mutual trust not only between judicial authorities, but also between citizens in the EU. As seen above, references to mutual trust have been used by the Commission in order to be able to justify EU competence to legislate in the field under Article 82(2) TFEU. However, the above passage goes beyond the Commission's statements in the Explanatory Memorandum to the victims' Directive, by focusing specifically on the link between the establishment of EU rules on the rights of victims and confidence in 'the very notion of justice'. As with the references to mutual trust, this passage is very vague and the link between victims' rights and the achievement of justice is not substantiated and appears tenuous, to say the least. What is noteworthy in the Commission's Communication on victims is that it does not attempt to place the development of victims' rights in the context of criminal justice in Europe within the general framework of the development of legislation on the rights of the defendant at EU level, legislation which has been long pursued by the Commission and achieved after the introduction of a specific legal basis in Article 82(2) TFEU.[133]

These broad references to the achievement of mutual trust and confidence in the very notion of justice have not survived the finally adopted Directives on victims' rights. The impact on the balance of powers in the criminal justice system of the current EU legislative framework on victims, and in particular of the Directive on the rights of victims, remains to be seen. The Directive does include a series of provisions related to victims' rights and puts forward a general objective that victims must receive appropriate information, support and protection and are able to participate in criminal proceedings,[134] an objective which must guide the implementation and interpretation of the Directive. However, as seen above, member states have been granted considerable discretion as to how to achieve this objective, with the enforcement of key victims' rights prescribed by the Directive being left to national law. The Directive thus attempts to achieve a delicate balance between introducing minimum rules on victims' rights at EU level while not distorting the balance of powers and the expression of justice thus far settled in the various domestic criminal justice systems of individual member states. When looking at the interpretation of victims' rights at EU level, it is essential not to view victims' rights in isolation but to interpret these in accordance with fundamental rights, in particular the rights of the suspect or the defendant. The Directive on the rights of the victim contains a number of references to the need

[132] ibid p 3.
[133] Mitsilegas, *EU Criminal Law,* ch 3.
[134] Art 1(1).

to respect defence rights in this context,[135] and consistent Court of Justice case law[136] has confirmed this need. The requirement to interpret victims' rights in conformity with fundamental rights and in particular defence and fair trial rights arises even more prominently in the post-Lisbon, post-Charter era. The Court's case law on the applicability of the Charter of Fundamental Rights,[137] calls for a systemic examination of national provisions on the position of the victim in criminal proceedings and their impact on fundamental rights, even if such provisions do not constitute a direct and specific implementation of the standards set out in the EU victims' rights Directives.

VI. CONCLUSION

The evolution of legislation of victims' rights at EU level reflects a clear political commitment by the EU institutions to be seen to be active in strengthening the position of the victim in the criminal justice process. The EU has legislated on victims notwithstanding the considerable limits of EU competence in the field and notwithstanding the considerable diversity in national legal systems with regard to the protection of victims and their place in the criminal justice process. The political imperative to legislate on victims' rights has thus taken precedence over considerations of legality and legal certainty. As has been noted with regard to the evolution of victims' rights in the US context, 'the symbolic strength of the term "victim's rights" overrides careful scrutiny: Who could be anti-victim?'[138] The translation of this political will into legal reality in EU law has led to a situation whereby the general objective of strengthening the position of the victim in criminal justice across the European Union is to be achieved either by a system of mutual recognition aimed at providing maximum flexibility to national criminal justice systems, or by the introduction of EU-wide minimum standards on victims' rights whose implementation depends largely on the specificities of the criminal justice systems of member states. The 'Lisbonisation' of victims' rights has not fundamentally changed the picture—at least as far as the drafting of EU law in the field is concerned—as regards legal certainty, some of the effects of Union law on national legal orders (in particular direct effect) and the degree of discretion left to member states. Key pieces of the puzzle of the interaction between EU and national criminal law on victims' rights will thus continue to be filled by the Court of Justice, which has already been faced with the significant challenge of ensuring

[135] According to the Preamble, the rights set out in the Directive are without prejudice to the rights of the offender. The term 'offender' refers to a person who has been convicted of a crime. However, for the purposes of this Directive, it also refers to a suspected or accused person before any acknowledgement of guilt or conviction, and it is without prejudice to the presumption of innocence—recital 12. See also Arts 18, 20 and 23 of the Directive.

[136] *Pupino*, para 59; *Katz*, para 48.

[137] See in particular Case C-617/10 *Fransson* (CJEU, 26 February 2013).

[138] LN Henderson, 'The Wrongs of Victim's Rights' (1985) 37 *Stanford Law Review* 937–1021, 952.

the effectiveness of EU law on victims while recognising national specificities and interests in the field of criminal justice. The Court of Justice—and national courts in their duties of ensuring the enforcement of EU law on victims at the domestic level and interpreting national law in conformity with EU law—will continue to face fundamental questions on the extent to which EU law on victims will change the balance of powers and the concept of justice at the national level. In this context, in the post-Lisbon era in particular, the judiciary is required to interpret provisions on victims' rights in conformity with fundamental rights and in particular fair trial and defence rights as enshrined in the Charter. Political discourse on the rights of victims as well as the piecemeal and functional characteristics of EU criminal procedure competence under Article 82(2) TFEU have led to legislation on victims' rights being developed largely in isolation from legislation on the rights of the defendant. If legislation on the rights of the victim aims to reflect broader concepts of justice at the national and EU level and their intersection, the need for a more holistic approach, viewing victims' rights in the light of fundamental rights and taking full account of the position of the suspect and the defendant in criminal proceedings is essential.

16

Responding to the Plight of Victims of Terrorism: European Approaches and Dilemmas

JESSICA ALMQVIST

I. INTRODUCTION

THIS CHAPTER CENTRES on the contemporary struggle of victims of terrorism for recognition and respect for their human rights. Special attention is paid to persons who have suffered from terrorist offences perpetrated in Europe or abroad when affecting European citizens. Following an analysis of the factors that attest to the vulnerability of this group of victims, the study examines how European states have sought to respond to the harms and sufferings of this group within established schemes of regional cooperation and integration. In this regard, it analyses and compares the somewhat different approaches that have emerged in response to the plight of these victims in the context of the Organization of Security and Cooperation in Europe (OSCE), the Council of Europe (COE) and the European Union (EU), respectively.

Recent law and policy developments of these regional organisations manifest a growing determination to advance common European standards of law and justice with regard to victims of crime, including of terrorism. At the same time, however, for reasons that will be pointed out, the process has been slow and the outcome remains unsatisfactory. In particular, even if the COE and the EU now regard victims of terrorism as representing a vulnerable group and, as such, ought to be given special protection, their acknowledgement is restricted, for the most part, to criminal proceedings. Even so, contemporary experiences reveal that the ability of courts to perform their functions in relation to terrorist offences varies widely depending on the nature of such offences and court capabilities. With time, European systems of criminal justice have become fairly viable with respect to the investigation and prosecution of crimes perpetrated by domestic actors; meanwhile, it has proven more difficult to bring the perpetrators of acts committed by international terrorist organisations and networks to justice. In this light, it is argued that further development of regional standards should adhere to pertinent international policy recommendations on the right to reparation if and when terrorist offences constitute gross violations of human rights and humanitarian law.

II. TERRORISM: CHANGING FACE OF VICTIMHOOD

Terrorism is not a novel problem for Europe. Several countries have decades of experience and advanced capabilities to tackle domestic terrorist organisations pursuing ethno-nationalist/separatist and ideological agendas and aspirations. However, the bombing of Pan Am Flight 103 over Lockerbie, Scotland, on 21 December 1988, which killed 270 persons, made the UK acutely aware of its lack of preparation to tackle and respond to international terrorist attacks that cause situations of mass victimisation. The catastrophic effects of the terrorist attacks of 9/11 in the US, causing 2,752 deaths and injuring 2,594 persons, transformed international terrorism to a global and European concern. The train bombings in Madrid on 11 March 2004 and the terrorist attacks on London on 7 July 2005, both connected with Al Qaeda, brought the threat of international terrorism to the forefront of the European security agenda. Both attacks demonstrated the readiness of international terrorist organisations and networks to cause mass destruction of life and property. A total of 192 persons lost their lives and 1,847 were injured in the Madrid bombings. In the London bombings, 56 persons, including the four suicide bombers, died and more than 700 suffered injuries.

However, contemporary experiences with situations of mass victimisation as a consequence of terrorist attacks are not limited to Al Qaeda or Jihad terrorism. In the Beslan School Massacre in early September 2004, 344 hostages died (including 186 children) and more than 700 were injured. The perpetrators, Islamist militants, demanded recognition of the independence of Chechnya with a subsequent Russian withdrawal. The attacks in Norway on 4 July 2011 claimed a total of 77 lives of mostly young persons, and caused critical injuries to 67 persons. The perpetrator, a Norwegian national, is a right-wing extremist, who acted on his own. The bombings at the 2013 Boston Marathon ended three lives and injured around 200, 17 among them severely. At least 13 had their legs amputated. The perpetrators, two brothers, one of them killed in the police chase, were US naturalised citizens with roots in Chechnya and Avar (Russian enclaves). Finally, in the shopping mall attacks in Nairobi with the siege that began on 21 September 2013 and ended three days later, at least 67 persons lost their lives and 194 were injured. Up to 25,000 were affected by the attacks and in need of assistance.[1]

The weapons and strategies employed in the major attacks that have taken place since the turn of the century, such as the use of improvised explosives and suicide bombers in crowded places, are not so different from attacks against civilian

[1] See information obtained by International Federation of Red Cross and Red Crescent Societies, available at: www.ifrc.org/docs/Appeals/13/MDRKE02702.pdf.

populations in war zones. The effects can be devastating, producing situations of numerous deaths and mass casualties among those who are targeted. Bomb blasts cause injuries that are especially severe and complex. Injuries to limbs can require amputation, while other trauma include lung injuries and respiratory failure, burns, global eye ruptures, brain and abdominal injuries, middle ear damages, concussion, and the penetration of foreign objects into body parts.[2] Medical centres have difficulty in tackling situations of mass casualties, not only because of the complex and technically challenging injuries, but also due to the large number of persons in need of immediate care.[3] Also the psychological impact tends to be significant, with lasting traumas and depressions among both direct and indirect victims. Terrorist attacks may also provoke anger among vicarious victims, ie eye witnesses or bystanders, who may be impelled to seek revenge and retribution through an increasingly hostile and violent behaviour against Muslim communities at home and abroad.[4]

Besides the vulnerability of victims of terrorism due to the severity of the crimes, responses to terrorist attacks can lead to 'secondary' victimisation if the plight of these victims is ignored or forgotten.[5] The 9/11 terrorist attacks in the US transformed terrorism into an international security threat. The UN Security Council took the lead in the Global Fight against Terrorism that was launched immediately following these attacks.[6] The main objectives of this fight are to prevent and combat terrorism. With these aims in mind, the Security Council has requested the adoption of extraordinary coercive measures—above all, targeted sanctions, including asset freeze and blacklisting, as well as legitimised the right of the US and its allies to use armed force as a matter of self-defence in response to 9/11. In the shadow of international law, states have pursued a range of illegal strategies to prevent and combat terrorism. The measures include prolonged or indefinite administrative detention of terrorist suspects, denying them access to justice, torturing them, or killing them.[7]

The global process consisting of the 'securitisation' of international terrorism has done little to assist the victims of attacks that have already been committed. The use of extraordinary and illegal measures with the involvement of national

[2] E Savitsky, B Eastbridge, Borden Institute and D Katz (eds), *Combat Casualty Care. Lessons Learned from Oef and Oif* (Wahington DC, US Department of the Army, 2012), esp ch 2.

[3] See information of American Trauma Society, available at: www.amtrauma.org/resources/tiide/index.aspx.

[4] A Pemberton, 'Al Qaeda and Vicarious Victims: Victimological Insights into Globalized Terrorism', in R Letschert and J Van Dijk (eds), *The New Faces of Victimhood: Globalization, Transnational Crimes and Victim Rights* (New York, Springer, 2011) 223–52.

[5] UNODOC, *The Criminal Justice Response to Support Victims of Acts of Terrorism* (Vienna, United Nations, 2011), para 6.

[6] UNSC Res 1373 of 28 September 2001, UN doc S/RES/1373/2001.

[7] Other tactics include the use of control orders as well as immigration and deportation laws to bypass the criminal justice system. See Briefing by the UN High Commissioner of Human Rights to the Counter-terrorism Committee on 24 October 2013, available at: www.un.org/en/sc/ctc/news/2013-10-31_UNHCHR_CTC_Briefing.html.

intelligence and security services as well as military troops has produced a heightened sense of secrecy, rendering access to information about cases involving terrorist acts especially difficult. Simultaneously, the role of the courts and the criminal process diminished. Though it is now possible to observe an increase in the number of terrorist trials leading to convictions, the object of these trials is to prosecute persons who are accused of terrorism for so-called 'victimless' crime. These trials are the result of the effective criminalisation of acts related to aiding and abetting in the financing, planning and instigation of the commission of terrorist acts even if never actually taking place. This reality means that the ordinary mechanism for obtaining justice and some truth about already committed terrorist attacks has been rather ineffective. More generally, the fight against terrorism is not so different from other fights (or 'wars') against crime. There is a risk that victims are treated as mere statistics or instruments to legitimise the need to allocate (more) resources and competences to relevant agencies and organs operating in these fights.[8]

III. BALANCING TERRORISM PREVENTION WITH VICTIMS' RIGHTS

Since the UN launching the Global Fight against Terrorism, European states have advanced regional frameworks and strategies to prevent or suppress terrorism, including international terrorism. With time, some consideration has also been given to the interests and needs of persons that have already suffered from terrorist attacks. Not only the OSCE, but also the COE and the EU now recognise the importance of the plight of these victims. At the same time, as will be explained in this section, there is no common ground among these organisations on what is owed to this group of victims, and the stress is still placed on preventing the next attack.

A. The OSCE Response

The OSCE, which comprises 57 states, was initially created to serve as a forum for dialogue and negotiation between West and East. Since the end of the Cold War, a new series of objectives has been defined. According to the Charter of Paris for a New Europe (1990), the defence and promotion of democracy, the rule of law and human rights as key to the provision of stability and security in Europe. This commitment involves the condemnation, as criminal, of all acts, methods, and practices of terrorism. In the Charter, the participating states expressed their determination to work for the eradication of terrorism both bilaterally and

[8] See eg Markus Dirk Dubber, *Victims in the War on Crime: The Use and Abuse of Victims' Rights* (New York, New York University Press, 2002).

through multilateral cooperation.[9] As a regional organisation recognised by the UN Security Council under Chapter VII of the UN Charter, the OSCE stood ready to contribute to the Global Fight against Terrorism once it had been initiated. As a first step, it adopted the Bucharest Plan of Action for Combating Terrorism in December 2001.[10] One year later, it also passed the Charter on Preventing and Combating Terrorism.[11] The two instruments reaffirm the UN understanding that acts of international terrorism amount to a threat to international security, which must be prevented and suppressed. In a similar vein, the OSCE Strategy to Address Threats to Security and Stability in the Twenty-First Century (2003) proclaims terrorism as 'one of the most important causes of instability in the current security environment'.[12]

None of the above-mentioned instruments consider the interests or needs of victims of terrorism. Rather, the question was dealt with in a separate decision in 2004,[13] which acknowledges the need 'to strengthen solidarity with victims of terrorism, who have suffered bodily injury or impairment of health, and with dependents of family members of persons who have died as a result of such attacks, in accordance with each State's domestic law'. In the same decision, the OSCE Permanent Council invites the participating states 'to explore the possibility of introducing or enhancing appropriate measures, subject to domestic legislation, for support, including financial assistance, to victims of terrorism and their families'. Moreover, it encourages these states to 'cooperate with relevant institutions of civil society in expressing solidarity with and providing support for the victims of terrorism and their families'. The Office of Democratic Institutions and Human Rights, which was asked to promote this decision has considered the matter as part of the 'human dimension' of the OESC contribution to the Global Fight against Terrorism. For example, in 2007, it organised a High-level Meeting on Victims of Terrorism in 2007, whose final report addresses the challenges of defining 'victim of terrorism' as well as victims assistance and support, including the role of NGOs therein.[14] In addition, one chapter of its manual on countering terrorism while protecting human rights is devoted to victims of terrorism.[15] However, though the manual affirms that the rights of this group are protected by human rights law, it also recalls that the participating states have not assumed any commitments relating specifically to compensation for victims of terrorism besides

[9] But note that several of its declarations prior to this date (from Helsinki to Istanbul) also proclaim a commitment to fight terrorism.

[10] Bucharest Plan of Action for Combating Terrorism, OSCE doc MC(9) DEC/1 4 December 2001.

[11] OSCE Charter on Preventing and Combating Terrorism, OSCE doc MC(10).JOUR/2 7 December 2002.

[12] OSCE Strategy Address Threats to Security and Stability in the Twenty-First Century, adopted at the 11th meeting of the Ministerial Council, Maastricht, 1 and 2 December 2003, para 10.

[13] Decision No 618 Solidarity with Victims of Terrorism, OSCE doc PC DEC 618, 1 July 2004.

[14] See Final Report of the OSCE High-Level Meeting on Victims of Terrorism, 13–14 September 2007, Vienna, Austria, OSCE, 14 February 2008.

[15] OSCE, *Countering Terrorism, Protecting Human Rights: A Manual*, OSCE, 21 February 2008, 27–29.

expressing solidarity with them.[16] Finally, the OSCE Consolidated Framework for the Fight against Terrorism, adopted in 2012, stresses activities to enhance cooperation and build capacity to prevent and combat terrorism, among other objectives, to 'place a focus on the role of victims of terrorism and their families, promoting best practices in the area of solidarity with them and ensuring that their voices are heard'.[17]

The OSCE does not pretend to further international 'standard-setting' with respect to rights of victims of terrorism, but rather to promote existing ones, above all relevant UN recommendations on this matter. Nevertheless, the UN approach is fairly weak. In 2004, the UN Security Council created a working group to explore the possibility of setting up an international fund to compensate victims of terrorist acts and their families.[18] However, the group that was established rapidly announced that the idea of such a fund was premature, and that the best way to protect victims is to encourage states to adopt suitable programmes of assistance.[19] The UN Global Strategy on the Fight against Terrorism, which was approved by the General Assembly on 8 September 2006, did not succeed in redressing the marginalisation of the matter. The main objectives of the strategy are to prevent, suppress, and combat terrorism. The situation of the victims becomes relevant only insofar as their dehumanisation is a condition that breeds terrorism. In this light, UN member states should considering 'putting in place, on a voluntary basis, national systems of assistance that would promote the needs of victims of terrorism and their families and facilitate the normalization of their lives'. The same Strategy also expresses a commitment to foster international solidarity with the victims. In particular, it encourages civil society to engage in a global campaign against terrorism.[20] Though reaffirming that the rights of victims of terrorism should be understood as a human rights issue, it refrains from detailing what their rights are.[21]

In 2008, the UN Counter-terrorism Implementation Task Force created a second working group related to the victims of terrorism. The initiative, which aims

[16] Ibid, p 29. Decision No 618 is also reaffirmed in OSCE/ODIHR Background Paper on Solidarity with Victims of Terrorism. Technical Workshop on Solidarity with Victims of Terrorism, Oñati, 9–10 March 2005; and OSCE/ODIHR Background Paper on Preventing and Combating Terrorism: The Human Dimension, OSCE Annual Security Review Conference, 29 June–1 July 2011, p 5. In the mentioned background paper, ODIHR furthermore recalls that it offers expert analysis and advice to OSCE participating states on key human rights issues that arise in the fight against terrorism, as well as on the conditions that may foster and sustain terrorism, including on the protection of victims of terrorism (p 7).

[17] Decision No 1063 OSCE Consolidated Framework for the Fight against Terrorism, adopted by the Permanent Council at its 934th Plenary Meeting, OSCE doc PC DEC/1063, 7 December 2012, p 5.

[18] UNSC Res 1566 of 8 October 2004, paras 9 and 10.

[19] Report of UNSC Working Group 1566 (2004), UN doc S/2005/789, 16 December 2005, paras 31 and 32. It thereafter reiterated the same position in Report of UNSC Working Group 1566 (2004), UN doc S/2007/755, 31 December 2007, para 6. In its most recent report, the members of the working group express doubts as to whether the topic of victims of terrorism still lies within its mandate as a result of the creation of another working group under the auspices of the UN Implementation Task Force. See Report of UNSC Working Group 1566 (2004), UN doc S/1010/683, 30 December 2010, paras 5–7.

[20] UN Global Strategy (2006), para 8.

[21] UN Global Strategy (2006), section IV.

at supporting and highlighting their conditions, reflects an effort to disconnect and relocate discourses and actions related to their plight from the security-driven fight against terrorism. The task force stresses the importance of soft and innovative measures to respond to the dehumanisation of victims of terrorism, underscoring dialogue and exchange of information.[22] While the initiative is novel, it is neither comprehensive nor legal in outlook and focus. Indeed, it is a striking fact that there is still no single international legal framework setting out the rights of victims of terrorist offences. In June 2012, the current UN Special Rapporteur on the promotion and protection of human rights and fundamental freedoms while countering terrorism lamented that 'despite the proliferation of international agreements concerned with the suppression of terrorism, there is none that specifically addresses the human rights of the victims and the corresponding obligations of States'.[23]

B. The Council of Europe

For the COE terrorism challenges the three fundamental values it cherishes: human rights, the rule of law and pluralist democracy. In a manner similar to the OSCE, this organisation with its 47 members has responded to the UN call for a 'role of the regional organisations, structures and strategies in combating terrorism'.[24] In particular, it contributes to the Global Fight against Terrorism through the provision of a forum for discussing and adopting regional standards and best practice. It also offers assistance to its members in improving their counter-terrorism capabilities. In a lead to strengthen its role in this fight, it drafted a new Convention on the Prevention of Terrorism.[25] The instrument, which was adopted in 2005 and entered into force in 2007, supplements existing multilateral anti-terrorist treaties.[26] Its main aim is to combat 'victimless' crime, above all,

[22] Report on Symposium on Supporting Victims of Terrorism (2008), available at: www.un.org/en/terrorism/ctitf/pdfs/un_report_supporting_victims_terrorism.pdf.

[23] Report of the Special Rapporteur on the promotion and protection of human rights and fundamental freedoms while countering terrorism, Ben Emmerson. Framework principles for securing the human rights of victims of terrorism. UN doc A/HRC/2014, 4 June 2012.

[24] See eg UNGA res of 29 June 2013, para 17.

[25] As of 20 April 2014, the Convention has been ratified by 25 states. An additional 15 states have signed but not ratified.

[26] According to Art 26 of the 2005 Convention, it supplements applicable multilateral or bilateral treaties or agreements between the Parties, including the provisions of the following Council of Europe treaties: European Convention on Extradition, opened for signature, in Paris, on 13 December 1957 (ETS No 24); European Convention on Mutual Assistance in Criminal Matters, opened for signature in Strasbourg, on 20 April 1959 (ETS No 30); European Convention on the Suppression of Terrorism, opened for signature, in Strasbourg, on 27 January 1977 (ETS No 90); Additional Protocol to the European Convention on Mutual Assistance in Criminal Matters, opened for signature in Strasbourg on 17 March 1978 (ETS No 99); Second Additional Protocol to the European Convention on Mutual Assistance in Criminal Matters, opened for signature in Strasbourg on 8 November 2001 (ETS No 182); Protocol amending the European Convention on the Suppression of Terrorism, opened for signature in Strasbourg on 15 May 2003 (ETS No 190).

acts of public provocation to commit terrorist offences as well as recruitment and training for terrorism.[27] In this sense, it secures the right of persons not to be a victim of terrorism in the first place. The COE understands terrorist offences as referring to the acts that have been criminalised in the 12 UN Conventions that were in force at the time of adopting the Convention, and specifically points out that the acts of public provocation, training or recruitment constitute offences regardless of whether a terrorist offence has actually been committed (Article 8). The Convention requests its parties to adopt such measures as may be necessary to establish as a criminal offence under its domestic law: a) participating as an accomplice in the public provocation, training or recruitment of terrorists; b) organising or directing others to commit any of these offences, c) contributing to the commission of one or more of these offences by a group of persons acting with a common purpose. Finally, the parties are also obliged to adopt such measures as may be necessary to establish as a criminal offence under its domestic law 'the attempt to commit' any such offence (Article 9). The Convention furthermore obliges parties to create liability for legal entities participating in any of the mentioned offences (Article 10). All offences must be punished with 'effective, proportionate and dissuasive penalties' and legal entities must be 'subject to effective, proportionate and dissuasive criminal or non-criminal sanctions, including monetary sanctions' (Article 11). The Convention also establishes the duty to investigate such offences (Article 15) as well as the duty to prosecute or extradite alleged offenders (Article 18).

The question of the rights of victims of already committed terrorist acts is understood as more appropriately addressed in the context of its work related to the rights of victims of crime. When addressing the plight of victims of terrorism, it thus recalls the European Convention on the Compensation of Victims of Violent Crimes (1983);[28] Recommendation R (85) 11 on the position of the victim in the framework of criminal law and procedure (1985); and Recommendation R (87) 21 on Assistance to Victims and the Prevention of Victimisation. Following the launching of the Global Fight against Terrorism, the COE has singled out the plight of victims of terrorism for special attention. From the outset, however, most attention was paid to the right to compensation. For example, in its Guidelines on

[27] The term 'public provocation to commit terrorist offences' means 'the distribution, or otherwise making available, of a message to the public, with the intent to incite the commission of a terrorist offence, where such conduct, whether or not directly advocating terrorist offences, causes a danger that one or more such offences may be committed' (Art 4). The term 'recruitment for terrorism' means to solicit another person to commit or participate in the commission of a terrorist offence, or to join an association or group, for the purpose of contributing to the commission of one or more terrorist offences by the association or the group' (Art 5). 'Training for terrorism', finally, means 'provide instruction in the making or use of explosives, firearms or other weapons or noxious or hazardous substances, or in other specific methods or techniques, for the purpose of carrying out or contributing to the commission of a terrorist offence, knowing that the skills provided are intended to be used for this purpose (Art 6).

[28] European Convention on the Compensation of Victims of Violent Crimes of 24 November 1983, ETS No 116.

Human Rights and the Fight against Terrorism (2002), the COE recalls the 'necessity of states, notably for reasons of equity and social solidarity, to ensure that victims of terrorist acts can obtain compensation'.[29] Moreover, it notes that in cases where compensation is not available through the confiscation of the property of the perpetrators, organisers or sponsors of terrorist acts, the 'state must contribute to the compensation of the victims of attacks that took place on its territory, as far as their person or their health is concerned'.[30] Compensation shall be given to those who have sustained serious bodily injury or an impairment of health directly attributable to an intentional crime of violence; and the dependants of persons who have died as a result of such crime.[31]

The First International Congress of Victims of Terrorism (Madrid, 26–27 January 2004) called on the COE to address the question of victims of terrorism in a more thorough fashion. Its first response was to include a provision in the European Convention on the Prevention of Terrorism (2005). Stressing in its preamble 'the precarious situation faced by those who suffer from terrorism', and in this regard reaffirming the profound solidarity of Council of Europe states with the victims and their families, the 2005 Convention requests the parties to 'adopt such measures as may be necessary to protect and support the victims of terrorism that has been committed within its own territory'. These measures may include, through the appropriate national schemes and subject to domestic legislation, inter alia, financial assistance and compensation for victims of terrorism and their close family members (Article 13). During 2005, the Committee of Ministers also passed a set of Guidelines on the protection of Victims of Terrorist Acts. Apart from staking out the meaning and scope of the right to compensation, these Guidelines provide a detailed account of the rights of victims of terrorism, including to emergency and continued assistance, to information about the act of which they have suffered, and to protection of their private and family life.[32] Most emphasis is placed on the role of criminal justice in making their rights effective. The Guidelines not only emphasise the duty of states to investigate the terrorist acts, to bring individuals suspected of terrorist acts to justice, and to access competent courts in order to bring a civil action in support of their rights; in addition, it is recommended that 'at all stages of the proceedings, victims of terrorist acts should be treated in a manner which gives due consideration to their personal situation, their rights and their dignity'.

Recommendation (2006) 8 of the Committee of Ministers to Member States on assistance to crime victims sheds more light onto the rights of victims of

[29] The Guidelines on Human Rights and the Fight against Terrorism were adopted by the Committee of Ministers on 11 July 2002 at the 804th meeting of the Ministers' Deputies.

[30] Guideline XVII of the Guidelines on Human Rights and the Fight against Terrorism (2002).

[31] NB that this provision is a restatement of Art 2 of the European Convention on Compensation to Victims of Violent Crime (1983).

[32] See Guidelines on the Protection of Victims of Terrorist Acts, adopted by the Committee of Ministers on 2 March 2005 at the 917th meeting of the Ministers' Deputies.

terrorism.[33] In particular, it responds to repeated calls of the European ministers of justice in 2003 and 2005, inviting the COE to adopt new rules concerning the support of victims of terrorist acts and their families. At the same time, the 2006 Recommendation is not exclusively concerned with the vulnerabilities of victims of terrorism but also of other types of crimes. Reflecting a growing concern about the need for a more balanced view of the rights of offenders and the rights of crime victims, the 2006 Recommendation directs attention to a range of interests and needs of crime victims that states and their agencies as well as workplaces have not taken into account. The notion of a 'victim' means a 'natural person who has suffered harm, including physical or mental injury, emotional suffering or economic loss, caused by acts or omissions that are in violation of the criminal law of a member state'. It includes, where appropriate, 'the immediate family or dependants of the direct victim'. The 2006 Recommendation provides a comprehensive account of the right to information of relevance to their case, including information on legal proceedings as well as the availability of legal aid. It furthermore details the meaning and scope of the right to effective access to remedies and the right to compensation which should cover treatment and rehabilitation for physical and psychological injuries, loss of income, funeral expenses, loss of maintenance for dependents, as well as for pain and suffering. As pointed out, state compensation becomes especially relevant when damages are not covered by other sources, such as the offender, insurance or state funded health and social provisions. Insurance policies should not exclude damages caused by acts of terrorism unless other applicable provisions exist.

Also underlined in the 2006 Recommendation are the vulnerabilities of some categories of victims who can benefit from special measures best suited to their situation, not only as regards assistance, but also when coming into contact with criminal justice agencies, including the police. In addition, special measures are needed by organisations providing health services, social security, housing, education and employment. Emphasis is placed on the importance of selecting and training personnel dealing with victims, which should include the raising of awareness of the negative effects of crime on persons; and how to avoid the risk of causing secondary victimisation, ie victimisation that occurs not as a direct result of the criminal act but through the response of institutions and individuals to the victim. Specialised training is desirable with respect to personnel working with especially vulnerable categories of crime victims, not only of terrorism, but also of domestic or sexual violence, crimes motivated by racial, religious or other prejudice, families of murder victims as well as child victims. The provision of victim-sensitive training of staff in criminal justice agencies, including the police, is important, and should extend to staff in emergency, health, social security and employment services.

[33] Recommendation Rec (2006) 8 of the Committee of Ministers to member states on assistance to crime victims, adopted by the Committee of Ministers on 14 June 2006 at the 967th meeting of the Ministers' Deputies.

C. The European Union

In a manner similar to the OESC and the COE, EU cooperation on counter-terrorism intensified following the 9/11 attacks. The Council Framework Decision on combating terrorism (2002) constitutes the legal framework common to all members and includes a harmonised definition of terrorist offences.[34] Besides requesting member states to criminalise acts of 'public provocation to commit a terrorist offence', 'recruitment for terrorism' and 'training for terrorism', it upholds that 'victims of terrorist offences are vulnerable, and therefore specific measures are necessary with regard to them'.[35] In this regard, it requests EU member states to ensure that 'investigations into, or prosecution of, offences covered by this Framework Decision are not dependent on a report or accusation made by a person subjected to the offence, at least if the acts were committed on the territory of the Member State'. In addition, it refers to the Council Framework Decision 2001/220/JHA of 15 March 2001 on the standing of victims in criminal proceedings, and also requests member states to take all measures possible to ensure appropriate assistance for victims' families (Article 10).

Following the Madrid bombings in 2004, and the London bombings in 2005, the EU adopted a Counter-terrorism Strategy.[36] The EU Strategy is unique among European responses to terrorism insofar as it is not exclusively focused on the need to strengthen state capacities in preventing and combating terrorism, but also in responding to terrorist attacks that have already been taken place. In particular, the EU Strategy expresses a commitment to 'manage and minimise the consequences of a terrorist attack by improving capabilities to deal with: the aftermath; the coordination of the response; and the needs of victims'.[37] In this context, it notes that the effects of terrorist attacks are not so different from natural disasters, and that member states must use and/or develop their capabilities to respond to emergency situations, including those produced in the wake of terrorist attacks.[38] Finally, according to the EU Strategy, 'the solidarity, assistance and compensation to victims and their families constitute an integral part to the response to terrorism at the national and European level'.[39]

[34] Council Framework Decision 2002/475/JHA on combating terrorism [2002] OJ L164/3. Also see Council Framework Decision 2008/919/JHA amending Framework Decision 2002/475/JHA on combating terrorism [2002] OJ L330/21. But note that the topic of terrorism had been on the EU agenda prior to this date, as indicated eg in the Action Plan of the Council and Commission on how best to implement the provisions of the Treaty of Amsterdam on an area of freedom, security and justice [1999] OJ C19/1. Also relevant are the Council Conclusions of 25 September 2001 and of the Extraordinary European Council plan of action to combat terrorism of 21 September 2001.

[35] Framework Decision of 2002, para 8.

[36] The European Union Counter-terrorism Strategy, Council of the European Union, EU doc 14469/4/05 REV 4, 30 November 2005.

[37] ibid, p 3.

[38] ibid, para 32.

[39] ibid, para 36.

The most significant European instrument on victims' rights to date is the recently adopted Directive 2012/29/EU of the European Parliament and of the Council of 25 October 2012 establishing minimum standards on the rights, support and protection of victims of crime,[40] which replaces Council Framework Decision on the standing of victims of crime in legal proceedings of 2001. The 2012 Directive is a follow-up to the Stockholm Programme—An open and secure Europe serving and protecting citizens, adopted by the European Council at its meeting on 10 and 11 December 2009,[41] in which the Commission and the member states were asked to examine how to improve legislation and practical support measures for the protection of victims. Of primary concern was to strengthen the support for and recognition of all victims, including the victims of terrorism.[42] In general terms, the EU Directive is meant to strengthen the rights of victims and their family members to information, support and protection as well as their participation in criminal proceedings. In a manner similar to similar COE initiatives, the EU Directive establishes provisions concerning training of professionals coming into contact with victims of crime, and encourages cooperation between member states as well as the raising of awareness on victims' rights.

Victims of terrorism are singled out for special consideration due to the particular nature of the crime that has been committed against them. According to the EU Directive, these victims 'have suffered attacks that are intended ultimately to harm society', which means that they 'can be under significant public scrutiny and often need social recognition and respectful treatment by society'. In this light, member states should take account of the needs of these victims, and protect their dignity and security.[43] The EU Directive stresses that victims of terrorism tend to experience a 'high rate of secondary and repeat victimisation, of intimidation and retaliation'. Special care should be taken when assessing whether such risk exists on the basis of a strong presumption that those victims will benefit from special protection measures, and should be offered such measures during criminal proceedings.[44] The EU Directive requests the member states to make a timely and individual assessment of the most vulnerable groups of crime victims, in accordance with national procedures, to identify specific protection needs and to determine whether and to what extent they would benefit from special measures in the course of criminal proceedings. Such individual assessment shall take into account: the personal characteristics of the victim; the type or nature of the

[40] Directive 2012/29/EU of the European Parliament and of the Council establishing minimum standards on the rights, support and protection of victims of crime, and replacing Council Framework Decision 2001/220/JHA [2012] OJ L315/57.

[41] The Stockholm Programme—An Open and Secure Programme Serving and Protecting Citizens [2010] OJ C115/1.

[42] ibid.

[43] ibid, para 16.

[44] ibid, 57–58. Also included in this category of victims are victims of human trafficking, organised crime, violence in close relationships, sexual violence or exploitation, gender-based violence, hate crime, and victims with disabilities and child victims.

crime; and the circumstances of the crime. In particular, attention must be paid to victims who have suffered considerable harm due to the severity of the crime (Article 22).

The EU Directive thus creates a legal foundation for the claim set forth in the 2009 Stockholm Programme, which acknowledges that there are categories of crime victims that are more vulnerable than others or who find themselves in particularly exposed situations, among them, victims of terrorism. As also mentioned in the 2009 Stockholm Programme, these categories are in need of special support and legal protection as well as social recognition.[45] A similar claim had been made in a roadmap for strengthening the rights and protection of victims, in particular in criminal proceedings, approved in 2011. In pursuance of this roadmap, some victims, including victims of terrorism, have specific needs based on the type or on the circumstances of crime they are victim of, given the social, physical and psychological repercussions of these crimes. It was suggested that their special needs could be addressed in specific legislation dealing with the fight against these types of crimes.[46]

The worth of the EU Directive from the standpoint of victims of terrorism varies from case to case, depending on personal characteristics and the nature of the crime that has been committed. In practical terms, it must be noted that the special protection measures it sets forth focuses on the conduct of interviews and hearings. However, such measures may not necessarily concern primarily victims of terrorism, but rather to assist other vulnerable groups, such as victims of sexual or gender-based violence, of violence in close relationships, or child victims. Of rather more relevance to the victims of terrorism are the provisions related to training of professionals likely to come into contact with victims, such as police officers and court staff (Article 25). While the adoption of the EU Directive represents an important legal development, there is still no common EU victim of terrorism policy that attends to the particular circumstances of victims of terrorism, including international terrorism. Depending on the nature of the acts and court capabilities, terrorist attacks pose special challenges for states in the process of conducting effective investigations and bringing the perpetrators to justice.

IV. REPARATION: AN INTERNATIONAL LAW PERSPECTIVE

Recent COE and EU efforts to advance regional standards of law and justice for attending to the circumstances of victims of terrorism reveal an interest in rebalancing the focus on the rights of alleged perpetrators and potential victims with a consideration of victims of terrorist offences that have already been committed.

[45] ibid, para 2.3.4.

[46] Resolution of the Council on a Roadmap for strengthening the rights and protection of victims, in particular in criminal proceedings [2011] OJ C187/01, p 5.

However, as we have seen, the approaches and standards diverge somewhat from one another for reasons related to differing mandates and competences.

The weakest response is that of the OSCE. As this regional arrangement is mainly concerned with terrorism as a transnational threat to security and as a source of regional instability, it has marginalised the question about the fate of the victims. It follows the UN in this area of law and policy and, thus, sees its role as limited to a pleading for solidarity with the victims and for the establishment of national schemes of compensation. The COE, in contrast, which unlike the OSCE is a regional organisation with a well-established human rights mandate, has been more active in seeking to develop regional standards to be applied in national contexts. Its 2006 Recommendation related to assistance to victims of crime represents an important achievement. Not only does it provide a detailed account of the meaning and scope of the rights to information and compensation; it also dwells on the relevance of raising awareness and sensitivity among professionals and sectors of society who interact with victims about their particular needs and interests. Nevertheless, just as in the case of the OSCE, COE norms related to victims are 'soft' in the sense of having no legally binding character. As such, these norms fall short of providing any legal basis for victims to vindicate the rights proclaimed in the 2006 Recommendation in situations where no information, compensation, or assistance are available.

So far, the EU stands alone in having created a set of legal obligations for its members that require them to give special protection for victims of terrorism before, during and following criminal proceedings. The recognition of these victims as belonging to the most vulnerable victims of crime is especially striking. The EU furthermore considers the problems facing victims who are foreigners, as it states that the rights set out in this directive must not be made conditional on the victim's residence status in their territory or on the victim's citizenship or nationality'.[47] At the same time, the EU Directive on Victims' Rights can be criticised for reflecting only 'minimum' standards.[48] A somewhat different concern is that it has drawn its main source of inspiration from contributions made in the field of victimology. Less interest has been given to international law and policy concerning the rights of victims. One possible reason for this stance is that relevant international policy recommendations in this area, which centres on the notion of reparation for breaches of international law, are more far-reaching. According to the UN Basic Principles and Guidelines on the Right to a Remedy and Reparation for Victims of Gross Violations of International Human Rights Law and Serious Violations of International Human Rights law, adopted in 2005, reparation includes restitution, compensation, rehabilitation, satisfaction and

[47] EU Directive on Victims' Rights, para 10.

[48] Carlos Fernández de Casadevante Romani, *International Law of Victims* (Berlin/Heidelberg, Springer-Verlag, 2012) 84.

guarantees of non-repetition.[49] Both material and moral injuries are repaired. Special attention is given to satisfaction, which is meant to cover moral injuries, and covers the right to truth and the right to memory, including commemoration, as well as public apology and acceptance of responsibility.

A second possible reason for not taking reparation fully into account is some hesitation or discord among EU members whether the international recommendations in question are meant to be applicable in the wake of terrorist attacks. As the UN Special Rapporteur, Ben Emmerson notes in his report submitted in 2012,[50] the claim that terrorist offences constitute gross human rights violations remains controversial since such offences are perpetrated by non-state actors and not by states. From this standpoint, it is essential to overcome in each case the difficulties of attributing such offences to a particular state or set of states. Nevertheless, this task can be painstaking due to the difficulties involved in obtaining clear and compelling evidence as regards the more concrete relation between states and terrorist groups. Besides, non-state actors might well be organised in an autonomous manner and perpetrate their acts without any deep involvement of states. In response to this dilemma, Emmerson stresses the importance of interpreting international law in the light of a changing environment lest victims of terrorism are to become victims of outdated doctrines about the position of the state and its monopoly of power in international relations. For him, what matters, in the end, is that if and when acts consist of the deliberate infliction of lethal force that result in death or serious physical and psychological injuries, such acts must be understood as constituting gross human rights violations, quite regardless of the question of direct and indirect state responsibility.[51] In this context, it is important to recall the developments with respect to the international criminalisation of grave crime, including of crimes against humanity. Depending on their gravity, some terrorist offences may amount to crimes against humanity.[52]

The EU may be moving in the direction of acknowledging the aggravating circumstances of persons who have fallen victims of terrorist offences when it declares that victims of terrorism are vulnerable not just because of the gravity of the psychical or psychological injuries suffered, but also because the harm that has been inflicted *is intended ultimately to harm society*. Still, it resists considering acts of terrorism as amounting to gross violations of human rights, and thus prefers not to differentiate between the rights of victims of terrorism as opposed to the rights of victims of other crimes with respect to determining what, if anything,

[49] Basic Principles and Guidelines on the Right to a Remedy and Reparation for Victims of Gross Violations of International Human Rights Law and Serious Violations of International Human Rights Law, UNGA Res 60/147, 16 December 2005, paras 15–23.

[50] Above, n 23.

[51] Ibid, paras 13–14.

[52] For a discussion of this claim, see MP Scharf and MA Newton, 'Terrorism and Crimes against Humanity', in L Sadat (ed), *Forging a Convention on Crimes against Humanity* (Cambridge, Cambridge University Press, 2011), 262–78.

is owed to this group of victims in addition to support, assistance, compensation and legal standing in criminal proceedings.

Regardless of what each of us think about the applicability of the international right to reparation in the case of victims of terrorism, including international terrorism, recent experiences reveal that a response that mainly focuses on the rights of victims in relation to criminal proceedings can be unsatisfactory. Though criminal justice is an important matter of principle, the ability of courts to perform their functions varies widely, depending on the nature and the kind of energy that drives the terrorist offences. It furthermore depends on court capabilities. Over time and as a result of the development of schemes of cooperation in criminal matters, European systems of criminal justice have become fairly viable with respect to the investigation and prosecution of crimes perpetrated by domestic terrorist groups; so far, however, it has proven more difficult, sometimes impossible, to bring the principal perpetrators of acts of international terrorism to justice. This challenge is the result of various factors, not only the use of suicide bombers but also the transnational and organised character of these crimes.[53] The latter means that the person or persons who ordered or induced a given terrorist offence may reside or hide in a country that is not likely to accept an extradition request.

Hundreds of terrorist trials have been held in the US since the time of the 9/11 attacks. The top charges have been general criminal conspiracy, material support for terrorists and material support for foreign terrorist organisations.[54] While these trials can reveal some of the truth of about the terrorist attacks of 9/11, the persons who carried out the attacks and who ordered or solicited the attacks will never be prosecuted.

The trial that was held in relation to the bombings in Madrid in 2004 has been the most effective and meaningful trial so far, in the sense that material authors of this attack were convicted as a result of this trial. It was found that the bombings had been planned and carried out by an Islamist cell. While seven of the accused were acquitted, three persons were convicted as the material authors of the bombings, and sentenced to more than 40,000 years in prison. The rest of the accused (19) were convicted of belonging to a terrorist organisation, for collaborating with such an organisation, and for supplying the explosives used in the bombings. Seven members of the Islamist cell, and the main suspects, committed suicide in Leganes when they were about to be detained. The victims were disappointed with the outcome of the trial, pointing to the acquittals and in particular the fact that the person accused of having masterminded the bombings

[53] EA Baylis, 'The Inevitable Impunity of Suicide Terrorists', in JT Parry, *Evil, Law and the State: Perspectives on State Power and Violence* (Amsterdam, Editions Rodopi BV, 2006), 111–26.

[54] Center on Law and Security, New York University School of Law, *Terrorist Trial Report Card: September 11, 2001–September 11, 2011* (New York, Center on Law and Security, 2011) 13–14, available: www.lawandsecurity.org/Portals/0/Documents/TTRC%20Ten%20Year%20Issue.pdf.

was not convicted.[55] Critical commentators stress that the verdicts reflected the difficulties faced by police forces and judges as they seek to imprison those accused of international terrorism: the preponderance of circumstantial evidence rather than concrete proof; problems related to evidence translated from Arabic and with evidence gathered by other countries; unreliable witnesses; and the lack of confessions.[56]

The London bombings on 7 July 2005 were also the subject of criminal proceedings. Since the persons who carried out the attacks were suicide bombers, the focus of these proceedings was on those persons who attempted (but failed) to perpetrate terrorist acts on 7 July and the subsequent attempt to strike on 21 July 2005. The three men who were charged in 2007 in connection with the bombings of 7 July were acquitted in 2009. Two men who were cleared of helping the 7 July bombers choose their targets were thereafter sentenced to seven years in jail for planning to attend a terrorist training camp in Pakistan. In July 2007, four persons were found guilty of attempting to detonate an explosive device or a bomb in connection with the attempted attack on 21 July 2005. Each of them was sentenced to life imprisonment with a minimum of 40 years. Following retrial, two more defendants were convicted of involvement in this plot. Survivors of the 7 July attacks and family members who lost their loved ones mean that this outcome strengthened the case for an independent inquiry into the bombings.

The trial in relation to the bombing of Pan-Am Flight 103 over Lockerbie, Scotland, on 21 December 1988, has been criticised for not meeting the expectations of finding out the truth about this horrific event. The trials at Camp Zeist in the Netherlands, which were concluded in January 2001, led to one conviction of murder and one acquittal of two Libyan nationals who were accused of having placed the bombs in the plane following orders by Muammar Gaddafi. Family members and friends of the direct victims are still searching for the truth. Even though Gaddafi eventually accepted responsibility for the Lockerbie bombing and paid compensation to the families of the direct victims, he maintained that he had not given any orders. As we know, Gaddafi, the person who allegedly ordered the bombing, was killed in 2011 in connection with the UN-authorised armed intervention in Libya.

In the light of this record, the worth of a focus on rights in relation to criminal proceedings depends on the nature of the acts. Depending on the gravity of the offences that have been committed, the development of regional standards related to victims of terrorism can benefit from international policy recommendations applicable in situations of gross violations of human rights. Unlike European responses, these recommendations consider a range of different measures besides the imposition of criminal sanctions to repair the harms and suffering of the

[55] F Halliday, 'Justice in Madrid: the "11–March" Verdict', *OpenDemocracy*, 5 November 2007, available: www.opendemocracy.net/article/globalisation/global_politics/11M.

[56] For an in-depth account of problems related to terrorist cases, see eg UNODC, *Digest of Terrorist Cases* (New York, United Nations, 2010) esp 8–20.

victims.[57] The right to the truth is not limited to criminal proceedings, but extends to the conduct of independent public inquiries, or so-called truth commissions. The concern expressed about the vulnerability of victims of international terrorism in relation to developing approaches to rights of victims of crime, including terrorism more generally, is not meant to downplay or treat as less important the plight of victims of domestic terrorism. For example, all victims of terrorism, as victims of violent crime in general, are owed short and long-term assistance, compensation, and support for the purpose of restoring their personal autonomy. There seem to be no relevant differences among persons who have been victims of terrorism, or of violent crime in general, which call for them to be treated differently in the process of implementing these rights. At the same time, experience over the last decade show that criminal justice now seems to work fairly well in relation to terrorist acts carried out by domestic terrorist groups and persons,[58] but remains less effective in relation to acts carried out by international terrorist networks and organisations.

V. CONCLUSION

Since the time of the proclamation of the Global Fight against Terrorism, the plight of victims of terrorism, including international terrorism, has been overshadowed by the urgency of preventing the next attack. The influence of victimology as a specialised branch of criminology has raised the importance of victims of crime, including of terrorist offences.[59] The move away from an exclusive focus on the rights of crime suspects and perpetrators towards a consideration of the circumstances of victims of crime has led European institutions to recognise victims' rights to assistance and compensation, and to promote a role for these victims in the criminal process.[60] Victims of terrorism have benefited from these developments. Nevertheless, as has been pointed out in this chapter, the European approaches to victims of terrorism do not consider sufficiently the prospect that criminal justice can fail, depending on the nature of the criminal act.[61] The right of legal standing and participation for victims in criminal proceedings becomes next to meaningless

[57] For a more cautious view of considering terrorism as a human rights violation, see eg C Warbrick, 'The European Response to Terrorism in an Age of Human Rights' (2004) 15(5) *European Journal of International Law* 989, 1006.

[58] See eg EUROPOL, *TE-SAT 2013, EU Terrorism Situation and Trend Report* (Van Deventer, European Police Office, 2013).

[59] H-J Albrecht and M Kilchling, 'Victims of Terrorism Policies: Should Victims of Terrorism Be Treated Differently?', in M Wade and Almir Valjemic (eds), *A War on Terror? The European Stance on a New Threat, Changing Laws and Human Rights Implications* (New York, Springer, 2010) 221–44, 221.

[60] C Hoyle and L Zedner, 'Victims, Victimization, and Criminal Justice', in M Maguire, R Morgan and R Reiner, *The Oxford Handbook of Criminology* (Oxford, Oxford University Press, 2008), 460–95, 487.

[61] See eg EUROPOL, *TE-SAT 2013, EU Terrorism Situation and Trend Report* (Van Deventer, European Police Office, 2013).

in cases where it is especially difficult, if not practically impossible, to bring the actual perpetrators of the crimes to be investigated and prosecuted to justice. While the effective functioning of criminal justice is an ideal to strive for, and efforts should be made to establish the conditions for a more central role for courts, cases of international terrorism are particularly challenging.

In the light of these findings, it has been suggested that European law and policy can benefit from the insights of contemporary international policy recommendations related to victims of gross violations of human rights and humanitarian law. Indeed, according to the present chapter, the deliberate infliction of lethal force that causes deaths and bodily injuries amount to such violations even if committed by non-state actors and in spite of the difficulties of attributing state responsibility. International law and policy concerned with the rights of victims of attacks on civilian populations understand grave breaches of human rights and humanitarian law as generating a right to reparation. Besides restitution, if possible, compensation, rehabilitation and guarantees of non-repetition, reparation extends to satisfaction. The latter recognises the importance of, and aspires to repair moral injuries. Satisfaction includes but is not limited to the imposition of criminal sanction but also covers the rights to truth and to memory as well as commemoration. The moral and social dimensions of reparation are growing in importance as indicated by recent efforts to involve victims of crime in criminal proceedings. Nevertheless, when such proceedings are not forthcoming, even if regrettable, alternative mechanisms must be established for the purpose of allowing victims to tell their stories, and to seek the truth about what happened to them or their loved ones.

17

Victims of Trafficking and Smuggling of Migrants in International and European Law[1]

JACOBO RÍOS RODRÍGUEZ

THE PHENOMENON OF trafficking and smuggling of migrants is serious, and impacts most states in the world. For example, an estimated 15,000 victims have been found dead at the borders of Europe since 1988, of whom a little more than a third have disappeared at sea.[2] According to the most recent UN data, the number of migrants smuggled from Latin America to North America will increase by 6.6 billion per year, entailing 3 million illegal entries into the territory of the United States.[3] Recent tragedies such as the Lampedusa incident in October 2013, with more than 300 victims, emphasise the human drama to which the law must provide an answer.[4]

However, from a legal perspective, the migration itself is unlawful only if it violates national laws of entry to a territory. Consequently, the first way to avoid this illegality and its side effects is to organise the movement of persons within the law. An example would include the agreement between Vietnam and the High Commissioner for Refugees, signed in 1979 to organise an orderly departure and a regular migration. It is a preventive approach that is not always sufficiently

[1] This chapter presents in English some extracts and ideas produced in previous works by the author, published initially in French, including: J Ríos Rodríguez, 'Le trafic illicite de migrants par voie maritime', in Société française pour le droit international, *L'État dans la mondialisation* (Paris, Pedone, 2013) 371–87; J Ríos Rodríguez, 'La lutte contre la traite et le trafic illicite de migrants: de la prévention des infractions à la protection des victimes', in C-A Chassin (ed), *Migrations contraintes* (Paris, Pedone, 2014) 163–77; and J Ríos Rodríguez, 'La maltraitance du migrant', in P Weckel, and G S Goodwin-Gill (ed), *Migrations internationales* (The Hague, Centre for Studies and Research in International Law and International Relations, The Hague Academy of International Law, not yet published).

[2] Fortress Europe, 'Forteresse Europe', 14 January 2010, available at: http://fortresseurope.blogspot.com/2006/01/forteresse-europe.html.

[3] Centre d'actualités de l'ONU, 'Crime organisé: face à un phénomène global, l'ONU sonne l'alarme', 18 October 2010, available at: www.un.org/apps/newsFr/storyF.asp?NewsID=23374&Cr=crime&Cr1=&Kw1=trafic&Kw2=migrants&Kw3=.

[4] 'Lampedusa: la communauté internationale appelle à des mesures' *Le Monde*, 12 October 2013.

exploited. The repressive approach, which meets the objectives of migration control, is the most used method.

Nevertheless, for its proper use, it is necessary to distinguish the object of repression. That is to say, to distinguish the organisers of the illegal transfer of people from the victim of their activities. To make such a distinction, one must still overcome some initial difficulties that influence the legal approach.

Prevention thus proves to be an integral part of the international (United Nations) norms and European protection—from both the European Union and Council of Europe—which should benefit victims of smuggling and trafficking, but it is also the weak point of many states. Jurisprudence provides examples that show that state condemnations are related to a lack of prevention thus causing a lack of effective protection of victims.

Despite the diversity of instruments and offences, the existence of a link between the texts must be assumed from the start, as border measures that states may adopt are the same in both United Nations Protocols established by their Article 11.[5] However, for a more straightforward analysis, it is necessary to focus on the offences themselves rather than be limited to preventive or repressive measures taken by the states.

What are the respective definitions of trafficking and smuggling? We will examine consecutively migrants as victims of trafficking and smuggling, both in specific international and European norms (section I) and in general treaty norms (section II), and then we address the practical issue of victims of maritime smuggling, distinguishing between whether it is a ship without a flag (section III) or with a flag (section IV), before describing the gaps and shortcomings in the protection of victims by states (section V).

[5] According to which: '1. Without prejudice to international commitments in relation to the free movement of people, States Parties shall strengthen, to the extent possible, such border controls as may be necessary to prevent and detect trafficking in persons. 2. Each State Party shall adopt legislative or other appropriate measures to prevent, to the extent possible, means of transport operated by commercial carriers from being used in the commission of offences established in accordance with article 5 of this Protocol. 3. Where appropriate, and without prejudice to applicable international conventions, such measures shall include establishing the obligation of commercial carriers, including any transportation company or the owner or operator of any means of transport, to ascertain that all passengers are in possession of the travel documents required for entry into the receiving State. 4. Each State Party shall take the necessary measures, in accordance with its domestic law, to provide for sanctions in cases of violation of the obligation set forth in paragraph 3 of this article. 5. Each State Party shall consider taking measures that permit, in accordance with its domestic law, the denial of entry or revocation of visas of persons implicated in the commission of offences established in accordance with this Protocol. 6. Without prejudice to article 27 of the Convention, States Parties shall consider strengthening cooperation among border control agencies by, inter alia, establishing and maintaining direct channels of communication'. V. Protocol against the smuggling of migrants by land, sea and air, supplementing the Convention against Transnational Organised Crime, signed on 12 December 2000, and Protocol to prevent, suppress and punish trafficking in persons, especially women and children, supplementing the United Nations Convention against Transnational Organized Crime, signed on 12 December 2000.

I. NOTIONS OF 'TRAFFICKING' AND 'SMUGGLING'[6]

Smuggling and trafficking are the subject of two Protocols of the UN Convention against Transnational Organized Crime.[7] However, the normative framework, international and regional is plural. It is mainly related to the application of the jurisprudence provided by judgments of international courts and shows a degree of prevention which paradoxically can be offset with the degree of protection offered to the victims of these activities.

According to the Protocol,

> 'Trafficking in persons' shall mean the recruitment, transportation, transfer, harbouring or receipt of persons, by means of the threat or use of force or other forms of coercion, of abduction, of fraud, of deception, of the abuse of power or of a position of vulnerability or of the giving or receiving of payments or benefits to achieve the consent of a person having control over another person, for the purpose of exploitation.[8]

Thus, three features will be essential in defining the relationship between the two offences: there is an absence of consent from the migrant to his or her trafficking, the goal is exploitation—a form of abuse—and may be international but also purely domestic, with a lawful or unlawful entry into the territory.

The Protocol on smuggling defines it as 'the procurement, in order to obtain, directly or indirectly, a financial or other material benefit, of the illegal entry of a person into a State Party of which the person is not a national or a permanent resident',[9] while at the same time stating that '"Illegal entry" shall mean crossing borders without complying with the necessary requirements for legal entry into the receiving States.'[10]

Consequently here the three different characteristics imply the existence of a consent of the migrant to his or her trafficking, no requirement of direct exploitation of the migrant and the international nature of traffic because it is necessarily accomplished by crossing a border.

In contrast, the approach of the European Union—inspired by and yet different from that of the United Nations—is more concrete, and less focused on the protection of migrants. There is a clear influence of the Protocol on both the

[6] See especially J Ríos Rodríguez, 'La maltraitance du migrant', in P Weckel, and GS Goodwin-Gill (eds), *Migrations internationales* (The Hague, Centre for Studies and Research in International Law and International Relations, The Hague Academy of International Law, not yet published).

[7] These recent norms show, despite the critiscism that will follow their introduction, some significant progress, demonstrating the international evolution on the matter. A former approach of a pre-contemporaneous international law can be found in L Varlez, 'Les migrations internationales et leur réglementation' [1927] 20(V) *Recueil des Cours de l'Académie de Droit international* 165–348.

[8] Protocol to prevent, suppress and punish trafficking in persons, especially women and children, op cit.

[9] Protocol against the smuggling of migrants by land, sea and air, op cit.

[10] ibid.

overall approach taken in European regional norms, particularly observable in the common definition of trafficking.[11]

Further to the Protocols of 2000, several European standards regulations were adopted, for example, the Council Framework Decision on combating trafficking in human beings,[12] the Council Directive 2002/90/EC defining the facilitation of unauthorised entry, transit and residence,[13] and the Council Framework Decision on the strengthening of the penal framework to prevent the facilitation of unauthorised entry, transit and residence.[14]

Council Directive 2002/90/EC, which is a European text intended to combat trafficking, has some interesting features.[15] It is immediately apparent that it does not mention the word 'illicit trafficking', but it states, in section 1.1, that:

> Each Member State shall adopt appropriate sanctions on: (a) any person who intentionally assists a person who is not a national of a Member State to enter, or transit across, the territory of a Member State in breach of the laws of the State concerned on the entry or transit of aliens; (b) any person who, for financial gain, intentionally assists a person who is not a national of a Member State to reside within the territory of a Member State in breach of the laws of the State concerned on the residence of aliens.[16]

In other words, the difference is that while the aim for profit is not required from traffickers to introduce migrant victims, it must exist in order to help them stay.[17]

It is certain that this goal is one of the main, but not exclusive, reasons for trafficking activities. However, the European Directive adopts a perspective which puts profit and non-profit activities on the same level, having no positive effect on the protection of migrants. The removal of the requirement of profit on the entrance of the migrant from the text of the United Nations 'a été essentiellement motivée par la volonté de lutter efficacement contre les filières de passeurs, plus

[11] A Weyembergh, 'La lutte contre la traite et le trafic d'êtres humains' [2006] 77(1–2) *Revue internationale de droit pénal: bulletin de l'Association Internationale de Droit Pénal* 214.

[12] Council Framework Decision on combating trafficking in human beings [2002] OJ L203/1.

[13] Council Directive 2002/90/EC defining the facilitation of unauthorised entry, transit and residence [2002] OJ L328/17.

[14] Council Framework Decision 2002/946/JHA on the strengthening of the penal framework to prevent the facilitation of unauthorised entry, transit and residence [2002] OJ L328/1.

[15] See for instance L Arroyo Zapatero, 'De la lutte contre l'esclavage et la traite des blanches à la proscription du trafic d'êtres humains', in M Delmas-Marty and J Lelier (eds), *Les chemins de l'harmonisation pénale* (Paris, Société de Législation Comparée, 2008) 117–19.

[16] Council Directive 2002/90/EC defining the facilitation of unauthorised entry, transit and residence, op cit.

[17] This text has been adopted further to a French initiative, as France did not want to take into account the profit motive as a constitutive element. See on this topic J Vernier, 'French Criminal and Administrative Law concerning Smuggling of Migrants and Trafficking in Human Beings: Punishing Trafficked People for their Protection?', in E Guild and P Minderhoud (eds), *Immigration and criminal law in the European Union: the legal measures and social consequences of criminal law in member States on trafficking and smuggling in human beings* (Leiden, Nijhoff, 2006) 8.

précisément par la volonté de contourner les difficultés éprouvées en pratique pour démontrer l'existence du but de lucre'.[18]

To distinguish activities that are done with the motivation of profit plays a dual role. On the one hand, its lack of mention for border crossing was justified because of the difficulty of proving it. It might be easier to target the trafficking if it is not necessary to provide evidence, often complex, of its profit-making nature.

On the other hand, and upon joint consideration of paragraphs 1 and 2 of Article I, it is clear that the possible criminalisation of humanitarian purpose of introducing people into a country diverts from the objective of protecting the victims. It seems that, despite the aim to facilitate the proof of traffic without requiring the presence of profit, the European regional framework which fights against such activities is less focused on the protection of vulnerable people than on the suppression of practices violating state sovereignty. Criticism was quickly raised, including from the United Nations High Commissioner for Refugees[19] and from the Commission of Civil Liberties, Justice and Home Affairs of the European Parliament.

There are other distinctions of principle between the two offences. Trafficking is an ongoing offence, which extends over time while the abuse continues. Smuggling for its part is an instant offence, which occurs as soon as the illegal entry is realised. But there are other more relevant features, focusing on the people involved in these activities.

At European level, we should also mention Directive 2011/36/EU on preventing and combating trafficking in human beings and protecting its victims, and replacing Council Framework Decision 2002/629/JHA.[20] While it is too early for a review, four innovative legal elements can be emphasised: predicting sanctions and the exclusion of their application to the victims,[21] the possible criminal responsibility of the users of services of victims of trafficking,[22] better protection

[18] 'Has mainly been prompted by the desire to fight efficiently against smugglers, and more precisely by the desire to by-pass the practical difficulties encountered in proving the existence of a profit-making objective' (our translation). A Weyembergh, 'La lutte contre la traite et le trafic d'êtres humains', op cit, p 219.

[19] J Vernier, op cit, p 10.

[20] Directive 2011/36/EU on preventing and combating trafficking in human beings and protecting its victims, and replacing Council Framework Decision 2002/629/JHA [2011] OJ L101/1.

[21] Art 8 of the Directive states that 'Member States shall, in accordance with the basic principles of their legal systems, take the necessary measures to ensure that competent national authorities are entitled not to prosecute or impose penalties on victims of trafficking in human beings for their involvement in criminal activities which they have been compelled to commit as a direct consequence of being subjected to any of the acts referred to in Article 2'.

[22] It still lacks precision but it remains possible. According to Art 18.4, 'In order to make the preventing and combating of trafficking in human beings more effective by discouraging demand, Member States shall consider taking measures to establish as a criminal offence the use of services which are the objects of exploitation as referred to in Article 2, with the knowledge that the person is a victim of an offence referred to in Article 2'. Ibid.

of victims, particularly in the case of children,[23] and possible extraterritorial application.[24]

Thus, their distinction, although recent, seems clear. However, the reality is more complex, and it is possible to build the link between them from a concept that connects smuggling and trafficking in law and in practice, beyond initial appearances. This is the concept of abuse.

It is a verifiable fact in trafficking: abuse constitutes an essential qualification, whether it is sexual abuse, forced labour or any other instance.

However, it is also a verifiable element in many cases of smuggling. Migrants often suffer abuse from the smuggler during their journey. This was reiterated by the Commission on Human Rights shortly after the adoption of the Protocols.[25] Such abuse can also be found in illegal migration.

Although it is not part of the qualifying elements of the offense of smuggling, abuse is nevertheless a part of this activity with a different purpose. In trafficking, there is an abuse of the individual, of the migrant, the direct purpose being exploitation. With smuggling, there is an exploitation of the situation and indirectly, as a means of achieving it, abuse of the migrant also exists. This sets a priori the purpose as distinct in each case of abuse, but the degree of severity may also be different, trafficking being the most serious violation in the basic offence. This different degree serves as a basis for the distinction within existing legal instruments.[26]

However, this approach does not withstand analysis. The link exists between trafficking and smuggling and is based on an element of mistreatment of the migrant. This connectivity allows some cases of smuggling to be considered to be of a much greater degree of severity than a basic trafficking offence. However, it is necessary for regulations to provide for this possibility. In this sense, Article 6 of the Protocol against smuggling provides as an aggravating condition '[circumstances that] endanger, or are likely to endanger, the lives or safety of the migrants concerned'[27] and 'that entail inhuman or degrading treatment, including for exploitation, of such migrants'.[28] Here is the only mention of such abuse

[23] Art 13.1 states that 'Child victims of trafficking in human beings shall be provided with assistance, support and protection. In the application of this Directive the child's best interests shall be a primary consideration'. Ibid.

[24] Many aspects of this topic are covered by Art 10, and more specifically in the second paragraph, which states that 'A Member State shall inform the Commission where it decides to establish further jurisdiction over the offences referred to in Articles 2 and 3 committed outside its territory, inter alia, where: (a) the offence is committed against one of its nationals or a person who is an habitual resident in its territory; (b) the offence is committed for the benefit of a legal person established in its territory or; (c) the offender in an habitual resident in its territory'. Ibid.

[25] Commission des droits de l'homme, Sous-Commission de la promotion et de la protection des droits de l'homme, *Point 6 de l'ordre du jour provisoire. L'introduction clandestine et la traite de personnes et la protection des droits fondamentaux de ces personnes,* doc E/CN 4/Sub 2/2001/26, 5 July 2001.

[26] L Arroyo Zapatero, op cit, p 116.

[27] Protocol against the smuggling of migrants by land, sea and air, op cit.

[28] ibid.

in the case of smuggling: illicit treatment can be performed by exploiting the migrant. The exploitation does not cover all the possibilities of abuse, it is only one of its forms. In this case, smuggling would be considered to be an aggravated offence where it entails a much more intrusive treatment of the migrant than that of its 'basic' equivalent. Nonetheless, the passive subject of trafficking, as configured by the Protocol, remains distinct from the migrant: it is sovereignty. Moreover, this concept of abuse as an aggravating circumstance is not accompanied, in the Protocol, by adequate measures to protect the migrant, compared to its counterpart.

II. CONVENTIONAL PROTECTION OF VICTIMS IN OTHER NORMS

Even when standards are applied within the European framework, we must go beyond the standards of the EU and the Council of Europe. The international law of human rights is also applicable to victims of trafficking and smuggling. For example, regardless of the specific texts of the Protocols,[29] it should be noted that 'many aspects of smuggling are already covered by international human rights law'.[30] It is the same for trafficking. Human rights are based on the obligation to protect the victims of such activities: 'This obligation is important because it reinforces a notion that smuggled people are also victims of human rights abuses, and therefore has the effect of redirecting smuggling into a human rights discourse.'[31]

Thus, whether in the Forced Labour Convention of 28 June 1930 (n° 29), or in the Convention for the Suppression of the Traffic in Persons and of the Exploitation of the Prostitution of Others of 2 December 1949, the obligation to protect is explicit.[32]

Whether by the Convention relating to the Status of Refugees of 28 July 1951 and its Protocol relating to the Status of Refugees, the Convention on the Elimination of All Forms of Discrimination against Women of 18 December1979 or by the Convention on the Rights of the Child of 20 November1989, minorities suffering violations of their rights by traffickers and smugglers became the subject of specific legislation. In addition, in Article 16.2 of the International Convention on the Protection of the Rights of All Migrant Workers and Members of Their Families of 18 December 1990, the obligation to protect is formulated thus: 'Migrant workers and members of their families shall be entitled to effective protection by the State against violence, physical injury, threats and intimidation,

[29] On the need to read the Protocols in combination with other instruments of migrant protection, see ONU, Comité spécial sur l'élaboration d'une convention contre la criminalité transnationale organisée et la justice pénale, Document A/AC 254/30, ninth session, Vienna, 5–16 June 2000, para 18.

[30] T Obokata, 'Smuggling of Human Beings from a Human Rights Perspective: Obligations of Non-State and State Actors under International Human Rights Law' [2005] 17 *International Journal of Refugee Law* 415.

[31] ibid, p 408.

[32] As set out in Arts 16, 17, and 19 of the conventions.

whether by public officials or by private individuals, groups or institutions.'[33] This Convention applies to regular and irregular migrants. The list can be long, also including the ILO Convention Concerning the Prohibition and Immediate Action for the Elimination of the Worst Forms of Child Labour of 17 June 1999, the Optional Protocol to the Convention on the Rights of the Child on the sale of children, child prostitution and child pornography, of 25 May 2000,[34] and, of course, the Council of Europe Convention on Action against Trafficking in Human Beings.

The existence of these obligations *erga omnes* overcomes the difficulty raised by the national margin of appreciation when it comes to demonstrating whether the elements that constitute the offence are met.

Facing the *erga omnes* nature of these obligations, the international practice still lists many examples of detention conditions that do not conform to those described. For example, Greece is the European Union state that is most affected by the phenomenon of migration, as it is a country of entry into the Union by the land border with Turkey. Conditions of detention of migrants there have been criticised by the UN Special Rapporteur on torture,[35] and the UNHCR also requested improvements.[36] The violation of these obligations is highlighted by the imprisonment of illegal migrants. The law and reality are then at opposite extremes: if one requires protection, the other adopts a punitive approach that goes against the norms. This is also the case in some African countries, among others, which has allowed the International Organization for Migration to find a 'manque d'harmonie'[37] in the fulfilment of state obligations.

III. MARITIME MIGRANTS PROTECTION: SHIPS WITHOUT A FLAG[38]

As is well known, one of the most difficult aspects of migration in Europe is the arrival of migrants predominantly via sea borders. Here the issue is the definition of the borders of the EU, within a framework of cross-border responsibilities.

[33] International Convention on the Protection of the Rights of All Migrant Workers and Members of Their Families, Arts 8, 9, and 10.

[34] The obligation to protect is explicit in the Convention on the Protection of the Rights of All Migrant Workers and Members of Their Families.

[35] Centre d'actualités de l'ONU, 'Grèce: inquiétudes sur les conditions de détention des migrants clandestins', 20 October 2010, available at: www.un.org/apps/newsFr/storyF.asp?NewsID=23411#.VGt9PfmsV7E.

[36] Centre d'actualités de l'ONU, 'Le HCR exhorte l'UE à aider la Grèce à réformer son système d'asile', 26 October 2010, available at: www.un.org/apps/newsFr/storyF.asp?NewsID=23473#.VGuCE_msV7E.

[37] 'Disharmony' (our translation). Organisation internationale pour les migrations, *In Pursuit of the Southern Dream: Victims of Necessity. Assessment of the irregular movement of men from East Africa and the Horn to South Africa*, April 2009.

[38] See especially J Ríos Rodríguez, 'Le trafic illicite de migrants par voie maritime', in Société française pour le droit international, *L'État dans la mondialisation* (Paris, Pedone, 2013) 371–87, *passim*.

Initially, we do not seek responses from Frontex or other similar systems, but in the overall international standards determining that the EU must respect the law of the sea. The 1982 Montego Bay Convention on the Law of the Sea[39] can serve as a general framework to complete gaps because its Protocol organises cooperation in the prevention and repression under general public international law which includes the law of the sea.[40] It is possible to find an inequality depending on whether the ship concerned has a flag or not, with varying degrees of repression.

In the case of a ship without a flag, there is a real fight against smuggling organised by international standards. In most cases, they are extremely fragile boats and subject to the vagaries of the sea journey. To reach their destination, they often cross the high seas before reaching national maritime space. It is necessary to distinguish the latter from the high seas.

If the ship is on the high seas, the state wishing to act has an initial choice: either to undertake collective action, requesting assistance from other states parties to stop the smuggling in the framework of international cooperation, or to attempt individual action to board the vessel and take 'appropriate measures in accordance with relevant domestic and international law'.[41] Article 8 of the Protocol provides that

> A State Party that has reasonable grounds to suspect that a vessel that is flying its flag or claiming its registry, that is without nationality or that, though flying a foreign flag or refusing to show a flag, is in reality of the nationality of the State Party concerned is engaged in the smuggling of migrants by sea may request the assistance of other States Parties in suppressing the use of the vessel for that purpose. The States Parties so requested shall render such assistance to the extent possible within their means.[42]

This possibility to adopt measures qualified as 'appropriate' without defining them is ambivalent: this stems from the Protocol, but its deliberately vague and imprecise formulation is questionable, because of its ambiguity. What measures are we talking about? Measures of domestic law? Measures of international law? The questions are numerous. The answers, for their part, are not specified in spite of some provisions.[43] There is no relevant international jurisprudence on

[39] United Nations Convention on the Law of the Sea, signed in Montego Bay on 10 December1982.

[40] R Goy, 'Le régime international des migrants illicites par voie de mer' (2002) 7 *Annuaire du droit de la mer* 255.

[41] Art 8.7 states that 'A State Party that has reasonable grounds to suspect that a vessel is engaged in the smuggling of migrants by sea and is without nationality or may be assimilated to a vessel without nationality may board and search the vessel. If evidence confirming the suspicion is found, that State Party shall take appropriate measures in accordance with relevant domestic and international law.' Protocol against the smuggling of migrants by land, sea and air, opcit.

[42] ibid.

[43] See for example Art 9 of the Protocol: '1. Where a State Party takes measures against a vessel in accordance with article 8 of this Protocol, it shall: (a) Ensure the safety and humane treatment of the persons on board; (b) Take due account of the need not to endanger the security of the vessel or its cargo; (c) Take due account of the need not to prejudice the commercial or legal interests of the flag State or any other interested State; (d) Ensure, within available means, that any measure taken with regard to the vessel is environmentally sound. 2. Where the grounds for measures taken pursuant

the matter for now,[44] which seems to give states a margin of interpretation with respect to the text.

While the most severe measure would probably be the use of force, which should be necessary, justified and reasonable,[45] and be preceded by a warning, other measures are more common in international practice. Confiscation of the vessel, together with the arrest of the traffickers, is the main option. However, the Protocol does not provide any guidance on what is to be done next, which raises the fundamental question of jurisdiction of the state to judge: is it competent to judge smugglers that have just been arrested? Or is it necessary to surrender them to their state of nationality? This question arises with particular force in the matter because the state from which the smugglers originate may not be inclined to exercise its jurisdiction, if the difference in living standards between the state of origin and the state of destination of migrants is so large that it promotes tolerance of such practices, regardless of the reprehensible or illegal activities of smugglers during the sea crossing.

The answer seems to be positive and supportive in principle of judgment in the courts of the state which have arrested smugglers on the high seas, but a variety of possible domestic solutions qualify the scope and basis of that competence. For example, it is possible to quote the decision of the Judicial Committee of the British Privy Council in the case of the British ship *Asya*.[46] It was indeed a ship without a flag, arrested on the high seas, with 733 illegal migrants; the British decision stated that the intervention was unlawful because no other state had jurisdiction. So the 'most competent' state, the one which believes it is competent, relies upon the lack of any claim for competency from other states, which could have taken the occasion to repress smuggling.[47]

to article 8 of this Protocol prove to be unfounded, the vessel shall be compensated for any loss or damage that may have been sustained, provided that the vessel has not committed any act justifying the measures taken. 3. Any measure taken, adopted or implemented in accordance with this chapter shall take due account of the need not to interfere with or to affect: (a) The rights and obligations and the exercise of jurisdiction of coastal States in accordance with the international law of the sea; or (b) The authority of the flag State to exercise jurisdiction and control in administrative, technical and social matters involving the vessel. 4. Any measure taken at sea pursuant to this chapter shall be carried out only by warships or military aircraft, or by other ships or aircraft clearly marked and identifiable as being on government service and authorized to that effect'.

[44] According to Philippe Gautier, Greffier du TIDM, it can be explained by 'infrequency of the use of judicial remedies in disputes relating to such materials'. P Gautier, 'Le rôle du Tribunal international du droit de la mer face à la violence en mer', in JM Sobrino Heredia (ed), *Sûreté maritime et violence en mer. Maritime security and violence at sea* (Bruxelles, Bruylant, collection de droit international, 2011) 483.

[45] R Goy, op cit, p 273.

[46] *Naim Molvan v Attorney General for Palestine (The 'Asya')* (1948) 81 Ll L Rep 277, United Kingdom Privy Council (Judicial Committee).

[47] ibid.

The same goes for the judgment of the Tribunale di Crotone of 27 September 2001 in the *Cemil Pamuk* case concerning a ship without a flag, arrested on the high seas, where the Italian Court confirmed its jurisdiction.[48] In contrast, however, a third illustration, from Spain, is rather paradoxical or surprising.[49] At stake here were three court orders of the Audiencia Provincial de Las Palmas, which, in 2006, refused Spanish competence regarding prisoners on the high seas and migrant smugglers because of the 'extraterritoriality' of the high seas, and this without even making an explicit reference to the Protocol: this is nothing less than 'non-recognition of extraterritoriality'.[50] This ruling absolutely disregards the Protocol against the Smuggling of Migrants, and furthermore does not seem to take into account the existence of rules outside the domestic territory. This ruling was later quashed by the Spanish Supreme Court,[51] although the latter rulings were not directly based on the Protocol but on the universal jurisdiction in force at the time for Spanish courts.[52] The Court could have founded its ruling more directly on the Protocol, an international treaty signed and ratified by Spain. This is just one example of domestic differences of opinion[53] that may distort the Protocol, or at least make its application less smooth.

If what has been discussed so far mainly concerns the high seas, ships without a flag engaged in human smuggling may also be found in national maritime waters. The issue of competence to act is then quickly resolved. In this case, the right of innocent passage through the territorial sea of the coastal state does not exist, because we cannot speak of an 'innocent' character when the ship does not announce its nationality: the absence of identification is itself a threat. The state must then take the necessary steps and intercept the boat when it is close to its coast.[54] In any case, and this is a new and important conventional gap, the Protocol is silent on the fate of ships and migrant victims after interception, which can facilitate the application of very different national measures according to the case.

[48] *Pamuk et al* (Tribunale di Crotone, 27 September 2001) [2001] *Rivista di Diritto Internazionale* 1155.

[49] About Art 318 bis of the Spanish penal code and its relations with internation texts, see eg MJ Guardiola Lago, op cit, pp 428–31.

[50] A del Valle-Gálvez, 'Mesures nationales sur le trafic illégal de personnes et la criminalité transnationale organisée', in J M Sobrino Heredia (ed), op cit, p 28.

[51] Tribunal Supremo, judgments 788/2007 (8 August 2007), and 1121/2008 (11 January 2008).

[52] J Ríos Rodríguez, 'La restriction de la compétence universelle des juridictions nationales: les exemples belge et espagnol', (2010) 114(3) *Revue générale de droit international public* 563–95.

[53] V Muntarbhorn, 'Combating Migrant Smuggling and Trafficking in Persons, especially Women: the normative Framework re-appraised', in TA Aleinikoff and V Chetail (eds), *Migration and international legal norms* (The Hague, TMC Asser Press, 2003)164.

[54] On interception at sea, see O Barsalou, 'L'interception des réfugiés en mer: un régime juridique aux confins de la normativité' (2008) 12(3) *Lex Electronica* 25.

IV. MARITIME MIGRANTS PROTECTION: SHIPS WITH A FLAG[55]

Whether on the high seas or in national maritime space, what if the ship has a flag? This is less of an EU issue, the EU generally being concerned with cases dealing with makeshift boats. The principle of exclusive jurisdiction of the flag state is prevalent, although a distinction can still be made according to the maritime area in question.

If the maritime space is not subject to the sovereignty of a state, the principle of exclusive jurisdiction of the flag state rules the case[56] as Article 8 shows. For example, if a state other than that of the flag has 'reasonable grounds' to suspect a case of smuggling of migrants, it must notify the flag state, and it may possibly take 'appropriate' measures, which indicates, once again, a vagueness:

> A State Party that has reasonable grounds to suspect that a vessel exercising freedom of navigation in accordance with international law and flying the flag or displaying the marks of registry of another State Party is engaged in the smuggling of migrants by sea may so notify the flag State, request confirmation of registry and, if confirmed, request authorization from the flag State to take appropriate measures with regard to that vessel.[57]

This principle depends on the will of the state to exercise its powers, and limits the possibilities of action of other states according to the action or inaction of the flag state.

Are these measures of national law or international law? Are they bilateral agreements between the state of origin and the state of destination of the migrants? In this context, naval patrols monitoring the coastline of the Mediterranean can be found acting in operations whose indefiniteness is permitted by the ambiguity of the Protocol. Bilateral agreements proliferate in this vague framework, for example, the US–Haiti exchange of notes of 1981,[58] the most recent 1997 Protocol between Italy and Albania,[59] or the much-criticised Italy–Libya agreement of 2007.[60] In other words, the collaboration of EU member states with non-member

[55] See especially J Ríos Rodríguez, 'Le trafic illicite de migrants par voie maritime', in Société française pour le droit international, *L'État dans la mondialisation* (Paris, Pedone, 2013) 371–87, *passim*.

[56] In an excessive way, as is emphasised by Rafael Casado Raigón. See R Casado Raigón, 'Trafic illicite des personnes et criminalité transnationale organisée', in JM Sobrino Heredia (ed), op cit, p 18.

[57] V Protocol against the smuggling of migrants by land, sea and air, op cit.

[58] See on this topic Inter-American Commission on Human Rights, Decision of the Commission as to the merits of case 10.675, United States 13 March 1997.

[59] See the Agreement of 18 November 1997 between Italia and Albania on seasonal workers. In the 1990s Italy also concluded readmission agreements with states including Albania, Macedonia, Romania, Croatia, Morocco, Tunisia and Algeria.

[60] See the Protocolli di collaborazione in materia migratoria, between Italya and Libya on 29 December 2007, as well as the Protocole Aggiuntivo tecnico-operativo. See also the Trattato di amicizia, partenariato e cooperazione tra la Repubblica italiana e la grande Giamahiria araba libica popolare socialista, signed between Italy and Libya on 29 Decembre 2007. See esp Art 19 which states that: '2. Sempre in tema di lotta all'immigrazione clandestina, le due Partì promuovono la realizzazione di un sistema di controllo delle frontiere terrestri libiche, da affidare a società italiane in possesso delle necessarie competenze tecnologiche. Il Governo italiano sosterrà il 50% dei costi,

states is sometimes involved, a collaboration which may even violate international standards.

The Protocol against smuggling includes an obligation to reply to a request for authorisation. This raises the question of the possibility of an implicit authorisation in the case of silence of the flag state, which again remains unanswered. Article 8.4 of the Protocol provides that

> A State Party shall respond expeditiously to a request from another State Party to determine whether a vessel that is claiming its registry or flying its flag is entitled to do so and to a request for authorisation made in accordance with paragraph 2 of this article.[61]

Implicit authorisation would seem to be contrary to the principle of exclusive jurisdiction of that state which manages most of the provisions. If we look at the Convention on the Law of the Sea, to which the Protocol refers in general, it is possible to clearly identify texts that inspired the latter in the fight against illicit trafficking, including the 1995 Agreement on illicit drug smuggling at sea: 'No such actions may be taken by virtue of this Agreement, without the authorisation of the flag State.'[62]

If these different aspects show an inequality according to the maritime space in question and the vessel concerned in the repression of smuggling of migrants, there is also a clear inequality between several offences under international conventions. Indeed, there is nothing on the right to seize the ship, nor on the trying of smugglers, while these possibilities are stated in the Convention of Montego Bay in the case of ships engaged in piracy.[63] In addition, the Convention on the Law of the Sea provides that in the case of the slave trade, visits and release rights

mentre per il restante 50% le due Parti chiederanno all'Unione Europea di farsene carico, tenuto conto delle Intese a suo tempo intervenute tra la Grande Giamahiria e la 'Commissione Europea. 3. Le due Parti collaborano alla definizione di iniziative, sia bilaterali, sia in ambito regionale, per prevenire il fenomeno dell'immigrazione clandestina nei Paesi di origine dei flussi migratori' ['2. Still on the topic of illegal migration, both parties encouraged the realisation of a control system of the Lybian border. Italian firms with required technological capabilities will be in charge of this. The Italian government will support 50% of the cost while for the 50% remaining, both parties request the UE to support them, taking into account the intepretations of the Lybian arab and of the European Comission 3. Both parties will collaborate to establish initiatives at the bilateral and regional level to prevent illegal migration in the countries of origins of the migration flows', our translation].

[61] Protocol against the smuggling of migrants by land, sea and air, op cit.

[62] See Art 6 of the Agreement on Illicit Traffic by Sea, implementing Art 17 of the United Nations Convention against Illicit Traffic in Narcotic Drugs and Psychotropic Substances, Strasbourg, 31 January 1995.

[63] Art 105 of the Montego Bay Convention is about the seizure of a pirate ship or aircraft, and states that: 'every State may seize a pirate ship or aircraft, or a ship or aircraft taken by piracy and under the control of pirates, and arrest the persons and seize the property on board. The courts of the State which carried out the seizure may decide upon the penalties to be imposed, and may also determine the action to be taken with regard to the ships, aircraft or property, subject to the rights of third parties acting in good faith'. The article is to be read with another, Art 106, to avoid arbitrary seizure: 'Where the seizure of a ship or aircraft on suspicion of piracy has been effected without adequate grounds, the State making the seizure shall be liable to the State the nationality of which is possessed by the ship or aircraft for any loss or damage caused by the seizure'. Montego Bay Convention, op cit.

exist even when it is a ship with flag.[64] Piracy and trafficking therefore benefit from a settlement allowing a better enforcement of the respective offences.

Moreover, and always on the high seas, the question of the right of self-protection also arises: can a state exercise this right to avoid the massive influx of migrants on its territory, and thus preserve its sovereignty? Some Anglo-Saxon states have claimed it unilaterally.[65] However, it seems difficult to recognise the validity of such a claim under international law. The matter was considered by the International Law Commission in 1956 at its eighth session, and taken away from the Geneva Convention of 1958.[66] In this regard, it is worth mentioning the judgment of the ECtHR of 23 February 2012, *Hirsi Jamaa and others v Italy*, in which the Court recalled that the principle of non-refoulement is applicable even extraterritorially, that is to say, on the high seas. The ECtHR asserts the principle of non-refoulement further to an interception on the high seas. The judgment quotes specifically from several texts and statements; a note by the UN High Commissioner for Refugees stating the items at stake, defining it as 'a cardinal protection principle enshrined in the Convention, to which no reservations are permitted',[67] and asserts that

> The International Law of Human Rights established the non-refoulement as a fundamental element of the absolute prohibition of torture and cruel, inhuman or degrading treatment. The obligation not to return is also recognised as applying to refugees regardless of their official recognition, which clearly includes asylum seekers whose status has not yet been determined … This includes the rejection border interception and indirect refoulement, whether an individual seeking asylum or a mass influx.

It has come to be considered a rule of customary international law binding on all states. In addition, international human rights law has established non-refoulement as a fundamental component of the absolute prohibition of torture and cruel, inhuman or degrading treatment or punishment. The duty not to refoule is also recognised as applying to refugees irrespective of their formal recognition, thus obviously including asylum-seekers whose status has not yet been determined. It encompasses any measure attributable to a state which could have the effect of returning an asylum-seeker or refugee to the frontiers of territories where his or her life or freedom would be threatened, or where he or she would risk persecution. This includes rejection at the frontier, interception and indirect refoulement, whether of an individual seeking asylum or in situations of mass influx.'[68]

[64] Art 110 of the Montego Bay Convention also states that 'Except where acts of interference derive from powers conferred by treaty, a warship which encounters on the high seas a foreign ship, other than a ship entitled to complete immunity in accordance with articles 95 and 96, is not justified in boarding it unless there is reasonable ground for suspecting that: (a) the ship is engaged in piracy; (b) the ship is engaged in the slave trade'.

[65] As for example the United States in 1981.

[66] Convention sur la haute mer, signed in Geneva, 29 April 1958.

[67] *Hirsi Jamma and Others v Italy* (ECtHR, 23 February 2012).

[68] ibid.

Above all, the ECtHR considers in this recent decision the various consecrations of this principle, to conclude that:

> Under the European Convention, a refugee cannot be subjected to *refoulement* to his or her country of origin or any other country where he or she risks incurring serious harm caused by any identified or unidentified person or public or private entity. The act of *refoulement* may consist in expulsion, extradition, deportation, removal, informal transfer, 'rendition', rejection, refusal of admission or any other measure which would result in compelling the person to remain in the country of origin. The risk of serious harm may result from foreign aggression, internal armed conflict, extrajudicial death, enforced disappearance, death penalty, torture, inhuman or degrading treatment, forced labour, trafficking in human beings, persecution, trial based on a retroactive penal law or on evidence obtained by torture or inhuman and degrading treatment, or a 'flagrant violation' of the essence of any Convention right in the receiving State (direct *refoulement*) or from further delivery of that person by the receiving State to a third State where there is such a risk (indirect *refoulement*).[69]

Moreover, critical to smuggling by sea and the possibily of state action, it also states: 'the procedural guarantee of individual evaluation of asylum claims and the ensuing prohibition of collective expulsion are not limited to the land and maritime territory of a State but also apply on the high seas.'[70]

If however it is national maritime space, whether territorial sea, inland waters or ports of a state, the question concerns the right of innocent passage of a ship with a flag suspected of being engaged in smuggling. The qualification of the passage as harmless or not is a decision made unilaterally by the coastal state. It will not be an innocent passage if there is a risk of threat or violation of law. Can one, however, take action without the consent of the flag state? The Protocol is not clear about this. It may seem difficult to adopt these measures unless we consider the possible adverse effects of this passage, or except when the ship leaves internal waters.[71] Regarding the port, the coastal state has a larger freedom: it may modulate access and closures, or direct boarded ships to the port, as Italy did in the affairs of and of *Cemil Pamuk*,[72] in the port of Crotone.

As can be seen when examining these many questions, inequalities, gaps and silences, the object of protection established directly by the Protocol is basically the sovereignty of states, while in this offence there is a main victim, the migrant.

[69] ibid.

[70] ibid.

[71] It is the right to pursue; see PA Fernández Sánchez, 'Tráfico ilegal de personas y cooperación marítima internacional', in JA Pueyo Losa and JJ Urbina (eds), *La cooperación internacional en la ordenación de los mares y océanos*, vol 1 (Madrid, Iustel, 2009) 384.

[72] *Pamuk et al* (Tribunale di Crotone, 27 September 2001).

V. PRACTICAL INEFFECTIVENESS OF VICTIM PROTECTION[73]

Some international courts have had the opportunity to further clarify the obligation of prevention when states do not comply with their conventional obligations.

Notably, the leading ECtHR judgment in the matter is the case of *Rantsev v Cyprus and Russia.*[74] In this case, according to the Court, Cypriot and Russian authorities failed to protect the victim, while they had evidence to assume that she was the object of trafficking. This was a violation by Cyprus of Article 2 of the European Convention on the right to life, for lack of effective investigation, and of Article 4 concerning the prohibition of slavery and forced labour, and by both Cyprus and Russia of Article 5 on the right to liberty and security of person.

The ECtHR considers this case a breach of the positive obligations of states, a failure of both protection and prevention. It thus links these two aspects, which only emphasises the problem raised when there is a gap between one and the other. As is pointed out,

> finally, the Court reiterates that its judgments serve not only to decide those cases brought before it but, more generally, to elucidate, safeguard and develop the rules instituted by the Convention, thereby contributing to the observance by the States of the engagements undertaken by them as Contracting Parties.[75]

The ECtHR thus relieves the states of the obligation to investigate the authors and terms of smuggling and trafficking activities. It is an obligation to act, a priori and a posteriori, preventive and repressive, which demonstrates the need for effective investigations, already stated in other previous judgments.[76] The judgment is based on Article 4 of the European Convention:

> In order for a positive obligation to take operational measures to arise in the circumstances of a particular case, it must be demonstrated that the State authorities were aware, or ought to have been aware, of circumstances giving rise to a credible suspicion that an identified individual had been, or was at real and immediate risk of being, trafficked or exploited within the meaning of Article 3(a) of the Palermo Protocol and Article 4(a) of the Anti-Trafficking Convention. In the case of an answer in the affirmative, there will be a violation of Article 4 of the Convention where the authorities fail to take appropriate measures within the scope of their powers to remove the individual from that situation or risk.[77]

It emphasises at the same time the obligation to set up an appropriate legislative and administrative framework, to take protective measures and to investigate the potential offence.

[73] See especially J Ríos Rodríguez, 'La lutte contre la traite et le trafic illicite de migrants: de la prévention des infractions à la protection des victimes', in C-A Chassin (ed), *Migrations contraintes* (Paris, Pedone, 2014) 163–77.

[74] *Rantsev v Cyprus and Russia* (ECtHR, 7 January 2010).

[75] ibid.

[76] *Kaya v Turkey* (ECtHR, 19 February 1998), § 107, and *Ergi v Turkey* (ECtHR, 28 July1998), § 82.

[77] *Rantsev v Cyprus and Russia* (ECtHR, 7 January 2010).

The question is otherwise outside the European area, either the EU or the Council of Europe. Other regional areas are less integrated, but do provide interesting and sometimes convergent examples. A judgment of the Court of Justice of ECOWAS on 27 October 2008 in the case *Hadijatou Mani Koraou v Niger* also qualified the 'responsibility for inaction' of that state, which had not done enough to prevent slavery suffered by the victim. Thus, the Court asserted that

> '[a]ttendu que la Cour relève que la République du Niger n'a pas suffisamment protégé les droits de la requérante contre la pratique de l'esclavage … Dit que dame Hadijatou Mani Koraou a été victime d'esclavage et que la République du Niger en est responsable par l'inaction de ses autorités administratives et judiciaires.[78]

According to the Court, the State is responsible for having failed to protect the victim, both from an administrative and judicial point of view: 'la situation d' esclave de la requérante, même si elle émane d'un particulier agissant dans un contexte prétendument coutumier ou individuel, lui ouvrait droit à une protection par les autorités de la République du Niger, qu'elles soient administratives ou judiciaires'.[79]

The application of the judgment by the states has not yet been successful, starting with the lack of definition of prevention, continuing with the non-application of treaty provisions in some cases, thereby producing failures in the protection of victims. The problem is complexified by internal difficulties. Some states do not differentiate between trafficking and smuggling offences. For example, Articles 318bis and 313 of the Spanish Penal Code[80] on the topic remain partial and confused. While these crimes have common points, not recognising their specificity can mean ignoring the international instruments that criminalise them and can cause problems with international coordination, the sentencing of concurrent offences, as well as a lack of general harmonisation, all of which only highlight the confusion of the objectives pursued.

[78] 'Considering that the Court notes that the Republic of Niger has not adequately protected the rights of the applicant against the practice of slavery. 4. As this situation of slavery caused her some physical, psychological and moral harms. 5. As the applicant is therefore entitled to a lump sum for restorative damages resulting from slavery … Says that lady Hadijatou Mani Koraou was the victim of slavery and the Republic of Niger is responsible for the inaction of its administrative and judicial authorities.' Cour de Justice de la CEDEAO, *Dame Hadijatou Mani Koraou c. la République du Niger*, ECW/CCJ/JUD/06/08, 27 October 2008. Translation by the author.

[79] 'The Court further considers that the applicant slave situation, even if it emanates from an individual acting in a supposedly customary or individual context, entitled her to protection by the authorities of the Republic of Niger, whether administrative or judicial. Consequently, the defendant is responsible both in internationaland domestic laws of any form of violation of human rights of the applicant based on slavery because of its tolerance, passivity, inaction and its abstention to deal with this practice'. Ibid.

[80] These two articles are currently being revised, but the project does not mention a distinction between the two offences. On Art 318 bis of the Spanish Penal Code and its relation with international texts, see for instance MJ Guardiola Lago, 'La traite des êtres humains et l'immigration clandestine en Espagne: réfléchissent-elles les prévisions des Nations Unies et de l'Union Européenne?' [2008] 79(3–4) *Revue internationale de droit pénal: bulletin de l'Association Internationale de Droit Pénal* 428–31.

If a partial or inadequate implementation prompts criticism, according to the US Trafficking in Persons Report (Department of State, 2014) quoted above, other states simply do not meet international standards.[81] In this repect, the report highlights Syria, the Czech Republic, Greece, Kosovo and Russia. However, among those on the list of complying states, judgments exist such as that in the case of *CN and V v France*,[82] condemning France for domestic slavery, servitude and forced labour as specific offences related to trafficking but, according to the Court, distinct and less severe. Servitude appeared as a particular type of exploitation in the UN Protocol, constituting a possible element of trafficking: in all servitude there is a service provided, the fact of living in the property of others and especially the impression that the status is immutable, helps distinguish it from forced labour and makes it worse.

The ECtHR has also found a breach of positive obligations by France, which has not set up an appropriate legislative and administrative framework for the fight against slavery and forced labour, in violation of Article 4 of the European Convention, which States: '1. No one shall be held in slavery or servitude. 2. No one shall be required to perform forced or compulsory labour.'[83] These obligations are to investigate effectively, and to criminalise and effectively penalise acts covered by Article 4. This second requirement was not respected by France[84] despite changes in its legislative framework in 2003 especially during the revision of several articles of the Penal Code.[85]

The gap between the prevention of illegal activities and the protection of victims thus promotes the unequal, partial and faulty application by states, including those who are otherwise shown to be consistent with international standards.[86] Examples are numerous and can be subject to particular studies. Obviously, it is up to the domestic courts of states to act in the first place and to apply international instruments where possible. However, it follows from an analysis of the current situation that too few cases reach court, most falling into a kind of oblivion or no man's land from which they never reappear.

[81] US Department of State, *Trafficking in Persons Report 2012*, available at: www.State.gov/j/tip/rls/tiprpt/2012.

[82] *CN and V v France* (ECtHR, 11 October 2012). See also A-K Diop, 'CEDH, esclavage domestique: Malgré l'adaptation de sa législation après l'arrêt Siliadin, la France une nouvelle fois condamnée dans l'affaire, CN et V c/France (requête n° 67724/09)', *Sentinelle*, n° 322, 4 November 2012.

[83] Convention européenne de sauvegarde des droits de l'homme et des libertés fondamentales, signed in Rome on 4 November 1950.

[84] France has already been condemned before in a similar situation. See *Siliadin v France* (ECtHR, 26 July 2005), and P Weckel, 'Cour européenne des droits de l'homme Arrêt du 26 juillet 2005 Siliadin contre France', *Sentinelle*, n° 30, 28 August 2005.

[85] This despite older and rather symbolic instruments like the Act ('Loi') 2001–434, 21 May 2001, which tends to recognise trafficking and slavery as a crime against humanity, *JORF*, 23 May 2001

[86] On a peculiar origin of immigration, see for instance OIT, Bureau international du travail, *Le trafic et l'exploitation des immigrants chinois en France*, report from G Yun and V Poisson (Geneva, 2005).

VI. CONCLUSION

Protection of the rights of migrants against abuse is therefore based not only on specific texts combatting against smuggling or trafficking, but also on the obligations *erga omnes* of states, articulated in a set of shared responsibilities. Members of the EU or the Council of Europe are bound by special obligations under regional law, but the general international law is not less binding, despite a less-developed capacity to implement the rules. Such rights must be reconciled with the desire of states to preserve the integrity of their borders, including the borders of the Union. Conciliation between human rights and security concerns is possible; it is, however, necessary that the second, no doubt legitimate, goal is not achieved at the expense of the necessary priority of protection of the human person.

In conclusion, there is an imbalance in the fight against the phenomenon of trafficking and smuggling. The presence of constraint seems clear in cases mentioned, as it is a form of migration in which the migrant suffers the imposition of the perpetrators' external will at different times. This fight is undoubtedly better organised, from a general point of view, than it was 15 years ago. However, the legal framework has shortcomings that the role of the courts cannot rectify. The courts can, at best, highlight the problems and correct them, but it is the states' responsibility to manage the prevention of these crimes and the protection of victims. This means improving the international and European legal framework, effectively implementing it and supplementing it with more material but effective operations, ranging from blocking payments and electronic transactions, a pragmatic use of new technologies, efforts in suppression of such activity, field checks and specifically the apprehension of criminals responsible for trafficking and smuggling.[87]

Indeed, effective combat against such crimes requires a real willingness of states to properly implement the international instruments at their disposal, even beyond the reform of the general system. This could lead to the possible improvement of international instruments or to a review of domestic law to progressively and explicitly incorporate the positive obligations stemming from international jurisprudence.

[87] See F Raach, 'Le HCR réitère son appel réclamant l'arrestation des trafiquants d'êtres humains qui opèrent depuis la Somalie', *Sentinelle*, n° 51, 29 January 2006.

V

Circumstantial Vulnerability

18

The Effective Supervision of European Prison Conditions

STEVE FOSTER

I. INTRODUCTION

INCARCERATED PRISONERS ARE particularly vulnerable to violation of their basic rights and human dignity.[1] Despite their detention being within the law, there may be a general reluctance on behalf of the state and the general public to offer them conditions which appropriately care for their health and well-being. This reluctance may stem from the general idea that prison conditions should be inevitably harsh, as part of their punishment, and is further defended by financial and resource arguments. Such detainees are, therefore, placed in an invidious and vulnerable position, often subjected to unsatisfactory, and sometimes, unlawful conditions, which fail to meet necessary standards with respect to matters such as accommodation, food, health care and recreation, together with more specific concerns such as the effect of solitary confinement on prisoners' mental and physical welfare.

Despite a plethora of international and regional instruments pertaining to basic prison conditions, the effective challenge to inhuman and degrading conditions in European prisons has been inconsistent and limited. In addition to the possibility of direct legal challenge via Article 3 of the European Convention—before the European Court of Human Rights or at the domestic level—there are regulatory schemes, such as the European Prison Rules (2006)—which lay down basic standards applicable to the confinement of both general and specific category prisoners. These can be augmented by monitoring processes carried out by agencies such as the European Committee for the Prevention of Torture (CPT), which not only allow for visits to and reports on places of detention, but which can also inform the decisions of European and domestic courts.

Each process, of course, has its limitations. The judicial method can only deal with cases that are brought before it and provide remedies to the applicants as victims; its role on standard-setting and education is thus restrictive. On the other

[1] S Foster, 'Automatic Forfeiture of Prisoners' Rights' (2007) 16(1) *Nottingham Law Journal* 1.

hand, European rules and monitoring processes are not, at least directly, legally binding, and are considered by the judicial bodies to a limited degree. A recent EU initiative in this area—the Commission's 2011 Green Paper on strengthening mutual trust in the European judicial area[2]—does at least provide a higher public profile to the problem, and it is hoped that this will encourage reforms at the domestic level as well as greater supervision at the European level.

II. PRISON CONDITIONS AND INTERNATIONAL HUMAN RIGHTS LAW

A primary objective of international human rights law is to prohibit the state's use of torture and other ill-treatment of human beings. This is expressed in absolute terms in Article 5 of the Universal Declaration of Human Rights 1948 and Article 3 of the European Convention for the Protection of Human Rights and Fundamental Freedoms (1950): 'No one shall be subject to torture or to cruel, inhuman or degrading treatment or punishment.'

Although these provisions are not expressly related to the treatment of prisoners, those in detention are particularly vulnerable to mistreatment and substandard and unacceptable conditions. Accordingly, a variety of international treaties and instruments are dedicated to imposing acceptable standards of treatment on those responsible for detaining individuals. For example, in addition to Article 7 of the International Covenant on Civil and Political Rights 1966, which repeats the general prohibition against torture and inhuman and degrading treatment and punishment, Article 10 makes specific reference to prisoners and declares that all persons deprived of their liberty shall be treated with humanity and with respect for the inherent dignity of the human person.[3]

There are a number of treaties and other international and instruments, together with monitoring bodies, established to set and enforce standards with respect to the treatment of prisoners.[4] However, these Rules are not intended to be directly and judicially enforceable, and have limited authority with respect to the case law of judicial agencies such as the European Court of Human Rights.[5] Nevertheless, the establishment of international bodies responsible for preventing ill-treatment in detention can inform the judicial challenge to unlawful prison conditions. Instruments such as the UN Convention against Torture and other Cruel, Inhuman or Degrading Treatment or Punishment 1984 (CAT) and the

[2] EU Commission, Green Paper on the application of EU criminal justice legislation in the field of detention Brussels COM (2011) 327 final.

[3] See S Joseph and M Castan, *The International Covenant on Civil and Political Rights: cases, materials and commentary*, 3rd edn (Oxford, OUP, 2013).

[4] N Rodley and M Pollard, *The Treatment of Prisoners in International Law*, 3rd edn (Oxford, Clarendon Press, 2009). Both the UN and the Council of Europe have passed Prison Rules establishing the minimum standards of the detention of prisoners (UN Standard Minimum Rules for the Treatment of Prisoners (1955), including the Basic Principles for the Treatment of Prisoners (1990), and the European Prison Rules 2006).

[5] S Livingstone, T Owen and A Macdonald, *Prison Law*, 4th edn (Oxford, OUP, 2008) 168.

European Convention for the Prevention of Torture and Inhuman or Degrading Treatment or Punishment 1987 (ECPT) establish Committees to monitor the prohibition of torture in member states. More importantly the ECPT establishes an independent Committee for the Prevention of Torture (CPT) which has the power to make visits to places of detention in each member state and to submit reports of those visits, reporting on any violation of Article 3 and the principles contained in the Torture Convention.[6] Although such reports are not strictly enforceable on the member state, they can inform domestic practice and have been used by judicial bodies such as the European Court of Human Rights to inform its jurisprudence in cases where prison conditions and practices are challenged under Article 3 of the European Convention on Human Rights.[7]

The *judicial* enforcement of acceptable prison conditions in line with internationally accepted standards faces a number of difficulties. First, the fact of lawful imprisonment itself might lead to a re-evaluation of the standards expected in prisons and the acceptability of certain practices such as social isolation, which outside the context of imprisonment might be regarded as inhuman and degrading. Secondly, and related to the first issue, judicial bodies might take into consideration the dangerousness of the offender and the need to guarantee prison order and public safety in assessing whether international standards have been violated. These factors may well compromise the absolute character of provisions such as Article 3 of the European Convention, and lead to the approval of conditions and practices which are inconsistent with the state's duty to treat individuals with due respect and dignity.[8] Thirdly, as acceptable and decent prison conditions depend essentially on economic resources as well as the willingness of the state institutions to abide by international human rights standards, judges may be reluctant to challenge conditions that are claimed to be in breach of those standards. These difficulties might lead to a conservative approach being adopted by the courts, whereby they will only intervene if the mistreatment of the prisoner is deliberate. It is with respect to the above difficulties that this chapter will now seek to analyse the jurisprudence of the European Court of Human Rights with respect to challenges of prison conditions and practices by, largely, lawfully incarcerated detainees.

As we shall see, effective judicial challenge to inhuman and degrading conditions in European prisons has been inconsistent and limited. Further, regulatory schemes, such as the European Prison Rules which lay down basic standards applicable to the confinement of both general and specific category prisoners, and augmented by monitoring processes carried out by agencies such as the European Committee for the Prevention of Torture (CPT), which not only allow for visits to and reports on places of detention, but which can also inform the decisions of

[6] R Morgan and M Evans, *Preventing Torture* (Oxford, OUP, 1998).

[7] J Murdoch, 'The impact of the Council of Europe's "Torture Committee" and the evolution of standard-setting in relation to places of detention' [2006] *European Human Rights Law Review* 159.

[8] S Palmer, 'A Wrong Turning: Article 3 ECHR and Proportionality' (2006) *Cambridge Law Journal* 438.

European and domestic courts, each have their limitations. The judicial method can only deal with cases that are brought before it and provide remedies to the applicants as victims; its role on standard-setting and education is, thus restrictive. On the other hand, European rules and monitoring processes are not, directly at least, legally binding, and are considered by the judicial bodies to a limited degree.

A recent EU initiative in this area—the European Commission's 2011 Green Paper on strengthening mutual trust in the European judicial area[9]—addresses both the effectiveness of the current processes for monitoring conditions of detention and the need for greater cooperation between those processes and greater dialogue between various states in this area. In this respect the initiative does, at the very least, provide a higher public profile to the issue of prison conditions, hopefully encouraging reforms at the domestic level as well as a more robust supervision at the European level, including from the European Court of Human Rights.

III. ARTICLE 3 OF THE EUROPEAN CONVENTION: THE WORK OF THE EUROPEAN COURT OF HUMAN RIGHTS

Article 3 of the European Convention, prohibiting torture and inhuman or degrading treatment or punishment, has enormous potential in challenging all aspects of detention.[10] In addition to its relevance to challenging general conditions of imprisonment, Article 3 can also be employed in respect of sentencing,[11] forced medical treatment,[12] and solitary confinement.[13] Traditionally, the European Court and Commission of Human Rights took a cautious approach in determining challenges to general prison conditions, and were reluctant to find states in violation of Article 3.[14] For example, in *B v United Kingdom*,[15] the European Commission held that although the conditions at the institution were 'unsatisfactory'—the applicant had been detained at Broadmoor for three and a half years at a time when there was evidence of serious overcrowding and poor facilities—they did not constitute a violation of Article 3.[16]

The reasons for this initial approach were both pragmatic and diplomatic, and are also relevant to both political initiatives such as the one contained in the

[9] EU Commission, Green Paper on the application of EU criminal justice legislation in the field of detention Brussels COM (2011) 327 final.

[10] For a comprehensive analysis of the terms employed in Art 3, see J Cooper, *Cruelty—An Analysis of Article 3* (London, Sweet & Maxwell, 2003), ch 3.

[11] *V and T v United Kingdom* (2000) 30 EHRR 121.

[12] *X v FRG* (1985) 7 EHRR 152.

[13] *X v United Kingdom* 21 DR 95.

[14] See B Dickson, *Human Rights and the European Convention* (London, Sweet and Maxwell, 1997), ch 3. See, for example, *Reed v United Kingdom* 19 DR 113.

[15] *B v United Kingdom* (1983) 5 EHRR 114.

[16] See also *Hilton v United Kingdom* (1981) 3 EHRR 104; *T v United Kingdom* 28 DR 5; *McFeeley v United Kingdom* (1981) 3 EHRR 161.

recent EU Green Paper, and the continued reluctance of the European Court to establish clear rules on many aspects of prison conditions. Thus, judicial bodies are in general reluctant to interfere with prison managerial decisions, particularly where any decision might affect the allocation of resources. This reluctance was heightened by the desire of the European Court and Commission to respect the member state's autonomy in respect to its own penal policy. In addition, in the absence of strict legal guidelines and standards with respect to prison conditions, the Commission and Court were wary of setting standards in this area, preferring to interfere only when there was evidence of systematic and deliberate ill treatment, and to leave standard setting either to the domestic authorities or other international or regional regulations, such as the European Prison Rules.[17]

Judicial regulation is still, however, beset by these difficulties and the limitations of judicial regulation. In particular, the European Court of Human Rights must be satisfied that a prisoner's treatment is serious enough to constitute a breach of the terms employed in Article 3.[18] Thus, it will have to distinguish treatment or conditions that are part and parcel of the harshness of incarceration from treatment or conditions which impose an unacceptable detriment on the detainee so as to constitute a violation.[19] This question will be one of degree and the Court will need to examine a variety of factors, some of which are not specific to the particular case and applicant's suffering, but which allow the Court to regard certain treatment and conditions as at least prima facie acceptable because they achieve certain penological benefits, and are adopted commonly among all member states. Thus, although, Article 3 is recognised as an absolute right, admitting of no exceptions or justifications, it is clear that not all forms of ill-treatment will be in violation of its provisions. Further, although any possible social or other benefits deriving from such treatment will not excuse treatment that falls within such terms, it is clear that in deciding whether the threshold under Article 3 has been met, the Court can take into account whether the treatment complained of is part and parcel of a necessary and civilised social order. Thus, although arrest, detention, and imprisonment may degrade a person, they are regarded as acceptable under the Convention. Equally, in deciding whether the circumstances of such actions cross the necessary threshold, the Court can take into account factors such as the victim's age and dangerousness.[20] This latitude allows the Court to impose a

[17] The European Prison Rules (2006), a product of the Council of Europe, and the UN Standard Minimum Rules (1955), which lay down guidance with respect to the treatment of prisoners and other detainees on matters such as general conditions, segregation, medical treatment and recreation.

[18] The definitions of the individual terms employed in Art 3 were explored in *Ireland v United Kingdom* (1978) 2 EHRR 25: inhuman treatment was that which was capable of causing if not bodily injury, at least intense physical and mental suffering and acute psychiatric disturbances, whilst degrading treatment was such as to arouse in their victims feelings of fear, anguish and inferiority capable of humiliating them and possibly taking away their physical or moral resistance (ibid, paras 167–68).

[19] See *Valasinas v Lithuania* App no 44558/98 (ECtHR, 24 July 2001), 12 BHRC 266.

[20] For example, in relation to the compatibility of handcuffing of prisoners: see *Ranimen v Finland* (1996) 26 EHRR 583.

margin of discretion, and although such a mechanism is inappropriate once the necessary threshold has been met under Article 3, such discretion is relevant in shaping the boundaries of acceptable treatment and, in this context, lawful and unlawful prison conditions.[21]

These factors are important in assessing both the limitations and effectiveness of the European Court's jurisprudence in this area, despite the important dicta of the Court in *Selmouni v France*,[22] where it took the view that the increasingly high standard being required in the area of human rights correspondingly required a greater firmness in assessing breaches of the fundamental values of democratic societies, and that certain acts which in the past were classified as inhuman and degrading treatment, as opposed to torture, could be classified differently in the future.[23] This dictum might mean that the Court could now consider conditions of detention, formerly considered unacceptable but without constituting inhuman or degrading, as being in violation of Article 3; although this potential is always circumscribed by the Court's reluctance to set specific standards or to question general penal policy.

Before examining the more positive approach taken by the European Court in this area, it is worth reiterating two factors which militate against the full protection of detainees' rights. First, it has been generally accepted that it is permissible to consider the dangerousness of the prisoner and issues of public and prison safety in determining whether the conditions were contrary to Article 3.[24] Accordingly, the Court will not decide a case solely on grounds of suffering and the unacceptability of certain conditions, but will take into account more objective factors which might, initially at least, justify those conditions.[25] Secondly, although the Court is now more willing to consider both the European Prison Rules and the findings of the European Committee on the Prevention of Torture (CPT) than the Commission used to,[26] it must be remembered that the Court is exercising a judicial function in finding that the threshold under Article 3 has been crossed, and cannot be swayed solely by the fact that such conditions

[21] See S Foster, 'Prison Conditions and Human Rights' (2008) *Web Journal of Legal Studies.*

[22] *Selmouni v France* (1999) 20 EHRR 403.

[23] ibid, para 101.

[24] *Krocher and Moller v Switzerland* 1983 34 D &R 24. In this case, two prisoners remanded on charges of terrorist murders were kept under constant surveillance in separate, isolated cells with the windows frosted over and allowed 20 minutes exercise per day. The Commission found taking into account that the terrorist environment justified severe security measures and that the conditions were relaxed after four weeks, there was insufficient evidence that they had been subjected to a form of suffering designed to punish them, destroy their personality or break their resistance.

[25] See, for example, *Hassan v Secretary of State for Justice* [2011] EWHC 1359 (Admin).

[26] In *Delazarus v United Kingdom* App no 17525/90 (ECtHR, 19 February 1993) the applicant claimed that his conditions in solitary confinement amounted to a breach of Art 3, relying on the findings of the CPT and the Prison Inspector in England that there was overcrowding, the use of chamber pots, and that prisoners were in their cells for 23 hours per day. The Commission declared the case inadmissible on the basis that being in solitary confinement, he could not complain of overcrowding and was less affected by the use of chamber pots.

are regarded as unacceptable within rules drawn up by bodies responsible for standard-setting in the area of prison conditions.

IV. THE EUROPEAN COURT'S CURRENT APPROACH TO ARTICLE 3 AND PRISON CONDITIONS

The Court's more positive stance with respect to Article 3 and prison conditions can be explained on a number of grounds. First, following its judgment in *Selmouni v France*,[27] the Court appears to have lowered its threshold with regard to the concepts of inhuman and degrading treatment, leading, incidentally, to a more proactive approach to matters such as poor prison conditions.[28] Secondly, since the creation of the full-time Court, prison conditions cases are considered by a judicial body, avoiding the allegation that was made in the past that admissibility decisions were often made by the Commission in a cursory fashion and, possibly, on policy grounds.[29] Thirdly, in recent years the European Court has considered a great number of claims concerning quite extreme prison conditions in Eastern Europe, thus providing it with the opportunity to condemn a variety of clearly unacceptable practices and to establish some minimum standards with respect to the treatment of prisoners in all jurisdictions within the Council of Europe. Finally, the Court has been willing to take into account the findings of the European Committee for the Prevention of Torture (CPT) in making a substantive determination under Article 3. Thus, despite the differences in judicial and standard-setting functions, there is now substantial evidence that the Court is prepared to be led by the Committee's findings and to feed those into their final judicial determinations.[30]

That the Court is now prepared to take a more robust approach to the challenge of prison conditions is evident in two cases involving prison conditions in Greece. In *Peers v Greece*[31] the applicant, a British national, had been arrested on drug-related charges, and complained about the conditions of his incarceration as a remand prisoner in a Greek prison. His complaints included that he had been detained, alongside one other detainee, in a cramped cell which had little natural light and no ventilation and which had an open toilet, which often failed to work, and that he had been provided with no access to vocational courses or activities

[27] *Selmouni v France* (1999) 29 EHRR 403.

[28] See Y Arai-Yokoi, (2003) 'Grading Scale of Degradation: Identifying the Threshold of Degrading Treatment or Punishment under Article 3 ECHR' (2003) 21(3) *Netherlands Human Rights Quarterly* 383, 404–10.

[29] See JP Gardner and CL Wickremasinghe, 'England and Wales and the European Convention', in B Dickson (ed), *Human Rights and the European Convention* (London, Sweet and Maxwell, 1997) 47–48; and S Livingstone and T Owen, *Prison Law* (Oxford, OUP, 1999) 182–85.

[30] See for example, *Peers v Greece*, considered below. See R Morgan and M Evans, *Preventing Torture: The European Convention on the Prevention of Torture and Inhuman or Degrading Treatment or Punishment* (Oxford, OUP, 1998) and R Morgan and M Evans (eds), *Protecting Prisoners: the Standards of the European Committee for the Prevention of Torture in Context* (Oxford, OUP, 1999).

[31] *Peers v Greece* (2001) 33 EHRR 51.

or a library. The European Court held that although there had been no evidence of a positive intention to humiliate or debase the applicant, the fact that the state authorities had taken no steps to improve the objectively unacceptable conditions of the applicant's detention denoted a lack of respect for the applicant.[32] Taking into account the fact that, for at least two months, he had to spend a considerable part of each day practically confined to his bed in a cell with no ventilation and no window, and had to use the toilet in the presence of another inmate (and be present while the toilet was being used by his cellmate), the Court was of the opinion that the conditions gave rise in him to feelings of anguish and inferiority, capable of humiliating and debasing him.[33] The conditions therefore amounted to degrading treatment within Article 3. In the second case, *Dougoz v Greece*,[34] the Court found that the detention of the applicant in an overcrowded cell with inadequate sanitation and insufficient beds where he was deprived of fresh air, daylight, hot water and exercise, constituted degrading treatment and thus a violation of Article 3. In coming to that conclusion, the Court noted that the CPT had corroborated the applicant's allegations.[35] Further evidence of this approach is evident from its decision in *Kalashnikov v Russia*.[36] In this case a remand prisoner complained, inter alia, that the conditions and duration of his detention (four years and 10 months) were in breach of Article 3. Upholding the complaint, the Court held that the duration of the applicant's detention, taken with the cramped and insanitary conditions in which he had been held, amounted to degrading treatment. In particular, it noted that he had been forced to endure overcrowding and poor sleeping conditions, and as a result he had contracted skin diseases and fungal infections over the period of his detention.[37]

These cases are usually decided on the basis of the cumulative effect of the conditions, rather than the breach of any standards relating to any particular aspect of such conditions, such as the minimum space that should be allowed to each prisoner. Thus, in the recent case of *Canali v France*,[38] the Court found a violation of Article 3, taking into account both the cramped conditions of the prison cell[39]

[32] ibid para 74. See also the Court's decision in *AB v The Netherlands* (2003) 37 EHRR 48, where it was held that the failure to implement urgent recommendations from the CPT meant that the applicant had no effective remedy under Art 13.

[33] ibid, para 75.

[34] *Dougoz v Greece* (2002) 34 EHRR 61.

[35] ibid, para 46. Contrast the older decision in *Delazarus v United Kingdom*, n 26 above. The European Court can also take such reports into account in determining whether extradition or deportation would subject the applicant to intolerable conditions or treatment. Thus, in *Hilal v United Kingdom* (2001) 33 EHRR 2, the Court gave strong weight to the evidence of deplorable conditions in the Republic of Tanzania's prisons.

[36] *Kalashnikov v Russia* (2003) 36 EHRR 34.

[37] ibid, paras 100–01.

[38] *Canali v France* App no 40119/09 (ECtHR, 25 April 2014).

[39] The size of the cell met the standards laid down by a recent CPT report, although the CPT had stressed that that finding was dependent on the prisoners being allowed sufficient time out of the cell, which was not the case in the present application.

and unsatisfactory sanitary facilities and hygiene. However, the European Court has been willing to intervene in cases of overcrowding and find a violation of Article 3 in cases where such overcrowding is caused by systemic problems inherent in that state. Thus, in *Torreggiani v Italy*[40] in a pilot judgment the European Court held that as the breach of the prisoner's right to benefit from adequate conditions of detention was not the result of isolated incidents, but arose from a systemic problem, which resulted in turn from a chronic malfunction particular to the Italian penitentiary system, then there had been a breach of Article 3.[41] It should be noted, however, that this judgment does not attempt to lay down any specific standards relating to overcrowding, and in *Achmant v Greece*,[42] the UK High Court stressed that the European Court had never purported to lay down a bright line rule for the amount of personal living space which, if fallen below, would result in a violation of Article 3.

Despite evidence of a bold new approach, the European Court has made it clear that it is essential for the applicant to prove that the conditions are so intolerable that they cross the threshold implicit in the wording of Article 3. In *Valasinas v Lithuania*[43] the applicant complained that in both the normal regime wing and in the separate segregation unit there was, inter alia, overcrowding, poor sanitation and washing facilities, poor catering, a lack of access to medical treatment and limited meaningful activities for prisoners, although there was access to books and newspapers and organised cultural and recreational events. The Court found that there was no breach of Article 3 in respect of the conditions of detention because they did not attain the minimum level of severity required to amount to degrading treatment within the meaning of Article 3. In the Court's view, the treatment had to go beyond the level that was inevitable upon the imposition of a legitimate punishment and that measures depriving a person of his liberty may often involve such an element; the duty on the state was to detain a person under such conditions which were compatible with respect for his human dignity so that the manner and method of the measure did not subject him to distress or hardship of an intensity exceeding the unavoidable level of suffering inherent in detention.[44]

The above cases, and the inherent restriction on a prisoner's dignity caused by incarceration, expose the limits of judicial supervision. The European and domestic courts are charged with finding a violation of Article 3—something that it will only do in exceptional cases where the necessary and high threshold has been met. Conscious of its judicial role and the dangers of taking on a legislative or

[40] *Torreggiani v Italy*, App nos 43517/09, 46882/09, 55400/09, 57875/09, 61535/10, 35315/10 and 37818/10 (ECtHR, January 2014).

[41] ibid, paras 87–89. This judgment was employed by the UK High Court in *Badre v Italy* [2014] EWHC 614 (Admin) in deciding that an individual would face a real risk of being subjected to a breach of Art 3 if he was extradited to Italy to serve a sentence in those overcrowded conditions.

[42] *Achmant v Greece* [2012] EWHC 3470 (Admin).

[43] *Valasinas v Lithuania*, n 19 above.

[44] ibid, para 102.

standard-setting function, it cannot possibly achieve what can be more reasonably expected of regulations laid down by agencies responsible for such standards and their monitoring. This dilemma is particularly acute in respect of vulnerable prisoners, who have special needs and require particular protection from unacceptable conditions of detention, and whose protection by the European Court will now be examined.

V. THE EUROPEAN COURT, ARTICLE 3 AND VULNERABLE PRISONERS

The detention and treatment of prisoners with physical, mental or other disabilities raises the question of whether such persons should be incarcerated in prison, and the appropriate standards of their treatment in prison.[45] In addition to concerns expressed by the CPT,[46] a number of decisions of the European Court have ruled on the treatment of such detainees and the compatibility of their detention and treatment with Article 3.[47] For the reasons already highlighted, the European Court's approach is to look at each case on its merits, and in *Grori v Albania*,[48] it was stressed that although there was no general duty to release prisoners suffering from serious illnesses, there was an obligation to ensure that a prisoner received adequate treatment or medication, and that *this* duty at least was not excused on grounds of expense.[49]

The European Court has taken a robust approach where vulnerable prisoners are subjected to harsh conditions of imprisonment and not treated in a manner that is consistent with their physical or mental state.[50] For example, in *Keenan v United Kingdom*,[51] it held that there had been a violation of Article 3 in respect of the manner in which the authorities had treated a mentally ill prisoner who was a known suicide risk. The Court found that the lack of effective monitoring of the prisoner's condition and the lack of informed psychiatric input into his assessment and treatment disclosed significant defects in the medical care provided to a mentally ill person with such a risk.[52] That approach was followed in *McGlinchey v United Kingdom*,[53] which concerned the standard of care and treatment of prisoners with drug addiction, and where the Court confirmed that the state had a duty to ensure that a person was detained in conditions that were compatible with

[45] S Foster, 'Disabled Prisoners and Human Rights Law: the jurisprudence of the European Court of Human Rights and the domestic courts (2011) *Prisoner Service Journal* 36.

[46] See J Murdoch, The Impact of the Council of Europe's "Torture Committee" and the Evolution of Standard-setting in Relation to Places of Detention [2006] *European Human Rights Law Review* 159.

[47] Foster, n 45 above.

[48] *Grori v Albania* App no 25336/04 (ECtHR, 7 July 2009).

[49] Ibid, para 131. See also *Akhmetov v Russia* App no 37463/04 (ECtHR, 1 April 2010), where the refusal to transfer a prisoner to a civilian hospital was held to be in breach of Art 3.

[50] Foster, n 45 above.

[51] *Keenan v United Kingdom* (2001) 33 EHRR 38.

[52] ibid, para 116.

[53] *McGlinchey v United Kingdom* (2003) 37 EHRR 41.

respect for human dignity, including the duty to make proper provision for the prisoner's health and well-being in the form of requisite medical assistance.[54] The Court thus concluded that the prison authorities had failed to comply with their duty to provide her with the requisite medical care and their treatment of her had violated the prohibition against inhuman and degrading treatment contained in Article 3.[55]

The Court has also, albeit indirectly, established principles relating to the standard of conditions concerning prisoners with long term or permanent physical disabilities. Thus, in *Price v United Kingdom*,[56] it was held that the detention of a severely disabled person in conditions where she was dangerously cold, risked developing sores because her bed was too hard or unreachable, and was unable to go to the toilet or to keep clean without the greatest of difficulty, constituted degrading treatment within Article 3.[57] Further, in *Vincent v France*,[58] the Court found a violation in respect of the treatment of a wheelchair-bound prisoner who had been detained for four months in a prison which had inadequate facilities to deal with his disability. The Court concluded that the applicant had been totally reliant on the authorities and had lost the ability to leave his cell or move about the prison independently, as a wheel had to be removed from his chair every time he entered or left his cell.[59]

The question is, therefore, whether the place of detention is adequately and appropriately sourced to accommodate the prisoner, and if this is not the case, then there will be a violation despite any practical security reasons for detaining the prisoner in a normal prison. Thus, in *Riviere v France*,[60] there had been a violation when the applicant, a long-term prisoner with a psychiatric disorder, had been detained in normal prison conditions without proper facilities for his disorder. In the Court's view he should have been detained in special conditions, irrespective of his offence or perceived dangerousness. However, the Court, unsurprisingly, has not laid down any bright rule about the acceptability of subjecting disabled prisoners to the normal harsh conditions of imprisonment. Thus, in *Gelfmann v France*,[61] there had been no violation when a prisoner, who had suffered from AIDS for nearly 20 years, had had his request for release on medical grounds refused. The Court stressed that was 'no general obligation to release a prisoner

[54] ibid, para 57.

[55] ibid, para 58. See more recently, the decision of the European Court in *Taddei v France* App no 36435/07 (ECtHR, 21 December 2010), where it was held that the failure by the prison authorities and the French courts to move an anorexic prisoner to a civilian hospital where she could be treated properly for her condition was in breach of Art 3.

[56] *Price v United Kingdom* (2002) 34 EHRR 53; see S Foster 'Inhuman and Degrading Prison Conditions' (2001) *New Law Journal* 1222.

[57] This case involved detention in a police cell, but is reliable authority in respect of general prison conditions

[58] *Vincent v France* App no 6253/03 (ECtHR, 24 October 2006).

[59] ibid, para 103.

[60] *Riviere v France* App no 33834/03 (ECtHR, 11 July 2006).

[61] *Gelfmann v France* (2006) 42 EHRR 4.

on health grounds or to transfer him to a civilian hospital, even if suffering from an illness that was difficult to treat, provided the prisoner is receiving *adequate* treatment in prison and his condition was being monitored by an outside hospital' (italics added).[62]

Decisions in cases such as *Keenan* and *Price* display a promisingly robust approach to the treatment of mentally ill or disabled persons in places of detention, the disability of the prisoner often making the Court more willing to rule on the compatibility of prison conditions with basic human rights. However, the Court is not prepared to prescribe general standards, preferring instead to consider the impact of the conditions on the particular prisoner. Thus, in *Aerts v Belgium*[63] it found no violation when a mentally ill prisoner was detained in what the Court conceded were 'unsatisfactory conditions' that were not conducive to his effective treatment. As there was no evidence of a deterioration of the applicant's mental health, it held that the prisoner had not been subjected to inhuman or degrading treatment.[64]

Similar issues are raised with respect to the detention of elderly and infirm prisoners, the European Court conducting a pragmatic balance between the functions of the criminal justice system and the human rights of the prisoners. Thus, the Court will determine a violation when such prisoners cannot be guaranteed adequate medical and other care while serving their sentence. For example, in *Mouisel v France*[65] it held that the failure to release a seriously ill prisoner from prison amounted to a violation of Article 3. In that case the prisoner had contracted leukaemia and complained of the standards of his treatment before his ultimate release. The Court noted that the prisoner was suffering from permanent asthenia and fatigue, that he was waking up in pain in the night and that there was a psychological impact of stress on his life expectancy. Decisively, the Court noted that the prison was scarcely equipped to deal with illness, and had failed to transfer him to another institution.[66]

In contrast, the Court has refused to intervene in cases where prisoners have made general claims based on their age and ill health. Thus, it adopted a 'hands-off' approach in *Papon v France (No 1)*,[67] where, in an admissibility decision it noted that although the Convention did not exclude the possibility 'that *in certain conditions* the detention of an elderly person over a lengthy period might raise an issue under Article 3, in the instant case the applicant's general state of health and his conditions of detention and treatment had not reached the level of severity' (italics added).[68] The Court noted that none of the member states had an upper age

[62] ibid, para 50.
[63] *Aerts v Begium* (2000) 29 EHRR 50.
[64] ibid, para 66.
[65] *Mouisel v France* (2004) 38 EHRR 34.
[66] ibid, para 47. See also *Farbtuhs v Latvia* App no 4672/02 (ECtHR, 2 December 2004).
[67] *Papon v France (No 1)* (2001) 39 EHRR 10.
[68] ibid, para 46.

limit for detention,[69] thus highlighting the need for legally enforceable and clear rules in these areas, where judicial intervention is, inevitably, limited. Similarly, in *Matencio v France*,[70] the Court held that there had been no violation of Article 3 when a prisoner suffered a stroke in prison and claimed that his detention and conditions of detention violated his Convention rights. In the Court's view he was offered adequate medical assistance and thus the threshold in Article 3 had not been reached.[71] The case law of the Court in this area remains cautious and highly dependent on the individual facts and it is clear that exceptional circumstances need to be present to find a violation of Article 3.[72] This again stresses the need for agreement at the European level that certain practices that threaten individual dignity should become unlawful, thus informing the Court's duty in interpreting Article 3, and thus strengthening the protection of vulnerable detainees.

A common European initiative would also be welcome in resolving the question of whether such prisoners should receive sentences of imprisonment, and the extent to which domestic courts should consider the prisoner's incapacities when considering just punishment. This initiative would strengthen the limited duty imposed by the European Court on domestic judges to carry out their functions consistently with Article 3, both at the initial sentencing stage and when asked to consider release or deferral. The European Court is prepared to intervene in appropriate cases, and in *Kupczak v Poland*[73] it found a violation of Article 3 when the Polish domestic courts continued to extend the prisoner's pre-trial detention, despite his ill-health and the lack of availability of a morphine pump to aid his chronic back problems. With respect to the UK, case law suggests that judges will take a cautious approach and that, as with prison conditions in general, will be primarily concerned with whether the prison has the necessary facilities to cope with the prisoner's disability rather than the more general question whether imprisonment would be an inhumane option for a person with such a disability. For example, in *R v Hetherington*,[74] the UK Court of Appeal held that although, following the European Court's ruling in *Price v United Kingdom* (above), the prison authorities had a duty to cater for a prisoner's disabilities, on the facts there was sufficient evidence that the prison could cater for the claimant's physical disabilities during his 18 months sentence.

[69] ibid, para 47.

[70] *Matencio v France* App no 58749/00 (ECtHR, 15 January 2004).

[71] This approach was followed by the UK courts in *R (Spink) v Home Secretary* [2005] EWCA Civ 275, where it was held that it was important to bear in mind that the claimant was a serving prisoner and that it is in general in the public interest that the allotted sentence is served.

[72] For example, in *Sawonuik v United Kingdom* App no 63719/00 (ECtHR, 29 May 2001), the Court held that the imprisonment of a 79-year-old war criminal was not, in the absence of other evidence of ill-treatment or exceptional hardship, in violation of Art 3, provided the prisoner was in receipt of appropriate medical care.

[73] *Kupczak v Poland* App no 2627/09 (ECtHR, 25 January 2011).

[74] *R v Hetherington* [2009] EWCA Civ 1186.

VI. CRITICAL OVERVIEW ON JUDICIAL PROTECTION

Although it clear that the European Court has offered some protection to vulnerable prisoners, the limitations of Article 3 claims are evident when the prisoner attempts to persuade the Court that a breach of specific standards relating to conditions of detention breach Article 3. This can be seen when examining decisions relating to whether inadequate in-cell sanitation could constitute a violation of Article 3. In *Napier v Scottish Ministers*,[75] the Scottish courts held that the subjection of the applicant to 'slopping out' in prison constituted inhuman and degrading treatment within Article 3. That decision however, did not establish any general prohibition regarding the adequacy of in-cell sanitation or the unacceptability of the 'slopping-out' procedure;[76] although the European Court has stressed that access to appropriate toilets and maintenance of good hygiene conditions are essential elements in an environment for humans, and that prisoners had to have easy access to sanitary facilities in which their privacy was protected.[77] Thus, in subsequent cases the UK domestic courts have made it clear that the slopping-out process is not automatically in violation of Article 3 and that each case will turn on its facts.[78]

Thus, judicial pronouncements on prison conditions are only obviously effective, ex post facto, for the specific victim, assuming they succeed. Further, both the European and domestic courts usually require a 'victim' before making such a pronouncement, and will not hear an application relating to 'academic' arguments on prison conditions if there is no identifiable prisoner who is suffering such conditions. This remains a limitation of the judicial method of monitoring prison conditions, despite the availability of pilot judgments of the European Court under rule 61 of the Rules of the European Court of Human Rights.[79] Further, such decisions often do little to establish acceptable standards of treatment to all prisoners, or prohibit certain practices which are regarded as unacceptable by rule makers and monitors, but which may not cross the judicial threshold necessary to find a breach of Article 3.[80]

There has undoubtedly been an increased willingness on behalf of the European Court of Human Rights to challenge prison conditions in accordance with international human rights norms. In particular it is now prepared to find violations of those standards in the absence of bad faith, deliberate

[75] *The Times*, 14 May 2004. Noted by Thomson in (2004) 17 SLT 103.

[76] See A Lawson, and A Mukherjee, 'Slopping out in Scotland' [2004] EHRLR 645.

[77] *Canali v France* App no 40119/09 (ECtHR, 25 April 2013). In that case the Court held that a toilet annex that was only partially closed off was not acceptable in a cell occupied by more than one person.

[78] *Grant and Gleaves v Ministry of Justice* [2011] EWHC 3379 (QB).

[79] That procedure was used in the recent case of *Torreggiani v Italy*, considered above, at n 40.

[80] See *R (Hall) v University College London Hospital NHS Foundation Trust and Home Secretary* [2013] EWHC 198 (Admin), where it was held that *it was not the court's role to assess whether the care provided to him fell short of the optimal or even a reasonable standard* (italics added); rather it must determine whether the treatment breached his human rights (para 32).

ill-treatment or any positive intention to humiliate, and by doing so is prepared to set some, albeit fluid, standards of acceptable treatment. Such standards were formerly the domain of each state government and guided by international guidelines from treaties lacking judicial enforcement, but recent case law suggests that the Court is prepared, albeit in quite extreme case, to enforce them.

However, given the open-ended wording of Article 3, as well as the variety of conditions and practices in member states of the Council of Europe, the case law of the European Court is, inevitably, inconsistent. Despite the absolute character of Article 3, the lack of uniform standards and practices on matters such as sentencing, security, and prison resources will lead to a wide level of discretion, in turn producing unpredictable case law. As a consequence, the European Court appears reluctant to make an authoritative ruling on specific aspects of prison conditions, such as solitary confinement, sanitary facilities, or even the incarceration of physically and mentally incapable prisoners, preferring instead to decide cases on an individual basis and concentrating on the impact of those conditions on the individual applicants.

However, the European Court has taken a more positive approach in the protection of vulnerable prisoners. Whilst not laying down any specific guidelines in these areas, cases such as *Keenan*, *Price* and *McGlinchey* have imposed strict duties on domestic authorities with respect to their care and treatment, thus protecting them from the harshness of general prison life that is likely to be felt more intensely because of their situation. These cases have given the European Court the opportunity to rule on prison conditions and at the same time have informed UK domestic law on the civil liability of authorities towards prisoners.[81]

VII. EUROPEAN PRISON RULES AND RECENT EU INITIATIVES

The latest version of the European Prison Rules (2006) was formulated by the Committee of Ministers of the Council of Europe in January 2006,[82] and provides guidance on the running of prisons in member states, and the treatment of prisoners and the protection of their human rights.[83] They are based on the United Nations Standard Minimum Rules for the Treatment of Prisoners (1987) and, although rule 1 of the basic principles provides that *all persons deprived of their liberty* shall be treated with respect for their human rights, rule 10.1 states that the Rules apply to persons who have been remanded in custody by a judicial authority or who have been deprived of their liberty following conviction.

[81] See, for example, *Reeves v Commissioner for the Police of the Metropolis* [2002] AC 283 on the duty of care owed by police and prison authorities in cases of suicides in detention in England and Wales. See S Foster, 'The Negligence of Prison Authorities and the Protection of Prisoners' Rights (2005) 26(1) *Liverpool Law Review* 75.

[82] Recommendation Rec (2006) 2 of the Committee of Ministers to member states on the European Prison Rules, adopted 11 January 2006.

[83] Previous versions of the European Prison Rules were formulated in 1973 and 1987.

Rule 4 then specifies that prison conditions that infringe prisoner's human rights are not justified by lack of resources,[84] and rule 5 that life in prison shall approximate as closely as possible the positive aspects of life in the community.[85] With specific reference to prisoners suffering from mental illness and whose state of mental health is incompatible with detention in prison, rule 12.1 provides that such prisoners should be detained in an establishment specially designed for that purpose, although rule 12.2 states that if such persons are exceptionally held in prison, there shall be special regulations that take account of their status and needs.[86] In addition, Rule 47.1 provides that specialised prisons or sections under medical control shall be available for the observation and treatment of prisoners suffering from mental disorder or abnormality who do not necessarily fall under the provision of rule 12. Further, rule 47.2 provides that the prison medical service shall provide for the psychiatric treatment of all prisoners who are in need of such treatment and pay special attention to suicide prevention. These principles are probably reflected by the current case law of the European Court, which insists that detention will be in breach of Article 3 if the necessary medical and psychiatric help is not available,[87] and which have found domestic authorities in breach of Article 3 if they fail to provide the necessary medical and psychiatric help to vulnerable prisoners.[88] Similarly, provisions in the European Prison Rules which state that prison authorities shall safeguard the health of all prisoners in their care,[89] and that health policy in prisons shall be integrated into, and compatible with, national health policy,[90] have been followed by the European Court, who insist that the detention and continued detention of disabled, ill and infirm prisoners remains compatible with Article 3 only if adequate medical and other facilities are available to such prisoners.[91]

Part II of the Rules lays down principles in respect of prison conditions, and rule 18.1 provides that the accommodation provided for prisoners, and in particular all sleeping accommodation, shall respect human dignity and, as far as possible, privacy, and meet the requirements of health and hygiene, due regard being paid to floor space, cubic content of air, lighting, heating and ventilation. As we have seen, these Rules have informed the decisions of the European Court

[84] See the decision in *Grori v Albania*, n 48 above.

[85] Rule 2 also provides that persons deprived of their liberty retain rights that are not lawfully taken away by the decision sentencing them, and r 3 that restrictions placed on such persons shall be the minimum necessary and proportionate to the legitimate objective for which they are imposed.

[86] In addition, r 47.1 provides that specialised prisons or sections under medical control shall be available for the observation and treatment of prisoners suffering from mental disorder or abnormality that do not necessarily fall under the provision of r 12. Further, r 47.2 provides that the prison medical service shall provide for the psychiatric treatment of all prisoners who are in need of such treatment and pay special attention to suicide prevention.

[87] See, for example *Grori v Albania*, n 48 above, and the other cases examined in this chapter with respect to the treatment of vulnerable prisoners.

[88] *Keenan v United Kingdom*, n 51 above.

[89] Rule 38.

[90] Rule 40.2.

[91] See, for example *Mouisel v France*, n 65 above.

of Human Rights under Article 3,[92] although the Rules are phrased more generally and generously, and do not require the breaching of the threshold of inhuman and degrading contained in that article. The Rules also insist that national law sets specific minimum requirements in respect of the requirements of rule 18.1, above, and for mechanisms to ensure that those standards are not breached by the overcrowding of prisons.[93]

The Rules also make specific reference to sanitation; rule 19.3 insisting that prisoners have ready access to sanitary facilities that are hygienic and respect privacy. Although the European Court has found a violation of Article 3 where sanitary facilities have been found to be inadequate and humiliating,[94] these findings are usually based on the cumulative effect of various conditions rather than the breach of this rule per se. Also, the UK domestic courts have made it clear that processes such as 'slopping out'—which appear to breach rule 19.3—will not result in an automatic breach of Article 3, but will depend on the circumstances of the cases and the effect of such conditions on the particular applicant.[95]

These Rules, together with the work and visits of the CPT, ensure that member states are aware of such standards and that they are encouraged to implement them in national policy and law. Together with the case law of the European Court of Human Rights—and the decisions of domestic courts that are informed by such jurisprudence—which make binding decisions in prison conditions claims and which are in turn informed by the European Prison Rules and the findings of the CPT—there exists a varied and reasonably coherent system for monitoring prison conditions and protecting prisoners' human rights and dignity with respect to their incarceration. However, recent EU initiatives, including the European Commission's 2011 Green Paper on strengthening mutual trust in the European judicial area[96]—and the European Parliament's resolution on detention conditions[97]—may provide a higher public and state profile to the problem and may encourage reforms in domestic law and practice as well as greater supervision at the European level.

The European Commission's Green Paper explores the extent to which detention conditions impact on mutual trust and mutual recognition and judicial cooperation within the European Union. The Commission, whilst accepting that detention conditions and prison management are the responsibility of

[92] *Peers v Greece*, n 31 above.

[93] Rules 18.3 and 18.4 respectively. In addition, many states have signed the optional protocol to the UN Convention Against Torture and Inhuman and Degrading Treatment or Punishment (OPCAT), which insists each state party establish a mechanism (a National Preventive Mechanism (NPM)) to undertake visits of places of detention and to report on such visits, with appropriate recommendations for improvement.

[94] *Peers v Greece*, n 31 above.

[95] *Napier v Scottish Minister*, n 75 above, and *Grant and Gleaves v Ministry of Justice*, n 78 above.

[96] EU Commission, Green Paper on the application of EU criminal justice legislation in the field of detention Brussels COM (2011) 327 final.

[97] European Parliament Resolution of 15 December 2011 on detention conditions in the EU (2011/2897).

member states, states its interest in the area of conditions because of the central importance of the principle of mutual recognition of judicial decisions for the areas of freedom, security and justice.[98] Although the Green Paper is concerned mainly with pre-trial detention, the Commission also considers the wider area of prison conditions in the EU in Part 6 of the Paper—'Improving Detention Conditions'. The Paper notes that the Stockholm Project states that 'efforts to promote the exchange of best practice should be pursued and the implementation of the … European Prison Rules supported', and that detention and best practices in prison management could also be addressed.[99]

It should be stressed, of course, that in addition to the limited scope of the Green Paper, above, the Commission are referring to conditions in EU states, whereas the European Prison Rules and other monitoring conditions extend to all Council of Europe states, many of which do not belong to the EU and possess the worst conditions of detention. Nevertheless, the Green Paper addresses general issues of prison conditions in Europe and stresses the importance of both various legal and non-legal procedures for regulating and monitoring conditions of detention,[100] as well as a number of prison-related activities via different financial programmes.[101]

In the Green Paper the Commission posed two questions for public consultation with respect to prison conditions:

1. (Question 9) How could monitoring of detention conditions by the member states be better promoted, and how could the EU encourage prison administration to network and establish best practice? And
2. (Question 10) How could the work of the Council of Europe and that of member states be better promoted as they endeavour to put good detention standards into practice?

In assessing the responses to those questions the Commission observed that a number of agencies had noted the persistence of poor prison conditions and the variation in detention conditions in the member states, and that many organisations had called for the adoption of *binding* EU minimum standards on detention conditions,[102] although, interestingly, the vast majority of member states did not support that recommendation.[103] It was also noted that although the respondents did not call for a new monitoring body at the EU level—believing that it would

[98] Purpose, at p 1.

[99] The Stockholm Programme [2010] OJ C115/1.

[100] Such as the European Prison Rules, the UN Standard Minimum Rules, the CPT and ECPT and the 2006 Optional Protocol to the UN Convention against Torture (OPCAT).

[101] Green Paper, 6.1 and 6.2. The various financial programmes are detailed in Table 2 of the Paper and include the Criminal Justice Programme on the study of detention in the EU, which was published in 2011 and reported on various aspects of prison conditions and prisoner health care.

[102] EU Commission 'Analysis of the Replies to the Green Paper on the Application of EU Criminal Justice Legislation in the field of Detention', p 16.

[103] ibid, p 18.

confuse and duplicate the work of the existing mechanisms—the EU should instead expand the level of financial and organisational support it offers to the existing systems.[104] This recommendation was also considered alongside the suggestion that the work of the existing monitoring bodies should be better coordinated, and the dissemination of their recommendations improved.[105]

With respect to the second question (Question 10), the Commission received a number of recommendations for greater collaboration between the EU and the Council of Europe in the area of prison conditions so as to ensure the respect and successful implementation of relevant European standards.[106] This included the recommendation that the EU should support the Council's activities by financial assistance for funding of projects aimed at improving standards in the field, training for prison staff, the further dissemination of knowledge regarding the Council of Europe's standards, and the creation of a European prisons cooperation network.[107]

It was also recommended that the decisions of the European Court of Human Rights on prison conditions should be disseminated broadly and that national governments should make their responses to national rulings.[108] It is suggested that this would be a positive move in promoting accountability and better conditions, despite the inherent limitations of such judicial decisions in setting standards in this area. The responses made little reference to specific aspects of prison conditions, although it was suggested that the maximum capacity of each individual detention establishment should be specified and that such minimum should be respected without exception.

VIII. CONCLUSIONS

Despite the plethora of international and regional instruments and agencies dedicated to the protection of individuals from inhuman, degrading and otherwise unacceptable conditions of detention, prisoners remain vulnerable to violation of their basic rights and human dignity. There is abundant evidence to support the claim that, despite these mechanisms, such individuals are often subjected to unsatisfactory, and often, unlawful conditions, which fail to meet necessary standards with respect to basic matters such as their accommodation. The effective challenge to and monitoring of inhuman and degrading conditions in European prisons, despite its variation, is limited and has not appeared to have improved prison conditions to a level that would satisfy standards laid down by international law. Direct legal challenge via Article 3 before the European

[104] ibid, p 17.
[105] ibid, p 16.
[106] ibid, pp 17 and 18.
[107] ibid, p 18.
[108] ibid.

Court of Human Rights, regulatory schemes such as the European Prison Rules (2006), and monitoring processes carried out by agencies such as the CPT, all have their limitations. In particular, the case law of the European Court under Article 3, although less difficult to predict than once was the case, shows that the European and domestic courts will continue to take a reactive rather than proactive stance, leaving the establishment and enforcement of strict guidelines to state authorities and the drafters and monitors of international rules governing conditions of detention. Notwithstanding this, recent case law does provide some evidence that prison conditions are most clearly a justiciable matter, and that state authorities are not to be left with unlimited discretion in this area.

Recent EU initiative in this area—particularly the Commission's 2011 Green Paper—helps provide a higher public profile to the problem of maintaining standards in European prisons, and it is hoped that the recommendations by various agencies, made in response to the EU Commission's request for public consultation, will encourage reforms both at domestic and European levels. However, without the adoption of binding EU rules in this area, it is suggested that the existing mechanisms will continue earnestly, although unsuccessfully in protecting human beings from substandard conditions of detention.

19

The Ultimate Social (or is it Economic?) Vulnerability: Poverty in European Law

KRISTA NADAKAVUKAREN SCHEFER[1]

I. INTRODUCTION

> 'Vulnerable' and 'vulnerability' as common terms in the lexicon of development, but their use is often vague. They serve are convenient substitutes for 'poor' and 'poverty', and allow planners and other professionals to restrain the overuse of those words. … Vulnerability, though, is not the same as poverty. It means not lack or want, but defencelessness, insecurity, and exposure to risk, shocks and stress. … Yet vulnerability, and its opposite, security, stand out as recurrent concerns of poor people which professional definitions of poverty overlook.[2]

Robert Chambers' words, written in 1989 in the context of development studies, seem to have had some effect. In Europe, no less than in the developing world, 'poverty' is understood as a multi-faceted condition that consists of a web of physical, psychological, educational, and social disadvantages—as well as economic ones. As a result, low income and a lack of assets is no longer the sole focus of European social policy and it is questionable whether it is even the primary focus of these policies. Income deprivation—in fact so easy to resolve through transfer payments—is rarely the only cause of a poor individual's vulnerability. Thus, in aiming to be more effective in reducing vulnerability, policymakers have terminologically joined social exclusion to poverty to ensure a more comprehensive attack on conditions that prevent individuals from realising their full potential. With 'social exclusion and poverty' the new catchwords of European social policy, 2010 was named the official European Year on Poverty and Social Exclusion, and a Platform on Poverty and Social Exclusion was launched as a 'flagship initiative' within the Europe 2020 framework.

[1] I want to thank Jasmin Häcker for her patient and able research assistance. Any mistakes are my own.

[2] Robert Chambers, 'Vulnerability, Coping and Policy' (2006) 37(4) *Institute of Development Studies Bulletin* 33 (originally published as 'Vulnerability: How the Poor Cope' (1989) 20(2) *IDS Bulletin*).

Legally, a provision in the Charter of Fundamental Rights recognises and respects measures to combat poverty and social exclusion, and a Social Charter right to protection against poverty and social exclusion exists for Council of Europe members. European courts, too, seem to have embraced the multi-faceted nature of social vulnerability. The European Court of Human Rights' attention to 'vulnerable groups' demonstrates that the judges recognise that factors other than income can make a difference to the enjoyment of protected human rights. The risk of social exclusion and poverty is greater for persons with disabilities, refugees, children, and the elderly, so individuals belonging to these groups receive particular legal protection.

But has the multi-dimensional concept of social vulnerability as a focus of policy-makers fostered legal decision-making in protecting the poor? Without explicit judicial references to 'social vulnerability' or to 'poverty', it is hard to say whether the advances in sociological and economic understandings of poverty's complexities have been sufficiently understood by the legal community, or whether they have not led to a diminishing of attention to the still-very-relevant condition of income deprivation alone.

The following pages set out a discussion of poverty in European law, recognising income deprivation as a core aspect of social vulnerability. Section II gives a brief background to the two concepts at the base of this study—social vulnerability and poverty—and sets forth a summary review of poverty levels in the European region. Next follows a description of the various legal instruments relevant to the protection of low-income individuals and the provisions' application, with a focus on the European Court of Justice's and European Court of Human Rights' handling of poverty. Section IV's discussion of the consequences of this jurisprudence follows. Section V offers some thoughts on whether the European legal system could improve on the social equality of its population by focusing its protections more directly on income disadvantages.

II. POVERTY AND SOCIAL VULNERABILITY

A. Poverty

'Poverty' is not a term favoured by lawyers and judges. Many characteristics of impoverishment, of course, are the subject of human rights law (access to food, water, adequate housing, health infrastructures), but there is no internationally recognised right to not live in poverty. Is this because poverty is commonly associated with low monetary income, and money itself is only one aspect of poverty? Perhaps. If this is indeed the case, then the law may be correct in its failure to specifically attend to the condition of income deprivation.

Other disciplines' views of poverty are more sophisticated. Economics studies on poverty (to measure it and assess its impacts on economies) have become progressively more elaborate, with debates over what should be measured and how. While the two basic approaches look to assess either income or expenditure (with disagreements as to the data necessary and the methods to be applied to do so), other theories try to capture the familial and societal aspects of poverty. The latter approach builds on sociological studies of poverty. These have exposed the relationships and networks that impoverished persons maintain to survive with few material assets. They also have highlighted the contributory effects of other deprivations on income poverty, showing that poverty is not just a cause of homelessness, disability, lack of education, and poor mental health, but is often a consequence of these.

Other scholars reject the primarily financial approach to defining poverty more fundamentally. The capability approach (that considers poverty an 'unfreedom') recognises that lives can be impoverished even where incomes are sufficient to cover material wants.[3] Income, Sen reminds us, is merely instrumental to well-being—people need more than wealth to be free.

Here, the scope of problems seems to escape clear definition. The impoverished individual is socially disadvantaged, set out against multiple hurdles to her full integration in the life of a community. The financial, physical, cognitive, or psychological weaknesses that characterise poverty may make individuals unable to participate fully or freely in activities that tie people together, providing them with a background against which to develop ideas about themselves and to determine their futures.

i. *Poverty Measurement in the EU*

The statistical information on poverty collected by the EU has integrated the broader aspects of poverty into the traditional economic frameworks. Using a multivariate approach in addition to absolute and relative measures, the EU hopes to capture the social exclusion aspects of poverty as measured by consumption patterns along with those that are income-focused.

The parameters to be assessed by Eurostat are set forth in Commission regulations to ensure comparability.[4] Currently, data is collected on both individuals and households by means of personal interviews.[5] These units will answer a set of questions relating to their social and cultural participation and on their level of material deprivation.[6] These questions try to capture whether social exclusion is voluntary, involuntary, and/or due to financial status. The periods over which

[3] Martha Nussbaum's and Amartya Sen's renowned idea of attending to an individual's particular needs when assessing what is required to make a life worth valuing considers poverty to have many aspects, all of which limit the capacity of the person to reach her full potential. Eg, Amartya Sen, *Development as Freedom* (New York, Alfred A Knopf, 1999) 14.

[4] See Commission Regulation (EU) 67/2014 implementing Regulation (EC) 1177/2003 concerning Community statistics on income and living conditions (EU-SILC) as regards the 2015 list of target secondary variables on social and cultural participation and material deprivation.

[5] Reg (EU) 67/2014, Annex.

[6] ibid.

the data applies are categorised as 'current', 'last 12 months', or 'usual', allowing the statistics to reflect adjustments in behaviour due to temporary income shortages and perceptions of vulnerability.[7]

ii. How much Poverty in Europe?

Going by the numbers, there is a modest amount of poverty in Europe. There are, for a start, few residents of Europe who are unable to survive due to a lack of resources. The 'absolute',[8] or 'extreme',[9] poverty that forces over one billion people worldwide to live without enough food, water, or shelter exists at minimal levels in Europe, where approximately 4 million survive at the edge of subsistence.[10] This number is low thanks primarily to the existence of multi-layered social assistance programmes and social insurance.

Relative poverty rates indicate, however, that there is a noticeable proportion of the population that suffers from restricted access to resources. The term 'relative poverty' refers to having an income that is a set percentage (Europe adheres to the World Bank's benchmark of 60 per cent) less than the median income in the community. This permits a comparison of wealth distributions across countries, even though it says little about the amount of resources available to the people in total.

The notion behind measuring inequality even in 'rich' countries is to underscore the value of social inclusion for individual well-being. While not physically life-threatening, great financial inequality can severely hamper a person's quality of life in a community. Persons with less than 60 per cent of the average financial resources available to their neighbours will be less able to choose how they live, what they eat, how they dress, which leisure activities they will take part in, and how much they participate in governing their town or country. All of these things are integral to social integration, thus making it a more accurate measure of poverty than the uniform standard of $1.25/day.

Officially, the EU looks at poverty from a more holistic perspective than income, focusing on degrees of 'material deprivation'. This single measure captures both a lack of resources and a risk of poverty. According to Eurostat, in 2012, there were 124.5 million people (24.8 per cent of the EU population) who were considered

[7] ibid.

[8] Defined by the World Bank as existence on $1.25 per day.

[9] The European Commission's report on extreme poverty calls the term 'absolute poverty' a 'marketing tool, a heuristic device, to provide an acceptable focus for world efforts to tackle poverty'. It therefore has adopted the term 'extreme poverty' to indicate a lack of resources such that subsistence cannot be assured. European Commission, Directorate-General for Employment, Social Affairs and Inclusion, 'The Measurement of Extreme Poverty in the European Union' (28 January 2011) (available at measurement_extreme_poverty-1.pdf).

[10] The World Bank's 2012 statistics of $1.25 per day populations show that nine European Member States have a percentage of their populations living in severe poverty. See The World Bank, 'World Development Indicators' (July 2012). Only Bulgaria (1.9 per cent of the population) has more than 0.5 per cent of the population living with $1.25 per day, with the others having significantly lower figures. Ibid.

'at risk of poverty or social exclusion' (ARPSE). Somewhat illogically, the ARPSE category includes those who live below the poverty line ('at risk of poverty'), those categorised as in a state of 'severe material deprivation',[11] and those in households with a 'very low work intensity'.[12]

Of those at risk of poverty, 17 per cent are still living below the poverty line after transfer payments. At approximately 10 per cent of the total population,[13] the average level of severe material deprivation assessed by Eurostat is modest, but individual country figures can vary significantly (up to 44 per cent in Bulgaria, and over 25 per cent in Hungary and Romania). The degree of low work intensity for those at risk of poverty was similar, at 10.4 per cent in 2012.

B. Social Vulnerability

Official poverty statistics are often contested, because measurement is based on statistics, and which statistics should be used, and how, is not accepted by all economists. The measurement of poverty in Europe depends on taking information about incomes and consumption from widely differing economies and cultures, requiring the compilation and cross-correlation of statistics that have been unified into equivalent units (normally Purchasing Power Parity, PPP) for comparison's sake. This can introduce multiple levels of inaccuracy, from the subjectivity of survey responses in collecting raw data to the use of inappropriate PPPs to the misinterpretation of the data by its final user.[14]

More importantly, even where the data and measurement methods are sound, assessing poverty requires the use of an accurate definition of what 'poverty' is. As Ravallion writes, 'Ambigous concepts make deceptive statistics',[15] and poverty is an ambiguous concept.[16] The European shift in focus from poverty to

[11] A person is considered to exist in this state when she cannot access four out of nine consumables contained on a list: 'Severely materially deprived persons have living conditions greatly constrained by a lack of resources and cannot afford at least four of the following: to pay rent or utility bills; to keep their home adequately warm; to pay unexpected expenses; to eat meat, fish or a protein equivalent every second day; a week holiday away from home; a car; a washing machine; a colour TV; or a telephone'. See Eurostat, Severely Materially Deprived People: Indicator Profile (http://epp.eurostat.ec.europa.eu/cache/ITY_SDDS/EN/t2020_53_esmsip.htm).

[12] This means that of the eligible working hours of the adults in the household, less than 20 per cent were actually worked.

[13] SILC, Material deprivation rate—Economic strain and durables dimension (17–02–2014) (available at http://appsso.eurostat.ec.europa.eu/nui/show.do?dataset=ilc_sip8&lang=en).

[14] See Sanjay G Reddy and Thomas Pogge, 'How Not to Count the Poor' in Sudhir Anand, Paul Segal, and Joseph E Stiglitz (eds), *Debates on the Measurement of Global Poverty* (Oxford, Oxford University Press, 2010) 42–85.

[15] Martin Ravallion, 'The Debate on Globalization, Poverty, and Inequality: Why Measurement Matters' in Anand et al (n 14) 25–41, 26.

[16] Ravallion takes a very different view of the World Bank's measurement methods than do Reddy and Pogge. See generally Martin Ravallion, 'A Reply to Reddy and Pogge' in Anand, Segal, Stiglitz (n 14) 86–101. He notes that the measurement of poverty is very difficult (p 97), but that efforts have improved data and methods (p 93).

social exclusion as the criterion for social vulnerability had much to do with dissatisfaction with economic poverty measurement methods.

By the early 1990s, sociologists had begun to criticise the fact that the then-major economic approaches to studying poverty centred on measuring income or consumption, and failed to take into account the non-financial aspects of poverty.[17] Attention to the social context rather than economic metrics alone allowed researchers to be more precise in analysing the lives of the poor. Looking at the poor's intra-household relationships, their social networks, and their environment, social scientists highlighted the ability of some economically vulnerable persons to access non-income resources and thereby avoid severe hardship.[18]

In the late 1990s, the basic idea of social vulnerability was opening up new angles of research in the economics literature itself. Replacing income-focused studies of poverty with studies on poverty dynamics (which try to measure the likelihood of a household's movement in and out of poverty),[19] assets (assessing, for example, how management of various assets can reduce vulnerability),[20] sustainable livelihoods (looking at the types and structure of risks to sources of household income and responses to the risks),[21] and food security (mainly looking at how to identify risks of not having access to food),[22] the multi-dimensional approach to poverty studies took hold internationally. The United Nation Development Programme's Human Poverty Index, with its aim of measuring 'human poverty' rather than 'income poverty', is witness to the need to look to social vulnerability as well as income deprivation.

i. Social Vulnerability from a Legal Perspective

Despite—or perhaps because of—its frequent use, social vulnerability is a term without a strict meaning. One set of authors defines it as 'a life-situation characterized by a multi-dimensional combination of factors of disadvantage and advantage, of inclusion and exclusion'.[23] With no precisely defined boundaries, social vulnerability subsumes factual disadvantages of many sorts—ethnic background, youth or age, gender, and socioeconomic status are clearly key,[24] but numerous other factors have also been set out as having a significant influence on whether an individual is at risk of suffering harm to her well-being (employment

[17] See Jeffrey Alwang, Paul B Siegel, Steen L Jørgensen, 'Vulnerability: A View from Different Disciplines', *Social Protection Discussion Series* No 0115 (Geneva, World Bank, June 2001) 17–18.

[18] ibid.

[19] ibid 7–8 (discussing the literature on poverty dynamics).

[20] ibid 9–10.

[21] ibid 10–13.

[22] ibid 13–17.

[23] Costanzo Ranci and Mauro Migliavacca, 'Social Vulnerability: A Multi-Dimensional Analysis' in Costanzo Ranci (ed), *Social Vulnerability in Europe: The New Configuration of Social Risks* (Basingstoke, Palgrave Macmillan, 2009) 219–49, 219.

[24] Susan L Cutter, Bryan J Boruff, and W Lynn Shirley, 'Social Vulnerability to Environmental Hazards' (2003) 84(2) *Social Science Quarterly* 243, 245.

status, education, legal status, physical condition, place of residence, and others).[25] Indeed, social vulnerability is essentially everything that could keep individuals from fully taking part in the life of the community. As a sociological concept, the breadth ensures a more comprehensive understanding of societal relationships. As an economic concept, the breadth assists in gaining a more accurate metric for assessing risks and results. Yet, this breadth makes 'social vulnerability' a very difficult concept to apply in law.

ii. Vulnerability

To be vulnerable means to be at risk of suffering harm. In the social sciences, vulnerability indicates a heightened risk of harm for particular individuals or groups. Thus, those who are more likely to face threats to their well-being, and those who face threats that are more likely to have serious impacts on their well-being than they would have on others, are 'vulnerable'. Under this view, individuals are vulnerable because of a personal characteristic, group membership, or due to the context in which they find themselves.

Researchers on vulnerability differ, however, on just how literally they approach the term. While some seem to consider those persons to be socially vulnerable who are experiencing deprivations on the basis of certain factors or conditions,[26] others insist that *actual* suffering and the *risk* of suffering must be kept separate. Chambers, for example, writes: 'Vulnerability, though, is not the same as poverty. It means not lack or want, but defencelessness, insecurity, and exposure to risk, shocks and stress.'[27]

This emphasis on exposure to risk is of particular importance to the legal analysis of vulnerability, for it underlines that the pool of 'the vulnerable' is much larger than the pool of the actually suffering. In fact, for vulnerability theorists such as Martha Fineman and Anna Grear, the pool of the vulnerable includes every human being. The main thrust of Fineman's path-breaking work in vulnerability is her emphasis on the idea that vulnerability is 'placed at the core of our understanding of what it means to be human', that it is constant, and that some forms are either impervious to human control (such as ageing) or are influenced by events beyond human control (such as natural disaster).[28] As a result, human rights law's focus on protecting the freedoms of the autonomous subject is misdirected, for every individual is dependent on others, and it is the protection of the

[25] See Cutter et al (n 24) pp 246–47 (table listing 17 factors of social vulnerability and the research done on each).

[26] This is the approach taken by the European Court of Human Rights, for example. See below section III.B.ii.a.

[27] Chambers (n 2) p 33.

[28] Martha Albertson Fineman, 'Equality, Autonomy, and the Vulnerable Subject in Law and Politics' in Martha Fineman and Anna Grear (eds), *Vulnerability: Reflections on a New Ethical Foundation for Law and Politics* (Farnham, Ashgate, 2013) 13–27.

individual that should thus be the measure of the relationship between the state and the person.

In the legal framework, as we shall see, a particularistic concept of vulnerability is gaining traction. This allows the idea of vulnerability to be brought into the human rights framework (instead of standing as an alternative to it), as the characteristic of being vulnerable may indicate discrimination. In doing so, vulnerability reveals humanity's unfailing ability to distinguish among those who are, from a human rights perspective, equals.

In the case of all of the recognised vulnerable groups (racial minorities, migrants, the disabled, children), however, the discrimination view of vulnerability often indicates the opposite side of discrimination—treating persons with different characteristics alike. Either form of discrimination (or, in the worst cases, both together) can limit the enjoyment of basic rights. The distinguishing factor of 'social' vulnerability for the law, therefore, is that being identifiably vulnerable (or belonging to an identified vulnerable group) limits the extent to which a person can enjoy the benefits of life in a community.

The multifaceted nature of social vulnerability poses a problem to courts where the interaction of factors makes distilling out a single aspect of discrimination difficult. The most obvious result of social vulnerability is income poverty, but income poverty is also a powerful factor of social vulnerability. Economic vulnerability in a world of markets heightens each type of vulnerability and can create vulnerability where it otherwise would not exist. Being 'poor', that is, can make finding a job even more difficult for the immigrant while a disabling accident can push a person into financial difficulty. This means that for courts attending to vulnerabilities, income deprivation ought to be considered on its own as well as in combination with other factors. So far, however, income poverty as a social vulnerability is rarely addressed directly.

III. POVERTY PROTECTIONS IN EUROPEAN LEGAL INSTRUMENTS

The region of the world where the emergence of poverty law holds greatest hope is Europe. The region's modern legal history demonstrates a greater commitment to protecting human dignity than do the world's other regions and its legal instruments have already gone further than other systems in offering protection against social vulnerabilities.

A. Policy Instruments

Numerous European political instruments over the years have challenged member states and the European institutions to assess and address the problems of the economically vulnerable within their territories. The EU's current political initiatives to address the multiple dimensions of poverty and the accompanying social vulnerabilities have been preceded by numerous programmes targeting income deprivation.[29] The first European Economic Community poverty programme began in 1975, with both comprehensive national reports on various metrics of poverty and cross-country topical studies on unemployment, social security, and poverty lending comparative insights.[30] The second programme, starting in 1986, saw the development of improved poverty indicators by Eurostat.[31] An 'Observatory' of policies was initiated during the third programme, but more noteworthy is the altered terminology—'social exclusion' replacing 'poverty' as the programme's focus.[32] According to one commentator, this switch could have had much to do with a cultural clash between the continental member states and the British over the concept of poverty. Whereas the British traditionally viewed and measured poverty as income (or consumption) deprivation, the French adhered to the more relational conception of deprivation. Today's policies seem to reconcile these approaches, attending to income deprivation by both supporting individuals' ability to earn wages but also by fostering social inclusion.

The oldest of the Union instruments to address vulnerability is the European Social Fund (ESF), which has been in existence since its 1957 establishment in the Treaty of Rome. The ESF is a structural financing programme that aims at promoting employment. Thus, it has traditionally focused on reducing income vulnerability, rather than relieving the most severe forms of actualised poverty. In its most recent form, the Fund is offering over 80.3 billion euros to member states for projects targeting growth and employment, with at least 20 per cent of this reserved for social inclusion programmes. A special fund within the ESF is the Youth Employment Initiative, which targets unemployed young people who are not in educational or other training programmes.

Whereas the ESF is truly focused on lessening economic vulnerability by enhancing employment opportunities, the new Europe 2020 Programme and the Platform Against Poverty are the most visible political initiatives to address poverty itself. Influenced heavily by the economic downturn of recent years, the 2020 Programme focuses on economic growth and aims to reduce the number of Europeans living in poverty by 20 million over the next six years.

Its 'flagship initiative', the European Platform Against Poverty and Social Exclusion, is one of the main vehicles to ensure that the soft targets of the Programme are actualised. To promote these, the Platform calls for the Commission to integrate the contributions of civil society as well as regional and local governmental authorities in its policy-making and to undertake studies and issue recommendations on a range of issues relating to poverty. The Platform

[29] For a concise overview of the pre-Millennial poverty programmes, see Joined Cases C-239/96 R and C-240/96 R *UK and Germany v Commission* 24 September 1996 [1996] ECR I-04475, §§ 14–27.

[30] Graham Room, 'Poverty and Social Exclusion: The New European Agenda for Policy and Research' in Graham Room (ed), *Beyond the Threshold* (Bristol, The Policy Press, 1995) 1–9, 2.

[31] ibid p 2.

[32] ibid p 3.

is notable for its direct references to poverty and income vulnerability, stating clearly in its list of rationales that there is both significant poverty and a substantial level of income vulnerability in the EU as well as a growing income gap between rich and poor,[33] that social inequalities are growing as a result of income inequality,[34] and that poverty 'can be classed as a human rights violation and is thus proof of the effort still needed to achieve the aims set out in Article 3(3)' of the TEU.[35] This turn-back to a clearer focus on poverty as an issue of income deprivation in policy-making is interesting, and opens the door to the possibility of sharpening legal instruments to address the lack of financial resources more explicitly as well.

B. Legal Instruments

Poverty, as a matter of social policy, is mainly left to the member states to regulate. The Treaty on the Functioning of the European Union classifies social policies as a matter of shared competences, but in fact has remained substantially out of the member states' way in their regulation of social assistance and social insurance programmes. With the implementation of the European Platform, the Parliament suggests a more unified approach to poverty reduction, but continues to mainly 'call on' the member states to take actions. Similarly, while the Commission stated its plans to 'step up efforts to combat poverty and social exclusion',[36] it continues to stress that 'essential policies to tackle poverty and social exclusion are primarily in the hands of member states'.[37]

A full discussion of poverty in the European legal system would have to examine each set of national laws and the courts' enforcement of these provisions. As such an undertaking would far surpass the scope of this author's expertise, the following will focus solely on the three most significant regional instruments: the consolidated treaties of the European Union; the Council of Europe's Social Charter; and the European Convention on Human Rights.

[33] C 153 E/60 at A.

[34] C 153 E/60 at F.

[35] C 153 E/60 at H.

[36] Report from the Commission to the Council and the European Parliament on the implementation, results and overall assessment of the 2010 European Year for Combating Poverty and Social Exclusion COM (2012) 107 final 4.2, p 10.

[37] COM (2012) 107 final 4, p 10. The Commission does acknowledge that the EU 'has a major role to play' and 'must live up to expectations', but the 'new instruments' to which it refers with which to fulfil this major role are those of Europe 2020 and the Platform—both of which are soft policy instruments rather than legal tools.

i. Poverty in the EU Treaties: Textual References and Jurisprudence

Originally conceived to protect economic freedoms in the hopes of defeating poverty and its political consequences, the agreements leading to today's European Union treaties[38] were focused on the protection of those aspects of life that were aimed at fostering the development of a single market (movement of goods, services, labour and capital) governed by common rules where necessary, but leaving member state authority intact where possible. Growing attention to human rights expanded the scope such that today's European Union framework includes a full Charter of Fundamental Rights (CFR) in addition to the Treaty on European Union (TEU) and the Treaty on the Functioning of the European Union (TFEU). The European Court of Justice (ECJ), as the highest juridical instance in the Union, decides on Member's compatibility with the rules of each of the European treaties.

Together with the TFEU, the TEU and the CFR demonstrate a clear recognition of the fact that there is a group of socially vulnerable persons which may require special attention from the government. Although the drafters did not use the term 'vulnerable', it is reasonably clear that those living in poverty and the socially excluded face particular risks in being able to achieve the 'well-being' the Union aims to provide its peoples.

a. TEU

The original liberalism of the Union's post-World War II founders incorporated goals of improved standards of living as a presumptive result of economic integration. Seeing economic growth as consequence of trading freedoms, the project of creating a common European market was an effort to restore prosperity. Thus, the Treaty's provisions on free movement of goods, services, and labour can be understood as implicitly aiming at poverty reduction. Yet, naturally, this assumption cannot be the basis of a legal obligation to notice poverty.

The post-Lisbon TEU, however, adds some language to which the ECJ might refer when interpreting other provisions. In Article 3 TEU, the aim of 'well-being' is explicitly set forth.[39] Moreover, the EU obliges itself to 'combat social exclusion and discrimination, and … promote social justice and protection' at home[40]—a much stronger call than that stated in Article 3(3)'s first paragraph, where the promise is to 'work for the sustainable development of Europe … aiming at full employment and social progress'[41] and that two paragraphs below, in which the Union promises to 'contribute to … eradication of poverty' abroad.[42] As aims, the

[38] All references are to the 2012 consolidated version of the treaties.
[39] Art 3(1) TEU.
[40] Art 3(3) TEU.
[41] Art 3(3) TEU.
[42] Art 3(5) TEU.

text of Article 3 is likely to be referred to by the Court for purposes of interpretation but is not firmly applied on its own. At the same time, these are not preambular paragraphs, and the clear separation of the Article 3(3) paragraphs ought to be given particular judicial attention. As yet, however, there have been no court decisions on the precise status of Article 3 TEU, so its relevance to the reduction of income poverty in Europe remains questionable.[43]

b. TFEU

The concepts of well-being and combating social exclusion are given further reference in the TFEU. Article 9 of that treaty notes that the Union's policy-making shall 'take into account the requirements of ... the guarantee of adequate social protection [and] the fight against social exclusion'.[44] By posing the Union as an opponent of 'social exclusion' and obligating itself to action to create a minimum of 'social protection', the TFEU underscores the implicit vulnerability of those who lack the resources or means to participate freely in society.

The significance of the TFEU to the law of income poverty is that it clearly establishes the competence of the Union to legislate for poverty reduction should it choose to do so. In Article 4 TFEU, 'social policy' is set out as an area of shared competence.

The further elaboration of the competences of social policy found in Title X ('Social Policy') is heavily based on policies in the area of labour rights. Certainly, this focus on ensuring an adequate level of labour rights, protections, and provision for social insurance is of clear benefit to the socially vulnerable (given the connection between employment and both poverty and social exclusion). By reducing the risks of becoming unemployed and those of falling into poverty should unemployment occur, the vulnerability of the worker is reduced. That the provisions could be interpreted as purely relating to labour rights is hardly conceivable, given the prominent place of social exclusion and poverty reduction on the EU's political agenda.

Even if Title X were to be restrictively interpreted, however, the TFEU affords further shared competences to the Union in the area of economic, social and territorial cohesion.[45] Article 174 TFEU commands that 'the Union shall develop and pursue its actions leading to the strengthening of its economic, social and territorial cohesion'. As there are significant differences in levels and intensities of

[43] Ian Manners' discussion of the normative power of the EU in international relations sheds a more hopeful light on the significance of Art 3(3). Manners asserts that the Union's obligation to apply its own principles to its external affairs can change international norms. See Ian Manners, 'The normative ethics of the European Union' (2008) 84(1) *International Affairs* 45, 48, 52–53. If this is true, the fact that Art 3(3) requires the Union to combat social exclusion and pursue social justice at home would mean that it must also do so abroad; this in turn could contribute to the development of a more general principle of combating social exclusion that would apply to all states.

[44] Art 9 TFEU.

[45] Art 4(2)(c) TFEU; Title XVIII TFEU.

poverty among the member states, this provision lends a hook for legislating on poverty alleviation. This is in fact what has occurred.

In May 2013, the European Parliament released a draft legislative resolution on the Council's 'proposal for a regulation of the European Parliament and of the Council on the Fund for European Aid to the Most Deprived'.[46] According to the first reading amendments, the law, if passed, would provide moneys to member states for the purpose of supplementing the European Social Fund's financial assistance with moneys to be used for offering food and non-food material assistance to those suffering most from poverty (named as the homeless and children in materially deprived households).[47] If adopted, this legislation would be a first step toward a clear Union programme to address income deprivation broadly, as the measure of 'material deprivation' would be based on a deprivation index that emphasises income and financial status—the absolute and relative income as well as 'the ability to make ends meet' and over-indebtedness.[48]

c. CFR

The EU's Charter of Fundamental Rights enhances the Union's legal framework significantly by incorporating the human rights recognised in the ECHR as well as the ECJ's case law. The CFR has an explicit provision on poverty and social exclusion in which these terms are separated from references to employment-based rights.[49]

CFR Article 34, 'Social security and social assistance', has three paragraphs, each of which implicitly indicates groups which are vulnerable and promises that the EU will respect any rights to financial resources they may enjoy. Paragraphs 1 and 2 speak of those who are easily recognised as vulnerable—whether because of physical condition (maternity, illness, or accident), age, dependency, or status as a foreigner. Those who have lost a job are also named.[50] While carefully caged so as not to give an independent right not to live a life of poverty, paragraph 3 states:

> In order to combat social exclusion and poverty, the Union recognizes and respects the right to social and housing assistance so as to ensure a decent existence for all those who lack sufficient resources, in accordance with the rules laid down by Union law and national laws and practices.

This provision is particularly noteworthy for underscoring the origin of the problems facing the both the excluded and the poor: a 'lack [of] sufficient resources'.

[46] [2013] OJ C133/62; see also COM (2012)0617—C7-0358/2012—2012/0295 (COD).

[47] See ibid proposed amendment to Recital 6, p 10.

[48] ibid proposed amendment to Recital 12(c), pp 14–15.

[49] While the Charter's Art 17 sets out a right to property, this, like the right in Protocol 1 ECHR, cannot be seen as offering protection against poverty outside of the unlikely event of a state expropriating so much of an individual's property that she would face impoverishment.

[50] Art 34(1) CFR.

It is unfortunate that there is no case law discussing Article 34, for this is the most promising provision yet for the furtherance of a general concept of poverty as a vulnerability—one that allows room for recognising that in some cases, the risks a poor person faces within a community are due solely to a failure of money and access to credit. Naturally, the wording allows for social exclusion and poverty to be seen as a single category. This would have the unfortunate consequence of seeing the two as synonymous, which, as will be discussed below, is not necessarily the case.

Before setting out my considerations of why discussions of social vulnerability in law should allow for a specific analysis of income poverty on its own, it is important to mention that the ECJ's jurisprudence to CFR Article 21 does not bring the discussion of poverty further. The prohibition on non-discrimination set out in Article 21 is similar to that of EMRK Article 14. The grounds mentioned are slightly different, with a substitution of 'disability, age or sexual orientation' for the 'other status' found elsewhere. These, as one can see, are in fact the European Court of Human Rights' (ECtHR) categories of vulnerable persons, and poverty is—not surprisingly—not among them. The list is inclusive, however, as indicated by the words 'such as' at the beginning of the sentence.

Case law on Article 21 so far does not show much promise for addressing poverty on its own. Given the high correlation between poverty and the other Article 21 categories, this may not be significant as a practical matter. Theoretically, however, it leaves the same issues open that the lack of reference to income deprivation by the ECtHR in matters of discrimination does.

While the provisions of the Charter appear to make it a promising instrument to address income poverty, the restriction of its effectiveness to Union legislation reduces its potency. Article 51 TFEU limits the applicability of the Charter's provisions 'to the institutions, bodies, offices and agencies of the Union … and to the Member States only when they are implementing Union law'.[51] Given the lack of Union law mandating that measures be taken to reduce income poverty or to afford income-deprived individuals with rights or protections based on their economic status, the CFR is likely to remain underutilised.[52]

ii. Protection of Poverty in the Council of Europe

Europe is not only one of the wealthiest regions of the world, it is also the region with the most developed set of rules to protect society's most disadvantaged. The idea of developing legal protections for the economically and socially disadvantaged persons in Europe stems from the earliest post-World War II years, but, like

[51] Art 51(1) TEFU.

[52] Eg, *Case of Ms NG v Sparkasse O*, Landesgericht Düsseldorf, 16 September 2011, 6 Sa 909/11, 10 (dismissing claim of a wrongfully dismissed employee that her dismissal violated CFR Art 21(1)'s prohibition on discrimination on the basis of property because the Art 21 prohibition only applies to member states when they are implementing Union law).

the UN Covenants, was considered separable from the protections of civil and political rights. Thus, the initial European human rights system consisted of the European Convention on Human Rights and Fundamental Freedoms (ECHR) on the one hand and the European Social Charter (ESC) on the other. Poverty, in the early days of the European region, was clearly a matter only for the latter. We have seen that the new Union focus on poverty and social exclusion has expanded the scope for legal protections of income poverty to emerge, but the bindingness of the provisions is low and the access to the ones that are binding is limited.

The instruments of the Council of Europe offer more promise to individuals affected by income poverty. Both the ESC and the ECHR provide for direct individual complaints and offer remedies in case a violation is found. We turn now to examine how these instruments have approached income poverty and the accompanying social vulnerability.

a. Poverty in ECHR Jurisprudence

The European Convention on Human Rights (ECHR), drafted parallel to the ESC, is focused on the protection of civil and political rights—the traditional, 'first generation' human rights. As such, it is not too surprising that ECHR judges recently noted that 'the Convention does not enshrine any "right not to be poor"'.[53]

Indeed, a quick run-through of the substantive rights set out reveals that they make no mention of *poverty* or *poor*, nor are the words *income*, *exclusion*, or *economic* to be found. *Social* is mentioned twice, although not in the sense of social exclusion as is found in the Charter: the Convention itself (Article 14) and Protocol 12 (Article 1) both refer to the prohibited grounds of discrimination on the basis of social origin. *Property* is mentioned in this context as well—Article 14 states that the rights and freedoms of the Convention are to be 'secured without discrimination' on grounds of property—and the protection of property is also found in Article 1 of the 1952 Protocol. Interestingly, while Article 14's use of the term has led to no significant protections of those without property, the right to property is commonly acknowledged as broad, including economic interests and claims along with tangible property.[54] Thus, the right to hold on to property is protected, but not the right to have any in the first place.

The Convention, it would appear, offers little if any protections against poverty—in either of its forms (income deprivation or as social exclusion). And, it seems, the Court knows it.

But the Convention's text is a product of its time, and that time was one not just of political division over the acceptability of denoting economic interests as 'rights', but also of broader disagreement over the definition of poverty. While

[53] ECHR Seminar Organizing Committee (Judges Laffranque, Raimondi, Bianku, Nussberger, and Sicilianos, assisted by R Liddell), Seminar Background Paper: *Implementing the European Convention on Human Rights in times of economic crisis* (25 January 2013), § 1.

[54] See, eg, *Fabris v France* App no 16574/08 (ECtHR, 7 February 2013), §§49–50.

there is still significant debate over the setting and use of poverty lines and the precise definition of content of a subsistence income, there is broad consensus around the idea that financial deprivation often has serious implications on the economic, social, and political opportunities available to individuals. The Court, therefore, seeing the Convention as an evolving document, has read the treaty's provisions as offering some protections against the worst consequences of economic deprivation.

Poverty and the Effective Enjoyment of Rights

A factual connection between financial status and civil rights was recognised as determinative in the Airey judgment in 1979. Discussed further below, the *Airey* Court's clear language providing an early basis for the comprehensive view of human rights currently applied. More recent cases demonstrate the Court's awareness of poverty's multiple dimensions, and its recognition of the vulnerability of impoverished claimants. This strand of judgments provides hope to some observers that the Convention can offer sufficient flexibility to judges to pursue the goals of vulnerability theorists in establishing institutions that are more responsive to the human needs of real people (and not just to the theoretical needs of the liberal subject of law).

Yet, what the Court has yet to do is clearly set forth income deprivation on its own as a characteristic of vulnerability. Thus, while it has intervened to protect particular individuals from the effects of poverty where the individual is in circumstances of dependence on the state and has also identified certain groups of individuals as 'vulnerable' and in need of particular attention to ensure their enjoyment of the Convention's rights, the Court does not offer much hope for those who object to the systematic, or institutionalised, division of wealth in European societies.

Article 6 and the Right to Access to Courts

The *Airey* judgment deserves particular comment, as it sets out a basis for regarding poverty through the Convention. In the case, Mrs Airey complained that she was unable to attain a legal order of separation from her alcoholic and abusive husband due to a lack of financial resources.[55] Her claim of a violation of Article 6 was upheld by the Court. The Convention's rights, wrote the majority, are not primarily aimed at protecting economic or social well-being, but the real enjoyment of the civil and political rights is to some extent connected to financial conditions.[56] Thus, where access to legal proceedings is impossible because a person is unable to afford such access, it is the state's obligation to support that person in order to ensure that the

[55] *Airey v Ireland* App no 6289/73 (ECtHR, 9 October 1979).
[56] ibid, § 26.

rights are 'practical and effective'.[57] Mrs Airey's rights under Articles 6 and 8 had been violated because the government had not done so.[58]

Article 3 and the Prohibition on Degrading Treatment

Interestingly, most of the poverty-related cases rest on the guarantees of Article 3 ECHR, the protection from torture. 'No one', states Article 3, 'shall be subjected to torture or to inhuman or degrading treatment or punishment'. Seeing poverty as 'inhuman' or 'degrading' would therefore open the way to protecting against this condition.

The ECHR has taken limited steps in this direction where an individual was under the state's control and her extreme poverty was clear and known to the authorities. In several cases the Court has indicated that it might find a duty on states to provide a person with medical care if the person were 'in circumstances wholly dependent on' the state.[59] In the case of *MSS v Belgium and Greece*[60] this suggestion was acted on when an asylum-seeker's plea was ignored by the state authorities for several months, leaving him with no financial resources, shelter, or sanitation. While his condition of 'most extreme poverty'[61] lasted only a matter of months, the lack of even a minimal level of state support, in combination with the failure to offer him any information as to when his request would be resolved, was found to be a violation of his rights under Article 3.[62] Because MSS was considered particularly vulnerable due to his condition as an asylum-seeker,[63] the Court presumed a positive duty on the state to ensure that he would not be faced with such feelings of degradation.

The *Budina* case raised a similar question as to the state's obligation to provide financial assistance to protect a person from suffering from degrading living conditions. In that case, Ms Budina, an elderly woman who was chronically ill with tuberculosis and mental health problems, complained that her pension was inadequate to allow her to live a dignified existence. The Court, while repeating its commitment to the possibility of finding a state duty to support her materially, denied her claim of Article 3 violation. The conditions in which she lived,

[57] ibid, § 24.

[58] ibid, § 28. See also *Annoni di Gussola and Others v France* App nos 31819/96 and 33293/96, ECHR 2000–XI, § 56 (the Court 'considers that the precariousness of the applicants' respective financial circumstances, which made it impossible for them even to begin to comply with the judgments of the courts of appeal, constitutes the decisive factor in the examination of the limitations on their right of access to the Court of Cassation').

[59] *O'Rourke v United Kingdom* App no 39022/97 (ECtHR, 26 June 2001); *Nitecki v Poland* App no 65653/01 (ECtHR, 21 March 2002).

[60] *MSS v Belgium and Greece* App no 30696/09 (ECtHR [GC], 21 January 2011).

[61] ibid, § 254.

[62] ibid, § 263.

[63] Judge Sajó dissents from this characterisation, arguing against categorical grouping of 'vulnerable persons'. See *MSS v Belgium and Greece*, Partly Concurring and Partly Dissenting Opinion of Judge Sajó. He also opposes the recognition of rights of asylum seekers to material subsistence to cover 'basic needs'.

the majority held, were not such as to be degrading. The language of the decision sheds light on the extent of income deprivation one must suffer to be considered eligible for protection under Article 3:

> [T]he Court notes that the applicant's income within the period in question was not high in absolute terms. However, the applicant has failed to substantiate her allegation that the lack of funds translated itself into concrete suffering. On the contrary, in her observations the applicant explained that in 2008 her pension was enough for flat maintenance, food, and hygiene items, but was not enough for clothes, non-food goods, sanitary and cultural services, health and sanatorium treatment. Of these latter items, it appears that the applicant was in fact eligible for free medical treatment. … Indeed there is no indication in the materials before the Court that the level of pension and social benefits available to the applicant have been insufficient to protect her from damage to her physical or mental health or from a situation of degradation incompatible with human dignity …. Therefore even though the applicant's situation was difficult, … the Court is not persuaded that in the circumstances of the present case the high threshold of Article 3 has been met.[64]

Individuals must suffer particularly extreme levels of material deprivation, it would appear, before Article 3 ECHR will offer protection.

Relative Poverty: Article 14 and Discrimination

Much of the poverty suffered in Europe is 'relative' poverty—the form in which an individual or family has enough resources to secure basic survival, but not enough to be able to fully partake of community life. Does the law regard the difficulties faced by these persons?

Even when an individual is not suffering extreme poverty, the Convention could help ensure that impoverished persons are not targeted for disadvantageous treatment. The protection most suited for those in relative poverty is that found in the prohibition on non-discrimination.

As a support to the protections guaranteed by the Convention, the Court may entertain a complaint based solely on the discriminatory application of a right or freedom on the basis of Article 14 ECHR or an Article 14 claim in combination with a claim of a violation of the underlying right/freedom. According to Article 14, the state may not distinguish, exclude, restrict, prefer, or otherwise differentiate ('discriminate'), or permit discrimination of, an individual in her enjoyment of the Convention's protections. Not an absolute prohibition, Article 14 sets out a number of possible characteristics upon which persons can be identified as deserving preferential or disadvantageous treatment and restricts their use as legal criteria. These prohibited grounds of discrimination are those of 'sex, race, colour, language, religion, political or other opinion, national or social origin, association with a national minority, property, birth or other status'.

[64] *Budina v Russia* (dec) App no 45603/05 (ECtHR, 18 June 2009) 7.

Overlapping with the grounds set out in Protocol 12 and the UN Covenants' Article 2, Article 14 offers little in the way of particular surprises (welcome or unwelcome) for poverty scholars. Whereas the potential for condemning practices that would unreasonably negatively affect impoverished individuals' or groups' right to life, liberty, family, or property exists, the Courts have refrained from wielding the offered tools to create an explicit prohibition on discrimination based on 'poverty'.

Relative Poverty on the Basis of Social Origin and Birth

There have been few opportunities for the Court to investigate the limits of 'social origin' or 'birth' as grounds of discrimination. Ensuring that hereditary social status, whether on the basis of class or caste, does not translate into legal differentiation, the prohibition integrates the idea that community perspectives and tradition should not determine an individual's position before the law. It is a small step from prohibiting a community-supported norm such as title to make a difference and seeing wealth—or the lack of it—as an equally illegitimate grounds to differentiate individuals in a legal system. Put forth as a possibility by commentators on both the ECHR and the ICESCR, this extension of 'social origin' or 'birth', however, has not yet been written into the Court's decisions.

Relative Poverty on the Basis of Property

The legal concept of property, as discussed below, is extremely complex. For purposes of discrimination law, however, the matter is simpler: the prohibition on discrimination based on property is a protection against differential treatment of individuals based on the amount of property they own. The Court's jurisprudence on property as a basis of discrimination is extremely limited: in *Chassagnou and Others v France*, the Court found in favour of complainants that alleged discrimination on the basis of property when they demonstrated that large landowners were privileged over small landowners by local rules requiring small holders to transfer public hunting rights but not large holders.[65]

Whether discrimination could be alleged on the basis of disadvantaging those with no property is conceivable, but as there is no right to acquire property set out in the Convention, the discrimination would need to affect the claimant's rights under a separate clause—such as that to family and home (Article 8) or physical integrity (Article 3). As yet, however, there are no such cases from which to extrapolate the impacts on poverty.

[65] *Chassagnou and Others v France* App nos 25088/94, 28331/95, and 28443/95 (ECtHR, 29 April 1999).

Relative Poverty: Other Status

Because Article 14's is an illustrative list (as indicated by the words 'such as' before the list begins), the 'other status' provision is not strictly necessary, but it does lend a contextual framework. The illegal grounds for discrimination are to be ones that lend 'status'—a characteristic that is either unchangeable or not easily changeable—to the individual. Thus, the Court has found disability, age, marital status, and place of residence (among others) to be such statuses.[66]

Interestingly, each of these recognised 'other status' elements is often found in combination with poverty—certainly increasing the risk of a person having both a low income and reduced social resources, disability, marital status, and even place of residence can also be a result of poverty. Yet, so far there has been little indication from the Court that poverty would be considered a 'status', the discrimination of which would be prohibited by Article 14. The Committee on Economic, Social and Cultural Rights, however, has written on this topic. General Comment 20 devotes one paragraph to the possible application of the non-discrimination obligation to individuals who are in 'a certain economic or social … strata within society'.[67] When a person is impoverished or homeless, the Committee points out, 'discrimination, stigmatization and negative stereotyping' can result in denial of numerous social or civil rights.[68] Without directly calling for a prohibition on such discrimination, the Committee clearly suggests that poverty could be considered a 'status'.[69]

The paucity of cases addressing poverty in the discrimination context prevents a full understanding of what the Court might do with Article 14's text in the future.

Right to Property under the Protocol

Protocol 1 to the ECHR, recognising the right to property, ensures that individuals are entitled to retain their possessions or be compensated for their losses incurred by the government's acquisition of their property. It does not lend a right to individuals to have or acquire property.[70] This, again, is a key limitation to its potential for addressing extreme poverty and unequal distributions of income.

[66] The Court has also found fatherhood, membership in an organisation, military rank, and the legitimacy of a child's birth (*Vermeire v Belgium* (1991) Series A no 214-C; *Brauer v. Germany* App no 3545/04 (ECtHR, 28 May 2009)) to be statuses protected by Art 14. See European Union Agency for Fundamental Rights, *Handbook on European non-discrimination law* (Luxembourg, Publications Office of the European Union, 2011) § 4.12, p 118 (with cases listed). The Committee on Economic, Social, and Cultural Rights has held up disability, age, nationality, marital and family status, sexual orientation and gender identity, health status, and place of residence to be candidates for 'other status' upon which states should not discriminate. E/C.12/GC/20, §§ 28–34.

[67] ibid § 35.

[68] ibid.

[69] ibid.

[70] *Fabris v France*, § 50 (also citing *Slivenko and Others v Latvia* (dec) [GC], App no 48321/99, § 121, ECHR 2002–II (extracts); *Ališić and Others v Bosnia-Herzegovina Croatia, Serbia, Slovenia and the former Yugoslav Republic of Macedonia* (dec) App no 60642/08 (ECtHR, 17 October 2011), § 52.

Still, the Protocol has been used effectively as a protective shield for impoverished Europeans. This has been put into effect in two ways: first, by finding that rights to social benefit payments are 'property'; second, the states are given significant margins of appreciation in defining their social and economic policy programmes.

As mentioned above, the Court has developed a substantial and consistent case law that defines 'property' broadly. An individual's legitimate interests in non-material benefits are considered as falling within the protections of Protocol 1, Article 1.[71] This exends to individuals who have a right to social security payments and unemployment benefits. While there is no obligation on states to offer social security payments, if they do offer such as a right, this right is protected under Article 1.[72]

That states have a margin of appreciation in determining their own economic and social policies is also firmly established and of clear benefit to poverty reduction programmes. A recent judgment repeated the Court's position on this:

> [A]cknowledging that the margin of appreciation available to the legislature in implementing social and economic policies should be a wide one, the Court has declared that it will respect the legislature's judgment as to what is in the 'public' or 'general' interest unless that judgment is manifestly without reasonable foundation.[73]

This obviously has important consequences in the area of taxation, where the Court has held that taxes may be collected for the purpose of redistributing income. It also can affect the availability of housing for the poor—although individual rent control policies have often been found to violate the property owner's rights, the decisions have been based on the government's failure to adequately balance the interests at stake rather than on a principled opposition to offering benefits to the poor at the cost of other private persons.[74] Indeed, the Court has stated explicitly that

> measures, implemented with a view to securing the social protection of tenants … aimed at preventing homelessness, as well as at protecting the dignity of poorly off tenants … had a legitimate aim in the general interest, as required by the second paragraph of Article 1.[75]

The Protocol, therefore, can support member states' attempts to reduce poverty. It does not, however, go further than member states themselves wish to regulate.

[71] *Fabris v France*, § 50.

[72] *Carson and Others v United Kingdom* App no. 42184/05 (ECtHR, 16 March 2010), § 64 ('if a State did decide to enact legislation providing for the payment as of right of a welfare benefit or pension—whether conditional or not on the prior payment of contributions—that legislation had to be regarded as generating a proprietary interest falling within the ambit of Article 1 of Protocol No. 1 for persons satisfying its requirements'); *Stec and Others v the United Kingdom* (dec) [GC], App nos. 65731/01 and 65900/01, ECHR 2005-X, § 54.

[73] Eg, *Bittó and Others v Slovakia* App no 30255/09 (ECtHR, 28 January 2014), §§ 96, 101.

[74] *Bittó*, § 116. See also *Ghigo v Malta* App no 31122/05, § 69 (ECtHR, 26 September 2006); *Edwards v Malta* App no 17647/04 (ECtHR, 24 October 2006) §78; *Hutten-Czapska v Poland* App no 35014/97 (ECtHR, 19 June 2006), § 224.

[75] *Edwards v Malta*, §§ 67–68.

b. European Social Charter (1996)

The 1961 adoption of the European Social Charter was intended to form the pendant to the ECHR's protection of civil and political rights by providing protections of economic and social rights. While it entered into force in 1965, however, it failed to live up to the hopes of its supporters. With states able to choose from among its provision those to which they would be bound, its Committee of Independent Experts subject to the CoE's Committee of Ministers, and no mechanism for individual complaints, the instrument remained weak and 'largely ignored'.[76]

As legal attention to economic and social rights in the wider human rights community began to develop in the 1990s, pressure grew for the Charter's rejuvenation. The ensuing revision process led to a more independent Committee of Experts and a mechanism for hearing 'collective complaints'—that is, charges brought by individuals or groups alleging a party's failure to adhere to the Charter obligations. Should such allegations be upheld by the Committee, it can call on the party to come into compliance.

While the process leading to the Revised Social Charter was mainly about strengthening the institutional framework, it also expanded the scope of the rights the Charter sets out to protect. Among the new provisions is Article 30, which contains an explicit reference to poverty and social exclusion:

1. Everyone has the right to protection against poverty and social exclusion.
2. With a view to ensuring the effective exercise of the right to protection against poverty and social exclusion, the Parties undertake:
   a. to take measures within the framework of an overall and co-ordinated approach to promote the effective access of persons who live or risk living in a situation of social exclusion or poverty, as well as their families, to, in particular, employment, housing, training, education, culture and social and medical assistance;
   b. to review these measures with a view to their adaptation if necessary.

The grant of a right to protection against poverty is particularly important given the strength of its wording. Defining 'poverty' as a 'deprivation due to a lack of resources',[77] the Committee takes the view that living in such a condition is a violation of human dignity.[78] The rights language is therefore a conscious decision to link economic conditions to the normative framework of human rights law. It also calls attention to the multidimensional aspects of poverty[79] and indicates that parties must address all of these in their programmes to ensure poor

[76] Olivier De Schutter, *International Human Right Law* (Cambridge, Cambridge University Press, 2010) 914.

[77] *Digest of the Case Law of the European Committee of Social Rights*, 1 September 2008, p 167 (text available at www.coe.int/t/dghl/monitoring/socialcharter/Digest/DigestSept2008_en.pdf). See also Conclusions 2005, France, p 261.

[78] *Digest* at 167. See also Conclusions 2003, France, p 214.

[79] ibid.

individuals' enjoyment of social rights.[80] Interestingly, too, the Committee stresses that financial resources are required to both fund poverty reduction programmes and to eliminate economic vulnerability of individuals: 'adequate resources are an essential element to enable people to become self-sufficient'.[81]

Does this signal a swing back to viewing poverty as a fundamentally income-based problem? It is too early to tell much, but perhaps it is indicative that the one judicial instance given clear language on 'poverty' has defined the notion in this way. We turn, then, to why I think this warrants attention.

IV. WHICH LEGAL APPROACH TO POVERTY?

> 'Law!' said Bunce, with all the scorn he knew how to command — 'law! Did ye ever know a poor man yet was the better for law, or for a lawyer?'[82]

It is particularly interesting when pursuing a European-centred examination of poverty law to see the difference between how sociological and economic views of the close relationship between poverty and social vulnerability have strongly influenced the politics of poverty reduction and how this relationship is addressed by the courts. Whereas there are numerous legislative reform efforts stemming from studies setting forth the concepts of social cohesion that places social exclusion and income deprivation as dual aspects of poverty, this combination of factors has remained largely absent from European human rights jurisprudence. Similarly, while the ECtHR has given some attention to aspects of social vulnerability as a factor relevant to a state's human rights obligations, income deprivation—and thus 'poverty'—on its own receives at most passing notice and the language of the CFR has not been addressed by the ECJ at all.

To the extent that the legal system does protect a person's social inclusion, the judges are to be commended for recognising that even where basic income is secured, the vulnerability of the person to violations of his human rights remains high when he is unable to access the non-financial resources that ensure his ability to fully participate in the life of the community. The idea of 'vulnerability' itself—the existence of an elevated risk of harm due to a certain condition—demands giving notice to the individual's ability to interact with others and to profit from public infrastructure and services. With 'social vulnerability' recognised as a multi-dimensional concept, the need for policy makers to attend to a variety of risks is absolutely critical, because income alone is insufficient to offset the various social risks faced by individuals and households. Ranci and Migliavacca name the stability of employment, housing, dependency, and the ability to balance care for children or elderly relations with work schedules as dimensions of social

[80] *Digest* at 168.

[81] ibid. See also Conclusions 2005, Slovenia, p 674.

[82] Anthony Trollope, *The Warden*, ch 4.

vulnerability that are in addition to the economic aspect of a low income and lack of assets.[83] With varying groups of the population exposed to different levels of each aspect of social vulnerability, and with cumulative effects as well as combined effects, measuring income deprivation alone would severely underestimate levels of overall social vulnerability.

At the same time, it is puzzling that a low income plays so little role in legal analysis, for the connection between low income and social vulnerability is an established one, with a 40 per cent probability of households with even temporarily low income experiencing other forms of vulnerability[84] and less than 25 per cent of impoverished households not experiencing other aspects of social vulnerability.[85] Perhaps more telling, of those families that suffer most from social hardship, nearly 60 per cent are income-poor.[86]

True, a lack of income alone may indicate very little about an individual's ability to live a life of dignity and fulfilment. Varying expectations, the context in which a person lives, the non-material resources available—all these can substitute for income's role in achieving dignity. Indeed, research suggests that housing deprivation (overcrowded or poor quality living space) creates greater social vulnerability than does low income alone,[87] suggesting that attention to the material conditions of shelter may be the most effective policy to take to address social vulnerability.

Even so, a lack of income is a severe limitation on an individual's freedom to choose how to live one's life. Without income, many opportunities to participate in the life of the community become more difficult to pursue and many possibilities are foreclosed. Income poverty is therefore an 'unfreedom', in Sen's terminology.[88] The instrumental nature of income does not take away from it its importance to the individual in her pursuit of a life worth valuing. The instrumental nature rather enforces the idea that level of income is not the *only* aspect of human rights significance when looking at poverty, but it is still a *part* of poverty.

For Europe, the existence of income poverty stands in the way of achieving the Union's goal of ensuring the wellbeing of all of its people. The literature attending to the opinions of poor individuals themselves is perhaps more telling than statistical compilations in this regard. Reading the results of the World Bank project, 'Voices of the Poor', it becomes clear that even where supplemented by non-monetary resources so that basic material needs are satisfied, the life

[83] See Constanzo Ranci and Mauro Migliavacca, 'Social Vulnerability' in Ranci (n 23) pp 219–49, 219–26.

[84] ibid, p 230.

[85] ibid, p 243.

[86] ibid, p 243 (noting that the rate of poverty in situations of 'severe hardship'—as opposed to vulnerability—is 57.8 per cent).

[87] Ranci and Migliavacca estimate that the probability of experiencing other social vulnerabilities increases three times if housing is inadequate than if it is sufficient. Ibid, p 230.

[88] Sen, of course, focuses his argument on the idea that low income is not the only form of 'poverty'. He does not deny, however, that income deprivation is also a form.

of an income-deprived person can be considered 'illbeing' and further research reinforces this finding. Shame, grief, and fear frequently accompany poverty, but frustration, anger, and the stress of constantly needing to think about finances do too, and are just as destructive to mental health. To ensure comprehensive wellbeing income poverty must also be addressed.

Why, then, do the European courts so rarely address income poverty directly?

The answer to this question must remain speculative beyond the obvious noting of an absence of explicit treaty text references to 'poverty'. This indeed is the most likely reason, in fact. With the exception of the CFR Article 34.3, the word simply does not appear in the widely applicable legal instruments. The EU, founded on the assumption that liberalised economic relations between its member states would lead to economic growth, *presumes* the subsequent elimination of poverty. Its provisions, therefore, did not need to specifically address it.[89]

Textual limitations cannot be the whole story, however, as there is enough open language in these texts to ensure that—at the very least—the state of impoverishment could be seen as a 'other status' for ECHR Article 14 (or come within the 'such as' of CFR Article 21).

Another plausible explanation would be that judges are not themselves experts of sociological and economic assessment methods. Given the undecided state (as well as the copious quantity and technical sophistication) of poverty research, judges are left with no authoritative measures for assessing poverty accurately and therefore prefer to refer to other descriptive criteria when applying the law to an individual's concrete situation.

A more subtle reason for not looking at income poverty directly is that the judges are looking past it. In this, the courts are applying only too well the lessons of the past two decades of poverty research. Given the firm evidence for the multidimensional nature of poverty and the elegant and convincing theories that value capacity and discount the role of mere financial deprivation in human dignity, there is perhaps an justified intellectual disdain of over-simplification being exhibited by the courts when they refuse to see an individual as harmed solely by the fact of not having sufficient income. Low income, they acknowledge, may worsen a person's deprivations in other areas, but with no independent right not to be poor, focusing on the other deprivations is more satisfying from the legal point of view (for the court does not have to resort to expansive interpretation of the treaty) and from the intellectual one. Clearly, this is a position that can be taken under European law because the income deprivation normally encountered by the courts is not that of extreme poverty, but rather relative poverty. (Indeed, where subsistence is threatened, such as in cases of refugees with no financial resources, the lack of financial means is often pointed out.)

[89] Jos Berghman 'Social Exclusion in Europe: Policy Context and Analytical Framework' in Room (n 30) pp 10–28, 12.

V. CONCLUSION: LEARNING FROM THE VULNERABILITY PERSPECTIVE

A. Vulnerability: the Vulnerable Subject or the Dignified Human?

Despite the ECtHR's use of vulnerability language in its recent jurisprudence, it is a human rights court and not a vulnerability court. This may make a difference—particularly in the area of poverty and income deprivation.

Martha Fineman's theorisation of 'vulnerability' reminds us that we are each vulnerable, that vulnerability is a universal characteristic of mortals because we are embodied. This fact of human vulnerability makes each of us dependent on others to a greater or lesser extent throughout our lives. Celebrating this mutual dependence, vulnerability is not seen as something only negative or limiting, as it 'is also in many ways *generative*: it forges bonds between human beings and leads us to create institutions'.[90]

Indeed, for Fineman, vulnerability drives societal formation itself: 'It is the recognition and experience of human vulnerabilities that brings individuals into families, families into communities, and communities into societies, nation states, and international organizations.'[91] Society's institutions should thus provide the 'assets' we need to be resilient—physical, human, social, ecological, and existential assets.[92] Because institutions themselves are vulnerable, the state must intervene when institutions fail to function for the good of individuals and society.[93] Thus the call for the dually 'responsive state': simultaneously assisting institutions and individuals in accordance with the principles of deep 'equality and open access and shared opportunity'.[94]

B. The Difference it Makes

The idea that social exclusion is preferred to income deprivation in European law relating to poverty appears to this author as problematic for the precise reason that it allows one to categorise those suffering from poverty as individuals or households who are unconnected, lacking social resources as well as material ones, and unable therefore to help themselves. While this may be the case for some of the poor, it is not the same for all. Seeing the income poor as vulnerable because of their lack of income, on the other hand, avoids such potentially denigrating

[90] Alexandra Timmer, 'A Quiet Revolution: Vulnerability in the European Court of Human Rights' in Martha Fineman and Anna Grear (eds), *Vulnerability: Reflections on a New Ethical Foundation for Law and Politics* (Farnham, Ashgate, 2013) 147–70, 149 (citing Fineman, '"Elderly" as vulnerable: rethinking the nature of individual and social responsibility' (2012) 20(1) *The Elder Law Journal* 101; emphasis in original).

[91] Fineman, 'Equality, Autonomy' (2013) (n 28) p 22.

[92] ibid, pp 22–23.

[93] ibid, p 25.

[94] ibid.

assumptions. Yes, the income poor are vulnerable, but they are vulnerable because they have low income. Period.

This thought is particularly important for Europe today, in the shadow of economic recession. Today's income poor—those who are unemployed or underemployed—may not be undereducated, they may not be untrained, and most importantly, they may not be socially excluded. They may, in fact, have good education, substantial training and experience, and wide social networks. In times of significant unemployment, however, they cannot find jobs and their networks may not be able to help them access employment or alternative financial resources.

The poverty as social exclusion view encourages the non-impoverished to consider the poor as a particular societal group. Tying social protections only to 'discriminations' and the visibly 'vulnerable' fosters the basic human rights premise of the liberal, autonomous person being the legal standard, with special help offered to the identifiably disadvantaged. Perhaps seeing the income-poor as persons with low income would help those of us who have never been faced with poverty to see them more as equals. As equally vulnerable, only differently so.

20

Irregular Migrants in Europe: Deprivation of Status as a Type of State-Imposed Vulnerability[*]

SARA IGLESIAS SÁNCHEZ

I. INTRODUCTION

THIS CHAPTER COVERS the legal status of foreign nationals who find themselves irregularly present in the country in which they reside. As such, the group of 'irregular migrants' covers a wide variety of individuals, such as those having irregularly crossed the border, those having overstayed their tourism or study visas, those having lost their residence permits for various reasons, those working illegally, those whose applications for international protection have been rejected, or those having already been identified as being irregularly present but who cannot be expelled for various reasons.[1]

Irregular migrants can be considered from the perspective of the vulnerability attached to not having the nationality of the state of residence.[2] Outside the European context, the mere condition of being a non-national as an element of vulnerability has been openly recognised by the Inter-American Court of Human rights and by the UN General Assembly,[3] as well as having been echoed in the preamble of the UN Convention on the Protection of the Rights of all Migrant Workers and Members of their Families.[4] The considerations of the

[*] The views expressed in this chapter are purely personal to the author.

[1] For a typology, see C Morehouse and M Blomfield, *Irregular Migration in Europe* (Washington, DC, Migration Policy Institute, December 2011). See E Guild, 'Who is an irregular migrant?' in B Bogusz et al (eds), *Irregular Migration and Human Rights: Theoretical, European and International Perspectives* (Leiden, Martinus Nijhoff, 2004) 3–28.

[2] On the vulnerable condition of 'non-nationals' see Part III of this volume.

[3] The General Assemby refers to 'the situation of vulnerability in which migrants frequently find themselves, owing, inter alia, to their absence from their State of origin and to the difficulties they encounter because of differences of language, custom and culture, as well as the economic and social difficulties and obstacles for the return to their States of origin of migrants who are non-documented or in an irregular situation', Resolution A/RES/54/166 on 'Protection of migrants' of 24 February 2000.

[4] This Convention mentions 'the situation of vulnerability in which migrant workers and members of their families frequently find themselves owing, among other things, to their absence from their State of origin and to the difficulties they may encounter arising from their presence in the State of employment.'

Inter-American Court in this respect are particularly enlightening, in that they emphasise the situation of disempowerment that usually accompanies a migratory experience. Indeed,

> Migrants are generally in a vulnerable situation as subjects of human rights; they are in an individual situation of absence or difference of power with regard to non-migrants (nationals or residents). This situation of vulnerability has an ideological dimension and occurs in a historical context that is distinct for each State and is maintained by de jure (inequalities between nationals and aliens in the laws) and de facto (structural inequalities) situations. This leads to the establishment of differences in their access to the public resources administered by the State.[5]

Beyond this reality, the particular vulnerability of irregular migrants adds to the effects of this 'dissociation between nationality and physical presence'.[6] Irregular migrants may be of any age, gender, race or sexual orientation. Theoretically, they may come from any economic or social background. From this perspective, the only fact that formally singles out irregular migrants as a group is the state policy choice to set up specific legal regimes which deny rights to and impose specific sanctions on those not respecting the administrative set-up designed to implement legal migration policies. Nonetheless, regarding irregular migration from a merely formalistic point of view would lead to a disingenuous conception of the vulnerable condition of individuals deprived of migration status. Indeed, it must not be ignored that irregular migrants are often affected by other particular circumstances, for example, an uncertain economic status, being a part of a racial or religious minority in their country of residence, or having suffered physical or psychological harm in their countries of origin or during their *parcours* to reach their destination countries. This makes irregular migrants a multifarious group in which vulnerability may arise out of different circumstances, which are usually compounded.

The conceptual delimitation of the source of vulnerability has important legal consequences. This chapter focuses on the emergence of a recognition of vulnerability linked to irregular status per se. Indeed, reality provides a blunt description: being deprived of migration status leads to living in precarious conditions, which include no social welfare, a lack of a minimum level of health care, exposure to exploitation in labour and other private relations, difficulties in securing accommodation, etc.[7] The fear of being reported entails not only a potential deprivation of basic goods and services, such as health or educational services, but also a complete disconnection from state authorities in cases where their rights are violated by other private parties. Moreover, this vulnerability

[5] Advisory Opinion on Juridical Condition and Rights of the Undocumented Migrants, OC-18/03, Inter-American Court of Human Rights (IACrtHR), 17 September 2003, 112.

[6] Commissioner for Human Rights, Council of Europe, 'The Human Rights of Irregular Migrants', Issue Paper, CommDH/IssuePaper (2007)1, 17 December 2007, p 7.

[7] See, at length, R Cholewinski, *Study on obstacles to effective access of irregular migrants to minimum social rights* (Strasbourg, Council of Europe, December 2005).

presents itself in varying degrees along the successive vicissitudes that may occur during the migration process, and is present upon arrival and during transit, stay, detention and removal proceedings.[8] In this regard, the most general element inducing a situation of vulnerability is the fact that the presence of the migrant in the state in which they reside is considered illegal: they are 'outlaws in the original sense of that term: they live outside the law, and outside its protection'.[9]

This is not the place to examine the debate on the paradoxes of the approach of liberal democracies towards migration, and on the impact of their policies on the legal status of irregular migrants.[10] Nonetheless, it is worth recalling that the existence of irregular migration itself is a legal construct that ensues from the existence of migration policies, which intrinsically entail the creation of a *legal other*, the establishment of boundaries between different categories of individuals, and the application of different legal regimes when it comes to the definition of their legal status and of their rights. International law has traditionally validated the sovereign right of states to deny entry and residence to foreigners who do not abide by their migration rules. This reaffirms the position of states not according residence rights to those irregularly staying within their borders. Since a lack of residence status irradiates in the enjoyment of the most basics human rights, the prerogatives of states to deny residence rights is inevitably in tension with human rights law. As a consequence, the lack of migration status emerges as the element that renders individuals powerless within state structures. It is precisely by virtue of the operation of the law, that the most fundamental differentiation between individuals has been created: 'the gulf between those with some kind of migration status and those without it is vitally important.'[11]

Europe, as a continent of migration, has seen a proliferation of regimes aimed at controlling migration. Despite a disparity in the figures,[12] irregular migration is regarded as a structural issue that affects differently, but generally, all European states. Even in times of crisis, irregular migration has proven to be one of the most resilient social features in the northern hemisphere, and will foreseeably continue to be at the heart of national debates. Against this background, European countries have put in place different migration systems when it comes to the consequences of a violation of their migration rules: whereas some of them rely on an administrative law approach, others have created criminal offences related

[8] For the analysis of vulnerability during all these stages, see Commissioner for Human Rights, Council of Europe, 'The Human Rights of Irregular Migrants', op cit pp 8–11.

[9] Commissioner for Human Rights, Council of Europe, 'The Human Rights of Irregular Migrants', op cit p 3.

[10] JH Carens, 'Aliens and Citizens: The Case for Open Borders' (1987) 49 *Review of Politics* 251–73; B Ackerman, *Social Justice in the Liberal State* (New Haven, Yale University Press, 1980) 93–95.

[11] C Dauvergne, *Making People Illegal* (Cambridge, Cambridge University Press, 2008) 21. See also S Sassen, *Losing Control? Sovereignty in an Age of Globalization* (New York, Columbia University Press, 1996).

[12] For an approach, see the results of the Clandestino Project (Final Report), at http://clandestino.eliamep.gr/wp-content/uploads/2010/03/clandestino-final-report-november-2009.pdf.

to irregular entry, stay and work, which can even entail penalties of deprivation of liberty.[13]

The role of EU law and the approach of the different institutions of the Council of Europe are crucial in this regard, in that they have contributed to fostering common approaches in the fight against irregular migration as a 'phenomenon' of common concern. Both organisations have also had a modest, but decisive, role in the last two decades in contributing to the determination of the legal status of irregular migrants.

Irregular migrants are undoubtedly a vulnerable group from a factual point of view. Nonetheless, whether they can be conceptualised as a vulnerable group, from a legal point of view under European law, remains a much more debated issue. Indeed, the legal implications of the recognition of a vulnerable group, from a legal point of view, are far-reaching, and seem to be somewhat be at odds with the policy objective of fighting illegal migration. With a focus on this tension, this chapter will provide a systematic and critical account of the legal engagement of the Council of Europe and the European Union with the status of *irregular* migrants, as a different and autonomous issue with respect to the 'fight against *illegal* migration'.

II. IRREGULAR MIGRANTS AND THE COUNCIL OF EUROPE

The Council of Europe has produced some of the legal instruments, which are currently of the greatest importance for the protection of irregular migrants. Nonetheless, despite the existence of a European Convention on the Legal Status of Migrant Workers,[14] this instrument only applies to legally resident foreigners who are nationals of the contracting states. This is also, in principle, the case with respect to the European Social Charter.[15] Without doubt, the European Convention on Human Rights (ECHR) constitutes the most powerful instrument applicable to irregular migrants.

Beyond the above-mentioned legally binding instruments, and before we analyse the decisions of the European Court of Human Rights (ECtHR) and of the European Social Committee (ESC), consideration of the political approach of the Parliamentary Assembly and of the Committee of Ministers gives us the policy framework necessary to understand the overall approach of the organisation.

[13] European Migration Network, *Illegally resident third-country nationals in EUMS: State approaches towards them, their profile and social situation* (European Migration Network, 2005). See also, on the approaches towards criminalisation, E Guild, *Criminalization of migration in Europe: human rights implications*, Issue Paper Commissioner for Human Rights, September 2009.

[14] 1977, ETS No 93.

[15] European Social Charter 1961, ETS No 35; European Social Charter (revised) 1996, ETS No 163.

A. The Political Approach

In the framework of the Council of Europe, the legal and social situation of irregular migrants has often been the object of concern at the political level. The Parliamentary Assembly and the Committee of Ministers have exposed their views on the challenges related to irregular migration in several soft law documents, which have proven influential, even though the issue of producing a legally binding document regarding irregular migration has remained an elusive question.[16] The role of the Parliamentary Assembly in this regard has been vital to introducing the issue of the dramatic situation of irregular migrants to the European political debate,[17] and has extended far beyond the political reaction to serious events and mounting migration pressure in the Mediterranean area,[18] examining all the central topics related to the challenges posed by irregular migration, such as the return and readmission of irregular migrants,[19] the situation of unaccompanied minors,[20] and immigrant detention[21] or regularisation.[22] In this regard, the Assembly has not shied away from the controversial debate on regularisations, putting forward, shortly before the EU Pact on Immigration and

[16] For a view of these approaches, including the Human Rights Commissionner, see S Tonelli, 'Irregular migration and human rights: a Council of Europe perspective' in B Bogusz et al (eds), *Irregular Migration and Human Rights* op cit, pp 301–09.

[17] See, on this issue H Surrel, 'Le Conseil de l'Europe et l'accès au territoire européen' in S Leclerc (ed), *Europe(s), Droit(s) et migrant irrégulier* (Brussels, Bruylant 2012) 43–59.

[18] Eg Resolution 1521 (2006) and Recommendation 1767 (2006), Mass arrival of irregular migrants on Europe's Southern shores; Resolution 1637 (2008) and Recommendation 1850 (2008), Europe's 'boat-people': mixed migration flows by sea into southern Europe; Resolution 1821 (2011) and Recommendation 1974 (2011), The interception and rescue at sea of asylum seekers, refugees and irregular migrants; Resolution 1805 (2011) and Recommendation 1967 (2011), The large-scale arrival of irregular migrants, asylum seekers and refugees on Europe's southern shores; Resolution 1918 (2013) and Recommendation 2010 (2013) Migration and asylum: mounting tensions in the Eastern Mediterranean.

[19] Resolution 1741 (2010) and Recommendation 1925 (2010), Readmission agreements: a mechanism for returning irregular migrants; Resolution 1742 (2010) and Recommendation 1926 (2010) Voluntary return programmes: an effective, humane and cost-effective mechanism for returning irregular migrants; Resolution 1788 (2011) and Recommendation 1956 (2011); Recommendation 2028 (2013), Monitoring the return of irregular migrants and failed asylum seekers by land, sea and air; Preventing harm to refugees and migrants in extradition and expulsion cases: Rule 39 indications by the European Court of Human Rights; Recommendation 2028 (2013), Monitoring the return of irregular migrants and failed asylum seekers by land, sea and air.

[20] Resolution 1810 (2011) Unaccompanied children in Europe: issues of arrival, stay and return. See also Recommendation 1969 (2011). Recommendation 1985 (2011), Undocumented migrant children in an irregular situation: a real cause for concern.

[21] The detention of asylum seekers and irregular migrants in Europe represents one of the most controversial topics. The action of the Assembly has been firm in this field, demanding the Committee to establish minimum guidelines (Recommendation 1850 (2008)), in line with the rules already elaborated by the Commission against torture (Resolution 1509 (2006)—See Normes—CPT/Inf/E (2002)1—rev 2010). See also Resolution 1707 (2010) and Recommendation 1900 (2010) establishig ten guidelines, and a demand to the Committee of ministers to establish a consultative group (28 January 2010).

[22] Resolution 1568 (2007) and Recommendation 1807 (2007), Regularisation programmes for irregular migrants.

Asylum closed files against these policies, a ground breaking approach in political terms, recognising the positive effects of regularisation programmes.[23] Moreover, the Assembly has maintained an open attitude towards the phenomenon of irregular migration, and has often expressed realistic views that are far from the official discourse of zero tolerance coming from states. The point of view of the Assembly has supported an approach to irregular migration that focuses on the need to increase the attention on the rights of individuals due to the particular conditions of vulnerability, upon the premise that 'living under clandestine conditions invariably deprives people of their fundamental and social rights and their human dignity and exposes them to insecure living conditions for as long as they remain clandestine'.[24]

In this regard, the Assembly has adopted one of the most firm and progressive positions with respect to the problems caused by the legal uncertainty surrounding the legal status of irregular migrants. Indeed, one of the major challenges regarding the legal situation of irregular migrants and a key element explaining their particular vulnerability is precisely the lack of a clear setting of the rights they enjoy, and of the state obligations towards them. The virtue of the UN International Convention on the Protection of the Rights of All Migrant Workers and Members of their Families is precisely its comprehensive scope of application, with its Part III encompassing the rights of migrant workers and their family members irrespective of their migratory status.[25] Nonetheless, this Convention has not been ratified by many of the state parties of the Council of Europe, and its material scope is limited to workers and their families, not covering therefore non-working migrants.[26] Against this background, the Assembly has been particularly active in emphasising the need to recognise and ensure the protection of human rights of irregular migrants, and has recommended the Committee of Ministers to elaborate a specific international instrument with regard to the situation of 'clandestine migration', putting forward, among other principles, that 'clandestine migrants should not be deprived of their rights, including the right to welfare for children, and particularly for vulnerable individuals, the right to emergency health care and the right not to be held in slavery or servitude'.[27]

[23] 'The Assembly recognises that regularisation programmes offer the possibility for safeguarding the rights of irregular migrants who are often in a particularly vulnerable situation. They also offer the possibility for member states to tackle the underground economy and ensure that social contributions and taxes are paid. However, the Assembly also recognises that there are concerns about regularisation programmes, particularly in that they may create a pull effect for further irregular migration.' Recommendation 1807 (2007).

[24] Recommendation 1449 (2000), Clandestine migration from the south of the Mediterranean into Europe.

[25] New York, 18 December 1990. Entry into force 1 July 2003, United Nations, Treaty Series, vol 2220, p 3; Doc A/RES/45/158.

[26] The members of the Council of Europe that have ratified to this date are: Albania, Azerbaijan, Bosnia and Herzegovina and Turkey. Armenia, Montenegro and Serbia have signed but not ratified the Convention.

[27] Recommendation 1577 (2002), Creation of a charter of intent on clandestine migration.

The Assembly was very explicit in this recommendation and pinpointed some of the most fundamental issues that remain unsolved: the existence of grey areas between asylum-seekers and irregular migrants, the almost exclusive focus on the fight against irregular migration and the lack of international attention to the situation of migrants themselves. For these reasons, the Assembly advocated a single and comprehensive pan-European instrument to establish some basic principles regarding irregular migration and the rights of irregular migrants. Nonetheless, in response to this initiative, the Committee of Ministers did not consider it opportune 'to elaborate a new international instrument on clandestine migration', underlining the fact that greater use of existing texts should instead be the preferred solution.[28]

Following this approach, the Parliamentary Assembly, in its Resolution 1509 (2006), explicitly recognised the vulnerability of irregular migrants as the basis for the need for particular protection of their human rights,[29] and invited member states of the CoE to ratify human rights instruments relevant to irregular migrants and to guarantee their minimum civil, political, economic and social rights. The legal uncertainty and lack of a specific legal instrument regulating the basic rights of irregular migrants has led to the idea of 'minimum rights', also present in Recommendation 1755 (2006) in which the Parliamentary Assembly proposes an exercise of identification of a set of minimum rights which should be respected.[30] As E van Thijn proposed in the report that served as the basis for this recommendation, even though there is a large number of disparate instruments that are relevant to the legal protection of irregular migrants, 'their varying degree of signature and ratification, lead to a web of uncertainty as to the minimum rights to be applied to irregular migrants'.

Even though the Committee of Ministers has not always followed the recommendations of the Parliamentary Assembly, the issue of the legal status of irregular migrants has gained importance over the years. In 1978, when considering the need for states to take restrictive measures concerning irregular migration, it was already considered necessary

> that foreign workers in breach of the law are allowed, even when repatriated, to retain the rights acquired in the course of their work in the matter of remuneration, social security and other benefits and that they receive legal aid in the event of litigation concerning the rights referred to in this paragraph.[31]

One of the most relevant statements of the Committee with respect to the legal status of irregular migrants is contained in Recommendation R (2000) 3 on the right to the satisfaction of basic material needs of persons in situations of extreme

[28] Reply from the Committee of Ministers Doc 9930 (2003).

[29] 'Irregular migrants, as they are often in a vulnerable situation, have a particular need for the protection of their human rights, including basic civil, political, economic and social rights'. Resolution 1509 (2006), Human rights of irregular migrants, of 27 June 2006.

[30] Recommendation 1755 (2006), Human rights of irregular migrants, of 27 June 2006.

[31] Resolution (78) 44, On clandestine immigration and the illegal employment of foreign workers.

hardship, where the Committee stated that the exercise of the right to satisfaction of basic human needs 'should be open to all citizens and foreigners, whatever the latters' position under national rules on the status of foreigners'. Moreover, the Committee has recognised that the vulnerability of irregular migrants is increased during immigrant detention,[32] and has adopted a set of guidelines on measures on forced return.[33] With respect to the issue of the clarification of rights of irregular migrants, the Committee proceeded, in 2011, to a codification of the Council of Europe standards and guidelines in the field of human rights protection of irregular migrants, based on the case law of the ECtHR and of the Social Committee.

The resulting approach seems to respect the basic understanding that there is no right of residence for irregular migrants in the state where they are physically present, but at the same time, there is a need to recognise a minimal protection which already resorts from international law.[34]

B. The European Court of Human Rights and Irregular Migration

Despite its enormous relevance, it is impossible here to give a complete account of the entire case law of the ECtHR that might have an impact on the rights of irregular migrants.[35] The point of departure in this regard is the consolidated recognition by the Court of the entitlement of states to control migration to and residence in their territories.[36] Nonetheless, this does not entail those who do not respect migration regulations being deprived of the protection of the Convention:

> [M]igrants do have rights protected by the Convention, regardless of their legal status in the host country. The fact that a migrant has not been authorised to enter or reside in a country does not deprive him or her of his or her human rights.[37]

Despite this statement, the Convention itself contains specific modulations that strongly affect the legal position of irregular migrants. First, the right of free

[32] Reply to Parliamentary Assembly Recommendation 1900 (2010), The detention of asylum seekers and irregular migrants in Europe.

[33] Committee of Ministers' 20 Guidelines on Forced Returns COM (2005) 40 final.

[34] JF Akandji-Kombé, 'Le Conseil de l'Europe et le séjour du migrant irrégulier: l'approche protectrice. Un droit européen protecteur des migrants irréguliers en matière de séjour?' in S Leclerc (ed), *Europe(s), Droit(s) et migrant irrégulier* (Brussels, Bruylant 2012) 95–116, 97.

[35] See N Blake, 'Developments in the case law of the European Court of Human Rights' in B Bogusz et al (eds), *Irregular Migration and Human Rights* op cit pp 431–51.

[36] *Abdulaziz, Cabales and Balkandali v United Kingdom* (1985) Series A no 94, p 34, para 67; *Boujlifa v France* (1997) EHRR 1997–VI 2264, para 42.

[37] Concurring opinion of Judge Pinto de Albuquerque, joined by judge Vučinić, *de Souza Ribeiro v France* (2012) EHRR 46.

movement only applies to persons in a regular situation.[38] Second, migration detention is expressly allowed by the Convention.[39]

In the absence of a right of residence and of a right of entry for foreigners, the ECtHR has nonetheless established important limitations to the powers of states to expel third country nationals when there exist a danger of violation of Article 2 ECHR (right to life), or of Article 3 (prohibition of torture and inhuman or degrading treatment) in the country of destination.[40] Moreover, the right to family and private life (Article 8 ECHR), cannot only prevent expulsion from the territory of a state party,[41] but also impose on the state positive obligations to authorise entry and residence,[42] leading to a path to regularise irregular stay.[43]

In the application of these principles, the ECtHR takes into account the particular situation of vulnerability of the affected individuals to determine the level of gravity in order to establish a violation of Article 3 ECHR. In any case, when the vulnerable position of a migrant has led the Court to find the existence of the an element of vulnerability suitable to affect the gravity test under Article 3 ECHR in order to prevent refoulement, the vulnerability emanated principally not from the irregular situation of individuals per se, but from other elements, such as very exceptional circumstances concerning the health condition of the applicant in relation to the health services available in the destination country,[44] or racial, ethnic or religious discrimination.[45]

[38] Art 2, Protocol 4.

[39] See Art 5, para 1(f), authorising 'the lawful arrest or detention of a person to prevent his effecting an unauthorised entry into the country or of a person against whom action is being taken with a view to deportation or extradition'.

[40] *Soering v UK* (1989) 11 EHRR 439; *Cruz Varas ea v Sweden* App no 15576/89 (ECtHR, 20 March 1991); *R v United Kingdom* App no 146/1996/767/964 (ECtHR, 2 May 1997).

[41] *Berrehab v Netherlands* (1988) Series A no 138, p 8, (1988) 11 EHRR 322; *Boultif v Switzerland* (2001) 33 EHRR 1179; *AA v United Kingdom* App no 8000/08 (ECtHR, 8 September 2011).

[42] *Sen v Netherlands* App no 31465/96 (2001) 36 EHRR 81; *Tuquabo-Tekle and Others v Netherlands* App no 60665/00 (ECtHR, 1 December 2005); *Osman v Denmark* App no 38058/09 (ECtHR, 14 June 2011); *Sisojeva and others v Latvia* App no 60654/00 (ECtHR, Chamber judgment 16 June 2005 and Grand Chamber judgment 15 January 2007).

[43] D Thym, 'Respect for private and family life under article 8 ECHR in immigration cases: a human right to regularize illegal stay?' (2008) 57 *International & Comparative Law Quarterly* 87–112.

[44] *D v United Kingdom* (1997) 24 EHRR 423, in which the applicant was in 'advanced stages of a terminal and incurable illness', being affected by AIDS. However, this solution is not applied when the illness has not attained such terminal stages, *Arcila Henao v Netherlands* (dec) App no 13669/03 (ECtHR, 24 June 2003); *Ndangoya v Sweden* (dec) App no 17868/03 (ECtHR, 22 June 2004); *Megnigan v Netherlands* (dec) App no 25629/04 (ECtHR, 25 November 2004). This approach was confirmed in *N v United Kingdom* App no 26565/05 (ECtHR [GC], 28 May 2008) *v*. The very exceptional circumstances were, nonetheless, not found in cases concerning mental health, *Bensaid v United Kingdom* App no 44599/98, ECHR 2001–I; *Samina v Sweden* App no 55463/09 (ECtHR, 20 January 2012) and in *Husseini v Sweden* App no 10611/09, (ECtHR, 8 March 2012); or in a case concerning a person who had suffered severe injuries and amputations, *SHH v United Kingdom* App no 60367/10 (ECtHR, 29 January 2013). An application based on the lack of education in the countries of destination was also declared inadmissible in this respect: *15 Foreign Students v United Kingdom* App no 7671/76 (ECtHR, 19 May 1977).

[45] *Cyprus v Turkey* (2002) 35 EHRR 30.

In cases regarding detention conditions the Court has recognised the particular vulnerability of asylum-seekers.[46] In this framework, the statements of the Court in the cases *Rahimi v Greece* and *Mubilanzila Mayeka and Kaniki Mitunga v Belgium* are particularly striking, since the Court, in order to highlight the particularly vulnerable condition of the applicants, referred to the fact that they were of 'very young age, the fact that [they were] *illegal immigrant[s] in a foreign land* and the fact that [they were] unaccompanied by [their] family from whom [they] had become separated so that [they were] effectively left to [their] own devices'.[47] As a consequence, the fact that they were in an 'extremely vulnerable situation … takes precedence over consideration of [their] status as an illegal immigrant'.[48] In *Ahmed v Malta*, the Court also stated that 'the applicant was in a vulnerable position, *not only because of the fact that she was an irregular immigrant* and because of her specific past and her personal emotional circumstances … but also because of her fragile health'.[49] In all these cases, irregularity stands out as an additional element that adds up to a serious situation of compounded vulnerability in which factors related to age or health play the primary role. However, irregularity does not seem to have reached the magnitude to be considered as an autonomous element to render an individual vulnerable. Indeed, despite the farreaching statements by the ECtHR in these cases, which seem to move from the condemnation of irregularity to an assessment of this condition as an element of vulnerability, this still seems far from advancing irregular migrants per se as a particularly vulnerable group. Moreover, it has to be taken into account that the applicants in these cases were asylum-seekers, and in one case, an unaccompanied five-year-old child.[50]

The presence of elements of special vulnerability can also integrate the analysis of the proportionality in cases relating the 'returnability' of foreigners. Indeed, among the elements enumerated in *Ünal*, there is room to consider the situation of the family, the circumstances surrounding children, and the solidity of social, cultural and family relations in the country of destination.[51] In *Kiyutin v Russia*, where the applicant had been refused a residence permit because of his HIV-positive status, the Court considered that people living with HIV are 'a vulnerable group with a history of prejudice and stigmatisation and that the state should be afforded only a narrow margin of appreciation in choosing measures that single out this group for differential treatment on the basis of their HIV status', and subsequently found a discrimination in violation of Article 14, taken

[46] *MSS v Belgium and Greece* App no 30696/09, (2011) 53 EHRR 2. See, on the discussion on asylum-seekers as a particularly vulnerable group, the separate opinion of Judge Sajó in this case.

[47] *Rahimi v Greece* App no 8687/08 (ECtHR, 5 April 2011). See also *Mubilanzila Mayeka and Kaniki Mitunga v Belgium* App no 13178/03, EHRR 2006–XI. See also *Kanagaratnam and Others v Belgium* App no 15297/09 (ECtHR, 13 December 2011); *Muskhadzhiyeva ea v Belgium* App no 41442/07 (ECtHR, 19 January 2010).

[48] ibid.

[49] *Aden Ahmed v Malta* App no 55352/12 (ECtHR, 23 July 2013).

[50] In this sense: JF Akandji-Kombé, 'Le Conseil de l'Europe et le séjour du migrant irrégulier ' op cit p 114.

[51] *Üner v Netherlands* App no 46410/99 (ECtHR, 18 October 2006).

in conjunction with Article 8 ECHR.[52] Nonetheless, the specific circumstances regarding the severe health conditions of a family member have not always led the Court to recognise that a violation of Article 8 ECHR has existed, as the case *Gül v Switzerland* made clear.[53] Indeed, the reaffirmation of the legitimacy of states implementing their own immigration policy seems to cancel out the value of irregularity as an element of specific vulnerability in cases where what is at stake is precisely the immigration status and/or the right to remain. In this regard, even though the Court takes into account the length of the irregular stay to evaluate the circumstances of the case,[54] the fact that the stay has been irregular,[55] and any immigration-related offences (such as forgery of passports), play to the detriment of the applicant.[56]

On another note, the Court has not adopted a univocal and definitive position as to the legality of discrimination on the basis of migration status. In *Ponomaryovi v Bulgaria*, the Court found a violation of Article 14 of the Convention in conjunction with Article 2 of Protocol No 1 (right to education), because the applicants, irregular migrants at the point of the facts that gave rise to the case, were charged fees for secondary education while other legal migrants and nationals where not. Nonetheless, in this case the Court very much emphasised the fact that the applicants had not entered the country illegally but had 'found themselves, somewhat inadvertently, in the situation of aliens lacking permanent residence permits', that the national authorities did not have the intention to expel them, and that they did not intend to abuse the educational system.[57] Indeed, the case confirmed that immigration status can be one of the grounds of distinction encompassed by the notion of 'other status' as mentioned in Article 14. Nonetheless, in *Bah v UK*, a case concerning access to a social housing benefit, the Court emphasised that

> Given the element of choice involved in immigration status … while differential treatment based on this ground must still be objectively and reasonably justifiable, the justification required will not be as weighty as in the case of a distinction based, for example, on nationality.[58]

This approach seems to depart from the reasoning of the Court in *Anakomba Yula v Belgium*, where it had stated, in a case concerning the access to legal aid

[52] *Kiyutin v Russia* (2011) 53 EHRR 364.

[53] *Gül v Switzerland* Reports of Judgments and Decisions 1996–I, 173–74.

[54] *Rodrigues da Silva v Netherlands* (2007) 44 EHRR 34; *Nunez v Norway* App no 55597/09 (ECtHR, 28 June 2011).

[55] See *Palanci v Switzerland* App no 2607/08 (ECtHR, 25 March 2014), in which 'the Court is therefore not willing to attribute the same weight to the duration of the applicant's stay in Switzerland as it would do if he had lived there with a valid residence permit throughout that period'. On the contrary, the fact that the residence has been legal leads the Court to state that only very weighty reasons can justify expulsion; see *Maslov v Austria* App no 1638/03, (2008) 47 EHRR 20, para 75.

[56] See, eg *Antwi and others v Norway* App no 26940/10 (ECtHR, 14 February 2012); *Darren Omoregie and Others v Norway* App no 265/07 (ECtHR, 31 July 2008), para 67.

[57] *Ponomaryovi v Bulgaria* App no 5335/05 (ECtHR, 21 June 2011). On discrimination on grounds of nationality, see inter alia *Gaygusuz v Austria* Reports of Judgments and Decisions 1996–IV, para 42.

[58] *Bah v United Kingdom* App no 56328/07 (ECtHR, 27 September 2011).

of an irregular immigrant in the framework of an action to contest paternity, that, in a case concerning serious issues of family law '[i]l fallait donc des raisons particulièrement impérieuses pour justifier une différence de traitement entre la requérante, qui ne possédait pas de carte de séjour, et les personnes qui en possédaient une'.[59]

C. Vulnerability: the Trigger for Activating the Protection of the European Social Charter

One of the most spectacular impacts of the notion of vulnerability has occurred with respect to the interpretation of the European Social Charter by the European Committee on Social Rights. The limitation of the personal scope of application of the Revised Social Charter, as operated by paragraph 1 of its Appendix, leads to the conclusion that this instrument would be of little impact in the situation of irregular migrants, since its provisions are only applicable to lawful residents who are nationals of the contracting parties.[60] Nonetheless, the Committee has adopted a far-reaching interpretation of this limitation based on teleological grounds, stating that 'such restriction should not end up having unreasonably detrimental effects where the protection of vulnerable groups of persons is at stake'.[61] In 2004, the Committee found in *FIDH v France*, relying on the link between health care and human dignity, that 'legislation or practice which denies entitlement to medical assistance to foreign nationals, within the territory of a State Party, even if they are there illegally, is contrary to the Charter'.[62] This approach was continued in *Defence for Children International v Netherlands*, this time regarding the right to shelter, which was again connected to the right to life and to human dignity,[63] and in *Defence for Children International v Belgium*, where the Committee offered a more substantiated reasoning. Indeed, in this last decision, the Committee established that the interpretation that makes the ESC applicable to irregular residents may only be applied in an exceptional manner, and only with regard to 'those provisions whose fundamental purpose is closely linked to the requirement to secure the most fundamental human rights and to safeguard the persons concerned by the provision in question from serious threats

[59] 'Very weighty reasons would have to be put forward to justify a difference of treatment between the applicant, who did not have a residence card, and those in possession of such document' (translation by the author), *Anakomba Yula v Belgium* App no 45413/07 (ECtHR, 10 March 2009).

[60] See, on this issue, JF Akandji-Kombé, 'La Charte sociale européenne et la protection des migrants en situation irrégulière', Memorandum, Commission des migrations, des réfugiés et de la population, AS/Mig/Inf (2005) 17.

[61] *Defence for Children International v the Netherlands*, Collective Complaint No 47/2008, Decision on the merits of, 28 October 2009.

[62] *International Federation for Human Rights (FIDH) v France*, Collective Complaint No 14/2003, Decision on the merits of, 8 September 2004.

[63] n 61 above.

to the enjoyment of those rights'.[64] This approach would lead to an analysis of each of the rights protected by the Charter, on the basis of their purpose to secure the 'most fundamental' rights. Taking into account the particular vulnerability of children who are irregular migrants, the Committee stated that the ESC requires states to fulfil positive obligations to provide accommodation, basic care and protection to children and young persons. The special vulnerability of children is the basis for the need of a particular protection,[65] which has led the Committee to overcome the limitations of the personal scope of application of the Social Charter: vulnerability seems to be the only way to make these rights relevant to irregular migrants.[66]

III. IRREGULAR MIGRATION IN THE EUROPEAN UNION

A. The Constitutional Framework

Illegal migration has been explicitly regarded as a phenomenon of 'common interest' among the states of the European Union since the Treaty of Maastricht. The explicit Community competence to adopt measures aimed at preventing irregular migration was introduced by the Amsterdam Treaty, leading to the adoption of a first generation of mainly restrictive measures. The current constitutional framework, put in place by the Treaty of Lisbon, further deepens the possibilities of engagement of the Union in the determination of the legal status of third country nationals, through the creation of a truly common immigration policy. The overarching principles that inspire this policy are contained in Article 79 of the Treaty on the Functioning of the European Union (TFEU), which restricts the application of the 'fair treatment principle' to 'third-country nationals residing legally in Member States'. Irregular migrants seem, therefore, to be excluded from this constitutional obligation to resort to considerations of 'fairness' when regulating their status at the EU level. This is a significant deficiency in the general framework offered by the Treaty and a first element that provides for an erratic approach of the EU towards the legal status of irregular migrants. However, it has to be noted that the relationship of these principles with Article 67 TFEU is not clear, since this last provision situates fundamental rights at the summit of the principles that should guide EU action in the Area of Freedom, Security and Justice, referring to the principle of fair treatment with regard to third country nationals without restriction based on their migration situation.

Article 79 TFEU also contains the basic elements of the EU approach to irregular migration: the Union shall develop a common immigration policy aimed at

[64] *Defence for Children International v Belgium*, Complaint No 69/2011, Decision on the merits of, 23 October 2013.

[65] On these decisions, see ch 2 in this volume.

[66] Akandji-Kombé, p 112.

ensuring 'the prevention of, and enhanced measures to combat, illegal immigration and trafficking in human beings'.[67] Nonetheless, the content of the EU competence towards irregular migration goes well beyond the prevention and combat of irregular migration. Indeed, Article 79(2)(c) TFEU, which confirms as a Union competence 'illegal immigration and unauthorised residence, including removal and repatriation of persons residing without authorisation', has an enormous potential. This is clearly a broad competence that encompasses not only restrictive measures aimed at removal and repatriation, but also measures that cover illegal immigration in general as well as 'unauthorised residence' in its broadest scope. As a consequence the competence of the Union with regard to irregular migration is potentially general, covering not only measures related to prevention at the border and return policy, but also comprising the regulation of the status of undocumented migrants.

With a broad set of issues related to the status of irregular migrants placed directly within the 'scope of EU law', the relevance of the Charter of Fundamental Rights immediately becomes a central element in the interpretation and application of EU instruments and connected national legislation.[68] Indeed, the Charter of Fundamental Rights does not generally (with some exceptions) distinguish on the basis of migration status for the entitlement to fundamental rights. It has already been effectively applied with regard to the interpretation of the Returns Directive, and should also be deemed to be applicable in border control situations governed by the Schengen Borders Code.[69] In this regard, the mandate established in Article 52, paragraph 3 of the Charter, to interpret this instrument in light of the ECHR, renders the case law and the approaches analysed in the previous section immediately relevant, as the minimum floor below which the EU standard cannot fall.

B. The Legal Approach to the Fight against Illegal Migration[70]

From the inception of the common migration policy, the fight against illegal migration has been conceived as one of the phenomena with regard to which member states should join their actions in order to accomplish more effective results. The incipient configuration set up by the Treaty of Amsterdam situated the then new competences of the European Community in the field of migration as closely connected to the objective of achieving the free movement of persons, allowing for the adoption of measures on 'illegal immigration and illegal

[67] A first element to highlight is the unfortunate choice of the term 'illegal immigration' by the Treaty itself, despite the general agreement of the scientific community on more suitable terminology, such as irregular or undocumented migration.

[68] See Case C-617/10 *Åkerberg Fransson* EU:C:2013:105.

[69] Case C-23/12 *Zakaria* EU:C:2013:24.

[70] Here, we refer to 'illegal migration', since this is the concept used by the Treaty and by secondary law.

residence, including repatriation of illegal residents'. Under this constitutional setting, the first generation of EU migration norms came into being, in the aftermath of 9/11 with an uncontested bias towards the securitisation of migration and the fight against illegal migration. The central position of the objective of the fight against illegal migration has also shaped connected policies such as the common visa policy or the policy regarding the control of the external borders of the Union,[71] occupying the leading inspirational role in the creation and development of the Agency of the EU for the management of external borders (FRONTEX).

From a policy point of view, the overarching premise, as stated in the Immigration and Asylum Pact, is that 'illegal immigrants on Member States' territory must leave that territory'. If before the Returns Directive, [72] EU law did not impose an obligation on member states to initiate return or expulsion procedures,[73] nowadays the exceptions provided for in the directive notwithstanding, 'Member States shall issue a return decision to any third-country national staying illegally on their territory'.[74]

The normative action of the Union has been directed at tackling irregular migration as a complex phenomenon, aiming at sanctioning the different actors involved and mainly, at removing irregular migrants from the territory of the member states. The first legal instruments adopted in this regard were designed precisely from the point of view of fostering the operational cooperation among member state authorities, with the absolute priority of fostering removal of irregularly present immigrants. As a kind of 'compensatory' rationale that would offset the elimination of control at internal borders, the first Directive enacted in this field established the mutual recognition of expulsion orders among member states.[75] Subsequently, a Directive on assistance in cases of transit for the purposes of removal by air,[76] and a decision on the organisation of joint flights for removals, were adopted.[77] The focus on removal has been furthered, moreover, by the adoption of a network of readmission agreements with third countries. In this sense, the Union has decidedly developed its external action, which has led to expressly recognising an external competence with respect to readmission

[71] See, for one of the most striking developments, the Commission Proposal for a Regulation establishing an Entry/Exit System (EES) to register entry and exit data of third country nationals crossing the external borders of the member states of the European Union COM (2013) 95 final.

[72] Directive 2008/115/EC on common standards and procedures in member states for returning illegally staying third-country nationals [2008] OJ L348/98.

[73] Joined Cases C-261/08 and C-348/08 *Zurita García and Choque Cabrera* [2009] ECR I-10143.

[74] Art 6, para 1 of the Directive.

[75] Council Directive 2001/40/EC on the mutual recognition of decisions on the expulsion of third country nationals [2001] OJ L149/34. See also Council Decision 2004/191/EC setting out the criteria and practical arrangements for the compensation of the financial imbalances resulting from the application of Directive 2001/40/EC on the mutual recognition of decisions on the expulsion of third-country nationals [2004] OJ L60/55.

[76] Council Directive 2003/110/EC on assistance in cases of transit for the purposes of removal by air [2003] OJ L321/26.

[77] Council Decision of 29 April 2004 on the organisation of joint flights for removals from the territory of two or more member states, of third-country nationals who are subjects of individual removal orders [2004] OJ L261/28.

agreements in the Lisbon Treaty. The centrepiece of the approach of the Union towards the return and removal of irregular migrants, the Return Directive, was approved in 2008.

The action of the Union in this field has further focused on the consolidation of an approach based on the punishment of any kind of collaboration or action directly contributing to the phenomenon of illegal migration through a legal framework based on sanctions to the actors involved in the migration process. The first instrument adopted in this regard was aimed at introducing obligations and sanctions to carriers.[78] The punitive approach was further deepened through an impulse to criminalise conduct aimed at facilitating any of the stages linked with irregular migration (entry, transit and residence).[79] Finally, the employers' sanctions Directive—a central piece in the effort to eliminate incentives of irregular migration—was passed in 2009.[80] All these measures, being directed at actors other than migrants themselves, have an important effect not only in that they discourage cooperative or negligent behaviour that may directly support illegal migration, but also because they contribute to isolate and reduce the social and economic universe of irregular migrants. In this sense, their 'impact' on the phenomenon that they intend to tackle translates into a direct contribution to induce 'self-deportation'. In this regard, the EU Fundamental Rights Agency (FRA) has advocated for a revision of the Facilitation Directive to prohibit the penalisation of actions that have been undertaken with a humanitarian aim.[81]

From this normative action, it is clear that the European Union, as an actor that has been empowered by states to share the exercise of their sovereign competences in this field, fully endorses the state objective to fight illegal migration as an undesired phenomenon, and enhances the legal and operational capabilities of states in this respect. In this regard, it is clear that irregular migrants are not approached as a vulnerable group in need of protection, but are placed in a situation in which the legal developments at the Union level significantly contribute to aggravate their vulnerability. True, the European Union has been active in the field of preventing trafficking in human beings,[82] but besides the specific group of trafficked persons, there is no general legal recognition of irregular migrants as a group deserving, per se, any special legal protection. On the contrary, the

[78] Council Directive 2001/51/EC Supplementing the Provisions of Article 26 of the Convention Implementing the Schengen Agreement of 14 June 1985.

[79] Council Directive 2002/90/EC defining the facilitation of unauthorised entry, transit and residence [2002] OJ L328 (Art 1, para 2: Any member state may decide not to impose sanctions with regard to the behaviour defined in paragraph 1(a) by applying its national law and practice for cases where the aim of the behaviour is to provide humanitarian assistance to the person concerned); Council Framework Decision 2002/946/JHA on the strengthening of the penal framework to prevent the facilitation of unauthorised entry, transit and residence [2002] OJ L 328/1.

[80] Council Directive 2009/52/EC providing for minimum standards on sanctions and measures against employers of illegally staying third-country nationals [2009] OJ L168/24.

[81] 'Fundamental Rights of migrants in an irregular situation in the European Union. Comparative Report', FRA, 2011.

[82] See ch 17 by Jacobo Ríos Rodríguez in this volume.

normative evolution of the fight against illegal migration has led to the adoption of border and sanctions policies that negatively impact the specific needs of the vulnerable group of asylum-seekers.[83]

In this regard, the deepening of European integration in the field of border and migration control has undoubtedly led to a strengthening of the conditions and requirements to flank European borders. The legislative action of the EU has been concentrated on the design of strategies and mechanisms for fighting illegal migration through removal and through punitive instruments, rather than on addressing the problems of exploitation, discrimination and status, undermining therefore 'the legitimacy of the entire AFSJ project as well as Europe's commitments to fundamental rights protection for all its residents, independent of their immigration and citizenship status'.[84] The image of Europe as a fortress has proliferated in the doctrine and in the press, and has been further buttressed by an erratic approach to the dramatic reality of immigration by sea.[85] The need for a clarification of responsibilities for rescue at sea led to the adoption to the Rules for sea border operations coordinated by Frontex, adopted in 2010,[86] reinforcing the need for respect for fundamental rights, and the explicit recognition of the need to consider the special needs of children, victims of trafficking, persons in need of urgent medical assistance, persons in need of international protection and other persons in a particularly vulnerable situation.[87] The decision approving these rules, originally adopted as implementing measures, was annulled in 2012 by the CJEU, on the grounds that these rules should have been adopted by the legislative procedure.[88] The procedural grounds on which this issue is based should not obscure the constitutional implications of this judgement, since it confirms that ultimate decisions on fundamental human rights issues on the control of external borders legitimately belong to the legislative branch.[89]

[83] See V Moreno-Lax, 'Must EU Borders have Doors for Refugees? On the Compatibility of Schengen Visas and Carriers' Sanctions with EU Member States' Obligations to Provide International Protection to Refugees' (2008) 10 *European Journal of Migration and Law* 315–64.

[84] S Carrera and E Guild, 'Undocumented migrants and the Stockholm Programme. Ensuring access to rights?' in S Carrera and M Merlino (eds), *Assessing EU Policy on Irregular Immigration under the Stockholm Programe* (Brussels, CEPS, October 2010).

[85] See, on this issue, Marcello Di Filippo, 'Irregular Migration across the Mediterranean Sea: Problematic Issues Concerning the International Rules on Safeguard of Life at Sea' (2013) 1 *Paix et Sécurité Internationales* 53–76; A Fischer-Lescano, T Löhr and T Tohidipur, 'Border Controls at Sea: Requirements under International Human Rights and Refugee Law' (2009) 21(2) *International Journal of Refugee Law* 256.

[86] Council Decision 2010/252/UE supplementing the Schengen Borders Code as regards the surveillance of the sea external borders in the context of operational cooperation coordinated by the European Agency for the Management of Operational Cooperation at the External Borders of the Member States of the European Union [2010] OJ L111/20.

[87] Rule 1(3).

[88] On this judgment, see M Acosta Sánchez and I González García, 'TJUE—Sentencia de 05.09.2012, Parlamento c. Consejo—C-355/10, Vigilancia de fronteras marítimas y elementos esenciales en los actos de ejecución' (2014) 47 *Revista de Derecho Comunitario Europeo* 267–84.

[89] See, particularly, point 77, C-355/10, Parliament/Council, EU:C:2012:516.

C. The Status of Irregular Migrants under EU Law

Despite this generally restrictive scenario motivated by the pursuance of the overriding objective, embedded into the treaties, of 'fighting against illegal migration', the impact of EU law on the determination of the status of irregular migrants has not been negative. Indeed, the Returns Directive of 2008 and the Employers' Sanctions Directive of 2009 both contain certain elements that make explicit a consideration of irregular migrants as individuals who deserve protection. Their vulnerability arises here as an underlying element that inspires the need to mitigate the effects of restrictive norms in the enjoyment of some basic fundamental rights. Moreover, the existence of a broad EU competence with regard to irregular migration and the development of secondary law in this field, situate a large part of this topic 'under the scope of EU law' for the purposes of determining whether particular actions of EU member states governed by the EU fundamental rights comply with standard of the Charter.

In this regard, it is to be noted that case law is progressively unveiling the protective function of the Returns Directive,[90] making clear that it has enhanced the legal status of irregular migrants beyond the minimum standard of the ECHR introducing limitations to detention periods that have been strictly interpreted by the CJEU,[91] establishing restrictions to entry bans,[92] and also conferring important powers on national judges in reviewing decisions on the extension of detention.[93] Despite the criticisms that this norm has received for its repressive character, its enactment has contributed (in a certainly limited manner) to the clarification of the legal status of irregular migrants. Indeed, the Directive enacts relevant procedural rights during return procedures. Nonetheless, in this regard, the CJEU, without examining this issue from the point of view of the vulnerability of immigrants kept in detention,[94] has declared that the violation of such procedural rights, even if it amounts to a violation of the right to be heard in the extension of detention, would not lead to the lifting of a detention measure unless the national jurisdiction finds that 'the infringement at issue actually deprived the party relying thereon of the possibility of arguing his defence better, to the extent that the outcome of that administrative procedure could have been different'.[95]

[90] In this sense, F Lutz, 'L'arrêt "Kadzoev": Un premier test pour la directive "Retour"' (2010) 2 *Revue du Droit de l'Union Européenne* 331–45.

[91] Case C-357/09 PPU *Kadzoev* [2009] ECR I-11189. Confirming that the directive does not apply to asylum-seekers: Case C-534/11 *Arslan* EU:C:2013:343. For a comparison with the ECHR standard, C Costello, 'Human Rights and the Elusive Universal Subject: Immigration Detention Under International Human Rights and EU Law' (2012) 19(1) *Indiana Journal of Global Legal Studies* 257–303.

[92] See, in this regard, Case C-297/12 *Filev and Osmani* EU:C:2013:569.

[93] Case C-146/14 PPU *Mahdi* EU:C:2014:1320.

[94] Mr G advanced an argument in this sense, see para 29 of the Opinion of Advocate General Wathelet in this case.

[95] Case C-383/13 PPU *G and R* EU:C:2013:533. For a substantiated criticism of the standard identified by the Court in this case, see R Alonso García, *El juez nacional en la encrucijada europea de los derechos fundamentales* (Madrid, Cívitas, 2014). See also F Gazin, 'Droit d'être entendu dans le cadre d'une rétention préparant un retour' (2013) n° 11, Novembre *Europe* 453.

The Returns Directive has also contributed to the emergence of an incipient legal regime for immigrants in return procedures, whose expulsion has been suspended, stating that member states have to take into account that family unity with family members present in their territory is maintained; emergency health care and essential treatment of illness are provided; minors are granted access to the basic education system subject to the length of their stay; and that the special needs of vulnerable persons are taken into account.[96] In this regard, vulnerable persons are defined as 'minors, unaccompanied minors, disabled people, elderly people, pregnant women, single parents with minor children and persons who have been subjected to torture, rape or other serious forms of psychological, physical or sexual violence'.[97]

Moreover, states have an obligation to provide a written confirmation to those whose return is pending, which constitutes a step towards legal certainty and contributes to granting irregular migrants legal recognition. Nonetheless, these developments are only applicable to those immigrants who have already been detected by the authorities and whose return is pending, and do not in any case amount to the recognition of a residence status to those whose return cannot be effectively carried out.[98] Indeed, the CJEU has recently confirmed that the Directive does not oblige member states to grant residence permits to those irregular migrants released from detention after it has been stated that no reasonable prospect for return existed, in the sense of Article 15, paragraph 4 of the Directive.[99] On another note, in the name of the effectiveness of the Directive, the CJEU has declared that certain national systems that establish criminal sanctions with regard to irregular migration, imposing imprisonment penalties and home detention sanctions, were not in conformity with EU law.[100] However, despite the indirect beneficial effect on irregular migrants, this case law does not find its foundations in a fundamental rights reasoning and does not take into account considerations of vulnerability,[101] neither does it seem to prevent the possibility of criminalising irregular migration, or imposing imprisonment sanctions after the return procedure has failed.[102]

Another relevant development in the determination of the rights of irregular migrants is the provision of the employers' sanctions directive that obliges member states to ensure that employers are liable to pay outstanding remuneration to

[96] Art 14 of the Directive.

[97] ibid.

[98] On this discussion, see D Acosta Arcarazo, 'The Returns Directive: Possible Limits and Interpretation', in K Zwaan (ed), *The Returns Directive: Central Themes, Problem Issues, and Implementation in Selected Member States* (Nijmegen, Wolf Legal Publishers, 2011).

[99] Case C-146/14 PPU, *Mahdi.*

[100] Case C-61/11 PPU *El Dridi* [2011] ECR I-3015; Case C-329/11 *Achughbabian* [2011] ECR I-12695; Case C-430/11 *Sagor* EU:C:2012:777; Case C-522/11 *Mbaye* EU:C:2013:190.

[101] For a criticism in this sense, B Bertrand, 'La Cour de justice et la directive Retour: la stratégie du Roseau' (2011) 4 *Revue des affaires européennes—Law & european affairs* 845–58, 856.

[102] This remains open to interpretation, but seems to be the conclusion that can be deduced from *Achughbabian*. See, in particular, para 32 of the judgment.

illegally employed third-country nationals. Even though this obligation is drafted in the form of an obligation directed to the member states, and is aimed at serving as a deterrent towards employers, its content gives rise to an important right for third-country nationals, which should be enforceable in horizontal relations through the implementing legislation of the states. The lack of transposing measures in this sense or their incorrectness would give rise to the responsibility of the given member state towards the third-country national concerned.

Finally, it is necessary to briefly mention the effects of EU free movement and of citizenship of the Union with respect to the irregularity of status of nationals of member states and the members of their family. Even though the citizenship right of free movement and residence remains subject to a number of conditions, the possibility that an EU citizen finds himself in a situation in which he may lose his rights of residence and subsequently be expelled have been progressively reduced, eliminating any possibility for the states to rely on formal requirements that may endanger the right of residence,[103] restrictively interpreting the public order exceptions, and strictly constructing the notion of a disproportionate burden on the level of social assistance of the member states.[104]

Most importantly, the fundamental place of free movement and EU citizenship in the legal order of the Union has led to a hierarchisation of priorities, making it possible to trump considerations based on irregular migration. After the dubious result of the *Akrich* case,[105] the CJEU confirmed in *Jia* and in *Metock*,[106] that the exercise of free movement for the purposes of placing a certain situation under EU law cannot be considered as 'abuse of rights'. There is no room for a punitive response to family members for having spent time as irregular migrants: as soon as they have recognised family ties with EU citizens and the situation is covered by EU free movement rules, their status should be 'regularised'. These effects go even further, even in cases that are not covered by EU free movement rules: indeed, following the line of precedent of *Chen*,[107] the *Ruiz Zambrano*[108] case provided for a new via of regularisation of parents of minor EU citizens, when the expulsion of the former would imperil the right to be present in the Union enjoyed by the latter. These cases provide a very important element to bear in mind when considering the legal approach of EU law towards irregular migration: the Court has solved the dilemma between the need for protection of European citizens and the fight against illegal immigration very clearly in favour of the former. This is

[103] Eg Case C-215/03 *Oulane* [2005] ECR 2005 I-1215.

[104] For the challenges posed to this scheme by the recent crisis involving Roma citizens, see ch 7 by Tawhida Ahmed in this volume. See, also, Case C-333/13 *Dano* [2014] EU:C:2014:2358.

[105] Case C-109/01 *Akrich* [2003] ECR I-9607.

[106] Case C-1/05 *Jia* [2007] ECR I-1; Case C-127/08 *Metock and others* [2008] ECR I-6241.

[107] Case C-200/02 *Zhu and Chen* [2004] ECR I-9925.

[108] Case C-34/09 *Ruiz Zambrano* [2011] ECR I-1177. The application of this line of reasoning has nonetheless been restricted in subsequent cases : see Case C-434/09 *McCarthy* (judgment of 5 May 2011); Case C-256/11 *Dereci and others* (judgment of 15 November 2011); Joined Cases C-356/11 and C-357/11 *O and S* (judgment of 6 December 2012); Case C-87/12 *Ymeraga* (judgment of 8 May 2013); Case C-86/12 *Alokpa and Moudoulou* (judgment of 10 October 2013).

very relevant, since the purpose of fighting illegal migration is enshrined in the Treaty and clearly spelled out as one of the inspiring principles of the common migration policy. This argument was put forward by many member states in their observations in the *Metock* or *Ruiz Zambrano* cases: giving residence rights to EU family members that were in an illegal situation, or granting them to parents of EU citizens that have never used free movement rights, would attract more irregular migrants given the easier path to regularisation. Despite this stringent argument, the Court has privileged a position that situates the rights of EU citizens at the centre stage, and in this way, a sort of 'constitutional' pre-eminence has emerged: considerations based on fundamental rights and on the protection of the basic status of European citizenship supersede the objective of fighting illegal migration.

IV. CONCLUDING REMARKS

Despite the undoubtable vulnerability attached de facto to the irregularity of the migration status, the notion of vulnerability is struggling to make its way in European law as a legal concept with concrete legal ramifications with regard to irregular migrants.

In the framework of the CoE, the vulnerability of irregular migrants has been firmly recognised at the political level by the Parliamentary Assembly, an approach which has been followed to some extent by the Committee of Ministers, undertaking a non-negligible action adopting soft law documents that tackle the situation of irregular migrants from a human rights approach. Nonetheless, the legal consequences of the vulnerability of irregular migrants in the case law of the ECtHR seem to still be under construction. A fundamental distinction of the role of irregularity can already be made. In cases regarding immigration status or the right to remain (cases involving expulsion, or a positive obligation to grant a residence permit, under Article 8 ECHR), irregular migration status is regarded as a contravention and not as an element of vulnerability, playing to the detriment of the immigrant's position in the examination of proportionality. Only other circumstances arising out of other vulnerability grounds, such as age or health, can serve to offset the legitimate prerogatives of states to control migration. On the contrary, in cases regarding access to and the enjoyment of other fundamental rights, as it has been clear in detention cases, irregularity plays the role of 'aggravating' the already vulnerable status under other circumstances such as health or age. Against this framework, irregularity does not yet seem to have emerged as an autonomous ground of vulnerability suitable to trigger, in isolation, the same legal consequences as other vulnerability grounds. Finally, the consideration of an irregular status as a suspect ground in discrimination cases seems to be variable, depending on the fundamental right at stake.

The most advanced approach towards an autonomous role of irregular status as an element of vulnerability appears in the framework of the European Social

Committee. Indeed, in recent cases, the connection to human dignity has been used to ensure the relevance of the most fundamental rights of the Charter to immigrants in an irregular situation, overcoming the limitations of the scope of application of the European Social Charter. Moreover, irregularity seems to be destined to play a role in itself not only as a preliminary hurdle to be overcome in terms of the scope of application, but as an element of vulnerability to be taken into account in the analysis that leads to overcoming such a hurdle.

In the framework of the EU, we can conclude that the approach towards irregular migrants does not follow the approach of considering them to be a particularly vulnerable group in need of protection. Even though the returns Directive and the employers sanctions Directive introduce relevant elements that contribute to enhancing the legal position of some irregular migrants, the absolute focus of EU migration policy continues to be the objective of 'fighting illegal migration', strongly embedded in the constitutional structure as set up by the Treaty. This approach has, so far, prevented the emergence of a general and comprehensive EU approach towards the legal status of irregular migrants. Nonetheless, the potential width of the EU competence could, in the future, well give rise to new secondary legislation, or to the reform of the existing instruments, with a perspective more inclined to taking into account the legal challenges that the lack of status entails for the enjoyment of fundamental rights.

In the EU framework, vulnerability, as was the case in the framework of the case law of the ECtHR, becomes relevant in several secondary law instruments, only to introduce the need to take into account the special situation of groups such as asylum-seekers, children and persons with special needs. Irregularity of status, in itself, is not recognised as an element suitable to trigger specific protection, beyond the guarantees provided for in the Charter and in secondary law. In this regard, it should be borne in mind that the scope of EU law relevant to the situation of irregular migrants does not end with the specific secondary law adopted under the legal basis of the common migration policy, but also encompasses other instruments under other policies, such as social policy or the anti-discrimination Directives.[109]

As a consequence, it would, at first sight, appear that there is an opposition between the 'two Europes', the Council of Europe's structures being more inclined to a fundamental rights approach, which recognises irregularity as an element of growing importance to determine the vulnerable position of individuals.[110] However, these different approaches are not so much inspired by radically different material positions towards the fundamental rights' protection that should be granted to irregular migrants, as by the different competences and tasks carried out by the two organisations. Granted, the EU, for the width of its competences

[109] See, in this regard, FRA report, op cit.

[110] In this sense JM Larralde, 'Les garanties au retour de la Convention européenne des droits de l'homme' in S Leclerc (ed), *Europe(s), Droit(s) et migrnat irrégulier* (Brussels, Bruylant 2012) 177–96, 177.

and the nature of its legal acts, likens its position of interest to that of the states, in the exercise of the sovereign competences conferred by them.

As the result of the principle of international law according to which states remain free to determine admission of foreigners, the existence of internal legislation limiting the possibilities of migration entails, as a necessary consequence, the existence of situations in which people do not comply with national migratory legal regimes. Having in mind the universalising aspiration of human rights and their implicit claim of equality and non-discrimination, migration law and human rights are intrinsically in tension, and the legislature and judiciary struggle to define the line between the acceptable differences in treatment, and between the core elements of rights that cannot be denied to irregular migrants. This debate seems to still be ongoing in both organisations. In this sense, the inspiration provided by the Council of Europe's approach can indeed lead to overcoming the view that the predominant objective of the 'fight' against irregular migration as an undesirable phenomenon prevents any possibility of actively regulating the status of irregular migrants. Indeed, as the Employers' Sanctions Directive has shown, enhancing the legal position of irregular migrants (through the right to back payment, in this case) cannot only contribute to diminishing their vulnerability and legal invisibility, but can serve as a relevant deterrent for those attempting to benefite from this vulnerable position.

Index

www.ingramcontent.com/pod-product-compliance
Lightning Source LLC
LaVergne TN
LVHW052215200926
848481LV00001B/112